Core

Sociological

Dichotomies

ONE WEEK LOAN

dichotomy 1 Division (esp. sharply defined) in two classes, parts, etc. L16. **b** A sharp or paradoxical contrast M20.

The New Shorter Oxford English Dictionary

Core Sociological Dichotomies

EDITED BY CHRIS JENKS

SAGE Publications
London • Thousand Oaks • New Delhi

First published 1998

SAGE Publications Ltd
6 Bonhill Street
London EC2A 4PU

SAGE Publications Inc.
2455 Teller Road
Thousand Oaks, California 91320

SAGE Publications India Pvt Ltd
32, M-Block Market
Greater Kailash – I
New Delhi 110 048

British Library Cataloguing in Publication data
A catalogue record for this book is available
from the British Library

ISBN 0 8039 7978 9
ISBN 0 8039 7979 7 (pbk)

Library of Congress catalog record available

Typeset by Mayhew Typesetting, Rhayader, Powys
Printed in Great Britain by The Cromwell Press Ltd,
Trowbridge, Wiltshire

Contents

Notes on Contributors

The Department of Sociology at Goldsmiths College, University of London, is one of the foremost departments of sociology in the UK. It has a considerable reputation in the fields of social theory, cultural theory and qualitative research as well as in a variety of substantive areas represented in this book. There are twenty-one full-time members of staff in the Department and a large number of visiting tutors. All of the people contributing to this volume are associated with the Department either as staff or as postgraduate students or, in some cases, as both. Although they are all leading research figures within the discipline, this book has been written with generations of students and their needs in mind.

LES BACK was both an undergraduate and a postgraduate student at Goldsmiths College. He is now Senior Lecturer in Sociology at Goldsmiths College. His most recent major publications are *New Ethnicities and Urban Culture* (UCL Press 1995), *Race, Politics and Social Change* (with J. Solomos: Routledge 1995) and *Racism and Society* (with J. Solomos: Macmillan 1995), and he awaits publication of *Racism* (with J. Solomos: Routledge). His current research focuses on cultures of racism in football.

JOANNE ENTWISTLE is currently Senior Lecturer in Communications and Cultural Studies at the University of North London, having completed her doctoral studies in the Department of Sociology, Goldsmiths College. She awaits publication of *Fashion, the Body and Identity* (Polity) and *Fashioning the Career Woman* (Berg). Her research interests are fashion, gender and the body.

PAUL FILMER is Senior Lecturer in Sociology at Goldsmiths College. He is co-author of *New Directions in Sociological Theory* (Collier-Macmillan 1972), *Problems of Reflexivity and Dialectics in Sociological Inquiry* (Routledge 1974) and *Working in Crafts* (Crafts Council 1983). He awaits the publication of *All Singin', Some Dancin': A Sociological Study of the Musical* (with V. Rimmer and D. Walsh: Mellen). His research interests are in art, literature and culture.

CHRIS JENKS is Professor of Sociology and Pro-Warden (Research) at Goldsmiths College. His most recent major publications are *Cultural Reproduction* (Routledge 1993), *Culture* (Routledge 1993), *Visual Culture* (Routledge 1995), *Childhood* (Routledge 1996) and *Theorizing Childhood* (with A. James and A. Prout: Polity 1998), and he awaits publication of *Subculture: The Fragmentation of the Social* (Sage) and *Transgressive Culture* (with C. Rojek).

JOSEP R. LLOBERA recently retired from the Department after sixteen years' service and is now Emeritus Reader in Sociology at Goldsmiths College. He has also been awarded the status of Visiting Professor of Anthropology at the University College, London and Visiting Professor at the Universitat Pompeu Fabra, Barcelona. His most recent major publication is *The God of Modernity: The Development of Nationalism in Modern Europe* (Berg 1995).

JEAN POPEAU is a Visiting Tutor in Sociology at Goldsmiths College, where he completed his doctoral studies. His current research interests are in the theory and literature of negritude and the theoretical possibilities of a black aesthetics, and he has publications in these areas.

CLIVE SEALE is Senior Lecturer in Sociology and Deputy Head of the Department of Sociology at Goldsmiths College. His most recent major publications include *Medical Knowledge: Doubt and Certainty* (with A. Pattison: Open University Press 1994), *The Year Before Death* (with A. Cartright: Avebury 1994), *Researching Society and Culture* (Sage 1998) and *Constructing Death: The Sociology of Dying and Bereavement* (Cambridge 1998). His research interests are in the field of death and dying, particularly hospice care and euthanasia.

DAVID SILVERMAN is Professor of Sociology at Goldsmiths College, and the longest serving member of staff in the Department. He achieved early recognition for his work with the publication of *The Theory of Organizations* (Heinemann 1970) and has continued as a prolific researcher and writer. His most recent major publications include *Interpreting Qualitative Data: Methods for Analysing Talk, Text and Interaction* (Sage 1993), *Organizations in Action* (with D. Boden: Sage 1996), *Discourses of Counselling: HIV Counselling as Social Interaction* and *Qualitative Research: Theory, Method and Practice* (Sage 1997). His most recent book is *Harvey Sacks* (Polity 1998).

DON SLATER is Lecturer in Sociology at Goldsmiths College. He has recently published *Consumer Culture and Modernity* (Polity 1997) and he awaits the publication of *Markets, Modernity and Social Theory* (with Fran Tonkiss: Polity 1998) and *The Business of Advertising* (with S. Nixon: Arnold). His research interests are theories of consumer culture, the sociology of economic life, information technology and visual culture.

SUE STEDMAN-JONES was previously Lecturer in Sociology at Goldsmiths College, specializing in the philosophy of social science. She is now a freelance researcher and writer living in Paris. She awaits publication of *Durkheim Re-considered* (Polity).

HELEN THOMAS has made the transition through undergraduate and research postgraduate in the Department to Senior Lecturer in Sociology and Head of the Department of Sociology at Goldsmiths College. Her most recent major publications are *Dance, Gender and Culture* (Macmillan 1993), *Dance, Modernity and Culture: Explorations in the Sociology of Dance* (Routledge 1995) and *Dance in the City* (Macmillan 1997), and she awaits publication of *The Body, Dance and Cultural Theory* (Macmillan).

FRAN TONKISS is Lecturer in Sociology at Goldsmiths College. She awaits publication of *Markets, Modernity and Social Theory* (with Don Slater: Polity). Her research interests concern urban issues and the sociology of economic life. She was previously a research postgraduate in the Department.

DAVID F. WALSH is Senior Lecturer in Sociology at Goldsmiths College. He is co-author of *New Directions in Sociological Theory* (Collier-Macmillan 1972) and he awaits publication of *All Singin', Some Dancin': A Sociological Study of the Musical* (with P. Filmar and V. Rimmer: Mellen). His current research is in the area of popular culture and music theatre.

Introduction

Chris Jenks

This book contains an invitation and a welcome, not just to an academic subject but also to a way of thinking about the world. Sociology, which is the discipline that has brought us all together, has a relatively short history, yet it has had a significant and growing impact on the culture, thought styles and public policy of contemporary society. We need to ask how this could have occurred, and what forms this influence might have taken.

While teaching sociology at a variety of levels for over twenty-five years I, like so many of the contributors to this volume, have noticed that the character of everyday life has changed quite dramatically. During the past quarter of a century social life has transformed in many ways, and continues to change increasingly quickly so that less and less about social life remains stable and predictable. During this same turbulent historical period it has also been noticeable that a popular interest in sociology has emerged, but particularly the interest of a growing number of under-graduate students. This interest continues to expand in both volume and intensity and it is reflected in your personal attraction to our shared subject.

We might suggest that the recurring alterations in the structure of our society over the recent past, and our shared desire for the relative sense of security that society once provided, have brought forth a collective response from people to try to understand more about the relationships that hold between them. Thus as we all feel potentially less structured in our social lives we seek to arrest this experience of lack of control through our own knowledge.

At a time when governments internationally are calling out for a higher level of recruitment to mathematics, engineering, physics and chemistry, and industry and commerce are demanding increased skills in technology and natural science, students are choosing in vast numbers to study the humanities, but more especially the social sciences.

Clearly we now appear more preoccupied than ever before with questions concerning our personal and social identities, and our collective responses to social pressures and constraints. The boundaries of our interest and inquiry are expanding and we are more amenable to receiving information about our social conduct and adapting our behaviour in response to it. So, if we take a few examples: the changing attitudes of men towards women; the interactions between different cultural communities; the way that children are taught and assessed in schools; the relations between the forces of law and order and the public; the manner in which doctors consult with their patients; and the strategies and programmes that politicians employ; these are all, at some level, coming to be informed by what we might call a 'sociological perspective'.

In the same way that it is possible to point to different areas of everyday life and suggest that sociology has contributed to their modern form, either directly or indirectly, we can also say with confidence that there is no area of collective life and no aspect of social action that sociologists themselves have felt unable or unwilling to explore. Everyone anticipates that sociologists will want to speak about issues to do with social class, which has always appeared as one of our most significant explanatory concepts. However sociologists are equally concerned to study football hooliganism, HIV infection, humour, dying, racial conflict, childrearing practices, popular culture etc.: the list is inexhaustible. All of the social world is our stage but, of course, we tend to be drawn to study some topics more than others and that is usually because some topics are of more pressing concern and call forth a greater moral commitment at particular historical moments. It would be hard not to be concerned with HIV infection in the modern world.

When sociology was new – and a variety of histories and commentaries will tell you that it found its origins towards the end of the nineteenth century – its concerns were quite different to those that preoccupy us today. Sociology was, at the outset, a particularly European way of thinking even though a large part of its tradition developed in parallel in the USA. Throughout the nineteenth century all of the major European countries were still experiencing the disruptive after-effects of the French Revolution of 1789. The inflexible politics of an old order of government and privilege that had for so long kept societies stable and unchanged was now being questioned. The Revolution had violently challenged the long-held assumptions concerning power, prestige, hierarchy and status and had produced an instability that required an adjustment to change. These social adjustments were now all guided by a philosophical concern with the principles of equality, freedom and altruism deriving from the new French Republic. At the same time technology was developing and the way that people produced things for use and consumption in society had changed. Farming and small-scale domestic manufacture were giving way to industrialization and mass production. People were moving from the countryside into towns, urban populations were becoming larger and denser, and, most significant of all, the structure of relationships between people was altering dramatically and irrevocably through new divisions of labour. Overriding and directing all of these changes a new form of political economy had evolved which, through a variety of mutations, was destined to rule our lives and contribute to major world threatening antagonisms up until the present day. This form is what we have come to call 'capitalism'. It is, in part, a mode of production but it is also a description of the way in which, at a more general level, all of social life becomes transformed into a market and thus all things, people and actions take on a quantitative value. This transformation through capitalism begins, in turn, to shape the way that people relate to one another and, subsequently, the ways in which their personal identities are formed.

All through our discipline's formative period sociologists selected their problems from the agenda of their day and treated them not simply as practical issues but also as moral issues, that is, as issues of value. So when Marx considered social stratification, Weber sought to explain bureaucracy and Durkheim investigated the social causes of suicide, they all did so with a larger view of what a 'good society' might be in mind, and they were all writing about problems that derive from capitalism. In the context of our society at the end of the twentieth century it is less and less easy to think about values that are shared or beliefs that are common. Sociology has adapted to this problem, in part, by beginning to find ways of addressing the personal experience of a whole range of different groups within the world of today. Now, even though we may not have abandoned our visions of the 'good society', as sociologists living in the present we tend to be concerned with more specific contexts. So, for example, we might wish: to express the politics and identities of people of different genders and different sexual orientations; to articulate the experience of people from a variety of ethnic groups and belief systems; to realize what it is to be a child rather than an adult; or to demonstrate the social constraints pressing on a person with 'special needs'. These examples, and there are many more, might indicate how our work as sociologists continues to have a general, and critical, appeal and application even in a modern society where it is increasingly difficult to spot the values or beliefs that people hold in common.

In this book we have chosen, quite specifically, to look at some pairs of ideas that we think will help you to understand sociology as a subject with a tradition but, more importantly, will help you relate to sociology as a relevant way of understanding your world today and your place within it.

HOW TO USE THIS BOOK

As a student of sociology, or indeed almost any subject at university, it is possible to fall into the trap of thinking that what you are studying always belongs to someone else. By this I mean that you arrive at a strange institution apparently full of learned and expert people who 'know' about sets of very complex ideas which they will 'tell' you about for the next three years. These elders (that is, the professors and lecturers) produce your knowledge through their research. Your textbooks, written by learned people, are full of ideas that you must collect and store for three years. These authors, researchers and teachers, ancient and modern, 'own' the subject. You, on the other hand, have little or no part in the subject, you assume that your role is to listen and collect and maybe copy these learned people: this makes your learning passive and your practice merely imitation. This kind of learning is something we pick up at home, through school and through the mass media: it is a difficult habit to break.

Adopting and retaining this passivity is, of course, no way to study and it is certainly no way to fill three years of your adult life while you are at university. You must engage with your subject, use your subject, address your own problems through the subject and, as I have said before, treat it as a way of seeing the world – your way of seeing the world. This book attempts to encourage your participation.

None of the authors writing here believe sociology is a museum that you should spend time simply walking around, looking at the dusty exhibits. We are all inviting you to join in and make your interests and perspectives relevant through our shared, and chosen, subject – sociology. Sociology is a living subject, a living practice and a living way of coming to know about the world. You as newcomers and enthusiasts are vital to that life, and your vitality feeds our shared tradition. Our chosen method for inviting you to engage with us in looking at modern issues in the modern world, which we all inhabit in our different ways, is by investigating pairs of ideas that we see as fundamental to sociological understanding. These we have called *core dichotomies*. Dichotomies are ideas that are divided into two parts and the parts usually stand in opposition to one another.

Let us take an example of dichotomous or binary thinking. If I decide to vote for a particular party at an election, I may do so because:

(a) I freely choose to *or* I feel constrained to do so;
(b) the party represents my interests *or* my parents always voted for them;
(c) I have decided according to the current state of the economy *or* I have been influenced by the media and propaganda;
(d) the party closely identifies with my own moral position *or* people of my social class always vote for this party,

and so on. These alternative pairs of reasons are dichotomies.

Now the first reasons in these pairs are explanations in terms of freedom, choice, individuality and free will; the second reasons are explanations in terms of constraint, determinism, social pressure and public opinion. As sociologists we might examine this problem through the core dichotomy of agency (first reasons) and structure (second reasons). Does somebody act according to the influence of either agency or structure? The answer will usually be somewhere in the middle. However, employing the dichotomy allows us to put exaggerated forms of the arguments on each side, or each end if we see it as a continuum, and the balance between the extremes often helps us to achieve a clearer answer in the middle ground. Of course the dichotomy of agency and structure, which is the first one discussed in this book, is not just about voting behaviour: it is about all social behaviour, from the most serious to the most trivial, from why I might commit a crime to why I might take up smoking or even wear a yellow tie! Remember, nothing escapes the interest of the sociologist.

So we reason in the form of dichotomies here because they enable us to establish arguments from two strong and opposite positions and because they will enable you also to engage with debates from both sides and to see the strengths of the arguments on both sides. In this way, we anticipate, you will not simply inhabit the debates or arguments that belong to other people; rather you will be in a position to make your own mind up or to reform the problem.

There are other good reasons for approaching sociology through core dichotomies. The first is to do with location, that is, your location and the character of your society. For years sociology spoke about the world from the perspective of the Western European and this caused it to be guilty of what anthropologists refer to as 'ethnocentrism'. Ethnocentrism means that a person has a set of ideas containing an attitude that his or her own race, nation or culture is superior to all others, and this can be achieved not only explicitly by judging other societies inferior but also implicitly by simply ignoring them and their differences. In a more modern context many feel that sociology has been further guilty of speaking about the world from the perspective of the Western European white male. We do certainly have to be increasingly conscious of the perspective we adopt and the partiality that our perspective reveals.

By analysing social events in terms of abstract dichotomies like agency and structure we are less likely to ignore the views and arguments of others not like ourselves. Indeed, by using dichotomous thinking we are more likely to provide a space from within which others' differences can emerge. It is also the case that your particular perspective as a reader of this book, perhaps as a woman, perhaps as a member of an ethnic minority, perhaps as a member of a working-class family, perhaps as a resident of New York, Melbourne or Manchester, will not be glossed over when we discuss the world through dichotomies in the way that it might be if I gave you my explanation, however clear, as a white, middle-class, British male, of, for example, the difficulties facing the modern family in London. What you would learn about is another person's experiences, perspective and social location. Dichotomies then have a relevance to people's social experience across different social locations and can therefore include us all, without any exclusion.

The second reason for approaching sociological issues through dichotomies is to do with history and time. We might rightly suppose that although sociologists from the early twentieth century would know nothing about the atom bomb, global warming or the influence of television on children, they would certainly be concerned with a different set of issues about class, solidarity, industrialization, and the influence of religion – all things that are less relevant to us now. However, just as we could place each one of our concerns within a dichotomous argument based on continuity and change or on fact and value, for example, so also could they. The dichotomies then are relatively timeless and will address problems stretching back to the origins of our discipline, but will also take us forward into a period when you, the readers, will be setting the problems for our discipline. In this way, to look at sociological issues through core dichotomies rather than through fashionable theories or perspectives alone will ensure that your thoughts and ideas will be timely, but simultaneously never out of date.

There is, however, one major drawback to arguing in terms of dichotomies which applies in specific cases. If we are looking at pairs of abstractions like the local and the global, or absolute and relative, then all of the advantages listed above accrue and we can extend our thinking about a topic. If, however, we are looking at substantive differences between people and placing them in oppositional pairs then we can create antagonisms and conflicts that may be unintentional, but are certainly divisive and potentially painful. Think, for example, of the pairings between: short and tall; able and disabled; gay and straight; or even bright and stupid. As sociologists we should recognize that these pairings, and many others, are constructed within our society and should therefore be critically investigated by us rather than reinforced in our discussions. To this end although we, in this book, recognize the absolute centrality of questions concerning 'gender' and also 'ethnicity' to understanding your own social identity and the social relationships that exist between people within the modern world, we do not set up our arguments as between men and women, or black people and white people. Both of these formulations you will recognize as having provided lasting social battlegrounds in terms of civil rights, the division of labour, differential life chances and notions of freedom and oppression. Rather we cover these two important topics through the less confrontational pairings of sex and gender, and race and ethnicity, which enables us to understand the different experiences of being gendered and belonging to a particular cultural group without setting these differences against one another. We trust that you will, in turn, be informed by these two debates but also recognize them to be substantive reworkings of the dichotomy between nature and culture.

Begin now, and remember that this book will provide you with a basis for the discussion of any of the interesting topics that appear in the other courses that you are taking, from methodology, through social structure, to all of the exciting and exploratory choices that you can make through your optional courses. It should also have an influence, at a later stage, if you are required to make a report or write a dissertation on a topic of your own. Here you will need to have developed a way of producing good arguments. Most specifically, on a day-to-day basis at university, when you are required to put a point in a seminar or a class, or just to express your point of view in a discussion with a friend, you will find that these basic dichotomies and the form of reasoning that they contain will predispose you for an active and fulfilling engagement in academic life.

Each of the authors contributing to this book has gone some way to helping you into their chosen dichotomy. We have all attempted to write in a manner that is user-friendly but not patronizing. You will find introductions to concepts and some concepts explained at length, but you will also find yourself, at times, involved in quite high-level and demanding theoretical questioning. Please do persevere. Remember, you are the 'active' learner and we are attempting to bring you into a way of seeing the world that is critical, valuable and rewarding – but never just simple. In addition, the authors have provided you with a list of **Key Concepts** for each chapter that you can look up and refer across your different courses. There is also a combined reference list for all the books and articles cited.

Best wishes.

Structure/Agency

David F. Walsh

The contents of this chapter are, in many senses, foundational to a lot of the arguments that follow within this book, as are many of the authors referred to.

Of all the concepts which sociology has developed to understand and investigate society, social structure is the most important and absolutely central to the discipline. The reason is simple. In order to conceive of society at all as a phenomenon which does exist objectively as a reality it is necessary to see that there is some definite form of organization to the way in which the persons who live in it relate to one another that shapes the nature of these relationships in particular ways. Society is these various patterns of social relationships that emerge and develop between its members, and social structure is the term (i.e. concept) that sociology uses to capture and describe the organization of these patterns and the shapes which they take.

It is not possible for sociology to think of society as simply an aggregate or collection of individuals *per se* because society consists of the ways in which they are collected together into a community of people. But it is at this point that the nature of what comprises social structure comes to constitute a problem for sociology and the issue of structure versus agency emerges as a central topic for the investigation of social life. Is the community which is society a collection of individuals who, as individuals, actively forge their relationships with one another and create society in the process of doing so? Or do the social relationships which make up society achieve an autonomous identity that establishes them as external conditions which determine the activities of the members of society as they enter into them? In both cases, society is seen to consist of relationships between its members which are structured, or organized, in particular ways and so has an objective existence. However, the first argument treats society and its structures as composed out of the actions of its individual members who are agents of their own actions and produce their relationships with one another in terms of this agency; whilst the second argument treats society and its structures as a **system** of relationships that determines the activities of the members of society through the ways in which it works as a system that conditions how people are able to behave within it. This is our dichotomy.

Both positions have been taken up in sociological theory, usually in opposition to one another, and the dispute between the two arguments continues to be an issue of contemporary debate. We may loosely refer to the two positions as individualistic, voluntaristic or action sociology as opposed to holistic, deterministic or structuralist sociology. However, what I want to suggest is that the assertion of one position rather than the other leads to irresolvable problems in both cases when one is attempting to deal with the actual nature of social relationships. Moreover, the effort to reconcile the two positions by arguing that social relationships are a product of human agency and also condition social activity within society often only restates the problem that social relationships are relationships between active individuals and an objectively existent society, without necessarily resolving it by showing how social action both produces and is a product of society at one and the same time. Let us outline first, then, the general features of the two positions as they argue about the nature of society, before moving into a more detailed investigation of the ideas of major sociological theorists who take up one or the other of these two positions or attempt to reconcile them as they seek to investigate and explain the nature of society and the bases of its organization (Cuff and Payne 1979).

The foundation of the **structuralist** position lies in the argument that human beings are essentially social creatures who by their very nature are made by their social habitat which is society. On this basis it makes no sense to talk of human beings as individuals as though they can and do exist independently of the social context in which they necessarily live together with one another. Indeed the very content and character of the interests, purposes and values which they espouse as persons, the motives which precipitate their actions, and the kinds of personality traits they develop can be seen to derive from the social world which they inhabit. Even individuality itself is argued to be a product of a certain kind of society – the modern industrial world – which generates a kind and sense of personal identity because of the way in which it is organized at the level of the social relationships of which it is composed.

What then is society in these terms? Essentially it is a phenomenon that exists as an autonomous reality in its own right: it is, as Émile Durkheim puts it, *sui generis* (existing in its own right) and irreducible to any other level of human existence, be it biological or psychological (Durkheim 1964a). Although, of course, society cannot exist without its individual members, it is not an aggregate of individuals but an emergent reality that results from the association between them, and the properties which it possesses stem from this association itself and not from the characteristics of the individuals who engage in this association. If it stemmed from the latter then society could be explained in terms of psychology, which structuralist sociology wants to argue that it cannot. Instead, structuralist sociology argues that human association, that is social relationships, creates a wholly new reality (as does, we might note, the right combination of oxygen and hydrogen in the physical world when water is created) which is a world of social facts. These social facts are the typical patterns of action and relationships that constitute the structures and institutions which make up society in the form of phenomena such as social class, the family, work, the state, etc. That these structures and institutions have a seemingly abstract character that makes them somewhat less visible than the individual by no means undermines their essential reality which can be detected and measured by the ways in which they determine the behaviour of the members of society. This is apparent from how the position of the individuals within these structures and institutions comes to determine what they can and cannot do and what in fact they do do, and the essential typicality of how all individuals in the same structural and institutional positions engage in the same (i.e. typical) kinds of actions as one another despite the fact that they are different people. This is easily evidenced by the invariant character of such behaviour which all of us as members of society commonsensically, let alone sociologically, rely upon in order to relate to one another at all and the world in which we live. For example, a lecture is recognizable as such by lecturers and students and participated in by both because it involves a typical form of behaviour on the part of both, irrespective of the personal idiosyncrasies of lecturers and students: if it was the latter that determined the nature of a lecture then it would possess an infinite variability of behaviour that would make it impossible to be a recognizable activity, namely a lecture, at all. These structures and institutions, then, play a regulative role in social life and they have a history and autonomy that transcend the purely personal to the point where they constrain the behaviour of the members of society as well as enabling them to interact with one another. They are conditions which govern social life, and the bases on which they emerge and work have to be understood in terms of what gave rise to them historically and what factors keep them in operation.

At this point different kinds of structuralist theories vary as to how they explain structures and institutions. On the one hand theorists of a Marxist and neo-Marxist persuasion argue that the structural organization of social relationships derives from the collective organization of the processes of production through which a material basis is provided for the existence of society, so that social relationships have an essentially economic foundation (Bottomore and Rubel 1965). On the other hand, culturalist theories such as those of Durkheim, and functionalism, argue that there are certain basic and environmentally determined conditions to which society has to adapt in order for social life to be possible, which it does through the cultural creation of institutions and structures that provide solutions to the problems that these conditions create. In both cases what emerges is a system of social relationships which has a fixed and determining character for the behaviour of the persons participating in them, either in terms of a particular mode of economic production in which the individual is constrained to engage in work and productive activity, and of how that mode of production is organized materially, technologically and managerially, or in terms of a culture with collective values and rules which are inculcated into the individual through a process of socialization as he or she enters into and progresses through society. In both cases, society is being treated as a system of structures and institutions in which its members take up particular positions in the form of roles which then determine how they can act within them, but it is the way that system works internally in terms of its own logic that is the basis of the social organization of society and therefore the determinant of the behaviour of the members of society. Indeed culturalist theories, such as those of the anthropologist Claude Lévi-Strauss, go even further than this to suggest that the very nature of culture itself which finds its expression in symbols and myths is a kind of language which has its own internal and underlying grammar that determines what kind of meaning can be imposed upon life and the world. So it is not that the members of society actively use the culture to make sense of life and the world for themselves, but rather that they are unconscious vehicles through which the culture speaks so that it determines how they are able to see and do things. At its most extreme, then, structuralist sociology treats society as an autonomous entity composed of structures and institutions that impose themselves upon and control the actions of the members of society by organizing themselves in terms of their own logic, which is dictated by the economic and cultural factors that have produced it and which are extra-individual. Thus the degree to which the members of society are agents of their own existence and their relationships with one another is quite minimal, since not only are their actions determined by their position within structures and institutions but so too are their thoughts, values and interests. If you like, then, the only agent of social action is structure itself (Cohen 1968).

The opposite action position in sociology rejects this systemic structuralism on the grounds that it leads to a dehumanized version of the social world through an illegitimate reification of society which completely objectifies structures and institutions and divorces them from the actual activities of the members of society as individuals within it. From this perspective society is not an immutable and determining force which externally conditions the lives of its members, but rather they are agents who produce and sustain it. Human beings can and do make themselves into what they are; they are able to take charge of their own lives and to shape the social world into forms which meet their own needs. History is not a matter of some inexorable and autonomous process of change; rather, changes occur because human beings make them occur. Society, then, consists of the deeds of its members and they are the authors of them. The starting point for the action position in relationship to the nature of society is the individual and his or her action, which is essentially and subjectively meaningful to the individual in the sense that it is directed and undertaken in terms of the interests, purposes, values and motives of the individual as a subject in the light of his or her needs. Social interaction and therefore social relationships arise from the fact that the satisfaction of need and the pursuit of interests requires the co-operation, collaboration or control of other individuals in a similar position. This leads to the development and construction of mutual forms of the regulation and organization of relationships between individuals that are based upon a reciprocity of understanding and expectations which then license and control their interactions with one another. So society emerges as a community of individuals which has an objective degree of autonomy in the sense that it consists of intersubjective relationships between its members based on collective understanding and expectation that are embodied in collective rules and forms of organization. But these understandings, expectations and rules and the forms of the organization of interaction which they produce, which are the structures and institutions of society, are not objects and forces in their own right which take on a life of their own quite independently of the human beings who act in terms of and participate in them. Ultimately structures are what people do together with one another. But to see the structures of society as things is a mistake: to talk of collective phenomena such as social classes, the family, the state, etc. is acceptable only as long as one recognizes that they are a shorthand way of referring to complex patterns of relationships between individuals. Of course these relationships entail typical ways of acting and so we are dealing with structured social activity, but this structuring of social activity takes place from the inside and is not imposed from the outside through the ways in which individuals organize their relationships with one another as agents of them and sustain them on that basis. How so?

Firstly, in order to organize their own actions and interactions with others, individuals have to define situations in particular ways: it is not simply that situations impose themselves upon individuals in some predefined fashion that determines how action and interaction will proceed. For example, it is not possible to understand criminal activity independently of how certain activities are defined as criminal by various people, groups and agencies in society and consequently dealt with on this basis by both criminals and the forces of law and order. Moreover, sociology needs to pursue this further by looking at how society's members go about connecting up and putting together different aspects of the social world to form a picture of events within it and so conduct their own activities and interactions in the light of and in relation to this. For example, when investigating suicide, as many sociologists have, it is necessary to examine how coroners piece together and decide upon the relevance of the different biographical and situational circumstances of the dead person to see how a verdict of suicide is arrived at, rather than one of accident or murder, and so how the fact of suicide is established and recorded as a fact.

Secondly, the organization of social action requires individuals to take decisions since all situations always offer a variety of possible choices of action within them, and to understand how structure and institutions work requires a knowledge of how this decision-making takes place. For example, it would be impossible to understand bureaucracy without investigating how bureaucrats interpret and choose to implement bureaucratic policies and objectives. Structures and institutions, then, when investigated entail complex and intricate interactions and relationships between human beings who are agents of what they do and not simply products of a system. The social environment is a world of possible and alternative ways of acting which requires decisions and choice on the part of its members as to what to do; and, in making decisions, its members make society as they arrange their relations with one another in the course of living their own lives. This they can and do in a whole variety of ways. However, this does not mean that society can be explained in terms of the psychology of the individual (action sociology is about social action and is not psychologistic); it means only that it is necessary to recognize that human beings are subjects and therefore agents of their actions and that society is an intersubjective world. In this sense society is not an object because social relationships come to be organized into particular forms and patterns through interaction that is based on mutual understanding and expectations which both facilitate and regulate the ways in which it takes place. Society, however, does have an objective existence of its own in the sense that it is an extra-individual phenomenon with a structure and organization that establish it as a reality which is different from the individual but not separate from the active agency of its members: it is how they act together in mutual and reciprocal ways to form a community that constitutes society.

Moreover, as such, society does have a history and force which helps to shape the conduct of activity within it. We are, as members, born into a social world which has been produced over centuries by the multiplicity of choices and decisions made by our ancestors, and we have to live with this inheritance and its effects in making our own choices and decisions. Moreover, we have to live with the fact that the intentions which were embodied in the actions of our ancestors have necessarily had unintended consequences which they could not and did not envisage, and yet have left a legacy of all forms of social organization in the contemporary world which helps to shape existence in it. History does weigh on the present and human agency does not necessarily entail control over the future. For example, Max Weber points out just how strategic the values and work ethic of ascetic Protestantism were for the contemporary Western world because of the role they played in the development of capitalism by fostering the whole ethos which facilitated its emergence and now sustains its legitimacy as a form of economic organization. Ascetic Protestantism had not intended to do this but was creating a religious ethic designed to assuage fears of damnation and hopefully secure a place in heaven for believers. But the fact that history weighs upon society and that action has unforeseen consequences does not mean that society has emergent properties and law-like qualities that separate it from the activities of its members as a system operating with a logic of its own and externally determining what they do.

The problem with the action approach, however, enters precisely here because in all this discussion of historical circumstances, unintended consequences and the organization of action on a collective basis, what is being tacitly acknowledged is a reality that is quite problematic to address in terms of the individual because it is extra- or supra-individual and clearly does have a degree of determination in relation to human action because it socializes it and in doing so organizes it in particular kinds of ways. The socialization and organization come from the existence of structures and institutions which have a regulatory and directive character that is enforceable, and they have an impersonal nature in themselves however personally they come to be inhabited. It is simply not true that society can be modified and transformed at the will of its members in any way that they want, because structures and institutions do have an organizational foundation which is rooted in things like economic conditions, power bases, administrative needs, environmental conditions and resources, technological developments, the biological and psychological parameters of human nature, the logic of forms of knowledge, historical events and circumstances and so on; none of these are necessarily individual and personal as such, and they give structures and institutions a degree of autonomy in terms of how they work. Moreover, this autonomy is recognizable in the fact that they cannot be reduced to and investigated at any level other than that on which they exist. The argument that structures and institutions like class, the family, the state, etc. can be replaced by and investigated at the level of descriptions of what individuals do falls apart when sociologists attempt to analyse them in these terms. This is because what individuals are doing only makes sense when we describe it in terms of the structures and institutions in which the activity is implicated. For example, what fathers do as fathers only makes sense in terms of the existence of the family of which the father is a part. As such, what this recognizes is that society is made up not simply of individuals but of people who occupy positions in the various structures and institutions of society which organize what they do, the ways in which they do it and so the typicality of their behaviour. The argument that people act in terms of their own needs, interests, purposes and values and that they are agents on this basis must also recognize how all of these too have much of their derivation in the culture of the society in which the individual lives and how that, however differentiated, is collective and operates at the level of communal meaning, symbols, myths, classification, schemes, etc. which are all embodied in and as languages whose organization and use are social and not personal (Rex 1961).

The problem of the issue of structure and agency in social life, then, is clear even if the resolution of it is not. On the one hand, society is not a system of immutable and reified structures and institutions operating as a law-like system of objectively organized relationships that determines all action within it. Human beings are not simply cogs in a machine or puppets on a string because they can and do make sense of their social environment, exercise choices in relation to it and modify it in a whole variety of ways, which makes them agents in the social world and creators of social structure. To repeat, social structures are what people do together with one another. On the other hand, they do it in the form of structures and institutions which are supra-personal entities with an organizational basis in conditions other than those simply a product of human need and interest; which cannot be transformed just at will by human beings; and which do have a regulatory and directive effect on human behaviour in society since they are the basis of its sociality. Now, having said this, is the problem of structure and agency one which can only be stated as a paradox, or one on which sociologists can only take sides, or are there ways of moving to some resolution of it, however limited this might be? The issue is crucial because more is at stake than just sociology: in the end it raises the question of what human beings are and what they can and cannot do in practice. What I want to look at now is how a number of major sociologies and sociologists have dealt with this.

Within classical sociology the tendency of various major thinkers has been to take sides, although built into these arguments has always been an undertow in the direction of the opposite position, however faint. On the structuralist side, we find the thought of Karl Marx, Émile Durkheim and the theory of functionalism (Cohen 1968). Marx's conception of society has its grounds in a theory of action: as he put it, human beings make their own history. But Marx goes on to argue that they do this in circumstances which are not of their own choosing, and he develops an analysis of how action is organized by these circumstances as material conditions of production which structure and determine the social relationships that are primarily generated by the particular material forces of production utilized, which include not only raw materials but also the technology which is used to extract and work them into products. So, historically, societies can be distinguished in terms of the particular material mode of production which is their foundation and which structures the social relationships between the members of a society on the basis of the division of labour which is entailed in it. This constitutes the historical and practical circumstances of social life from which arise the forms of consciousness, culture and institutions of society, i.e. the superstructure of society. As the mode of production produces a surplus of products and wealth in society, so the structure of productive relationships within it (the social structure) that emerges is a hierarchical structure of ownership and control over the forces of production which creates different classes in society (primarily a ruling class who own the means of production and a subordinate class whose labour is either owned by or sold to the ruling class for its use in production). These classes, in turn, have objective and opposing interests by virtue of their position within the social relations of production which determines their consciousness. Futhermore the ruling class, by virtue of its ownership of the means of production, owns the means for the production of ideas and institutions in society too, and these are produced in terms of the interests of that ruling class and legitimate its position of ownership and power in society both institutionally and ideologically.

So, for Marx, the material forces of production create a mode of production which is a system of social relationships that is determined by it and which generates the whole institutional and cultural framework of society. At the heart of this social system is the class structure of society which differentiates its members into opposed social groups with competing interests, and this determines how individuals participate in society and the ways in which they act within it; processes of historical development are propelled by the struggles between classes that the changes in the mode of production induce. Capitalism, as a mode of production, is an economic system of manufacture and exchange which is geared towards the production and sale of commodities within a market for profit, where the manufacture of commodities consists of the use of the formally free labour of workers in exchange for a wage to create commodities in which the manufacturer extracts surplus value from the labour of the worker in terms of the difference between the wage paid to the worker and the value of the commodity produced by him/her to generate that profit. So, Marx argues, the labour of the worker is objectified through its sale to and use by the manufacturer, and thus the worker is alienated from his or her own existence as a subject and the life of the worker is determined by the fate of the commodities which he or she produces for the market, which is governed by the laws of supply and demand and the search for profit on which the manufacture of commodities depends in the capitalist system. Thus the capitalist system of production creates a market economy in which a hierarchical class structure emerges, consisting of a ruling capitalist class (the bourgeoisie) who own the labour of a subordinate exploited working class (the proletariat) who live in a situation of impoverished and alienated conditions which shape their lives and actions since these are enforced upon them by the capitalist system itself. As such the interests of the bourgeoisie and the proletariat are necessarily opposed and this sets up objective conditions of conflict and struggle between them into which both classes are inevitably drawn by the way in which the capitalist system works as structures of exploitative and alienated social relationships.

In these terms then it is clear that, for Marx, human action as productive activity is circumscribed by the material conditions within which it takes place and which establish its organizational limits and structure the social relationships that emerge between the members of society and the institutional forms which they can take. Any attempt to explain capitalism as relationships of economic exchange based upon the pursuit of individual self-interest, leading to the creation of a division of labour and contractual relationships between the members of society based upon the co-operation and free exchange of goods and services between them which they created through their labour, has to face the fact that the relationship between worker and employer is located in a whole system of economic production which determines how labour is sold and utilized in productive activity by a market economy that is geared to profit. Neither the worker nor the capitalist is free to organize their activities within a capitalist market system: rather the market system demands that the worker sells his or her labour on the basis of what the employer is prepared to pay for it and this, in turn, is determined by the need of the employer to produce a profit in the production of commodities in the face of the competition from other capitalist producers in the market. Both worker and employer are caught up in the way that the capitalist market works, and their respective interests and actions are dictated by the position which they occupy within it. It is not individual self-interest which determines their actions but the market-place itself which structures what those interests are and how they can be pursued at the level of action: in the one case it is the ever more determined need to make a profit and in the other it is the ever more determined need to earn a living wage. But the market opposes these two needs to one another since profit can only be achieved by minimizing the costs of production which entails controlling and reducing the cost of labour, i.e. wages.

Yet, of course, Marx as a revolutionary needs to argue that this capitalist system is one which human beings can change and so he needs to bring back human agency into his account of economic activity and the material work of production which structures the social relationships of society. He does this by arguing that, ultimately, the conditions which govern social relationships within a particular mode of production can be changed by human activity once it is recognized by those who are subject to it – that the mode of production is not a naturally given phenomenon but a historical product. To do this the members of society must become conscious of how, by organizing the mode of production on a particular basis, they become subject to its forms of determination over their lives and so develop new forms of production which generate social relationships that meet their own needs and interests. Note, however, that this requires collective and not individual action on the basis of a new organization of the mode of production which restructures social relationships according to the new material conditions which it produces. But this change is only possible if the forces of production have themselves begun to change: in the case of the transition from capitalism to socialism the change is only possible because capitalism is already a mode of production based upon the social organization of labour power as the basis of manufacture which makes possible the social control of production by producers themselves, i.e. the workforce or the proletariat.

So, for Marx, the basis on which the proletariat can become agents of the creation of a society which meets and expresses their needs is still conditional on the emergence of a system of production which creates the conditions in which they can become agents of their own lives, namely a productive system in which the co-operative exercise of their labour power is the objective material basis of social life. That is why, for Marx, capitalism was the necessary precursor of socialism. It created the material conditions for the emergence of socialism in which human beings could seize control of their own labour power since it was that on which capitalist production was based: all that was needed was that the private ownership of labour power be replaced by the collective control of labour power by the labour force itself. Through this the proletariat could seize control of their own lives and create a society tailored to their own needs. In this sense, then, agency re-enters Marx's account of society in the sense that he sees the possibility of a society whose structures and institutions are produced and sustained on that basis, but it is necessary to recognize that it only becomes possible in terms of the advent of a particular form of material production which opens up the possibility that human beings can collectively control the co-operative use of their labour. At no point does Marx suggest that the human actor is an agent of his or her action but only that social conditions of production can emerge in which actors can become agents. The human actor is a thoroughly social creature whose status as an agent of action is a creation of certain kinds of materially generated social relationships which form his or her personality. The individualism of capitalist society is a false subjectivity promoted by the relations induced by the competitive conditions of the sale of labour and the ownership of wealth and property which the market society of capitalism promotes. A genuine subjectivity can only emerge when human beings control the use of their own labour, but that too depends on a social organization of production in which each produces according to his or her own ability and receives rewards according to his or her own needs. The subject as agent is then a creation of particular social relationships of production that have a material foundation and not the progenitor of them: for Marx, it is that socialist relations of production create individuality and not that individuality exists *per se* (Bottomore and Rubel 1965).

Durkheim, even more than Marx, provides a structuralist theory of society. His very starting point is to distinguish the nature of society from the individual by arguing that human association creates an entirely new level of reality with its own properties. This realm of reality consists of social facts which are typical forms of the action of human beings, and they derive not from the individual who engages in them but from society itself, which is an external and constraining force upon the individuals who live within it. The original foundation of society is a collective consciousness – a collective body of ideas, values and norms – which binds the members of society into a community through their essential resemblance to one another, as the consciousness of the individual is only a reflection of the collective consciousness installed in each person. Thus Durkheim argues that the nature of social solidarity in simple societies is 'mechanical' and finds its expression and institutionalization in the detailed and comprehensive regulation of the activities of societal members through religiously based and repressive norms and values that sanction their behaviour on a penal basis. There is no individuality in this kind of society, so agency in regard to their own actions is not possible for its members: action is a totally communal phenomenon. However, in a process of historical evolution precipitated by population increase and new forms of communication in society, the nature of social relationships changes as an adaptive response through the emergence of the division of labour which differentiates out social activity within society and ties its members into reciprocal and contractual relationships in terms of the functional interdependence that arises between these activities. Thus a new form of social solidarity emerges, characteristic of complex industrial societies, which is 'organic' and entails a society whose members are bound together as a community by the social and economic ties of exchange that emerge from the performance of tasks and activities within the organizational system of the division of labour. The collective consciousness now shrinks and reduces its role in society as an adaptive response to the emergence of the division of labour to become the normative and regulative framework through which contractual relationships of exchange are established and sustained.

So, in the Durkheimian model of modern society, a system of social relationships is produced by the division of labour and the members of society come to participate in it by taking up positions and roles within it in terms of the tasks which it involves. They are, then, the functionaries of these roles and their actions are determined by how the performance of these roles is dictated by the institutional structures to which they belong through normative regulations and sanctions which are inculcated into the individual through processes of socialization and external constraint. The agency of the actor is confined to the performance of roles within an institutional context that regulates it. Yet Durkheim now comes to argue that the social differentiation produced by the division of labour in terms of the creation of specialized tasks and activities within society must of necessity create individuality since the performance of specific and special-ized activities by its members now comes to distinguish each member from any of the other members. Moreover, the weakened state of the collective consciousness in alliance with this can only create a degree of individual consciousness that is personal and not communal. Modern industrial society responds by elevating and institutionalising the value of individuality to give it a central position within its culture.

But Durkheim does not draw the conclusion from this that society and its structures and institutions are now constructed on the basis of individuals pursuing their own interests as agents of their actions. Rather he argues that just as individuality is a social fact that has been structurally produced through the division of labour, so the preservation of society depends upon the constraint of the individual and the control of the pursuit of self-interest. Too great an autonomy of the individual from the social group precipitates the disintegration of the community which depends on communal values and normative regulation to maintain the social ties between its members, and can even lead to the destruction of the individual himself or herself on the basis of suicide. Social relationships can only be maintained if the freedom of the individual is curtailed through the insti-tutional and normative regulation of social action by the community exercising constraint over the individual that ties him or her back into group life. The foundations of group life, then, are distinct from the indi-vidual and self-interest and are not dependent on the latter; and social existence, therefore, requires that the group remains external and controlling in respect of the behaviour of individuals within it through its structural organization and normative regulation of action. Agency, then, must give way to structure if society is to exist and maintain itself, which entails social control over the individual by society through an organized division of labour that maintains a particular structure of social relation-ships and that is underpinned by a collective consciousness as a regulatory framework for the activities and tasks performed within it.

Functionalism takes the Durkheimian argument about the systemic nature of society as an external and constraining force over the activities of its members even further in a structuralist direction. For functionalism, the structures and institutions of society emerge as an adaptive response to environmental conditions such as the scarcity of material resources, the unsocialized biological and psychological nature of the child, the problems of co-ordinating activities in a social way, etc. produced by the common culture of society in which the structures and institutions that emerge function to meet these conditions. It is not human agency, then, which creates structures and institutions but processes of natural selection in relation to the environmental conditions that generate them, and together they interlock into an autonomous system that is guided, through culture, by the logic of the adaptation of the social system to its environment. It is the functionality of structures and institutions in these terms that governs the ways in which they work and change, and social relationships are formed between the members of society through them as members come to participate in them by taking up positions and roles in their organization. The performance of roles is governed by institutionally based rules and expectations which are inculcated into individuals through processes of socialization and external sanction so they act in accordance with them. So structures and institutions are part of a larger system operating with its own functional logic that governs how activity is arranged within them, and the agency of individuals is constrained by the organizational and normative regulation of action within them on the basis of the sanction and reward of individuals for conformity. This is built into the individual through socialization processes. Without this conformity, structures and institutions would cease to function in a way that adapts society to its environment. Human agency, then, is required but its organization must necessarily be structurally determined in terms of the needs of the social system as represented by its institutional framework. Other than that, agency threatens a form of deviant action which could only attack the existence of society by undermining the necessary forms which the structural and institutional organization of social relationships takes and on which their functionality depends (Giddens 1976).

In contrast to systems theory in classical sociology with its emphasis on the autonomy of structures and institutions is the work of action theorists who emphasize the voluntaristic and interactional nature of social organization. Of these Weber is the chief protagonist. Weber argues that, ultimately, society is a collection of individuals whose **interactions** with one another constitute social life. Action is by its very nature subjectively meaningful to the actor in the sense that it is determined by the interests, purposes and values of the individual actor and it leads to social interaction only in so far as these are orientated to the actions of other individuals and conducted by them on this basis. So interaction, and therefore social relationships, are organized and thereby structured through shared interests, purposes and values and shaped by actors interacting with one another on this basis. In this way they come to form a community based upon such social organization. Institutions, then, such as the state and social classes are a way of talking about relationships among individuals and the kinds of ways in which as individuals they act, and are not autonomous entities. They have their basis in a shared orientation to the world which leads to the organization of action in terms of a particular rational organization of it which entails the selection of particular means to attain the ends of actors. It is the particular form in terms of which actions are organized on a means/ends basis that constitutes social structure, and institutions are the ways in which collectivities of actors establish fixed patterns of relationships between one another. So actors come to act in typical ways in terms of these institutions which are legitimated by their shared interests and values which motivate how they act.

Note that it is not socialization which mediates the relationship between institutional arrangements and the typical actions that take place within them, but a common commitment to shared values, interests and purposes (i.e. culture) on the part of actors which leads them to regulate and organize their interactions on a shared motivational basis. Consequently Weber is able to move from this discussion of the various ways in which action and interaction comes to be organized on a means/ends basis through shared interests and values on the part of actors to a discussion of larger-scale structures, institutions, societies and civilizations. Each of these social forms is a culturally and communally organized complex of social interactions that has been established historically on the basis of particular ways of formulating and legitimating interests in terms of values and constructing particular means by which they can be achieved. Indeed, Weber's interest in Western civilization consists in demonstrating how a particular form of the organization of action on an institutional basis grounds the nature of its structure and institutions, and he locates its sources in the Judaeo-Christian values of that civilization and its effects upon the understanding, formulation, creation and resolution of the practical problems of economic organization and political administration that the members of Western society necessarily had to engage with on a historical basis. But they did this as historical agents of their own lives, taking decisions and organizing their social activities on the basis of their own values, purposes, interests and needs. There is no direction to history other than that which emerges from the interaction of individuals as they pursue their interests and values and take decisions in the light of this, and human existence has no meaning other than that which the individual can give to it in terms of the values which he or she espouses and acts upon.

Yet Weber is forced to admit – and here a sense of the autonomy of *structure* emerges – that the outcome of purposeful action does establish patterns of its organization that were not necessarily intended by actors which shape the possibilities of consequent activity, and that, once in place, historical forms of the social organization of action may enforce themselves upon actors in society. The work ethic of ascetic Protestantism that was induced by the religious directives of a calling and predestination which created a disciplined way of life amongst Protestants, and that helped to create a basis for the rational organization of the capitalist economy, may have been an option for Protestants but is now enforceable on the inhabitants of capitalist societies by virtue of its legitimation within capitalism and the organization of economic and social life in terms of it. Equally so the technical efficiency and superiority of the bureaucratic administration of the organization of complex modern societies, once established, presents the members of such societies with no alternative and they must of necessity accept the basis on which bureaucratic administration works in terms of the organization of their activities. That social structure and institutions are a product of human agency on a historical basis, and are sustained by a continuous commitment to the values and forms of social action which they entail, does not preclude them taking on their own life and structuring social life in terms of this. Weber recognizes as much in his critical assessment of the rationalistic and bureaucratic nature of Western society which reduces its members to cogs in the machinery of the social organization which has been created by this civilization. Even for Weber, then, once structures and institutions have been created by human activity they establish conditions for action within it and cannot simply be changed at the will of actors. Yet ultimately they are what actors do together with one another on the basis of shared beliefs, purposes and means of organizing their relations amongst themselves. The autonomy and objectivity of institutions lies only in their interactional and therefore supra-individual character and not in their existence as entities which have some reality outside of this.

Simmel shares a similar position to Weber. Society is the web of interactions between its members that has its ultimate basis in their purposes and interests as individuals. But the realization of these through interaction organizes it into forms and patterns that achieve a quasi-autonomy over the ways in which individuals act. Although interaction always depends on the fact that individuals influence and are influenced by one another, this congeals in the reciprocal typification of one another's nature and activities on a shared and group basis that structures social relationships. Consequently social action is dictated in terms of these typifications as interactants see and are seen by one another as types of persons engaged in particular forms of action. In this sense the form of the organization of interaction structures the ways in which individuals relate to one another, and the more complex that form becomes within the major institutions of society the less individualistic are the ways in which it can be inhabited and the more impersonal are the relationships which constitute it. So the individual becomes a representative of the institution, occupying a niche within it. As social interaction is organized, identity becomes fixed by it and shapes relationships with others (Runciman 1978).

With symbolic interactionism (which is fully discussed in the chapter 'Active/Passive'), the organization of social life in terms of the subjectively meaningful nature of action and social relationships becomes more closely focused and analysed around the issue of how they are constructed and determined at the level of meaning by the actor as an agent of his or her own behaviour. But it is this paradoxical relationship between both the individual determination of action and its socially structured organization as the basis of the formation of community that becomes the starting point of two major attempts by sociological theorists to reconcile agency and structure with one another, namely the work of Talcott Parsons and Alfred Schutz.

Parsons begins by arguing that social life has its foundation in the goal-directed action of the individual which gives it subjective meaning for the actor, and it is directed and organized by the normative orientation of the actor, i.e. by the norms and values in terms of which the actor selects ends and chooses means for their achievement. So action is purposeful and rationally organized by the actor as an agent on a means/ends basis. But the isolated actor is a theoretical fiction because empirically human beings always live in society. Consequently human action can only be understood in terms of the fact that it takes place in the social context of the action of other actors. Necessarily these are interlinked because actors in the pursuit of their goals must face the fact of others in pursuit of the same, but under the conditions that actors need to gain one another's assistance and co-operation to achieve their goals because of the scarcity of resources relative to the wants of all actors. Consequently actors have to find a way of orientating and relating to one another which, Parsons argues, they come to do by developing reciprocal expectations about one another's actions. The more they interact, the more these expectations become fixed and standardized to the point at which they achieve an institutionalized status which now places the actors in a situation of double contingency *vis-à-vis* one another, namely that each actor must orientate not only to his or her own expectations of other actors but also to their expectations of him or her. These two sets of expectations interlock and so come to be the basis on which they interact.

In this way interaction turns into a self-sufficient and regulating system: it develops its own equilibrium because the interactants have a vested interest in maintaining the form of their relationship, for they derive rewards from it in terms of the satisfaction of their goals and this internally sanctions the system; and it has its own boundaries since the interactants will want to keep one another in line in order to maintain it, which gives the system external sanctions that are built into it. In these terms, then, the normative orientation through which actors organize their actions becomes communal in the form of an institutionalized set of reciprocal expectations, and their actions are regulated by this and actors are socialized into acting in accordance with it: this is the nature of the social basis of social action, i.e. the foundation of society. But more, this social organization of action has emergent properties which constitute it as a reality distinct from the individual and produce society, which are:

1 *culture* – a common set of norms and values shared by the interactants;
2 *structure* – an organized pattern of relationships between interactants in which they occupy positions and roles on the basis of how that culture prescribes their rights and obligations *vis-à-vis* one another and so shapes their actions; and
3 *personality* – selves formed by socialization in terms of the internalization of their rights and obligations.

Society works on the basis of a common culture which structures social relationships between its members and is maintained through ensuring its members' conformity through socialization backed by reward and punishment. Social action, then, is the product of society which has its foundation in voluntaristic interaction but is also a regulatory agency of action in itself because of the autonomy of the culture and structures that emerge through interaction.

Having established how interaction produces a system which is society, Parsons goes on to address its nature as a system and the logic in terms of which it works, which takes him in the direction of functionalism. He argues that it is located in an environment which is characterized by conditions of scarce resources, the unsocialized individual, the coexistence of individuals and the legitimation of norms and values which pose it with problems (what Parsons calls functional prerequisites) that have to be resolved for society to exist and maintain itself. This it does by developing specific institutions such as economic arrangements, political arrangements, religion, the family, etc. through its culture that function to satisfy these prerequisites, and these interlock in the ways in which they function to ensure that society is an integrated and functioning whole. Society, as a system, is adapted to its environment and changes as environmental conditions change. What is problematic, however, in this attempt to reconcile agency and structure is that, in treating society as an autonomous and regulatory system operating according to its own logic, Parsons comes to see action within it as determined by the system and the way in which it works. It is no longer the actor who is in charge of his or her actions: rather they stem from his or her position and role in institutions and structures which normatively determine action through socialization and external sanctions. Indeed agency must be controlled and set within certain limits by society because it poses the threat of deviant behaviour which would undermine the system and the conformity with collective norms and values on which it depends (Hamilton 1973).

The solution proposed by Schutz to the problem of the relationship of agency and structure in many ways follows Parsons but poses the societal institutionalization of social action in a different way that avoids treating society as a system which ultimately undermines the idea that human agency plays a part in its organization. Schutz offers a phenomenological reworking of action which concentrates on the way in which action is subjectively meaningful and how society is organized through intersubjective and shared meanings. What characterizes human action is its basis in the consciousness of the actor in which the action is determined and organized in terms of the project which the actor is seeking to fulfil through it and which arises from the biographical situation of the actor which is personal to him or her. This is what gives action subjective meaning. However, the actor is always situated in a social world which he or she recognizes as being composed of other actors and social scenes which are taken for granted as the natural and factual environment of his or her actions and into which action has to be fitted. Yet the factual nature of society, however much it is taken for granted by actors and accepted as a real world of facts and events by them, is actually created in terms of how they make sense of it and conduct their social relationships on this basis. What sustains its reality for them is the language which they use to describe and make sense of the social world and the ways in which this provides for a common sense of it, i.e. provides for a shared consciousness of it. Using language, the members of society are able to typify their experiences of the world and so construct the actions and events within it as realities. But in order to interact with one another, actors must arrive at a shared sense of the social world which typifies events and circumstances in the same way and so establish a common reality in which they can participate together. This they achieve in the form of common sense which is embodied in language and its use, and which creates a reciprocity of perspectives between actors which is able to discount the biographical differences between them and their personal consciousness to achieve a common consciousness of the world. This constitutes the knowledge of any person in the community about the social world, as opposed to the particular knowledge of particular people which derives from their personal biographical situations. This common consciousness is what counts as a common sense in society.

So the particularity of the consciousness of the individual is overcome by common sense through the use of language which allows the members of a linguistic community to recognize and account for the events of the social world in the same way and so to erect, typify and construct them as the facts of the social world which all of them share. So a shared consciousness, produced through the use of language, leads to the social construction of reality and establishes this reality as the objective environment for action within it through the social distribution and use of common-sense knowledge by the members of society. Using this common-sense knowledge, the members of society collectively type social scenes and one another in terms of their relative degree of familiarity and anonymity. They organize their relationships with one another in terms of reciprocal motivation, where the motivation of one actor to achieve his or her own end motivates the other actors to act in accordance with it in order to achieve their own ends. Common-sense knowledge provides a social vocabulary of typical motives in terms of which actors can understand one another's actions and their motivation and so make sense of them and consequently organize their social relationships.

Yet this social world which is constructed through shared common-sense typifications of it, and organized and structured as a world of interaction on that basis, can never become a reality that detaches itself from its interactional and constructed basis, however much it is taken as being an objective environment of facts, events and actions by its members. This is because, ultimately, the nature of social scenes is always a matter of negotiating their reality by the members of society as they interact with one another on a common-sense basis; and because interactants, however they organize action on the basis of reciprocal motivation, can never comprehend the actions of one another beyond the point of knowing and engaging with one another for all practical purposes. In other words, interaction and social life are always a continuous achievement on the occasion of inter-action, in which a practical sense of the situation and the actions taking place within it is arrived at by participants that is sufficient for them to organize and manage social relationships between themselves, but this does not eliminate the fact that ultimately action is motivated by the biographical situation of the actor which lies behind and goes beyond this. That actors can and do engage in intersubjective relationships which are socially organized on the basis of common-sense knowledge does not make them something other than individuals too, at the same time, with their own motives and purposes. It is only that they achieve them together through the use of common-sense knowledge which creates a shared sense of the reality of the social world, but this reality is negotiated and constrains action only on this basis of its negotiated character. So, for Schutz, society is indeed an objective, real and communal world for its members but it is actually constituted by its members on a continuous basis through the use of common-sense knowledge, as embodied in language, which they share with one another and bring to bear on one another's actions and the social scenes in which they take place on a practical day-to-day basis. It has a structure because the members of society structure the events within it and organize their relationships with one another through their common ways of making sense of it. It is the real and objective world in which they live but it is produced by their activities (Schutz 1972).

However, contemporary sociology would argue that the phenomenolo-gical sociology of Schutz offers an account of society which is altogether too subjectivist. It too turns to language to explain the organization of social life, but it tends to eliminate the subject altogether in terms of its sense of how social life is organized on this basis by emphasizing the determining character of language. Both structuralism and post-structuralism (which are more fully discussed in the chapter 'Modernity/Postmodernity') argue that human beings are communicating creatures using language. In these terms the world is a linguistic invention as language is a grid imposed upon the chaos of appearances. In this sense language does not correspond to things but is an arbitrary system of signs which only make sense within a total linguistic system, and linguistic systems differ from one another in terms of the codes on which they are based. Moreover, it is not that we speak language; rather it precedes and speaks to us as we learn it and thus determines our consciousness as human beings but unconsciously. It is not the intention of the speaker which determines what language means but the structure of that language, and this structure is based on an organized system of oppositions between words which determines their meaning in terms of their contrast with other words, e.g. red is red because it is not green, blue, etc., and not because it captures some essential reality which is redness. What can be said and have meaning in language is what the structure of that language permits, i.e. it is determined by the grammar on which that language is based. The relationship between words as signs and what they signify, then, is entirely arbitrary and constituted by language itself: it is part of the code with which that language operates and thus how that language codifies things and gives them meaning and reality.

Using this, and drawing upon Durkheim's late work which focuses upon the symbolic organization of social life, Lévi-Strauss treats culture as a language which structures and organizes society through representing its nature for its inhabitants and so determining the ways in which they can relate to one another. It is a language of mythology whose grammar constructs things in terms of the binary oppositions between events – the living versus the dead, human versus animal, male versus female, etc. – in which these contrasts allow the members of society to culturally represent and practically resolve the contradictions and conflicts that exist in their lives and their world. The meaning of these myths, then, is determined by the oppositions which are built into every myth and the oppositions between each myth and all of the other myths of a society's mythological system. It is the logic in terms of which they are organized as myths that gives them their meaning. So what the inhabitants who tell and listen to these myths think about them is irrelevant to their meaning since this is determined by their internal structure which gives them meaning through the pattern of oppositions which is generated by and in them. They have their own laws and these speak through the people who tell them and listen to them and thus organize their lives in ways of which they are unaware because they are subject to these laws. The source of the laws which govern mythology – the mytho-logic of myths – lies not in the intentions and consciousness of people, according to Lévi-Strauss, but is a function of the nature of the human mind itself which naturally thinks in terms of binary oppositions: the human mind is a mythological mind by its very nature because this is how mind works. Society is a product of an underlying system of relationships between its material and cultural elements that is mythologically languaged and thus structures and controls social relationships within it on this basis.

In contrast to the cultural structuralism of Lévi-Strauss, Louis Althusser produces a materialist structuralism which reconstructs Marxism in these terms on the grounds that it represents the true nature of Marx's thought. He argues that the social formations of society which constitute it are produced by the underlying system of interrelationships between its economic, political and ideological structures. Society, then, has a material existence. In this the culture of society may play a part in creating and reproducing the structures of society but as a material structure itself. Culture is the system of representations secreted by society: it expresses the way the members of society live, the social conditions of their existence, and so it determines their consciousness and subjectivity. But culture is ideology, and it is real but ideological because it is necessarily a false representation of existence. Although human beings cannot live without a representation of their world and their relationship with it, yet this social totality is opaque for the inhabitants who occupy a place within it, and so it needs to be represented mythologically in order to ensure the social cohesion of society. Ideology as culture is the social cement which binds the whole structure together by assigning specific roles in the political economy to individuals and getting them to accept and fill them and so become agents of it. But ideology is given to individuals in the same way as their economic and political relationships, and through its theoretical practices it operates as a structural condition which constitutes them as subjects in the social world by generating the form and content of their subjectivity. Ideology emerges from the mode of production of society and the class struggle and is an agent of class domination within society where the economic, social and political relationships of society can only maintain themselves under the forms of ideological subjection. In capitalist society, this maintenance of the social totality is achieved through the state apparatus (the bureaucracy, the judiciary, the military, etc.) by the ideological state apparatus (education, the family, etc., i.e. civil society): the former secures the political conditions for the operation of the latter. The ruling ideology of capitalism is concentrated in the latter which socializes and interpolates individuals into the existing economic, social and political relationships of capitalist society. Through this socialization, individuals participate in the ideological apparatus of capitalist society and become constituted as subjects through their subjection to ideology by their incorporation into its theoretical practices. The subject, then, disappears and with it human agency in society, since the individual is a product of the system and how it works and not a producer of it through his or her own conscious and purposeful activity.

Poststructuralist theory, such as that of Jean Baudrillard and Michel Foucault, retains this sense of the materiality of language and consciousness and the conditioning part it plays in the generation and construction of social reality, but it radically historicizes it. In doing so it rejects the conception of a unitary human nature to which structuralism commits itself and substitutes instead a conception of human nature as historically produced by the particular economic, political and social conditions of society which generate their own forms of life, knowledge and consciousness with their own internal constitution, logic and validity. In particular poststructuralism rejects the idea of the transcendent, conscious and self-determining subject, which lies at the heart of modernist Enlightenment and scientific thought, who constitutes the basis for the development of a universal and objective reason and knowledge and who is the agent of historical change. This is the version of individuality to which modern Western society subscribes.

udrillard, contemporary society is a postmodern society which is no
structured by production in which the individual conforms to its
eeds but by symbolic exchange. It is a heterogeneous society of different
groups with their own codes and practices of everyday life at the level of
discourse, lifestyle, bodies, sexuality, communication, etc., and it involves
the rejection of the logic of production and its instrumental rationality that
dominated the modernist society of capitalism. Capitalism now has been
replaced by a consumer society which is characterized by a proliferation of
signs, the media and their messages, environmental design, cybernetic
steering systems, contemporary art and a sign culture. It is a society of
simulations based on new forms of technology and culture. Signs now take
on a life of their own and come to be the primary determinants of social
experience. Signs and codes replace reality and the world is experienced
through images (simulation) to the point where the real as something
different from the image disappears. A world of hyper-reality is created in
which everything in the world is simulated in the sense that models created
by images replace the real, e.g. ideal sex in sex manuals replaces sex,
television news replaces the real news events themselves, politics is the
packaging of candidates etc.

So implosion is the key to the postmodern world in which a process of
entropy sets in: meanings and messages neutralize one another in a constant
flow of information, advertising, entertainment and politics. People are
sucked into a black hole of messages trying to solicit them to buy, consume,
work, vote, register an opinion, participate in social life, etc., to the point
where social divisions and distinctions are no longer evident. So the postmodern world is a world of simulation with no structures and boundaries,
an artificial creation in which reality disappears into a haze of images and
signs. Human agency disappears under the weight of signs and images
created by the technologies of postmodern society which function as mechanisms of social control over its inhabitants. Yet, even so, Baudrillard
suggests the possibility of agency in this kind of society through a counter-
cultural politics, particularly by marginal groups, that creates new cultures,
codes and everyday practices to challenge and change this society. But
ultimately he rejects politics (and, with it, human agency) on the grounds
that once knowledge entailed a demystification of reality, whereas now all
knowledge is simply interpretation with no secure foundation. All political
action could do is lead to a cancerous growth of interpretations which only
increases the hyper-reality of society. Nihilism and political cynicism, then,
are the only response that is possible for its inhabitants to adopt in such a
society as nothing of account can really be said and done in it (Bauman 1992).

From the perspective of Foucault, Baudrillard's focus upon the media,
consumption, fashion, leisure, etc. as contemporary mechanisms of power
and social control and reproduction really leaves the important structures of
postmodern society under-characterized. There is more to power and social
control than this. So, whereas Baudrillard shows how social differentiation

implodes through semiotic and media power, Foucault shows how discipline and power in modern society segregate, differentiate, hierarchalize, marginalize and exclude people in it. All societies are organized in terms of discursive practices which are knowledge-based systems of language embodied in social practices that have their own rationality and a historical foundation and constitute the basis of administration and control in them. So knowledge is power and a form of governance. Foucault calls postmodern society a carceral society based upon a moral technology of social control embodied in Enlightenment and scientific discourse and its practices, which submit the inhabitants of society and their bodies to control through their minds on the basis of particular ideas that are treated as possessing an objective universality and moral necessity. The form which this power takes is embodied in supervision and surveillance which exacts control through enforcing discipline on people. It entails a panopticon vision which, through its practices of organizing all social activities spatially (workshops, cells, hospital wards, etc.), collectively (factories, schools, barracks, etc.), controlwise (timetabling, scheduling, regularizing, etc.) and in terms of a hierarchy of supervision (delegation, ranks, etc.), creates a disciplined social environment that forms docile bodies by producing order through the supervision of every fragment of the lives of people in it via formal regulations and informal surveillance to make sure everyone conforms. This discipline, which is disguised in and by utopian values, is designed to create a moral transformation of the individual which makes him or her the hard-working, conscience-ridden and useful creature that is required by the tactics of production and warfare in the rational, efficient and technical contemporary society. It is a form of discipline and technology of control that thrives on normalizing judgement based on the rational and scientific knowledge perpetuated by academics and professionals, which analyses and categorizes human beings in particular ways and into which they are inculcated by its disciplinary and supervisory practices. It carries with it the right to punish people who do not fit into its categories of normality and sociality.

So knowledge and power come together in the production of the disciplined individual in all social activities in contemporary society through its discursive organizational practices, and this is the form of governmentality in it. Moreover, this disciplinary organization of contemporary society in terms of surveillance is anonymous, dispersed and comprehensive: it is not in the hands of any particular groups within society and all within society are subject to it. So knowledge is power and creates the subject (the individual) through its rituals of truth and practices of discipline and governance: it generates technologies of the soul through which the members of society inhabit it in terms of the enforcement and internalization of normalcy. There is no subject, then, other than that which the discursive practices of society produce, and so the idea of agency in the creation of society by individuals in terms of their conscious, purposeful actions is both naive and mistaken.

Yet Foucault is forced to recognize the possibility of resistance to the discursive practices of contemporary society and its forms of government by exploding the bases of the objectivity and legitimacy of the knowledge on which they are based, by showing its historical contingency and by demonstrating the power which is embodied therein. This entails the possibility of agency and self-determination in relationship to the discursive practices of modern society. It involves creating a discourse politics in which marginal groups can contest the straitjacket of normal identities imposed by hegemonic discourses to release differences that articulate people's needs and demands, and a bio-politics that reinvents the body by creating new modes of desire and pleasure. Both strategies risk marginalization and exclusion because the norms and rules of the dominant discourse define what is rational, sane and true, but both strategies carry the potential of new forms of subjectivity and values.

Moreover, in his late work, Foucault begins now to examine how individuals can transform their own subjectivities through techniques of the care of the self in which discipline may no longer necessarily be an instrument of domination. In this he contrasts Graeco-Roman ethics, in which desire was an area of human existence requiring moderation and self-control because of its potentially self-destructive nature, and in which it was admirable to turn one's life into a work of art through self-mastery and ethical stylization, with Judaeo-Christian ethics, which saw desire as evil by its very nature and as needing to be renounced and thus policed it through ethical interactions and rigid moral codification. Modern Western culture has perpetuated this in a new scientific mode. The former, then, entails an attempt to constitute oneself as a free self, and Graeco-Roman ethics offers us, in contemporary society, a model which can be drawn upon but not exactly repeated for the reinvention of the self as an autonomous and self-governing being as opposed to the self produced by the coercive and normalizing institutions of contemporary society. In arguing this the subject is not seen by Foucault as having an inner essence: it is still discursively and socially conditioned and situated within power relations. However, he now argues, individuals do have the power to define their identities, master their own bodies and desires and forgo practices of freedom for themselves but in a dialectical relationship to a constraining social field that seeks to impose limits on the individual. Self-mastery and stylized existence are how one can potentially maintain self-autonomy in relation to it, but this involves, too, the formation of oneself as a critical thinker and moral agent.

So the issue of agency and structure continues to remain a topic of contemporary sociological debate in the sense that every conception of social structure must ultimately reduce to what people do in society, yet society always consists of particular and institutionalized forms of the organization of these actions. These cannot work, however, without the commitment of actors to them. The question of structure and agency then is whether this commitment is simply enforced or entirely volunteered, and how it is possible for it to be a combination of both so that social structure is both achieved by and constitutive of social action. The point is: under what conditions and how does this occur?

KEY CONCEPTS

STRUCTURE This concept is central to sociology, it is usually employed to refer to any recurring patterns of social behaviour. Such behaviour, because it is common and regular, has a constraining effect on other people and we all tend to act in accord with the pressures exercised by social structure, e.g. we stand in queues; our relationships follow a common pattern.

AGENCY This concept is used to express the degree of free will that is exercised by the individual in their social action. We express our agency according to the degree of constraint we experience from the structure. Some people have less agency than others because of structural factors like poverty, and some circumstances create less agency for all, like an oppressive political state.

System A term usually used to describe a theory. Systems theory supposes that the social world is organized in terms of overlapping and interlocking systems that operate in a reciprocal manner. Thus society comprises the political; educational; occupational; economic; family and kinship systems and so on, and they all contribute to the whole. Such a theory implies a grand plan.

Structuralism This is a complex social theory that crosses a number of disciplines. It rests on the belief that at a fundamental level of mind all people share identical qualities. Thus whatever differences we produce, across space or time, in our languages, kinship patterns, myths, and customs, these are only surface differences. At a deep structural level all behaviour is reducible to a similar set of causes.

Functionalism This is an influential theory that developed in sociology and anthropology before the 1960s. It supposes that all social action and all social institutions operate with a purpose, that is, they function to the benefit of the totality. The causes of all behaviour can thus be explained in terms of function. Such a theory has trouble explaining behaviour that it sees as deviant, destructive and therefore dysfunctional.

Interactionism A social theory that does not presuppose the nature of society, rather it believes that people create meanings and reality in their day-to-day interactions and that such meanings depend upon affirmation in interaction.

Continuity/Change

Fran Tonkiss

How do societies change? Is there a set of principles which govern processes of change in different societies? Do changes in society *make sense*? Sociologists are continually setting themselves problems about social change – most of them not as abstract as these. When we examine the reorganization of family life, or analyse the role of women in the workforce, we are asking a set of questions about (amongst other things) social change. When we consider styles in fashion, or in cinema or in music, we are considering processes of social change. When we think about our object of study as *modern* society, or when we consider *traditional* institutions such as the Church or the monarchy, we are employing an implicit set of categories based on conceptions of social change and continuity.

This chapter considers different approaches within sociology to questions of continuity and change. The discussion is in three sections. It begins by looking at how the emergence of sociology as a discipline was closely tied to the recognition of a distinctly 'modern' society, one which was marked off from traditional forms of social life and was itself characterized by rapid and endemic processes of social change. Different theorists analysed the special character of modern society on the basis of certain axial principles – the key factors, that is, that shaped modern social forms.

Sociologists have developed a number of formal systems within which processes of change and mechanisms of continuity might be understood. The central part of this discussion identifies four broad 'models' for analysing change. Three of these – evolutionary approaches, functionalist approaches and conflict approaches – represent accounts which have been most influential within sociology. The fourth model – non-linear approaches –

indicates a more recent challenge to conventional methods of understanding social change, history and transition. This alternative way of viewing continuity and change poses a new set of problems for social analysis (Abrams 1982).

The final part of the discussion returns to the character of continuity/ change as an organizing dichotomy for sociological thought, and places this in the context of contemporary concerns and critiques. While classical theorists identified different precepts for the analysis of modern society, they shared a commitment to an idea of social progress. Descriptive accounts of social change were in this way set within an overarching narrative of progress in modern societies. This central notion has been seriously questioned within recent social theory.

While the validity of large-scale models of transition has been widely challenged, recent social analysis evinces a new concern with change in late modern societies. In particular, theories of post-Fordism and postmodernism have identified pronounced shifts in the spheres of economics and culture. Given the effects of globalization in each of these domains, it is unlikely that such changes will be confined to the societies of the capitalist 'core'. This presents contemporary sociology with something of a paradox. On the one hand, recent critical arguments have put into question sociology's attempt to impose analytic order on a rather disorganized social world. On the other, processes of change in an increasingly global society appear ever faster, more far-reaching, and more in need of analysis. It is in terms of such a paradox that the problem of continuity and change must now be placed (Giddens 1984).

SOCIOLOGY AND MODERN SOCIETY

The analysis of how and why societies change is one of the most basic and the most difficult concerns for sociology. As a discipline, classical sociology set itself the task of explaining the emergent form of modern society. Thinkers such as Comte, Marx, Durkheim and Weber sought in different ways to capture the specific character of the **modern**, and suggested how this might be distinguished from **traditional** ways of life. Our 'myths of origins' for modern society frequently involve seismic shifts in the organization of social life: the French Revolution, the Industrial Revolution, and the 'great transformation' from feudalism to capitalism in Western Europe. The fact that the latter two of these involved rather slow, incremental and patchy processes of change may immediately suggest some of the difficulties in analysing social change over a long period and on a large scale.

Many of the key categories which have informed sociological analysis – industrialization, urbanization, rationalization, technological innovation – centre on processes through which forms of social life come to be modernized. A twin concern with social *change* – the processes through which social forms are transformed – and *continuity* – the processes which maintain and reproduce a stable social system – has been an important feature of sociological analysis since Comte. Comte conceived of these dual processes in terms of laws governing social *dynamics* (producing change) and laws governing social *statics* (maintaining stability).

If classical sociology evinced a fascination with the rapid social changes brought about by industrialization and technical innovation, this was matched by a concern with social stability and order. Moreover, theories of change implied an interest in the future of societies, as well as in the relationship between past and present. The concept of **progress**, in particular, involved the projection of changes into the future, and was often linked to attempts to regulate and stabilize social change in this regard. This entailed a special role for the social sciences. If modern society was characterized by rapid and widespread changes, rational social science promised to render these observable, comprehensible and controllable. Social change, that is, might be harnessed in the interests of social improvement.

Such a concern with processes of social change and continuity has both descriptive elements, and logical or formal elements. In descriptive mode, sociologists provide practical accounts of the processes and effects of change in society. In formal mode, sociologists identify the structural properties or characteristics which work either to promote change in social forms, or to preserve their stability. A descriptive analysis of particular social changes, then, frequently draws on a more formal understanding of why societies do, or indeed do not, change. For this reason, the way in which we conceive processes and mechanisms of social change will be closely tied to how we conceptualize the formation of society and social structures.

Classical approaches to social change shared two general principles. The first of these related to the *scale* on which change occurred; the second concerned the *direction* of social change. Each was based on a particular conception of society, and a particular view of history. Nineteenth-century social theory conceived of society as a complex whole – a unitary, structured form. Thinkers such as Marx and Durkheim sought to identify the enduring and distinctive structures and institutions around which dynamics of change and stability might be modelled: in Marx's case, the mode of production; in Durkheim's, the division of labour. While different theorists focused on different elements as the catalysts for change or the mechanisms of social order, the assumption that change and continuity obtained at the level of a social *system* was generally shared. This assumption led sociologists to look for regular patterns of change in different societies, as well as laying the ground for large-scale comparative analysis.

The second conception shared among theorists of social change concerns the direction in which change takes place. A conviction that processes of change tend towards the improvement of the conditions of social life and the refinement of social forms is based on two major influences in the development of sociology. The first of these is an Enlightenment philosophy of history, particularly evident in the work of Comte. In this view, the present is located within a linear movement of history towards a future which is 'perfectible'. Human society, that is, is getting better all the time. This tradition of Enlightenment thought sees the development of human knowledge and the application of reason to human affairs as the basis for social progress.

The other influence derives from the impact of Darwinism on nineteenth-century social theory, offering an account of how social systems 'evolve' in terms of increasing complexity, differentiation and adaptation. These conjoined influences – theories of progress and evolutionism – were most apparent in the work of such classical thinkers as Spencer and Durkheim. While other approaches to social change and reproduction, particularly those influenced by Marxism and centring on issues of conflict and crisis, tend to reject an evolutionary and incremental model of social transformation, they nevertheless tend to rely on a linear conception of the direction of social change. Societies are seen to move *forward* through the development of instrumental capacities, social institutions and enlightened social values. Classical sociology in these ways placed dynamics of change and reproduction in modern societies at the centre of its analytic agenda. It also established a framework for analysis based on a large-scale or 'macroscopic' perspective, and an orientation to linear, progressive change. These core elements provide the backdrop against which we might examine different models for the analysis of continuity and change.

MODELS OF CONTINUITY AND CHANGE

For the purpose of this discussion, I have grouped approaches to social change and continuity within four broad categories. These categories are rather artificial, and are not mutually exclusive. I use them here as 'sorting' devices for a range of ideas about social transition and stability. The four categories are:

1 evolutionary approaches;
2 functionalist approaches;
3 conflict and agency approaches;
4 non-linear approaches.

Evolutionary approaches to social change

The most influential account of social change within classical sociology was one modelled on the natural scientific theory of **evolution**. Within this perspective, society is viewed as a complex totality whose parts are subject to a process of increasing differentiation, adaptation and specialization. Such an approach was an explicit response to the emergence of new social forms under industrial capitalism in Western Europe and North America. The two key processes involved in social change in this account are growth and integration. As a society 'grows' in population size and concentration, economic output and technical competence, different parts of the system become more highly specialized in terms of their function. Crucially, for evolutionary social theory, it is precisely this process of differentiation which integrates modern societies. As different functions, for example those relating to production and those relating to government, become more specialized, society is constituted as a system of interdependent parts, each fulfilling its necessary role.

For theorists of social evolution, increasing complexity at the level of social systems represents a logic of progress in human societies, in a manner which is analogous to the way that successful biological species adapt to changing conditions. Theorists such as Spencer, Durkheim and Hobhouse offered linear models of change marked by increasing adaptability and differentiation within social forms. For Durkheim, the complexity of modern society is based on an advanced division of labour, where work is broken down into a multiplicity of different activities, and individuals come to play quite distinct roles within the system of production.

In his account in *The Division of Labour in Society* Durkheim (1964a) argued that individual roles were becoming more highly differentiated as an outcome of social and economic development. Modern society was characterized by an increased 'moral density', where the social interactions of its members become more numerous, more frequent and more specialized. Such moral density promotes, for Durkheim, a form of 'organic solidarity' which holds society together as a complex totality. This is in distinction to the 'mechanical solidarity' typical of premodern societies, whose members are integrated in terms of very set social roles and a more basic structure of authority.

While these models are rather rudimentary, Durkheim did not see this transition in social forms simply as a 'great transformation' from traditional to modern society. Rather, the development of industrial society involved an ongoing process of differentiation, which at an extreme threatened to isolate individuals and dissolve the social bonds between them. At this point, social science had a role to play in suggesting mechanisms through which these processes could be controlled. Durkheim saw the advanced division of labour as creating a more complex network of social interdependencies, but he also identified the associated dangers of anomie, individualism and disorder which needed to be regulated by positive social policy reforms. Processes of change and differentiation in modern social forms, that is, needed to be managed in the interest of preserving social stability.

Although an evolutionist notion of social progress has been something of a guiding spirit for the development of theories of change, evolutionary models themselves have come to be held in disfavour. Two important strands of criticism have been levelled at evolutionary approaches to social change: the first is a political critique, and the second an analytic critique. Firstly, the idea that a more complex society is necessarily a more 'advanced' society, and the conflation of models of social and human evolution, establishes sometimes quite explicit hierarchies between different societies and social groups. 'Advanced' societies may be distinguished from 'backward' societies both in social structural terms and in cultural terms. Not least of the criticisms which may be levelled at social evolutionary principles is their use to legitimate certain racist and nationalist claims to superiority.

Aside from the pernicious political purposes which social evolutionism has at times served, at an analytic level evolutionary models have been challenged on the basis of their intrinsic theory of social forms. Evolutionary models posit a unified social totality: society, that is, is understood as a distinct and coherent entity. While society is seen as increasingly complex and highly differentiated, different levels of social reality are abstracted in the form of a unitary *system*. Evolutionary approaches are in this way committed to a large-scale or macroscopic view of changes within a social system, which cannot always account for changes at a more local level. The idea that societies advance via a smooth, linear logic of progress depends on taking a rather long view of social change. Taking a 'multi-linear' approach, on the other hand, highlights the uneven and often unequal manner in which change may occur, and puts into question a larger notion of 'progress'. We might consider this point in relation to different perspectives on industrialization. The conflation of modernity with progress, for example, tends to obscure the fact that there is no necessary link between the modernization of economic structures and the improvement of political systems or basic living conditions in many developing societies.

A macroscopic perspective may also miss the way that the effects of progress are not usually distributed or experienced equally within a social system. A feminist analysis of industrialization, for instance, would argue that women's labour was not decoupled from the household in the same manner, or at the same rate, as men's labour. And an emphasis on technological innovations, such as the spinning jenny or the lathe (or, indeed, the personal computer), reveals the 'lag' between changes in material culture and larger changes in social and cultural organization. Each of these perspectives challenges the even, linear account offered by evolutionary approaches to social change.

Functionalist approaches to social change

Evolutionary approaches, while they have been subject to serious criticism, have exerted a profound influence on the analysis of society and social change. The conception of society as a complex totality is perhaps the most important principle of sociological analysis which may be traced back to an evolutionist perspective, together with the latter's emphasis on linear social progress. A major offshoot of evolutionist theory in this century is represented by the functionalist account of social change.

Functionalist models of social change draw on a metaphorical comparison between social systems and biological organisms. The existence of a whole organism or system may be explained in terms of the relationship between its different organs or parts. Functionalism, that is, concerns the interrelationship between parts and wholes. Functionalism is not always demarcated from evolutionism, but may be distinguished in terms of its preoccupation with mechanisms of social order rather than logics of social change. While Spencer and Durkheim are seen as the classical forebears of functionalist thought, within twentieth-century sociology functionalism is most closely associated with the work of Talcott Parsons (Parsons 1966). Cybernetic and 'chaos' theories, which view social forms as complex, self-regulating systems, provide the most contemporary version of a functionalist social analysis.

In functionalist accounts, society is viewed as a self-equilibrating system, displaying an internal tendency towards social stability or balance. Parsons divides this system into distinct but interdependent structures or subsystems, each fulfilling a different role in the reproduction of social order: those geared to adaptation, goal attainment, integration and latency (the AGIL model). We might broadly, but usefully, think about these different subsystems as corresponding to the economy, the political system, social institutions and culture. Modern societies are in this way assumed to be constituted in similar ways, and to share a structural tendency towards equilibrium.

In a complex society, these subsystems are highly differentiated one from another, in terms of both the social functions they perform and the clarity of the boundaries between them. In modern societies, for example, the economic system is more clearly separated from the family than is generally taken to be the case in traditional societies (although this claim would be challenged by many feminist thinkers). Similarly, rational, technocratic government is rigorously demarcated from the realm of cultural values. For example, the government of a nuclear state may make a decision to conduct nuclear tests explicitly on technical and scientific grounds, setting aside ethical questions about the possession of such weapons.

Parsons distinguishes between processes which preserve and reproduce a stable social system, and those which transform social structures. Functionalist analysis has a special concern with those processes which maintain **equilibrium**, or *homeostasis*, within a social system. These processes involve the adaptation of particular subsystems to changing conditions, and the maintenance of distinct boundaries between them. Parsons suggests that homeostatic processes allow a social system to adapt to external changes (which might include interaction with other societies, or a changing economic environment) without radical social upheaval.

An example of the way in which particular subsystems adapt in a functional manner to change at another structural level is evident in Parsons's account of the nuclear family. Parsons argues that the small, loosely integrated unit is the typical family form in modern, industrial societies. This change in the social institution of the family is in line with two sets of conditions relating to the economic sphere. Firstly, within an industrial division of labour, production shifts away from the household as the basic economic unit. The space of the family and the space of work are separated. Secondly, economic roles and status increasingly come to be acquired through training, qualification and work experience, rather than being passed on through family structures. The individual gains greater economic independence from the extended family, and as a result extended familial bonds weaken.

As well as being an example of functional adaptation between different social structures (economic forms and the social institution of the family), Parsons's treatment of the family offers a linear model of social change – where economic modernization corresponds to more 'modern' social institutions. However this model, based on a study of North American society, may be challenged using comparative data. Ethnographic and historical accounts may be used to argue that the 'modern' conjugal family form was equally common in pre-industrial societies, both in East Asia and in Europe (see Chirot 1994: 126–7). While it may be true that the nuclear family form is well suited to the division of labour in an industrial economy, this does not simply indicate a logic of social progress.

Functionalist accounts may be criticized on four important levels. Firstly, they conceive of society as a bounded system. Societies are not organisms and do not have natural 'boundaries'. The use of a biological metaphor neglects the differences and fragmentation which occur *within* social groups, such as class and power relations, as well as patterns of interaction and exchange between societies. The second line of criticism targets the conservative nature of functionalist explanation. Functionalist analysis is chiefly concerned with processes which secure social continuity and equilibrium. On these grounds, it is unable to provide an adequate explanation for social change. What is more, by defining society in terms of homeostasis or equilibrium, functionalist approaches tend to preclude the possibility of radical change altogether.

Functionalism has been criticized, thirdly, for its relationship to a crude form of social evolutionism. In this connection we might refer to Parsons and Smelser's (1956) distinction between the characteristic structural formation, or 'pattern variables', of industrial and pre-industrial societies. The evolutionary impulse within many functionalist accounts has been well suited to a view of non-Western culture as premodern, pre-literate or pre-scientific. Fourthly, functionalism provides an 'over-determined' model of the individual, endowing them with minimal agency within a complex but ultimately self-regulating social system. It is this conception of agency, together with the functionalist emphasis on continuity rather than change, that is challenged by conflict theories.

Conflict and agency approaches to social change

The most vigorous challenge to functionalist accounts has come from conflict theories. This dynamic approach to change stresses social disorder and crisis, in contrast to functionalism's concern with order and balance. It also stresses the importance of social agents in bringing about change. Conflict models have been closely associated with Marxist analysis. Marx's own work was infected by a nineteenth-century conception of progress which he shared with the social evolutionists, and Marxist history is generally linear in orientation. However, Marx's account of systemic contradiction and revolutionary transformation marks his work off clearly from other nineteenth-century thinkers who viewed change as smooth, naturalized and cumulative. Later Marxists developed a notion of 'uneven development' to explain how societal transition did not occur at the same time, at the same rate, or to the same extent in different national and regional contexts.

A further strand of Marxist theory draws on Marx's concept of class struggle as the basis for social change. This recalls Marx and Engels's statement in *The Communist Manifesto* that 'the history of all hitherto existing society is the history of class struggle.' While conflict is embedded in the economic structure of class, it is realized in the practice of real social agents. Conflict theory has taken up this dynamic conception of social change, albeit in a context where Marx's own model of history and class conflict has been widely questioned.

An important intervention in these debates was signalled by Ralf Dahrendorf's *Class and Class Conflict in Industrial Society* (1959). Dahrendorf argued that Marx's model of class antagonism was no longer adequate for the analysis of modern industrial society. However, he retained the key concepts of class and conflict to analyse the more complex economic and social relations typical of advanced capitalism. Dahrendorf's work represented a critique of the conservative nature of functionalist analysis, as well as its tendency to locate change at the level of social structures rather than that of social actors.

Approaches to change which stress the role of human agency are not confined to class analyses. Indeed, liberal social theory places the rational individual actor at the centre of social processes, whether these involve change and transformation or the upholding of tradition and order. Other accounts of change stress collective action which is not reducible to class. The respective struggles of women, black women and men, and colonized peoples provide alternative models of resistance and change. Theories of 'new social movements' have developed since the 1960s in order to analyse such collective agents as peace, environmental and gay rights movements. These draw at least as much from feminist and civil rights models as they do from class theory. The widely celebrated role of 'people power' in the collapse of Soviet communism, however partial an explanation, provides a clear example of the importance of human agents in effecting social change.

These alternative models of agency depart from a class-based approach not simply in identifying a different set of actors, but also on a more fundamental level. Marxist analysis remains wedded to an overall logic of change, located in the economic structure of class. However, theories of new social movements, of popular struggle and especially 'people power', are less firmly grounded in a general explanation of how and why societies change. If the working class, or (less often) women or black people, have been seen as the agents of a historical process which is in some sense over-determined, social movements which form and reform around single issues, shared lifestyles or social networks put into question this larger logic of social change.

Non-linear approaches to social change

Evolutionary, functionalist and conflict theories bring important differences in emphasis and analysis to the study of social continuity and change. Evolutionary theories focus on a smooth and cumulative model of progress; functionalism emphasizes the processes which maintain social order and adaptation between parts; conflict theories stress the dynamic and dis-ruptive character of social change, including the role of social actors. What these approaches share, however, is a linearity in the *direction* of change. In each case, processes of social change and mechanisms of social order are located within a general logic of progress.

The fourth category under which we might consider theories of con-tinuity and change – that of non-linear approaches – is a particularly diffuse and disparate grouping. These approaches are defined more clearly in terms of their resistance to a logic of social progress than on the basis of a common theory of change. They may also be more useful for explaining apparent 'reversals' or 'declines' as aspects of social change.

These types of explanation construct models alternative to those based on a linear conception of progress. Cyclical and 'rise-and-fall' theories, for instance, offer a different way of describing the patterns in which change occurs. Such models have been most widely used to explain economic cycles or 'waves' – as in the Great Depression, or the boom–bust cycle of successive periods of growth and recession since the Second World War. While these models allow a sharper analytic focus on distinct cycles in economic development, they do not in themselves disrupt a larger logic of progress in capitalist societies. However, it may be possible that other cyclical approaches to social change are becoming more relevant and more useful for contemporary sociological analysis in ways which put into question the long-held association between change, modernity and progress.

Notions of 'progress' have been seriously challenged on both conceptual and political grounds, and these criticisms appear to gain increasing support from a range of social and cultural changes in contemporary life. To take a large-scale example, the collapse of communism in the Soviet Union has been followed by a process of what is frequently called nationalist or ethnic 'revival' – a *return*, that is, to what are construed as traditional or premodern customs, affiliations, languages and practices. On a similarly large scale, religious revival may be seen as a global phenomenon, not only in terms of the growth of fundamentalist groups within the major world religions, but also with the proliferation of diverse sects and alternative forms of spiritualism.

These non-linear approaches to social change operate on different scales and in a number of social domains. Aspects of the environmental movement are associated with a return to premodern values which suppose a more holistic relationship between people and nature than that typical of technical, scientific and rational modern society. In the 1980s, the British government encouraged a return to a system of 'Victorian values' which would place greater emphasis on family life, personal industry, charity and civic principles than was thought to be evident in the late twentieth century. The recent 'backlash' against feminist ideas and programmes in a number of Anglophone societies involves a critique of 'progressive' views of gender roles and relationships.

This is not to suggest, in any of these cases, that the traditional values and practices which are being 'revived' are necessarily more authentic or more socially desirable than the effects of 'progress' which they displace. Indeed, the notion of tradition does not simply indicate a self-evident realm of values, attitudes and behaviour, but emerges in response to a particular representation of the ways that society has changed. However, each of these examples puts into question our attitudes to the present, our relationship to the past, and our ways of imagining the future. The language and the categories of analysis which we use to understand and explain our social experiences are challenged.

This observation raises a further issue about the manner in which change is conceived and represented within social theory. Do non-linear approaches suggest that the nature of change itself has altered, or is it the case that change in society will appear differently depending on how it is filtered through particular analytic models? The primary mode of explanation within sociological accounts of change has been concerned with questions of causality, seeking to identify the conditions or factors which produce processes of change. A logic of cause and effect, however, is put into question by a non-linear approach to social change.

An emphasis on the 'discontinuity' of social change is particularly associated with the work of the French philosopher and historian Michel Foucault (Foucault 1984). While Foucault had an interest in the differential character of historical periods – the ancient, the classical and especially the modern – his concern was not to locate these as phases in an overarching logic of social progress and transformation. Rather, these might be seen as historical moments which evinced particular constellations of ideas, practices, institutions, and what Foucault called 'discourses' – the formal systems of knowledge which help to organize different domains of social life. Foucault's analyses, which have gained increasing influence within sociology in recent years, concentrated on such domains as medicine, psychiatry, deviance and punishment, and sexuality. In each of these cases, Foucault examined the local processes, structures and ideas which formed and transformed these domains within the early modern period.

This approach issues a serious challenge to the notion of historical explanation in social science. Foucault's work does not simply offer a local analysis of social changes which may be inserted into an overall systemic logic. Rather, he rejects the emphasis on large theoretical systems, and stresses instead the irreducible character of distinct patterns of disruption and change. For example, while Foucault suggests that nineteenth-century transformations in the regulation of people's bodies (in relation to such things as their health, their hygiene and their sexual conduct) helped to produce a sober and industrious workforce, he is opposed to the idea that these social changes may be explained as effects of capitalist development. In rejecting the relevance of causal explanation for his own form of analysis, Foucault subverts the central mode of explanation in the social sciences: that which seeks to establish a relation between social causes and effects.

In this approach, change might be thought of in terms of *discontinuity*: disruptions and alterations in social organization which are not easily reduced to an underlying causal logic. Social change, in this conception, is seen as arbitrary, accidental or unpredictable. What, then, might be the implications for a contemporary sociological account of continuity and change? (Crook et al. 1992).

CONCLUSION: A 'FUTURE' FOR SOCIAL CHANGE?

The challenge to linear conceptions of social change fits in with a more general critique of the idea of progress (Hall and Gieben 1992). To a significant degree, theories of social change have been developed within sociology in relation to processes of modernization, and have taken the characteristic features of modernization as the central elements of their models. The transition from feudalism to capitalism, the social effects of industrialization and urbanization, and the systemic upheavals associated with periods of revolution have been centrepieces of analysis of social change.

This concern with logics of continuity and change has served to reinforce certain assumptions that have helped shape sociology as a discipline. If modern society was characterized by the classical sociologists in terms of rapid, complex and radical change, its implicit 'other' was a premodern society which was understood to be fixed, simple and unchanging. This distinction served to underpin discourses of 'backwardness' in relation to non-Western societies and to promote Western models of industrial development. It also produced a particular account of modern society which did not always recognize the coexistence of 'traditional' and 'modern' elements, or the manner in which change may occur in quite unpredictable and even regressive ways.

An interest in processes of social change has, arguably, gone into something of its own decline within contemporary sociology. This is clearly not because social change no longer takes place (although theories about the 'end of history' have enjoyed a certain vogue of late), but because sociologists have become subject to a kind of scepticism about their ability to analyse large-scale processes of change. The construction of 'grand' theoretical models for explaining social change (such as that offered by Marxist historical materialism) is generally not considered viable as an analytic tool, being too abstract, too unwieldy, too insensitive to the richness of social detail, too arrogant in the assumption of its own explanatory power. The 'order' which is established by the use of such theoretical constructs is seen to derive from the model itself, rather than accurately representing any underlying pattern of social progress. Such analytic models, that is, impose order on a world which might be better understood in terms of disorder, disjuncture and accident; and which is in any case irreducible to a single axial principle, such as the system of production.

Is there, then, a 'future' for theories of change? Problematics of continuity and change continue to preoccupy sociological analysis. Is consumer capitalism fundamentally different from industrial capitalism? Are we, or are some of us, now living in a postmodern age? Is the nation-state still relevant? How is new technology reshaping social forms?

These questions are large ones, but if a set of principles were to be established for how they might be studied, perhaps most importantly this would involve a sensitivity to questions of *scale*. An interest in the local effects of social change, in the diverse connections between different factors, places and agents, offers a descriptive richness which can be missed by broad-brush theories of change.

The other principle of analysis which may have to be reconsidered concerns the *direction* of change. A more developed focus on the cycles, rhythms and contingencies of social change departs from a universal logic of progress. This would avoid a tendency to see local continuities in terms of social stasis or inertia, of conservatism or 'backwardness'. Other factors which did not appear to fit a linear model, such as religious revival in secularized societies, would not appear as aberrations or historical hangovers within a larger pattern of forward movement. Questions of scale and of direction, therefore, remain central to sociological accounts of change. However, criticisms of large-scale attempts to analyse social transitions suggest that each of these principles should be approached in a quite flexible manner. Patterns of change tend to look the same only when viewed from a great height; more particular and contextual analysis stresses the distinctive and irreducible character of social events, processes and actors. Social change is still a key concern for sociology; it does not, however, always happen in the image of sociological models.

KEY CONCEPTS

CONTINUITY The state or quality of things being continuous in society. The idea that we can rely on a certain stasis and stability in the order of things from one day to the next. Our laws, rules, means of communication and forms of understanding depend on this.

CHANGE The idea of discontinuity between historical moments. Of course change is happening all of the time in as much as what I do today is not the same as I did yesterday, but some change is more significant and some more lasting than other change e.g. revolution; war; votes for women. Sociologists study the causes and significance of change.

Modern This is largely a way of describing societies that have evolved through industrialization, urbanization and capitalism. Apart from these major structural changes we also note a change in the attitudes and beliefs of modern societies.

Tradition This is a way of referring to pre-modern societies, the ancient and the feudal. Tradition is also a way of referring to those elements of the past that are important and kept alive in the present. Thus all academic disciplines have traditions otherwise we would only be studying yesterdays findings.

Progress The idea that change is for the good. To progress is to move forward positively. A problem with evolutionism is that it confuses growth and progress.

Evolution A theory originally developed by Darwin to account for the way that organisms change strategically in order to adapt to changes in their environment, those that do not change do not survive. In relation to societies the theory implies that we are all adapting to social change in the same ways. In an earlier stage of social science people believed that 'simple' or 'primitive' societies were evolving towards 'civilization'.

Equilibrium   The state of affairs where all parts of a system are perfectly balanced and thus ensuring the perfect functioning of that system. Any one sided development or malfunction within a system can cause the system to change, distort or collapse.

Fact/Value

Sue Stedman-Jones

> Whether he wants it or not, or whether he is aware of it or not, anyone who spends his life studying society . . . *is* acting morally and usually politically as well.
>
> C.W. Mills, *The Sociological Imagination* (1970: 90)

The fact/value dichotomy is one of the most fundamental in the social sciences: it enters into the issues of objectivity and commitment at all levels of methodological, theoretical and moral practice of social science. Sociologists are interested in accurate, unbiased descriptions of social phenomena, in a theoretical framework that reveals the social world in its true nature. To present one's own values as fact is bias, if not propaganda, whilst to confuse fact with value is prejudicial to the interests of objective research. Sociologists are concerned about the moral implications of their outlook and practice. Does their research support illegitimate regimes? Does their theory support the status quo and justify sexism and racism? It is clear that the issue of value and fact raises questions central to a human science: those of **objectivity** in scientific knowledge and the basis of critique and practical activity.

A PRELIMINARY DEFINITION

But what is meant by fact and what is meant by value? It is important in this area to start with a simple definition that can help us in the discussion.

A classic factual statement is 'It is raining outside.' This statement is either true or false according to a certain state of affairs, which is independent of the statement and which can **confirm** or disconfirm it. It is an observational statement: it is based on evidence that is observable. Further it is **empirical**: the state of affairs, the rain outside, is evident to our senses; we can see the rain, and if we were to go outside we would get wet. This state of affairs is neutral *vis-à-vis* my feelings about it. It just is so: it is what the philosopher Hume called a brute fact. I could be glad about it after a long period of drought, or I could be annoyed because I wanted to play tennis. Neither of these make any difference to the truth of the statement. Most importantly, it is independent of any decisions I may make about rain. Give or take the value of raindances, it doesn't actually make any sense to say that I have decided that it should rain this afternoon; one may hope, but one's decision cannot bring about the rain. Finally this state of affairs is shared and public: we are all getting wet in the bus queue. The nature of a fact is shown by these features of a factual statement: it is observational, empirical, independent of feelings, decisions and choice, and is public and shared.

These are in contrast to certain features of values and value judgements. Values range from simple preferences, through aesthetic judgements, to supreme moral and political choices that are crucial both to our life and to the maintenance of society. A preference could be, for example, 'I prefer cherries to apples.' This refers to a liking for one fruit rather than another; I like cherries, but Jane loathes them. There is nothing inherent in the nature of cherries that entails that one person loves them and another person hates them. This variability of taste preferences leads to the adage *de gustibus non est disputandem*, 'there can be no dispute about taste.' Many believe that this can be generalized to cover all value judgements. Already we can see that there is a difference from a fact here. No one would doubt the judgement of someone who hated cherries, in the way they would doubt the judgement or indeed sight of someone who denied that it was raining when it was. There would appear to be nothing in the nature of the object referred to that authorizes or legitimizes only one valid response to it.

This quality becomes more problematic when we move on to aesthetic judgements. I may say that Picasso is the greatest of painters or that Bach is the greatest of composers. I may cite certain features of *Guernica* – the lines, the form, its political and moral strength – as support for my judgement. Equally I may cite certain features of the 'St John Passion' as evidence of Bach's compositional skills. Indeed many people would agree with me. But there is nothing to prove that someone who holds the opposite view is quite simply wrong or needs to visit a doctor. Disputation about the greatness of artists is a central part of disputation about the nature of aesthetic values and ideals. David Hume said:

> Euclid has fully explained all the qualities of the circle, but has not in any proposition said a word of its beauty. The reason is evident. The beauty is not a

quality of the circle. It is only the effect which the figure produces upon the mind, whose peculiar structure renders it susceptible of such sentiments. (1961: 291)

I have a right to my opinion, which has something to do with my outlook, my judgement and the choices which I make. So when we come to what Max Weber called ultimate evaluations there is a strong element of choice: if I decide that life is worth living, I have chosen to hold the value of optimism. If I have decided that I would rather die than submit to tyranny or oppression, then I have chosen the values of freedom and democracy over life itself. This element of choice is central to moral and political choice. I choose whether to vote Labour or Conservative – and if I can choose then I must be free in some way. But there is a further element of moral and political values that some have argued is their defining feature. We think here that something ought to be the case: governments ought not to oppress their people, democratic values ought to prevail in the world. I think that I ought to tell the truth and I ought to repay debts. This quality of 'ought-ness' about moral values means that the logic of moral values is quite distinct from empirical judgements and indeed aesthetic values. It is the quality of obligation that for the philosopher Kant in the eighteenth century indicated the area of morality and is proof of its reality. So for Durkheim obligation is a defining feature of morality.

The concept of value thus covers a wide range of cases, from simple and unimportant preferences to supreme moral and political choices that lie at the heart of one's life. The quality of value is indicated by the nature of moral judgement. Here we are apparently in the presence of a judgement rather than a statement. And this judgement expresses either a preference or a choice. This means that in contrast to a classic observation statement, these judgements are subjective in the sense that they have something to do with me as a person – my tastes and my choices – and therefore they are not necessarily public or shared in the same sense as an observation state-ment. Not everyone likes cherries, admires Picasso or is a democrat. That is, values are in some sense connected to my subjectivity, my individuality and to choices and decision in a way that factual matters are not. Lastly and most importantly there is a strong emotive component to values that is absent from factual areas. We care passionately about moral and political values.

The difference between these two types of things means that we should really keep them separate in our thought and reasoning. But do we?

In every system . . . which I have hitherto met with . . . I have always remark'd, that the author proceeds for some time in the ordinary way of reasoning . . . when of a sudden I am surpriz'd to find, that instead of the usual copulations of propositions, is and is not, I meet with no proposition that is not concerned with an ought, or an ought not. This change is imperceptible, but it is, however, of the last consequence. For as this ought, or ought not, expresses some relation or affirmation, 'tis necessary that it should be observ'd and explain'd; and at the same time that a reason should be given, for what seems altogether inconceivable, how this new relation can be a deduction from others, which are entirely different from it. (Hume 1967: 469)

This statement from the eighteenth-century philosopher, has acquired axiological status in almost all discussions of the relation between fact and value. It has become known as Hume's law. It tells us two things. Firstly, we must not confuse fact and value: they are two quite different things in relation to propositions and reality. Secondly, we cannot derive values from facts. These raise two quite separate problems for the social sciences. The first is part of the problem of objectivity. It raises the question of what are facts and what are values and how they can be kept separate in theory and research. The second relates to the problem of **commitment** – theoretical, moral or political. But if values are not to be derived from facts, where do they come from and how do we justify them?

Is the relation between fact and value dichotomous? Dichotomy means an unbridgeable logical gap. Here, it indicates a logical gap that is crossed at one's scientific and moral peril. But, as such, it is a dichotomy that many philosophers and social theorists have attempted to at least justify, if not modify or even transcend, in the interests of morality and social science. The issues raised are these. If fact and value are not connected, why do we point to certain states of affairs to justify our moral beliefs? Can any one seriously look at the Holocaust and its untold suffering and its millions of deaths and not morally condemn fascism? Is there not here demonstrated an essential connection with certain facts (the condition of people in concentration camps) and certain moral judgements (that this is to be condemned as inhuman and barbaric)? Are there no values associated with the empirical practice of social science? Are there any further moral and political values to being a sociologist? Or should sociology be value-free? That is, it raises the problem of the relation between values and social research in its broadest aspect.

MAX WEBER: FACT/VALUE AND VALUE FREEDOM

Max Weber established the classic position of the dichotomous nature of fact and value in the elaboration of his doctrine of value freedom (*Wertfreiheit*), in 'The Meaning of Ethical Neutrality in Sociology and Economics' (1917). Weber holds that there are two distinct spheres: that of facts and that of values. This is for him a metaphysical position which entails a logical disjunction between statements of fact and statements of value. The sphere of facts, whether relating to the physical or the social, is the subject matter of science, because it can only be dealt with by the observational methods of science. Questions relating to the sphere of facts and therefore the empirical sphere of science include: what phenomena exist in the world, what law-like relations exist between them, and what explains them? On the contrary, 'Value judgements are to be understood, where nothing else is implied or expressly stated, as practical evaluations of the unsatisfactory or satisfactory character of phenomena subject to our influence' (Weber 1949: 1). What follows from this

> is the intrinsically simple demand that the investigator and teacher should keep unconditionally separate the establishment of empirical facts (including the value orientated conduct of the empirical individual whom he is investigating) and his own practical evaluations i.e. his evaluation of those facts as satisfactory or unsatisfactory (including among those facts evaluations made by the empirical persons who are the objects of investigation). (1949: 11)

This follows because 'These two things are entirely and logically different and to deal with them as though they were the same represents a confusion of entirely heterogeneous problems' (1949: 11). All evaluations about the facts must be excluded from the sphere of science; all recommendations for action must be presented as extra-scientific.

These issues were developed in his earlier article '"Objectivity" in Social Science and Social Policy' (1904). This article was written partly in relation to questions of editorial policy of the journal *Archiv für Sozialwissenschaft und Sozialpolitik*, which raised the question of the relation between value judgements and empirical material. He supports 'The logical distinction between "existential knowledge" i.e. knowledge of what "is" and "normative knowledge" i.e. knowledge of "what should be"' (1949: 51). In this Weber opposes objectivism in general and historicism in particular. The first is a general position that is maintained by a number of thinkers in various ways. It holds that what is 'normatively right' is identical with 'the immutably existent' (1949: 51). The second holds that what is right is identical with what emerges in the historical process. Giddens (1993) maintains that Weber was in particular attacking theories of natural right and Marxist theories of history. These two positions confuse fact and value. And further they derive values from facts: that is, they believe that principles of right action should be derived from facts. For Weber, 'It can never be the task of an empirical science to provide binding norms and ideals from which directives for immediate practical activity can be derived' (1949: 52). Theories of natural right and Marxist theories of history each involve an illegitimate extension of empirical knowledge. The distinction between fact and value is associated with the distinction between means and ends. Empirical knowledge can help us determine which means might be the best way to achieve any end: it can help us to decide on the practicality of any means or indeed the consequences of following any particular line of action. It can never determine ends of action for us. Final or ultimate evaluations can only be the lonely and subjective decision of each individual thinker.

The distinction between fact and value is especially important in the social sciences, for Weber, because these concern human action. Whatever our preferences we must acknowledge the existence or truth of certain forms of social life. The study of human action rapidly becomes political when moral judgement is applied to it, and in the interest of the dispassionate study of the social we must avoid the emotional pressures involved in the political. This was particularly important in the German universities during the First World War when Weber's article was written. Gouldner (1973) argued that Weber was concerned with the freedom of action and integrity of the state and particularly the university, as part of Western rationalism. The state might be impelled into censoring the university, and therefore compromising its autonomy, if political judgements were expressed from the university platform. It is interesting to note that Weber, who might otherwise appear a liberal in moral and political views, argues, according to Gouldner, that professors are not entitled to freedom from state control in matters of values, because these do not rest on academic specialism (1973: 9).

Weber is keen to distinguish himself from 'pseudo-ethical neutrality'. He does not hold that the teacher or the thinker should have no values: unfortunately he is often portrayed in this fashion. Ethical neutrality in the strictest sense would indicate a thinker who had not developed an ethical position, and for Weber this would be a person who had forfeited the necessity for rational moral self-determination. This latter concept is an important element of Weber's position. He believed that real ethical decision is private, individual and lonely. In other words, showing that all evaluation is extra-scientific for Weber does not entail moral indifference: 'An attitude of moral indifference has no connection with scientific objectivity' (1949: 60). It does follow from his views that someone with no principles or values and with an indifference to suffering or the great importance of human life, for example, is going to be a more objective researcher. Indeed for him the logical separation between facts is the precondition of both meaningful moral argument and scientific objectivity. It is because morality is so important to him that it must be kept separate: it is a matter of individual subjective choice, for the thinker concerned.

Rather, the factual and the evaluative must be kept clearly separate, because only the sphere of fact is capable of objectivity and can therefore be part of science. Weber insists that evaluations, in both teaching and research, must be shown to be the choice and determination of the thinker concerned. Good teaching and research involve the clearest exposition of the empirical material and clearest representation of the values of the thinker and the 'value relevance' that governed the choice of empirical material.

There are certain issues that clearly immediately stem from this. Firstly, is Weber's characterization of moral decision accurate: does it imply the irrationality of ethics? Secondly, how sociological is the separation? And thirdly, is there really a strictly empirical, value-neutral realm of fact that constitutes the kernel of a science and is the cornerstone of its objectivity?

VALUES AS IRRATIONAL?

Firstly, this view of the nature of moral decision was influenced by different philosophies. Giddens (1993) believes that it was Kant rather than Hume who influenced Weber. On the contrary, I suggest that it was neo-Kantian German thought that influenced him, rather than Kant himself. It was a tendency of neo-Kantian thought in Germany to more greatly emphasize the split between science and values than Kant. Both science and ethics were aspects of reason for Kant. Reason was not limited to science; he did not make morality the matter of subjective choice and faith that is finally irrational for Weber. He held that certain ethical positions could be established objectively, i.e. as universally shared by all rational beings. For him this follows from the nature of practical reason (Kant 1964). This is quite different from Weber's position which holds to the subjectivity of values and their irreconcilable nature.

Brubaker in *The Limits of Rationality* (1984) shows that Weber's position leads to 'the ethical irrationality of the world'. The subjectivity and relativity of value orientations leads to a value clash, because values are inner to individuals: they are subjectively generated and therefore can only claim subjective validity. This clash of value orientations is part of the struggle for meaning in the modern world. That there is no rational resolution of value conflict is part of Weber's dark vision of the modern world. Giddens points out that value conflict is in turn associated with his stress on the primacy of power and power struggles in social development. Different systems of cultural values cannot be resolved by a demonstration of the rational superiority of one over the other, but only by the power of a group to impose its will on those different from itself. This conception of ethical irrationality is for certain thinkers (Kant and Durkheim, for example) a major problem, not the solution to modern moral and political dilemmas.

THE PHILOSOPHICAL BACKGROUND TO THIS DEFINITION OF VALUE

The other features of Weber's thought were certain elements of empiricist and positivist thought. From Hume in the eighteenth century to the twentieth century, a characteristic of this is that only logical and empirical statements are capable of any verification and therefore of objectivity. Values are therefore subjective and non-verifiable. Added to these influences is that of Nietzsche and existentialist thought, where it is held that morality is a matter of individual faith or affirmation. Wilhelm Hennis argues that Weber was influenced by Nietzsche's 'ethic of distinction' (1988: 150). If it is indeed the case that Weber was influenced by Nietzsche's 'genealogy of morals', then he cannot have failed to note the distinction between slave morality and the free affirmations of those who have lost guilt and bad conscience.

Under this interpretation, there is a huge difference between Weber and Kant and Durkheim. Weber, like Kant, believes that we must be free when we decide on a moral action. However for Kant this freedom is rational in the sense that the action must be compatible with a rule that could be undertaken by all: it must make sense as a general rule of behaviour. On this basis, lying cannot make sense as a general rule of action for it cannot be consistently acted on. Further for Durkheim all morality must be considered in terms of solidarity. The total moral relations between persons in society make up the 'objective sphere' in which all moral judgements must be finally assessed. Here then heroic affirmations must be subject to a wider court of appeal. This consideration must limit features of subjectivity and loneliness that characterize Weber's account of moral decision-making. Further if there are considerations that go beyond the subjective loneliness of the moral agent, then we have to consider whether the radical split between value and fact can be maintained, in the sense that value is subjective and fact is objective.

From a philosophical point of view, much work in modern moral philosophy has denied the logical gulf between fact and value that Weber's distinction so relies upon. Certain general lines of argument establish that there can be no absolute gap between what is evaluative and what is factual – particularly in relation to morality. Morality concerns some fundamental conceptions, like goodness or welfare or even happiness, that are not reducible to the private choice of the individual. These constitute limits on what can plausibly be called moral action. These thus constitute 'bridge notions' between values and facts, and allow one to derive values from facts in certain instances.

HOW SOCIOLOGICAL IS THE DISTINCTION?

It is important to consider just how sociological this account of value is. It is characteristic of a Protestant culture, which stresses the individual conscience as the arbiter of values at the expense of wider institutional frameworks of value authentication. If Weber's account bears such cultural baggage, it would be simply ethnocentric to take this as the arbiter of all accounts of value and its social relations. For Durkheim values are part of a wider framework – the totality of social relations – and as such the validity of each value decision must to some extent be arbitrated in terms of a wider framework than my own private choices. For this reason, he disputes the separation of fact from value in his paper 'Value Judgements and Judgements of Reality' (1911): 'There is not one way of thinking and judging for dealing with existence and another for estimating value' (1974b: 95). Both are aspects of judgement and all judgement involves ideals. 'The function of some is to express the reality to which they adhere. These are properly called concepts. The function of others is, on the contrary, to transfigure the realities to which they relate, and these are the ideals of value' (1974b: 95). Ideals are not cold abstractions which the individual determines alone, for behind them lies the power of the collective. For this reason they are dynamic and capable of transforming reality (1974b: 93).

COMMITMENT AND SOCIAL ANALYSIS

One of the most important conclusions of Weber's position is that considerations of justice in society must be excluded from the objective and empirical aspect of sociology, which must be value-free. In this Weber is in direct contrast to Durkheim, who in *The Division of Labour in Society* argues that the search for justice must be a primary task of modern societies. Charles Taylor (1994) in 'Neutrality in Political Science' argues against the conception of value neutrality, and therefore the separation between facts and values, because to say that something fulfils human wants and needs is a *prima facie* reason to call it good. That is, goodness cannot rely solely on my decision which is arbitrary in relation to facts. A central fact that governs my choice must be certain considerations about the human condition. That is, the concept of good has an objective connection with human welfare, and cannot be reduced to my individual choice. What Taylor argued for political science we can adapt to social science: 'A sociological (political) framework cannot fail to contain some, even implicit conception of human needs, wants, purposes' (1994: 568). This would commit sociology to value commitment and not value freedom.

THE NEUTRALITY OF FACTS AND SOCIOLOGY

The other aspect of Weber's position implies that there is a value-neutral area of facts, discoverable as empirical regularities, and this constitutes the scientific kernel of any science. It is this claim that is particularly

57

contentious in the social sciences. Whether there are any absolutely value-neutral facts is the key issue of the social sciences. The example of an empirical proposition is simple and clear: unfortunately there are few examples of such value-neutral empirical material in the social sciences. This follows not because of the biased nature of sociology, but because of the material it studies. It concerns reality as given to different conceptual systems and different value schemes. Reality as it is 'in itself' is not sociologically significant, because what is important is the belief system, the code, the representation that each particular group or culture makes of the world, and how this affects their behaviour and social action. What is important is that an unbiased account of this is given. Of course Weber recognized the problems here and established classic positions in relation to concept formation both at the level of agent and culture and at the theoretical level. Can we achieve a description of these 'forms of life', as Wittgenstein called them, in a value-free and empirical way? Can we get inside other cultures and value systems in a value-free way? Can we represent action and systems of action in our own culture or society in a value-free way?

MORAL OBJECTIVISM AGAINST WEBER

This raises the question of whether there is any set of facts whose truth logically compels a certain set of value responses, and which is central to a human science. That is, could the social sciences counter Weber with a new-found objectivism? For Weber the essentially subjective nature of moral judgement means that there is nothing inherent in the facts to logically compel us to hold a particular view: for him we are here in the sphere of ultimate evaluations, and these are a matter of faith and not reason (Weber 1949: 14, 55). Leo Strauss in *Natural Right and History* (1953) argued for a position of moral objectivism against Weber's subjectivist view of ultimate evaluations. He argues that this theory is a central component of Weber's value-free doctrine. If we can establish that this ethical subjectivism is wrong then a central component of his value-free doctrine will fall, and with it Weber's claim that we can only have objective knowledge of empirical value-free facts. Thus Strauss challenges Weber's implication that there can be no knowledge, only faith about ultimate evaluations. We know that tyranny and cruelty are wrong, and we have no difficulty in recognizing them when we see them. Indeed he goes further and claims that it is simply unscientific to not describe them as such: to avoid these judgements is to be unscientific. To do so is to fail to see the social phenomena for what they are. Thus the Nazi concentration camps, as a matter of science and sociological truth, must be described as evil. One of the consequences of Weber's position is that all evaluations must be excluded from the sphere of science. It follows that questions of justice in society must be excluded from all objective considerations in social science. For Strauss objective moral descriptions of moral phenomena should be central to a morally committed social science.

Theodor Adorno, although from a different logic and politics, pursues a similar line of reasoning: 'Society, the knowledge of which is ultimately the aim of sociology if it is to be more than a mere technique, can only crystallize at all around a conception of the just society' (1976: 118). It follows that knowledge of society does not imply value-free knowledge. He disputes the disjunction between objectivity and value, and therefore the equation of the social scientific with value freedom. Indeed this disjunction, together with the distinction between means and ends, is part of a societal process. This split was not found at a certain moment of history and philosophy: it is not found in Kant and Hegel. Rather it is found in a type of society characterized above all by the exchange relation. This leads to 'dissections of abstraction'. All judgement about reality is made on the basis of certain essential features about that reality and is therefore tied to that reality; it is not based on an arbitrary standpoint or privately and absolutely autonomous choice of values. We are parts of a totality and therefore theory, action and value cannot be 'exhausted in a subjectively irrational decision' (1976: 119). Indeed he argues, with Karl Popper, that value-free sociology is not thereby objectivist, but is subjectivist because essentially psychologist. Sociology should establish knowledge of those institutions that surround the individual, it should focus on the 'socially active environment' which is found in institutions: these are independent of the choice of value relevances and the ultimate evaluations of the individuals concerned or even the sociologists and their framework of interpretation. He thus denies the philosophy and the sociology of the standpoint. 'The experience of the contradictory character of societal reality is not an arbitrary standpoint, but rather the motive which first constitutes the first possibility of sociology' (1976: 120). Thus value-free sociology conceals the antagonistic character of reality.

Popper (1976) from a different position argues that the science of sociology actually requires not value freedom but the implementation of a certain type of value. It is a mistake to assume that the objectivity of science rests on the objectivity of the scientist: on this basis the natural scientist must always be more objective than a social scientist, because by definition s/he is more 'detached' from the subject matter, and therefore more value-free. For Popper the objectivity of science rests on the 'critical method'. This he contrasts to inductivism which assumes that science must start with neutral, empirical observations, and progress from there to the accumulation of data through induction to generalizations and to the establishment of a law. On this model only in the rarest cases can scientists detach themselves from the values of their class and culture, and therefore establish a 'value-free' social science. The critical approach admits that we must always start with a hypothesis and that our approach to the facts is always dictated by this: there are no theory-neutral or value-free facts *per se*. Rather what we must ensure is that our hypothesis is subject to all possible disconfirmation at the hands of experience. In particular we must search for criticism within the tradition of scientific research. For Popper objectivity rests solely on pertinent mutual criticism. With Weber, he recognizes the paradoxical nature of value freedom – that it is itself a value. What we must search for are social values that enable the critical tradition to flourish. We can then isolate the social values that help foster objectivity. These are competition (of individual scientists and various schools), tradition (namely the critical tradition), social institution (publication, congresses), and lastly the power of the state (its tolerance of free discussion). Thus there are values of the highest order which are associated with relevance, significance and the search for truth.

WEBER'S DOCTRINE IN SOCIOLOGY

Nevertheless Weber's position on value freedom has been taken in a particular way in sociology – not simply in the illusion of purely empirical objectivist sociology that ignores his reminder that all empirical material is gathered in terms of 'value relevance', but mostly in terms of a morally neutral apolitical theory. As Gouldner said in 'Anti-Minotaur: The Myth of Value-Free Sociology':

> What to Weber was an agonizing expression of a highly personal faith, intensely felt and painstakingly argued, has today become a hollow catechism, a password, and a good excuse for no longer thinking seriously. It has become increasingly the trivial token of professional respectability . . . the gentleman's promise that boats will not be rocked. (1973: 6)

The doctrine has had good as well as bad effects on sociology. On the plus side it benefited the autonomy of sociology: it freed it from Church and state, and gave the subject the freedom to pursue its own theoretical concerns. And it freed sociologists from the 'moral compulsiveness' of their own locality or 'tribe'. On the negative side it contributed to the increasing professionalization of the subject as just one more element to be sold to the highest bidder in the marketplace. 'Thou shalt not commit a critical or negative value-judgement – especially of one's own society' (1973: 14). It is associated with the sociological 'classicists' who are committed to the rituals of the craft to the extent of emptying it of significant truth. In contrast to these are the Romantics who prefer the 'vivid ethnographic' and 'sensuously expressive' to 'dull taxonomy' and 'formal questionnaires' (1973: 18). Further Gouldner points out that the value-free doctrine is subject to political pressures: whilst many were prepared to adopt it before Hiroshima, after they were not so sure.

It is quite clear that Weber has given a warning for social science that is of permanent value. Certain social theories that have presented themselves as the most objective can be seen to have concealed value premises that are presented as either factual or objective or scientific, when in fact they represent the value preferences or class outlook of the thinkers/system concerned. Marxism presented itself as an objective, scientific view of history and society. A central component of its theoretical equipment is the concept of contradiction. The philosophical background to Marxist thought is Hegelianism: here the concept of contradiction implies an insufficiency, an imperfection. Socialist society is non-contradictory, in contrast to capitalist. Capitalist society cannot survive because it is inherently contradictory; there are forces released which are mutually incompatible. For Engels the fundamental contradiction is that between socialized production and capitalist appropriation: that is, production is co-operative and social, but the fruits of this labour is appropriated by just a few individuals, the capitalists. As Lessnof (1974) shows, this cannot mean a logical contradiction. Rather it is a combination of two elements: firstly, this state of affairs is unjust (a value judgement); secondly, it leads to conflict between wage-earners and capitalists (a judgement of fact). For Weber the first, as a value judgement, should be presented as a value choice of the thinker and not as part of an objective process of history, and should not be confused with the second which is factual. To confuse these two different types of statement in a single term 'contradiction' offends against Weber's prescription.

Lessnoff also rightly points out that functionalism also contains a concealed value premise that is dressed up as a factual statement. There are two types of function in relation to a social system: 'institutional relational functionalism' means that which contributes to maintaining the social system in its existing form; 'societal survival functionalism' means that which maintains the social system in any form whatever. Both are factual meanings, but there is implicit a value judgement that this is a desirable effect of a social practice, that this is the effect a social practice ought to produce. I will not discuss whether or not there is an essential link between conservatism and functionalism. Gouldner's 'Coming Crisis' has documented a link. We can at least raise the question of whether conservative thinkers conceal their political preferences under descriptions of 'objective' functional relations. Most recently, feminist thought has shown us that what is presented as an objective viewpoint on social relations can conceal a patriarchal view, which does not just imply the subordination of women, but takes its own masculinist bias as identical with the real. All of these are bad sociology: not only are they theoretically inadequate in relation to the empirical material, but the thinkers concerned are identifying the real with their own values. All would have benefited from the frank admission of the proponents of their own political preferences.

Finally, as Gouldner shows in 'The Sociologist as Partisan' (1973), however much we reveal our commitments and empathies in sociological research, the problem of objectivity remains an essential goal in the pursuit of truth. And for this reason Weber's dichotomy, despite its difficulties, remains a heuristic, a dynamic ideal in the Durkheimian sense, which functions to stimulate research. It would seem to be a dichotomy we cannot live with, but cannot function without.

KEY CONCEPTS

FACT   A fact is what is said to be the case and it is associated with observation and experiment. All high status forms of knowledge, like science, try to deal in facts. Facts are supposed not to be negotiable, they are lasting and they are not open to question. Science not only determines facts it also, at its best, challenges them.

VALUE   Values are statements which are supposed to be much more tied up with judgement and subjectivity. Values are suppositions, they are not objective and they do not apply to all people. That 'this is a blue door' is a fact; that 'I like blue doors' is a value. However, if I say 'the Holocaust was evil' is that a fact or a value?

Objective   This is a state of affairs having to do with the qualities of the object in reality or the object as perceived as opposed to qualities in the minds of the people perceiving them. Objectivity is another way of claiming status for a statement, if it is objective it is not open to interpretation.

Confirmation   This is a method of science that seeks to show that a statement or a state of affairs is true. If I seek to confirm something then I seek to show that it is true, often by repeating an experiment.

Empirical   Facts or beliefs that are usually based wholly on experiment and observation. Most sciences claim that their knowledge is empirical and thus based on practical scientific knowledge of the world.

Commitment   A willing acknowledgement of an individuals faith or belief in another or in an idea. A commitment implies an unequivocal acceptance of a person, their theories, or a set of beliefs.

Local/Global

Les Back

At its most fundamental globalization refers to the interconnection of regions, nation-states and continents through economic, technological and political means. Anthony Giddens has pointed out that modernity is 'inherently globalizing' (1990: 63). In our current informational age new technologies like the Internet and the fax machine make it possible for me sitting here in London to bounce messages around the globe and access information from archives in places as remote as North America, India and Brazil. But the notion of globalization means more than just interconnectedness. It enables us to think about the relationship between time and space and how societies in a particular locality are affected by political and economic changes elsewhere. Giddens attempts to identify this through what he refers to as 'the intersection between presence and absence' (1991: 21). Put another way, global social relations are integral to the nature of local circumstances even though they may remain latent. In this sense we cannot neatly separate the global from the local: these two notions together constitute a *relationship* rather than a dichotomy.

With the emergence of electronic media it became possible to communicate and share intimate dialogue while remaining at a physical distance. Marshall McLuhan summed this up in a famous passage from his book *Understanding Media*:

> After three thousand years of explosion, by means of fragmentary and mechanical technologies, the Western world is imploding. During the mechanical ages we have extended our bodies in space. Today after more than a century of electric technology, we have extended our central nervous system itself in a

global embrace, abolishing both space and time as far as our planet is
concerned . . . As electrically contracted, the globe is no more than a village.
(1964: 11–12)

Yet, global interconnection cannot completely integrate human societies
that remain spatially dispersed. Something distinctly local remains, or may
even be being fostered, within the global circuits of capital and culture. I
want to try and unpick these complex relationships by looking at a particular locality, namely the area known as Deptford, South London in
which Goldsmiths College is located and from which I am tapping out
these thoughts.

FROM THE CRADLE OF EMPIRE TO THE HEART OF DARKNESS

Every morning as I walk down New Cross Road to my office I pass
Deptford Town Hall, an elegant Edwardian structure built in the early part
of the twentieth century (Figure 1). This building is a monument to South
London's maritime past. It is modelled on a the hull of a ship, and four
statues of British admirals adorn the front of the building and look down
on passers-by. At the top of the building above a clock tower is a weather-
vane in the form of a ship. In 1994, when the building was being renovated,
some heartless villain or anarchist guerrilla stole the original. During the
year it took to replace the wrought iron miniature my walk to work was
not quite the same. Somehow Deptford doesn't make sense without its ship.

The galleon was the technology *par excellence* of the imperial age and it
was here on the banks of the Thames that these vessels were constructed at
the King's Yard established by Henry VIII in 1513 (Steele 1993). Deptford's
local culture cannot be understood without an appreciation of its maritime
history and the global connections that were established through ships and
the local people both notable and destitute who sailed in them. Indeed,
Goldsmiths College, where many of the sociologists contributing to this
book work, was a boarding school for the sons of officers in the Royal Navy
and Royal Marines until 1889 (Firth 1991).

The official guide to the borough published in 1915 describes the significance of the national heroes celebrated in stone at the Town Hall:

> Sir Francis Drake with a globe in the background suggests the first circum-
> navigation of the world. The gallant [Robert] Blake, with 1652 underneath his
> effigy, recalls that admiral's first engagement with [the Dutch admiral] Von
> Trump in that year. On the opposite side of the oriel window the figure of
> Nelson, with the date of Trafalgar 1805, is a reminder of the appropriate opening
> of the Town Hall on the centenary of the famous action. The fourth admiral is a
> conventional representation of a British admiral of the recent period. (Bingham
> 1915: 25)

FIGURE 1 *Maritime connections, Deptford Town Hall, 1 August 1996*

Blake was not only renowned for his battles against the Dutch but travelled extensively to the Caribbean to raid the Spanish colonies. The Town Hall was opened on 19 July 1905 with the Fabian reformer Sidney Webb present. Every surface of the building is adorned with maritime emblems including dolphins, shells, cables and anchors, tridents and windlasses. The souvenir brochure published to commemorate the occasion emphasized the figurative portrait of history in the design:

> The note of symbolism is maintained down to the smallest trifle, as is illustrated by the wreaths under the admirals. Thus amid the foliage in the wreath under Admiral Drake is hung a cluster of beads and trinkets as well as a chalice and crucifix, which suggest the spoils of a Spanish galleon, or the plunder of some Spanish church, while among the oak leaves under Admiral Blake is a clasped Bible in allusion to his puritanism. (Borough of Lewisham 1905: 23)

The Town Hall was once described as 'obscene', not because of its imperial imagery but 'because its luxury contrasted so strongly with the poverty of the borough' (Coulter 1990: 114) (Figure 2). It was the first time that this district had been granted its own local form of government. Local identity is symbolized in a very self-conscious way through allusions to exploration, passage, and international conflict. Global relationships are thus sedimented in 'the local' setting.

In 1553 *The Primrose*, built at Deptford, was part of a small fleet which established the first contact between the English and the African kingdom of Benin. Indeed key figures in the emerging slave trade like John Hawkins, Treasurer of the Queen's Navy, were closely connected with the Deptford yard. Joan Anim-Addo comments in her excellent history of black South East London:

> John Hawkins, who lived in the Treasurer's House at Deptford Dockyard, could be considered the 'English Father of the Atlantic Slave Trade'. On his first slaving trip in 1562 Hawkins was able to combine trading activities for the two chief commodities of the period. He took gold from Lower Guinea and at least 300 slaves from Upper Guinea, 1,000 miles away. (1995: 8)

Travelling on to the Caribbean Hawkins traded his human cargo for pearls, ginger, sugar and hides. Thus was established the triangular trade that would be so devastating for the African chattel, yet lucrative for London's merchants. Hawkins flaunted his success in slaving. His coat of arms showed three black men shackled with slave collars and his crest showed a captive slave tied and bound (1995: 9). Indeed, on his third slaving trip in 1567 he was accompanied by none other than Francis Drake whose memory is celebrated in stone at Deptford Town Hall. This part of London was to provide an important base for the city's expanding commerce. There

FIGURE 2 *My walk to work as it would have been about 1910 (published with permission of Lewisham Local Studies Archive)*

was little distinction in this community of seafarers between the maritime adventurer and the ignominious slaver. Joan Anim-Addo concludes: 'The ships themselves, the majority built or fitted out at Deptford for the maiden voyages, often returned to Africa after repair in the area's dockyards' (1995: 12). These histories, often hidden within the public versions, provide an important reminder of how this particular locality both affected and was affected by the early forms of European expansion. All this makes me think of the traces of a different past every morning as I gaze upon the miniature iron galleon which sits on top of my favourite 'local' building.

Joseph Conrad in his novella *The Heart of Darkness* captures these international connections between the imperial metropolis and the colonial hinterland. The book is about a voyage that starts in London and ends in the African interior, as Marlowe – the book's protagonist – searches out a brutal colonial administrator called Kurtz. Written between 1898 and 1899 the following passage describes the departure:

> The old river in its broad reach rested unruffled at the decline of day, after ages of good service done to the race that peopled its banks, spread out in the tranquil dignity of a waterway leading to the uttermost ends of the earth . . . And indeed nothing is easier for a man who has, as the phrase goes, 'followed the sea' with reverence and affection, than to evoke the great spirit of the past upon the lower reaches of the Thames. They had sailed from Deptford, from

Greenwich, from Erith – the adventurers and the settlers; kings' ships and the ships of men on 'Change; captains, admirals, the 'dark interlopers' of Eastern trade, the commissioned 'generals' of the East India fleets. Hunters for gold or pursuers of fame, they all had gone out on that stream, bearing the sword, and often the torch, messengers of the might within the land, bearers of a spark from the sacred fire. What greatness had not floated on the ebb of that river into the mystery of the unknown earth! . . . The dreams of men, the seed of commonwealth, the germs of empires. (Conrad 1990: 136–7)

What Conrad captures in this passage is the role that the river played in establishing the routeways of European expansion and the effect this had on the 'race that peopled its banks'. It also draws a clear connection between **empire** and exploration. Francis Drake – after his forays in slaving – circumnavigated the globe aboard the *Golden Hind* and looted the Spanish Empire along the way. He was knighted by Queen Elizabeth I on the deck of the *Golden Hind* at Deptford in 1581. Drake died in the Caribbean in 1595 along with his fellow traveller and slave trader John Hawkins.

London emerged as 'a kind of Emporium for the whole Earth' (Joseph Addison, quoted in Porter 1994). Peter Linebaugh comments in his seminal study of eighteenth-century London society:

The Thames was the jugular vein of the British Empire. London the largest city in the western hemisphere, containing by 1800 nearly a million souls, was both the capital of England and the centre of the Empire that embraced the work-shops of Bengal, the plantations of the Caribbean, the 'factories' of West Africa and the forests of North America . . . Through these waters passed the wealth of the Empire. (1991: 409–10)

Along with the flow of commodities came migrations of people from various hinterlands: Jews came to London from Poland and Germany, and French Huguenots came fleeing religious persecution. It is also little known that from the middle of the eighteenth century there were between 5000 and 10,000 Africans living in London, of whom some were seamen but most were transported to Britain as servants and chattel (Fryer 1984). London provided the financial centre from which Britain's slave trade was funded and it was developed economically from the fruits of slavery. From the late eighteenth century London's population, and in particular its working classes, may be likened to a popular drink of the time called 'All Nations': this intoxicating mixture sold in 'dram shops' was made up of the dregs of different spirits (Linebaugh 1991: 358).

The great imperial companies of the era established themselves on the banks of the Thames. To the north the West India Company built large dock complexes in the last years of the eighteenth century. It was from here that sugar – the fruit of Caribbean plantocracies – was unloaded and popularized amongst London's citizens regardless of class. Indeed, so prized were these Caribbean spoils that a River Thames Force was established in the late eighteenth century as the first force in London's history to command centralized state authority, responsible for the payment of the West India Fleet's 'lumping gangs' and dockside workers (1991: 433). South of the river the East India Company – founded in Deptford – traded silver to Chinese merchants, and brought home among many other items tea, which became a favourite English drink in the eighteenth century (Rediker 1987: 39; Dews 1971; Steele 1993). Some of the most quintessential icons of Englishness – like the cup of English tea – barely dissolve the sweet traces of an imperial legacy (Hall 1991b; 1992a). It is crucial to stress here that the development of London and its localities has depended on flows of commodities and labour for at least 300 years. Even fish and chips, the most evocative culinary emblem of 'native London life', conceals a translocal cultural history. Popularized in the late nineteenth century, fish and chips was the result of the fusion of French styles of preparing fried potatoes and an East European Jewish tradition for frying fish (Malvery 1907; Walton, 1992).

The relationship between imperial expansion and culture is central to the story of what it means to be part of English society in general and London in particular. Equally, the historical denial of the long-standing presence of Africans and South Asians has meant that their contribution to English society has been ignored. London has a global, **multicultural** past to be recovered but the historical traces of this history have been bleached from public memory. English culture, whether embodied in the 'afternoon cup of tea', the Friday night 'fish and chips supper' or the 'jovial London Bobbie', is part of the story of imperialism. Yet these global processes also brought the children of slavery and empire 'up river'.

Ignatius Sancho, one of the first black writers to emerge from this part of London, was born during the middle passage on a slave ship in 1729. Joan Anim-Addo documents this extraordinary life in her book *The Longest Journey* (1995). Sancho was bought by a family in Greenwich as a servant for three young sisters. His thirst for learning and education brought him into conflict with his mistresses. Eventually, he ran away and made his case to the Duchess of Montague who employed him as a butler. In the Montagues' library Sancho taught himself to read and write. The Montagues were involved in the plantation system in the Caribbean but they were also philanthropic and keen on 'racial experiments':

> The Duke of Montague had previously involved himself in the education of Francis Williams, a boy born of free blacks in Jamaica. Wishing to see if education would affect a black child in ways similar to a white, the duke had provided for the young Francis to be educated at a grammar school and then at Cambridge . . . It is likely that local black people would have seized any opportunity to exchange news and stories, particularly about sympathetic whites. (1995: 48)

This 'local knowledge' enabled Sancho to become one of London's earliest black writers. The *Letters of Ignatius Sancho* – his first publication – became a bestseller and captured a national audience. Olaudah Equiano was another black literary and political figure who was brought to Deptford and resold into slavery there. Later after buying his freedom he campaigned for the abolition of slavery and wrote *The Interesting Narrative of the Life of Laudah Equiano or Gustav Vassa*: this autobiography documented in detail the experience of slavery from the slave's point of view. The stories of Sancho and Equiano mark the beginning of an intellectual movement that needs to be understood in both local and international terms. The unintended consequence of imperial expansion was that it allowed intellectuals like C.L.R. James – who spent the last years of his life in the neighbouring district of Brixton – to use the metropolis to transform the cultural legacy of empire and to challenge the very forms of knowledge that were produced in its institutions.

Thinking about the river as the routeway for modernity and imperialism's globalizing impulses helps us bring into focus the historical processes which existed prior to the current period where the relationship between the local and the global have become more intense. Paul Gilroy has reminded us that the relationship between contemporary London and the global colonial hinterlands is not an 'other story' which should be seen as some kind of appendix to London's official story: it is an integral part of *the* story (1993a: 84). Edward Said in his book *Culture and Imperialism* sums this up beautifully:

> Far from being unitary or monolithic autonomous things, cultures actually assume more 'foreign' elements, alterities, differences, than they consciously exclude. Who in India or Algeria can confidently separate out the British or French component of the past from present actualities, and who in Britain or France can draw a clear circle around British London or French Paris that would exclude the impact of India and Algeria upon those two imperial cities? (1993: 15)

Said argues persuasively that in this context we need to see imperialism not merely as an economic and political phenomenon but also as embodied within culture and enshrined within art, ideas, science and architecture. The prime meridian fixed at Greenwich in 1884 – just a few miles from Deptford – is the place from which time is measured (i.e. Greenwich Mean Time). It is also the point from which everywhere else in the world is plotted: the cartography of empire was drawn from a hill in South London. In 1894 a small group of London anarchists attempted to blow up the first meridian. This incident is dramatized in Joseph Conrad's brilliant novel *The Secret Agent*, first published in 1907 just two years after Deptford Town Hall was opened. Maybe there is a connection between the Greenwich bomb, anti-imperial sentiment and the recent theft of the Town Hall ship.

From its high perch this symbol of Deptford's imperial past oversaw the breakup of the dockyards, the dismantling of empire and the settlement of three generations of post-colonial subjects from the Caribbean, Ireland, Africa, South East Asia and Cyprus. Such diverse communities give this part of London an intensely multicultural and international resonance, and the combination of these differences refashioned the social landscape yet took on a distinctly local form. Deposited within 'the local' are present global relationships, but also we can find there the historical imprint of past connections. In his *Prison Notebooks* the Italian thinker Antonio Gramsci – who was incarcerated by Benito Mussolini for his leftist politics – argued that the starting point for any critical understanding of our place in the world involves a kind of archaeology of everyday life. He wrote that we are a 'product of the historical process to date which has deposited in you an infinity of traces, without leaving an inventory' (Gramsci 1971: 324). We can extend this principle to the local context in which past and present global interconnections are registered and begin the processes of building an inventory of local/global relationships.

'FROM ROOTS TO AERIALS': SPACE, CULTURE AND TIME

The Brazilian musician Gilberto Gil has suggested that we live in an age where roots have been replaced by aerials (see Back 1996: 218). He captures the sense here that within the informational age the relationship between space, culture and time has been radically reconfigured. It took Francis Drake three years to circumnavigate the globe by ship and sail. Today through electronic media one can make the same trip through virtual means within a fraction of a second. In the context of these technological forms of integration the relationship between local and global has become more intense and immediate. It is this traffic that Gilberto Gil attempts to name. He prioritizes the importance of being 'tuned in' to the global networks that are made possible by informational **technologies**. The electronic highways of the late twentieth century have exceeded infinitely their maritime counterparts. Iain Chambers (1994) has recently argued that in contemporary societies social forms are fluid and itinerant and produced within global *routeways*. From this perspective local rootedness has been superseded by global interconnection.

This brings us back to Marshall McLuhan's visionary comments about the globe being reduced to an electronically created **global village**. David Harvey has referred to this process of reordering temporal and geographical relationships through the notion of 'time–space compression' (1989: 240). He emphasizes that under the pressure of economic and technological change, spatial and temporal distance is collapsed so that people within remote localities can be brought together without moving physically. In the context of financial markets this has clear consequences because changes in Japan's financial centre will immediately impact on its counterpart in Britain or the United States. Harvey also argues that this process of contraction is not smooth and lineal. Rather, he suggests that the restructuring of capitalism produces intense episodes of time–space compression where economic and social processes are 'speeded up'.

All technologies which enable travel or communication change the relationship between space and time. What makes the current period distinct is the intensity of the shift. Kevin Robins sums this up neatly: 'Globalization is about the compression of time and space horizons and the creation of a world of instantaneity and depthlessness. Global space is a space of flows, an electronic space, a decentred space in which frontiers and boundaries have become permeable' (1991: 33). The interpenetration of the local and global has a long history but today new technologies are accelerating this process at heightened frequency.

Important questions are raised here. Who is using this technology? What global geometry of power has resulted from these new and highly efficient informational networks? Does this merely result in the spread of so-called Western culture? Some have argued that these developments produce a form of *cultural imperialism*. This perspective is related to the 'dependency paradigm' associated with figures like André Gunder Frank and Walter Rodney. It suggests that international flows of technology and media hardware strengthen the dependency relationship between the West and the former colonial peripheries and promote a form of cultural homogenization. One of the criticisms of this model is that it obscures the deep effects of imperialism itself. In the same way that the culture of metropolitan London is deeply imbued with global traces, so too are cities like Bombay and Kingston, Jamaica, in part the product of the export of European religion, education and other values which long ago and perhaps irretrievably altered the cultural milieu of the colonized (Bhabha 1994).

Annabelle Sreberny-Mohammadi (1991) argues persuasively that emphasizing the Western domination of media and communication technologies masks the fact that the nations of the South are producing more and more complicated forms of media. Within the current situation complex forms of media flows are occurring. For example TV Globo, a major Brazilian network, exports its programmes to 128 countries including Cuba, China and Germany. It even exports its programmes back to its former colonizer – Portugal. The station produces more programmes than any other channel in the television world (Tracey, 1988). Equally, India's Bombay film industry – or 'Bollywood' – is the largest in the world, producing over 1000 films per year distributed throughout the South Asian diaspora including Britain, Canada, the United States, Scandinavia and Africa. These examples disrupt any simple notion that the global culture is being homogenized through processes of cultural imperialism.

Arjun Appadurai has attempted to explain these complex flows of culture and translocal relationship through developing a new way of describing how social relations are expressed and formulated spatially: 'The new global cultural economy has to be understood as a complex, overlapping, disjunctive order, which cannot any longer be understood in terms of existing centre–periphery models (even those that might account for multiple centres and peripheries)' (1990: 296). Here the notion of a 'disjunctive order' is crucial. What he means by this is that the processes of globalization are not smooth and integrated. Rather what exists within these new configurations of time, space and culture are distinct landscapes that may function in a way that remains distinct from other aspects of global culture. Appadurai argues convincingly that the process of globalization is complexly variegated. He attempts to develop a language whereby we can begin to specify and theorize the distinct forms of globalization. He refers to this as an 'elementary framework' which he defines as consisting of five spatialized units or 'scapes'. The distribution of technology he refers to as *technoscapes*; networks of international finance he calls *finanscapes*; patterns of media dissemination he designates as *mediascapes*; spatial distributions of images and meaning becomes *ideoscapes*; and finally, he names 'landscapes of persons' like tourists, immigrants, refugees, exiles and guest workers as occupying a transnational *ethnoscape*. What is useful within Appadurai's approach is that he provides a series of concepts which enable us to describe how complex social relationships are sustained through time and space. More recently Appadurai has argued that the nature of these connections means that the local or regional setting becomes little more than the arena in which transnational, religious, economic and political forces are played out (Appadurai 1995).

The intensifying of global interconnection has not resulted in the flattening of cultural difference. Indeed, one might even speak of a kind of 'corporate multiculturalism' that can be found within the advertising imagery of companies like Benetton, Philips and Sony (Solomos and Back 1996: 185). Rather than a reduction of cultural diversity within commercial cultures we have seen a fascination with difference and a marketing of ethnicity and otherness (Hall 1991a). Kevin Robins has shown that globalization does not obliterate local cultures but rather packages them: 'The local and exotic are torn out of place and time to be repackaged for the world bazaar. So-called world culture may reflect a new valuation of difference and particularity but it is also very much about making a profit from it' (1991: 31). Drawing on the work of Theodore Levitt (1983), in particular his notion of the 'global standardization of segments', Robins describes the ways in which the plurality of cultural segments are expanded to world-wide proportions within the context of global markets.

One of the things which both Robins and Levitt underestimate is the flexibility that transnational corporations can have with regard to cultural difference. Advertisers are willing to integrate all kind of notions of difference as long as they serve their purpose. An example is Nike sportswear's use of the black director Spike Lee in their commercials. The aesthetic of urban blackness can quite comfortably be assimilated in Nike advertising because such imagery appeals to the youthful audience – both in the United States and globally – that the company is trying to attract. Yet, at the same time, the kinds of cultural representations that make it into the 'world bazaar' are highly selective. These images have to be saleable within a cultural supermarket that in large part remains dominated by a Western clientele. Stuart Hall reminds us: 'If you want to sample the exotic cuisine of other cultures in one place, it would be better to eat in Manhattan, Paris or London than in Calcutta or Delhi' (1992a: 305). The point here is that globalization can go hand in hand with the commercialization of exotic local cultures.

The growing international forms of technological integration do not necessarily undermine the potency of nationalism or other forms of localism. Globalization can strengthen local identities while still operating within the logic of time–space compression (Hall 1992a). Through the Internet electronic messages, texts and symbols can be circulated throughout the globe and accessed by anyone who has the appropriate computer hardware. Ultra-right-wing political movements seem able to combine a transnational technology with xenophobic nationalism without any contradiction. These nationalist groupings are using this technology to redraw their maps of belonging. A good example of this syndrome can be found on the American neo-fascist website The Aryan Crusader's Library (ACL), which is run by Reuben Logsdon. Beneath the title of The Aryan Crusader's Library is a map of the United States. Inside the map are the words 'Keeping America White'. Figure 3, taken from ACL, maps all the key sites of American neo-fascist activity. This includes Stormfront in West Palm Beach, the Institute of Historical Review in California, Resistance Records in Detroit and the Zündelsite across the border in Toronto, Canada. This image works at two levels. Websites and net activists are mapped within the borders of the American nation. Beyond this it plots the utopian networld of American nationalists. The image is placed within a specific territory. Yet, it is equally the embodiment of a racist utopia which is entirely dependent on cyberspace to give it meaning: Greater White Amerikkka is a virtual home. The Internet provides these groups with an arena in which utopian and racially exclusive nationalism can be expressed in an unregulated fashion. These patterns disrupt received understandings of globalization and localization. The Internet serves to reinforce rather than threaten the intense forms of localization at the heart of ultra-right nationalist ideologies (see Back et al. 1996).

Returning to Gilberto Gil's prophetic comment about 'aerials' and 'roots', it is clear that the technologies of cyberspace will not necessarily undermine the 'rootedness' that is so closely related to the ideologies of nationalism and xenophobia. The progression towards a 'global village' is unevenly

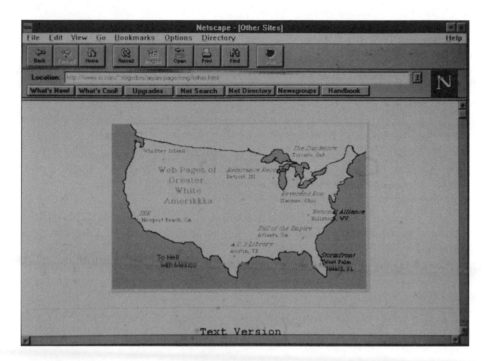

FIGURE 3   *Key sites of American neo-fascist activity*

developed. The technological revolution of our current informational age has radically reordered the relationship between social and economic life, time and space. Yet, this does not automatically eclipse the importance of local patterns of culture and identity.

CONCLUSION

To summarize, globalization is an uneven process in term of both its episodes of time–space compression and the communities it involves and affects. Doreen Massey (1991) has argued that an emergent 'power geometry' exists within the new global technologies. She contrasts the 'jet-setters', who are sending and receiving faxes and e-mail, controlling the news, writing books, organizing investments and international currency transactions, with 'The undocumented migrant workers from Mexico, crowding into Tijuana to make a perhaps fatal dash for it across the border into the United States to grab a chance at a new life. Here the experience of movement, and indeed the confusing plurality of cultures, is very different' (1991: 26). While the power geometry of the present age does not exactly replicate those of the imperial past, it still retains some aspects of Western domination.

75

I have tried to stress the importance of looking at the local/global as a relationship and not a binary opposition. Regardless of the current, and sometimes excessive, commentary on the impact of information technology on our lives, the virtual world always exists in a relationship with its non-virtual counterpart. In this sense neighbourhoods and regions provide the nodal points where cultural routeways converge. When this happens something new is produced that cannot be reduced to the sum of its global parts. In this sense localities matter for they provide the context in which people make sense of their sometimes confusing world. For all of their volatility, the notions of solidarity which are established within particular places provide a power means to express collective identities.

As I make the return walk from my office down Lewisham Way to New Cross Gate station, I see not only the traces of London's imperial past but the signs of its post-colonial present. This is registered in the plantain and yam sold by the South Asian grocer; the English 'fry-up' served at Gem's, a Turkish Cypriot owned café; and the Caribbean 'fried chicken' available from the Cummin' Up takeaway. These transnational flavours serve a complex local community that has been brought together in a particular place. In order to understand such communities we need to identify the global in the local and the local in the global.

KEY CONCEPTS

LOCAL This is a concept that sociologists use to refer to that which is close, parochial, part of a community or a society. The local is the experience of nearness, intimacy, shared assumptions and a common pattern of communication.

GLOBAL The global is a way of speaking about the wider picture, that which is beyond the local. It is also a way of referring to the modern tendency, through technology, communications and economic forces, of the world becoming smaller and faster and having more in common, in some senses!

Multiculture A society where people from a variety of different cultural and ethnic backgrounds live in a proximity, and with a degree of interaction, is a multicultural society. Such a society makes no guarantee of integration between the groups but it has to be achieved at some level, usually that of a common language.

Technology Modern electronic means of production and communication which accelerate all social processes by enabling quicker forms of output and more rapid relationships. Technology also facilitates the exercise of power.

Global village   This is the idea that through technology and new converging forms of economy and political state that the world is shrinking and diminishing the importance of peoples differences. It also means that local differences become subservient to global decisions and global power.

Empire   This refers to a state that rules and combines many territories usually brought together by defeat or capture. An empire names a cluster of societies brought together not by choice but by a dominating power. See the Roman Empire, the British Empire.

Qualitative/Quantitative

David Silverman

The choice between different research **methods** depends upon what you are trying to find out. For instance, if you want to discover how people intend to vote, then a quantitative method, like a social survey, may seem the most appropriate choice. On the other hand, if you are concerned with exploring people's wider perceptions or everyday behaviour, then qualitative methods may be favoured (Gilbert 1993).

However, other, less practical questions arise when you choose between 'qualitative' and 'quantitative' methods. The researcher has to bear in mind that these methods are often evaluated differently. This is shown in Table 1 which is drawn from the terms used by speakers at a conference on research methods. The table shows how imprecise, evaluative considerations come into play when researchers describe qualitative and quantitative methods. Depending on your point of view, Table 1 might suggest that quantitative research was superior because, for example, it is value-free. The implication here is that quantitative research simply objectively reports reality, whereas qualitative research is influenced by the researcher's political values. Conversely, other people might argue that such value freedom in social science is either undesirable or impossible.

The same sort of argument can arise about 'flexibility'. For some people, this flexibility encourages qualitative researchers to be innovative. For others, flexibility might be criticized as meaning lack of structure. Conversely, being 'fixed' gives such a structure to research but without flexibility.

However, this is by no means a balanced argument. Outside the social science community, there is little doubt that quantitative data rule the roost.

TABLE 1 *Claimed features of qualitative and quantitative method*

Qualitative	Quantitative
Soft	Hard
Flexible	Fixed
Subjective	Objective
Political	Value-free
Case study	Survey
Speculative	Hypothesis testing
Grounded	Abstract

Source: Halfpenny 1979: 799

Governments favour quantitative research because it mimics the research of its own agencies (Cicourel 1964: 36). They want quick answers based on 'reliable' variables. Similarly, many research funding agencies call qualitative researchers 'journalists or soft scientists. Their work is termed unscientific, or only exploratory, or entirely personal and full of bias' (Denzin and Lincoln 1994: 4).

For the general public, there is a mixture of respect for and suspicion of quantitative data ('you can say anything you like with figures'; 'lies, damn lies and statistics'). This is reflected by the media. On the one hand, public opinion polls are treated as newsworthy – particularly immediately before elections. On the other hand, unemployment and inflation statistics are often viewed with suspicion – particularly when they appear to contradict your own experience (statistics which show that inflation has fallen may not be credible if you see prices going up for the goods you buy!).

By the 1990s, in many Western countries, the assumed reliability of quantitative research was beginning to be under significant threat. In Britain, for instance, the ways in which inflation and unemployment were calculated during the Thatcher era were regularly changed. This suggested to some that such indices might be being 'fixed' in order to cast a favourable light upon these matters. Similarly, the failure of surveys of voting intention in the British general election of 1992 (almost comparable to the similar failure of US polling studies in the 1948 Truman–Dewey presidential race) made the public a little sceptical about such statistics – even though the companies involved insisted they were providing only statements of current voting intentions and not predictions of the actual result.

But such concerns may constitute only a 'blip' in the ongoing history of the dominance of quantitative research. Qualitative researchers still largely feel themselves to be second-class citizens whose work typically evokes suspicion, where the 'gold standard' is quantitative research.

STRUCTURE AND ARGUMENT

This chapter is organized in terms of the following five issues which are treated in consecutive sections, namely:

1   the nature of quantitative research;
2   the nature of qualitative research;
3   the critique of qualitative data;
4   the critique of quantitative data;
5   validity in qualitative research.

Readers should be aware that even textbooks cannot offer purely 'neutral' treatment of the topics they cover. Much will depend upon the material included (and excluded) and upon the particular position of the author: we all have our own 'axes to grind'. Underlying my presentation is the following context. I write as someone who has been associated with qualitative work. However, unlike some qualitative researchers, I have used quantitative measures where appropriate. This is because I share quantitative researchers' aim to do **science** (loosely defined as critical sifting of data, leading to cumulative generalizations which can always be later refuted).

In relation to this book, I argue that most dichotomies or polarities in social science are highly dangerous. At best, they are pedagogic devices for students to obtain a first grip on a difficult field: they help us to learn the jargon. At worst, they are excuses for not thinking, which assemble groups of sociologists into 'armed camps', unwilling to learn from one another.

However, so far we have been dealing with little more than empty terms, apparently related to whether or not researchers use statistics of some kind. In the next two sections, I address in rather more detail what social scientists mean by quantitative and qualitative research.

VARIETIES OF QUANTITATIVE RESEARCH

Bryman (1988) has discussed the five main methods of quantitative social science research and these are set out in Table 2.

To flesh out the bare bones of Table 2, I will use one example based on the quantitative analysis of official statistics. The example relates to data taken from the General Social Survey (GSS) carried out every year by the US National Opinion Research Center (NORC) and discussed by Procter (1993). Procter shows how you can use these data to calculate the relationship between two or more variables. Sociologists have long been interested in 'social mobility' – the movement between different statuses in

TABLE 2 *Methods of quantitative research*

Method	Features	Advantages
Social survey	Random samples Measured variables	Representative Tests hypotheses
Experiment	Experimental stimulus Control group not exposed to stimulus	Precise measurement
Official statistics	Analysis of previously collected data	Large data sets
Structured observation	Observations recorded on predetermined schedule	Reliability of observations
Content analysis	Predetermined categories used to count content of mass media products	Reliability of measures

Source: adapted from Bryman 1988: 11–12

TABLE 3 *Respondent's occupation by father's occupation (%)*

Son's occupation	Father's occupation	
	Non-manual	**Manual**
Non-manual	63.4	27.4
Manual	36.6	72.6

Source: adapted from Procter 1993: 246

society either within one lifetime or between generations. The GSS data can be used to calculate the latter, as Table 3 shows.

In Table 3, we are shown the relationship between father's and son's occupation. In this case, the father's occupation is the 'independent' variable because it is treated as the possible cause of the son's occupation (the 'dependent' variable). Table 3 appears to show a strong association (or 'correlation') between father's and son's occupations. For instance, of the group with non-manual fathers, 63.4% were themselves in non-manual jobs. However, among sons with fathers in manual occupations, only 27.4% had obtained non-manual work. Because the sample of over 1000 people was randomly recruited, we can be confident, within specifiable limits, that this correlation is unlikely to be obtained by chance.

However, quantitative researchers are reluctant to move from statements of correlation to causal statements. For instance, both father's and son's occupation may be associated with another variable (say inherited wealth) which lies behind the apparent link between occupations of father and son. Because of such an 'antecedent' variable, we cannot confidently state that father's occupation is a significant *cause* of son's occupation. Indeed, because this antecedent variable causes both of the others to vary together, the association between the occupation of fathers and sons is misleading or 'spurious'.

Along these lines Procter (1993: 248–9) makes the interesting observation that there appears to be a marked correlation between the price of rum in Barbados and the level of Methodist ministers' salaries, i.e. in any given year, both go up or down together. However, we should not jump to the conclusion that this means that rum distillers fund the Methodist Church. As Procter points out, both the price of rum and ministers' salaries may simply be responding to inflationary pressures. Hence the initial correlation is 'spurious'.

While looking at Tables 2 and 3, you may have been struck by the extent to which quantitative social research uses the same language that you may have been taught in say physics, chemistry or biology. As Bryman notes: 'Quantitative research is . . . a genre which uses a special language . . . [similar] to the ways in which scientists talk about how they investigate the natural order – variables, control, measurement, experiment' (1988: 12). Sometimes, this has led critics to claim that quantitative research ignores the differences between the natural and social world by failing to understand the 'meanings' that are brought to social life. This charge is often associated with critics who label quantitative research as 'positivistic' (e.g. Filmer et al. 1972). Unfortunately, 'positivism' is a very slippery and emotive term. Not only is it difficult to define but there are very few quantitative researchers who would accept it (see Marsh 1982: Ch. 3). Instead, most quantitative researchers would argue that they do not aim to produce a science of laws (like physics) but aim simply to produce a set of cumulative generalizations based on the critical sifting of data, i.e. a 'science' as defined above.

As I argue, at this level, many of the apparent differences between quantitative and qualitative research should disappear – although some qualitative researchers remain insistent that they want nothing to do with even such a limited version of science (see Phillips 1974). It follows that, when we compare the two kinds of research, the most we should be looking for are different emphases between 'schools' who themselves contain many internal differences.

VARIETIES OF QUALITATIVE RESEARCH

Qualitative researchers often assume that a dependence on purely quantitative methods may neglect the social and cultural construction of the 'variables' which quantitative research seeks to correlate. As Kirk and Miller (1986) argue, 'attitudes', for instance, do not simply attach to the inside of people's heads, and researching them depends on making a whole series of analytical assumptions. They conclude: 'The survey researcher who discusses is not wrong to do so. Rather, the researcher is wrong if he or she fails to acknowledge the theoretical basis on which it is meaningful to make measurements of such entities and to do so with survey questions' (1986: 15).

According to its critics, much quantitative research leads to the use of a set of *ad hoc* procedures to define, count and analyse its variables (Blumer 1956; Cicourel 1964; Silverman 1975). On the basis of this critique, qualitative researchers have preferred to describe how, in everyday life, we actually go about defining, counting and analysing. The implication is that quantitative researchers unknowingly use the methods of everyday life, even as they claim scientific objectivity (Cicourel 1964; Garfinkel 1967).

Qualitative researchers go on to argue that we should not assume that techniques used in quantitative research are the *only* way of establishing the validity of findings from qualitative or field research. This means that a number of practices which originate from quantitative studies may be *inappropriate* to field research. These include the assumptions that social science research can only be valid if based on experimental data, official statistics or the random sampling of populations and that quantified data are the only valid or generalizable social facts.

Critics of quantitative research argue that these assumptions have a number of defects (Lipset et al. 1962, and see Cicourel 1964; Denzin 1970; Schwartz and Jacobs 1979; Hammersley and Atkinson 1983; Gubrium 1988). These critics note that experiments, official statistics and survey data may simply be inappropriate to some of the tasks of social science. For instance, they exclude the observation of behaviour in everyday situations. Hence, while quantification may *sometimes* be useful, it can conceal as well as reveal basic social processes.

Consider the problem of counting attitudes in surveys. Do we all have coherent attitudes on any topics which await the researcher's questions? And how do 'attitudes' relate to what we actually do – our practices? Or think of official statistics on cause of death compared with studies of how hospital staff (Sudnow 1968), pathologists and statistical clerks (Prior 1987) attend to deaths. Note that this is *not* to argue that such statistics may be biased. Instead, it is to suggest that there are areas of social reality which such statistics cannot measure. So the methods used by qualitative researchers exemplify a common belief that they can provide a 'deeper' understanding of social phenomena than would be obtained from purely quantitative data. Some of these methods are set out in Table 4.

The methods presented in Table 4 are often combined. For instance, many qualitative case studies combine observation with interviewing. Moreover, each method can be used in either qualitative or quantitative research studies. As Table 5 shows, the overall nature of the research **methodology** shapes how each method is used.

Table 5 shows that methods are techniques which take on a specific meaning according to the methodology in which they are used. To take just one example, although there are quantifiable, standardized observation schedules, observation is not generally seen as a very important method of

TABLE 4 *Methods of qualitative research*

Method	Features	Advantages
Observation	Extended periods of contact	Understanding of subcultures
Texts and documents	Attention to organization and use of such material	Theoretical understanding
Interviews	Relatively unstructured and open-ended	Understanding experience
Audio and video recording	Precise transcripts of naturally occurring interactions	Understanding how interaction is organized

TABLE 5 *Different uses for four methods*

Method	Methodology	
	Quantitative research	**Qualitative research**
Observation	Preliminary work, e.g. prior to framing questionnaire	Fundamental to understanding another culture
Textual analysis	Content analysis, i.e. counting in terms of researchers' categories	Understanding participants' categories
Interviews	Survey research: mainly fixed-choice questions to random samples	Open-ended questions to small samples
Transcripts	Used infrequently to check the accuracy of interview records	Used to understand how participants organize their talk

Source: Silverman 1993: 9

data collection in quantitative research. This is because it is difficult to conduct observational studies on large samples. Quantitative researchers also argue that observation is not a very 'reliable' data-collection method because different observers may record different observations. If used at all, observation is held to be only appropriate at a preliminary or 'exploratory' stage of research.

Conversely, observational studies have been fundamental to much qualitative research. Beginning with the pioneering case studies of non-Western societies by early anthropologists (Malinowski 1922; Radcliffe-Brown 1948) and continuing with the work by sociologists in Chicago prior to the Second World War (Thomas and Znaniecki 1927), the observational method has often been the chosen method to understand another culture.

The Chicago School tradition continued for two decades after the Second World War. In the 1950s, Becker (1953) conducted a classic observational study of drug use. He was particularly concerned with the relationship between marihuana smokers' own understandings and the interactions in which they were involved. He discovered that people's participation in groups of users taught them how to respond to the drug. Without such learning, novices would not understand how to smoke marihuana or how to respond to its effects. Consequently, they would not get 'high' and so would not continue to use it.

Becker outlines a number of stages through which novices pass on their path to becoming regular smokers. These include:

1   Direct teaching: e.g. being taught the difference between how to smoke marihuana and how to smoke tobacco; learning how to interpret its effects and their significance.
2   Learning how to enjoy the effects: through interaction with experienced users, the novice learns to find pleasure in sensations which, at first, may be quite frightening.
3   Resocialization after difficulties: even experienced users can have an unpleasant or frightening experience through using a larger quantity or a different quality of marihuana. Fellow users can 'cool them out', explaining the reasons for this experience and reassuring them that they may safely continue to use the drug.
4   Learning connoisseurship: through developing a greater appreciation of the drug's effects, becoming able to distinguish between different kinds and qualities of the drug.

Becker stresses that it is only in the context of a social network, which provides a means of interpreting the effects of the drug, that people become stable marihuana users. It is unlikely that such a network could have been identified by, say, survey research methods concerned with the attitudes of marihuana users. However, this is not to rule out the value of quantitative social surveys to test how widespread are the features Becker describes (e.g. among different groups of users).

Just as quantitative researchers would resist the charge that they are all 'positivists' (Marsh 1982), there is no agreed doctrine underlying all qualitative social research. Instead, there are many 'isms' that appear to lie behind qualitative methods, for example interactionism, feminism, postmodernism and ethnomethodology (the nature of these diverse approaches lies beyond the scope of this chapter).

In spite of this diversity, qualitative researchers are seen by Hammersley (1992) to share a set of preferences which I set out below:

1   a preference for qualitative data – understood simply as the analysis of words and images rather than numbers;
2   a preference for naturally occurring data – observation rather than experiment, unstructured versus structured interviews;
3   a preference for meanings rather than behaviour – attempting 'to document the world from the point of view of the people studied' (1992: 165);
4   a rejection of natural science as a model;

5   a preference for inductive, hypothesis-generating research rather than hypothesis testing (cf. Glaser and Strauss 1967).

Unfortunately, as Hammersley himself recognizes, such a simple list is a huge over-generalization. For instance, to take just item 5 above, qualitative research would look a little odd, after a history of over 100 years, if it had no **hypotheses** to test (see Silverman 1993: 26)!

Nonetheless, if we take the list above as a reasonable approximation of the main features of qualitative research, we can start to see why it can be criticized. As already noted, in a world where numbers talk and people use the term 'hard' science, a failure to test hypotheses, coupled with a rejection of natural science methods, certainly leave qualitative researchers open to criticism.

Of course, many scientists themselves reject the wilder dreams of positivism, for instance the search for laws based on laboratory experiment as the 'gold standard' of good science. Nonetheless, we are still left with this troubling question: why should we *believe* what qualitative researchers tell us? How can they demonstrate that their descriptions are accurate and that their explanations hold water? It is to these questions that I now turn.

THE CRITIQUE OF QUALITATIVE DATA

As already noted, qualitative research is, by definition, stronger on long descriptive narratives than on statistical tables. The problem that arises here is how such a researcher goes about categorizing the events or activities described. This is sometimes known as the problem of *reliability*. As Hammersley puts it, reliability 'refers to the degree of consistency with which instances are assigned to the same category by different observers or by the same observer on different occasions' (1992: 67). The issue of consistency particularly arises because shortage of space means that many qualitative studies provide readers with little more than brief, persuasive, data extracts. As Bryman notes about the typical observational study: 'field notes or extended transcripts are rarely available; these would be very helpful in order to allow the reader to formulate his or her own hunches about the perspective of the people who have been studied' (1988: 77).

Moreover, even when people's activities are tape-recorded and transcribed, the reliability of the interpretation of transcripts may be gravely weakened by a failure to record apparently trivial, but often crucial, pauses and overlaps. For instance, a recent study of medical consultations was concerned to establish whether cancer patients had understood that their condition was fatal. When researchers first listened to tapes of relevant hospital consultations, they sometimes felt that there was no evidence that the patients had picked up their doctors' often guarded statements about their prognosis. However, when the tapes were retranscribed, it was demonstrated that patients used very soft utterances (like 'yes' or, more usually 'mm') to mark that they were taking up this information. Equally, doctors would monitor patients' silences and rephrase their prognosis statements (see Clavarino et al. 1995).

Some social researchers argue that a concern for the reliability of observations arises only within the quantitative research tradition. Because what they call the 'positivist' position sees no difference between the natural and social worlds, reliable measures of social life are only needed by such 'positivists'. Conversely, it is argued, once we treat social reality as always in flux, then it makes no sense to worry about whether our research instruments measure accurately (e.g. Marshall and Rossman 1989).

Such a position would rule out any systematic research since it implies that we cannot assume any stable properties in the social world. However, if we concede the possible existence of such properties, why shouldn't other work replicate these properties? As Kirk and Miller argue:

> Qualitative researchers can no longer afford to beg the issue of reliability. While the forte of field research will always lie in its capability to sort out the validity of propositions, its results will (reasonably) go ignored minus attention to reliability. For reliability to be calculated, it is incumbent on the scientific investigator to document his or her procedure. (1986: 72)

A second criticism of qualitative research relates to how sound are the explanations it offers. This is sometimes known as the problem of 'anecdotalism', revealed in the way in which research reports sometimes appeal to a few, telling 'examples' of some apparent phenomenon, without any attempt to analyse less clear (or even contradictory) data (Silverman 1989). This problem is expressed very clearly by Bryman:

> There is a tendency towards an anecdotal approach to the use of data in relation to conclusions or explanations in qualitative research. Brief conversations, snippets from unstructured interviews . . . are used to provide evidence of a particular contention. There are grounds for disquiet in that the representativeness or generality of these fragments is rarely addressed. (1988: 77)

This complaint of 'anecdotalism' questions the *validity* of much qualitative research. 'Validity' is another word for truth: 'By validity, I mean truth: interpreted as the extent to which an account accurately represents the social phenomena to which it refers' (Hammersley 1990: 57). Sometimes one doubts the validity of an explanation because the researcher has clearly made no attempt to deal with contrary cases. Sometimes, the extended immersion in the 'field', so typical of qualitative research, leads to a certain preciousness about the validity of the researcher's own interpretation of 'their' tribe or organization. Or sometimes, the demands of journal editors for shorter and shorter articles simply mean that the researcher is reluctantly led only to use 'telling' examples – something that can happen in much the same way in the natural sciences where, for instance, laboratory assistants have been shown to select 'perfect' slides for their professor's important lecture (see Lynch 1984).

Despite these common problems, doubts about the reliability and validity of qualitative research have led many quantitative researchers to downplay the value of the former. This means that in many, quantitatively oriented social science methodology textbooks, qualitative research is often treated as a relatively minor methodology. As such, it should only be contemplated at early or 'exploratory' stages of a study. Viewed from this perspective, qualitative research can be used to familiarize oneself with a setting before the serious sampling and counting begin.

This view is expressed in the extract below from an early text. Note how the authors refer to 'non-quantified data' – implying that quantitative data is the standard form:

> The inspection of *nonquantified* data may be particularly helpful if it is done periodically throughout a study rather than postponed to the end of the statistical analysis. Frequently, a single incident noted by a perceptive observer contains the clue to an understanding of a phenomenon. If the social scientist becomes aware of this implication at a moment when he can still add to his material or exploit further the data he has already collected, he may considerably enrich the quality of his conclusions. (Selltiz et al. 1964: 435, my emphasis)

Despite these authors' 'friendly' view of the uses of 'non-quantified' data, they assume that 'statistical analysis' is the bedrock of research. A similar focus is to be found, a quarter of a century later, in another mainly quantitative text: 'Field research is essentially a matter of immersing oneself in a naturally occurring . . . set of events in order to gain firsthand knowledge of the situation' (Singleton et al. 1988: 11). Note the emphasis on 'immersion' and its implicit contrast with later, more focused research. This is underlined in the authors' subsequent identification of qualitative or field research with 'exploration' and 'description' (1988: 296) and their approval of the use of field research 'when one knows relatively little about the subject under investigation' (1988: 298–9). However, as we shall see below, this kind of 'damning by faint praise' has been more than balanced by criticisms of quantitative research offered by many qualitative researchers.

THE CRITIQUE OF QUANTITATIVE DATA

The critique of purely quantitative research has a long history beginning in the 1950s. C. Wright Mills (1959) criticizes the atheoretical character of much quantitative research which he calls 'abstracted empiricism'. Blumer (1956) had noted how the attempt to establish correlations between variables depended upon a lack of attention to how these variables are defined by the people being studied. Finally, Cicourel (1964), influenced by Schutz (1964a) and Garfinkel (1967), draws attention to how the choice of a purely mathematical logic can neglect the common-sense reasoning used by *both* participants and researchers.

Let me try to concretize this critique by means of a single example. More than twenty years ago two American sociologists, Peter Blau and Richard Schoenherr conducted a study of several large organizations. The study is interesting for our present purposes because it is explicitly based on a critique of qualitative methods. In these authors' view, too much research in the 1960s had used qualitative methods to describe 'informal' aspects of organization – like how employees perceive their organization and act according to these perceptions rather than according to the organizational 'rulebook'. Blau and Schoenherr (1971) suggested that the time was ripe to switch the balance and to concentrate on 'formal' organization, like how jobs are officially defined and how many 'levels' exist in the organizational hierarchy. Such features can then be seen as 'variables' and statistical correlations can be produced which are both reliable and valid.

Let us see how such an apparently simple, quantitative logic worked out in practice. Blau and Schoenherr used as their data organizational wallcharts which show hierarchies and job functions. Unfortunately, from their point of view, as a revealing early chapter acknowledges, these wallcharts are often ambiguous and vary in structure from one organization to another. Consequently, it was necessary to discuss their meaning in interviews with 'key informants' in each organization. Using this information, Blau and Schoenherr constructed standardized measures of various aspects of organizational structure such as 'hierarchy' and 'job specificity'. The result of all this was a set of statistical correlations which convincingly show the relationship between the variables that Blau and Schoenherr constructed.

Unfortunately, given the indeterminancy of the data they are working with, the authors engaged in a series of sensible but undoubtedly *ad hoc* decisions in order to standardize the different forms in which people talk about their own organization. For instance, they decided to integrate into one category the two grades of 'clerk' that appear on one organization's wallchart of authority. This decision was guided by a statistical logic that demanded clearly defined, 'reliable' measures. However, the researchers' decision has an unknown relationship to how participants in the organization concerned actually relate to this wallchart and how or when they invoke it. Indeed, Blau and Schoenherr are prevented from examining such matters by their decision to stay at a purely 'structural' level and to avoid 'informal' behaviour. This means that their own interpretation of the meaning of the statistical correlations so obtained, while no doubt statistically rigorous, is equally *ad hoc*.

What we have here is a nice case of 'the cart leading the horse'. Blau and Schoenherr adopt a purely statistical logic precisely in order to replace common-sense understandings by scientific explanations. However, despite themselves, they inevitably appeal to common-sense knowledge both in defining their 'variables' and in interpreting their correlations. So the quantitative desire to establish 'operational' definitions at an early stage of social research can be an arbitrary process which deflects attention away from the everyday sense-making procedures of people in specific milieux. As a consequence, the 'hard' data on social structures which quantitative researchers claim to provide can turn out to be a mirage (see also Cicourel 1964).

This brief (non-random) example should allow you to understand the kind of criticisms that are often directed at purely quantitative research by more qualitative 'types'. Because space is short, let me try to summarize these criticisms by means of the following list:

1   Such research can amount to a 'quick fix', involving little or no contact with people or the 'field'.
2   Statistical correlations are provided but they are based upon 'variables' that, in the context of naturally occurring interaction, are arbitrarily defined.
3   After the fact speculation about the meaning of correlations can involve the very common-sense processes of reasoning that such science tries to avoid (see Cicourel 1964: 14, 21).
4   The pursuit of 'measurable' phenomena can mean that unperceived values creep into research by simply taking on board highly problematic and unreliable concepts such as 'delinquency' or 'intelligence'.
5   While it is important to test hypotheses, a purely statistical logic can make the development of hypotheses a trivial matter and fail to help in generating hypotheses from data (see Glaser and Strauss 1967).

It should be noted that the list above contains simply some complaints made about *some* quantitative research. Moreover, because quantitative researchers are rarely 'dopes', many treat such matters seriously and try to overcome them. So, for instance, epidemiologists, who study official statistics about disease, and criminologists are only too aware of the problematic character of what gets recorded as, say, 'cause of death' or a 'criminal offence' (see Hindess 1973). Equally, good quantitative researchers are only too aware of the problems involved in interpreting statistical correlations in relation to what the variables involved 'mean' to the participants (see Marsh 1982: Ch. 5).

In the light of this qualification, I conclude this section by observing that an insistence that any research worth its salt should follow a purely quantitative logic would simply rule out the study of many interesting phenomena relating to what people actually do in their day-to-day lives, whether in homes, offices or other public and private places. But, as the next section shows, a balanced view should accept the strengths, as well as the limitations, of quantitative research.

VALIDITY IN QUALITATIVE RESEARCH

As earlier sections have made clear, quantitative measures offer no simple solution to the question of validity. As Fielding and Fielding point out, some interpretation takes place even when using apparently 'hard' quantitative measures:

> ultimately all methods of data collection are analysed 'qualitatively', in so far as the act of analysis is an interpretation, and therefore of necessity a selective rendering. Whether the data collected are quantifiable or qualitative, the issue of the *warrant* for their inferences must be confronted. (1986: 12, my emphasis)

So qualitative researchers should not be overly defensive. Quantitative researchers have no 'golden key' to validity. Nonetheless, qualitative researchers remain troubled by two problems:

1   How can they claim that their findings are 'representative', given that they are unlikely to use random samples (the problem of 'representativeness')?
2   How can they base their findings on more than one or two favourable 'examples' (the problem of 'hypothesis testing')?

I will begin with the problem of *representativeness*. Qualitative studies often draw their data from only one or two settings (e.g. a school or a prison). It is unlikely that these settings will have been selected on a random basis. For instance, in observational studies, a setting may be chosen because it allows access. This gives rise to a problem familiar to users of quantitative methods: 'How do we know . . . how representative case study findings are of all members of the population from which the case was selected?' (Bryman 1988: 88).

The problem of representativeness is a perennial worry of case study researchers. Let me outline two ways that we can address it. The first is by inferring from one case to a larger population. Hammersley (1992) suggests three methods through which we can attempt to generalize from the analysis of a single case:

1   obtaining information about relevant aspects of the population of cases and comparing our case to them;

2   using survey research on a random sample of cases;
3   co-ordinating several ethnographic studies.

Through such comparisons with a larger sample, we may be able to establish some sense of the representativeness of our single case.

Even if the qualitative researcher is only working with a single case, (s)he should be addressing the problem of sampling by means of constant comparisons. Miles and Huberman illustrate this point very well, using the example of qualitative research on police work:

> sampling means . . . just taking a smaller chunk of a larger universe. If I focus on one precinct station and one kind of police officer making one kind of booking, I can make few legitimate claims about other precincts, or about other officers and bookings within the precinct I have studied. If, on the other hand, I hang around one precinct long enough and track a variety of arrests and bookings, I will probably have a large enough sample of settings, actors, and events to make confident claims not only about these variables but also about how laws are enforced and interpreted within the precinct. (1984: 38)

The second way to address the problem of representativeness is to make generalizations in terms of theories. It is important to recognize that generalizing from cases to populations does not follow a purely statistical logic in qualitative research. As an example, Bryman uses Glaser and Strauss's discussion of whether (and, if so, how) hospital patients become aware of their impending death:

> The issue of whether the particular hospital studied is 'typical' is not the critical issue; what is important is whether the experiences of dying patients are typical of the broad class of phenomena . . . to which the theory refers. Subsequent research would then focus on the validity of the proposition in other milieux (e.g. doctors' surgeries). (1988: 91)

Bryman thus argues that:

> the issue should be couched in terms of the generalizability of cases to *theoretical* propositions rather than to *populations* or universes. (1988: 90, my emphasis)

As our understanding of social processes improves, we are increasingly able to choose settings and cases on theoretical grounds – for instance, because the case offers a crucial test of a theory. This leads directly to our second issue: how we can test hypotheses in qualitative research.

A solution to the problem of *hypothesis testing* is simply for qualitative researchers to seek to refute their initial assumptions about their data in order to achieve objectivity. As Kirk and Miller argue: 'The assumptions underlying the search for objectivity are simple. There is a world of empirical reality out there. The way we perceive and understand that world is largely up to us, but the world does not tolerate all understandings of it equally' (1986: 11).

Kirk and Miller remind us of the need for 'objectivity' in qualitative research. One way of being critical is, as Popper (1959) has suggested, to seek to refute assumed relations between phenomena. This means over-coming the temptation to jump to easy conclusions just because there is some evidence that seems to lead in an interesting direction. Instead, we must subject this evidence to every possible test. Then, only if we cannot refute the existence of a certain relationship are we in a position to speak about 'objective' knowledge. Even then, however, our knowledge is always provisional, subject to a subsequent study which may come up with disconfirming evidence. Popper puts it this way:

> What characterizes the empirical method is its manner of exposing to falsi-fication, in every conceivable way, the system to be tested. Its aim is not to save the lives of untenable systems but, on the contrary, to select the one which is by comparison the fittest, by exposing them all to the fiercest struggle for survival. (1959: 42)

As we have seen, quantitative researchers attempt to satisfy Popper's demand for attempts at 'falsification' by carefully excluding 'spurious' cor-relations. How can qualitative researchers satisfy Popper's criterion?

One solution is to employ the constant comparative method. This means that the qualitative researcher should always attempt to find another case through which to test out a provisional hypothesis. For instance, when I was studying what happened to Down's syndrome children in a heart hospital, I tested out my findings with similar tape-recordings of consul-tations involving children without that congenital abnormality (Silverman 1981). Even when there is no comparative group available to test hypoth-eses, qualitative researchers can isolate deviant cases in a single data set and use them to refine their initial hypotheses (Silverman 1993: Ch. 8).

Equally, there is no reason why qualitative researchers should not, where appropriate, use quantitative measures. Simple counting techniques can offer a means to survey the whole corpus of data ordinarily lost in inten-sive, qualitative research. Instead of taking the researcher's word for it, the reader has a chance to gain a sense of the flavour of the data as a whole. In turn, researchers are able to test and to revise their generalizations, removing nagging doubts about the accuracy of their impressions about the data (Strong 1979).

In a study of cancer clinics (Silverman 1984), I used some simple quan-titative measures in order to respond to some of these problems. The aim was to demonstrate that the qualitative analysis was reasonably represen-tative of the data as a whole. Occasionally, however, the figures revealed that the reality was not in line with my overall impressions. Consequently, the analysis was tightened and my characterizations of clinic behaviour were specified more carefully.

CONCLUSION

The use of quantitative measures in qualitative research shows that the whole 'qualitative/quantitative' dichotomy is open to question. Ultimately, objectivity should be the common aim of all social science (see Kirk and Miller 1986: 10–11). As Hammersley argues: 'the process of inquiry in science is the same whatever method is used, and the retreat into paradigms effectively stultifies debate and hampers progress' (1992: 182). This means that, if we wish to establish criteria for distinguishing qualitative research, we will need to understand the similar issues faced by any systematic attempt at description and explanation, whether quantitative or qualitative.

In principle, there is no reason to prefer any form of data. I conclude, therefore, with a statement which shows the absurdity of pushing too far the qualitative/quantitative distinction:

> We are not faced, then, with a stark choice between words and numbers, or even between precise and imprecise data; but rather with a range from more to less precise data. Furthermore, our decisions about what level of precision is appropriate in relation to any particular claim should depend on the nature of what we are trying to describe, on the likely accuracy of our descriptions, on our purposes, and on the resources available to us; not on ideological commitment to one methodological paradigm or another. (1992: 163)

KEY CONCEPTS

QUALITATIVE A methodology which privileges material drawn from non-quantitative sources. Thus any work in the social sciences that collects and analyses its material in the form of conversations; written or recorded responses to questions; sections of books, reports or newspapers; attitude tests; focus group discussions and so on. A methodology that focuses on the texture and the value qualities of its data.

QUANTITATIVE A methodology in the social sciences that uses numerical data to reach its findings. Thus any statistical techniques for the collection and analysis of material; any transformation of human behaviour into the form of numbers. Statements in the form of '85% of people say that . . .' are quantitative, they tend to be of higher status than qualitative statements, and they tend to be regarded as fact.

Method   This is a specific research technique like: ethnography; participant observation; surveys; questionnaires; observation; interviews, etc.

Science   Science describes the dominant form of understanding in western society throughout modernity. Science has provided most of the things that we regard as good and essential to our society, like engineering and medicine. Science is also a way of talking about a critical sifting of data, leading to cumulative generalizations which can always be later refuted.

Methodology   This is a general approach to studying research topics; it usually involves both a perspective and a chosen style of analysis, like quantification for example.

Hypothesis   An hypothesis is a testable proposition. If I say 'all swans are white' this is an hypothesis and we can go out and test it by looking at swans, but particularly by looking for black swans. If we find none then the hypothesis becomes an empirical generalization.

NOTE

I am most grateful for the comments of Clive Seale on an earlier draft of this chapter.

Normal/Pathological

Clive Seale

DURKHEIM AND NORMALITY

Normality and pathology are terms which initially might seem better applied to matters of health and illness than to social life. The speciality of pathology within medicine is devoted to seeking out abnormalities (pathologies) of body organs that cause disease. Historically, amongst sociologists Durkheim comes closest to a view of society that parallels this medical perspective on the body. He tended to see the sociologist as a sort of diagnostician of the ills of society, skilled in identifying social pathology (such as an unusually high crime rate) and in recommending restorative treatment for implementation by politicians. Unlike scholars of medicine, though, who tend to see the normal body as a fixed entity, duly described in anatomical textbooks, Durkheim had a surprisingly relativistic[1] view of what constituted normality. Thus he believed that what counted as normal in a particular society might not be normal for another. Nevertheless, Durkheim felt that it was possible to judge what was normal for a given society at a particular point in time by applying an objective knowledge about laws of social development according to which societies could be ranked and categorized.

Durkheim's sociology in this area has been quite extensively criticized (e.g. Giddens 1986). In particular, his view that what was generally the case in a particular 'type' of society (e.g. a particular class of acts are designated as 'crimes') was therefore normal for that society has been said to support a rather conservative approach to normality. Additionally, the view that societies can be ranked and categorized as if they were biological organisms in some sort of evolutionary family tree is now regarded as rather outdated (Lukes 1973). These criticisms, however, should not obscure Durkheim's contribution, which stems from a desire to explore quite fundamental aspects of social organization. In particular, Durkheim was interested in the basis of social solidarity, the desire of people to feel bound together in a common enterprise, seeing this as the source of moral and social order. For Durkheim, pathological social forms involved the loosening of such solidarity. In such circumstances, individuals in increasing numbers feel detached from social norms, which are the moral rules that regulate conduct and promote a sense of solidarity, this in turn leading to a general increase in anomie, of feeling outside society. This is the root of Durkheim's interest in suicide as an indicator of social breakdown, and in religion as a moral and integrative force.

Any discussion of normality and pathology as sociological concepts must locate itself in relation to this Durkheimian vision, and acknowledge the linkage of the concepts to ideas about social solidarity and **membership**. As in Durkheim, this chapter will seek to understand the idea of normality in terms of the forces that bind people together, that drive them to seek membership in each other's society. Pathology, conversely, will be understood as the forces that divide people from each other. In contrast to Durkheim, however, the chapter will focus on the active construction of normality, using examples from medicine in particular. The power to define what counts as 'normal', and the role of statistical thinking in the **social construction** of normality, will be addressed. The chapter will also explore the consequences of living in a late modern age where the rules that govern what is to be counted as normal are widely discussed and debated. Before considering these matters, however, we will explore the roots of the desire to be normal.

MEMBERSHIP: WANTING TO BE NORMAL

Human social life, the capacity to communicate with language, to pass understandings between people, even to recognize each other as people rather than some other class of being, depends on our capacity for a basic sense of trust. The development of trust begins in early childhood. The baby must trust that the parent will return when he or she leaves the room, and sometimes experiences difficulty in this. A basic sense of optimism about continuing in life depends on a perception that there is an order and a meaning to life, in which the person has a secure place. Giddens has described these first stages in the formulation of self-identity as 'a sort of emotional inoculation against existential anxieties – a protection against future threats and dangers which allows the individual to sustain hope and courage in the face of whatever debilitating circumstances she or he might later confront' (1991: 39). Thus an orientation towards life rests on what Giddens (deriving the term from psychoanalysis) calls 'ontological security' – a security about being in the world. Durkheim's concept of anomie (as well as his concept of egoism) can be opposed to this, representing the breakdown of ontological security as a sense of aimlessness overwhelms the individual. Significantly, this points the individual towards death, and Durkheim (1897) documents 'anomic' suicide as the consequence of such a dissolution.

In other parts of his work, Durkheim (1912) was concerned to show how religious ritual helps social groups to defend against disintegration and promote solidarity. Religious rituals in their original ('elementary') forms were not simply matters of affirming belief, but were occasions for the generation of emotional energy. In such rituals sacred objects or symbols ('totems') are invested with the values of the community involved. Such rituals are of particular importance at times of major transformation such as birth, puberty, marriage and death, as is shown in the chapter 'Life/Death'. The Durkheimian anthropologist Van Gennep (1909) made a special study of these, calling them 'rites of passage' to indicate their capacity to generate new social identities for individuals involved. In Giddens's terms, one might understand such occasions as generating optimism by reinforcing the ontological security of members.

Later sociologists have extended the Durkheimian interest in the major ceremonies of traditional social groups to an analysis of the small-scale interactions of everyday life. Thus for Goffman (1967) ritual permeates daily social life, indicating, for example, status divisions by words and body movements that convey deference, or demonstrate membership of particular groups by styles of dress, manners or displays of 'right' attitudes. Garfinkel (1963) has exposed the precarious nature of the agreements on which everyday social interaction is based in a series of 'experiments' designed to disrupt expectations. Thus, he reports the following interaction:

S: [*waving his hand cheerily*] How are you?
E: How am I in regard to what? My health, my finance, my school work, my peace of mind, my . . .
S: [*red in the face and suddenly out of control*] Look! I was just trying to be polite. Frankly, I don't give a damn how you are.

(adapted from Garfinkel 1963: 222)

The second speaker (E) disrupts the ritualized greeting that is expected by the first speaker (S) by contradicting taken-for-granted assumptions about normal behaviour. Norms of conduct guard against such 'misunderstandings' by indicating agreed definitions about the meaning of particular actions or forms of words. By demonstrating their understanding of such 'agreements' people indicate their membership in the social group amongst whom such agreements are current.

The sociology of Talcott Parsons (1951) tends to depict social norms as static, independent entitles, commanding widespread consensus and exerting a constraining influence on the individual, being rules to which people either subscribe or do not. This is inappropriate for understanding late modern social conditions, where self-identity is actively constructed through the strategic selection of a multitude of available memberships. For example, disavowing a norm can be a means of asserting membership elsewhere, as in the following interaction, where an adolescent responding to a parent's question conducts a Garfinkel-like experiment to reject the norms of family membership in favour of an alternative identity:

P: Where are you going?
A: Out.
P: What are you going to do?
A: Nothing.

(adapted from Giddens 1989: 96)

However, broadly speaking everyday social interaction can be seen as a continual negotiation of membership through interaction ritual, routinely contributing to the ontological security of members who thereby reinforce their own and others' agreement to continue in the enterprise of normal social life.

PATHOLOGY AND SOCIAL EXCLUSION

Because of the capacity of sociology to expose what lies behind everyday social consensus, and to make explicit the rules which normally bind people together, it has tended to attract individuals who are particularly interested in exploring marginal situations. Studying people who stand outside the group, who challenge the norms held by the majority, or who are strangers, is attractive to the individual sociologist who may identify aspects of his or her own biography with that of the marginalized (e.g. Becker 1963). The study of people who break or do not know rules can provide moments of particular analytic insight (e.g. Schutz 1964b). Making what is 'normal' seem strange is a fundamental methodological orientation in sociology and anthropology, and has led at times to quite extreme positions about the nature of knowledge and morality, implying the impossibility of sustaining universal standards of truth or goodness.[2]

The variability of norms is demonstrated in the development of 'manners', documented by the historical sociologist Norbert Elias (1939), whose investigation of this apparently minor aspect of social life has revealed that the standards expected at the dinner tables of modern society are historically and culturally specific, suggesting a raising in the threshold of shame and disgust over a period of centuries. This is shown in a series of quotations from European books on manners, presented with dates of authorship:

1558   It does not befit a modest, honourable man to prepare to relieve nature in the presence of other people. . . Similarly, he will not wash his hands on returning to decent society from private places, as the reason for his washing will arouse disagreeable thoughts in people.

1560   It is a far too dirty thing for a child to offer others something he has gnawed, or something he disdains to eat himself, unless it be to his servant . . . he must not lift the meat to his mouth now with one hand and now with the other . . . he should always do so with his right hand, taking the bread or meat decently with three fingers only.

1672   If everyone is eating from the same dish, you should take care not to put your hand in it before those of higher rank do so.

1714   Wherever you spit, you should put your foot on the saliva . . . At the houses of the great, one spits into one's handkerchief. (from books on manners, quoted in Elias 1939: 107, 74, 75, 127)

All of these describe behaviour that today would be considered abnormal, marking out a person as socially inferior, blameworthy and in need of correction. Yet they were taken from books that were trying to show their readers the standards of behaviour necessary to gain entry to the highest social circles, showing that norms considered acceptable in one society are not necessarily appropriate in another.

The existence of books on manners also reveals that norms can become matters for debate and reflection, and their manipulation can become a part of an individual's strategy for seeking social advantage. Thus the social climber seeks to learn the behaviour considered appropriate in the group to which he or she aspires, and the snob specializes in identifying the marks of bad behaviour that reveal inferior social origins. **Stigma**, the deliberate marking of an individual as offensive, inferior and blameworthy, is a type of inflicted social pain. It is commonly used by individuals to affirm their own membership of a desired group and thus sustain their own ontological security. As described in the chapter 'Life/Death', the application of stigma can be understood as a minor rehearsal for killing, part of a victorious affirmation of survival which depends on the identification of an enemy who carries the burden of death on behalf of the 'normal' person.

Stigma is therefore a strategy of power, and its workings have been described in detail by Erving Goffman (1968). The stigmatized individual may be chosen on the basis of blemishes of the body (e.g. leprosy), of character or of behaviour (e.g. alcoholism), or some tribal stigma may be gained by virtue of belonging to some disfavoured social group (e.g. Jews). The stigma applied to people with AIDS is unusual in combining all three of these: the physical appearance of illness, allegations of promiscuity, and membership of what doctors call the 'risk' groups for AIDS: homosexuals, drug users and prostitutes, who are already stigmatized. A 'master status' or 'label' is bestowed upon the person thus stigmatized, which 'spoils' all other aspects of identity. Once known, the label confirms that all aspects of the person's behaviour can be understood as being due to this new identity. Thus if people with mental illness become angry it is understood as a sign of their illness rather than being due to some other cause (Rosenhan 1973). A variety of subterfuges may be engaged in by individuals with stig-matized conditions, involving passing as normal, covering up stigmas, controlling information and, ultimately, seeking consolation and com-panionship in subcultures of others (one's 'own') with the same condition (e.g. the leper colony, the self-help group).

TOLERANCE

In late modern social conditions, however, tolerance is a widespread social value. The unpleasant effects of stigma are widely recognized and stigma champions (whom Goffman 1968 called the 'wise') rapidly arise to combat the marginalization of the stigmatized. Tribal sentiments are generally condemned as primitive, and laws to promote social harmony and inclu-sion (e.g. race relations law, equal opportunities) command general sup-port. Softer social labels have emerged to describe categories of person previously referred to by words such as 'blind', 'deaf', 'feeble minded', 'retarded', 'mad', 'cripples', 'idiots' or 'bastards'. Once considered accept-able, these labels now too nakedly convey connotations of inferiority. As a further example, the case of AIDS is again illustrative. The homophobic sentiment generated by newspaper headlines (e.g. 'the gay plague') has attracted official opprobrium, and the medical profession and government have united to propose a more 'tolerant' view, that will not 'drive it underground'.[3]

In these circumstances people have difficulty in finding safe enemies to hate. One or two still surface from time to time (e.g. child abusers), and particular efforts may be devoted to stigmatizing the intolerant (e.g. racists), but the individual in late modern society is constantly confronted with potential enemies whose basic humanity threatens to surface and generate feelings of sympathy. If this does not happen straight away, supporters and explainers will emerge, suggesting psychological motives for bad behaviour that induce the listener to see things from the other's point of view. The political debates about criminality reflect this basic tension: is the criminal bad and therefore worthy of punishment, or is the criminal motive understandable in the circumstances, the product of nurture rather than nature, and the criminal therefore deserving of rehabilitation, inclusion and a renewal of social membership amongst the 'normals'?

The historical growth in empathy (the capacity to see things from others' point of view) in European societies has been described by Norbert Elias (1939) as a part of a great 'civilizing process'. Associated with the monopolization of the means to violence by central authorities, firstly by powerful kings, then by democratically elected states, disputes between individuals have gradually come to be settled by means of words rather than resort to violent assaults. The means to power for the medieval knight depended on bodily strength and his readiness to use martial skills to physically subdue enemies. With the development of courtly society (which depended on regal powers to inhibit such violent behaviour), manners, artifice, strategy, calculation and manipulation came to govern individuals' relations with each other. Whereas the traditional individual led the life of a warrior, the modern person came to lead the life of a diplomat, carefully negotiating a myriad of complex norms, weaving in and out of different groups, strategically claiming membership according to taste, lifestyle or personal advantage. This way of life requires finely tuned social skills, and the stress of failure in this complex enterprise has become the subject of psychological expertise. Stress, in fact, has become a catchword of our times, seen as causing all manner of modern ailments, and standing as a metaphor for the difficulties of modern living.

The path of the **deviant**, however, is not always one that is conferred or adopted by human agency. People are sometimes marginalized through no actively applied stigma, nor through more or less conscious decisions to break rules, but by virtue of the deterioration of their bodies. The problem of embodiment has only recently become a topic of major sociological concern (e.g. Turner 1984; 1992), but it provides an additional insight into the nature of pathological social identity, exclusion and inclusion.

PAIN AND THE UNMAKING OF THE WORLD

Phenomenological sociology aims to explore the way in which human consciousness constructs meaning from an otherwise undifferentiated, chaotic stream of experience (Berger and Luckmann 1966). Berger (1969), for example, describes how individuals use religion to construct worlds of meaning. Making a world of meaning contrasts with the 'unmaking' effect of certain illnesses, which threaten the individual with a resurgence of chaos and the destruction of meaning. Illness, in fact, can be understood as a sort of Garfinkel-like 'experiment' with shared meanings, threatening to disrupt these and force the individual to reassess his or her relationships with others. Examples of this can be found by studying people with chronic pains.

Chronic pain differs from the normal pain of which we all have experience in that it does not cease once tissue damage has healed, and no obvious physical cause can be found. It commonly attracts labels such as 'low back pain' or 'chronic pain syndrome' which are residual categories used by medicine in which to place problems that are ill understood and for which there is no evident remedy. The lack of an established medical cause can be profoundly disturbing, as is demonstrated in the words of some sufferers:

> When my leg went numb in March of '77, then . . . it really hit me. I almost flipped out, in a sense, because I knew that there it was again, and it would be like a sore tooth. It would never go away. That's when it really threw me in an emotional turmoil – [a] crisis. (Hilbert 1984: 367)

> I honestly don't know what it is. And *that's* pretty frustrating a lot of times. Just the fact that *I* don't know what it is, you know. I've been frustrated with that. Well, what *is* this goddamn thing? Why do I *have* these headaches? (1984: 368)

This experience gives people the feeling that they are experiencing their bodies incorrectly. When others begin to find the chronic nature of the pain puzzling this can lead to a degree of intolerance that is akin to stigma. Constant unexplained pain produces feelings of isolation and difference from others who inhabit a more normal world. Here are the words of another person with chronic pain:

> Sometimes, if I had to visualize it, it would seem as though there there's a ah . . . a demon, a monster, something very . . . horrible lurking around banging the insides of my body, ripping it apart. And ah, I'm containing it, or I'm trying to contain it, so that no one else can see it, so that no one else can be disturbed by it. Because it's scaring the daylights out of me, and I'd assume that . . . gee, if anybody had to, had to look at this, that . . . they'd avoid me like the plague. So I redouble my efforts to . . . say . . . I'm gonna be perfectly contained about this whole thing. And maybe the less I do, the less I make myself known, and the less I . . . venture out . . . or display any, any initiative, then I won't let the, this junk out. It seems like there's something very, very terrible happening. I have no control over it. (Good 1994: 121–2)

Hilbert, a sociologist who has studied people with chronic pains, has described their experience as 'continuously approaching the amorphous frontier of non-membership . . . They are falling out of culture' (1984: 375). These troubles represent an extreme end of our experience of embodiment. For the most part we possess adequate 'explanations' for physical pains, these being powerfully underwritten by scientific narratives. In fact, the institutionalized narratives provided by medicine are actively sought out and appropriated in the world-making activities of individuals concerned to discover a meaning to the experience of bodily suffering. Medical narratives in modern society have in general taken the place of religious narratives in explaining the problem of human suffering, and in sustaining the hopes of the suffering individual to claim membership and assert normality. Medical treatment – whether technically successful or not – can be understood as a ritual of inclusion, proceeding by documenting the varieties of the pathological so that concepts of normal illnesses can be sustained, generating new membership categories for people's use. Medicine is therefore a key institution for defining normality and for distinguishing and containing pathological conditions. Its power to define what counts as normality means that it is implicated in strategies of power.

GOVERNING NORMALITY

It will be clear now that the achievement of membership by espousing normality is a basic feature of social life. It is threatened by actively applied stigma or, as in the section above, by illness. It is also the case that what counts as normal is socially constructed, and that different versions of normality are actively appropriated into individual projects of self-identity. Sustaining particular definitions of what is normal, and the gathering (or coercing) of people's allegiance to one's definition, is an aspect of power. People can be encouraged to participate in a disturbing range of behaviour on the grounds that this is 'normal'. Thus the Nazi bureaucrats who organized transportations to concentration camps were 'normal' citizens with 'normal' families and lives, doing a 'normal' job (Bauman 1989).

The very word 'normal' is itself used strategically to gain power. Ian Hacking has made a particular study of the statistical construction of normality as it has been applied to social life, commenting that: 'the benign and sterile-sounding word "normal" has become one of the most powerful ideological tools of the twentieth century' (1990: 169). He points out the role that numbers and statistics have played in regulating European populations since the early nineteenth century. Counting aspects of social life, particularly those which threatened social order, such as suicide, crime, vagrancy, madness, prostitution and disease, became very widespread, and was carried out by government agencies (as indeed it still is today). This led to a particular style of reasoning based on statistical probabilities, so that the likelihood of crime, the risk of suicide, the potential for madness, were all subject to rational calculation, representing a taming of chance and a gain in control and predictability. These became deeply embedded in the mentality of government, and increasingly entered the thinking of citizens.

Auguste Comte (1798–1857), who coined the term 'sociology', derived his inspiration from an emerging medical view of the body and disease. His 'positive philosophy' portrayed society as an organism continually aspiring to a state of normality. Coupled with emerging statistical ideas about normality, this type of thinking came to be associated with a view of pathological states as progressive deviations from the norm, which was itself often defined in terms of statistical averages. The word 'normality' increasingly came to conflate what *is* the case with what *ought* to be (a linking of fact and value). Thus the average life, defined as an absence of pathology, was increasingly seen as desirable, and sociology in its origins was implicated in promoting these conservative ideals. Indeed, Durkheim played a part in this progression of ideas.

SOVEREIGN POWER AND DISCIPLINARY SURVEILLANCE

In conjunction with the rise in statistical definitions of the normal was a shift in the manner in which power was exercised. This has been described by the French social theorist Michel Foucault, who distinguishes between two forms of power: *sovereign* and *disciplinary*. Sovereign power was characteristic of the sixteenth- and seventeenth-century rule of European kings. Under this regime, power depended on physical coercion and public punishment for wrongdoing. Ceremonies of punishment and retribution, such as public executions, demonstrated to the population at large that criminal acts were understood as an assault upon the authority of the king, and were duly punished by exacting revenge upon the body of the criminal. For the witnesses of public executions, the criminal was thereby defined as the other, placed outside humanity, devoid of the rights of membership as an example of pathology. Public executions strengthened the allegiance of the population to the king (who was also a god) by providing a safe enemy to stigmatize and kill.

In various ways this type of regal authority had declined in European countries by the nineteenth century (the French cut off the head of their king), and was replaced by a new form of disciplinary power. This operated by constructing and promoting, with the aid of statistical information, particular definitions of normality. From being coerced to follow the will of the king, citizens learned to survey themselves as bearers of normality. Foucault illustrated this by referring to the panopticon (meaning 'all-seeing'), Jeremy Bentham's design for a prison which symbolized the new form of power. The design of this prison is such that the guard in a central tower can observe the inmates' actions without being seen by the prisoners themselves. The prisoners, then, survey nothing but their own selves, thereby becoming their own jailors. Foucault is particularly critical of people advocating 'humane' penal regimes. In relation to the supposed liberation of the insane from their chains in Parisian asylums in the eighteenth century, for example, he argues that these substitute for what he calls the 'free terror of madness, the stifling anguish of responsibility' (Foucault 1967, reprinted in Rabinow 1984: 145). Self-surveillance involves the internalization of standards of normality, so that under disciplinary power people constantly monitor themselves for signs of pathology. Thus people draw upon a widespread knowledge of what it is to be sane, healthy and good, and of their opposites, madness, disease and criminality. The role of psychology in promoting particular versions of mental hygiene, and a particular view of the good life, has been documented extensively by Rose (1989). A particular technique of disciplinary power is the confession, whereby people admit to bad (or 'unhealthy') behaviour, thus speaking themselves into a discourse about what it is to be normal. Rose regards psychotherapy as a form of such confession.

While definitions of normality are clearly implicated in strategies of power, the accounts provided by Foucault and his followers often lack analysis of how particular definitions further the interests of particular social groups (beyond some vaguely defined 'government'). Power appears to be diffused so widely, and constructed so readily in discourses that often appear to come from nowhere, that the term loses its capacity for indicating a technique for gaining social and material advantage over others. Indeed, in recent formulations, disciplinary power is equated with the creative expression of novel forms of selfhood.

THE ROLE OF MEDICINE

It was shown earlier that medical analogies have influenced the development of ideas of normality in sociologists such as Durkheim and Comte. Foucault (1967; 1976), too, pays particular attention to the role of medicine in defining what it is to be normal. As a social institution, medicine can be seen as having taken over from religion in a process of secularization, becoming increasingly influential in defining the good life (Turner 1987). Doctors play an important part in policing social pathology.

This was first described by Parsons (1951) in his account of the 'sick role'. Basically, doctors are entrusted with distinguishing malingerers from the 'truly' sick, acting as gatekeepers to legitimate entry to the socially accepted sick role, which itself contains certain rights and responsibilities (for example, to try to get better). It was shown earlier that the experience of pain can be experienced as a fall out of membership. Doctors, in a sense, 'catch' the falling individual by providing legitimating labels for the sick which satisfactorily explain their condition in the eyes of others – justifying, for example, failure to carry out 'normal' activities such as going to work. The problem for some individuals with chronic pains is that some doctors believe them to be malingerers, so that not only do they face the existential terrors of a body beyond their understanding or control, they may also experience stigma.

Parsons presented an analysis that was basically supportive of doctors, assuming a consensus about their altruistic motives. Subsequent critics (e.g. Freidson 1970; Navarro 1976) have noted that medical definitions of normality – the criteria by which doctors police the sick role – are often distorted by professional interests and by the state using the medical profession to promote its interests against those of patients. Thus doctors may be more likely to admit for treatment an 'interesting' case that is likely to result in a satisfying cure, and less likely to admit a person who is incurable or otherwise troublesome. The state may try to exert a particular influence to restrain doctors from signing too many sickness notes to allow people to avoid work or claim benefits.

More broadly, medical knowledge and practice play a part in categorizing, ordering and containing a variety of pathologies – in other words, constructing them. The application of Foucauldian ideas suggests that medicine plays an important part in making available to people ways of thinking about pathology. Foucault paid particular attention to the role of hospitals and asylums in dividing different categories of deviance, and in constructing statistical definitions of normality. Thus the distinction between mental and physical illness, and the distinction of madness from badness (criminality), only emerged gradually, and under medical supervision. Surveys of institutions of confinement existing previous to these divisions revealed how thoroughly mixed these categories once were:

> In 1690 a survey of 3000 internees at Salpêtrière . . . revealed that the majority of them were paupers, vagabonds and beggars, while the rest were, in the terminology of the survey, 'ordinary folk', 'prisoners of *lettres de cachet*', 'decrepit women', 'infirm and dotty old women', 'epileptics', 'innocent dwarfs and deformed', 'feeble minded', 'violent mad', and 'incorrigible girls'. Almost a century later, in 1781 . . . in a Berlin workhouse 'idlers', 'rogues and libertines', 'infirm and criminals', and 'destitute old women and children' all mixed together. (Cousins and Hussain 1984: 110)

Diagnosis, as a 'dividing practice', represents the application of medical categories which are now used to separate classes of the people described above. The advantage of the Parisian hospital system, Foucault (1976) argues, lay in the fact that large numbers of relatively powerless patients were congregated in one place. Doctors could therefore begin to see their patients as 'cases' or 'numbers', carriers of diseases rather than unique individuals with unique diseases. Disease was therefore separated from the patient, studied, ordered and categorized in its own right, exhibiting characteristics that were separate from the biography of individual patients. Statistical norms concerning the frequency of disease and its appearance in the body could then be constructed.

This style of thinking helped to make people's behaviour (their disease) into a thing, with a rule-governed life of its own, that people 'caught' (as in infectious diseases) or fell into (as in categories of madness). In the field of mental illness, many categories used in the past have come to be regarded as ideological constructions of pathology, serving the interests of social control. Thus there is an extensive critique of the diagnosis of hysteria as a device constructed by a patriarchal medical profession to pathologize and thus control women rebelling against the restrictive Victorian norms governing appropriate female conduct (summarized in James 1994).

CONCLUSION

In this chapter it has been argued that the desire to be normal, and to exclude and stigmatize the abnormal or pathological, is linked to the desire for membership and security that is a basic motive for participation in social life. Durkheim's sociology is centrally preoccupied with issues of social solidarity and social order, but is itself somewhat normative in spite of its analytic strengths. Thus Durkheim paid scant attention to the role of power in the social construction and manipulation of standards of normality. Durkheim himself adopted a statistical definition of normality as the average, a perspective that must be seen in the context of his own times.

Defining normality and pathology, and the widespread diffusion of such definitions, so that people come to judge themselves according to such definitions, is an important feature of disciplinary power, often exercised on behalf of professions or by the state. Sociology possesses the capacity to reflect upon these strategies of power, and the chapter has sought to provide the outlines of sociological perspectives on medical definitions of normality. This should not obscure the fact that other institutions (e.g. law, religion, the penal system, armies, schools) can also be analysed in this way.

KEY CONCEPTS

NORMAL Normal phenomena in social life are usually the most stable and enduring ones, things that last the longest and provide most continuity – this does not mean that they are necessarily 'good'. Attitudes that last can be racist, sexist and prejudicial but their endurance can make them seem normal.

PATHOLOGICAL Pathological phenomena in society are usually the most fleeting or transitory. This does not mean that they are sick or injured but that they do not have a lasting impact on the social structure. Thus their pathology stems from their instability.

Membership   Sociologists use membership to imply belonging to a society, group or culture. That belonging means that the member will be conscious of all of the rules and expectations that hold that group together as that group. Membership therefore indicates that becoming a member requires social learning and not just a natural development.

Social constructionism   This is a fairly recent form of social theory which derives from phenomenology. It suggests that social phenomena are made up according to the times and places in which they occur thus their meaning has to derive from their social context. So, for example, there has always been child abuse, for what reasons are we so concerned with it at the current time?

Stigma   This concept came into sociology through the work of Erving Goffman. He produced the thesis that some people suffer from spoiled person-alities because of disabilities, special needs, malformations or incapacities which they carry with them as if they were bearing a 'stigma'. A stigma, then, is anything that impedes the full integration of the self into the collectivity.

Deviance   This is a way of talking about behaviour that breaks normal rules. In societies rules breakers are usually punished and thus the normal features of a society are upheld. Deviants are not, however, a constant group, as you move through history in our own society you will find that actions once regarded as crimes are no longer thought of as such e.g. homosexuality, and as we move across societies you will find variance in their definitions of what counts as deviant e.g. use of marijuana.

Surveillance   This is a concept that has come into social theory through the works of Michel Foucault. It means that power operates in a modern society through the strategies we have developed for watching each others performance and also the socio-psychological ways in which we have come to watch ourselves through guilt and shame.

NOTES

1   See the chapter 'Relativism/Absolutism' for a definition.
2   This is the position of relativism, discussed in the chapter 'Relativism/ Absolutism'.
3   Durkheim would have understood these exhortations to altruism as an appropriate balance to the excessive egoism found in late modern society.

Culture/Nature

Helen Thomas

Sociology's concern to establish itself as a legitimate scientific mode of investigation in the late nineteenth century centred on a rejection of the positivist claim that human activity could be understood in terms of a causal biological explanation. At the same time, sociology maintained that the natural world is moulded by society and is transformed through human behaviour and social processes. In other words, the social is not reducible to the biological, and the natural world is constituted through the social. The clearest example of this position can be found in Émile Durkheim's approach to sociology. Durkheim (1982) maintained that society constituted a reality in its own right. He argued that in order to establish itself as a credible scientific discipline, sociology had to have its own subject matter which would delineate it from the other sciences such as biology and psychology. Although Durkheim considered that sociology should conform to the canons laid down by the other more established natural sciences, he insisted that it should have its own order of facts – *social facts*. Social facts, for Durkheim, have three characteristics: they are *external* to the individual, they are *typical* throughout society, and they *constrain* the individual to act in particular ways. Sociology's task, Durkheim argued, is to examine, classify and provide a causal explanation of the emergence and establishment of social facts and the function they perform in maintaining social order. Although Durkheim in his early work, in line with the positivist philosophy of Auguste Comte and Herbert Spencer, sought to establish that social facts were subject to laws, it is important to note that he maintained that the law-like characteristics of social facts had their own specificity, which was constituted by and through the social, and these were not reducible to physical or biological laws. The idea of nature in Durkheim finds its expression in the *nature of society*, as the following quotation demonstrates:

> It was not sufficient to establish that social facts had their own laws. It had also to be made clear that they have their own laws, specific in nature and comparable to physical or biological laws, without being directly reducible to the latter. (Durkheim 1982: 178)

The opposition between the world of nature and that of culture also finds an expression in the German tradition of sociology through, for example, the work of Max Weber and the neo-Kantian tradition of thought. Positivism, which took its starting point from the natural sciences, did not gain such a strong hold in German cultural and historical thought as it did in France and Britain in the nineteenth century. The idealist philosophy of Immanuel Kant (1724–1804) retained a dominant influence in German cultural thought from the middle of the eighteenth century through to the Revolution of 1848. F.W.D. Hegel's (1770–1831) philosophy, generally regarded as the culminating point in the development in post-Kantian thought, was based on the idealist premise that the true reality of our knowledge of the world is founded on the 'spirit' or the 'idea' as opposed to sensory perception, as the English empiricist philosophers such as David Hume (1711–76) had postulated. This emphasis on the spirit or the *Geist* separated Germany from the mainstream of European social thought. In German historical and social thought the world of the natural sciences and the world of human activity were presumed to be radically different. The natural sciences were concerned with the phenomenal world, while the cultural sciences dealt in the spiritual world (consciousness). Facts were the stuff of the natural sciences, while values were the stuff of the cultural sciences. As a result of the emphasis on the *Geist*, the Germans came to draw a sharp distinction between the natural sciences (*Naturwissenschaften*) and the cultural or historical sciences (*Geisteswissenschaften*). Because the two scientific fields had different objects, it was argued that the cultural sciences could not take their starting point from the natural sciences as the positivists had advocated. This left the exponents of the cultural sciences with the vexing problem of how to develop an approach towards an understanding of human (spiritual) behaviour that was not grounded in a mechanistic or naturalistic model. As H. Stuart Hughes (1974) notes, the result was the development of the method of interpretive understanding, or *verstehen*. The method of *verstehen* was formulated explicitly by the philosopher Wilhelm Dilthey in the 1880s but it received its greater elaboration in Weber's sociology which was directed towards an interpretive understanding of social action with a view to coming to an understanding of their significant causes. Although Weber was concerned to generate a scientific sociology, he nevertheless maintained the strict fact/value distinction which is the cornerstone of the *Geisteswissenschaften* tradition. The rigid separation between the social and the biological and individual psychology which lies at the heart of the classical tradition of sociology, for the most part, has formed the basis of modern sociology. As Paul Hirst and Penny Woolley have noted:

> Sociologists have, on the whole, energetically denied the importance of genetic, physical and individual psychological factors in human social life. In so doing they have reinforced and theorized a traditional cultural opposition between nature and culture. Social relations can even be seen as a *denial* of nature. (1982: 22)

There are a number of topics that could be used to explore further the cultural opposition to nature that has continued to haunt foundationalist approaches to sociology (see, for example, the chapters 'Sex/Gender' and 'Culture/Nature' in this volume). The topic under discussion in this chapter, however, is that of the body. The subject of the body as a topic of inquiry in its own right, until quite recently, has largely been ignored by sociology. That is, sociology has paid scant attention to the singularly most apparent fact of human life, which is that human beings *have* bodies that are both physically delimiting and enabling and that, to a certain extent, they *are* bodies (Turner 1984). It is, after all, through our bodies that we feel, see, smell, touch, speak and experience the world.

Although the fact of embodiment was not placed at the centre of the discourses of sociology, not all the human sciences ignored the body or kept it hidden from direct view. The study of the body, like the study of dance in society (Thomas 1995), has been the focus of attention of anthropologists and ethnographers since the late nineteenth century (see Polhemus 1975 for a detailed discussion of the various phases of development in the anthropology of the body). A consideration of the reasons why the body was featured in the discourses of anthropology as opposed to sociology in the first instance will shed some light on the nature/culture division within sociology.

According to Brian Turner (1991) there are a number of related reasons why anthropology developed a research interest in the body while sociology did not. In its initial stages in the nineteenth century, anthropology was concerned to consider the universal state of humanity. That is, philosophical anthropology within the context of European colonialism and cultural imperialism needed to consider what human beings had in common (the universals) in relation to wide ranging cultural differences of social relations. As a result the ontological importance of the fact of embodiment became a site of universality. This led to a consideration of what were the minimum social and cultural conditions required for the maintenance and continuation of the species. Thus, in part, according to Turner (1991) the body featured in the initial stages of anthropology because it provided one answer to the vexing question of cultural relativism. That is, despite the wide ranging observable differences between cultures, human beings at root were deemed to share certain common characteristics which made the survival of the species possible. The concern, here, then, centred on the age-old question of 'What is man (*sic*)?' The answers ranged from 'man' as a tool maker to 'man' as a creature with a memory, language, culture etc. (Turner 1991: 2).

Another reason why anthropology generated a strong research interest in the body, as Turner (1991: 6) demonstrates, lies in the fact that often in premodern societies the body (the decoration or mutilation of it) plays a central role in the rite of passage between different social statuses. The tattoos, scarification, body decorations etc. are public signifiers of the individual's status, age, family, sex, and tribal affiliation. Although it is also the case that in modern cultural formations dress, demeanour and cosmetics are important indicators of lifestyle and social class, and women are constantly being invited to transform themselves by doing something to their bodies, the body in premodern societies is a more universal site for public symbolization through ritual, and anthropology did start out in the nineteenth century by studying premodern societies.

The incorporation of evolutionary theory, particularly social Darwinism, into anthropology in the nineteenth century provided yet another line of development which contributed to the anthropological study of the body. Charles Darwin's (1969) study of *The Expression of the Emotions in Man and Animals*, first published in 1872, in which he argued that bodily expression is either innate or biologically determined and that it is cross-culturally universal, has been influential in the development of anthropology, although this influence has largely been of the negative kind. As Polhemus (1975) has pointed out, responses to Darwin's thesis led to the development of a nature/culture debate on the character of bodily expression within anthropology, namely the **universality** of bodily expression versus its cultural variability. The universalist position maintained that bodily expression is the same in all societies whilst the relativist position claimed that it is culturally variable. Anthropologists and ethnographers from the American tradition of 'cultural' anthropology in particular, which has its roots in Tylor's (1958) concept of culture, were concerned with the cultural aspects of human behaviour and therefore tended to adopt the cultural variability thesis (Hall 1969; Kroeber 1952; La Barre 1978). The followers of Darwin's position, however, were interested in the natural (non-social) aspects of behaviour and in order to establish the validity of their proposition they adopted the universality thesis. Over a period of time, this nature/culture debate developed into a second related debate, namely the *learnt* versus the *innate* character of bodily expression, or the nurture/nature dichotomy. Two major landmarks in the **nurture** side of the debate published in the 1940s were David Efron's *Gesture, Race and Culture* (1972) and Gregory Bateson and Margaret Mead's *Balinese Character* (1942). These studies influenced subsequent pioneering work in the field in the 1960s, such as Ray Birdwhistell's (1973) study of 'kinesics' (routine everyday movement) and Edward Hall's (1969) work on 'proxemics' (the study of interpersonal social space). Hall's work focused on the 'language of space' to demonstrate the congruences and differences in proxemic behaviour between different cultures. Birdwhistell attempted to treat the body movement as a distinct mode of communication which is learnt within a particular cultural context. Neo-Darwinists such as Paul Ekman (1977) and Ireñaus Eibl-Eibesfeldt (1972) on the other hand, rejected the nurture argument. On the basis of comparative studies of animals and humans they have argued that there is a high degree of association between the primary (natural) affects of anger, fear, surprise, disgust, happiness and sadness and the similar facial gestures that express them and that these are not culturally variable. The neo-Darwinist position also finds expression in more popular contemporary contributions such as Desmond Morris's *Intimate Behaviour* (1979). The notion of the 'human animal' exemplified in the naturalistic approach to the body has had an impact on and to a certain extent has reinforced contemporary popular perceptions of the body as the biological basis upon which the individual and culture are built (Thomas 1995). Social hierarchies and social divisions between groups and individuals, in this view, are not socially constructed but are an outcome of natural, biological or genetic programming. This form of reasoning also finds expression in the recent development of sociobiology (see Hirst and Woolley 1982: 66–89). However, as Turner (1991) notes, physical anthropology as a strand of anthropology has been slow to develop in comparison with the culturalist approach, and the most dominant theoretical trends in both anthropology and sociology have been concerned to focus on culture as opposed to nature.

There are several reasons why classical sociology did *not* give rise to a sociology of the body. To begin with, classical sociological theorists like Weber, Durkheim, Georg Simmel and Ferdinand Tönnies were concerned to define and understand the character of industrial urban societies rather than the differences between human beings in terms of social evolution. The more general philosophical question which sociology posed centred around the problem of *social order* in industrial societies. That is, it asked how it was possible for people to survive in a rapidly changing and alien social environment. For Weber, for example, industrial capitalist society is characterized by a particular form of action: rational action in relation to a goal, or instrumental rationality. He perceived that the bureaucratic social order to which capitalism gave rise would penetrate the very fabric of everyday life and this would lead to a loss of ultimate evaluations and the 'total disenchantment of the world'. That is, everything would be subsumed under instrumental reason. Thus, the issue of social action in German sociological theory, as Turner (1991) argues, came to be treated in terms of the most efficient means to attain a given end. The question of the ontological status of social actors remained *hidden* under the models of law and economics that served to formulate the concepts of the actor, agency, choice, attitudes and goals. Hence, as Turner points out: 'whereas the body had entered anthropology at the fundamental level of ontology, sociology, partly evolving theoretically along the notion of rational economic action, never elaborated a sociology of the body' (1991: 8).

Moreover, while anthropology was concerned with the issue of culture/ nature, sociology centred on the question of historicity (Turner 1991: 8). That is, classical sociological theorizing was concerned with the stages of development of societies, particularly their emergence into modernity or industrial capitalist society. Thus, Marx posed the question of historical development in terms of stages of production which culminated in capitalism, while Durkheim examined the transition from mechanical to organic solidarity, from a previous form of society founded on similarities to the emergence of industrial society founded on differences, and Weber considered the effect of puritanism on the development of modern capitalism. Capitalism, however, as Turner (1991: 8) notes, has distinctive qualities that separate it from other stages of development. Unlike the other older forms of socio-economic organization, capitalism achieves global proportions and in turn drags other forms of societies with different social and economic organizations, such as those in Asia and Africa, into its all-encompassing frame. Consequently, the central problematic of what is nature that had moulded anthropology, as the quotation from Hirst and Woolley (1982) cited earlier emphasizes, became absent in sociology. Sociology has privileged and thus reinforced the key features of mind over body, reason over desire, culture over nature, inscribed in the modernity project (see the chapter 'Modernity/Postmodernity' in this volume). It is important to note that it is precisely at the moment when these predominant ideas that shaped and moulded sociology began to be called into question in the 1980s, through the critiques of feminism and postmodernism, that the question of the body as a historical concern is brought back into the sociological frame: 'However, through most of its short history, sociology has been fundamentally a historical enquiry into the conditions for social change; it never successfully posed the question of the body as a historical issue' (Turner 1991: 8).

It is hardly surprising, then, that anthropology, rather than sociology, focused its attentions on the body. The major concern within the dominant 'cultural' anthropological avenue of research until the mid 1970s, as discussed earlier, has been to show that the ways in which we perceive our bodies and the ways in which we move are not just 'natural facts of existence', but rather are socially constructed. Thus, the aim has been to demonstrate that our routine bodily behaviours are relative to the culture in which they are performed and that they are learnt as opposed to being 'natural'. The cultural anthropological approaches mentioned above, such as those of Ray Birdwhistell and Edward Hall, however, did not develop their insights into the culturally variable and learnt character of bodily behaviour towards a specifically sociological approach to the study of the human body. Although Birdwhistell (1973), for example, argued that you cannot understand bodily behaviour unless you relate it back to the total context of the situation in which it is expressed and performed, he did not attempt to push his analysis further towards a discussion of the relationship between bodily behaviour in specific micro-social contexts and the wider macro-societal level. That is, Birdwhistell did not consider how the body is viewed and represented in society and how in turn this might affect the ways that individuals conduct and manage themselves bodily in everyday life. For the most part, cultural anthropologists have been over-concerned to demonstrate the validity of their case over and above that of exponents of social Darwinism rather than directing their findings towards a more sociological approach to the body in which the body is treated as a symbol of society (Polhemus 1975).

A major exception to this rule within the dominant American tradition on the body can be found in the work of the sociologist Erving Goffman. In *Relations in Public* (1972), Goffman attempted to uncover the 'social rules' for appropriate bodily behaviour in public places and spaces. Goffman, whose main body of work can be located within the symbolic interactionist tradition of thought, pointed out in *Relations in Public* that he owed much of his insight into the social rules and norms of bodily behaviour to the Durkheimian tradition of thought. Within the European Durkheimian tradition, writers like Robert Hertz (1973) in 1909, Marcel Mauss (1973) in 1934 and much later Mary Douglas in the 1970s have pointed the way to secure a sociological approach to the study of bodily expression. Their concerns have centred on an exploration of the social aspects of human bodily expression in order to elucidate, and say something significant about, the rules and the categories that are expressed in the social body or society. Although this tradition of **body symbolism** has its roots in Durkheim's sociological theory, in light of the discussion of sociology's opposition to nature and its concern with historicity, it should come as no great surprise to find that when a sociological study of the body did begin to develop, it came out of social anthropology which had been influenced by Durkheim's ideas, as opposed to sociology itself.

Although Durkheim was not concerned particularly with the body, for the reasons given above, nevertheless it was his claims regarding the social construction of knowledge in *The Elementary Forms of the Religious Life*, first published in 1915, that provided the impetus for this social constructionist tradition of the body within anthropology. As suggested at the beginning of this chapter, Durkheim was concerned to demarcate the study of the social world from that of biology or psychology. He sought to demonstrate how society moulded the individual in its own light. Durkheim maintained that the whole (society) is always greater than the sum of its parts (social institutions and individuals). Society, according to Durkheim, constitutes a reality in its own right (*sui generis*) and he maintained that social relations are different from and not reducible to individuals or other non-social factors. He sought to demonstrate the power of the social by focusing on such topics as the division of labour, suicide, and knowledge and beliefs In *The Elementary Forms of the Religious Life*, Durkheim (1976) set out to demonstrate the social basis of knowledge by seeking to explain the origin of religious beliefs from an examination of Aboriginal classificatory systems and Amerindian religions (in keeping with the nineteenth-century unilineal theory of history, these contemporary non-literate cultures were viewed as standing for earlier, more 'primitive' forms of social organization). Here, he argues that it was humanity's innate sociality that led to the development of a common set of symbols (language, rituals, rites). According to Durkheim, each individual contains a part of society within him/her. In order to become conscious of it and thereby organize themselves collectively, individuals had to communicate with each other. Symbolic forms and their potential for communally shared knowledge of the world have their roots in the social nature of human beings. Durkheim treats primitive belief systems as cosmological systems (systems of knowledge concerning the structure of the universe, creation and so forth). They constitute forms of knowledge that stem from the social realm. This is important because what Durkheim is saying is that knowledge, far from existing independently of the social realm, is generated from within the society itself; it is socially constructed.

Durkheim, however, did not apply his insights into the social construction of knowledge in 'primitive' belief systems to 'modern' industrial, scientific systems of thought (Douglas 1975). The reasons for this are twofold. First, as suggested above, he considered that 'primitive' societies were completely different from 'modern' industrial societies. The former corresponded to 'mechanical solidarity' and the latter to 'organic solidarity' (Durkheim 1947). Second, he believed that science, unlike primitive systems of knowledge, constituted an objective form of knowledge. Nevertheless, as Douglas (1975) has pointed out, despite his concern to exclude scientifically oriented forms of knowledge from his analysis, the theoretical impact of Durkheim's work remains, particularly if we refocus our attention and view ourselves in a similar light as the traditionally perceived denigrated 'other': primitive cultures. That is, forms of knowledge do not exist outside society: they are generated from and organized within the social realm and they are voiced in and through the various aspects of everyday experience.

'What,' we might ask, 'has this got to do with perceptions of the body?' Hertz (1973) and Mauss (1973), and latterly Douglas (1970; 1973; 1975), sought to apply Durkheim's ideas on the social construction of knowledge to the study of the body. Hertz turned his attention to the study of left/right body symbolism. He began from the proposition that the right hand and the left hand were classified and regarded differently in society: the right hand was elevated and the left was lowered in the eyes of society.

Hertz argued that there was no significant 'natural difference' between the two hands and that the clearly observed distinction between the right and the left was caused by the coercive power of society and maintained by the rules and the restrictions that surround it. Thus, just as Durkheim argued that society shapes the individual in its own image, so Hertz argued that the body is socially constructed. Hertz's perceived hierarchy of the right hand over the left, in turn, gave rise to a great deal of debate and refutation in French anthropology, although the principle that the body was symbolized by society was upheld (see Needham 1973). So, despite the fact that the validity of Hertz's observation of the 'pre-eminence of the right hand throughout society' was called into question, his theoretical premise that society gives meaning to and constrains the way the body is perceived was upheld. According to Hertz, the body has certain natural characteristics – left side and right side, back and front, top half and bottom half, hair, nails etc. – to which society can and does give meaning. The features of the human body are given a symbolic loading by society although for all practical purposes they are conceived as 'natural' (non-social).

Mauss (1973) focused on the learnt character of everyday techniques such as swimming, running and walking. He sought to demonstrate that our ordinary routine bodily behaviours, from waking to sleeping, from movement to stillness, are socially controlled. He also maintained that what we ordinarily conceive as 'natural' behaviour in relation to the body is also socially bound, such as the right amount of sleep the body requires to stay healthy. Although he considered that as he was concerned with movements of the body, the biological and psychological aspects must be considered, he nevertheless concluded that techniques of the body are governed by society through the educational process. Like Hertz, he adopted a social constructionist model.

The body, for Hertz (1973) and Mauss (1973), then, is a microcosm of society, and as such it is an appropriate area of sociological inquiry. The implications of this are that by focusing on bodily expression, the sociologist can draw out a number of layers of insight into our everyday experiences in society. This is particularly the case, Mauss (1973) argued, in relation to gender. All societies (as far as we know) seek to make distinctions between the sexes; and precisely because the body is an 'image of society', according to Mauss, it is an appropriate area to investigate the social construction of gender (see also the chapter 'Sex/Gender'). Although Hertz and Mauss indicated their intention of taking the 'nature' (of the body) into account, their social constructionist approach ultimately reinstated and sustained the culture/nature dichotomy in sociology. The concept of a 'natural' body is partially redundant in this view.

Douglas's (1970; 1973; 1975) work on the body draws on and extends the analysis put forward by Hertz and in particular by Mauss. Like Hertz (1973) and Mauss (1973), Douglas sees that the body is always treated as an image of society. While Hertz, in line with Durkheim, restricted his study to the analysis of 'primitive' classification systems, both Mauss and Douglas draw from a range of cultures, including 'modern' industrial societies. Indeed, Douglas (1970) argues that ritual is not simply a feature of 'primitive' societies but cuts across the traditionally perceived divide between 'us' (modern industrial formations) and 'them' (primitive cultures), and that this may be clearly seen in the rituals enacted on the body. She attempts to demonstrate that the way we perceive our bodily functions, boundaries and margins mirrors the type of society we belong to.

> The body is a model that can stand for any bounded system. Its boundaries can represent any boundaries that are threatened or precarious. The body is a complex structure. The function of the different parts affords it a rich source of symbols for other complex structures. (Douglas 1970: 138)

For Douglas, the body symbolizes society and society symbolizes the body. This is not a one-way process from society to the body or vice versa; rather, there is a degree of reciprocity at work so that each body, the physical body and the social body, reinforce each other. This reciprocity is implicit in the way we use our bodies in everyday life and in the attention we afford them.

In *Purity and Danger* (1970), for example, Douglas considers the symbolic load carried in attitudes towards bodily waste, urine, faeces, nail parings etc. There she draws particular attention to boundary maintenance and social forces that influence pollution ideas in society. She argues that the social system's concern to maintain itself in its boundaries is reflected in the care taken by society to maintain the body's boundaries. Douglas proposes that by examining the care taken towards the body's boundaries and margins, we should be able to say something significant about the idea that a particular social system has of itself. She suggests that people come to know their own society through the rules and rituals that are routinely enacted on the body and are expressed in the care and attention that is afforded it.

In *Natural Symbols* (1973) Douglas develops her approach to body symbolism further, and is there concerned to provide a method for analysing ritual and body symbolism that would enable comparisons to be made between groups that share the same social environment. In this work and in *Implicit Meanings* (1975), Douglas expresses a concern to get away from the culture/nature hierarchy in anthropology and sociology in order to demonstrate that we are not quite as different from others as we might imagine: 'we must lower the fence between us, ourselves, and them, the primitive tribes, and between us, humanity, and them, animals' (1975: 212). In order to do this she seeks to distinguish what she terms a 'natural tendency' to represent situations of a certain kind in an 'appropriate bodily style' (1973: 97). Mauss (1973) had proposed that there is no such thing as a natural body. Douglas maintains, however, that the body is symbolized by all societies and as such, she argues, it is a 'natural symbol'. At the same time, however, she argues that the ways in which the body is expressed and the meanings that surround it are culturally specific. 'The social body,' according to Douglas, 'constrains the way the physical body is perceived' (1973: 93). Since this natural expression is culturally determined, Douglas (1973: 97) insists that any consideration of the body as a natural symbol would entail paying careful attention to the 'social dimension'. Therefore, although she might start with the proposition of a 'natural body', the concern is always directed towards understanding of the particular social formation which the body expresses and through which the body is symbolized. As a result of her concern with the social body, as Chris Shilling (1993) points out, the individual body (that is, 'the ways in which people live, experience and perceive of their bodies') is in danger of collapsing 'into the positions and categories made available by the social system'.

Thus, the theoretical framework within this Durkheimian influenced tradition of the body is constructed in such a way as to examine the *social* aspects of human bodily expression in order to elucidate and say something significant about the rules and the categories that are expressed in the social order. It presents a sociological approach to the study of the body wherein the human body is treated as a symbol of society. This social constructionist approach has proved influential in anthropology. Its import for sociology has to do with the fact that it demonstrated that the body is a legitimate topic for sociological analysis. Since the mid 1980s, the body has emerged as an important topic of inquiry across the spectrum of the social sciences and the humanities. Sociologists, on the whole, have not drawn on the work of Douglas or Mauss and, as Shilling notes, 'have tended to look elsewhere for resources to assist their investigation of the body as a socially constructed entity' (1993: 73).

Feminist incursions into the social sciences, which have led to a rethinking of issues of culture/nature *vis-à-vis* gender inequalities, have proven important in the re-evaluation of the role of the body in large-scale industrial societies (see the chapter 'Sex/Gender'). Feminists from different theoretical perspectives have argued for the reclamation of women's bodies from the hands of patriarchal discourses, and have insisted that women be treated as agents of knowledge. Emily Martin's study *The Woman in the Body* (1989), for example, demonstrates that the ways in which women feel about their bodies in the contexts of their experiences of menstruation, giving birth and so on are often quite contrary to the assumptions made about women encapsulated in medical texts by medical science. These medicalized discourses on women's bodies, which are taken as a yardstick for measuring reality, are not value-free, as medical science would maintain. Rather, according to Martin (1989), they are ideological and oppressive to women and have wide ranging social consequences. Other developments in social theory, such as the analysis of class, status and consumption, have also led to a reconsideration of the role of the body in society. In Pierre Bourdieu's (1984) analysis, for example, the body turns out to be more than a written-on page: that is, it is not like a set of clothes that you can put on or take off at will. Rather, ideologies of class, gender and race are inscribed onto the anatomical surface of the body. Moreover, the current popularity of Foucault and the centrality of the modernity/postmodernity debate in the arts and the cultural sciences have led to a plethora of books and articles on the body in recent years. Foucault's (Rabinow 1991) radical anti-humanist approach to the body has been highly influential in sociology. His analysis has illuminated how bodies have been objectified and subjectified through a range of discursive practices. In fact, the body is not simply endowed with social meanings by these discursive practices, rather it is wholly constituted by them. The result is that the biological entity of the body simply 'disappears and instead becomes a socially constructed product which is infinitely malleable and highly unstable' (Shilling 1993: 74). In a sense, Foucault takes the social constructionist approach to its logical conclusion: the disappearing body. It is somewhat ironic that just as the body is brought into the discourse of sociology, the major theoretical influence in the area renders the fact of embodiment as a fiction. In Foucault's analysis the concept of nature is redundant, as it too is constituted through discourse.

Whilst it is important to note that social constructionist views of the body have tended to overemphasize the social at the expense of the natural, it also needs to be said that naturalistic conceptions of the body, for the most part, have been used to shore up and sustain continuing structural inequalities, such as inequalities of gender and race (1993: 55–60):

> The naturalistic focus on the body has proved unsatisfactory for most socio-logists . . . For sociologists, naturalistic views of the bodies of black people tended to say much less about what might be termed 'corporeal reality', than about the enormous utility of the body as a highly malleable ideological resource. (1993: 68–9)

In the battle between culture and nature in sociology, then, culture continues to have the last word.

KEY CONCEPTS

CULTURE   Culture is a term often used in the place of society. It is a concept that describes the symbolic world that we inhabit when we are members of a social group. So each different society, big or small, has a different culture, different symbols, different rituals and different ways of expressing itself. Any culture can, itself, be divided internally so that there exists a stratification of culture within a society, e.g. Bingo and the opera.

NATURE   Nature is the natural state of being in the world before human kind exercises its influence upon it. As soon as a human being takes a leaf and cooks it, dresses in it or builds a shelter with it, it becomes a cultural object. Humans transform nature into culture.

Universality   This concept means that a statement of a state of affairs has the same meaning and significance wherever and whenever it occurs – it is universal.

Nurture   Nature exerts a natural force on human beings so part of us might be driven by physical forces that are natural to our bodies like hunger, sleep, and sexual desire. Nurture is the process through which the social world exerts a pressure upon our natural instincts and desires and makes them cultural. These two forces are important causal opposites in explaining behaviour – is someone criminal because of their genetic structure or because of their upbringing?

Body symbolism   The human body is a natural thing that presents itself in the social world in cultural and symbolic ways. Body symbolism addresses that presentation. Think of: short skirts; high heel shoes; leather jackets; pin-stripe suits; body piercing; tattoos; hair fashions, etc. and you will begin to see the different messages that we can send by the way that we present our body in society.

Relativism/Absolutism

Sue Stedman-Jones

This dichotomy is one of the most fundamental of the antitheses of the social sciences: it becomes evident in the problem of understanding different cultures. Clifford Geertz says that the problem of culture clash that was familiar to anthropologists is now becoming common for everyone with the 'deprovincialisation of the world' through the global phenomena of immigration and refugees and via television which brings us news of other people and their often 'repellent beliefs' (1995: 44). The dichotomy has been present since the formulation of the concept of sociology in the nineteenth century and is present with us now at the end of the twentieth century. From Comte to postmodernism, sociologists embrace a form of relativism and oppose it to conceptions of the absolute for different reasons. At this moment, with postmodernism and poststructuralism, relativism is embraced on the basis that it leads to tolerance, and absolutism is condemned for underpinning terror and oppression. Certainly the worst oppressors of the twentieth century, Hitler and Stalin, claimed a fixed and absolutist point – the master race and its historical destiny, or revolutionary scientific socialism achievable through the laws of historical necessity – from which to eradicate all elements of **difference**.

The problem is, how do we characterize the absolute and the relative? Can relativism be coherently formulated and does its triumphant assertion guarantee tolerance? Does it help with the methodological and epistemological problems of a social science in understanding other cultures – in understanding difference?

A PRELIMINARY DEFINITION

The absolute can be defined as that which has unconditioned existence, that which is not conditioned by or relative to anything else. An example of this might be the Christian idea of God. In nineteenth-century philosophy, the German idealist movement made free use of such a concept – particularly Hegel's idea of spirit (*Geist*) as a spiritual self-moving, self-knowing principle that underlies all things, but reveals itself in the different moments of culture and history. The latter are the changing and relative and the former the absolute. Marxism developed out of Hegelianism, in part by introducing historical determinism and relativism, and so denying that there is anything fixed and unchanging in history. Modern forms of relativism, in postmodernism for example, also establish relativism by rejecting Hegel and the conception of the absolute.

In contrast to the absolute, the relative is that which has conditioned existence, that which depends on something else. It is thus finite as opposed to infinite, contingent as opposed to necessary, dependent as opposed to independent, **variable** as opposed to invariable, and changeable as opposed to eternal. However the concepts 'finite', 'contingent', 'dependent', 'variable' and 'changeable' are associated with the relative but are not one and the same as the relative. Thus one could say that the proposition 'It is raining today' is contingently true because tomorrow it will not rain and therefore it will not be true. But it is not relative because it does not depend on my perception of judgement; it is a state of affairs, and thus its truth is not relative to me.

What does 'relative' as opposed to the absolute mean? We could say 'relative' means 'relative to': it is an incomplete term. This concept of *relative to* must be regarded as the core of relativism. However we have still not arrived at relativism, because it could still be argued that X is relative to Y, and Y is something fixed. Thus we could argue that cultures are relative to needs – biological, psychological – and these are fixed and universal amongst all human beings. But the true doctrine of relativism is the denial that there are any fixed terms at all. Cultural relativists would argue that we can only understand needs through the lenses of culture, and cultures vary: therefore there is no fixed point from which to determine need. Relativism is thus associated with the perspectival: what is true is relative to **perspective**, and perspective varies. In this sense relativism is linked with the observation of **diversity**. We must recognize what Geertz calls 'unabsolute truths' (1995: 44).

We can see the difference between the absolute and the relative in terms of morality. Moral absolutism is the doctrine that certain actions are always wrong no matter what the circumstances and no matter what the consequences. Even more strongly, certain actions are held to be intrinsically wrong and this stricture cannot be overridden by considerations of circumstances. Moral relativists will on the contrary say it is precisely the circumstances that determine what counts as right or wrong. Thus Émile Durkheim (1974a: 43) argued that it is society that determines whether an action will be judged as right or wrong: murder in time of war is justifiable homicide, whilst in peace it is condemned and punished. This shows the variability in both definition and regulation of action. Thus action is right or wrong according to culture, and culture will vary. Enormous weight is thus put on the propositions that cultures determine what counts as true and right, and that cultures vary. These two propositions are the central pivots of cultural relativism. They are taken as establishing the variability of truth and morality. But is the concept of culture hard or clear enough to establish and justify relativism in terms of morality and knowledge? That female infanticide has been routinely practised for centuries in certain parts of the world is surely not enough to justify it.

There is however a paradoxical quality to the central proposition of relativism: all is relative. Firstly, it has a peculiar ring of absolutism about it. How can it be asserted so absolutely that all is relative? Most importantly, what kind of proposition is this? Is it empirically true? If so, its truth depends on a patient observation of all cultural, social, moral and political forms. In this case it cannot yet be said to be conclusively proved. However, secondly, the empirical nature of the relativist case is important: it is the observation of difference that is the strongest case for the relativist. Yet if the central proposition of relativism is not empirical, what kind of proposition is it? It is not logically true, for we are not involved in a contradiction if we deny that everything is relative. It thus has a peculiar epistemological status.

It is clear that it is easier to define relativism negatively, by denying the absolute, than by saying positively what relativism is. However, generally, relativism can be taken to mean that there is no absolute definition of truth or reality; thus what is true and what is real is simply what people claim to be so. It means that there is no divine, cosmological or universal arbiter of the competing claims to truth and reality: there are no absolutes. This claim has moral and cognitive dimensions, and in the social sciences it has methodological dimensions which must be evaluated before relativism is accepted.

COMTE: THE RELATIVE AND THE ABSOLUTE

Auguste Comte claimed that 'all is relative' is the only absolute proposition. He has the honour of founding sociology, or more accurately devising the name. (It is still too early to say whether he did this in one of his periodic attacks of insanity.) In the 48th lesson of his famous *Cours de philosophie positive* (1830–42) he declared that 'the inevitable passage from the absolute to the relative constitutes one of the most important philosophical results of each of the intellectual revolutions which have successively led the different orders of our speculation from the purely theological and metaphysical state to the truly scientific' (1975: 203). He opposed the ancient manner of studying being in terms of first and final causes, which is absolute, by the scientific approach of studying law and phenomena, which is relative. It is clear that he does not mean relative in the sense of relative to each person and their 'subjective' viewpoint. Objective knowledge is possible for him, and this consists in the grasping of the laws of reality which is immanent in the structure of the world, and as such bypass the human subjective viewpoint. Laws are relations between facts, and these must be observable: there can be no knowledge of essences. In sociology, the last of the positive sciences to develop, knowledge is governed by the historical method, which says that all forms of thought and historical period pass through three stages: the theological, the metaphysical and the positive. Thus although Comte pointed to historical variability and difference between epochs epistemologically and politically, he postulated one invariable law that governs this. Durkheim in Chapter 5 of *The Rules of Sociological Method* rejects the claim that there is one invariable law which governs all of human development and that there is one humanity to which it applies: instead we must recognize that there are diverse types of society and that they thus have their own individuality.

THE GREEK EXPERIENCE: NATURE/CULTURE

As Geertz shows it is the experience of culture contact that forces the awareness of diversity. The ancient Greeks as a trading nation were the first to experience culture contact. They grew to reflect on the phenomena of culture or 'civilization' through their contact with the civilizations of Persia, Babylon and Egypt, but also the more 'primitive' Scythians and Thracians. They were inclined to dismiss most as 'barbarians', in contrast to Hellenism. But this contact eventually led to questions as to whether various ways of life, religions and ethical codes were merely conventions, and therefore non-natural. Did Hellenism have a sacred ordinance, in contrast to the barbarians?

They formulated these questions into theoretical reflections fundamental to both sociology and philosophy. Lévi-Strauss argued that the distinction between nature and culture is essential to the foundation of a human science. Here we have a first definition of the relative and the absolute: we can define nature as what is necessary, unchangeable and universal and culture as that which is made by human beings, and therefore variable, contingent and changeable.

The Sophists, in Greek philosophy, were the first relativists (Guthrie 1971). They came to treat of culture and human beings in a microcosmic rather than a macrocosmic way. Sophism has been described as the process of human beings becoming self-conscious. They acknowledged the presence of the subject in the determination of reality and argued that what is real is determined by the subject of perception. They rejected the old 'theological' way of doing philosophy amongst the thinkers who are now known as the Presocratics – that is to find one ultimate constituent to reality (fire, earth, air, etc.) and one principle by which it can be explained. In contrast to this monistic theoretical tendency, the Sophists observed a wide diversity of facts, particularly about human beings and their beliefs. From this they concluded that what is true is relative to the perception of the human being, and what is just and morally right is relative to the interest or power of the person.

PROTAGOREAN RELATIVISM

Protagoras is the most famous of the Sophists and his statement the most famous statement of relativism: 'Man is the measure of all things: of the things that are, that they are, of the things that are not, that they are not.' How is this statement to be interpreted? Does 'man' here mean the individual, the group or the species? These entail three different types of relativism. But each of these types constitutes a rejection of the concept of truth *simpliciter*, and thus any conception of an absolute truth. Truth always means 'truth for': truth is always true for the individual, the group or the species (Guthrie 1971: 181–92).

Species relativism

This is really a form of humanism, and it stands opposed to forms of deism and the absolutism entailed by the conception of a God. Nietzsche's famous statement 'God is dead' means that human beings are alone in the cosmos, and we only have ourselves to guide us. The claim that all truths are human truths is central to the humanism of Feuerbach, which so influenced Marx. Although this contains the essential element of relativism that 'true' does not stand alone, but means 'true for', it could entail a universal truth – that which is true for humanity. Thus 'true for' here does entail the kind of relativism that we will look at later.

We have seen that Comte developed the idea that knowledge and science are relative to humanity, and that what counts as true is relative to the stage of history and intellectual development which humanity has reached. However the knowledge of the positive stage for Comte is more adequate and comprehensive, because it is scientific and deals with phenomenal realities and not fictions: it is thus the final stage of the process. The philosopher Kant in the eighteenth century argued that all knowledge is relative to the faculty of understanding; there is no knowledge of 'the thing in itself', but an objective knowledge of reality is still possible because of human reason. Further, a universal ethic is possible because of the activity of human reason.

Kantian ethics develops the conception of what is true for humanity in an ethical sense: right action is universal. This conception of true for humanity could entail a standard for universal human rights now, just as it constituted a standard for the socialist humanism of many nineteenth-century figures, Marx included.

Individual relativism

However, Protagoras's statement could also mean 'man' as individual human being. Thus it means that truth means 'true for' the individual; knowledge means knowledge for the individual; and morality means morality for the individual. This is pervasive in a certain contemporary common sense, for example the debate stopper 'It all depends on what you mean by' or 'It's up to the individual.' The conclusion of this is that the individual is the sole judge of what is true, what is right, and that logically there are no standards beyond this that can be invoked as a critique or as a standard of truth or morality, whereby certain positions can be judged false or inadequate. It means there are no general epistemological or moral standards, beyond what people may happen accidentally to agree on. It was this particularly that enraged Plato and triggered his attack on Sophism, and indeed founded Western rationalism.

Plato's response

Through his mouthpiece in the dialogues, Socrates, Plato argues that knowledge is real and it is founded on general definitions. Individualist relativism is thus self-defeating because to make any claim to knowledge is to invoke a criterion that the individual did not invent. Plato's argument against this type of relativism particularly occurs in the dialogue the *Theaetetus*, where his method is to extract the full implications of the argument, and then to show that this is incompatible with the criteria of knowledge which must be (a) infallible and (b) of 'what is'. Amongst his arguments are the following, which could be adapted to the situation of the social sciences.

Firstly, Plato argues that if knowledge is relative to the individual, then no person is wiser than any other, and then no one has any justification for setting themselves up as a teacher, and in particular for taking money for it. Here he is attacking not just the logical side of Sophism, but the commercial aspect of their teaching, the 'art and control of life'. This argument could be adapted against those who purport to teach and therefore impart knowledge, and use ratiocination to do both, but undermine this possibility by arguing that reason is either masculinist oppression or Enlightenment terror.

Secondly, he argues that if knowledge is relative to the individual and their perceptions then I could never be mistaken. But we know that it is possible to believe something to be true, which in fact turns out to be false. Thus, for example, the belief that the earth was flat later turned out to be a mistaken one. That there was a British Flat Earth Society long after the invention of the telescope is testimony to the power of belief over evidence. However, many of the beliefs that occupy social scientists do not have such possibilities of testing; and indeed it may be that testing them is strictly irrelevant to the sociological interest in them. Thus whether witches really exist is irrelevant to an interest in the role of witchcraft beliefs in any particular society.

Thirdly, Plato argues that a great part of knowledge consists in judgements which do not rely on individual perception or assent at all. Plato's clearest example is in mathematics. It does not matter what I feel or think about parallel lines: it is still true that they never meet. Equally whether I know anything about black holes, they still exist. Further, to make any claims about them I must invoke certain criteria or terms by which I identify them which are not reducible to my judgement, for example certain features of space, time, causality. Thus knowledge has certain features which means it transcends my judgement. Plato developed this into his theory of forms of reality which are eternal cognitive absolutes on which all knowledge rests. Aristotle developed Platonism into the claim that far from our perceptions and judgements being the measure of reality, it is reality which must be the measure of the amount and worth of our cognition. This division between reality as it is and appearance is central to the concept of ideology. And this Aristotelian realism has entered into Marxist philosophies of science in the twentieth century.

One of the main conclusions of sophistic relativism is that morality and justice are not real in the sense that they imply something beyond the interest or power of the individual. Thus justice is simply power, and in particular established power. The character Thrasymachus in Plato's *Republic* represents this view. Plato argued against this that the concept of justice involves a non-relative standard. For him this implies an absolute standard of justice. This in turn should be the foundation of the social order. For Plato, this was not present in any contemporary society. In the *Republic* he founded the concept of social organization and indeed societal critique on a non-relativistic conception of justice.

Social and cultural relativism

The third way in which we can interpret Protagoras's statement is that 'man' means the culture or society. This constitutes social or cultural relativism, which is central to the human sciences to the extent that it now seems almost a truism. Logically this develops Socrates's arguments about general definitions as lying at the heart of knowledge, but adds that it is the culture or society which establishes the general definitions. Thus, this form of relativism says that there are many and varied forms of general definitions, and that this variety depends on the variety and extent of 'conceptual schemes' or 'cultural codes' or social systems. 'True for' means true for the conceptual scheme or culture; there are no shared meanings or moral standards between groups. Plato moved from general to universal real essences. However this version of relativism avoids universalism by identifying meaning as that which is shared between a number of persons. For the social sciences it is the group or the society which is the foundation for general definitions, and thus the foundation of knowledge. That which is general or shared is the foundation of knowledge. This stands as a critique of individualist relativism, for each person can only make sense of reality or make moral decisions by reference to shared standards.

Geertz in *Local Knowledge* (1993) argues that the truth of cultural relativism is that we can never apprehend another culture as though it were our own. We can only look at such cultures by looking through and not behind the 'significative systems' of culture, which consists in 'the tangle of hermeneutic involvements' (1993: 45). That is we are always involved not just in seeing how they see the world, but in the problem of interpreting their systems of beliefs.

The clearest definition of social cultural relativism is that offered by Peter Winch in his book *The Idea of a Social Science* (1958), which applies the ideas of the later Wittgenstein to the methodological problems of the social sciences. The conception of meaning is central to Winch's analysis and involves conventions and rules that are shared and unique to the culture or society from which they derive. It follows then that we can identify the action of agents only by employing the concepts used in that culture. We cannot understand the action of the agents using concepts that are not used by the agent or not available to the culture or society concerned.

Peter Winch develops this to a logical form of conceptual relativism which argues that the very acts of judgements of identity and reality are made in a 'form of life' which is shared between a number of persons. It follows that it is these shared cognitive relations which define what is true and what is real. Thus truth and reality are strictly relative to a form of life and there are many forms of life. And since what is true and what is real can only be determined from within a form of life, it makes no sense to argue for a comparative position between forms of life. In particular we cannot use concepts and methods drawn from Western science to understand non-scientific cultures. This is the case for the above philosophical reasons, but of course it follows from the logic of his argument that there are no transcultural concepts that can be applied from one form of life to another.

Winch applies these concepts in his article 'Understanding a Primitive Society' (1970), which became a central plank in what is now known as the rationality debate. One argument here is that Western science is held by some to provide a non-context-dependent access to reality. Winch criticizes Evans-Pritchard in this paper. Evans-Pritchard argues that a scientific approach is as much a function of our culture as a magical approach is of certain other cultures, and acknowledges that there is no superiority for scientific thinking. Indeed he ran his household according to the Azande way and found it as satisfactory as any other. However, Evans-Pritchard does assume that there is a checking point for the real that is independent of cultural form. In this he assumes it has 'absolutist' status. He assumes that scientific notions are in accordance with objective reality. For Winch, on the other hand, we can only talk of the real through language and its concepts: reality is not what gives language sense, it is language that give reality sense, and this is formed in diverse kinds of life.

Contemporary relativists argue similarly in terms of the concept of 'conceptual scheme': it is impossible to understand or communicate anything without employing either a language or a conceptual scheme. Any language, or indeed science, is dependent on such a conceptual scheme. Conceptual schemes vary and there is no vantage point independent of such a scheme by which we can judge the scheme itself. A radical version of this is that these schemes are 'incommensurable' with each other. We find this line of thinking in the writings of Feyerabend, Kuhn and Whorf.

SOME PROBLEMS WITH CONCEPTUAL RELATIVISM

Firstly, conceptual relativism in practice would appear to be contradicted every time we try to understand a culture or science or historical period different from our own. It would appear to be contradicted each time scientists build on past scientific theories. According to this position it finally makes no sense to try to understand another conceptual scheme – let alone succeed, even if only partially. One couldn't say 'I don't think I have grasped all the concepts of Tibetan Buddhism.' We can have no sense of adequacy or even failure of our attempt to do so. Further we are by implication prisoners of our own conceptual scheme. We cannot move on, change or disagree. A radical sociological and conceptual determinism is entailed by this position. Questions like 'How did this scheme originate?', 'How adequate is it?', 'What interests or needs does it serve?' are apparently impossible to formulate, because they imply what is denied: a vantage point independent of the scheme. But it is precisely these kinds of questions that are central not only to an adequate sociological investigation, but to a perfectly human reflection on our own variety as a species and indeed evaluation of different forms of belief – perhaps even with a view to adopting such alternative ways of life as one's own.

Methodological critiques of Winch argue that this position, rather than showing how sociological understanding is possible, entails that it is impossible. Most strongly, it fails to show how we move between forms of life. But even if we could, how do we match concepts from different forms of life? We may have interests that are not necessarily at one with any of the forms of life we are studying. Is sociology a form of life itself? Even so, there is no explanation of how it applies to other forms of life with different assumptions from its own. Nor is there any clear sense of what a form of life is. In like manner MacIntyre (1970) criticizes Winch because the social sciences must be able to call on concepts that do not form part of the linguistic rules of a group – the concept of the unconscious, for example.

Ernest Gellner (1974) argues that relativism is a problem for the social sciences, not a solution to its difficulties. How can we get to know other cultures without using concepts that imply some non-relativist, transcultural criteria? He argues that science requires 'one world'. He is particularly opposed to Winch's 'symmetrical relativism', which assumes all cultures have equal cognitive power. Here he has in mind the Western industrial system as having greater capacity to answer need than pre-literate, pre-industrial societies. Thus it is in this, if not in any other way, not of the same cognitive status as other cultures.

CAN RELATIVISM BE CONSISTENTLY FORMULATED?

It has been remarked that no one lives as a relativist. We look left and right before we cross the road even if we are in Katmandu. We are appalled by the atrocities of Saddam Hussein against his own people. It is in the seminar or lecture room that relativism has its most persuasive force.

Mandelbaum (1982) uses the expression 'conceptual relativism' to indicate the view that statements are relative to an intellectual and conceptual background against which they make sense. It involves a distinction drawn by the philosopher Kant in the eighteenth century between the data of sense, which is given to the faculty of sensibility, and the organization of these data by the faculty of understanding. Now Kant did not infer the relativity of knowledge from this. Rather he argued that all people share certain fundamental concepts, 'categories', such as causality or quality. All knowledge and reality were possible on this basis, and therefore this knowledge is universal. However, in the nineteenth century thinkers argued that the concepts which order the data of sense differ, particularly from society to society and from historical epoch to historical epoch. Durkheim (1964b) in particular argued that categorial schemes vary according to society. It is then argued that each different conceptual scheme employs different criteria of truth and reality. So what counts as true or as real varies from scheme to scheme.

Donald Davidson, in his famous article 'On the Very Idea of a Conceptual Scheme' (1986), argues that the conditions that establish the radical relativism of a conceptual scheme can never be achieved. Davidson argues that the idea of a conceptual scheme itself is not coherent. He raises the question as to whether the argument for absolute difference of conceptual scheme be made. That is, can we prove that they are 'incommensurable' with each other? This involves the claim that if such schemes are languages (they could equally be scientific theories for Thomas Kuhn), they are not translatable into each other. A relativist will argue that there is no fixed stock of meanings or a theory-neutral reality which is a ground of comparison between these schemes. However, there is for Davidson a paradox about this version of relativism, which entails that it cannot be clearly formulated and therefore must fail. We can only establish that we have radically different conceptual schemes if we fail to translate. And if we get near enough to another language to say, for example, 'Well, they describe chairs differently from us', then this is a language like our own, or like enough for the non-translatability thesis to fall. That is, we have failed to show that it is radically non-translatable.

And there is this further paradox: we can only make sense of different points of view if we can agree on 'a common coordinate system on which to plot them'; and 'The existence of a common system belies the claim of dramatic incomparability' (1984: 67). Thus for example in terms of comparing different forms of the family, anthropologists compare different ways of childrearing only because they can identify the child and the parent in the first place. That is, they can only identify difference in families because they accept certain fixed data (the child) as that to which different practices attach. Thus there is no failure of translation or understandability between cultures here, even though there is difference.

This argument involves what Richard Rorty (1972) calls a 'verificationist' view – that is, that there is some stuff of the world, be it things or events, which are the condition for truth. And without this we cannot have a criterion for the difference of conceptual schemes – or their success or failure of translation. Rorty argues however that the difference between the ancient Greeks and ourselves does amount to a difference in conceptual schemes, because there are radically different concepts involved, i.e. there are non-translatable features of it. Mandelbaum (1982) argues that a consistent version of conceptual relativism can never be made, for all relativists have to implicitly make non-relativist assumptions. For example, Kuhn was forced to admit that rival scientific theories referred to the same set of facts, and without this they could not have been rivals. So Whorf, in his conception of comparative linguistics, assumed that different language users were referring to the same objects. Thus scientific theories and languages are not self-enclosed systems but refer to aspects of a world that is independent of the system of reference. So scientific disagreement is possible only because they can refer to the same set of facts over which there is disagreement.

Bernard Williams (1972) argues that there is a type of vulgar relativism which is self-contradictory. It maintains firstly that 'right' means 'right for a given society'. And secondly, that it is wrong for people in one society to condemn or interfere with the moral actions or values of another culture. But in the first claim it says all uses of 'right' are relative to a society, whilst in the second it uses 'wrong' in a non-relative way.

IS RELATIVISM ITSELF RELATIVE?

The doctrine of relativism now appears to be axiomatic for the social sciences. This has not always been so; the theory of relativism is stressed or downplayed, and thus is itself relative to social and historical factors. That is, the acceptance of relativism itself is socially and historically specific. We have seen that relativism as a theory grew under certain conditions in ancient Greece. Specifically, this was the period covering the end of tribalism. Alvin Gouldner in *Enter Plato* (1967) argued that this marked the end of a period of certainty about what should be done and believed. The rules which established social practice were themselves to be defined by consensual definition and not referred to tradition.

So also at the end of the Victorian era, there was a rejection of its imperialist absolutes: Sumner's adage 'the mores make anything right' reflects this rejection of absolutes. And after the experience of German fascism in World War II, there was in anthropology a turning away from relativist definitions of culture: Kroeber and the concept of universal categories of culture reflects the attempt to find what all human beings share.

TOWARDS AN EVALUATION OF RELATIVISM

In attempting to evaluate the various types of relativism in the context of the social sciences, it is worth bearing in mind the following reflections.

Firstly, is it true that because beliefs are held by people, this *ipso facto* makes them right? Clitoridectomy is practised widely in the world: the consequences are pain and mutilation for the women of those societies. Are there not criteria other than habit and tradition for the maintenance of a belief system?

Secondly, are cultures and historical periods self-contained moral and epistemic units, about which nothing further can be said or done? Might it not be the case that the cultural relativist is paradoxically introducing culture or society as a fixed term by which to establish relativism? It is the axiom of the social sciences that all is relative to culture or society. But if these are not fixed entities then we cannot coherently close any argument that a practice must be justified because it is relative to the culture? What are cultures? And are the limits of cultures and historical periods the limits of rational and moral discourses? If so, then German fascism was one such unit, and thus just a different morality. The way the world is moving now, the concept of a self-contained cultural unit is part of history.

Thirdly, the unacceptable face of moral relativism is that it appears to entail no critique of fascism. A relativist could of course argue that what was wrong with fascism is precisely that it didn't recognize and respect difference. Here the acceptable face of relativism is that it tolerates difference and diversity in ways of living and being. But this relies on the universal proposition that we should respect difference in other people. That is, we can only accept the relative because of an absolute moral value of respect for difference.

Fourthly, is there nothing that human beings everywhere share cognitively and morally? Winch must, like Dilthey, hold implicitly to some form of philosophical anthropology, which assumes certain central features of a common humanity. For Winch this must be the capacity to make sense of the rules. Does this not constitute a form of bridge notion between forms of life? This may of course be the basis for examining difference, but it could also point to a limitation of radical diversity of forms of life. We know what need and desperation look like even if we do not share witchcraft beliefs with a culture we might be trying to help. Winch himself clearly does not want to accept the unacceptable consequence of social/conceptual relativism, that of moral relativism. And in 'Nature and Convention' (1978) he argues that there are certain features which are essential to the very condition of a society. In the world situation today there is widespread abuse of human rights, but at the same time a recognition of the existence of universal human rights.

Fifthly, is it not the case that examining social beliefs to some extent involves going beyond them, to look for their extent, influence and social foundation? In other words, surely social beliefs are the data for the social scientist, not the final court of appeal? They can be analysed, explained, not always necessarily justified, simply because they exist.

Sixthly, Comte introduced an anti-absolutism and thus a form of relativism, but nevertheless introduced the comparative method, which was influential on Durkheim and subsequent sociology.

BY WAY OF A CONCLUSION

Finally, 'so the question is what do we do' (Geertz 1995) in this sea of 'unabsolute truths'? Does the recognition of difference establish tolerance or does it underwrite the conflict between religions, cultures, classes, races and sexes? Relativism is not just an issue of judgement but also one of practical consciousness, for it is a matter of what we do and believe. Can we not hold on to an ideal of what human beings all share rather than what differentiates them from each other? Durkheim introduced cultural relativism into the social sciences. He can have the last say here with his universal ideal of humanism, that is the last absolute that can be discovered in difference.

> Thus we make our way, little by little, towards a state, nearly achieved as of now, where the members of a single social group will have nothing in common amongst themselves except their humanity, except the constitutive attributes of the human person in general. This idea of the human person, given different nuances according to the diversity of national temperaments, is therefore the only idea which would be retained, unalterable and impersonal, above the changing torrent of individual opinions . . . Consequently nothing remains which men can love and honour except man himself. (Durkheim 1973: 51–2)

KEY CONCEPTS

RELATIVISM   Any theory in the social sciences is said to be relativistic if it cannot provide truth criteria independent of or outside of itself; that is, it is self-sustaining. Similarly if we seek to justify the practices that exist within a particular society because that is the ways that they have always done them we are similarly being relativistic. Relativism is an extremely tolerant way of understanding things but it allows no criteria for judging what is good or bad; true or false.

ABSOLUTISM   In philosophy absolutism is the form of belief that argues in terms of the existence of absolute qualities. These might crystallize around an idea of God, or they might be more secular and contain formal and uncontestable notions of truth and falsity; rightness and wrongness; good and evil, and so on. Absolutisms tend not to be open for negotiation.

Difference   Difference is a more formal idea than diversity and it implies that there is a categorical segregation between particular social forms. People relate not so much according to a recognition of the diversity but in accord with an acknowledgement of their identity and difference.

Variable   A variable is a conceptual feature of an analysis. In real life all kinds of things influence our behaviour but as sociologists we have to restrict our explanations to two or three causal features that are common to social groups not just individuals. I might, therefore, explain someone's behaviour in terms of their class, their gender and their ethnicity. These are three variables. They vary because one may have more influence on action than another in any particular circumstance.

Perspective   This term is used widely in sociology to talk about different ways of seeing, different ways of interpreting and different ways of experiencing social reality. So you might suppose that a Marxist and a non-Marxist have different perspectives on things.

Diversity   This concept implies a wide range of forms or manifestations of a social phenomenon. Social class appears in this society but in a diversity of ways; that is, there are some things in common to them all but there is variance between them.

Public/Private

Don Slater

The public/private dichotomy was as crucial to ancient as it is to modern thought and society. The fact that it disappeared during the feudal period in between gives us a clue as to its most basic meaning: the public/private distinction largely registers the separation of the 'household' from institutions which represent general or collective social interests. Under feudalism, all of what we might now call 'society' was understood in terms of kinship or kin-like bonds of loyalty or fealty on the model of the patriarchal household. The onset of both Western modernity and its public sphere is often identified with the separation of 'public' finances and institutions in the form of 'the state' from the 'private' coffers and household of the monarch.

For ancient Greek and Roman society, the public sphere – the *polis* or *res publica* – was the realm of free association between free citizens. It was in public that men (and only men) could be their true selves and achieve virtue and fame through competition in such things as sports and rhetoric. Men were deemed free in the *polis* not because it was unregulated but because it was kept rigidly separated from the private sphere of the household and domestic economy (*oikos*): the domestic sphere was regarded as the realm of mere physical reproduction and therefore of the compulsion and slavery of needs (particularly bodily), of immersion in the trivial, industrial and 'merely' private. The public sphere depended on the private sphere, and this was clearly recognized: to be a citizen one not only had to have wealth but actually to be the head of a household in which women, children and slaves attended to one's individual and particularistic needs, thus freeing one to move from the private world (the mundane, temporary, needy, natural) to the public world (a realm of culture, achievement and the hope of enduring fame) (Habermas 1991). Obviously household members other than the head could not enter the public sphere because they were slaves to necessity and therefore could not attain that state of freedom which was a *precondition* of citizenship. However, although public life depended on the private, private life was felt to have no intrinsic value and existed *only* to support the 'good life' lived in public: a life spent in privacy was by definition 'idiotic' (Arendt 1958: 37).

Modernity has in some respects reversed these valuations: as we shall see below, the private world of the individual, family and intimacy is now commonly regarded as the primary source of authentic values. Yet in many respects, the modern distinction runs in parallel to the ancient. One major meaning of the private/public distinction for example is the opposition between economy (*oikos*) and politics (*polis*) (as in privatization versus public ownership). The political should, by its very nature, constitute a sphere of general interest through sociable discourse and consultation as well as by virtue of an institutional distance from the ignoble (and self-interested) pursuit of private gain. Conversely, the economy is particular, individual and bound up with survival rather than goodness or virtue. Quite literally, 'privatization' means to return enterprise from the general interest of the political sphere to the private interests represented in economic action.

However, modernity has complicated the public/private divide in other ways. Above all, ancient thought and life ascribed *all* economic endeavour to the private household where it was carried out by women and subordinate (or enslaved) men. Modernity, on the other hand, divides economic activity itself between a public and private realm: we distinguish between the public world of work, production and enterprise on the one hand, and the private world of domestic life and *re*production on the other. Moreover, the public/private and production/reproduction divisions are conventionally understood in terms of a gender division of labour: in the conventional view, paid work outside the home is part of men's participation in public life as well as essential to their public status as 'breadwinners' for the private household of dependants; these dependants then belong to an unpaid and private world.

Hence, the modern public/private distinction is not one but (at least) two distinctions. Firstly, it refers to a very broad distinction between the general interest and that which pertains to particular interests. In this sense, the state is public (hence, an employee of the state is a 'public servant' rather than one who serves particular interests), whereas 'civil society' indicates that realm in which individuals come together on the basis of their private interests. Secondly, both the state and civil society, as well as the world of work, can be seen as a public sphere populated largely by men who are deemed able to operate outside the 'private' realm of the domestic household to which women and children are largely confined. In this distinction, the private also marks a realm of personal intimacy, of relationships which are to be defended from public scrutiny or interference, of values which cannot or should not be experienced in public life. These two sets of distinctions are interrelated and often confused in various ways. However, to begin with we will look at each one separately.

ECONOMICS AND POLITICS

In modern times, the public/private distinction arises originally, and most vividly, through early liberalism and utilitarianism. From Locke onwards, various concepts of privacy are used to restrict, resist and discipline the state (first the monarch, then modern political institutions). Liberalism's fundamental commitment is to liberty, which is conceived as the individual's right to pursue their privately defined desires. Modern liberalism starts, morally and philosophically, from the idea of sovereign individuals who are endowed with various needs (for example, for life, liberty and the pursuit of happiness), who have knowledge of those needs and who possess *reason*. They are thus defined by their rational pursuit of 'self-interest', and this is taken as the central definition of the private domain. From Hobbes onwards it is argued that society (let alone mere government) only arises when these sovereign individuals come together for various self-interested reasons (such as avoiding the 'war of all against all' or defence against external threats). Public institutions, in this account, only arise to defend private individuals and these individuals may legitimately dissolve public institutions if they contravene private interests. Liberalism carries this ethical position right through into contemporary thought: public institutions are to be entirely accountable to (and theoretically reducible to) the voluntary associations of private individuals pursuing their particular, rather than general, interests. When Margaret Thatcher declared that 'There is no such thing as society; only individuals and their families', she was articulating the classical liberal notion that the private has analytical and political priority over a public sphere which can only emerge through the voluntary association of individuals. This attitude to collectivities and to the very idea of social relations is profoundly consequential for social thought. This is most clearly expressed in the division between 'methodological individualists' for whom social structures can have no real existence except as the (generally unintentional) outcomes of a multitude of individual actions, and those such as Durkheim for whom society involves a publicly binding moral order.

The liberal view of the relation between public and private is often articulated as a relation between the state and 'civil society'. As we have noted, civil society labels a peculiarly modern notion of privacy: not the household but the realm of voluntary associations in which people come together in pursuit of their own political or economic interests. The most complete and complex version of this image of society is undoubtedly the market as portrayed in neo-classical economics. The market (as defined from the time of de Quesnay and Smith) is not a public institution at all or even a public sphere, properly speaking. It is simply what happens when a large number of individuals come together on the basis of private interests which they each rationally pursue through calculations of supply and demand, profit and utility reckoned in the common denominator of price. This multitude of calculations is indeed 'private' in that we need know nothing about what people want or why they want it: we (theorists and economic actors) merely watch people's behaviour (how much they are willing to buy and sell at various prices), observe the prices that result, and then orient our own actions accordingly. If this behaviour is allowed to carry on unimpeded, it will naturally produce 'welfare' (via Smith's 'hidden hand' of the market). However, if people's pursuit of their private desires is interfered with in the name of any public interest (for example, a belief that the state could manage things more efficiently, or a collective, publicly enforced notion of 'what people really need') then disaster will ensue in the form of both loss of liberty and economic inefficiency. Hence, a cornerstone of modern political ideology is the privacy of needs: for example, the concepts of consumer choice and consumer sovereignty express the view that my choices are private and unquestionable, that no one can legitimately tell me what I want or need or what I *should* want or need. For the ancients, the public sphere was to be defended from the private household on which it depended. Liberalism reverses this: the private is now the source of all ethical value and defines 'man's' liberty and true self. At the same time, the rise of this essentially bourgeois sphere (and concept) of civil society and private association has been continuously bound up with the creation of new forms of public sphere, and above all with ideas of 'public opinion', public information and communications, news and media. It is recognized from the eighteenth century onwards that private freedom as well as private commerce require an informed and involved citizenry, one that takes a public role and can enforce public accountability. For example, Tocqueville was concerned that when a people are entirely immersed in the pursuit of private interests they will leave public matters to professionals who, unchecked, can become tyrants. 'Publicity' – in the sense that some actions be carried out under the cold scrutiny of the collective citizenry – is crucial to democracy. And yet with another turn of the screw, modern thought has been obsessed with the freedom and independence of the organs of public opinion themselves: can commercial (i.e. privately owned) media, or media controlled by government (i.e. pursuing the particular interests of state institutions), truly inform or give voice to public opinion as opposed to manipulate and orchestrate it for private ends?

Private and public merge confusingly into one another in a further sense: privately owned productive forces can constitute huge social organizations with public functions and consequences. Unlike the household economy devalued by classical thought, modern production is carried out outside the home, within organizations and social relations (factories, division of labour, labour contracts and markets, capital and money as social relations) which are social rather than domestic or familial in character and are therefore 'public'. Marx clearly recognized the public status of private capital (and accords it a progressive role) in the sense that it constantly intensified the socialization of the labour process, collecting workers in ever greater numbers in ever larger units of production. Though still privately employed by private capital, the workforce could begin to see itself as a public body of interdependent social beings who could then take control through collective ownership in order to bring the forces of production clearly into the realm of the public and of politics. Some modern thinkers have emphasized the relative size and power of 'private' enterprise *vis-à-vis* the public domain: it is hard to apply the notion of 'private pursuit of individual interest' to a multinational corporation with a turnover dwarfing that of many states and employing hundreds of thousands within a complex technical division of labour. Similarly, the symptomatic modern fear of advertising and marketing technologies concerns the ability of private firms to invade and manipulate the private realm of the individual, and to mould private needs into appropriate forms of effective (public and collective) demand. As Leavis and Thompson (1933: 30–1) put it, 'A mass-production plant can be worked profitably only if it is worked to its full capacity, and only if its full output is absorbed by the market. That is to assume (output being so large in relation to population) something like the status and function of a public national organ.'

Progressive social theory and practice attacked the public/private division – which it associated with exploitation and alienation – arguing that private interests should be brought under the control of the public interest, that individual desires should form into a collective will, that the economy should be subsumed within the polity. It was thus relatively close to ancient thought which gave priority to an idealized *polis* over a devalued *oikos*. Hence, the familiar debates between 'privatization' and 'public ownership' in which private ownership mediated through markets is regarded as both anarchic and oppressive, whereas public ownership is identified with both democracy and reason because it brings both the means and the ends of economic life under public scrutiny and control. The dominant liberal-democratic version of this involved a measured compromise between public and private interest within a mixed economy: some needs are both private and best filled privately (highly particularistic consumer needs where choice is paramount); other needs are seen as universal and entailing an obligation on the part of society (in the form of the state) to its members, or are seen as essential to the continuance of society itself (hence, health, education and basic minima of food, clothing and shelter).

On the other hand, conservative, anti-modern thinkers from Burke onwards have also wished to overturn the public/private distinction, but they have tended to advocate a return to an (idealized, even feudalist) premodernity in which the political and the economic are integrated within traditional agrarian life. At the extreme point, fascism seeks to fashion a single people, the national community as a single family or household under the patriarchal guidance of party or paternalist firm. In this conception, the idea of 'culture' is often advocated as a way of transcending both economy and politics, to bring private and public together again within an organic 'way of life' and values which are to unite public and private behaviour.

THE PRIVATE HOUSEHOLD AND THE INTIMATE WORLD

The private sphere of civil society came to be viewed as the ethical centre of the modern world, but not everyone could enter it. When Locke talked of 'man's' natural liberties it is fairly clear that the apparently universalistic meaning of the word 'man' as usual cloaked its exclusionary character: Locke actually meant males who were white, adult and property owning. Only such people were deemed sufficiently able to know their own interests and pursue them rationally so that they might enter the sphere of civil society as voters, as 'public opinion' (in the media, the coffee houses, the intelligentsia), as economic agents in their own right with power of disposal over money and property (as opposed to consumers spending money earned by the head of household). Hence, that sphere which was private for empowered men was a prohibited public world for women and subordinate males who were restricted – as in ancient days – to the household, to the *oikos* whose private labour subsidizes the public life of men.

From the outset of modern social thought, then, the identification of public and private with state and civil society already assumed a further, underlying distinction between the world of the household and that outside it. This distinction was profoundly bound up with a gender division of labour between production and reproduction, and the gradual separation of paid, 'productive' labour from the home. In the premodern world production and reproduction were largely undifferentiated and carried out as household production; exchange of goods was a marginal or superficial feature. Modern economic relations on the other hand sharply distinguish public from private labour. On the one hand, social value, status and power depend on work which is carried out in socially organized institutions, which is 'productive' (contributes to the production of socially recognized forms of value such as profit) and which is consequently paid. Reproductive labour within the home, on the other hand – the work of maintaining body and soul through such things as cooking, cleaning, sewing; socializing and educating children; keeping up the practices and rituals of the culture and community – is treated as private labour and is unpaid. This version of the public/private distinction is clearly bound up with a gender division of labour which is exacerbated over the modern period as women are increasingly excluded from the public sphere of paid work and associated with the unpaid labour of maintaining the private sphere. Women (and children) are restricted in belief and practice to the private world of the family which is subordinate to and ruled (through the male breadwinner) by the public sphere. This exclusion has very direct material consequences: being confined to the private sphere means having neither the power and independence nor the status and equality that go with having money or property. It also means exclusion from civil rights such as the right to own property or to vote which are granted to participants in the public sphere. Finally, the original public/private distinction between production and reproduction is developed, in the twentieth century, into a distinction between (public) work and (private) *consumption*. Perhaps the high point of this process is the 1950s image of the middle-class family in which the father goes out to do publicly valued work, bringing home a wage which is spent by the mother as an expert in consumption, shopping and even 'domestic science' (a subject taught at school).

However, the distinction between the private household and the public world is bound up with considerably more than a distinction between paid and unpaid work. Rather, it seems to organize a very wide range of social distinctions and dichotomies, to assign different terms and experiences to different social spaces. Hence, when we think of privacy as the domestic, intimate and familial world, we associate it with (for example) emotion rather than reason, affection rather than competition, nurture rather than manufacture, substantive values rather than instrumental reason, personal rather than monetary or material bonds. Public and private are seen as different realms of experience and value, spatially and temporally separated and epitomized by different sorts of people and roles. Moreover, because these different worlds were seen in terms of gender division (as well as the distinction between adult and child, and between the biologically 'natural' family unit as opposed to the voluntary associations of men in business or politics) they were also seen to exemplify the most fundamental of modern distinctions, that between the natural and the social, between nature and culture. The private realm of the family, as well as the intimate world of the romantic couple, were anchored on the 'naturalness' of women, above all in their reproductive functions of bearing children and caring for men; the public sphere reflected the man's 'natural' capacity for reason, production and self-consciousness. Ironically, the distinction of public from private based on the closeness of one gender to nature is not very far removed from ancient thought (not surprisingly given the powerful influence of classical revivals amongst the Enlightenment expounders of such ideas): in ancient times, men could constitute the *polis* because they could both separate themselves from the necessities of physical life and at the same time dominate those who attended to them. Similarly, it is argued, in modernity women have been closely associated with nature and with domination by their bodily and emotional needs (their 'nature' as childbearing, nurturing, natural). They are therefore located in the private realm while masculinity is held to transcend the particularistic needs of the body and to be capable of a 'universalism' appropriate to the public sphere: it is able to 'separate itself and dominate nature' (Gatens 1991), to transcend the particularity of the body and enter into the (disembodied) universality of reason. Men can enter the public realm by virtue of being disembodied, while women are confined to the natural, to the bodily and hence the privacy of childbirth and childrearing.

The private sphere and its inhabitants can be treated as subordinate and inferior to the public, literally as 'dependants' who may serve but not accompany those who operate in the public world. Some of the most powerful modern movements (for example against sexism and racism) have taken the form of struggles for civil rights on the part of those who have been confined to the domestic world on the grounds that they have not the qualities required for public life: women and ethnic minorities campaigning for equality of wages and job opportunities, for the vote, for education, and so on. And yet, at the same time, the idealization and defence of the private sphere has been a central theme of modernity: Western culture has projected onto it an enormous range of values and experiences which seem to have been lost from public life yet to be essential to personal life. One starting point for this is the idealization of childhood from the eighteenth century onwards. As recounted by Aries (1973), premodern biographies did not include a separate stage of childhood, rather seeing the young as little adults whose activities and obligations were not radically differentiated from those of bigger adults. From the eighteenth century, childhood comes increasingly to be seen as both different and special, characterized by notions such as goodness and innocence, play, asexuality, love and affection. Especially in Rousseau, children – in common with noble savages – represent the natural values lost to artificial modern society. The private sphere is now meant to nurture and defend the child's innocence against the corruption of public life while the child comes to symbolize the innocence and beauty of the private sphere of the family itself. In Victorian society, this idealization comes to be central to a cult of the family, to the cloying sentimentality through which the 'pure' child (and pure woman) is to be utterly separated and defended from work, sexuality, knowledge, evil. Similarly, the increasing confinement of middle-class women within the private household is intricately bound up with idealizing them, 'placing woman on a pedestal', whereby she is excluded from public life because she is deemed irrational, incompetent and incapable of rising above 'nature' yet is also worshipped for exactly the same reasons.

The bourgeois idealization of the private was bound up with the idea of home as 'haven' from the public world: especially during the Victorian era, it came to be seen as virtually a sacred place which was filled with all the emotion, security, solidarity, continuity, substantive values and moral cohesion that had been squeezed out of the public world of instrumental reason and utilitarianism, of insecurity and constant change, of competitive individualism and of formal calculation. Indeed for many Victorians, the public/private division was closer to a division between sacred and profane, religion and reason. The idea of home as haven extended to the realm of the 'intimate', affective bonds between individuals (usually a man and a woman, or mother and child) which could be neither constituted nor even properly understood by the public. Perhaps one of the most extreme moments in this development was the ideal of romantic love, a notion of privacy that contested even domesticity as too determined by public considerations: the idea that the central human relationship was an entirely private relation of 'love' between two people, isolated from all other social relations and public considerations was inconceivable to the premodern world. Before the modern separation of public from private the formation of familial bonds was a matter of calculation and social strategy. The idea that one's choice of partner, or one's affective bonds, and marriage should coincide and be equally matters of private and irrational choice was a modern notion. In fact, the idea that one's intimate affections could be held to no public account (they were irrational, 'subjective', private to the 'reasons' of the heart) and should transcend all public concerns (for example, should not involve consideration of public advantages or advancement) was central to romantic rebellions *against* bourgeois society.

The idealizations of private family life were defined in relation to the life of the emerging bourgeoisie and articulated through its public discourses (religion, education, social sciences, state policy) as well as private behaviour. Indeed, a central development of the nineteenth century was the emergence of the notion of 'respectability', which not only required appropriate public behaviour but also stressed the propriety of the publicly visible tips of the private iceberg: language and accent, dress, cleanliness, home décor, etiquette – all ensured a rigid separation of private and public life (above all, the complete privatization of sexuality) and provided signs that private life conformed (or aspired) to middle-class standards. The informal public norms of 'respectability', however, could also mutate into public policy and scientific discourses about how private life should be led. The private lives of social classes other than the bourgeoisie were viewed as either dangerously secretive or probably degenerate: in both the nineteenth and twentieth centuries, many 'explanations' of modern social ills have focused on such failures to match the ideals of private life as maternal deprivation, fallen women, dysfunctional families, intemperance. While bourgeois private life was to be defended, the private lives of others could be the objects of social research and theory, as well as state policies. For example, the welfare state could be seen as helping people maintain certain minimum requirements of private life (as well as gaining opportunities of work and citizenship in public life). It could also be argued that in the process of doing so it defined the requirements of private life by codifying the mores of middle-class private life into public norms. For example, in many aspects of social provision, welfare states still assume a nuclear family (heterosexual, focused on childrearing, married). Moreover, the welfare state had also to define rules as to when it could offend against the general modern premise that a man's home is his castle. Hence, there is much concern to define the point at which private life has sufficiently failed in relation to norms of family life that the state can or must take children into care, enforce public health regulations, step between husband and wife and so on.

The difference from the ancient view is instructive: for the Greeks, one could only be free and therefore authentic in the public world; the private merely secured freedom from necessity. One could only really be someone in public. Much the same view pertained to eighteenth century society (at least as experienced through the Enlightenment and its revival of these classical themes): convivial public sociability (for example, the coffee-houses and inns) epitomized both the good life and authentic being. It is really only with Romanticism, inaugurated by Jean-Jacques Rousseau from the 1750s, that this view comes under attack: 'society' comes to be seen as an alien force or pressure, badgering people into conformism through the tyranny of fashion, etiquette, social scrutiny and so on. In contrast to the Greek (and neo-classical) view, society was now precisely the place where one could *not* be oneself. But in private one could: Rousseau quite revolutionized our view of the private by inventing it as the realm of the *intimate*, in which the truth of the self was to be discovered, experienced and treasured. Above all, truth was to be found in the self and in the intimate world which expressed and nurtured it, whereas in modern society, 'to be and to appear became two entirely different things, and from this distinction arose ostentatious display, deceitful cunning, and all the vices that follow in their train' (Rousseau 1984: 119). Rousseau's position involved an implicit injunction: the falsity of public life and the social world was to be judged by the authenticity of the intimate self, and there was a new ethical obligation to make one's public face conform to one's private self, to be *authentic*. Hence, the profound symbolism that Rousseau wrote the first autobiography: he aimed to write a truthful account of his intimate experience *in public*.

BLURRING THE DISTINCTION

Rousseau's romantic concern that public life should be governed by the values of the private self raises another set of issues. We have been concerned so far with the separation of public and private in the modern world. However, many social commentators have been more concerned with the confusion or blurring of the public/private division in both thought and practice. For example, Richard Sennett (1977) argues that Rousseau and Romanticism have promoted a situation in which the intimate values of the private world – above all the injunction to authenticity – have unwarrantedly invaded the public. Eighteenth-century members of the bourgeois public sphere were expected to perform through emulative consumption, adoption of fashionable manners, expressions and activities and so on. However, Sennett argues, such performances did not need to be 'authentic': it was not believed that this public behaviour expressed, or even should express, a true self; it was a performance, and a performance carried out 'at a distance from the self'. 'Seeming' and 'being' were separate issues and could live in comfortable discordance. Increasingly, however, a culture of authenticity has arisen in which we are expected to really be what we seem to be, and must appear (in public) as we really are (in private).

Sennett's argument stands in marked contrast to the more common argument that public values and institutions have invaded private life. For example, a variety of Marxist authors – probably best exemplified by the Frankfurt School or Lefebvre – have been concerned that 'private life' is becoming increasingly fictive or ideological with the expansion of both capitalism and the bureaucratic state. Whereas family life, leisure and consumption have been presented as sacred and as autonomous spheres of freedom, they have in fact become the objects (and vehicles) of modern forms of social control such as advertising and marketing, state policy, bureaucratic rationality. For example, Adorno argues that the ostensible privacy of leisure has become integrated as a functional part of capitalist reproduction, carrying out the public functions of increasing commodity consumption, enabling workers to recuperate their energies for further work, and ensuring political passivity through a policy of bread and circuses. Similarly, the private family can be understood in terms of its public function of reproducing labour. Hence, private life appears free yet has in fact been colonized by public commercial and political institutions.

Finally, a range of postmodern arguments stress the breakdown of the public/private distinction alongside most other spheres differentiated under modernity. The arguments for this are various and reprise many of the themes we have looked at. Firstly, public and private domains were partly established through the separation of work from the home and the distinction of production from reproduction. Yet these divisions are under attack. The former is threatened by new work structures involving short-term contracts, freelancing, home working and the mobility of work due to new technologies. The latter is threatened by a long-term move to service industries and to the management of people in work: more and more work and commodities provide goods which might once have belonged to the private sphere. For example, the rising therapeutic and counselling professions, consultancies, publications and businesses transform a vast range of private concerns into matters of public contractual relations, expertise, social institutions.

Secondly, new social movements such as feminism, anti-racism, movements for the rights of children or old people, environmentalism – all focus on the public political features of private life and tend to argue that treating private life as private is a way of allowing oppressive power to continue. For example, domestic violence is not a private matter for a woman or child who feels that the violent behaviour of a male head of household is being ignored and therefore implicitly condoned by the law, police and welfare institutions. The slogan that 'the personal is political' involves a recognition that private and public life interpenetrate in complex ways and that their separation itself has political significance. An interesting recent example involves childhood which, as we have seen, has often represented the purest sense of privacy: whereas previously state intervention in the private family was justified only by concern for the child's safety or normal development, a few recent cases have involved children using the public sphere of law to sue their own parents. The underlying argument is that children both can but also *should* have civil rights in the public sphere, and that personal relations within the family can properly be politicized.

Finally – and somewhat ironically – neo-liberalism, privatization and increasing commodification seem to undermine the public/private distinction between state and civil society through which liberalism originally launched this entire train of thought in the first place. More and more institutions which carry out major public functions (health service, education, etc.) are either private or increasingly made up of privately sub-contracted labour. At the same time, the scale (as well as the public role) of many private enterprises has involved increasing government participation or co-operation. An interesting example involves the fate of many inner cities. In ancient times, the centre of the *bios politikos* or public life of citizens was the *agora* which was also, in fact, the marketplace. Throughout history, indeed, the identity of cities and regions has been bound up with 'city centres', usually marketplaces, in which a range of economic, political and cultural activities can be carried out on a public stage. Yet recent 'postmodern' urban planning which centres on the city as a space of consumption and leisure has often taken the form of the private development of shopping malls and precincts. These can entirely take over the function, or the actual space, of the city centre, literally taking over the very symbol of the public sphere. The mall still fulfils many public functions (a place to congregate, to observe an assembled public and representations of the public nature of the society), yet it is constructed by and for private interests (commerce), and it allows private finance to appropriate public space and to police it (people can be excluded if they look as if they might disturb commerce: the young, the poor, the old). It could be argued that the shopping mall indicates the most profound contemporary confusion of public and private: it is a private development which 'simulates' a public sphere which has all but disappeared from contemporary society.

KEY CONCEPTS

PUBLIC   Social life is explicable in a number of ways and we inhabit it in a number of different places. The public is that part of life that is shared, visible and accountable. Public life is that which is governed by common norms, rules and values. The public is the realm that is controlled by the state but this is constantly encroaching on the private.

PRIVATE   The private is that realm of social life which is most intimate, inward, and concerned with personal identity. It is in the private where the individual can explore that which is non-normative or simply non-consensual. However, within a modern society we can only provide the private with so much sovereignty, we cannot let people cause each other physical damage albeit 'in private'. The private remains, however, the space for the exercise of free will in an increasingly public world. The private world is increasingly penetrated by forms of mass media and communication – people now carry mobile phones so they can be reached 'anywhere'!

Sex/Gender

Joanne Entwistle

All societies make the distinction between two sexes, male and female, a fact that begins from the recognition that men and women occupy different bodies. This recognition of bodily difference results in all cultures marking the difference in various ways; men and women assume distinct characteristics and perform different roles. How the line is drawn between men and women varies a great deal from culture to culture and so too the different characteristics and roles that get assigned to men and women. In the West this process starts from the moment a baby is born and continues throughout the lifespan. As well as being dressed differently, pink for a girl and blue for a boy, baby boys and girls are almost immediately assigned distinct traits and characteristics: boys in our society are frequently described as 'aggressive' and 'assertive', whilst girls are frequently described as 'passive' and 'gentle'. Western society makes a sharp distinction between men and women and brings into play a number of other binary oppositions: reason/emotion, culture/nature, mind/body; in each case, man is identified with the former and woman with the latter. These characteristics are assumed to predispose men and women to special roles later in life; in the West, for example, men's assertive nature is supposed to make them better able to operate in the world of business and politics whilst women's gentle and nurturing characteristics would seem to make them the 'natural' carers of babies and children in the home and predispose them to the so-called 'caring professions', jobs such as nursing and teaching. However as well as acknowledging a difference between the sexes, it would seem that a feature of most if not all cultures is that they give more value to the characteristics and roles associated with men than those that are associated with women.

Thus as Sherry Ortner has noted, 'the secondary status of woman in society is one of the true universals, a pan-cultural fact. Yet within that universal fact, the specific cultural conceptions and symbolizations of woman are extraordinarily diverse and even mutually contradictory' (1974: 72).

This dividing of the sexes raises two important questions. First, are these differences the result of fundamental biological differences between men and women, i.e. are they *natural*, or are they the result of social organization, and in effect *cultural*? Second, why is it that, in almost all cultures, the things associated with women are given lower social status than the things associated with men? (Tong 1994).

These questions have resonated in many areas of academic and social life and been the source of much intellectual debate. However they are of particular interest to feminists who are concerned to explain and challenge the low status of women in society. How these questions concerning sexual difference are answered is of fundamental political importance to feminism. Any account which calls on biology or nature to explain the position occupied by men and women in the social world is seen as problematic to a great many feminists who argue that this can lead to the assumption that sexual inequality is a 'natural' thing. Biology limits the possibilities for change because nature itself is largely impermeable to change; as Steven Rose et al. put it, 'there can be no argument with biology, it is unchangeable' (1984: 6). Accounts which focus on culture and not biology offer greater possibility for change in the status of women. Drawing a distinction between biology and culture is therefore one way for feminists to proceed in their analysis of women's subordination, and this is the purpose of the sex/gender dichotomy. A large number of feminists, including Ann Oakley (1974) and Michelle Barrett (1988), would argue therefore that a distinction needs to be drawn between the biological facts of difference, namely *sex*, and the social meanings that come to be attached to this fact, namely *gender*. Thus as Oakley puts it,

> 'sex' is a word that refers to the biological differences between male and female: the visible difference in genitalia, the related difference in procreative function. 'Gender' however is a matter of culture: it refers to the social classifications into 'masculine' and 'feminine'. (1974: 16)

In this way, biological material determines sex, making us male and female, but does not determine the traits of 'masculinity' and 'femininity' which are the products of culture. Thus as Oakley argues, a fundamental task of her book *Sex, Gender and Society* is to 'disentangle "sex" from "gender" in the many fields where the existence of natural differences between male and female has been proposed' (1974: 17). Those adopting this position point to the fact that there is no natural link between biological characteristics and social ones. Whilst all societies refer to biology in their accounts of gender difference and all believe their definitions of gender are natural, no two cultures would agree on exactly what distinguishes men from women. Anthropological evidence from across the world has shown the great degree of difference in how biology is interpreted, with characteristics ascribed to men and women different from our own. Margaret Mead in her classic study *Sex and Temperament in Three Primitive Societies* (1935) looked at three New Guinea tribes, the Arapesh, the Mundugumor and the Tschambuli and gave evidence of the degree of cultural variability in the interpretation of sexual difference. In the Arapesh tribe, she found men and women adopting characteristics which Western cultures would recognize as 'feminine'; in the Mundugumor, both sexes adopted characteristics which we would see as 'masculine'; whilst in the Tschambuli she found that women adopt 'masculine' traits and men 'feminine' ones. This lack of any universal correspondence between sex and gender means that there is no 'natural' link between the biological categories of 'male' and 'female' and the cultural characteristics of 'masculine' and 'feminine'. Further evidence that sex does not determine gender in a 'natural' way can be found in studies of people who have biological disorders, sometimes referred to as hermaphrodites. Oakley (1974) summarizes the findings of some of these studies. Boys born without penises can go on to assume typical 'masculine' characteristics whilst girls born with 'penises' but without ovaries go on to acquire 'feminine' characteristics and traits. Studies of hermaphrodites give us evidence that the acquisition of 'masculinity' and 'femininity' is not 'natural' or purely 'biological' but is the result of socialization – parental and cultural expectation. Similarly, the existence of transsexuals gives further evidence of the discontinuity between sex and gender. Transsexuals are born with the biological characteristics of one sex but identify with the gender characteristics of the opposite sex. As Oakley notes, 'to be a man or a woman, a boy or a girl, is as much a function of dress, gesture, occupation, social network and personality, as it is of possessing a particular set of genitals' (1974: 158).

The dichotomy of sex and gender has not been adopted by all feminists and in recent years the issue of whether a clear line can be drawn between biology and culture has been questioned. However, it still remains a good starting point for the 'denaturalization' of gender roles and characteristics, which, as will be discussed, 'common-sense' and sociological theories have tended to take for granted as natural.

FEMINISM, BIOLOGY AND SEXUAL DIFFERENCE

At the centre of debates about sexual difference is the body. What status does the body have in the social world? What is the significance of the fact that men and women occupy different bodies and play different roles in the reproductive process? The body, according to B. Turner (1984), has occupied a 'cryptic' place within sociology: as an object of sociological investigation it has been largely neglected but, given the fact that the social world is a world of bodies, it has been implicit within sociological theory. There are also examples within philosophical and social theory where the body is evoked explicitly as a way of explaining social phenomena. Explanations of social phenomena which depend on biology are commonly referred to as *biological determinism* or *biologism*. In the 1970s sociobiologists such as E.O. Wilson attempted to bring biology and sociology into direct contact. Books such as Richard Dawkins' *The Selfish Gene* (1975) and Desmond Morris's *The Naked Ape* (1976) have been popularly received partly because they have a 'common-sense' appeal. Many sociologists, however, are sceptical of sociobiology. Barrett (1988) gives some examples of these accounts within the social sciences, as well as outlining the problems endemic to them. Criminal behaviour, intelligence quotient or IQ, mental illness, the 'capabilities' of different races and sexes, have all been studied with reference to biological characteristics and body types: hormones, genes, chromosomes, and sometimes even facial and scalp formations. This analysis usually results in the classification of 'human nature' into 'types'. Rose et al. (1984) argue that biologist explanations are problematic and can be challenged on a number of grounds. Biologism is philosophically reductive and often methodologically crude: biological determinists subsume complex social and historical relations under biology, directly correlating biological evidence with the social world to explain the differences found there. A further problem is that biological accounts are conservative: they tend to result in things being seen as 'natural' and unchanging, 'you can't change human nature.' They have also been discredited by many sociologists on political grounds: biologism has sometimes led to discrimination against particular races, in particular Jews and blacks, and indeed against women.

Despite the problems with biologism, the biological facts of the body and more particularly the different reproductive abilities of men and women have been frequently evoked in everyday life and in philosophy and the social sciences to explain social differences in men and women. Biology is the edifice upon which ideas about men and women are built. Biology as 'this is how things are' is also a powerful way of legitimating existing social divisions between men and women. Differences in chromosomes, hormones and genitalia are given as 'facts' which make men and women what they are. McNay summarizes the ways in which the body has been held responsible for character traits in men and women, noting that often 'masculine characteristics can be seen to be related to dominant perceptions of the male body, i.e. firmness, aggression, strength' (1992: 17). Often male hormones are held responsible for men's aggression, thereby making aggression a 'natural' feature of masculinity rather than something social. The characteristics attributed to femininity also correspond to dominant perceptions of the female body: the 'feminine' is seen as 'soft', 'gentle'.

Along with this, the possession of ovaries and a womb which produce the female hormones are held responsible for women's so-called 'maternal instinct' and supposedly produce a feminine nature which is 'gentle', 'sensitive', 'nurturing' and better suited for the primary care of children

The question of what importance to give sex or biology as an explanatory factor in the making of men and women is a particularly difficult one for feminists. On the one hand, feminists must recognize the body and its biology since bodily difference is the foundation upon which the oppression of women is built. On the other hand, many feminists do not wish to resort to biological arguments to explain women's oppression because such arguments are generally conservative and provide fewer options for social transformation. The ways in which feminists have taken account of the body are varied, and the degree of status accorded to the body as an explanatory factor in women's oppression is one source of division amongst feminists. Whilst all feminists recognize the importance of social and symbolic forces in the construction of men and women, some do give biology a certain degree of importance as a factor, whilst others focus on the cultural symbols of masculinity and femininity. A fundamental division within feminism has opened up between those feminists who call themselves or have been called *social constructivists* and those who call themselves or have been called *essentialists*. Social constructivists are sceptical of any account of gender difference which relies on biology, whilst essentialists make claims that 'true womanhood' is located in female biology. The difference between this form of essentialism and the biological arguments discussed above is the political desire of radical feminists to alter women's status rather than use biology to legitimate the low status of feminine traits and characteristics. Given that feminist theory and philosophy have developed not in a vacuum but in response to mainstream (male) theory and philosophy, this discussion will first consider the ways in which sexual difference has been constructed within classical social theory today before discussing feminist theory in more detail.

SOCIOLOGY AND SEXUAL DIFFERENCE

The body has been at the centre of the sociological tradition's account of men and women in society, sometimes 'cryptically', sometimes referred to directly by philosophers and sociologists to explain the characteristics and roles of men and women in the social world. In particular, a woman's reproductive role has been very often given as the reason for her confinement to the home. There are many examples in this intellectual tradition of how male/female difference in reproductive function (sex) is used to explain and to justify social differences between men and women (gender). R.A. Sydie notes:

> The appeal to a 'natural' difference between men and women based on the reproductive capacity of women has provided the framework for dichotomised views of the nature of the sexes and the assumption that hierarchical relations of male superiority and female subordination are justified by the dichotomy. (1987: 2)

If women's subordination is universal but is not due to any biological or 'natural' inferiority on the part of women, the explanation needs to be found elsewhere. Ortner (1974) locates the problem of sexual asymmetry at the level of cultural ideology and symbols and asks, what is common to every culture which might explain the ubiquitous nature of female oppression? The answer she comes up with is that of 'nature': all cultures make a distinction between culture and nature and all see women as closer to nature than men. Moreover, the products of culture are generally considered superior to those of nature. Ortner gives two reasons for these associations of women with nature. First, because of their role in reproduction, women appear closer to nature and women's creativity is seen to be fulfilled through the process of giving birth; whereas men, on the other hand, have to find other outlets for the creativity, through the making of things, invention, technology, etc. Second, because of their role in reproduction, women have found their social functions limited to those of the domestic sphere, in particular childrearing, a role which is seen as 'natural' and 'animal' rather than social. Like women, children are also posed as closer to nature since they start out as unformed and uncultured beings unable even to talk. Since women spend so much time in the company of these unsocialized beings, the role of being a mother appears to bring them closer to the 'natural' and 'animal' world. The net result is that women are thought to be confined by their biology and are positioned in the private/domestic realm for longer periods than men who are free to operate in the public domain. Ortner's account does not argue that women actually *are* closer than men to nature, but that cultures produce symbols and ideas that make them appear so.

Sydie (1987) argues that understanding how this dichotomous view of the world has underpinned European thought is essential if one is to produce a critique of sociology. From Aristotle to the Enlightenment thinkers such as Locke and Rousseau, and sociologists such as Durkheim and Weber, male and female reproductive roles have been evoked to explain the positions men and women assume in the social world. Moreover, the Enlightenment, out of which sociology emerged, saw the rise of science and the triumph of reason over God, superstition and nature, a dichotomous split which was implicitly gendered since sociology took for granted the dichotomy of men to culture, women to nature.

The sometimes metaphoric identification of women with nature was a source of celebration for some philosophers who saw beauty in nature. Women were seen to be important to men: the association of women with the natural world supposedly gave men an insight into the divine plan. This train of thought runs through the work of the Romantic philosopher Jean-Jacques Rousseau. Rousseau (1972) saw the separation of men and women into public and private spheres as an essential aspect of social order. His ideas about the differences in the sexes are laid out clearly in *Émile*. In her analysis, Gatens (1991) discusses in detail Rousseau's characterization of the sexes in this text. He argues that the separation of men and women into different spheres is a 'natural' one: men and women are fundamentally, i.e. 'naturally', different creatures. Man is associated with the mind, he has a capacity for *reason* which makes him suited to the public sphere; whilst a woman is identified with her body, and her role in the reproductive process gives her an insight into the passions and makes her fit to perform in the private, domestic realm. Rousseau believed that man is born twice, once into existence, and a second time as a man. Woman, however, is only born once: she never rises from the natural state of existence. Thus whilst a man can transcend his sex, a woman is confined to hers. According to Rousseau, 'the male is only a male now and again, the female is always a female' (1972: 324). As Moira Gatens (1991) notes, in Rousseau's philosophy women are expected to provide a 'natural' foundation necessary for the security of the social contract. The private sphere provides the emotional and mental stability necessary to public and civic life, and marriage is the means by which men have access to the private sphere and therefore to 'nature'. Marriage also ensures men a domestic republic and female submissiveness. Women's confinement in the private sphere is therefore part of a 'natural hierarchy' which is necessary for social order. To stray too far from this natural organization would destroy social life. For Rousseau, the consequences of women entering the public sphere would be either that they become men and upset the balance between nature and culture, or that they stay female and corrupt the public sphere.

However there was also a more negative positioning of women as a force of nature. For many the female body, in particular the uterus, was a source of irrationality, and this fear of irrationality in the age of reason was just one justification for the exclusion of women from the public sphere. Thus as Sydie argues, 'whatever the interpretation, women were men's opposites, and the opposition was a necessary but potentially negative one' (1987: 5).

Sydie (1987) gives a detailed discussion of how this dichotomous split has operated within sociology to the detriment of women. At its inception, sociology made claim to be a science concerned with the social and not the natural world. Furthermore, since the nature/culture dichotomy was one of asymmetry rather than equality, the world of the social was seen to have a 'natural' right to control and dominate the world of nature. This characterization of the world in terms of nature/culture, whilst ostensibly gender-neutral, at closer inspection turns out to be biased towards men since, as we have seen, only men were placed on the side of culture. She argues that Durkheim, for example, whilst considering marriage and family structures as socially and not biologically organized, falls into biological arguments when discussing the different roles men and women adopt in society. The division of labour results in women's increasing confinement to the home but this division has organic and physiological dimensions: both sexes have different capacities which make them suited to their roles. Thus Durkheim saw the division between men and women as necessary and functional to society.

FEMINISTS TAKE ON THE ACADEMY

This acceptance of the nature/culture dichotomy on the part of sociology had tangible implications for sociological research. If the private sphere of women is treated as 'natural' then it was largely outside the realm of a sociology which concentrates its attention on social phenomena found in the public realm. In focusing on the public realm, the realm of society and culture, sociology effectively dealt largely with men's experiences and rendered invisible the experiences of women in the home. Thus, for a long time, housework and childrearing were conceived of as 'non-work', as 'natural' or 'animal' functions. As feminists such as Oakley (1977), Sydie (1987) and Barrett (1988) have shown, far from being gender-neutral, the early sociologists suffered from gender blindness: the generic 'man' of early sociology was shown to stand for 'men'. Breaking the association of women with nature is seen by many feminists to be an important strategy. In recent years feminists such as Oakley (1977) have challenged the view that women's work is natural, pointing instead to how housework and childcare are socially organized labour, as much a part of the social world as the paid work and activities of men outside the home.

Given the way in which the Western philosophical and sociological tradition has perpetuated the idea of women's 'natural' inferiority to men, feminists have been eager to challenge in various ways the dichotomies of nature/culture, mind/body, reason/passion, public/private. Whilst all feminists share a desire to change women's status of subordination, there has been no consensus amongst feminists about what theoretical and political strategies might best achieve this. There are various ways of categorizing feminists, however, and amongst the main categories are liberal, radical, Marxist, psychoanalytic and postmodernist and poststructuralist. These different schools of feminism have disagreed on what emphasis to place on biology as an explanatory factor in accounting for difference between men and women. Broadly speaking, the response to this issue has resulted in two major lines of argument that cut *across* the various schools of feminism. The first theme is that of transcendence of the body. Many feminists have argued that women's emancipation can only be achieved when they can move outside the confines of their bodies and reproductive functions. This theme can be found in liberal and Marxist feminist accounts and can be traced through to the work of contemporary postmodernist and poststructuralist feminists. It is, however, also found in some but not all radical feminist writings. In general, this line of thought is one which aims to see the eradication of difference and the emergence of an androgenous society where sexual difference has no meaning. Exactly how women can move beyond the body is a point of disagreement amongst these very different schools of feminism, with each proposing different theoretical and political strategies for the movement of women out of the confines of their sex. The second theme which has emerged in response to women's association with nature and the body has been the celebration of the female body and its properties. This celebration of the female body can be found in some contemporary radical feminism where there is a tendency to collapse sex and gender: the female sexual characteristics are seen to be a source of 'feminine' characteristics such as nurturing or passivism. Essentialism is also associated with the so-called 'French' feminism that adopts psychoanalysis to theorize the 'feminine' as a textual and political strategy for the understanding of woman as 'other' to man.

Not all schools of feminism have therefore challenged the pairing of women with nature and men with culture. Gatens (1991) argues that a number of different schools of feminism, in particular liberal, existential and radical feminism, take for granted the assumption that the female body positions women closer to nature. She suggests that it is only in recent years that the assumption of a 'natural' basis for the division of labour between the sexes has been challenged. However, whilst liberals, existentialists and radicals often begin by leaving the nature/female, culture/male distinctions in place, they differ on the *value* they give to nature and culture and also what can be done about altering the situation.

LIBERAL FEMINISM

Mary Wollstonecraft's now classic *Vindication of the Rights of Woman*, first published in 1792, is a good example of the arguments put forward by liberal feminists and how they maintain the body/mind, nature/culture, private/public distinctions, albeit with some modifications. Wollstonecraft addresses herself to Rousseau's philosophical position, particularly the ideas he laid down in *Émile*. What Wollstonecraft takes issue with in Rousseau is his positioning of women and men on opposite sides of each of these dichotomies. Her aim, according to Gatens, is to 'desexualise reason and passion, nature and culture; to lessen the importance of sexual difference in the structuring of subjectivity and social role; and to *humanise* (or sexually neutralise) both the private and the public spheres' (1991: 21).

Rather than seeing men and women as fundamentally (or naturally) different, as Rousseau does, Wollstonecraft argues that there is an essential similarity between all men and women. In this way, Wollstonecraft asserts the idea of an *a priori* genderless subject. Men and women are not different creatures with different characteristics but are fundamentally the same in that both sexes are capable of passion and reason. However, unlike Rousseau who saw the necessity of both reason and passion, Wollstonecraft places greater value on reason and argues that it must be brought to bear in order to control passion. The development of reason is not just possible and desirable in men, as Rousseau argues, but for Wollstonecraft can and must be cultivated in both sexes. To desexualize reason and make it a trait of men *and* women means giving women the same rights to education as men and allowing them to enter into public life. Wollstonecraft's feminism therefore assumes that the root of women's oppression lies in their confinement to reproduction and thus the private sphere, the life of the body and passions. In celebrating the life of the public realm Wollstonecraft proposes that reason and the mind must rule the body. Female emancipation therefore depends upon women *transcending* the confines of the female body which position them in the home/private realm. If women can achieve this transcendence (and it must be noted that she did not see all women able to do so) then an androgenous society would emerge where no distinctions are made between men and women on the basis of their sex.

The main problem with Wollstonecraft's argument is that it leaves intact the distinction between nature/culture, mind/body and public/private as taken-for-granted facts of life. She takes for granted women's confinement to the body and, as a corollary to this, the fact that women's private work in the home is 'natural'. Her argument with Rousseau is simply about the way in which he organizes these two domains in terms of the sexes. The liberal feminist celebration of reason and the public sphere as the root of female emancipation may ostensibly be gender-neutral, but the result is that it implicitly supports the view that the things men do are superior to the things women do. In terms of sociological research, it means devaluing of things which women do in the home and not recognizing that what women do in the home is also of *social* value.

EXISTENTIAL FEMINISM

The theme of women's transcendence of the body is one that links other feminists, for example existential feminists like Simone de Beauvoir (1972) and the radical feminist Shulamith Firestone (1970). One tenet of existentialism is a profound disgust of the body and the desire to transcend it. The body is seen as a problem to existentialists because it limits freedom in life and carries us to our death. This theme can be found in de Beauvoir's classic account of women's oppression in *The Second Sex*. For de Beauvoir, reproduction is one of the 'natural' facts of a woman's life which serve to limit her. She places no positive value on these facts; instead, pregnancy and childbirth are ugly and distasteful and the role of a mother is ultimately limiting and alienating to women, a source of unfreedom. The aim for de Beauvoir is for women to transcend their bodies. Fundamentally a *social constructivist*, de Beauvoir does not say that biology is the sole cause of women's oppression. However, as Gatens (1991) points out, her adoption of the existential framework is a problem for feminism. The existential framework is not gender-neutral, as de Beauvoir assumes it is, but is inflected with a masculinist bias which assumes that nature and the 'mere existence' of the body are negative aspects of life. Jean Bethke Elshtain (1981) is also critical of de Beauvoir's general attitude to the body because it ultimately results in a *greater* mistrust of the female body. De Beauvoir's feminism requires that a woman rejects her body and its reproductive abilities in order to become a free self, but this rejection of the body is more costly to women. Men can remain men during and after sexual intercourse, whilst a woman who becomes pregnant, according to de Beauvoir, loses her freedom and sense of self. Thus in de Beauvoir's account, a woman's reproductive capacity makes her more confined to her body than a man – a point that echoes philosophers like Rousseau.

How much significance should feminists give to the fact of reproduction? Barrett (1988) argues that undoubtedly the biological facts of reproduction do exert some restrictions on women: childbirth is painful and dangerous. However she suggests that it is necessary to look at the social meanings given to these 'facts' since there are culturally variable ways of dealing with reproduction. She suggests that the biological liabilities of reproduction for women need to be examined in the light of other biological limitations which affect men to a greater extent. Barrett asks, 'is a planned pregnancy for a thirty five year old more or less disruptive to her work life than an unplanned heart attack of a man of the same age?' (1988: 75). There is also no necessarily biological reason why women's childbearing role should mean that women are the primary carers of children, yet in most cultures they are. Gatens (1991) argues that it is not the fact of a woman's body *per se* that is the root of her oppression, but how it is constructed socially. In reproducing these values, Gatens argues that de Beauvoir's account does not provide a solution to the problem.

RADICAL FEMINISM

Whilst by no means a unified approach, one thing linking radical feminism has been the tendency to focus on the body and in particular on women's reproductive capacity in their accounts of oppression. Radical feminists have therefore emphasized the power men have over women's bodies: some like Firestone look at men's power over reproduction, whilst others like Susan Brownmiller (1975) and Andrea Dworkin (1981) look at rape and pornography. Firestone's (1970) account borrows from Marx's historical materialism but imposes sex not class as the motor of history. Men and women each make up a sex class and this biological division is the most fundamental one in history and the source of men's systematic subordination of women. Like de Beauvoir, Firestone is repelled by pregnancy which she argues is 'barbaric', but unlike de Beauvoir she goes as far as to see women's subjection rooted entirely in their biological role and thus presents a biological determinist account. Unlike liberal feminists, she does not see entry to education or the public sphere as effecting a transformation in women's low social status. Instead, women's emancipation can only take place through a biological revolution which would free them from the constraints of their bodies. The transcendence of the female body is made possible through the use of new reproductive technologies: contraception, sterilization and abortion, as well as technologies of artificial insemination, *in vitro* fertilization and so on which were in their infancy when Firestone was writing. Echoing Marx's call for the proletariat to cease the means of production, she argues that women must cease the means of reproduction. In this 'brave new world' women would not have to give birth to babies and, once the shackles of pregnancy and labour are removed, so too will be the 'common-sense' claim that women's 'natural' duty is to care for children.

This position has been challenged by other radical feminists. A number of radical feminists, amongst them Mary Daly (1978) and Adrienne Rich (1976), have pointed out the problems of placing such faith in science and technology. Given the history of science, it is more likely that reproductive technologies would fall into the hands of men than women, giving them another means to control women's bodies. Furthermore, the rendering of pregnancy, childbirth and childrearing as negative aspects of a woman's life has been challenged. Many radical feminists have argued that the problem is not that women give birth, but that giving birth is treated as a problem by a male-dominated society. Since Firestone, many radical feminists have chosen to see female biology and reproduction positively, as a source of strength for women. Rich (1976), for example, argues that it is men's jealousy of women's reproductive capacity that makes them control it. Male gynaecology and obstetrics now control women's reproduction where once female midwives did. In this way, men have also come to control how women feel about reproduction and alienated women from their own experience. For Rich, giving back to women control over pregnancy and childbirth would result in these things attaining a positive value. Radical feminists have therefore sought not to challenge the association of women with nature and men with culture, but to change the *values* given to these, inverting the hierarchy which places culture as superior to nature: the associations of women with nature, passion, carnality are posed as traits to be valued above those associated with men. Radical feminists produce an essentialist account since they argue that the traits women exhibit in the world are rooted in their biology. By mapping femininity directly onto 'female', and likewise 'masculinity' onto 'male', radical feminists do not divide sex from gender but collapse the dichotomy (Haraway 1990; 1991).

Are women closer to nature than men? Gatens (1991), Ortner (1974) and others would argue that they are not, but that the symbols a culture produces make it appear so. To assume that women are closer to nature is to conflate biological functions with social characteristics, which, as has been argued here by Oakley and Barrett, is highly problematic. These three approaches – liberal, existential, radical – in different ways leave in place the nature/women, culture/men dichotomies. Wollstonecraft, de Beauvoir and Firestone take for granted women's connection to nature and do not see this association as socially constructed. Likewise the radical strategy to change the values associated with nature and culture also simply leaves the structure in place. This is problematic to those feminists like Gatens who argue that the association of women with nature and men with culture is not 'natural' but socially constructed.

THE PROBLEMS OF THE SEX/GENDER DICHOTOMY

In recent years, a number of challenges have been made to the sex/gender distinction. Barrett (1988), in her later preface to *Women's Oppression Today*, points out some of the problems of separating sex and gender. Social constructivist feminists (like herself) have tended to overemphasize social forces and neglect biology and the real limitations that reproduction has placed on women in times of limited contraception. Moreover, although social constructivists tried to ignore, neutralize or transcend the body, the fact remains that the female body is the ontological ground of feminism since, as a political project, feminism depends on the idea of a biological woman. A further problem with the sex/gender distinction is that it assumes that a clear line can be made between biology and the social world: it is assumed that sex is an unadorned 'fact' of nature, a pre-social state onto which a social meaning is pinned. However, a point made strongly by poststructuralism is that biology and nature do not stand outside culture as 'raw facts' which then acquire a social meaning: biology and nature are themselves socially constituted. In the light of poststructuralism and in particular the work of Michel Foucault, the body has now ceased to be something taken for granted as 'natural' matter outside the social and thus unchanging, and has become the topic of historical and cultural analysis. Foucault's (1977; 1979a) analysis recognizes the concrete material existence of bodies in history but he does not acknowledge the body as having any essential qualities. Foucault's *anti-essentialist* position means that he considers how bodies acquire different meanings and are subject to historical forces of power at different times. Although Foucault does not address the question of sexual difference in his work, many feminists have turned to his analysis because it enables them to analyse the body as a concrete entity, shaped by social forces, but without having to acknowledge any essential or universal meanings of male and female bodies. It enables feminists to ask how particular meanings get attached to the female body at any one time and how these *come to be seen* as 'natural'.

CONCLUSION

The division between social constructivists and essentialists is, if anything, greater today than ever before. Feminists disagree on what significance to attach to the body, and the two trends – one towards transcendence of the body and nature, the other towards celebration of the body and women's connection to nature – can be mapped today onto the division between social constructivist and essentialist feminists. The former approach is currently campaigned by new postmodern feminists such as Sadie Plant and Donna Haraway, who in different ways celebrate technology: Plant looks to the disembodied space of the Internet as a potential source for transcendence of the body; Haraway looks to the unnatural cyborg as the means for women to rise above the female body and its oppressive connection to nature. The essentialist celebration of the feminine is now lodged within radical feminism and the 'French' feminism associated in particular with Luce Irigary and Hélène Cixous. The problem of how to interpret biology, what status to accord the body in social life, remains a matter of intense feminist debate. The sex/gender dichotomy, whilst useful, has not solved the problem of how to consider the relationship of biology to culture.

KEY CONCEPTS

SEX   This term is used in sociology not to describe the procreative act between people but rather to understand the natural disposition and physical configuration of the individual. By and large people are men or women, this is their sex.

GENDER   Gender is sociology's concept for distinguishing between our sexual identity and the social identity that has become historically and culturally attached to it. It does not follow from being sexually a woman that you are either good at or motivated to do housework. It is the case that only women can give birth, this is a natural and sexual difference, it is not the case that only women can engage in child care, this is a gender difference.

Race/Ethnicity

Jean Popeau

A dichotomy is associated with a division of a class or category into two mutually exclusive subclasses, yet race and ethnicity are not popularly regarded as mutually exclusive concepts. In the field of multi-ethnic education it has apparently become standard practice to substitute the term 'ethnicity' for 'race' in publications carrying government approval: 'ethnicity' is the more polite and less controversial term for 'race' in the thinking of certain bureaucrats. Where matters of classification according to ethnic origins are concerned for official enquiries, ethnicity is often regarded as determined by geography, by country of origin rather than 'race', thus giving ethnicity a geographical connotation not usually associated with 'race'. However, historically the major 'races' are associated with the natural peopling of certain parts of the earth: Africans, vaguely with the area south of the Sahara; Asians, or 'the yellow race', with the continent of Asia; whites or Europeans with the Caucasus (a geographical area comprising the mountains between the Black and Caspian Seas). Ethnicity is popularly seen as a matter of cultural plus geographical cohesion: 'ethnies' live in tightly knit cultural groups who sometimes seek to defend their territory by establishing boundaries with other 'ethnies' – boundaries which are sometimes fiercely defended, as in the former Yugoslavia, though they may form the area across which commerce between groups occurs (Barth 1969). 'Ethnicity' is associated with cultural unity, a cohesive *Weltanschauung* which seeks to define itself in relation to other value systems proclaimed by different groups.

In this chapter I shall examine the concepts of 'race' and 'ethnicity' individually, prior to an examination of the possible dichotomies between them.

RACE

The term 'race' is often placed within cautionary inverted commas to indicate the dubious scientific meaning of the concept. Modern genetics avoids reference to 'races': there has been so much sexual interaction between human populations that it would be meaningless to talk of absolute divisions between 'races'. The distribution of hereditary physical traits does not recognize clear divisions between populations: there is often greater variation within a 'racial' group than between two different groups.

Although based upon a 'biological fiction', the huge sociological ramifications of 'race' are however generally recognized by theorists. Howard Winant declares that 'race has become a fundamental organizing principle of contemporary social life' (1994: 270), and many social scientists would recognize some value in Winant's statement when faced with raging controversies surrounding race and intelligence, race and criminality, race and the ability to hurl a cricket ball at ninety miles an hour. The complexity which is 'race' does not deter the adoption of popular and journalistic assumptions based upon some vague notion of the importance of 'race', while the difficulties of the issue seem to fuel, rather than add an element of caution to, such opinions. Thus Winant's declaration of the fundamental importance of race for modernity is simply the reiteration of a social fact. In the metropolitan areas of the USA, France and Great Britain, to name but three countries, 'race' has begun to assume great categorial importance even where it is disguised by reference to 'ethnicity', 'multiculturalism', 'ethnic minorities' and 'other cultures'.

In order to appreciate the importance of race in Euro-American culture, it is necessary to examine the history of the concept. The debate surrounding race in Britain, Robert Young (1995: 118) notes, was initially based on liberal ideas of universal brotherhood stemming from the Enlightenment, and Biblical notions placing the origins of all races in one source. The diversity amongst peoples was explained in terms of culture rather than race. The values of the abolitionists of slavery and this liberal theorizing on race coincided with, and was strengthened by, the publication of Harriet Beecher Stowe's anti-slavery novel *Uncle Tom's Cabin* in 1852. However developments in the British Empire, and elsewhere, with racial themes, saw the political tenor of the debate move from paternalistic liberalism to a hard-edged racial superiority. The Indian 'Mutiny' of 1857, the American Civil War (1861–5) and the Jamaican Insurrection of 1865 were incidents in whose scenario race was important. The publication of Robert Knox's *The Races of Men* in 1850, which Robert Young terms 'the first substantively racialist scientific work in Britain' (1995: 119), saw the entry of 'race' as a concept into the popular imagination in Britain kindled by the new theory of 'scientific racism'. Similar developments had taken place on the European continent with the publication of works by Gobineau of France and Carus of Germany, all treating race as a fundamental cultural,

167

sociological and ultimately scientific explanation of human differences. 'Scientific' explanation had come to replace theological explanation in the theory of 'race':

> The new racialism could be described, therefore, as the overdetermined product of the conjuncture of a loss of belief in Biblical explanation and its replacement by apparently authoritative scientific laws, a sense of European cultural and technological pre-eminence, accompanied by working class unrest at home, revolution and colonial rebellion abroad and a civil war in the United States focussed on the issue of slavery. (1995: 120)

The term 'race' in its modern sense is associated with the publication of Gobineau's *Essai sur l'inégalité des races humaines* which appeared in 1853–5. Collette Guillaumin (1991: 10) notes that Gobineau gives no definition of 'race' in the work yet his idea of 'race' came to dominate the nineteenth and early twentieth centuries. Gobineau had been familiar with the writing of his British and American contemporaries who had linked race with history, as well as those who, like the American craniologist S.G. Morton, used empirical science in the formulation of their racial theories. Gobineau's theory differed from that of Josiah Nott, Henry Hotze and other **polygenesists** in its propagation of the fertility of hybrids, the result of the interbreeding of the different races. The racialist ideas of the American and British theorists depended on the belief in the infertility of hybrids for its thesis that the races were really separate species – so separate that hybridity was bound to be disastrous. As with most racialist ideas, fact was never a barrier to the popularization of tendentious theorizing: the fact that hybridity flourished in the colonies of Britain and the slave plantations of America did not affect the fervour with which this theory was propounded. Gobineau's theory was a peculiar mixture of negative and positive in its attitude to hybridity. For Gobineau hybridity was bound to lead to degeneration yet the production of civilization depended on it.

In Gobineau's system the sexualization of race manifests as the division of peoples into 'masculine' and 'feminine' races; the strong 'masculine' races (white Aryans) are associated with utilitarianism, materialism, technological progress, aggressive conquest; the 'feminine' races (black and yellow) with intellectuality and spirituality. Civilization or culture depends upon the mixing of the 'masculine' and 'feminine' races initiated by the sexual attraction of the white males for black and yellow females, to the ennoblement of the latter. The mixture of the white and black races produces great art and literature.

The prospects for miscegenation filled Gobineau with fascinated horror despite his recognition of its inevitability; for him, it was bound to lead to cosmopolitan metropolises, democracy, anarchy and violence. All civilization emanates from the white male's tendency to fuse with females of other

races, a process which leads inevitably to the degeneration of the
in the very production of civilization.

The concept of 'race' as a mixture of phenotypical, mental
characteristics passed in Europe from Gobineau's idea to the adv
ideology and their inauguration of the 'Nuremberg Laws' whic
the concept of 'race' in the German legal system (a similar con
be followed later by the South Africans in their apartheid system). This
action of the Nazis led to a debate about 'race' amongst social scientists,
who, while disowning the Nazi connection between **phenotype**, culture,
and psychology, attempted to redefine the centuries-old meaning of the
concept. Collette Guillaumin (1991: 11) notes that the American Anthropological Association's declaration of 1938, for example, implicitly rejects
the connection between phenotype, culture and psychology. The debate
which followed the dissolution of the Nazi regime saw the publication of
UNESCO's 1978 document *Déclaration sur la race*, which attempted a
definitive examination of the meaning of 'race'. The document rejected
popular and common-sense notions while accepting that there is such a
'thing' as 'race'.

The phenomenon of **class racism** suggests that the whole notion of 'race'
may have begun as a prejudice based upon class before it became one
based upon phenotype and colour. 'Class racism' began in Europe as a
feeling of superiority by the privileged and educated classes who
advocated policies to 'stop the lower orders breeding defectives' and to
promote the breeding of the 'best' members of 'the race'; this feeling later
manifested as the theory and political movement of 'eugenics' (Hayes 1994:
180). In Britain such figures as Francis Galton and Marie Stopes believed
that the 'genius' of the 'British race' should be perpetuated in its eminent
families, and the 'lower classes', representing the 'inferior' members of
society, should be discouraged from breeding and 'mongrelizing' the
population. Francis Galton believed in the relationship between phenotypical and mental characteristics, that human beings could be classified
according to the upper limits of their physical capacity, and that 'if this be
the case with stature, then it will be true as regards every other physical
feature – as circumference of head, size of brain, weight of grey matter,
number of brain fibres, &c.; and thence, by a step on which no physiologist
will hesitate, as regards mental capacity' (Galton 1869, quoted by Nicky
Hayes 1994: 183). Only a brief step is required to make the connection
between physical, mental and cultural characteristics, manifesting as a
belief in 'race', and the belief, like Galton's, in the hereditary transmission
of 'racial characteristics' with the accompanying idea that only the
aristocracy can carry the 'best' characteristics of the nation. Indeed, as
Guillaumin (1991: 12) notes, in France until the eighteenth century 'race'
was a term used to refer to the great families of the aristocracy; no one
outside the royal lineage could be said to belong to a 'race'. The nineteenth
century saw the formulation of today's popular association between

phenotype and mental and cultural characteristics which is vaguely known as 'race'.

Gobineau was instrumental in the development of the concept of racism from 'class racism', that is, racism within the same population or ethnic group, to a racism based on colour, or phenotype, across populations and continents. According to this formulation, civilization is as unknown to the 'lower races' as to the 'lower classes'. Gobineau makes a Manichaean division between the purer lineage of the upper classes (achieved through interbreeding) and 'the degenerate, miscegenated anarchic working class, with its materialistic democratic tendencies' (Young 1995: 114). Just as it would be impossible to change a member of the 'lower class' into an aristocrat, so it would be impossible to alter the status of a member of the 'lower races' to a position of equality with a 'race' of higher rank: the races are basically unequal and no amount of education will close the gap between them. This position of Gobineau's was echoed by the American educational psychologist Arthur Jensen in the 1970s, who justified his stance against improvements in black education by citing the Negro's hereditary difference in intelligence compared with whites, which no improvement in Negro education would bridge or reduce (Hayes 1994: 208–10).

Thus 'race' is defined in terms of lineage and kin solidarity, but also with the idea of superiority and inferiority between groups or classes within the same ethnic group or nation, and between nations and continents.

ETHNICITY

As a term, 'ethnicity' is recognized by sociologists as having relatively recent coinage. Eriksen (1993: 3) cites Glazer and Moynihan as noting that the word's first appearance was in the *Oxford English Dictionary* of 1972. The word 'ethnic' is derived from the Greek *ethnos* (in turn derived from *ethnikos*), originally meaning 'heathen' or pagan. It was used in this sense from the mid fourteenth century until the mid nineteenth century, when it gradually began to develop 'racial' connotations (to be linked with lineage and kin solidarity). As was noted earlier, ethnicity is often associated with geographical and cultural integrity.

Ethnicity theory is sometimes divided between 'primordialists' and 'instrumentalists'. The primordialist position defines ethnicity as a funda-mental, indefinable aspect of populations: primordialists like Van den Berghe (1981) and Clifford Geertz (1973) see ethnic identity as an essential aspect of human populations. Van den Berghe, whose theory we shall examine later, regards ethnic identity as a basic biological tendency. Geertz conceives ethnicity as an inchoate but powerful characteristic of human life: 'These congruities of blood, speech, custom, and so on are seen to have an

170

ineffable, and at times overpowering coerciveness in and of themselves' (1973: 259). In this concept 'race' (euphemistically termed 'blood' in Geertz's formulation) is subsumed within ethnicity which, as we shall see later, is the relationship between 'race' and 'ethnicity' formulated by other theorists (Balibar and Wallerstein 1991; Van den Berghe, 1981).

Instrumentalists define ethnicity as an instrument for the pursuit of material interests by competing cultural groups within complex societies. Abner Cohen is regarded as propounding an extreme example of 'instrumentalism' in his severing of the tie between ethnicity and culture; he conceives of ethnicity solely as a means for the pursuit of political objectives in the contemporary world, and therefore needing no historical or cultural explanations (Eriksen 1993: 55). In Cohen's (1974a; 1974b) notion that London stockbrokers constitute an ethnic group, no question of an atavistic, ineffable residue of sentiment and 'blood' manifests as an element of cohesiveness within the group; rather, the binding relationship is based on naked political self-interest. Cohen's position has been criticized for its failure to consider what constitutes the factors which enable ethnic groups to define themselves in relation to other ethnic groups and maintain their ethnic identity in the face of social and political developments (Eriksen 1993: 55). Most theorists take Milton J. Esman's middle position between that of Geertz and Cohen in regarding ethnicity as a dynamic element of social and political relations which maintains some form of identity through time (Esman 1994: 9–14).

Ethnicity was regarded in the America of the 1920s as a phenomenon associated with the European minorities who had come to the United States in the nineteenth and early twentieth centuries and had eventually 'assimilated' into white Anglo-Saxon America. Omi and Winant (1994: 16) refer to the confusion in the minds of the Chicago School – the originators of the 'ethnic paradigm' – between ethnic inequality and racial equality, ethnicity and race. The Chicago School's ethnicity theory could be divided into two concepts propagated by two groups of theorists: assimilationism and cultural pluralism. Both concepts used Anglo-Saxon America as the paradigm or standard by which the new immigrants from Europe – Irish, Italians, Jews, for example – were to be judged. Both groups of theorists used the new European immigrants as the basis for their empirical studies. The assimilationists stressed the possibilities of ethnic assimilation into Anglo-Saxon America; the cultural pluralists emphasized the acceptance of different immigrant cultures. Both sets of theorists concentrated on 'ethnic minorities', that is, minorities based upon white ethnic groups from Europe, and tended to ignore the experience of racial minorities, that is, black, brown, red and yellow peoples.

The 'melting pot' theory of ethnic relations, in which each ethnic group is regarded as an element which will eventually assimilate into the dominant culture, envisaged the demise of the 'Negro' and therefore of the 'race problem', according to its own 'ethnic paradigm' theory. Blacks were regarded as another ethnic group who would follow the pattern of the other ethnic groups through a process of assimilation. The theory failed to account for the differences between ethnic minorities and racial minorities, based as it was on a concept of ethnicity whose elements did not share the experiences of blacks and other racial minorities in the United States. It failed to take account of the experiences of blacks rooted in institutional structures of discrimination and a history of slavery, and the resulting tendency amongst blacks to defend a concept of black culture and to resist absorption into the dominant culture. It suggested that blacks' failure to assimilate into the dominant culture was due not to these structures of discrimination and exclusion but to inherent weaknesses in black 'norms' (lifestyles, families) resulting in a failure, unlike other ethnic minorities, to use their opportunities. The theorists of the 'ethnic paradigm' thus seemed to have failed to distinguish between 'race' and 'ethnicity', between the experiences of racial minorities and those of ethnic minorities.

RACE/ETHNICITY

The difficulty of distinguishing between race and ethnicity is acknowledged by most theorists. Eriksen notes that their separation 'is a problematic one' since ethnicity manifests in many forms, and 'ethnic ideologies tend to stress common descent among their members' (1993: 5). Banton's dichotomization of 'race' and 'ethnicity' by reference to 'us' and 'them' (1983: 106), in which ethnicity is a means of categorizing 'us' and race is a categorization of 'them' or 'the other', has some plausibility when placed in the context of the Chicago School's ethnicity theory which, as we noted earlier, was based on a categorization of the ethnic groups familiar to them, that is, the white European immigrant groups settling in North American cities in the early twentieth century. The Chicago School's tendency to theorize black and Asian groups *en masse*, as 'races', suggests an instinctive tendency to theorize those groups unfamiliar to 'us' as 'them', or 'other', that is, in racial terms.

Van den Berghe's theory of ethnicity sees it as consisting of linguistic and kin solidarity. For Van den Berghe (1981: 241) racism is the result of a particular case of ethnic solidarity based on phenotype as an ethnic indicator. In his theory it is ethnic solidarity which is the more 'natural' and atavistic mark of group solidarity, not race, which is a 'relatively uncommon and recent indicator of common descent' (1981: 240). His theory suggests a nature/culture divide between ethnicity and race, with ethnicity assuming the role of the 'natural element' in this relationship. Racism is a 'cultural invention', although ethnocentrism is 'inborn' or natural (1981: 240). His is a variation of sociobiology in which human action is analogized to that of animals: the human world with its complex cultural configuration is compared to the animal world at the level which they are both assumed to share – that is, the biological. At that level humans are instinctive agents of their 'selfish genes' who wish to maximize the value of their genes, either through interbreeding and co-operation with those who share them, or through coercion of groups who do not share their genes in a form of a parasitism which ensures the maximum well-being and survival of those genes. This tendency towards genetic or group solidarity leads to nepotism: ethnocentrism assumes the role of nepotistic solidarity with those who share the same ethnic descent as yourself. Given the 'natural' origins of this solidarity it is assumed to be inevitable and worthy. Racism, which is nepotistic solidarity with those who share the same phenotype (physical features including skin colour) as yourself, is relatively recent, a 'cultural invention', and not as worthy as ethnocentrism.

The implied dichotomy between race and ethnicity here arises out of the ramifications of Van den Berghe's theory. Ethnocentrism, kin solidarity based upon kin selection from shared genes, is 'natural', that is, a propensity shared with the other animals of nature, according to the terms of Van den Berghe's theory. Racism, a particular form of ethnocentrism which for Van den Berghe arises out of contact between groups with very different phenotypes, and continues only until interbreeding has blurred such phenotypical divides, is 'cultural', and not a characteristic shared with the rest of nature. Earlier in his book Van den Berghe (1981: 240) states that ethnic markers, that is, the outward signs by which kin solidarity is recognized, are all cultural in origin; therefore ethnocentrism, no less than racism, is based upon cultural norms.

Van den Berghe's attempts to formulate ethnicity in terms of genetics emerge as flawed in the light of the fact that 'ethnicity' like 'race' is a socially produced concept which cannot simply be reduced to a 'biological' content which it is assumed will give it greater rigour. The vague, complex and dynamic aspect of ethnicity which resists attempts at essentialization is a reflection of the reality of the operation of 'ethnicity' as a concept in society. It is necessary here to reaffirm the Wittgensteinian idea that the meaning of a word is its use (Wittgenstein 1968: 175–6), not that which the specialist would like to give it, especially when that word depends for its very sustenance on its social construction.

Unlike that of Van den Berghe, Etienne Balibar's formulation of ethnicity recognizes its complex social and cultural connotations. He conceives of race and ethnicity as engaged in a symbiotic relationship in which the 'fictive' construct of ethnicity is produced out of a combination of 'language' and 'race' in the creation of the ideal, the 'nation'. Balibar's term **fictive ethnicity** is modelled after Benedict Anderson's (1983) notion of ethnicity in terms of the sum of a collection of people who form 'the nation', very few of whose members they will know individually, and who therefore must base their sense of 'the nation' upon an imagined ethnic solidarity. Ethnicity must be 'produced' in Balibar's theory; it is a 'fictive'

173

construct which must nonetheless be seen as having 'the most natural of origins' (Balibar and Wallerstein 1991: 96). Language and race are the two routes to this production. Language and race appear at once as both 'natural' accepted givens in the order of nature, and transcendent: they constitute two ways of rooting historical populations in a fact of 'nature' (the diversity of languages and the diversity of races appearing predestined), but also two ways of giving a meaning to their continued existence, of transcending its contingency (1991: 96–7).

The modern idea of 'race' is based upon a monoracial system to which members of the nation are thought to belong; this idea of racial solidarity within a national context (for example, 'the French', 'the Germans', 'the English') is used to overcome class differences in the production of the national ideal. For Balibar and Wallerstein the nation is the authentic representation of the racial community rather than the clan, the neighbourhood community or social class. It is when nationals can marry and engage in sexual relations across social class or other local allegiances that the racial community becomes real at the national level. Ethnicization occurs at the level of the nation and ethnicity is produced out of a sense of racial solidarity which likens the nation to 'a great family' (1991: 100). Thus here the relationship between 'race' and 'ethnicity' is not dichotomized. Rather, 'race' is one of two elements involved in the production of ethnicity; 'race' is itself a cultural concept utilizing the idea of 'nature' or 'the natural' in the creation of its notion of spiritual and kin solidarity.

In the next two sections we shall examine two recent divergent views of the relationship between 'race' and 'ethnicity', those taken by minority groups and the new right respectively.

'BLACKNESS', 'RACE' AND 'ETHNICITY'

In the form in which ethnic groups from South Asia, Africa and the Caribbean came together to affirm their solidarity in the face of marginalization, and to fight for their political rights, the concept of blackness in Britain in the 1970s and 1980s embraced a political programme. The term 'black' here assumed a political rather than a 'racial' connotation in which individual ethnic differences were deferred for the 'bigger prize' of political and social justice. Here the term 'black' covers a diversity of cultural groups and experiences and is therefore a formulation with a wide political rather than racial reference, as Stuart Hall defined it, '"black" is essentially a politically and culturally *constructed* category, which cannot be grounded in a set of fixed transcultural or transcendental racial categories and which therefore has no guarantees in Nature' (1992b: 254).

Later developments find certain members of these ethnic groups challenging the terms of this 'solidarity', calling for recognition of the specificity of the experiences and values of each ethnic group. These developments represent a movement in the political history of British ethnic minorities in which 'race' no longer plays the same role as during the period of political solidarity, and rights do not have to be fought for under the former racial banner. The ethnic groups are able to affirm the uniqueness of their own cultural and social needs while coming together in solidarity with other politically marginalized groups such as gays, and single parents, where the political need arises.

The point is reached for the affirmation of what Stuart Hall calls 'new ethnicities', which, as Hall observes, beckon away from the essentialized 'racialized' construction of the black subject, with its negative colonial connotations, towards an 'ethnic' construction which acknowledges the role of history, culture and politics in the construction of the subject. Hall maintains: 'If the black subject and black experience are not stabilized by Nature or by some other essential guarantee, then it must be the case that they are constructed historically, culturally, politically – and the concept which refers to this is "ethnicity"' (1992b: 257). Hall seems to gesture towards the traditional nature/culture difference which associated blackness and therefore 'race' with nature, and 'ethnicity' with culture, in the process of denying the validity of that difference. We are moving, in Hall's formulation, away from the racialized notion of blackness with its suggestion of fixity and essentialism, towards the more dynamic concept of 'ethnicity' which recognizes the role of various social and political forces in the formation of the subject.

'ETHNICITY', 'RACE' AND THE NEW RIGHT

The new right is also aware of the social movement away from the biological and colonial connotations connected with the old meaning of 'race', towards the present championing of the rights of ethnic groups, and the recognition of the unique right of minority groups to affirm their religion, language and morality, in short their difference, manifest in 'multiculturalism'. Since the 1970s the right has seized on the notion of 'difference' and used it to propagate the old racism in the new guise of 'cultural difference'. It asserts that minority cultures are different, especially minority cultures of people of colour, so different that this difference is, and is likely to remain, permanent: therefore they should not be allowed to mix with the culture of the majority. As Collette Guillaumin puts it: 'apartheid is a form of institutionalized difference and "separate development" is a form of the right to be different' (1991: 12).

'Ethnicity' as an idea has been used by the new right to refer to concepts associating nation, race and colour in a sinister *mélange* in Britain. The new right's notion of 'ethnicity' would, for example, link 'Englishness' with a mixture of nationalism (being part of the English nation), racism (it is impossible to be black and English), and xenophobia. In a discourse employing the culturalist definition of 'race', a form of what David Gillborn (1995) refers to as 'deracialized talk', 'ethnicity' is employed by the new right as a reference to 'race' in which 'race' is present by its absence, in which the coded reference to 'culture' masks an incipient reference to 'race'. Margaret Thatcher's pre-election speech to the 1987 Conservative Party conference is a typical example:

> people are really afraid that this country might be swamped by people with a different culture. And, you know, the British character has done so much for democracy, for law, and done so much throughout the world, that if there is fear that it might be swamped, people are going to react and be rather hostile to those coming in. (Margaret Thatcher, January 1978: quoted in Gillborn 1995: 27)

Racist theorizing has developed in France, Balibar notes, into an attempt to justify and explain the spontaneous aggression of the 'masses', or proletariat youth, in terms of an instinctive awareness of the effects of 'unfair' and 'unnatural' mixing of cultures as proposed by anti-racists or 'the anti-racist industry'. The neo-racist attempts to employ the 'turnabout' effect, that is, a ruse by which he uses the arguments of anti-racists against their intentions. Anti-racists have hitherto demanded respect for dominated cultures against the oppressive universalism of the West, or, as Balibar and Wallerstein term it, 'the hegemony of certain standardizing imperialisms' (1991: 21). Anti-imperialists such as Lévi-Strauss have argued for the preservation of the integrity and difference of minority cultures, that all civilizations are complex and necessary for the preservation of human thought. They now find their theories 'turned about' by this new racism, calling itself not so much a 'racism' but a bias in favour of its own ethnic group, nation, culture and 'fundamental way of life', all of which are threatened by the presence of alien immigrant cultures, leading understandably, as they see it, to spontaneous violence against certain immigrant sections of the population. If racism is associated in the thinking of liberals and humanists with moral obloquy, the new right argues for its 'naturalness' and therefore its value. 'What's wrong with racism?' Enoch Powell asks, and he defines 'racism' not in terms of irrational hatred of blacks or Asians but as the instinctive and 'natural' desire to preserve the ethnicity and national character of the United Kingdom threatened by alien cultures.

What Hall refers to in his use of the term 'ethnicity' is its reclamation from the right for the purposes of a positive celebration of difference:

> The fact that this grounding of ethnicity in difference was deployed, in the discourse of racism, as a means of disavowing the realities of racism and repression does not mean that we can permit the term to be permanently

colonized. That appropriation will have to be contested, the term disarticulated from its position in the discourse of 'multiculturalism' and transcoded, just as we previously had to recuperate the term 'black', from its place in a system of negative equivalences. (1992b: 257)

This celebration of diversity and difference would involve a recognition of the cultural, historical and political forces which form individuals, positively breaking away from old racial stereotypes: in this guise 'ethnicity' could also embrace gender and sexual orientation as other elements to be considered in the formation of someone's individuality.

CONCLUSION

'Race' and 'ethnicity' have historically been synonymous in Europe. In European terms it is possible, for example, to regard Wales as a Celtic nation, to talk of the Welsh 'race', of 'Welsh' as an ethnic category without contradiction: 'race' and 'ethnicity' embrace in the concept of 'nation'. Banton (1983: 64) observes that 'nation', 'race' and 'ethnic group' have until recently been used in Europe to denote groups of the same order of magnitude and not segments of one another. As Robert Young (1995: 93) notes, the terms 'ethnicity' and 'race' were often used interchangeably in nineteenth-century Britain. Following the turbulence created around 'race' by the policies of the German Nazi regime of the 1930s, J.S. Huxley and A.C. Haddon proposed the use of 'ethnic group' as a substitute for 'race' based on its original ancient Greek connotation which designated a self-governing political unit (Banton 1983: 64).

The modernist connotation of 'race' and 'ethnicity' sees 'race' either subsumed in 'ethnicity', or referred to euphemistically through 'ethnicity'. We are returning to the nineteenth-century dynamic relationship between the two concepts in which 'race', 'nation' and language intermingle in the complexity which is the idea of 'ethnicity'.

KEY CONCEPTS

RACE Race is a concept that has long been used to ascribe natural differences to people from different cultural backgrounds. It has always operated as an explanatory device to confuse physical differences with cultural, intellectual and moral differences. Race is a crude attempt at a biological explanation of human difference whereas ethnicity speaks of the social differences between groups.

ETHNICITY   A term coined by Van den Berghe (1981) to characterize an ethnic group, that is, a collection of culturally related people living within a designated ethnic boundary.

Polygenesis   The theory that the various races are derived from different and unrelated origins, as opposed to monogenesis, the theory that the races are derived from the same origin.

Phenotype   The physical constitution of a person or ethnic group based upon the interaction between their genetic constitution and the environment, normally associated with outward physical characteristics.

Class racism   Class prejudice based upon a belief in the inferiority of those regarded as 'the lower orders' in the same ethnic group. The belief that they are so inferior as to constitute a separate 'race'.

Fictive ethnicity   Ethnic solidarity based upon an imagined relationship with members of the same national community who are thought to constitute one racial community.

Idealism/Materialism

David F. Walsh

The controversy between idealism and materialism enters sociology because organization becomes embodied in the actions of individuals at a conscious level in terms of the motives, interests and values which these individuals espouse. The issue, then, is in what way consciousness enters into social organization and social action. In this respect idealist sociologies place consciousness at the very core of social relationships and treat them as primarily established on this basis, whilst materialist sociologies argue that social relationships have their real foundation in economic, political, technological and environmental conditions which, in turn, create the ideas, values, purposes and motivations, i.e. the consciousness, of the members of society.

IDEALISM

Idealism, which entails the philosophical argument that ideas are a central part of reality, entered into sociology primarily through the influence of the eighteenth-century philosopher Kant or major sociological theorists such as Durkheim, Simmel and Weber. What Kant did was to reject the empiricist position which argued that the world consisted simply of physical objects that were knowable exclusively by the direct sensory experience of them in the form of sense perceptions. This for Kant ignored the role which the mind of the observer necessarily played in any knowledge of reality since, as he argued, the sensory experience of reality can only be apprehended and the objects of which it is composed can only be established on an empirical basis through the use of mind and its capacity to apprehend sensory experience in terms of categories such as time, space and causality. In this way mind introduces an order into sensory experiences that gives them a definite form and nature and so establishes the objective character of the phenomena that sense experience yields up. For Kant, then, mind is an essential basis for any knowledge of reality and it has its own intrinsic and categorizing nature. But Kant proceeded further to argue that the phenomenal world of facts established by the categorization of experience must be separated from the noumenal world of the human self to which the faculty of mind belongs. This noumenal world is a world of values and freedom of action in relation to them on the part of human beings in which reason becomes the basis of action, as opposed to the phenomenal world of facts which is a world of causal necessity. In this, facts and values are necessarily separate from one another: so facts cannot determine values and therefore cannot determine human life, which is a matter of values, reason and purposive action.

Taking up Kant's position, idealist sociologies argue that the social world must be distinguished then from the natural world as a subjective world of culture, consciousness and purposive action which is governed by the ideas, values and interests of its members, and sociology must understand and explain it in these terms. However, the sociological interest in culture, consciousness and purposive action, consists in showing how these have emerged historically and collectively as the common and ideational foundation for society, which allows its members to socially organize their actions and interactions with one another in terms of the common ideas, values and interests which they share with one another but on an intentional basis as agents of their own actions. Society, then, is an intersubjective world of social interaction which is organized and structured in terms of a social consciousness which is shared by its members, and therein lies its objective constitution and existence.

But it is precisely on the issue and fact of the historical emergence and collective formation of social consciousness as the basis of the social organization of society that idealist sociology becomes problematic. That actors are conscious and purposive agents in respect to their own actions, but act socially in terms of shared ideas, values and interests that have emerged historically and been established collectively and thereby institutionalized by the society in which they live, raises the issue of how, what and why the specific ideas, values and interests in a particular society, of whose culture and consciousness they are a part, together with the modalities of action and interaction, come to be established. And here, it becomes necessary to recognize how material factors and changes – economic, political, environmental, technological, etc. – clearly play a role in situating, creating and shaping social ideas, values and interests as an emergent if not entirely determined response to them. Some idealist sociologies do recognize this but argue that, ultimately, the material structures of society can only be engaged and realized organizationally and existentially in terms of consciously understood and purposive action and interaction. Idealist sociologies such as those of symbolic interactionism and phenomenology seek to take up the nature of consciousness and the social and cultural organization and enactment of social life and carry it through to an examination of how this is itself essentially productive of society and the social order of its relationships at an internal level of the social construction of the events, structures and institutions of which it is composed, rather than a matter of the social order being produced externally by material conditions of social organization. This, in turn, has led to a consideration of the central role of language in the constitution of society and the organization and structuring of social relations; and in so considering, these latter idealist sociologies, whatever their limitations, confront materialist sociologies with the need always to consider the fact that society necessarily exists in the social interaction between its members, which entails subjective and intersubjectively meaningful processes of negotiation, definition and decision-making on the part of the interactants.

But sociologies of action, meaning and the intersubjective constitution of society represent only a direct form of idealism in sociology. Indirectly idealism and the questions it raises for consciousness and culture in the organization of society enter into a variety of other sociological ways of theorizing, from those of specifically idealistic sociologies such as action theory and phenomenology even to what are primarily materialist sociologies, because they necessarily have to engage with the enactment of structure and institutions in the lives of the members of society. In this respect, many sociologies treat culture as an active ingredient in the organization of society in terms of the ways of life which develop within it. Functionalism treats culture as the mechanism by which society institutionalizes the structural adaptation of the social system to its environment. Durkheim and structuralism treat culture and consciousness as systems of symbols, knowledge and morality that are structurally constitutional of the existence of society and determinative of membership within it. Marxism addresses cultural and social consciousness in terms of ideologies which both legitimate the social structures of society and provide a major means for them to function effectively. And postmodern and poststructural sociologies enter their arguments about the nature and organization of society in terms of language, signification and discursive practices.

What the rest of this chapter will do, then, is to investigate how the idealist issues of culture, consciousness and action are taken up in sociology in relation to the materialist issues of economic, political, technological and environmental conditions of social life, to outline the various different theoretical positions which attempt to oppose or reconcile them, and to examine the strengths and weaknesses of their positions. I will argue that neither a wholly idealist nor a wholly materialist theory can adequately deal with and explain the nature of society, because ultimately culture, consciousness and action have a historical and material location and situation, both structurally and institutionally: yet structures and institutions cannot be realized without purposive action which entails consciousness, meaning and understanding (Filmer et al 1972).

IDEALIST SOCIOLOGIES

Within sociology, the idealist perspective emerges first with the development of action theory, which has its major foundation in the work of Weber (Rex 1973). But Weber does not subscribe to a purely idealist position, for two reasons. Firstly, he seeks to create a science of action which not only attempts to understand the meaning of action but sets out to explain it causally, and in the latter he is introducing a positivistic dimension into his sociology. And secondly, Weber, although he rejects any form of economic determinism in relation to the nature of social action – this is his objection to Marxism – argues that ideas, values and consciousness are co-determinants of social life along with material conditions, which they do not simply reflect but conjoin with as intertwined elements in the historical processes of the development of human civilization. However, in other respects, Weber's sociology has a distinctively idealist character. For him society is grounded in the subjectively meaningful action of its members as individuals and is, therefore, a world of culture as opposed to the meaningless world of objects that comprises nature. What distinguishes human action is that it is purposive conduct, and so the beliefs, values and interests of the actor determine its nature. Action becomes social when individuals orientate their actions to one another in terms of shared beliefs, values and interests and so organize their conduct in these terms, and this is the basis of the social organization of society. Historically, the mutual orientation which is the cultural foundation of society develops and institutionalizes itself within societies to form and organize (i.e. structure) action within it in collective and typical ways in the various arenas of social existence. Material changes are crucial to this process but not the exclusive determinants of it, as culture and consciousness shape and are shaped by them. So, for example, Weber argues that modern industrial capitalism appeared in Western civilization in the form of a highly rationalized organization of economic activity that depends on the calculative use of human and material resources to produce and sell commodities on a market for profit. But this rationalism and instrumentalism which are central to capitalism depended on the emergence of a cultural sense and a mental attitude to life of the same kind, as well as on material and political changes such as the growth of trade, the development of the city and the emergence of the state, before capitalism could occur. This cultural sense

and mental attitude came from the religious beliefs of Calvinist Protestantism which fashioned a rational and self-disciplined life and organization of
the world in a calling on the part of its members which produced the
rational and instrumental ethos of capitalism. So, for Weber, ideas and
values are central to the process by which the material basis of society
becomes embodied in the structural and institutional organization of it
(Outhwaite 1987).

Thus, for Weber, the material of society is action. It is consciously and
purposively conducted by the actor, and this means it has to be understood
from the inside in terms of the actor's beliefs, purposes and motives before
it can be explained, and it cannot be treated as just externally determined
by society. However, Weber seeks an understanding of action which is
objective in order to construct a sociological science of it, which means, to
him, an understanding of how it is caused at the level of purpose and
motivation which can be empirically verified. His solution is to argue that
the purposive nature of all action can be understood causally and explained
if action is seen as being motivationally organized by the actor in terms of
the ends which the actor pursues and the means which he/she selects to
pursue them, and this means–ends organization is seen as taking particular
forms which have been culturally, socially and institutionally established.
So individual action as purposive conduct is socially tied to the socio-
cultural structure of the society in which it takes place. By developing a
conceptual scheme of action in these terms – using ideal types – concrete
action can be empirically investigated in terms of causal hypotheses about
its determination that can be verified in the light of evidence about the
nature of concrete actions and the way they take place.

So Weber's position is that the members of society are actually producers
of society through their actions and not just products. However, his science
of action creates a problem, for his investigation of how action is socio-
culturally produced by society. His ideal types of action are constructed in
terms of a logic which produces a particular scientific way of understanding them, so the socio-cultural organization of action is supplanted by
the positivistic, causal, scientific explanation of them. The result is that the
internal organization of action at a culturally conscious and purposive level
by the actor must disappear. In other words, what is central to the idealist
position, namely that action has a rationale of its own at the level of ideas,
beliefs, values and purposes within a cultural and social setting operating
according to its own logic, is undermined by the causality of positivism
(Albrow 1990).

Weber's contemporary Simmel avoids this problem in his action theory
because he argues, unlike Weber, that action becomes socially organized at
the level of shared orientation and meaning through culture, which typifies
and makes sense of it, but on an intersubjective level, and this constitutes
the basis of social interaction and not the interests or purposes of the
individual. Society is their common realization and the forms it takes are

183

not a matter of individuals *per se*. Actors interact and society is produced on the basis of and through the use of these social and cultural typifications, which objectify the meaning of action for interactants so that they can establish it and their identities in cultural and social terms and organize their relationships together on this basis. So society is the myriad forms of association between its members that have been culturally generated in this way, however much it ultimately depends upon the minds of individuals to create and participate in it. Society is a matter of mutual consciousness, and the institutionalization of such, which is culture, constrains and organizes the social relationships of which society is composed and the actions within it. But the point for Simmel about social existence too, which is crucial to it, is that as individuals we are subjects as well as societal members: so our social lives carry this duality with them in the sense that our individuality stands in relationship to our sociality in our actions and shapes our human experience of the world in terms of the degree of participation in and withdrawal from the conduct of social relationships as we engage in them. Society is a matter of differential participation within it because social relationships are formed around different kinds of organizations which culturally require different types, degrees and amounts of participation in them. Sociology can really only consider the latter, but to take up the issue of the cultural nature of social life – which is the idealism in Simmel – is to recognize the rich warp and weft of the relationships and experiences that are entailed within it in terms of the relationship between the subjective lives of its individual members and the intersubjective social world in which they participate (Cohen 1968).

So, for Simmel, the major issue of the modern capitalist world (and here we can see the *rapprochement* of his ideas with postmodern sociology) is the cultural meaning of money and the forms of social interaction and social life which are produced on this basis, because it creates new relationships of freedom and dependence between the members of society as it objectifies, anonymizes and materializes their relationships and generates the covetous mind in the individual. But this leaves a problem for Simmel which a consideration of the materialist dimensions of capitalism alone can rectify, namely an analysis of the economic conditions of the emergence of money and the money economy and the effects of the organization of social relationships within modern society that the material structure of the money economy establishes in terms of things such as production, work, consumption and social inequalities.

However, action theory as it has developed in sociology has moved not to a *rapprochement* with materialism but towards a reconstruction of idealism to give it greater sociological credence. The objection to Weberian action theory in this lies in his attempt to combine the meaningful nature of the organization of the social world with a causal explanation of it on two counts. First, as I have previously argued, the causal rationality of science imposes its own structure of the meaning and understanding of action upon it that is based on the logic of scientific explanation, whereas the socio-cultural organization of society and the action within it has its own logic and rationale which structure the nature of social life. Secondly, meaning and causation are irreconcilable and belong to and entail two different orders of life, namely culture and nature. To treat action which is meaningful in causal terms, in the way Weber does, requires the meaning of action to be separated from the action itself and to be treated as the antecedent conditions which produce it. But the meaning of an action is inseparable from it in this way, since an action's very nature is dependent on its articulation through the meaning which is given to it, and this articulation is a matter of how the action is described and thus established as what it is. An action is what the person who is engaged in it understands themselves to be doing and so its sense, in these terms, is in its nature, i.e. the phenomenon that it is. Immediately, then, this raises the issue of language as the vehicle of human consciousness, meaning and sense in relationship to action, and it is to a consideration of this that idealist socio-logies move, not only because the organization of action at the level of sense is a product of the use of language and the rules which govern its use and so generate sense in language, but also because language is an eminently social phenomenon in itself. So the social organization of action and society in terms of the intersubjective constitution of social relationships, via culture and consciousness, can be taken up in terms of language and its constructive properties. But, in this, language is to be seen not in pictorial and correspondential terms, i.e. where the meaning of linguistic descriptions is treated as a product of the things they describe, but in reflexive terms, i.e. where language through its way of making sense and describing things actually generates and produces them as the things they are.

Symbolic interactionism does this in two ways in respect of its theory of society as a socially organized world of meaning and conscious action. Firstly, it sets out to show how society is generated and organized as a world of shared meaning. Secondly, it attempts to demonstrate how the individual becomes lodged into society and acts as a conscious agent within it through the formation of a self that is constituted in terms of incorporating the social meanings on which society and social life are based into himself or herself. But it approaches the role of consciousness and language in this not so much from the action theory of European sociology but from the American philosophical pragmatism of thinkers such as Dewey and Pierce. Pragmatism argues for a continuity between animal and human behaviour in the sense that, in both cases, it consists of an adaptive problem-solving response to the environment in which they live. But human behaviour is qualitatively transformed and distinguishable from animals, because it proceeds through the use of mind which turns human beings into conscious and sentient creatures acting on this basis and turning their environment into a symbolic universe which they engage with in terms of their understanding and not their senses. However, the social life of human beings like that of other animals is a matter of interactive communication conducted at the level of mutual gesture and response between them. In human beings, communicative interaction in terms of gesture and response is conducted through mind and not instinct, which turns it into a genuine and meaningful conversation. This conversation proceeds through reading an intention into gesture as a condition of responding to it, e.g. the meaning of shaking one's fist depends on an interpretation of what is intended by it (and therefore the action which it entails) before it can be responded to (and interaction take place). So human conduct has a symbolic character.

From this it follows that what permits human beings to interact and form social relationships and society is their ability to understand one another's gestures and so bring one another's actions into alignment, and this is procured through the mutuality of shared symbols that are embodied in a common language shared by them. Language is a system of significant symbols where the meaning of words is determined by the actions for which they stand. It is the shared (and thus social) vehicle through which human beings are able to give the same meaning to one another's gestures and responses, because it permits the individual to form the same response to his or her own gesture as he or she forms to that of the other, and so to interpret and define it in the same way. Taking the role of the other then in relation to oneself is what human relationships depend on. In this way social interaction becomes possible at the level of intercommunication through language, and society is socially organized and structured on this basis. The social world is a world of symbolic interaction.

But, in these terms, social behaviour is not just a simple matter of learning to gesture and respond linguistically, because to do this requires the incorporation of the other in oneself to do it. In this the self of the individual is constructed through symbolic interaction in which the individual internalizes the other's definition of his or her behaviour and defines it in this way too. So to inhabit human society is to acquire a self as a result of its basis in symbolic interaction and this, again, distinguishes human beings from all other animals. Psychologically, within the individual, self-formation is generated in terms of a dialogue between two parts, an 'I' and a 'Me'. The 'I' is the physiological and psychological impulses that produce gestural behaviour in the individual, but the 'Me' is the response of the other as this interprets and defines what the individual builds into himself or herself to produce a similar but this time internal response. So the individual, through the development of a self, becomes a society in miniature in which the symbolic interaction of society is mirrored and reproduced in the psychological interaction of the self. And, in this, mind and symbols are the basis of both the external and the internal interaction. Indeed this psychological interaction which the individual has with himself or herself is precisely what being a human is, and it provides for the conscious inner experiences which human beings have and which, unlike animals, are central to their actions, since human behaviour is largely covert and intentional rather than overt in nature. That is, human beings, because of mind, constantly consider, think and weigh up the possibilities of action in relation to their sense of society before acting, whereas animals respond instinctually to environmental stimuli. The self of the individual emerges in stages from childhood to adulthood in which the individual learns to master and incorporate the roles which others play in society by acquiring, through language, the meanings and definitions which are entailed in their performance. But more, because social life and action are a learning process of this kind, it is a never-ending thing, so individuals can and do change their selves as they enter new situations, interact with new others and acquire new social meanings.

So symbolic interactionism points to how human beings inhabit the world consciously which entails acting in a purposive fashion. But they do this socially, and it is the social and symbolic system of language that provides them with the means for organizing their actions collectively but in terms of the meaningful definition and negotiation of social situations. But what is problematic in symbolic interactionism is the lack of any materiality in its account of either the structure of society or the structure of the self. In the former this is noticeable: symbolic interactionism is unable to build up an understanding of the macro-organization of society from its micro-studies of social interaction or to show how historical, economic and political factors may be generative of the macro-circumstances within which micro-interaction takes place, e.g. the institutional official curriculum and the practice of teaching and learning that take place within the classroom. The materiality of the self is largely ignored by reducing the psyche not only to consciousness alone but to a socially framed consciousness which ignores the physiological and psychological structures of instinct, need and feeling. This is a process not of learning to internalize the other but of learning which involves a tense and conflictual process of projection, introjection, identification and rejection in the relations between the self and others. And by treating language as a system of significant symbols that constitute a fixed repertoire of meanings, even the negotiated interpretational character of life in society at the level of meaningful action becomes problematic to explain.

But it is in reference to this latter that phenomenological sociology finally comes to what must ultimately be the project of idealistic sociology, namely to show that the reality of society is socially constructed because the human social world is a world of culture, consciousness, meaning and action. Phenomenology argues that the world is experienced through consciousness, so subject and object are not separate from one another. Nor is the relationship of subject and object in consciousness a matter of the correspondence between the former and the latter, as positivism would argue; rather consciousness is intentional in the sense that it reaches out to grasp the objects of the world through experience by making that experience meaningful. In this way, then, the objects of the world are understood and typified in particular ways and their concrete reality is established on that basis. But everyday consciousness grasps and experiences the world in the natural attitude and treats it as a world of objective and pre-given facts. This is the common-sense attitude of daily life and it is essentially social in character too, i.e. the natural attitude assumes that the world is shared with other human beings who see and understand it in the same way. What then goes unnoticed in the natural attitude is its intentional and reflexive nature, i.e. its role in the typification and construction and the objectivity and reality of the world and its character as an intersubjective (i.e. social) consciousness. A phenomenological sociology, then, seeks to examine how society and social reality have their foundation in the reflexive and intersubjective nature of the natural attitude as it is embodied in the common-sense knowledge which the members of a society share with one another, in terms of which they socially understand the reality of their world and organize their actions together with one another within it. It investigates how the social world, through the common-sense organization of its life, is internally structured from within as the members of society use their common-sense knowledge of social reality as the basis of and for their daily lives. But whereas the members of society see this common-sense knowledge as practical knowledge about the facts of social reality, phenomenological sociology sees it as constructing the facts of social reality through its own way of making sense of the scenes of everyday social life and action within them and thereby typifies and objectifies them as facts.

Schutz takes the lead in this to argue that whereas the action of any particular individual stems from his or her unique biographical situation and is conducted in terms of a personal project which gives it a subjective meaning to the actor, yet their biography is formed in relation to a social and historically given setting (i.e. society) which they share with others and know in common through the common-sense knowledge which society equips them with as the basis of membership in it. So the consciousness of the individual is neither solitary nor solipsistic even when action has a unique or personal meaning to him or her because it is conducted in a social world with others that is known and shared with them on a common basis. Common-sense knowledge entails a shared and social consciousness which it achieves by creating a reciprocity of perspectives between individuals – an intersubjectivity that overcomes their subjectivity. It does this by building the assumptions into itself that, firstly, if individuals were to change places with one another they would see the world in the same way as one another, and, secondly, that individuals can discount their biographies from the point of view of making the world relevant to their lives and participating in it. So common-sense knowledge creates a knowledge which is that of any person and which permits the typification of the events of the world to become a social process rather than a matter of private experience of them. And this common-sense knowledge of the world then, by its very intersubjectivity and sociality, is the realm of objective meaning (i.e. culture) in terms of which society, social relationships and social life are organized (i.e. structure) and conducted (i.e. action).

Common-sense knowledge, then, takes the form of social typifications of the world and society (note the connection between Schutz and Simmel here) and it is embodied in natural language which socially organizes and distributes it throughout society. Using it, the members of society are able to interact with one another because it establishes for them what are the facts of the social world which they share together. However, since action is purposively conducted in terms of a project by the actor which motivates it, interaction between actors (the social) is dependent on the ability of them to produce an interlock of their actions. This, Schutz argues, occurs because social action is based on a reciprocity of motives in which the 'in order to' motives in terms of which actors pursue the achievement of their projects become the 'because of' motives in terms of which other actors comply with those actions by gearing their own actions to them, e.g. one actor's desire to eat becomes another actor's desire to produce a meal. But this reciprocity of motives is only possible because of the reciprocity of perspectives which common-sense knowledge entails in terms of the vocabulary of motives which is socially established by it and which allows actors to socially attribute motives to one another's actions and comply with them. Moreover, the organization of interaction on this basis is simply and only a social and practical matter of being able to accomplish the interaction, i.e. maintain a relationship, and never entails a complete understanding of one actor's action by another actor, because each individual's action has a unique and inpenetrable subjective meaning which is personally located in the specific biographical situation of each individual. It is in terms of objective, i.e. social meaning of action, that the members of society interact, and this is provided by the common-sense stock of recipe knowledge which actors share as members of the same society about typical motives, typical actions, typical events and typical situations that are its nature. So this common-sense and social knowledge of reality (culture and its social consciousness) is the basis of the organization of social life and action and interaction in it.

Moreover in its use on a practical basis as the foundation of social life, common-sense knowledge has its own rationality which is precisely that and which is not the same as science, so the cultural organization of social life must be treated and explicated in its own terms and not subjected to a scientific representation and explanation of it in science's causal terms. This does not prevent the empirical investigation of the cultural organization of social life at the level of the interactional and common-sense construction and organization but it does preclude the use of the hypothetico-deductive reason of science to do it. In this investigation, ethnomethodology has established the nature of the empirical programme. Taking common-sense knowledge of the facts and events of the social world and its embodiment in natural language, it investigates how the members of society draw upon this knowledge to conduct their daily lives together in terms of the socially organized ways in which they linguistically describe and account for the nature of life and social scenes of society and thus inhabit it and act within it. This knowledge they take for granted as fact and they use it in a practical and unreflexive fashion, so what remains unnoticed to them is its artful and interpretive use by them in which they are constantly negotiating and making sense of the social scenes and actions which they encounter and organizing their own actions in terms of this. So these scenes and actions are constructed as realities (the reflexivity of accounts). But this they do contextually (and here is the departure over language by phenomenological sociology from symbolic interaction) in the sense that any account of social scene or action draws upon its specificity to establish its factual reality (the indexicality of accounts). So language, as it is used, is socially organized by the members of society to make sense of their social world in terms of it, and the cultural knowledge which it embodies and establishes is constructive of social reality for its users. The members of society, then, are not dopes who know nothing about their world and their actions but culturally competent users of common-sense knowledge engaging and practising in the organization of their world through the practices in terms of which they account for and inhabit it. However they do it unreflexively and practically (i.e. in terms of the natural attitude) and so the constructed nature of social reality goes unnoticed by common-sense knowledge when it is used commonsensically.

But in addressing the production of society in terms of its intersubjective construction alone, phenomenological sociology, like all idealistic sociologies, is forced against the limits of its explanation of social life. What is missing is how the contextual nature of social situations is not simply an issue of how their objective reality is established through the negotiation and construction of them from within. They also have a historical location, a material foundation and an institutional existence which externally constrain the activities of people within them. The strength of idealistic sociology is to show that structures and institutions depend upon their articulation and enactment in practice but this takes place in the social space which, to a large extent, they circumscribe and establish. This then gives them an irreducible reality which is more than that of their intersubjective constitution and it is this reality which materialist accounts of society treat as central about its nature.

MATERIALISM

Unlike with idealism, it is not possible to define materialism in some very precise and specific way. The reason for this is that what materialist sociologies treat as the material conditions and character of the social world varies from one materialist theory to another, as does the extent to which different theories treat material factors as determining of social relationships and how they take up conscious and social action and position it in relation to them. What all forms of materialism then, in the last analysis, subscribe to is more a question of rejecting idealist conceptions of social reality which insist that its nature resides exclusively in human consciousness and the organization of action and social relationships in terms of this. Instead, materialism insists on treating the existential location of society as central to the determination and organization of social life, but what constitutes its existential location and its material foundation is distinguished differently within different sociologies.

MATERIALIST SOCIOLOGIES

One major strand of materialist sociology stems from the early positivistic position of Durkheim and the proto-functionalist model of society that inheres in this and which functionalist sociology proper develops in its own right. But, within this positivistic-functionalist framework, culture too is given a formative role in relation to the material processes of the social organization of society as a basis on the level of collective beliefs, values and norms for the instantiation of its structures and institutions. Durkheim argues that society exists as a separate reality in its own right which consists of social facts. These social facts are typical ways of acting, thinking and feeling which characterize the nature of social existence, and they stem not from the nature of the individuals who engage in them but from the structure and institutions of society which externally impose themselves on its members and constrain and determine their actions and relations with one another. Moreover, because the social facts of society have these three intrinsic characteristics of typicality, externality and constraint, they have the reality of things in the same way as the facts of nature are things and so can be observed and studied empirically as objective data on the same basis. So society is a reality which has its foundation in the constitution of group life and the social solidarity this produces in its members which comes materially from the form and density of the relationships between them (the morphological basis of society) and symbolically from the common beliefs, values and norms which they share (the collective consciousness or culture of society). Materially society is organized in terms of the existential forms which social activity entails (production, reproduction, and administration, government, etc.) and the functionally determined institutional arrangements in terms of which they are socially co-ordinated and structured (kinship, gender, age, economy, polity, etc.).

But this material and morphological foundation of society is sustained culturally by the collective beliefs, values and norms that symbolize, regulate and organize the social relationships of which these institutional arrangements are composed. So, Durkheim argues, the morphological structure of the social division of labour creates a specialization of activities in society and relationships of functional interdependence between them which produces a society in which social relationships become relationships of exchange and contract between its members. But this new form of society can only achieve real communal and solidary existence on the basis of contract and exchange if the functional interdependence produced by the division of labour is underpinned and realized by collective beliefs and values (i.e. culture and collective consciousness) that socially regulate the contractual relationships of exchange by establishing and determining the terms and conditions of their organization. Otherwise the specialization of social activity introduced by the division of labour would fragment the structure of society and foster a completely egotistical individualism in its members. So culture and consciousness are central to Durkheim's sociology but only in terms of their relationship to and realization of the social organization of the material and morphological conditions of their existence. And this material basis to society is further clarified in his argument that what precipitates the emergence of the social division of labour as the foundation of the modern world is the destruction of segmental societies by population increase in relation to better forms of communication and transportation. This bursts through the existing institutional and primarily kinship structures of simple societies to create a conflict over environmental resources between them and their different elements which only a reorganization and restriction of their use differentially by specialized social organs on an interdependent basis can resolve. That is, the economic, the political, the religious, etc. spheres of life need to separate out from one another and organize themselves institutionally and interdependently through the use of different resources for society to survive, and this is what a society based on the social division of labour entails and what its solidarity is now based on.

What is valuable in Durkheim's position is that he shows how the culture of society (its cognitive and moral ordering in terms of a collective consciousness) is central to its institutional organization, but that any sense of the nature of culture and its role in social life must necessarily relate it to its existential location *vis-à-vis* the material and morphological conditions of society. But this is achieved at a major and problematic cost to the analysis of social life. Firstly, it entails the objectification of social structures, institutions and consciousness to the point at which their activation on an interactional level by the members of society in terms of their actual conduct remains unaddressed. Durkheim, quite rightly, shows that individuality and the development of a personal consciousness require a society based upon the division of labour in which its members can distinguish themselves from one another because structurally they occupy different positions in society and engage in specialized and differentiated activities that require specific talents and abilities and make for a sense of identity. But how the members of society act in these terms is covered by a structural account of their position in the institutional organization of society and the external and constraining character of this on action and social relationships. For Durkheim, action is treated primarily as a result of social structure, rather than society being realized in terms of conscious and purposive action on the part of its members. Secondly, even at the level of the material and structural organization of society, Durkheim's examination of this and its historical formation is completely general and theoretical rather than specific and concrete. If in idealistic sociologies the micro-analysis of the intersubjective relationships between the members of society cannot address the macro-organization of the social world in which they are conducted, so, in Durkheim, the macro-analysis of structure and institutions does not address how their externality and constraint are internally organized and realized at the level of the interactional and purposive relationships between the members of society. Even though consciousness is introduced into the analysis of the organization of social life in terms of culture, it is entirely in terms of its normative and legislative nature and not in terms of its interpretive and creative uses.

Functionalism replicates these problems. In Durkheim's early work, society is conceived of as a system which is like an organism and, just like any other organism, its social organization is a product of its adaptation to the environment within which it is located. In terms of this then it becomes possible to specify what constitutes healthy or pathological states of the social organization of society in terms of whether they successfully adapt society to the conditions of its environment and thus preserve and maintain it or whether they undermine its stability and social order. Functionalism adopts this organic model of society and produces a version of the material foundations of society and its social organization in terms of the needs which these conditions pose for societal existence and which are met, and society is established and maintained through the development of its structural and institutional organization on a functional and adaptive basis *vis-à-vis* environmental conditions. The relationship between the social organization of society and the environment is both general and specific: general in the sense that the environmental conditions of society are universal, which explains the emergence of certain general structures and institutions in all societies; but specific in the sense that these conditions have localized character in their existence which explains the particular forms which these general structures and institutions take in particular societies. But although environmental conditions are real in themselves, they are not entirely material in a strict sense because they entail organizational and symbolic conditions too. Moreover, culture is the primary adaptive mechanism through which society as a system is able to generate and organize functional social and institutional structures, so the ideational enters into the social organization of social life through the way that structure and culture are tied together in the processes of the adaptation of society to its environment.

Within functionalism, Parsons develops the most sophisticated position. For him, the environment of the social system consists of physical, cultural and psychological conditions which impose functional needs (functional prerequisites) which have to be resolved structurally and institutionally in order for the social system to emerge and sustain itself (i.e. in order for society to be possible). The physical environment is the reality of scarce resources which have to be utilized, organized and allocated in society as its material basis of production and reward, which requires the development of economic institutions. The cultural environment poses the reality of the need for co-operation between the members of society, which requires a common value system in terms of which common goals and means can be specified to which they can subscribe. This provides the basis for authority and the distribution of power in society (the polity) which co-ordinates the activities of societal members and organizes the production and allocation of economic and symbolic resources in it. But additionally the cultural environment poses the need for collective values to be legitimated if the political and economic system of society is to be accepted by its members, which requires religion or a secular ideology. Finally, the psychological environment is one of unsocialized individuals with biological and psychological needs who have to be socialized into acting in accordance with society's requirements, which requires agencies of socialization and primarily the family. But what makes society a system of structures and institutions is that all of these environmental conditions and the institutional structural-functional solutions to them interlock with one another and operate in tandem and, as they interlock, so structures and institutions become environments for one another too, to which they must adapt.

But Parsons's theory of the social system also moves – and this is the sophistication that distinguishes it from other functionalist theories – to a consideration of the interactional level of its organization as well as its institutional organization and connects them through the normative order. Ultimately human life entails action which is motivated and determined on the basis of need, but socially this takes place in a situation of scarce resources and other human beings in pursuit of their needs. What then is a potential situation of conflict can only be resolved from the point of view of the establishment of social order and society, as opposed to warfare and chaos, if co-operation is produced between individuals in their actions. Such is achieved through the cultural and institutional organization of action by society on a social basis in which a central value system establishes normative control over the conduct of its members at the level of rules and expectations that govern the performance of social roles within society. So society exacts conformity to its value system on the part of its members through socialization and social control but it motivates them to accept it and rewards them with economic and symbolic resources which satisfy their needs on the basis of their social conformity in the performance of social roles. The actor in society becomes the social actor who organizes his or her actions in a societal rather than an individual way. So social action, the structure and institutions of society and the environment are functionally dovetailed into one another as a materially, culturally and normatively organized system.

The emphasis on environmental conditions and the functional needs of society, then, brings materialism into functionalist theory, and the cultural and normative organization of action within society is located existentially in terms of this. What is problematic, however, is the generalized conception of environmental necessity with which functionalism works, which, whilst capturing a vital sense of why certain kinds of structures and institutions may have a tendency to be universal because of their functionality, fails to examine the historical specificity of their generation and the unique forms which they take in different societies. It is not enough to localize the environment in relation to the social organization of a society; it is also necessary to address this historical interplay and conjunction of material conditions in terms of the dynamic interplay between them and emergent forms of socio-cultural consciousness as distinctive processes of change that are specific to the concrete organization of specific societies. Otherwise society is completely reified and removed from a historical and existential location in the world. But more: the culturalist element of functionalist theory which emphasizes the normative and regulative character of the institutional organization of action on the basis of common values ignores the extent to which competing values exist within society, which are tied to the interests of different groups within it on the basis of their structural location and pursued and enforced on the basis of power struggles between them. Authority has a coercive as well as a consensual role, and values are enforced as well as accepted. But at the level of interaction, the legislative nature of norms and values and the performance of social roles in terms of them are unavoidably subject to interpretation and decision-making by actors and not a matter of their programmatic instillation by society. Otherwise, why would deviance, conflict and creativity be part of social existence as well as duty, consensus and conformity?

If positivistic and functionalist sociologies develop a form of materialism, the major materialistic position in sociology is that of Marxism. Marx embraces materialism specifically as a rejection of the idealism of his mentor Hegel. Hegel argued that human life and the society in which it is organized form a world of consciousness and ideas that progressively develops in a rational direction over the course of history. Marx rejects this position for a historical materialism on the grounds that Hegel's theory robs the world of any real, objective and historical foundation. For Marx it is not social consciousness which determines social existence but the reverse, and social existence has a material foundation in the social organization of production through which human beings, in terms of their labour, create the physical and concrete basis of society. In this they establish their primary social relationships with one another as relations of production which are historically determined by the form and mode which production takes, as this is shaped by the particular material forces which it utilizes and organizes. The history of society is one of the dynamic, conflictual progressive movement of society from one stage to the next as the mode of production on which it is based changes, and so societies can be distinguished in terms of the mode of production by which they are socially organized (Bottomore and Rubel 1956).

But this analysis of society in terms of this mode of production by Marx and Marxism lends itself to two competing tendencies: one is praxiological and makes action a central part of social existence, and the other is systemic and moves the materialism in the direction of economic determinism (Benton 1975). In both cases the issue revolves around the nature of the organization of production and how social existence is formed and established by it. In the systemic model Marx distinguishes between the real and material base of society, which is the forces of production and the mode of production which is organized upon them, and the legal and political superstructure of society, which is the institutions and culture of society that are generated and determined by the material base. The argument here is that the particular form of social production (e.g. agriculture, industry) entails a specific division of labour between producers which forces them into definite spheres of labour. This, then, is the genesis of their actions and social relationships with one another. As production produces a surplus, so what surfaces is a particular structure of ownership and control which is central to its organization. This transforms the relations of production into class relationships of domination and subordination between a ruling class who own the forces of production and a subordinate class who do not. So the productive system realizes itself structurally in society as class and the institutional organization of society is based on this. In turn this class structure objectively establishes the social interests and determines the social actions of the members of society, but since the class structure is a hierarchical structure of domination and subordination the interests of different classes stand in opposition to one another and the relationships between them are conflictual as they struggle to realize them. The legal, political and cultural superstructure is simply the extension of the economic mode of production and the class structure which it creates into all the other spheres of social life.

The legal and political institutions of society are the forms of administration of government through which the ruling class organizes life within it to promote its interests and preserve its control over society. The culture and social consciousness of society (i.e. its ideas and values) take the form of a dominant ideology which reflects, masks, legitimates and reproduces the class relationships of society. As Marx puts it, the ruling ideas of an epoch are always the ideas of the ruling class who, through their ownership of the means of production, also own the means for the production of ideas, and these are a reflection of their own interests. But in so far as a dominant culture is established on this basis, so the ideas and values which it establishes are universalized throughout society and, by subscribing to it, the subordinate classes in society develop a false consciousness of themselves and their position and interests within it which makes them agents of and collaborators in their own subordination. However, since the system of production, through the private ownership of the forces of production, is a class system of domination and subordination, it has an inherent tendency to break down because it cannot ultimately contain the contradictions and conflicts within it that this produces and which lead to class conflict and class struggle, which become the motor of historical change through the revolutionary transformation of society. But revolution, in turn, is dependent upon the development of new forces of production which undermine the existing forces of production and the mode of production which is based upon them, and lead to the emergence of new classes who control them with the power to challenge and overthrow the existing ruling class as a result.

The capitalist system of production entails the industrial production of commodities to be sold for profit in a market. But the basis of industry is the use of labour power as the force of production which entails its commodification and sale by the labourer to produce profit. So a class structure is established in which a capitalist ruling class (the bourgeoisie) who own labour power and subordinate and exploit the workers who sell it (the proletariat). Furthermore, because the labourer loses control of his or her labour as it is commodified and utilized in the division of labour that is entailed in the industrial processes of manufacture, so the labourer is alienated from his or her own human being which lies in the capacity for creative and self-directed labour. Instead the fate of the worker is determined by the commodity which he or she produces. The whole system of capitalist production, then, is a system which is based upon the commodification of labour, and the capital which gives the bourgeoisie their ruling position in society is nothing more than the congealed fruits of the labour power of the proletariat which has been acquired through its ownership and exploitation by the bourgeois class. In capitalism, then, it is the system of production which determines life within it, and what this produces is a world of commodified, exploitative and alienated social relationships between its members. The dominant culture of capitalism ideologically legitimates this by presenting the market as the natural and necessary condition for economic production, which disguises how it is a historical and socially determined form of production that depends upon a particular organization of social relationships between producers through the sale of labour and its use for profit-based activity that dehumanizes them as it commodifies them. As profit becomes the basis of production in society, so it is this and not human need around which capitalist society is organized. But, for Marx, the commodification, exploitation and alienation of labour in capitalist manufacture is inherently contradictory, as profit opposes need, and its relentless pursuit in a competitive market forces the capitalist to reduce the cost of labour by lowering wages and creating unemployment in order to secure it. Not only does this lead to a degenerative cycle of booms and slumps in production as production and consumption fail to match up, but it polarizes the class structure into a small and ruling bourgeoisie class and an ever growing and subordinate proletariat who become an increasingly pauperized majority, and their objective interests stand in opposition to one another. Finally, Marx argues, this polarized class structure and the opposition of interests that the contradictions within the capitalist productive system produce can only intensify as these contradictions necessarily deepen to the point where class conflict must break out openly, leading the proletariat to organize itself politically against the bourgeoisie and to seize control of the productive system for themselves and in terms of their own collective interests since it is based on their labour. In this revolutionary struggle, then, socialism will come to replace capitalism and human and social need will replace profit as the basis on which labour is organized to generate the productive system of society.

But it is precisely this account of the transition from capitalism to socialism through revolutionary class struggle that shows up the problematic character of a systemic Marxism, since it assumes an important and determining role for consciousness and action in class organization, class struggle and political revolution which an intransitive and deterministic model of society that constructs it in terms of base and superstructure cannot provide for. What is valuable about treating production as a system is that it shows the constraints upon action that inhere in its organizational structure. Undoubtedly capitalism is based upon the logic of profit and the market and the material generation of an economic existence for the members of capitalist society in these terms. But this, as praxiological forms of Marxism particularly as developed by Gramsci point out, does not create a social world in which relationships are simply reducible to their economic determination. If this were so then Marx's predictions about the collapse of capitalism and the triumph of socialism would have been borne out historically, whereas it is socialism that seems to have collapsed and capitalism that has survived, mainly by changing its nature from a system of production to a system of consumption in which any utilitarian conception of need as the basis of human social existence has been replaced by the cultural construction of social existence in terms of the symbolic use of commodities as the basis of styles of life and sources of identity.

In this Marxism must confront what its systemic and economistic version of labour and production tends to ignore, which is the conscious, creative

and purposive nature of human labour through which the social organization of production is already a cultural as well as a material phenomenon,
as Weber argues. In this the superstructure of society is not generated by
the economic base but, from the very beginning, plays a vital role in
organizing it. It is not just that the productive system of capitalism provides
a material and existential basis for social divisions in society at the level of
class, but that the members of society must identify themselves consciously
and collectively in these terms if social relationships in society are to be
organized around this. This Marx recognizes but fails to grasp. That they
are not exclusively organized in terms of class in modern society points
towards other sources of social differentiation and power in society such as
status, gender, ethnicity and age, which are only tangentially related to
economic position in its system of production. Moreover the market
position of any group in capitalist society is a highly differentiated and not
a closed class situation: the possession, control and marketability of skills of
certain groups prevent their complete contractual monopolization by the
managers of industry. Indeed even the management of industry has
separated from its entrepreneurial control through joint stock companies,
and the move from secondary to tertiary service industry has created a
wholly new middle class as well as fragmenting the proletariat into skilled
and unskilled workers. The result for social stratification in the modern
world is a differentiation of groups within the capitalist productive system
who have different positions in it, different interests from one another,
different access to rewards from it and very different ideological and
pragmatic commitments to it as a result. In this sense, participation in the
capitalist world is very much a matter of different forms of conscious and
purposive engagement with and location in its structures and not just a
matter of coercive repression and false consciousness. Moreover, whatever
hegemony capitalist culture has achieved for itself in terms of the legitimation of the market it has paid for by having to incorporate the interests
of the proletariat as well as the bourgeoisie into its economic and political
organization through the industrial distribution of material rewards, the
control of economic policy, the welfare state, parliamentary democracy and
trade unions.

That it could do so is partly a reflection of technological development
that increases the productivity of labour and therefore wages but also the
flexibility of its ideological and political institutions which provide for a
redistribution of power within it. That capitalism works is because it is able
to harness the interests of the members of society and provide the rewards
in terms of which they commit themselves to it. But, if it is the material
organization of capitalist society which creates and organizes work, life and
reward within it, it is culture and ideology (i.e. social consciousness) that
sanctions, legitimates and commits its members to this on a pragmatic,
interested and purposive basis. So revolution or commitment is not a
matter of economic determination but a judgement of advantage in relation

to economic and social conditions by the members of society. Emancipation and progress, then, may be what people themselves decide they want and on the terms in which they see it, and this has proved to be, in capitalist society, what its members conceive themselves as getting from it and not what Marx theorized as their interests. In this, of course, the desire for commodities and its satisfaction cancels whatever forms of exploitation and alienation have been presented as the conditions in terms of which capitalism can make this work, but then this, in turn, raises the issue of whether a society which satisfies its members' desires and commits them to it in this way is entirely exploitative and alienating. That capitalism transforms human needs into material demands is the strength of Marx's materialism and his analysis of capitalist society in terms of it. That this transformation has now taken on a symbolic and cultural character as opposed to a merely utilitarian and material one is not something that Marx addresses. But that this only dehumanizes human beings and commodifies social existence is, however, disputable since it is a claim that legislates for need and human nature and ignores and denies the validity of its cultural and conscious expression. On the other hand, where the Marxist analysis of capitalism begins to bite differently and more powerfully is in the ways in which capitalism has developed as a world system, in which the workings of an international market now become a major determinant of and limit upon state sovereignty and the government of national state economies rather than a structure of class relations.

The concept of society as a system, which is there in Durkheim, functionalism and Marx, reappears in structuralism but now differently and with a realist philosophical stance which is closely allied to materialism in terms of its commitment to the objectivity of the world and its scientific study but rejects the positivism, empiricism and historicism of traditional forms of materialism. For **realism**, the reality of the world cannot simply be reduced to the empirical observation and perception of it and so explained in terms of the causal relationships between its phenomena that have been established factually on this basis. This would be to confuse reality with human perception and experience and make the events of that reality a product of them. Rather reality must be understood as existing separately from its surface appearances in these terms and consisting of its own objective and structural organization which generates the nature of phenomena and events of the world in terms of the modalities and processes through which this structural organization works. This reality can only be grasped through a theoretical and not an empirical understanding of its nature which observes the events and phenomena in terms of how their character is necessarily produced by the ways in which reality is structured. It is in these terms that structuralism understands society as a system in which its social formations and social relationships are determined by the logic of its underlying and real structural organization as a system. However, with sociological structuralism, the model of the system which is applied to society is one which is drawn from the semiotic conception of language as a system of signs whose meaning is governed by the underlying and determinative rules of organization which are the basis of the system.

Within sociology, structuralism has largely been associated with the ideational although not idealistic position of the late Durkheim and Lévi-Strauss and the Marxist materialist position of Althusser. Durkheim's position argued that, ultimately, the sociality of society depends on a sense of communal existence by its members and an organization of this structurally which requires the collective symbolic, cognitive and moral ordering of social life, i.e. a collective consciousness and collective representations of society and the world through which it is understandable, experienceable and organizable in communal terms. So a common culture is necessary for the existence of society, but this, in turn, arises from and within the morphological and material structures of society on a concomitant basis and in relation to which culture provides the means for their instantiation on an institutional and conscious basis within it. Symbolically, the collective representation of society and the collective moral and cognitive systems which it produces are presented in the form of God but, as society becomes more complex and the division of labour becomes its material foundation, reason and science replace religion as the basis of knowledge in society and secular ideologies replace religion as its moral foundation. Society, then, is a system whose reality and identity is composed of the underlying relationships between its structure and culture.

Lévi-Strauss takes this further by bringing a specifically linguistic model of system to bear upon society. Unlike Durkheim, he argues that the systemic interrelations between the symbolic and structural elements of society are not those of diachronic and causal determination but are structured and synchronic relationships of meaning. Just as a language is a meaningful system of signs which is structured by its own underlying grammar which gives signs their meaning, so society is a system of social organization which possesses an underlying grammar, the rules of which generate the institutional forms, social relations and social consciousness that this social organization takes. This social grammar is the grammar of mythology and, ultimately, it is a grammar that stems from the nature of the human mind itself. All societies are encultured and organized through a dominant mythology (which is the collective consciousness of society) that generates the sense, meaning and nature of life for its members, and this is because mythology constitutes the way in which the human mind thinks (even science has a mythological character). Because of this, mythology, despite the variety of forms of its expression, reveals a common basic structure, and it is the scientific understanding of this that reveals the nature of the social organization of society since this is its underlying and real foundation. So, in these terms, Lévi-Strauss engages in a cross-cultural analysis of the mythologies of societies to reveal the common structural form of myths and their determination of social life as a cultural relation with the natural world, and the problems of such for human and social existence within it that myths structurally symbolize and resolve. In this, mythology and its structuring and organization of social existence is presented by Lévi-Strauss as a synchronic system of relationships of proximity and coincidence in terms of the relationship between the structural and symbolic order of society and not a diachronic relationship of history and causality. Society, then, is like a language with an underlying grammar, and like language it forms a system that determines the organization of its social relationships.

In contrast to Durkheim and Lévi-Strauss, Althusser constructs a specifically materialist form of structuralism which draws upon the distinction that Marx makes in *Das Kapital* between the essence of the capitalist system and its empirical formation in terms of its underlying organization of production. But in this, Althusser rejects the base/superstructure distinction made by Marx in favour of a materialist conception of society as the total system of economic, political and cultural institutions and formations which are structurally organized and shaped by the relations of mutual determination and autonomy that exist between them as a system, and in which the economic is an overall determinant only in the final analysis. In these terms, the culture and collective consciousness of society too comprise a structure that is determined and determining in relation to the other structures of the system. In this it constitutes an ideological set of representations – images and concepts – which cement society together by creating a sense of their nature that would otherwise be opaque for its members, and this integrates them into it by forming their subjectivity and producing in them an acceptance of the economic and political roles that society allocates to them.

The ideological character of culture lies in the fact that it disguises the conditioning role that it plays in society as it mythologizes the reality of the system as opposed to offering knowledge of its nature. Culture and consciousness, then, as in all structuralist theory, are not a vehicle of subjective articulation and creative action on the part of individuals but a structure which imposes its own form of subjectivity and consciousness upon them. And, for Althusser, it is part of the material organization of production of society in the same way as its economic and political structures are, and it fulfils the ideological role of representing, articulating and legitimating them by structuring the consciousness of the members of society in accordance with their requirements. For Althusser, then, capitalism has to be seen as a class-bound system of production in which social relationships are generated and class rule is maintained by the underlying structural organization that the mode of production creates. But this organization is instantiated not just in its economic structures but also through the necessary and interrelated political institutions of coercion (the state and its apparatuses) and the ideological means of subjection (the dominant culture and the agents of its dissemination, namely the family and education) which are also a necessary part of this organization and its maintenance. So the former translates economic relationships into relationships of political power in society, and the latter creates the willing acceptance of life and labour within it. So the exploitative economic and social system which is capitalist society and the class structure in terms of which this manifests itself are both politically enforced and simultaneously disguised on an ideological level. Only through a structuralist scientific analysis which theoretically understands and empirically reveals the underlying nature of the structural organization of the capitalist system is it possible to penetrate the ideological disguise beneath which capitalism hides. This, then, will become the only weapon for a revolution against capitalism and the transformation of society to socialism (Cuff and Payne 1979).

For structuralism, then, society is a system of real and objective structures which has its own logic of organization that determines and shapes the nature of the social formations and relationships of which it is composed. The problem with this is that it objectivates society to the point at which it severs its organization from any form of historical and human agency within it; it eliminates history, subjectivity and action from its portrait of social life in favour of the economic, political and ideational determination of every aspect of social existence at a structural level by the social system as a system, which is the only reality that society possesses. Its members, then, have no identity, life and world apart from that which the system gives them.

POSTMODERN SOCIOLOGIES

With postmodern sociologies the idealism/materialism debate as such disappears since science itself is now in contention, let alone a sociological science of society. Postmodern sociologies attack the whole idea of truth, universality, certainty and objectivity which any form of science and scientific knowledge proposes. And with this, they reject systemic and structural understanding and analyses of society, arguing for a thorough historicization of it which sees its different forms of consciousness, knowledge, identities, significations, organization, etc. as historically produced and relative. And, in doing this, the whole idea of the individual as an autonomous subject, as the source of reason and knowledge in the social world produced by purposive action, which is the foundation stone of idealism, is rejected. Materialism doesn't entirely disappear in postmodern sociologies but surfaces in the **constructionism** that lies at the heart of their approach to society, in which language and discourse are treated as reflexively generative of the processes of social life in terms of their historical, political and cultural construction of identity and the social formations of society. But, in terms of this, society is no longer conceived of as a unified totality that has an underlying systemic and structural organization (Bauman 1992a).

Baudrillard is a major contributor to postmodern sociology. He argues that contemporary society has now become a postmodern world which is no longer structured by production and relations of economic exchange (the modern world) but exists in terms of symbolic exchanges. It is now a consumer society of heterogeneous groupings which is culturally differentiated through the proliferation of signs and significations generated by new technologies and systems of information production within it. In these terms signs have now taken on a life of their own and become the primary determinants of social experience. Signs, and their codes of representation, replace reality by images (what Baudrillard calls a process of simulation) to the point at which the real disappears into the image as opposed to being something separate from it. So a world of hyper-reality has been created which implodes into a black hole of meanings and messages that neutralize one another in a constant flow of information, advertising, politics, entertainment, etc., which sucks in the members of society as this solicits them to buy, consume, work, register an opinion, participate in society, etc. So the contemporary world is a world of simulacra with no structures and boundaries – an artificial creation in which reality disappears into a haze of images, signs and meanings. Under the weight of this, human agency is eliminated because images and signs control its practice, and action only generates more signs, images and meanings which only add to the hyper-reality since they have no more claim on the real than any others.

That the contemporary world is an information bound and flooded world in which consumption is crucial to its life is an important issue. Signs and signification are a central part of its organization and function on an ideational level particularly in terms of the role of consumption for the definition of self and social identity. But Baudrillard overdraws the picture of hyper-reality. Social reality has not disappeared into signification but continues to exist in political and economic organizations, social divisions, technological and administrative practices, etc. What Baudrillard's sociology lacks is any real conception of structure because he fails to address the economic and political bases of signs and signification except in terms of a rather crude, material and technological determinism which focuses upon the place of information systems within the contemporary world. Moreover, because of this, his negative estimation of the possibilities of action ignores the chance of a critical engagement with signs and significations in terms of an understanding of their relationship with a dependence on the structural organization of society. The relativization and dissolution of reality into signification is not justified empirically in terms of the structures which its members actually recognize and experience as conditions of and constraints upon their actions.

Some of these problems recur with Foucault's specifically poststructur-alist sociology. He moves away from Baudrillard's argument about the power, social control and reflexive production exercised by signs and images in the contemporary world to a consideration of the nature of the power and control that are exercised by its forms of discipline and govern-mentality. For Foucault, the organization of society lies in the discursive practices that are its mode of government, i.e. the historical, political and economically located systems of thought that are embodied as a social understanding of social life and the associated technologies which they produce for organizing it. These have their own internal rationality and they establish regimes of the governmentality of society. Discursive prac-tices then are forms of power through which self-identity, social relation-ships and social life are historically generated, constructed and produced. And, in this sense their organizational genealogy historically unearths the emergent systems of thought and its practices as epistemes constituted in terms of the determinative rationality with which they reflexively organize knowledge and produce their form of governmentality of the world. But the historical emergence of such epistemes is seen by Foucault not as a process of ongoing and continuous development, but as a series of dis-continuities and disjunctions between epistemes. There is, then, no grand narrative structure in terms of which the history and development of society can be understood, as classical sociology has attempted to produce. Moreover, science too is only another episteme which is reflexively grounded in its own organizational form of rationality and is not an absolute, objective and universal form of knowledge. Instead it constructs and produces its own regimes of power in terms of its own discursive practices.

On this basis, Foucault argues that the contemporary world is a carceral society based on a moral technology of social control produced by Enlightenment and scientific discourse and practices, which submits its members and their bodies to government through their minds and souls on the basis of knowledge and ideas that make a claim to universal objectivity and moral necessity. The form which this power and governmentality take is one of the constant and systematic supervision and surveillance of social life which enforces an exacting discipline on people. It entails a panopticon vision that regulates and schedules all social activities spatially, hier-archically and collectively to create a disciplined environment in which order is produced through the control of every fragment of the lives of people, in terms of formal regulation and informal surveillance to ensure conformity. This discipline extends into the person and is designed to create docility through a moral transformation of the individual into a hard-working, conscience-ridden and useful creature who meet the needs of production and warfare in a rational, efficient and technical society. It is a discipline with a technology of government that thrives on normalizing conceptions of identity and sociality which derive from rational and scientific knowledge and its professional use, which carry with them the right to punish people who do not fit into its categories of normality. Morever, this disciplinary organization of contemporary society is anonymous, dispersed and comprehensive: no one owns it but everyone is subject to it. The subject, then, is created in terms of the regimes of discipline and governance and the rituals of truth embodied in Enlightenment and scientific knowledge which sustain them. He/she now has no inner essence but is discursively and socially conditioned and situated with the power relationships and their technologies of the soul which enforce versions of normality on the person and which he/she internalizes. So, for Foucault, discipline and power in the contemporary world are determinative of its nature and the subject within it.

The problem, however, is the absolute nature of Foucault's constructionist position which is not and cannot be the comprehensive portrait of the contemporary social world that is claimed for it. The treatment of society in terms of its discursive formation alone carries its own limits along with it, in which the problems addressed by materialist and idealist sociologies resurface. Firstly, the genealogical analysis of the emergence of the contemporary Western world that Foucault produces in terms of the historical discontinuities and disjunctions in its governing episteme is partial, highly selective and empirically problematic in the light of the economic, political and other conditions which it excludes. Secondly, by emphasizing the decentralization and anonymity of power in the contemporary social world, Foucault misses other and crucial things about it which demonstrate that it is also structured in relation to social divisions in society; tied to ownership and control by dominant social groups in which it serves their interests and maintains social hierarchies; and concentrated economically and politically in the various institutional organizations of society. Finally, the disappearance of human agency is a major problem of Foucault's position. For Foucault, the subject is a product of the discursive regimes of the government of the body and soul of the individual, but he undertakes no *verstehen* or analysis which would concretely demonstrate this. Instead the subject is theorized out of his analysis by the commitment to constructionism. Yet, in the end, even Foucault is forced to recognize that reason and scientific knowledge are not merely power and regulation but can be utilized for purposes of autonomous self-control, which brings the individual as agent back into the picture of social life.

The problem with postmodern thought is that, by entirely replacing a consideration of society in terms of structure and agency by construction, signification and discourse, this leaves the production of social life with neither a concrete nor an interactional location but primarily a theoretical one. This constitutes not the conclusion of the historical narration of society but only a new, different and relativistic form of it which is highly problematic, particularly when the empirical has been placed in parentheses.

KEY CONCEPTS

IDEALISM   The argument that the social world is an intersubjective and cultural world of consciousness, meaning, values and purposive action on the part of its members, which has to be understood in order to be explained.

MATERIALISM   The argument that society consists of real and objective structures and institutions which have a historical, economic, political, technological and administrative foundation of their organization which determines their nature and which produces the social activities that take place within them.

Realism   The argument that social reality exists independently of our empirical perception of it, and has underlying, essential and objective structure which consists of a systemic and productive organization that determines the social formation and social relations within it and which must be grasped theoretically in order to explain them.

Constructionism   The argument that social reality is historically and reflexively constructed and produced through the systems of signification, knowledge and discursive practices in terms of which it is represented, organized and enacted.

Nationalism/Internationalism

Josep R. Llobera

Nationalism and internationalism are modern categories which have their roots in the Enlightenment. It was in Western Europe during the second half of the eighteenth century that love of nation and love of mankind came to exist as aspects of the same philosophical movement. Over the next two centuries, however, nationalism was to have the upper hand, spreading in different forms all over the world. In this chapter the main focus will be on the concept of nationalism.

PRELIMINARIES

Nationalism is, along with liberalism and socialism, one of the most powerful ideologies of modernity. I use the word 'ideology' in a minimalist, neutral sense to mean a system of ideas and values prevalent in a given milieu or social environment. In Durkheimian terms, nationalism as an ideology is a set of collective representations which are typical of modern societies. Two main factors explain the salience of nationalism in the world in which we live: first, the sacred character of the nation, borrowed from religion; and second, the will of the people to defend their sense of cultural community. I shall come back to these issues.

Nationalism is an ambiguous word, with a variety of mostly pejorative meanings. In everyday usage, but also often in the scholarly literature, nationalism is preferentially employed as a term of abuse; it refers to an irrational and extreme love of nation, to which everything else is sacrificed.

The emotions involved in nationalism are of the most elementary type (hence the label 'tribalism' often attached to it); people are willing to die, but also to kill, for their nation. I do not have to remind you of the everyday litany of horrors emerging from the former Yugoslavia – a conflict which media and politicians alike relish to present as a consequence of unchecked nationalist rivalries.

There are other ways, of course, of defining nationalism. If we equate nationalism to the love of one's nation – for which the term 'patriotism' is often used – the pejorative dimension may be somewhat neutralized, and a different picture of nationalism emerges. In this conception nationalism would incorporate sentiments which could be channelled in a productive and positive direction, be it at the material level (the economy) or at the spiritual level (the arts and literature), not forgetting the political domain of nation-building.

I would insist, then, that nationalism has no predetermined content; as a container of meaning, nationalism can refer to both the good and the evil realities of the nation. There is a liberal and democratic conception of the nation, just as there is one tainted with totalitarianism (of the communist, fascist or religious fundamentalist varieties). 'The task of a theory of nationalism,' as Tom Nairn reminded us some years ago, 'must be to embrace both horns of the dilemma. It must be to see the phenomena as a whole, in a way that rises above these "positive" and "negative" sides. Only in this fashion can we hope to escape from a moralizing perspective' (1977: 332) and rise to a more scientific one. As social scientists we should 'spend less time decrying it – which is a little like cursing the winds – and more in trying to figure out why it takes the forms it does and how it might be prevented from tearing apart even as it creates the societies in which it arises, and beyond that the fabric of modern civilization' (Geertz 1973: 254).

DEFINITIONS

As a working definition of nationalism I propose the following: 'Nationalism is a doctrine and a movement designed to promote and to safeguard the existence of a nation' (Seton-Watson 1986: 19). This is a rather simple but nonetheless useful definition provided that we are aware of the historical implications of such a statement.

Any attempt at coming to terms with the concept of nationalism requires the clarification of some basic terms, and particularly of the following: state, nation, ethnic community (ethnie) and nation-state. But a word of caution. There is no agreement about how to use these terms – the word 'nation' being especially controversial.

Now, 'state' is perhaps the easiest term to define and the one that creates the least divergence. I define the state as a centralized, territorially defined, sovereign polity. By 'centralized' I mean the existence of a single centre of power; by 'territorially defined' I refer to the existence of clearly defined physical borders; and by 'sovereign' I simply mean an autonomous, non-dependent entity. Finally, 'polity' is simply another word for political organization. This is, I think, an economical but nonetheless accurate definition of the state.

Now, of course, we could add other features to define the state. Max Weber referred to the monopolization and concentration of the means of coercion, that is, the monopoly of force as a key feature of the state. We could also mention bureaucratization, that is, the existence of a permanent body of officials, what we call in modern terminology a civil service. Again, legitimation is an important characteristic of the modern state, as is, at least ideally, cultural and linguistic homogenization.

When it comes to define the nation the problems begin. The term 'nation' is much more vague and ambiguous than the term 'state', with which it is sometimes confused, both in common parlance and in the scientific literature. Part of the confusion arises from the fact that we have inherited, from the late eighteenth century, two major definitions of the nation: one political and one cultural.

Rousseau was the founder of the political conception of the nation in so far as he equated nationhood with the expression of a people's collective will. In Rousseau's definition, which was adopted by the French Revolution, the emphasis is on the conscious, subjective element. Nationality and citizenship are coterminous, which is why, in the English, American and French traditions, the nation is essentially viewed as the liberal-democratic state.

The German philosopher Herder was the founder of the cultural conception of the nation. Herder equated nationhood with the ethnic characteristics of a people. In this case, the emphasis is on objective criteria, namely common descent, common culture and common language. Other factors can also be brought to bear: history, religion, race, law, territory, character, etc. Nations and ethnies are closely related; for Smith an ethnie is 'a named human population with shared ancestry myths, histories and cultures, having an association with a specific territory and a sense of solidarity' (1986: 32). While ethnies are ubiquitous historically and spatially, nations are essentially a modern phenomenon.

One of the most popular definitions of the nation to have emerged in the past years is that of Benedict Anderson (1991). He characterizes the nation as 'an imagined political community – and imagined as both inherently limited and sovereign' (1991: 6). By 'imagined' Anderson means the fact that 'the members of even the smallest nation will never know most of their fellow-members, meet them, or even hear of them, yet in the minds of each lives the image of their communion' (1991: 6).

Another feature of Anderson's definition is that nations are finite, have boundaries; in other words, no nation can encompass the whole of mankind; a nation assumes the existence of a world of nations. The sovereignty of the nation refers to the fact that the nation legitimates itself, without any reference to a divine order (the people are the nation, as the French revolutionaries boldly asserted in 1789, and no divinely ordained monarch could stop them). As to the idea of the nation as a community it points to an essential element of nationhood: the belief in a sense of fraternity or 'horizontal comradeship', with independence from other considerations (class, gender, etc. which may separate individuals) (1991: 7).

We are now in a position to define the commonly found expression 'nation-state'. In theory a nation-state is a state which is a nation; that is, a state which comprises a nation. But since we have two definitions of nation, we also have two definitions of nation-state. Let us take the example of the United Kingdom. According to the 'political nation' principle the UK can be envisaged from the perspective of its citizens, or crown subjects, who have a sense of loyalty towards the monarchy and the British state. In this sense we can say that the UK is a nation-state. However, if we adopt the 'cultural nation' principle, we find in the UK four historically constituted communities which have their own distinct identity expressed in a variety of ways, by reference to a number of ethnic markers (language, culture, history, etc.). In this second sense, we would refer to the UK as a multi-national state. In a well-publicized article (originally published in 1978), Walter Connor suggested that 'a survey of 132 entities generally considered to be states as of 1971', produced the surprising result that 'only 12 states (9.1%) could be justifiably described as nation-states' (1994: 96).

Unfortunately, in real political life things are more complicated, they are never so clear-cut, because historically, after the French Revolution, there has been an interpenetration between the two conceptions of the nation, with two general consequences. On the one hand, so called multinational states have tried to become proper nation-states through a process of nation-building, which essentially consists in an attempt at a cultural and linguistic homogenization and uniformization of the different, usually subordinated cultural nations. A key element in this process of homogenization is the educational system, which promotes the official language and the dominant culture of the state. Surprisingly enough, states have not always been successful in this endeavour, otherwise we would not have the great variety of minority nationalisms that we have in Europe, and elsewhere, today.

On the other hand, nations, that is, cultural nations, have tried to obtain more and more parcels of autonomy, and in the final instance have aimed at constituting themselves as sovereign states, when feasible. The principle of self-determination, so typical of modernity, is one of the consequences of this state of things.

Since the French Revolution, the nation (particularly in the cultural sense of the term) has become the highest value of modernity, and hence a highly desirable thing to have or to boast about. The recent events in Eastern

211

Europe, particularly since 1989, show that this principle is far from being obsolete. Even the European Community does not herald the end of national identities (in the cultural sense), but the very opposite: the flourishing of the submerged identities of the small, suppressed nations of Europe. I tend to use the word 'nation' mostly in its cultural sense, and reserve the expression 'nation-state' to those cases where state and nation coincide.

THE DEVELOPMENT OF NATIONALISM IN MODERNITY

1789–1870

The French Revolution and the Napoleonic invasions heralded and to a great extent triggered off the advent of modern nationalism in Western Europe, putting an end (at least temporarily) to the aristocratic conception of the nation prevailing in the *ancien régime* and modernizing the state, as well as generating sentiments of political independence and cultural autonomy among the affected countries (Greenfeld 1992). In Latin America, the Declaration of Independence of 1776, the French Revolution and the Napoleonic invasions were influential factors in generating successful movements for national independence in the first third of the century.

The post-Napoleonic period had started, however, in a most inauspicious way. The Congress of Vienna, which in 1815 had brought together the leading European states to decide on the future of the continent, resolutely opposed the emerging Italian and German nationalisms (as well as the Polish one). The independence of Greece in 1830 was seen as the first major success of the nationalist principle. There soon followed Belgium's independence. In any case, very few nineteenth-century political thinkers managed to grasp the enormity of the nationalist avalanche, seeing it at most as a passing fad. This also accounts for the paucity and poverty of theoretical statements on the national question. Of the three most powerful ideologies of the nineteenth century – liberalism, socialism and nationalism – identified with the emergence of modernity and the subversion of the *ancien régime*, nationalism is the one which was the least appreciated as an *idée-force* at the time of its appearance. Following ideas expressed a long time ago by Carlton Hayes and Hans Kohn among others, it is customary to see the development of nineteeenth-century and twentieth-century nationalism essentially in dichotomous and moralizing terms. Prior to 1870 there was a nationalism which was democratic, progressive and humanitarian; after 1870 nationalism became imperialist, authoritarian and chauvinist.

The first thing worth mentioning about the German-Italian model of nationalism is that it appears to combine state-building with nationalism. In a nutshell, the model assumes a unity – an 'Italian' and a 'German' nation – which would have existed since the medieval period and which expressed itself in a language, a culture and a common descent. Owing to a combination of internal factors (disorganization, selfishness, etc.) and external ones (foreign domination), the nation had been unable to flourish adequately in the past. The only way of doing that was for the nation to control its own affairs in the context of a modern, centralized state. This required a process of unification of the different independent or subjected political units which shared the same nationality. However, in both cases we can observe that in the process of national state-building the lead was taken by the most dynamic (either politically or economically) of the existing states in each civilizational area, that is, Prussia in Germany and Piedmont in the Italian case.

The French model of nationalism starts at the very opposite end of the spectrum, with the existence of a state with fixed, stable boundaries and in which the nation is envisaged as a manifestation of the free will of its citizens. In Pflanze's words: 'common sovereignty provided common institutions and a common political tradition from which emerged a sense of nationhood which transcended cultural differences' (1966: 139). Whether by historical accident or not, the French model incorporates two separate elements: popular sovereignty and historical state. And while the former acted as a catalyst in corroding autocratic monarchies, the latter had to face the onslaughts of cultural nationalisms, with varying effects and responses depending on a constellation of factors. The French model, while generally relying on Renan's idea of the nation as a spiritual principle, characterized by a common heritage of memories and a desire and will to live together, involved also the recognition of achieving cultural and linguistic homogeneity. There was a conscious attempt to attain these objectives by state-generated nationalism. Through the compulsory educational system both the medium (language, culture) and the message (civic values) were transmitted.

The third model could perhaps be called the Irish model of nationalism. It involves a culturally defined nation, usually associated with a historical territory within a given state (or states). By choosing Ireland to represent the third model, the case with the utmost complexity in terms of the relations between an oppressed nationality and its oppressor has been selected. The actual independence of Eire and the fact that Northern Ireland remained in the UK was one of the possible solutions to the bitter historical dispute between the Irish and the British government: these solutions ranged from limited autonomy to full territorial independence for Ireland. Although presenting some parallelism with the German-Italian model, the third model refers usually to small national units that try to break away from an existing multinational state or empire, rather than small states coming together to form a larger, nationally based state. The objectives of the nationalisms against the state vary from cultural demands to autonomy, from federalism to outright independence. In theory all units can progress from cultural demands to demands for independence (Hroch 1985).

That there is a contradiction between the expansionist tendencies of the state and the nationality principle is most obvious. The doctrines of political and cultural nationalism encouraged the creation of true nation-states, that is, states which contained a single nation (whichever way the latter was defined); realities were, however, rather different. Many nationalities never succeeded in creating their own state; many states were nation-states only in appearance. The state did not change its character because of the nationalist onslaught, but had to adapt to the new times and had at least to create the pretence of being a nation.

1870–1918

One area in which practically all Western European states coincided was in enhancing their prestige, their *grandeur*, by the possession of overseas colonies. It is somewhat ironic that at the time when the idea of self-determination was gaining ideological ground, the most intense colonial expansion overseas was taking place. This imperialist phase in European history was often justified in terms of a civilizing mission of superior races over inferior races. Imperialist countries had a 'national mission' to fulfil. The idea that the so-called inferior races could have the right to national emancipation was considered totally ludicrous by Western states.

What in fact predominated after 1870 was the naked power politics of the big states. In this context nationalism means an extreme form of patriotism, with clear jingoistic and chauvinistic characteristics within the overall framework of an imperialist policy. One could say, paraphrasing Lenin, that imperialism became the highest stage of nationalism. For the new breed of state nationalists 'the possession of an empire was an essential precondition for the free development of one's own national culture in time to come' (Mommsen 1974: 126). This is not to disregard the economic reasons for imperialism: the need to export excess capital and excess human resources to other territories. In addition, the vested interests of the colonial bureaucracy helped to perpetuate the system.

The development of imperialism reinforced the determination of Western European states to contain their internal national minorities or emerging nationalisms against the state by engaging ever more actively in policies of national homogenization, as well as in outright repressive measures against the cultural and political manifestations of the awakening nationalities. By 1913 the idea that small nations could achieve independence by insurrectional or any other means was considered improbable. The model of the unitary state was pervasive. Measured in terms of national independence, for example, only Norway was a successful case of self-determination in Western Europe in the period between 1870 and 1914. However, the First

World War changed things again. The collapse of empires in Central and Eastern Europe, and President Wilson's commitment to see national self-determination on the agenda, produced a remarkable flurry of small independent states, even if it did not solve the national question owing to the recalcitrant problem of the disadvantaged minorities in the new states.

1918–1945

Fascism was the culmination of state nationalism. All Western European countries developed radical nationalist movements that could be labelled, following Charles Maurras's felicitous expression, 'integral nationalisms'. They represented reactions against the new bourgeois democratic and liberal order that was emerging, and in which the working classes and the socialist parties were playing an increasingly important role. They were movements which tended to emerge as a result of a major crisis of confidence in the nation-state (international humiliation following military defeat or unsatisfied imperialist appetites). They appeared as movements of renewal, of revitalization of the perceived morbid organism. Both Nazi Germany and fascist Italy fit the case well. Fascism focused on the supremacy of the nation conceived inseparably from the state. Benito Mussolini expressed this thought when he said that fascism considered the state as an absolute. In this conception of the state the individual was seen in a totally subordinated position. As Anthony D. Smith has rightly noted, fascism 'tends to view the nation in instrumental terms, as a "power-house", a repository and weapon for the exercise of will and force' (1976: 56). Some authors, including Carlton Hayes and Anthony D. Smith, have been reluctant to accept that there is a close connection between nationalism and fascism. Although they are right in emphasizing the specificity of fascism, by failing to see a continuity between integral nationalism and the fascist conception of the nation-state they are in danger of ignoring a major dimension of fascism.

In the interwar period the fascist model of nationalism spread in one form or another all over Europe. Whether in power or in opposition, fascist movements were present in most countries. Where it was politically triumphant, fascism pursued to their extreme the policies of nation-building, in an attempt at creating the national homogeneity that was required to keep the masses of the country tuned into the mythical, often mystical, ideas of the nation. Fascism indeed emphasized the myths and symbols of the national community and made sure that the distinction between the public and the private spheres was all but wiped out. Fascism, based on a combination of terror and consensus, insisted on the participation of the masses in cults which would generate a sense of belonging to the nation and which allowed the individuals to feel that they were involved in its affairs. As an extreme form of nationalism, fascism has coloured the perception that the twentieth century has had of nationalism. In the war period some minority nationalisms, particularly in German-occupied territories, allowed themselves to fall under the spell or control of fascist ideologies, with predictable consequences for the postwar period.

1945–1989

The collapse of fascism in 1945 seemed to put an end to the era of nationalism in Europe. In its fascist form, nationalism took a totalitarian look which was seen as anathema in the postwar period, which saw Europe essentially divided along ideological lines. The Cold War and the policy of the blocs left no room for nationalist adventures. Between 1945 and 1989 borders were sacrosanct, inviolable.

On the other hand, a different kind of nationalism was developing outside Europe, reflecting the desire of colonial peoples to become independent, even if that represented at times a violent confrontation with the metropolis. Colonial imperialism began to crumble.

It would be Eurocentric to assume that terms like 'nation', 'nationalism', 'national sentiments', 'national consciousness' and so on, which in their modern form originated and developed in Western Europe, can function as universal concepts. There is, of course, a limited way in which they do, but the cultural diversity underlying the different civilizational spaces makes the nationalitarian convergence unlikely.

The burden of the proof is on those who proclaim, for example, that Sinhalese, Kurdish and Scottish nationalisms are essentially the same. Religious beliefs, kinship conceptions and ideas of territory are among the factors that play a fundamental part in the way in which the nation is conceived. Buddhism, Islam and Christianity involve different world views which radically affect the conceptualization of the nation. Bruce Kapferer (1988) shows how, in the the case of Sinhalese nationalism, Buddhism permeates the way in which political realities (including a demonic conception of evil) are perceived.

As John Armstrong (1982) has convincingly shown, sedentary populations tend to have a concept of territorial boundary which is totally absent in nomadic peoples. Finally, the form in which the community is envisaged is often a projection into a wider social space of kinship conceptions, with in some cases a strong emphasis on 'blood' or common descent. While anybody can become a Scot provided that they live in Scotland and identify with the Scottish nation socially and to a certain extent culturally, there is only one way of becoming a Kurd: by being descended from Kurds, that is, by being born a Kurd.

Around the 1960s, and generally speaking since, Third World nationalisms fall into two major categories: those inspired by religious traditions (Islam playing an important role here) and those based on Marxism-Leninism or on a native type of socialism.

In most cases the borders of the newly emerging states were determined by the colonial powers and reflected the old colonial delineation. In the making of the newly independent states no consideration was given to the issue of whether they were ethnically or linguistically homogeneous This was particularly the case in Africa. Third World nationalisms, hence, tend to belong to the type in which the state builds up the nation, or to be more precise, they try to do so. It is not surprising to observe that the number of successes has been rather limited; after all, in Western Europe the processes of converting multi-ethnic states into nation-states have taken hundreds of years.

It has been the role of the Westernized elites in the Third World to try to provide the masses with a consciousness of their unity, cohesion and identity in spite of the existing glaring ethnic, linguistic and religious divisions. Hence nations were invented out of thin air, communities were imagined where only diversity and dispersion existed, and narratives were created to sustain the whole wobbly edifice. In addition, this nationalism legitimated also the monopoly of power exerted by the elite.

An important contradiction which existed in Third World nationalisms was that while they presented themselves as anti-European, yet they had to rely on alien concepts such as the nation, the state, the constitution, developmentalism, etc. to realize their objectives. In a word, Third World countries had to come to terms with modernity (either of the liberal-democratic kind or of the socialist kind); in fact they were left with very little space for economic, political and cultural manoeuvring.

In his recent work, aptly subtitled *Africa and the Curse of the Nation-State*, Basil Davidson remarked that 'the acceptance of the postcolonial nation-state meant acceptance of the legacy of the colonial partition, and of the moral and political practices of colonial rule in its institutional dimensions' (1992: 162).

Furthermore, Third World leaders had often to combine modernity with tradition. This created a rather schizophrenic situation. Because popular support was weak and national integration only very precarious, many Third World countries developed authoritarian patterns in which the cult of the state, which was identified with the nation, was paramount. What emerged out of the post-colonial order, particularly in Africa, was, in the words of Crawford Young (1994: 288), a kind of 'integral state' in which the ruling groups exerted a total domination over the society at large. This state was the mirror image of the colonial one but was often taken to an extreme.

What characterizes the post-colonial state in the Third World is its multi-ethnic nature; within the borders of most states live together populations with different languages, religions, cultures, etc. In many cases the only thing that united the population of a colony was the desire to overthrow alien rule. After independence, the first and foremost task of the state was its feverish attempt to engage in more or less aggressive policies of nation-building, usually favouring the dominant ethnic group.

However, the results have been rather poor and there have been increasing demands for further autonomy or outright independence from the subordinated regions and ethnies. The fact that the developmental policies of most Third World countries have failed has not been a good omen for legitimizing these states. The growth of ethnic politics reflects, at least in part, the disenchantment with the economic bankrupcy of many Third World states; on the other hand, these states have shown very little inclination to satisfy ethnonational demands. In the long run, violent conflict of a separatist kind has become endemic and in fact very few states can boast of having solved the problem. Nonetheless, a superstitious respect for the internationally agreed borders of colonial times has been a principle to which most states have adhered, no matter how hypocritically.

1989–present

One of the effects of perceiving the Soviet Union as an anti-colonialist state was not only that the making of the Russian Empire up to 1917 was glossed over, but more importantly that the colonial structure of the Soviet Union rarely came under scrutiny. With the collapse of Soviet bloc in 1989 and the disintegration of the Soviet Union in 1991–2, these issues have come to the forefront. Suddenly, a state which had repeatedly claimed to have solved the national question exploded apparently as a result of nationalist pressures. To account for this cataclysmic event, two main types of explanation have been put forward (Suny 1993):

1   The first type envisages the Soviet Union as a reservoir of frozen nationalities, defrosted by the warmth of Gorbachev's *perestroika* (economic restructuring) and *glasnost* (transparence). In this perspective the emphasis is squarely on the pre-Soviet past, that is, on the formation of the Russian Empire in modernity and its inability to assimilate an array of very different peoples.
2   The second type focuses on the nationality policies of the Soviet Union and considers the extent to which it shaped the future nations of the 1989 Revolution.

In spite of its bad name, and against the predictions of most politicians and social scientists, nationalism made its reappearance in Western Europe in the form of minority nationalisms against the state in the 1960s, and has persisted unabated until the present (Smith 1981; Tyryakian and Rogowski 1985). This has been a source of political destabilization affecting most countries. All ethnonations try to preserve a sense of national identity and rightly believe that this can only be achieved in the framework of a state that provides them with a substantial degree of political autonomy.

Much has been made of the imitation effect of Third World movements of national liberation on Western European ethnonationalisms. That there was perhaps a rhetorical influence is undeniable, and in some cases organizational forms may have been borrowed. To what extent the anti-colonialist wave may have affected the timing of minority nationalisms in the West is open to debate. In any case, the major cause of ethnonational revival is to be found in the ever growing process of the imposition of the model of an alien nation-state on the everyday life of the subjected nationalities. The two major political objectives of the ethnonationalist movements are: the right of a community (big or small) to be different; and the right of a community to control its own affairs within a given territory. As predictable, ethnonationalist movements tend to occur in areas of high ethnonational potential. Most of these movements are not new. Since 1989 there has been a recrudescence of ethnonationalism in the West which has been often attributed to the 'Baltic effect' (independence of the Baltic countries). In many cases what we simply have is an opportunistic repackaging of long-standing demands.

The postwar period in Western Europe has been characterized by an extreme stability of political borders. Most of the states have come to the conclusion, no matter how reluctantly, that it was in their economic and military interests to create a united Europe, even if some political concessions in terms of state sovereignty had to be made. How far they are prepared to go to construct a politically unified Europe is not yet clear. And can a sense of European identity be created transcending, or maybe superseding in the Hegelian sense, the state and national divisions?

In the aftermath of the ideological thaw in Eastern Europe, the *de facto* Western European monopoly on the idea of Europe was challenged by peoples from this region and will no doubt be challenged by other nations. This brings to the fore the question: what is, then, Europe? A unique civilizational area or just a geographic denomination? An entity of the past, of the present or of the future, or maybe just a utopia? The anarchist dream of a federation of European peoples or a type of Hitlerite nightmare, a federation of European peoples large and small or a centralized, bureaucratic and uniform state? A common economic market or a unified polity? A social-democratic Europe or a free-for-all capitalist Europe? In conclusion, there are four major problems besetting the idea of a European supernation-state: the sovereignty of the states, the nationalism of the peoples, the integration of the non-European ethnic groups and the incorporation of non-Western European countries. As a consequence, its future is problematic; it will have to proceed at a rather slow pace and probably dilute many of the unitary aspirations (Garcia 1993).

The 1960s and the 1990s represent high points in the process of self-determination. The 1960s was the time of political independence for Third World countries freeing themselves from European-style colonialism; the 1990s have seen the collapse of the Soviet bloc and the disintegration of the Soviet Union and of other Eastern European states (Czechoslovakia and Yugoslavia) into a number of successor states. The process of self-determination of nations is far from completed. There are still a large number of extant ethnic and national claims. In the Third World, the post-colonial political structures are far from stable; ethnic/national separatism plagues many African and Asian countries. In the ex-Soviet world fissiparity is likely to continue, and the collapse of the Russian Federation cannot be excluded. Finally, the Western world is not totally impervious to these trends which could affect the Canadian, Belgian and Ukrainian states among others.

CLASSICAL SOCIOLOGY AND THE NATION

The reasons for the inability of social scientists to come to terms with the national question have their origins in the cosmopolitanism of the Enlightenment, but find their specific roots in the intellectual traditions of the recognized nineteenth-century founding parents of the social disciplines. The underlying political philosophies of the social scientific projects of the nineteenth century were based on either liberal or socialist conceptions of the world. No matter how different these conceptions might be, liberalism and socialism are both universalistic in nature, and hence they consider nationalism as a transient phenomenon. Only conservative and romantic thinkers perceived, in all its uncontrollable turbulence, the force of nationalism in history, but they were interested not in explaining its origins, character and development but rather in asserting its eternal reality.

It is an idle occupation to look for a theory of nationalism among the founders of the social sciences. At best, Marx, Durkheim and Weber made occasional remarks on the nation, but on the strength of these elements it is extremely difficult, if not altogether impossible, to build up a theory of nationalism.

The founders of historical materialism were certainly well aware of the nationalist phenomenon. As politically committed young intellectuals, Marx and Engels lived through the troublesome 1840s – a period in which nationalist struggles ravaged the European arena. In their formative years, then, they had to confront the nationalist demands of a variety of European peoples. To understand their attitude towards nationalism it is essential to know that they subordinated the survival of nations to the progressive march of history: some peoples were fossils from a long-gone past and were therefore objectively counter-revolutionary. These reactionary nations had to be sacrificed to the altar of the mightier national states. In the articles written by Marx and Engels for the *Neue Rheinische Zeitung* (1848–9), the national question was often present as part of the political scenario, but there was no attempt to explain the phenomenon except perhaps in terms of crude stereotypes of national character. It is obvious that for Marx and Engels the nation was not a central category of social existence, but rather a transitory institution created by the bourgeoisie; hence the passage in *The Communist Manifesto* to the effect that the 'proletariat has no fatherland'

At the turn of the century the vindication of the rights of nations changed the political panorama to the extent that to the Marxists of the Second International the national question was central to their political agenda. However, it was only within the Austro-Marxian tradition that a serious attempt was made to come to terms with the theoretical problems of the nation. Otto Bauer's *Die Nationalitätenfrage und die Sozialdemokratie* (1907) presented a theory of nationalism based on the idea of national character and of national culture, though he also used the dubious idea that nations have a historical destiny to fulfil. A much better known and more influential contribution from this period is, of course, Stalin's *Marxism and the National Question* (1913). In his definition of the nation, Stalin required the simultaneous coalescence of four elements (language, territory, economic life and psychic formation) in a historically constituted community of culture. As to Lenin, he adopted a more flexible definition of the nation, and although he was in favour, like most Marxists, of the creation of large political units, he endorsed the principle of self-determination of oppressed nations, at least in theory (Connor 1984; Nimni 1991).

As a whole the Marxist tradition has been extremely suspicious of nationalism, though for tactical reasons it has often made use of national sentiments to achieve socialist objectives. In any case, within Marxist theory the nation is not a significant concept that can help to explain the dynamics of modern history. I would tend to agree with Tom Nairn's sweeping statement that the 'theory of nationalism represents Marxism's great historical failure' (1977: 329). The extraordinary developments of the 1960s and 1970s in which socialist countries fought bitterly against each other along nationalist lines opened the eyes of some Marxists to the reality that national interests are, in the final instance, more important than socialist internationalism. The collapse of the Soviet Union and of Yugoslavia after 1989 has represented the nail in the coffin of Marxist pretences on nationalism. Whether this is the beginning, within Marxism, of a genuine interest in the theory of nationalism remains to be seen.

Émile Durkheim's silence on the national question is quite intriguing considering that in his formative period, in the 1880s, he was asking the same question that Renan had formulated in 1882: *Qu'est-ce qu'une nation?* In his early writings, mostly in the form of long book reviews, Durkheim made an inventory of a number of authors (Fouillée, Schäffle, Tönnies, Gumplowitz) who had contributed to the study of how national consciousness was created and maintained. The concepts that Durkheim evolved over this period – especially *conscience collective* and *représentation collective* – cried out to be applied to the study of national consciousness in contemporary societies. But towards the late 1890s Durkheim operated a double shift, which led him to an increasing concern with primitive societies and to the *refoulément*, to use B. Lacroix's expression, of the political sphere. The result was that the two basic concepts mentioned above were never put to the test for the study of modern nations.

We have to wait until the publication of a wartime pamphlet – *L'Allemagne au-dessus de tout* (1915) – to find Durkheim expressing an interest in the theory of the nation. The work was basically a tract against Treitschke and other German theorists who had deified the state and were objective accomplices of the expansionist policies of Kaiser Wilhelm. In opposition to Treitschke, Durkheim praised the German tradition of the *Volksgeist* (Savigny, Lazarus, Steinthal) because in their conception of the nation they took into account the impersonal forces of history (myths, legends, etc.). In other words, they assumed that a nation had a 'soul', a character which was independent of the will of the state. It is somewhat surprising, then, that when Durkheim proposed a definition of the nation – as a 'human group whose members, either for ethnic or simply for historical reasons, want to live under the same laws and constitute the same state' (Llobera 1994b: 156) – he was unable to clearly distinguish between nation and state. Could this oversight be a reflection of Durkheim's role as one of the committed ideologists of the Third Republic?

The First World War, with the collapse of socialist internationalism and the rallying of the working-class parties to the interests of their respective national states, was undoubtedly the catalyst that compelled many social scientists to think about the nation. Within the Durkheimian School, this led to a number of discontinued and failed attempts to incorporate the nation into sociological theory. In 1920–1 Marcel Mauss started to write a monograph on the nation, which he never completed (Llobera 1994b). From the scattered fragments that are extant we can conclude that his standpoint was not different from that of Durkheim in that he never solved the antinomy between state and nation. The problem with Durkheim and Mauss is that they had the French historical experience of a national state too much at heart to pay enough attention to alternative conceptions. Another Durkheimian, Maurice Halbwachs, although not directly concerned with articulating a theory of the nation, was nonetheless interested in the study of one of the key elements in any definition of the nation: the idea of collective memory. His work, however, had limited diffusion, and his refined conceptual tools were applied to a variety of groups (family, class, etc.) but not to the nation.

Wolfgang Mommsen (1984) has empirically established for liberal and democratic ears the unpalatable truth not only that Weber was a German nationalist, but that for him the national state was the 'ultimate value'; in other words, that in the final instance, the interests of the national state should prevail over any other interests. Although in *Economy and Society* Weber defined the nation as a community of sentiment based on some objective common factor (language, traditions, customs, social structure, history, race, etc.) and the belief that this factor generated values which were worth preserving against the encroachment by other communities, he insisted in creating an indissoluble bond between nation and state. To all practical purposes the nation, that is the cultural values of a community, could only be preserved in the framework of a purpose-built state. On the other hand, Weber knew very well that the modern state could not achieve its aims exclusively by brute force. The loyalty of the individual to the state depended on the existence of a national sentiment: hence the centrality of the equation of nation equals state.

There is little doubt that Weber's understanding of the nation was far superior to that of Marx or Durkheim. For one thing, he was well aware that national sentiments were not the creation of the rising bourgeoisie, but were actually rooted in the population of a country as a whole. Because *Kultur* was the distinctive feature of a national community, Weber was very interested in the question of its preservation, transmission and change. In this context he considered crucial the role played by the intellectuals in creating a literary culture. It is unfortunate that Weber did not write, as he had actually planned to do, a history of the national state.

MODERN THEORIES OF NATIONALISM

A comprehensive theory of nationalism should provide us with the following answers:

1   an account of the genesis and evolution of the idea of nation in Western Europe, as well as of its diffusion world-wide;
2   a spatio-temporal explanation of the varying structures, ideologies and movements of nationalism in the modern period;
3   an understanding of the collective feelings or sentiments of national identity along with the concomitant elements of consciousness.

How do different sociological theories approximate these lofty objectives? Generally speaking, most studies of nationalism are superficial descriptions of concrete cases or comparisons *à la* Frazer; as to point 3 it is practically *terra incognita*.

Among the few universalist theories of nationalism one should mention the primordialist and the sociobiological perspectives. Primordialism assumes that group identity is a given – that there exist in all societies certain primordial, irrational attachments based on blood, race, language, religion, region, etc. They are, in the words of Clifford Geertz (1973), ineffable and yet coercive ties, which are the result of a long process of crystallization. Modern states, particularly but not exclusively in the Third

World, are superimposed on the primordial realities which are the ethnic groups or communities.

The sociobiological approach starts with the assumption that nationalism is the result of the extension of kin selection to a wider sphere of individuals who are defined in terms of putative or common descent. Sociobiological explanations are not necessarily articulated in terms of genetic determinism, although it may be heuristically useful to make such an assumption. Most sociobiologists do not suggest that nationalism can be explained solely in terms of genetic mechanisms, that is, without linking them with the results of the human and social sciences. The sociobiological approach insists that nationalism combines both rational and irrational elements, that is a 'primitive mind' with modern techniques. The word 'nationalism' expresses different realities: a love of country, the assertion of national identity and national dignity, but also the xenophobic obsession to obtain these things through violence and sacrificing other nations. Nationalism builds on ethnocentrism towards the in-group and xenophobia towards the out-group.

It has been suggested that nationalism gives rise to a pride and dignity, within the members of a group, which in turn provides a moral and philosophical ground on which to militate for political sovereignty. Nationalism has its roots in the past, but it is a contemporary vehicle to vent out human propensities to war. It is important in this context to emphasize the psychological dimensions of nationalism: a bond is established between the individual and the nation based on the idea that the latter is a family writ large. The individual identifies with the nation and hence tends to prefer it to other nations. The extensive use of kin terms to refer to the nation reflects this psycho-affective reality that Edgar Morin has called 'matri-patriotic', with an associated fraternal/sororal component.

Sociobiologists often fail to account for the formation, evolution and eventual disappearance of nations; in this respect the historical and social sciences have an essential role to play. However, sociobiologists, by identifying certain human propensities for conflict and warfare which have served *Homo sapiens* well as a successful inclusive fitness maximizer, point out that these mechanisms, useful at an early stage of development, today risk the global annihilation of the human species. Recognizing these propensities can be the first step towards their neutralization.

Perhaps the best known and most impressive study of nationalism by a social scientist is that of Ernst Gellner (1983). He has gone a long way in providing a reasoned account for the emergence and pervasiveness of nationalism in modern times. His idea that the roots of nationalism are found in the structural needs of industrial society has appealed to a wide range of social scientists and historians, modernization theorists and Marxists alike.

The Gellnerian model asserts that it was the development of industrial capitalism and its unevenness that triggered off the development of nationalism. There was nothing prior to the industrial order (what Gellner refers to as agrarian society) that can be equated to nationalism because political units were not defined in terms of cultural boundaries. Besides industrialization Gellner mentions the impact of modernization (population growth, rapid urbanization, labour migration, etc.) on the development of nationalism at the global level.

Gellner's insistence that nations are invented (a position shared with all modernists) has also been widely accepted, perhaps because, among other things, it confirms the generalized perception among social scientists that nationalism is best explained in a reductionist fashion, i.e. subspecies economics. Not surprisingly, Gellner has little to say about national sentiments and consciousness. His sociological structuralism is also oblivious to history. Gellner states that the explanatory power of his theory is comprehensive, but not exhaustive. Among other things, it does not account for the virulence of fascist nationalisms. Nonetheless, he insists that his theory explains why nationalism has emerged and why it has become so pervasive. However, he tends to ignore state-generated nationalism and minimizes the role of the state in general. Nationalism is directed not only against internal low cultures, but also against other established state nationalisms.

Between the generalities of universalism and the limitations of modernism, there is room for a third type of theory which could be called evolutionary. It is true that as a mass phenomenon nationalism is a product of modern times, but in Europe the roots of nation as an 'imagined community' (Anderson), of national identity and even of incipient patriotic nationalism are firmly anchored in the medieval period (Llobera 1994a). There is, however, a conceptual gap between the medieval and the modern ideas of the nation; and that is why national identities had to be 're-created' or 'reinvented' in modernity. However, the crucial thing is how to account for the transition from the classical ethnies into modern nations (Smith 1981; 1986; 1991), and why this process took place originally in Western civilization. Only a theoretical framework which incorporates a variety of factors, not only economic (industrial capitalism), social (classes) or political (modern state), but also ideological (nationalist ideas), is likely to approximate the explanation needed given the complexities of the phenomenon (Llobera 1994a).

KEY CONCEPTS

NATIONALISM This concept describes the burgeoning tendency throughout modernity for states and nations to develop insular and protective identities, to

225

prescribe geographical and cultural boundaries around themselves and to detach from any wider collective interests except in the names of trade or alliance. Nations also patrol their boundaries jealously.

INTERNATIONALISM Is an ideology that has never really achieved its potential, rather it has become locked in particular political creed such as socialism. It speaks of the idea of cross nation and cross cultural co-operation and integration. Ironically the nearest approximation to an international community is contained in the common market ideal of the European Union, a community forged on international capitalism.

Theory/Practice

Paul Filmer

The relation between theory and practice is central to sociology. It is to be found at the origins of the discipline, at the beginnings of what Habermas (1987) has termed the 'unfinished project' of modernity. Indeed, when Talcott Parsons (1902–79) sought, in the middle of the twentieth century, to establish an encyclopaedic synthesis of theories of society (Parsons et al. 1961), the origins of modern social theory were located in the work of Nicolo Machiavelli (1469–1527) on how the new city states of Renaissance Europe could most effectively be governed according to the secular principles of their rational humanist culture. And as Bierstedt (1959; 1978) has noted, there has been no interruption to the propensity of successive generations of 'modern' social theorists to locate their work in the dominant Western mythological traditions of both Judaeo-Christian and Graeco-Roman thought. All human societies that have left records of their practices show a preoccupation with the condition and character of themselves as societies – a tendency to speculate about the adequacy of the general principles in terms of which they are organized. This preoccupation is what is meant by social theory and it is undertaken most actively as a social practice at times when societies are most concerned about the stability of their collective condition, the times at which societies undergo change.

Reasons for the active pursuit of theory as societies change are not hard to find. When members of societies recognize that the interactional structures through which they are related to one another are changing they recognize also the fragility of society, because it is an *idea*. Berger (1966) puts the issue in an interesting light when he differentiates between two related concepts to which the idea of society is fundamental: those of the 'individual in society' and its converse, 'society in the individual'. Society both produces the individual and is produced by it. Society itself is a concept, an idea, a product of theories generated and sustained in practice by the actions of individuals and groups (Schutz 1971). Thus, the specific and observable practices of social action and interaction are grounded in a fundamental, dichotomous and dialectical relation with their more general, abstract and theoretical origins in the idea of society. What is often termed the classical tradition in sociological theory (see, for example, Nisbet 1966; Truzzi 1971; Lemert 1993) is organized around this dichotomy and can be recovered in terms of it through an examination of three approaches to the construction of sociological theory and the ways in which they conceptualize social practice. The approaches are those of holism, individualism and Marxism, and each will be discussed in turn below. Before proceeding to this, however, it is worth noting several further implications of the dichotomous relation between theory and practice in sociology.

SOME IMPLICATIONS OF THE THEORY/PRACTICE DICHOTOMY

First, *theory implies comparison*, in two senses. The first of these has already been invoked: the *comparison with practice*. For sociological theory, the idea of society is tested for adequacy according to the extent that it can be put into practice and thereby realized as a way for individuals and groups to live an ordered and collective life. The second sense follows from this, and is itself a form of practice which stems from the origins of theory in thought and ideas. Because theories are generated through speculative thought, there is no necessary limit to the potential number of alternative theories that might be created in this way. Whether a theory can be realized in practice is an important test of its adequacy because it is one way in which a limit can be set on the number of theoretically possible forms of society that are worth conceptualizing. Theories, thus, can be *compared with one another* in terms of their adequacy to the tasks which they are required to perform (Layder 1994; Waters 1994).

This introduces the second implication: *theory implies method as a form of practice*. If theories are to be tested in practice, in order to decide on their adequacy, and if they are to be compared with one another on that basis, then the means by which such tests and comparisons are to be conducted have to be developed in relation to the theories. This necessity gives rise to a specialist form of theory, termed **methodology**, which is concerned with fundamental logical and philosophical questions which underlie the testing and application of theory in its relations to practice (Runciman 1983). The conduct of such testing and application is through research, which depends in turn on a central methodological concern of sociological theory with the status of sociology as a science. This concern is located in questions of what counts as adequate evidence in scientific sociology; how far scientific methods of sociological research match those of the natural and physical sciences; and how far, therefore, it is possible to formulate general propositions about the structure and processes of the social world which match the predictive accuracy of those which can be formulated about the natural world.

This methodological concern with scientific sociology, however, stands to some extent in tension with a third implication of the theory/practice dichotomy: *theory is critical*. Sociological theories are formulated not only to explain and analyse reality; they can be formulated also to *change* the structure and institutional order of society. Moreover, such change can be proposed in pursuit of particular interests that are present in existing societies but which are not yet dominant in them. This characteristic of theory as **critique** implies not only the critical formulation of a new, alternative social order, but two further critical qualities of theory as well. It implies, first, the means by which the new social order will be achieved in practice – that is, a *theory of social change*. This can involve a gradual and active piecemeal engineering of the transition from one societal condition to another (social reform), an inductive theory of the inevitability of the process of change according to some overarching historicist design (social evolution), or the accomplishment of a more radical, rapid and hence unpredictable transformation (social revolution). Secondly, and as a feature of theorizing change, critical theory is concerned also with the justification and **legitimation** of new social orders, and it is here that it can be seen to be in tension with the methodological concerns of sociology as science. For the principal means by which theoretical conceptions of alternative societal forms are elaborated is through the **ideologies** implied by social and political philosophies. There is, thus, an important relation between critical theory and ideological practice which leads Blum (1970), for example, to argue that the body of theoretical knowledge that any society holds about itself is what he terms a 'normative order' of thought for that society. That is to say, it does not just *inform* members about the condition of their society and the interactional relations which constitute it. It operates also as a set of *constraints* on their practices to ensure that they continue to reproduce the conditions which make possible the continuation of that society as one which knows and reproduces itself in that way. This feature of the practice of theory is often termed its **reflexivity** (Garfinkel 1967; Heritage 1984).

This point returns us to the beginning of the discussion, where it was noted that the centrality of the theory/practice dichotomy in sociology is related to the origins of the discipline itself in the formulation of the concept of 'modern' society. Societies which see themselves as modern are, by definition, societies that have to justify themselves in terms of a theory of change and a theory of order that is not available from any source other than the practice of their own reflexive theorizing – the theorizing which they undertake about themselves. Because they are modern, they cannot be explained in terms of tradition, since to be modern is to be differentiated from the past, from history and its prior determinations. Similarly, modern societies are utterly contemporary, and cannot be allowed the theoretical luxury of indulging in a future predicated, with an inevitable continuity, on a present determined by its past. The practical implications of this for conventional theory have led to the formulation of a theory of postmodern society (see chapter 'Modernity/Postmodernity'). This is the most recent instance of the necessity of theory to an understanding of the complex practices that are the routine existential experience of the individuals and groups which constitute modern societies. Earlier instances of the same tradition are those of holism, individualism and Marxism, which can now be considered in further detail.

HOLISTIC THEORY AND SOCIOLOGICAL FUNCTIONALISM

Holistic theories are so termed because they are based on the contention that the relation between the individual and society is set by the structural character of society itself, since human individuals are essentially social beings, conceived, born and brought up in a network of interactional human relations. At their most general level of discourse, holistic theorists argue that all human societies are composed of an effectively infinite number of such networks, each of which is organized analytically by a structurally identical ordering principle, and is a microcosm of larger structures (social institutions). These larger structures are, in turn, inter-related as whole societies which determine the common interactional order of the microcosmic networks which make them up.

The leading nineteenth-century exponent of **holism** was Émile Durkheim (1858–1917) who argued that sociology's scientific task is to study the causes and functions of what he termed social facts – social, that is, as opposed to physical or psychological facts about human actions. Physical facts are determined by the substantive activities of which the human organism is capable through the operations of its neuro-muscular physique, and psychological facts are the individual manifestations of the electro-chemical operation of its neuro-physiological structure. Both types of facts, moreover, are properties of the human species and can be generalized about, with few variations, between different cultures and across historical periods. Social facts, by contrast, cannot be reduced to physical or psychological actions and processes, and thus cannot be explained causally in terms of them.

Durkheim argues that social facts are the emergent properties of human actions and interactions. Rather than being expressive manifestations of the physiological properties of the human species, they are made manifest and observable as the structures of constraint that regulate the relations between human individuals and groups: they are the products of the ability of human beings to communicate with one another and to structure their interactions and interrelations. They are, that is to say, theoretical and abstract ideas. It is for this reason that Durkheim (1938) insists, as a rule of scientific sociological method, that they must be studied *as if they are things* (*comme les choses*). Durkheim goes on to classify them in order of increasing generality and abstraction, from informal rules of conduct, such as interactional etiquette and manners, to the formal laws which order whole societies and the overarching institutions of government and judiciary which establish and administer them. The enormous trans-historical and cross-societal variety of these institutions, as well as the range of differences in their interpretation and application within large-scale modern societies, support Durkheim's contention that social facts cannot be reduced to the universal characteristics of human physiology and psychology. But this very argument makes problematic the realization of the central aims of general theory in a scientific sociology. These aims seek to formulate general propositions about the fundamental characteristics of human societies: how they provide for their collective material needs, how they regulate and award priorities to the pursuit of the competing interests of differentiated groups of members, and how they maintain the coherence of their institutional structure and the integrity of their geographical and political boundaries. The sheer variety of effective solutions to these problems that have been accomplished by different societies over time suggests that such general propositions are difficult to establish, and even more difficult to test, in the way required by the conception of scientific method of the natural and physical sciences which Durkheim sought to adapt to the study of society. But this difficulty itself exemplifies the relation between sociological theory and its operationalization through the practice of sociological method. Sociology's claims to be a science are themselves a product of theories which determine how social scientific research is to be practised.

From amongst the considerable number of practical solutions to the fundamental problems of human society that can be adduced from historical and comparative sociological research, Durkheim (1933) argues that two types of societal forms predominate. He identifies these, in terms of the principles through which they cohere as structural wholes, as types of solidarity: mechanical and organic. *Mechanical social solidarity* is produced by replicating the fundamental social interrelationship of nuclear family kinship in marriage and parenthood, which produces sets of extended interrelations of consanguinity (shared blood) within and between several generations of families. These elaborated family networks are called clans, and are themselves interrelated in turn into tribes – which is the typical form taken by mechanically solid societies. Each clan is self-sufficient and consists of self-contained extended families; and each tribal society is composed of self-sufficient clans, all elements of which are effectively iden-tical in structure. *Organic social solidarity* is produced, by contrast, through differentiation rather than identity. The fundamental social relations

231

between individuals are based no longer on the ascribed status into which they are born as members of a consanguine, tribally contained and clan-based family. They are based instead on the socially regulated contracts which they are able to make with one another from the social positions which they have achieved by their own actions. Durkheim argues that these positions stem from a non-consanguine structure of social interrelations of interdependency, which are based upon a differentiation of the specialized skills of material production and social administration which he terms the *social* division of labour. This is quite different from what may be termed the *natural* division of labour in mechanically solid societies, which is limited largely to the natural specializations of skill that result from differences in age (physical maturity) and biological sex, and which reinforces the relatively unspecialized social solidarity achieved through replication of structurally identical social relations.

The change from mechanically to organically solid societies is proposed by Durkheim as an evolutionary one of the development of societies from structural simplicity to structural complexity. It is a manifestation, thus, of a holistic theory of social structure and a correlative theory of social change. Durkheim sees the change also as one of social progress. Organic solidarity is the normal structural condition of modern society, since the scale of structural interrelation is limited only by the possibilities that can be developed in terms of rational, secular human interests. The social and political orders of human communities are no longer limited necessarily by the belief systems and traditions of myth and religion. The increasingly large-scale and complex integration of modern societies results from the interdependence on one another of the individuals and groups which constitute them for the performance of the multifarious specialist tasks which fulfil the range of their various needs. Whereas mechanically solid societies are characterized structurally by primary groups whose members are routinely in face-to-face interaction with one another, organically solid societies proliferate through the development of secondary associations, such as bureaucracies, which facilitate interrelations between large and diversely differentiated groups in pursuit of their collective interests without necessarily requiring their members ever to be in face-to-face interaction. Durkheim argues further that this produces a new social morality which is grounded in the altruism that is generated by the interdependence between individuals and groups which is characteristic of the social division of labour. It is for this reason that structurally complex societies are described as organically solid: in theorizing their social structure, Durkheim makes a metaphorical comparison between the structure of complex, modern society and that of a biological organism, just as the type of structure which characterizes premodern societies, in being termed mechanical, is likened to a machine in the predictability of its operation. In organically solid societies, all parts are interdependent in their contribution to the well-being of the whole and are unable to function independently of the overall structure of interrelations in which they are implicated. It is the normal structural and processual condition for human societies that all recurrent, patterned activities of social interaction operate as functional parts of the whole which, in turn, acts the structure of their patterned character and ensures their recurrence and, like an organism, enables them to adapt to and alter their environment in order to sustain and develop themselves. Any recurrent activities that fail to contribute functionally to the continuing welfare of the social whole risk introducing pathological societal conditions, such as that of anomie, a condition which Durkheim terms *le mal de l'infini* (the sickness of infinite possibility), in which individuals are unable to accept or understand the need for their actions to be determined and regulated by collective principles which express the structural needs of society as a whole. Another example of such pathology offered by Durkheim is class conflict, which occurs as a result of members of a specific socio-economic group (class) putting their collective interests above those of society as a whole.

It is because of this theory of the determining relations between social structures and practical interactional processes that the school of holistic sociological theory based upon Durkheim's work is termed *structural-functional analysis* (see Merton 1957). It is also the basis for what later comes to be termed *systems theory* (Parsons 1951; Buckley 1967), since the determining relation between social structures, institutional processes and interactional practices is developed in terms of the theoretical principle of their reciprocal functionality for one another. This principle is proposed as common to all human societies, whatever their historicity or culture, and hence what identifies them as manifestations of the irreducible system of the universal collective (that is, social) condition of humankind.

Sociological holism, thus, is a critical theoretical analysis and explanation of the structure of relations between the individual and society. It accounts for the forms that the collective institutional orders of these relations take in practice, how they differ in comparison to one another between cultures and how they change over time. It proposes also a set of methodological practices by which these issues are most appropriately studied. In addition, to the extent that such studies are critically adequate, it can provide criteria in terms of which it is possible to identify the most effective structural forms of society from the point of view of the differing political and economic interests and moral ideals of the members of the groups which constitute them.

SOCIAL ACTION THEORY AND METHODOLOGICAL INDIVIDUALISM

Social action theorists, in contrast to functionalists, contend that the individual/society relation can only be analysed and explained through the practical social actions of individuals themselves, since only individuals actually exist as material, physical realities. Rather than seeing society as an institutionalized structure of relations which determine individual actions, social action theory argues that it is a concept generated by the theories, ideas and beliefs which individuals hold in common, and represents the stable, institutional basis which makes it possible for them to do so. It is this insistence on making the individual member of society the basis of sociological explanation that leads the practice of theorizing in terms of social action to be termed methodological **individualism**.

The major nineteenth-century exponent of social action theory and its concomitant individualist method was Max Weber (1864–1920). Weber argued as strongly that the social actions of the individual could *not* be reduced to determination by society as Durkheim argued the opposing position, that the actions of individuals *are* societally determined. And like Durkheim, he found it necessary to pay careful attention to the identification and definition of the proper topic of scientific sociological inquiry – not society, or even the individual as such, but the specific phenomenon of *social* action. Weber (1947) differentiates social action from individual action, which he sees as the conscious purposive behaviour of a particular individual motivated by his or her own interests. Action is, in turn, differentiated from behaviour, which he treats as an essentially psychological phenomenon occasioned by neuro-physiological reflexes such as a sneeze, a cough or a blink. Finally, action is differentiated from conduct, which Weber terms habitual action that has been learned and practised routinely to the extent that its performance no longer requires conscious reflection on the part of the actor. Social action is different from all of these phenomena because, unlike any of them, it takes account of the actual or potential presence in or relevance to the action situation of other individual social actors or groups of them: it is socially oriented. Like action itself, it is conscious and it has a purpose in being oriented to the accomplishment of a goal. But it is the focus on the actual, potential or even symbolic relevance of others to its conditions and consequences that identifies it as the proper topic of sociology. This topic is generated from the individualist theory of social action just as social facts are generated from the holist theory of structural functionalism. Both exemplify how theory generates the manner in which research is designed to test its adequacy in practice.

The conscious and purposive character of social action is, for Weber, the key to analysing its rationality; and it is through analysis of the rationality of social action that Weber develops an individualist theory of social structure. Society represents an institutionalization of the dominant mode of rationality of the social actions of its members. Thus the dominant form of institutional organization of a society is a manifestation of the dominant mode of rational consciousness amongst its members. Weber develops a method of classifying sociological phenomena into types according to the formal characteristics of their rationality as modes of action, which he terms *ideal types*. He identifies four of these ideal types of rationality: formal/legal rationality, value rationality, traditional rationality and affectual rationality. Each of them articulates a relation between the means and ends of purposive action and thus provides a basis in terms of which social actors can negotiate together a meaning to their actions which they can share in common. Formal/legal rationality proposes an instrumental mode of action in which the most causally efficient means are employed to achieve an end. For value rational action, by contrast, the selection of means by which to pursue a goal is governed by a code of ethics. The means chosen will not necessarily be the most efficient but are intended to be the most morally appropriate. The relation of means to ends in traditional rationality is not always explicable analytically, though it can always be described. The means of achieving goals in this instance are prescribed by custom and precedent rather than by any criterion that can be established by either inductive or deductive explanation. Affectual rationality articulates the criteria of selection of means to pursue ends in terms that are governed by the near-subjective rationality of feeling and emotion and represents those cases in which it is most difficult for actors to negotiate common meanings for their social actions.

Weber terms these types of rationality ideal because none of them will be found to be the sole mode of accounting for rational social action in any particular society or group. Nor could any particular social action be explained exclusively in terms of any one of the four types. But they do enable Weber to develop a concept of social structure from his theory of social action by making possible the explication, in methodologically individualist terms, of a differentiation between two types of society, each of which is characterized by the predominance of different types of rationality. Weber develops them from the work of Ferdinand Tonnies (1855–1936), who terms them *Gemeinschaft* (community) and *Gesellschaft* (association). They are structurally similar to the mechanically and organically solid types of societies identified by Durkheim: *gemeinschaftlich* societies are based on consanguine relations, primary groups and face-to-face interaction, whereas *gesellschaftlich* societies are characterized by more impersonal, large-scale secondary associations. Societies based on community are typically premodern and characterized by traditional rationality, complemented by both value rational and affectual action. In modern societies based on association, by contrast, the dominant mode of rationality is formal/legal, complemented by the occurrence of instances of all of the other three types. The structure of such societies is dominated by the bureaucracies of the modern state and the national and multinational corporations of industrial production and administration. These formal, rational-legal organizations are the institutional social manifestation of the dominant mode of rationality, which Weber sees as encroaching increasingly on the individual's freedom of action and expression, threatening to standardize human individualism into a calculative and dehumanizing impersonality.

It is this rational intellectual consciousness which is the basis of Weber's theory of social change. Unlike Durkheim, who argues that social change occurs as the structures of societies change through a process of differentiation and elaboration which he likens to the evolutionary growth of organisms, Weber (1930) sees social change as a result of conscious innovation through social action in the pursuit of the collective interests of dominant groups and which are legitimated through systems of *belief*. These processes are not necessarily general or typical of groups of societies, but occur under particular social, political, economic and cultural circumstances and, therefore, are characteristic of specific historical periods. Thus the mercantile and industrial forms of capitalism which come to dominate first Northern European and then global economies from the sixteenth to the early twentieth centuries, and are accompanied by the reciprocal political individualism of modern societies, are an institutional manifestation of the instrumentalism of formal/legal rational action. These forms of political economy and social order are themselves, to some extent, *theorized in advance* as a condition of social life to be brought about – that is, as a goal for the collective social action of those groups whose beliefs will legitimate the new order. In the case of the Northern European mercantile capitalism of the sixteenth and early seventeenth centuries, Weber argues, the ascetic, sectarian theology of Protestant Christianity played a crucial role by providing a belief system which legitimated the practices of individual entrepreneurialism and reinvestment through which the new economic institutions were established.

Social action theory provides a critical analysis of the structure and institutional processes of society in terms of the practices of its individual members. It shows a clear contrast to the critical *theoretical* emphasis on social structure that is characteristic of sociological holism, by giving a comparable emphasis to the *practices* of social actors. But this emphasis is complemented by the typical character of the *theorizing* that social actors have to undertake in terms of both the need to establish a coherent, rational relation between the ends that they act to achieve and the selection of the means which are socially available, or which they need to create socially to pursue them. It places the conscious practices of rational thought at the centre of human social action, which becomes identifiable as the topic of sociological inquiry as much in terms of its *meaningfulness* as by what *causes* it. The causes of social action, therefore, are not explicable primarily in methodologically holistic, social structural terms through their functions for the reinforcement of recurring social institutional processes. Instead, they are to be found in the methodologically individualist, shared social and cultural meanings of motive and intention through which social actors make sense for themselves and to one another of their interactional practices (Weber 1949). These meanings are a product of values and beliefs as much

as of reason and science. This important theoretical difference between the methodological perspectives of holism and individualism can also be discussed, in parallel substantive terms, as the sociological dichotomy between structure and agency (see chapter 'Structure/Agency').

MARXISM: PRAXIS AS THE PROPOSED UNITY OF THEORY AND PRACTICE

Karl Marx (1818–83) argued a different relation between the material conditions of social life and human consciousness, and hence between theory and practice. The method by which Marxist sociologists have studied this relation, termed *dialectical* or *historical materialism*, seeks to put an equal causal emphasis in sociological explanation on theory and practice. Social actions produce and are regulated by the institutional structures through which human beings pursue their material interests collectively in competition and conflict with one another. Their interests are generated by their fundamental organic needs to feed, house, protect and reproduce themselves. Marx argues that conflict is generated initially in prehistoric and structurally simple societies, where the natural provision of the means to fulfil these needs may be in short supply. However, he claims that human beings evolve an ability, early in their history as a species, to develop and apply skills of manufacture to the resources of their natural environment and thus to transform it into the goods necessary to provide for their needs. Thus, by co-operating socially, they are able to produce these goods more efficiently. Where the resources for the production of goods remain in short supply, however, such co-operation by one group of producers protects the resources from encroachment by others. And where there is an ample supply of resources, co-operation by one group to exclude access to them by others gives the excluding group power over them because it is able to control the ability of the others to provide for the fulfilment of their material needs.

These linked practices of cooperation and conflict over material production both *precipitate* the generation of theory to devise the techniques and technology of production, and are *justified* by it, through political ideologies and jurisprudential principles which legitimate the more or less exclusive ownership and control of natural resources by some groups as their *private property*. Marx theorizes a concept of social structure, therefore, which is composed of social groups that are differentiated from one another in terms of whether or not they own and control the means of production for the fulfilment of needs required by all members of society. Marx terms these groups *classes* in modern societies. They are involved in an inevitable conflict with one another which can only be

resolved by a common recognition that their fundamental interests in the fulfilment of needs are held in common, and are pursued more effectively by co-operation rather than competition. But the competition between social groups for scarce resources that produces the conflict of interest between classes is seen by the classical theorists of political economy, led by Adam Smith (1723–90), as the basis of the entrepreneurial drive of capitalism and its progressive innovations which generate economic wealth.

This leads Marx to develop what he terms a *critique of political economy* in the form of a theory focused on three distinct issues. First, it reinterprets human historiography in terms of the universal, epochal struggles of class conflict. Secondly, it reinterprets the ontology of the human species in terms of a conception of human beings as workers, whose essential activity is the transformation of their natural environment through their labour to fulfil their material needs. Thirdly, and most importantly, it proposes a new social order, that of communism, to overthrow and replace the exploitation of one class by another that is characteristic of industrial capitalism. The processes of social change which will bring about this new order will take the form of a political and economic revolution that originates, according to Marx, in the social structural contradictions of capitalism and their accompanying conflicts. Despite the methodological insistence of historical materialism that the practical social relations of production determine the legitimating theories of social and political order, it is clear that the revolution which will bring about the overthrow of capitalism starts life as a theoretical idea. Revolution, for Marx, is a realization of theory in practice, a praxis in which the distinction between theory and practice is dissolved. The revolution is accomplished by the proletariat of industrial workers who are able to unite as one because, as Marx states, they have nothing to lose but the chains of their exploitation by their opposing class, the capitalist bourgeoisie. And they are led in their revolutionary practice by the theorists, both of revolution as a process of change and of the new egalitarian political economy of communism.

Marxist theory proposes a dichotomy between theory and practice which, in many respects, parallels and offers an interesting instance of that between idealism and materialism (see chapter 'Idealism/Materialism'), not least because where revolutions have occurred that have matched the theoretical order of communism in practice, they have been brought about by causes other than the structural contradictions of capitalism. And the advanced industrial capitalist societies, which Marx predicted would be most susceptible to revolutionary overthrow *because* of their internal structural conditions, have proved to be the ones most immune to it. Marxist critical social theory has preoccupied itself with this problematic of its own for much of the twentieth century. In doing so it has, ironically, reinforced the very dichotomy between theory and practice that Marx himself sought to resolve through the concept of praxis.

A further dimension to the development of Marxist critical social theory, however, is the extent to which it has explored quite explicitly the relation between the practice of theory and the pursuit of interest. This was the basis of its critique of classical political economy. By contrast, the preoccupations of both holists and individualists with establishing methodologies appropriate to a scientific sociology led them to promote a concept of theory which was essentially abstract and general and, to that extent, divorced from routine, everyday social practices, no matter how exhaustively it sought to explain them. Marxism had its own version of social science – what came to be termed scientific socialism – which treated sociology as itself a form of critical theoretical practice. This has been termed subsequently (Althusser 1971) a science of social formations, committed to changing the social situation in which it was located through a revolutionary programme based upon a systematic inquiry designed to reveal and apply the historicist laws which ordered the dynamics of social processes. Indeed, it was partly in response to the revolutionary engagement of Marxist social theory that the sociologies of Durkheim and Weber developed their more abstract concepts of theory in terms of later, positivist conceptions of science. The social systems theory, referred to above, that had been developed by the middle of the twentieth century through attempts to synthesize these concepts of theory (Parsons 1937; 1951; Merton 1957; Demerath and Peterson 1967; Alexander 1987) had become increasingly abstract and disengaged from social practice. Inevitably therefore, new concerns have been developed in social theory which are oriented more directly towards the principal changes in the interactional practices of contemporary societies (Giddens and Turner 1987).

CONTEMPORARY ISSUES IN THE THEORY/PRACTICE DICHOTOMY: POSTSTRUCTURALISM, FEMINISM, MULTICULTURALISM AND POST-COLONIALISM

Whilst Marxism may provide an example of critically engaged theory, the new concerns of theory with contemporary social practices are not necessarily formulated in Marxist terms. However, some have in common with Marxism the need for theory to engage in a critique of existing social, political and economic institutional orders which are experienced by significant groups of their members as exploitative and oppressive. The reflexivity of critical theory requires that it addresses itself also to the issue of the extent to which theory has disguised its own ideological role in *legitimating* those orders, and this has led to a further concern in contemporary theory with its practice as **discourse**.

Two major examples of the concern of contemporary social theory with exploitation and oppression are its critiques of the traditions, first of *patriarchy*, the construction and perpetuation of gender inequality through the domination of women by men, and its problematic correlate of *sexism*, the reduction of explanation of human action to biological sexual determinants; and, secondly of *ethnocentricity*, the interpretation of the activities of different, often socially divided groups in terms of the ethnic culture of one, or a minority of them which is dominant over the others and the imposition of this interpretation over all others, and its problematic correlate of *racism*, the reduction of explanation of human action to determinants attributed to racial characteristics. These traditions have been criticized, respectively, by feminist and multiculturalist theoretical perspectives. Their development as core dichotomies in contemporary sociology are discussed elsewhere in the chapters 'Sex/Gender' and 'Race/Ethnicity'. But two general characteristics of the relation between contemporary theory and practice should be noted.

First, both feminist and multicultural theoretical perspectives are generated from the historical particularity of cumulative collective experiences of exploitation and oppression. These experiences have occurred both within and between different societies and cultures. Both theoretical perspectives are, therefore, essentially critical both of the *substantive social and cultural orders* which have generated them, and of the *institutional structure of power relations* through which they have been sustained. Secondly, as a result of this essential feature of critique, the two perspectives have generated both substantive topics and structural orientations which have redirected social theory in the late twentieth century away from the abstraction and over-generality of its traditional normative concerns.

Feminist theory has argued that contemporary social theory should be located on three new sites in particular: gender as a criterion of social division; the human body as a mode of non-verbal social and cultural expression; and structures of emotion and feeling as means of acquiring and expressing knowledge. To address gender as a form of social division is to make explicit, and thus accessible for criticism and change, the consequences of patriarchal history which privileges the interests of men over women as a matter of normative social institutional practice. In doing so, it exposes the implicitly ideological character of analyses of social division based upon class. Whether these analyses are orientated, like classical Marxism, to the revolutionary overthrow of industrial capitalism in favour of a classless society, or, like the liberal-conservative reformism of modern functionalism, to the amelioration of class conflict through the affluent egalitarianism that is supposedly characterized by a growing middle class, they remain unequivocally patriarchal. Feminist theory points out that to address social division exclusively in terms of class, however critically and with whatever revolutionary or reformist enthusiasm, leaves untouched the problems of inequality and exploitation of women sustained through patriarchy. Moreover, since patriarchal relations are in important respects economic relations between men and women, and are exploitative in refusing to recognize the full economic value of much of what is treated normatively as women's work (childcare and domestic housekeeping, for example), they are implicated in, and thus reinforce, the inegalitarian structure of the distribution of wealth which is a feature of capitalist political economy (Haraway 1991; Milner 1994).

To topicalize the body as a medium of expression is to focus on one fundamental site of patriarchal appropriation of female identity. Through the unremarked upon and unremunerated physical labours of childbirth, motherhood and domestic work, women's bodies have been used as a fundamental means of the social and cultural reproduction of patriarchy. This use has, in effect, been an expropriation of women's bodies by men. Informed by feminist theory, women's movements have acted in practice to reclaim power and identities through the exercise of choice in how to articulate their interests in and through their own bodies. The implications of this have contributed significantly to the burgeoning sociological concern with the body as a medium of expression (Turner 1984; Featherstone et al 1991; and Shilling 1993) and to the significance of the heterogeneity of human sexuality to social identity and personality (Fuss 1991; Giddens 1991; Weeks 1991).

The specifically differentiated character of feminist epistemology, with its emphases on the eroticism and sensuality of human feeling, has been developed, in important respects, in terms of the methodological concerns of poststructuralist theory, which is discussed in more detail in the chapter 'Modernity/Postmodernity'. This conjunction marked a reflexive turn in feminist theory, away from the critical sociological concern with the political economy of patriarchy, towards issues of feminist culture – specifically, with a distinctive feminist discourse. Rather than continuing to concern itself primarily with how patriarchy has pre-empted women's articulation of their experience as part of its structural positioning of them in subordinate social status and roles, poststructuralist feminist theory has deployed the method of **deconstruction** to address a different set of issues (Nicholson 1990). These are focused on the ways in which women as writers, readers, speakers of their own distinctive (non-masculine, anti-patriarchal) gendered languages have (re-)produced their own discursive culture of experiential texts as a resourceful articulation of their resistance to patriarchy (Spender 1980; Weedon 1987; Milner 1994). Among the several consequences for the theory/practice dichotomy in sociology of this feminist approach is the way it has addressed the problem of subjectivity. The resistant culture of feminism has been sustained not only in texts, but through the practices of resistance on which, often metaphorically, they reflect. This has produced a concept of personal identity in feminist theory which is fragmented – the consequence of the alienation of the expropriated subject in a socio-cultural structure of hostile domination.

In this respect, poststructuralist feminism has some concerns in common with **multiculturalist** theory. Just as modern Western societies have been distinctively and, until recently, for the most part unreflexively patriarchal and sexist in character, they have also been ethnocentric and racist. And the consequent phenomenon of personality fragmentation, which poststructuralist feminists argue has been experienced by women, has been experienced also by members of those populations which have been subjected to the economic exploitation and political domination of imperialism and colonialism. These practices have been legitimated invariably by epistemologically specious racist differentiations, grounded in the ethnocentrism of the imperializing/colonizing societies, which have asserted the innate superiority of white European over non-white, non-European physiology, consciousness, culture and social structure. Those individuals and groups subject to such racial domination in the USA developed what W.E.B. Du Bois (1868–1963) has termed double consciousness (Du Bois 1989), a concept which has been applied more recently by Gilroy (1993b) to analyse the multiple, fragmented identities of the Anglo-Caribbean/Afro-American diaspora that he terms the black Atlantic. In a parallel sense, following Said's (1978) analysis of Western conceptions of non-Western cultural identities, Spivak (1988) has identified one legacy of colonial subject constitution under capitalist imperialism, particularly in India, as the historically muted subaltern woman. Minh-ha (1989) has taken this deconstruction of the post-colonial, Third World female subject still further in arguing that she is constituted of infinite layers of identity differentiated by experience.

Multiculturalist theory has displaced the traditional sites of modern social theory, away from those of the dominant ethnocentric interests of Western industrial capitalist societies, by exposing the extent to which their development depended upon imperialism and colonialism. This displacement has produced a type of socio-cultural practice that has been termed post-colonial, and which is committed to a decentring of the dominant, concentric model of metropolitan European societal structure. **Post-colonialism** represents, instead, an inevitably uncentred, because diasporic, subversion of concentric metropolitan society by a structure of dispersed, peripheral groupings. Instead of a controlled heterogeneity of relatively uniformly structured subcultures, post-colonial society is multicultural in character and challenges the hegemonic historical narratives of globalism which have been developed as the postmodern equivalent of the historicist metanarratives of imperialism and colonialism (Ashcroft, Griffiths and Tiffin 1989; Adam and Tiffin 1991; Bhaba 1990). Both post-colonialist and multiculturalist theory are poststructuralist in character and are grounded, as is that of poststructuralist feminism, in the sustained, collective experience of subordination of self through the imposition of an identity as other – as subject to oppression. All three forms of contemporary theory show clearly the extent to which it is both dependent on, and necessary for, the reflexive ordering of the eclectic variety of interactional practices in the postmodern social world.

KEY CONCEPTS

THEORY   Theory is the realization and construction of the world in thought. The theoretical life is not simply one of contemplation for the anticipation is that theory constitutes changes in human conditions and particularly critical theory and action theory which are dedicated to the production of social change.

PRACTICE   Practice is seen as human intervention in the social process, a dynamic involvement and commitment on the part of people to change their circumstances. It is difficult to conceive of practice uninformed by theory, but also vice versa.

Methodology   The branch of sociological theory which is concerned with the most adequate and efficient ways of applying and testing theory in practice. It involves both the study of method against criteria of its adequacy as discourse and its application as a means of testing the explanatory claims of theory and their range of practical application.

Critique   The practice of formulating social theory which seeks not only to explain the structure and processes of the society(ies) to which it refers, but also to provide a diagnosis of its/their organizational and ethical shortcomings, a design for an alternative and a proposal of the changes required to implement it.

Legitimation   The practices by which a society justifies a particular order of institutional and interactional relations. These are routine practices for all societies and usually take a number of forms, such as a dominant set or system of beliefs, a set of statutes and their administration which regulate important (e.g. political and economic) relations, and a system for the reproduction of culture.

Ideology   A set of ideas, beliefs, values and concepts organized coherently into a persuasive account of the causes, conditions and directions of societies – often as important features of their cultures. Ideology has often been contrasted with theory, in senses in which the latter is tied to science for its meaning, on the grounds that whereas theory is concerned with *truthful* explanation, ideology offers explanations in terms of partial interests.

Reflexivity   A property of theory because it is an essential feature of language, reflexivity is that constitutive quality of language in use that resists its reduction to a medium of correspondence. Language not only describes what it refers to, but constitutes it reflexively. This is accomplished in terms of the user's intended meaning, the additional meaningful connotations that are available in the language through its cultural location, but which have not been intended, and the interpreter's selective understanding of the intended meanings and unintended connotations.

Holism An approach to sociological explanation that identifies its proper topic of inquiry as society as a whole, composed of interdependent and functionally reciprocal parts. Two significant consequences of this are, first, that it implies a socially determinist view of the individual as a product of society; and secondly, that societies are essentially conservative in developing recurrent institutional practices which are functionally necessary to their continued existence.

Individualism An approach to sociological explanation that, in contrast to holism, identifies its proper topic of inquiry as the individual member of society, conceived as a social actor in the Weberian sense – that is, whose actions take account of the actual or symbolic presence of others in the situations in which they occur. Societies, thus, are seen as the dynamic creations of individuals, despite the fact that the institutional structures through which societies are organized constrain individual freedom of action.

Discourse A term used by poststructuralists, especially Derrida and Michel Foucault (1926–84), to characterize a system of (usually verbal) semiotic practices of writing, reading and expressive and interpretive communicative exchange. Discursive interpretations are characterized by their explicit, reflexive attention to the ideological character endemic to the signs employed, and thus implied in the meanings which the signs are deployed to construct (Derrida 1978; Foucault 1972).

Deconstruction A method of interpretive reading of texts developed by the poststructuralist Jacques Derrida (1930–). It is based on a concept of language as decentred in the sense of not being dominated by a prescriptive set of preferred meanings. Reading of linguistic texts, therefore, is an exploration of the play of differences in the meanings reflexively available in the texts' constitutive words and the interrelations between them.

Multiculturalism A mode of contemporary social theory which conceptualizes late (or post-) modern societies as composed inevitably of a multiplicity of culturally differentiated groups. Many of these groups exist in a subversive relation to the traditional forms of societal domination and social order on the grounds of earlier experience of exploitation and oppression by or within them.

Postcolonialism A mode of contemporary social theory, closely related to multiculturalism, but focused initially and specifically on non-European societies which had been subjected to colonization and, more recently, modernization through the imposition of Eurocentric institutions and culture. These impositions were made by displacing the institutions and cultures of the indigenous peoples. With the ending of colonialism, which usually results from struggle, the formerly colonized society moves to recover its displaced institutions and culture – particularly its language and customs – and, in doing so decentres the imposed Eurocentrism.

Civil/Political

Fran Tonkiss

What sociologists commonly think of as 'society' has frequently been defined in contrast to another realm called the 'state'. The former is understood as a domain of *civil* activity – activity that is essentially private and freely chosen – while the latter is conceived as a *political* realm, concerned with public affairs and formal processes of government. Such a distinction between civil society and the **state** preoccupied the major theorists of modern society as new political structures emerged in Western Europe and North America after the mid seventeenth century. This chapter outlines the ways that the civil and the political have been conceptualized within modern social thought, and examines how a distinction between them has shaped such related conceptions as citizenship, power and rights.

The civil/political dichotomy raises questions about the precise limits and form of the relations, affiliations, structures and institutions which are grouped together under the rubric of 'society'. This term is often used to refer to the totality of interactions and institutions which individuals engage in on a collective basis. Theorists of civil society, however, wish to separate out those activities and associations in which people engage as 'free' or 'private' individuals, from those which concern their 'public' role as members of a political community. We might think about this as a split between a civil realm within which we govern ourselves, and a political realm in which we are governed by the state.

A separation between political and civil domains may be analysed in both a historical and a critical way. The first part of this discussion provides an overview of key approaches to this field dating from the mid seventeenth to the mid nineteenth century. As modern societies developed democratic political structures a number of theorists sought to delimit the proper role which the state should play in the lives of its citizens. They asked questions about the limits of political authority, and about the rights and liberties which were due to free citizens. While certain of these ideas may appear rather abstract or rooted in the political events of their time, theories of civil society helped mark out the space in which sociologists would later map the formation of society. In this sense, the assumption that it is possible to distinguish political from civil life, or that the state stands apart from and in contrast to society, has shaped sociological understandings of the social.

The later part of the discussion examines these assumptions in relation to more contemporary debates about **citizenship** and the nature of political power. There are two broad lines of argument to consider here, which problematize both sides of the core dichotomy. Firstly, these debates put into question the way in which 'politics' is defined. The civil/political split may itself may be seen as highly *political*, as it consigns an extended range of social relations and institutions (including the family, the workplace, the market and the church) to a 'private' realm of activity. Secondly, it is argued, the formal equality of citizenship may disguise deep inequalities within civil society. Such inequalities may prevent certain people from exercising their political rights in a free or informed way. Recent debates have sought to extend the definition of the citizen beyond formal legal and political rights, to consider how questions of citizenship might address power relations within civil society, whether these are economic in character or based on social divisions and differences.

These arguments bring a critical perspective to bear on conventional theories of civil society and the state. In particular, they reveal that the latter offer only a limited model of political agency, based on the person of the male citizen. However, such arguments also seek to move beyond critique, to think about social membership and political action in ways which transcend a simple civil/political split.

THEORIES OF CIVIL SOCIETY

Like many objects of sociological analysis, 'civil society' does not have an agreed definition. One of the difficulties in understanding a distinction between the civil and the political derives from the quite different ways in which various thinkers have understood 'civil society'. Common meanings may act as a guide here. At certain times civil matters are defined in contrast to religious ones, as in civil marriage ceremonies. At others, the 'civil' is contrasted to the military, as in civil defence or the term 'civilian'. The 'civil service' refers to those public departments which carry out the policies of elected governments, but are not themselves political in character. 'Civil law' is concerned with private rights, rather than with criminal or public offences. Perhaps most commonly, to be 'civil' means to be polite, agreeable, reasonable, *civilized*.

Broadly speaking, accounts of civil society have focused on two key realms, the economy and the household. However, the term extends to the range of associations and institutions which operate beyond the structures of the state – religious groups, the press, welfare and voluntary associations, schools, guilds, unions, campaigning organizations and so on. However defined, different theories of civil society have sought to delineate its relation to the formal political realm of the state. In the following sections, I consider classical approaches to civil society under three headings. Firstly, I examine those early thinkers who saw civil society in terms of a political community of male individuals. This group includes Hobbes, Locke and Rousseau. The second group comprises a diverse group of liberal theorists who made a more clear distinction between civil society as a realm of free association, and the state as a realm of public regulation. This group includes Paine, Ferguson and Tocqueville. Thirdly, I turn to the critique of civil society offered in the early work of Karl Marx. Marx understands civil society as a specific social form which emerges at a certain moment of historical development. In Marx's account civil society is both constituted by, and serves the interests of, bourgeois economic relations.

CIVIL SOCIETY AND POLITICAL COMMUNITY

Civil society appeared as a domain of enquiry in a period during which political structures in Europe and North America were rapidly reformed. Processes of democratization and the development of constitutional governments raised serious questions about the role and powers of the state in relation to its subjects. Whereas the absolutist state of the fifteenth to eighteenth centuries had concentrated authority in the hands of the sovereign (as exemplified by the absolutist monarchs of France in this period), changing state forms involved a more mutual relation between rulers and ruled based on new models of representation and citizenship.

The emergence of the modern constitutional and democratic state in Europe involved a questioning of the limits of political rule over free individuals. In what manner, and to what extent, may political authorities intervene in the workings of civil society and in the private activities of citizens? Constitutional forms, such as those established during the English Revolution (1640–88), placed clear limits on the scope and functions of state power. Central to constitutionalism is the principle that the state exists in order to protect and preserve the rights of its citizens, without infringing on the individual's freedom to act in their own interests.

Early conceptions of civil society in the liberal political philosophy of the seventeenth and eighteenth centuries see this in terms of a political community which is distinct from a state of nature. The civil and the political are at this stage viewed in terms of a formal unity, rather than a structure of opposition. For thinkers such as Hobbes, Locke and Rousseau, civil society refers to the contractual and formal arrangements by which adult men organize themselves as a community, subject to certain laws and restraints and in receipt of certain rights and securities. Hobbes's argument in *Leviathan* (1651) is that the state of nature which exists prior to the formation of human societies is one of fundamental and continual conflict: each person is in 'war' with all others for survival and power. The function of society is to place constraints on these 'natural passions' by organizing such fierce individual wills into a formal and general will. Each person gives up their rights and their freedoms to a sovereign political power, which offers its subjects protection, security and common defence. Civil society in this account is identical to the state and its system of laws.

Both Locke and Rousseau differ from Hobbes's model of civil society in that they locate political power with the body of men, rather than with the formal entity of the state. Locke, in his *Two Treatises of Government* (1690), sought to set constitutional limits on state power in a way which marked it off from the community of citizens. Whereas Hobbes invested authority with the state, Locke recognized the sovereignty of the people as a political community. Locke's work provides one of the central arguments for a set of constitutional 'checks and balances' which renders state power accountable and mediates relations between the state and civil society. Ultimate power rests with the people and the state rules only with their continuing consent. In Locke's account constitutional government rules in trust for and as the representative of the sovereign people, who may reclaim this power for themselves if the government fails properly to represent their interests.

Rousseau's work sustains a more clear distinction between the state and civil society. Like Hobbes, he sees civil society as emergent from a state of nature; unlike Hobbes he sees this natural state as one of essentially free and equal persons. The entrance into society may be conceived of as a 'social contract' between free individuals, where each gives up their individual wills in favour of the common will. For Rousseau, however, sovereignty remains indivisibly with the people. The state should be merely a formal expression of the popular will. Where state power extends its legitimate reach and 'enslaves' the free members of civil society, the latter must take power back for themselves. Rousseau's ideas, developed in *The Social Contract* (1762), were an important influence on revolutionary thinking in France and helped to shape the crucial notion of the 'citizen' as the member of the sovereign political community. This suspicion of state power as infringing on the sovereign rights of citizens is developed in the work of the second group of theorists under consideration here, who sought to demarcate the limits of state action at the boundaries of civil society.

CIVIL SOCIETY AND THE STATE: LIBERAL MODELS

One of the key thinkers to strictly mark off the state from society was Thomas Paine. In his *Rights of Man* (1791–2), Paine warns of the dangers of the political state, which should be an instrument of civil society, assuming a form of despotism over it. Paine views the state as a 'necessary evil' which exists to preserve social peace, but argues that its actions should be limited as far as possible. The best system is one where groups in civil society govern themselves, free from unnecessary intervention by the state. Paine was a radical and republican figure, whose critique of the constitutional monarchy in Britain made his ideas popular in North America and France.

Paine is sharply opposed to the Hobbesian idea that the political state represents a peaceful and civilized response to social conflict between individuals and groups, arguing that modern European societies were *uncivilized* to the extent that they concentrated power and privilege with the political apparatus of the state. Moreover, state tyranny underpinned injustice within the patriarchal household (for example, through property and inheritance laws), and within wider civil society, through unfair taxation and the defence of the rich. The state, in this account, becomes the *source* of social conflict, rather than its cure. A fierce advocate of the American Revolution, Paine argued that citizens must oppose state power wherever this threatens their civil liberties. All people were fundamentally equal, with equal rights and liberties. The proper form of the state was a minimal political body which governed on the basis of popular consent, and was grounded in certain fundamental civil rights such as freedom of speech, conscience and association.

Paine's ideas were based on a clear distinction between civil society and the state which was not evident in the work of Hobbes or Locke. These earlier thinkers saw the political community and civil society as being inseparable: the state, that is, was the formal expression of relations in civil society. For Paine, these realms were sharply delineated and mutually opposed. Human societies in Paine's view were naturally given to co-operation, free association and harmony, and only the most limited form of the state was required to govern this system. The state in this model becomes a simple administrative instrument in service to the spontaneous, natural and harmonious associations within civil society.

Such an emphasis on the forms of association which make up civil society is also evident in the work of the Scottish philosopher Adam Ferguson. Rather than focusing on the limits of state power, Ferguson examines the anatomy of civil society as an autonomous and complex realm. Ferguson differs crucially from earlier thinkers in arguing that civil society is not distinct from a state of nature. Human society is itself a *natural* arrangement. In *An Essay on the History of Civil Society* (1767) Ferguson dismisses the competing versions of the state of nature as a condition of either perpetual enmity (Hobbes) or essential equality (Rousseau), by remarking that people 'are to one another mutual objects both of fear and of love' (Section I, III). And these relations are always social. 'Society,' Ferguson writes, 'appears as old as the individual' (Section I, I); if a pre-social state of nature existed, 'it is a time of which we have no record, and in relation to which our opinions can serve no purpose, and are supported by no evidence' (Section I, I). Ferguson uses this argument as the basis for a study of civil societies throughout history and in different cultures, a project which can be viewed as one of the earliest exercises in comparative sociology.

Following Montesquieu's statement that 'Man is born in society and there he remains', Ferguson goes on, in a manner which appeals rather strikingly to modern social thinking, that 'Of all the terms that we employ in treating of human affairs, those of *natural* and *unnatural* are the least determinate in their meaning' (Section I, I, emphasis in original). To live in society is itself the natural state of human individuals. Furthermore, Ferguson does not view civil society as a set of formal relations and obligations which set constraints on human passions. Rather, civil society is the setting within which people's essential moral and social character can be positively realized:

> the experience of society brings every passion of the human mind upon its side. Its triumphs and prosperities, its calamities and distresses, bring a variety and a force of emotion, which can only have place in the company of our fellow-creatures. It is here that a man is made to forget his weakness, his cares of safety, and his subsistence; and to act from those passions which make him discover his force.

In depicting the political functions of the state Ferguson uses a language of 'liberties' rather than one of 'constraints'. Free nations, he writes, serve to protect the interests of their citizens and this security is considered a principal civil right (Part III, Section VI). In this context, liberties and rights are understood in a particular way. Ferguson recognizes that the concept of liberty and the proper means of securing it are subject to different interpretations. 'Liberty', that is, is seen as an essentially social concept, rather than simply a natural condition. Natural liberty consists in the freedom to act in any way one chooses, so long as this does not encroach on the freedom of others. Systems of law are developed in order to protect people from such infringements within a social framework. Specifically, the law exists to protect the citizen's property, life and liberty from the actions of others.

In addition to *civil* liberties relating to one's property, person and individual freedom, the state enshrines certain *political* rights. These promise the citizen a political and legal status and a share in the government of their society. Ferguson offers a pluralist model of civil society comprising diverse and often antagonistic interest groups. The more that 'every order of the people' has been included in the political and legal process, the more 'fortunate' is the nation. In a society made up of various classes and orders, of numerous parties and associations, each group must defend its own claims within the political realm. In this context, the system of law may rightly be thought of as a 'treaty' between different interests, which secures social peace by taking into account and settling their competing claims. Ferguson argues that justice resides not merely in the system of laws, but in the popular powers which lie behind it and on whose support the law depends. The protection of property and the person, as well as the political rights of representation, should not be left simply to the rule of law, but must be secured and strengthened by active participation in public life – by 'the vigour and jealousy of a free people' (Part III, Section VI).

Such arguments about pluralist political democracy are developed by the later thinker Alexis de Tocqueville. In *Democracy in America* (1835/40) Tocqueville makes an interesting move in examining the forms of despotism which can emerge within democratically elected governments. Tocqueville argues that political power must be dispersed and limited in important ways. Governments must be subject to regular elections. Executive and judiciary powers (that is, the government and the legal system) must be clearly separated, so that the system of justice operates independently from the interests of the government of the day. Tocqueville requires an active and mature form of citizenship: formal political representation is not enough. Like Ferguson, Tocqueville calls for the participation of the citizen *within* the institutions of the state – for example in the jury system, where citizens' judgements of their peers are guided by a notion of how they themselves would wish to be judged. Whereas Ferguson takes his examples from Roman and English law, Tocqueville refers to the jury system in the United States. Tocqueville is interesting, furthermore, in anticipating the bureaucratic modern society which was to preoccupy Weber's social theory. The extension of the regulatory powers of public institutions into the domains of policing, health, education and business produces a kind of administrative 'torpor' in civil society. His argument is for more vigorous and self-governing civil associations and the preservation and extension of this realm of freedom from state intervention.

CIVIL SOCIETY AND THE STATE: MARX'S MODEL

Classical views of civil society tend to be marked by a deep naturalism. While all of the thinkers that have been discussed so far were profoundly influenced by the concrete political circumstances in which they wrote – the English Revolution (Hobbes and Locke), the *ancien régime* in France

(Rousseau), the American and French Republics (Paine, Tocqueville) – their responses to these social contexts were framed in terms of a 'natural condition' of human social life, which was by definition timeless. If many societies *currently* took the form of a despotic state system, to take the example of Paine's argument, this was in conflict with the natural harmony of civil society. While these thinkers varied in the way they defined civil society and the mechanisms through which it should be secured, they commonly grounded their different conceptions in ideas about the natural and therefore universal condition of 'man'. The single exception to this rule is Adam Ferguson – strikingly modern in dismissing the distinction between 'natural' and 'unnatural' in relation to human societies.

A quite different argument appears in the works of the German philosophers Hegel and Marx. Hegel argues in the *Philosophy of Right* (1821), and Marx follows his lead, that civil society is a construct that appears at a specific stage of historical development. It represents a distinctly modern sphere, which is located between the domains of the household and the state. Civil society in Hegel's account comprises the economy, civil law, organized social classes, welfare associations, religious institutions and so on. For Hegel, the role of the modern state is to unify and transcend the conflicts of private interest within civil society and in this way realize a true political community. The crucial difference between Hegel's theory and that of Hobbes, for example, lies in the idea that the universal state represents a specifically *modern* moment in historical development and, what is more, a perfection of social forms through the triumph of reason in political affairs.

Marx follows Hegel in conceiving civil society as a historical construct which emerged in modern Europe in the eighteenth and nineteenth centuries. Such a move opens up a valuable political space for Marx, in shifting civil society from the realm of natural order to one in which it might be historically analysed and contested. Marx was extremely critical of the distinction between state and civil society, on the grounds that it supposed a split between a limited political community and a private and selfish realm of individual conduct. Marx's theory of civil society is developed through a rigorous critique of Hegel's *Philosophy of Right*. Marx wished to dissolve the distinction between political community and civil society not in order to realize a universal form of the state, but so as to demolish both conceptions entirely.

Marx develops these ideas in a series of early writings in which he was still deeply engaged with contemporary German debates and philosophy, in particular in his work of 1843: the critique of Hegel and the journal article, 'On the Jewish Question', where he intervenes in a debate over the Christian state in Germany (Marx 1977). In these pieces, Marx argues that modern bourgeois society is distinctive in effecting a separation of political and civil life which was absent in feudal society. Under feudalism, for example, the domains of work and household did not constitute some sort of private sphere of activity, but were fully integrated into a political structure of estates and corporations. The interests of any person were tied into those of the associations to which they belonged (Tester 1992).

Bourgeois civil society appears in the modern context as a sphere of private interests and rights. At the centre of this conception is the notion of the individual as one who possesses certain political rights and who otherwise acts freely in an economic sphere which is organized by private interests. This division of the political state from civil society is less an enduring or universal structure, and more a product of a historical process of class struggle in which the bourgeois class gains ascendancy over a feudal order. Rather than representing a system of natural liberty where men can go freely about their private business unfettered by the activities of the state, bourgeois civil society is marked by deep class divisions. For Marx, civil society is shaped by unequal relations of production: its sole freedoms are the bourgeois freedoms to buy and sell, its only rights the bourgeois rights of private property.

This account of civil society as a class order based on production, rather than a natural order based on human freedom, leads Marx to produce a rather different theory of the state from earlier liberal theorists. Whereas the state had been seen as a desirable force for order or a necessary evil, Marx sees the modern state as a system of political and legal mechanisms which are designed to protect the economic interests of the bourgeois class. Instead of representing a set of constraints on people's private interests and impulses, Marx argues that the capitalist state serves to secure and promote the interests of capital. The nature of the state is to be grasped in terms of the material conditions which are present in civil society, not in a study of the law or in discourses of political philosophy.

This model of the state is quite different from that of Hobbes or Locke and departs radically from that of Hegel in rejecting the idea that the state is a separate and an independent entity from civil society, let alone a rational and universal form that perfects a fragmented and conflictual private sphere. For Marx civil society is based on the system of private property, and the state functions as the political form of bourgeois authority in order to preserve property rights. In this view, other institutions and collectivities within civil society – such as families, guilds, churches and associations of various kinds – are simply reducible to (or diversions from) the logic of capitalist social relations.

'Civil society' in this conception is largely equated to the sphere of private economic activity undertaken by atomistic individuals. In seeking to preserve this realm from state intervention, argues Marx, theorists and advocates of civil society serve only to preserve the economic arrangements through which the bourgeoisie assumes domination over the proletariat. The distribution of wealth in capitalist society is fundamentally unjust; consequently, a properly free society would require a new division of property. The existence of the state as an independent entity grants certain individuals the formal equality of citizenship, while disguising the unequal (and ultimately more meaningful) economic relations within civil society.

The grounding of Marx's theory of state and civil society in class relations made him very sceptical of democratic reform. Campaigns of universal suffrage – claiming the rights of all adult men (and, later, adult women) to vote – the struggles for a free press, or the right to join a trade union, were seen by Marx as ultimately rather cosmetic reforms in capitalist society. A democratic state was not enough: real democratization had to occur at the level of civil society through the negation of unequal class relations. Indeed, the democratic reform of the state might only serve, through an illusory language of 'citizenship', to disguise the fundamentally unequal material relations in society.

Marx's contribution to debates about state and civil society is an extremely important one. In particular, the shift to a perspective which sees civil society as a historical form rather than a universal condition opens up room for rigorous sociological analysis as well as political critique. However, Marx's perspective may be criticized on the grounds that it reduces relations in civil society to economic ones. In arguing that civil society is structured by relations of production, Marx underplays the importance of other associations and institutions, social movements and corporations which are not political in a formal sense and are not wholly circumscribed by economic forms. Examples of these might include pressure groups and campaigns, clubs and institutions, a free press, reform movements, charities and voluntary associations. The structure of civil society, that is, can be seen as rather more complex than that offered by a simple model of class.

NEW DEFINITIONS, CONTEMPORARY DEBATES

The range of classical ideas on civil society and state power which have been considered in this discussion constitute and problematize a civil/political dichotomy in various ways. There are nonetheless some common grounds for critique. The discussion in this final section takes up two broad lines of argument. Firstly, it is argued that the customary model of state and civil society simplifies the manner in which political power is organized in modern liberal societies. Secondly, I examine the different sorts of 'rights' which citizenship may involve, and how these might affect people's access to equal civil and political status.

Mapping power and defining politics

A simple split between civil society as a private sphere of activity, and the state as a public sphere of regulation, produces a rather limited understanding of what constitutes 'politics'. It does this in two ways. It tends to simplify, firstly, the complex organization of state power and to neglect the networks of regulation which are established 'below' the level of the state. Secondly, it overlooks the *political* nature of many relations and associations within civil society, both as sites of repression and as sites of resistance.

If civil society has been generally conceived as a complex and diverse realm of interaction and organization, the state as its 'other' has too often appeared as a monolithic structure. Sovereign in its authority, drowsy with bureaucracy, the state in such a conception represents the central site of political power in society. However, this depiction gives too little weight to the complexities of state power, and to the way it links up with private forms of regulation. The modern state is not simply a massive 'leviathan' but is made up of a plethora of actors and institutions. Networks of public power extend through the fields of welfare, education and health, as well as through the military, the law and government. State power may be experienced at certain moments as benign, for example in the protection of individual rights under the law or the provision of welfare; and at others as quite brutal, as in the suppression of dissent or the harsh treatment of 'aliens'.

The limits of the state, which in an era of privatization are increasingly hard to define, do not in any case represent the limits of power. Within civil society, networks of employers, doctors, accountants, lawyers, teachers, planners, psychiatrists and other 'experts' trace diverse patterns of regulation and control. While the influence of such figures is frequently organized within a legal framework, and in this way underpinned by the authority of the state, they do not represent 'political' or even public agents in any formal sense. If I rent my house from a private landlord, the terms of our economic arrangement are governed by a bundle of legislation. The rather powerful position my landlord occupies in relation to me as a tenant derives from a mesh of economic and legal relations which are neither public nor wholly private, neither civil nor clearly political in character.

Such questions as to where power resides are linked to another set of questions about how 'politics' should be defined. A number of critics have argued that the political/civil distinction is based on a false claim that the private or social realm is somehow non-political. One of the most important lines of argument here involves a feminist assertion that activities in the 'private' realm of the family and gender relations are profoundly political in character (see Bock and James 1992). Such an observation has led to changes at the level of the state – for example, through the development of equal opportunities legislation, the provision of public nursery education, or (as in the early 1990s in the UK) the criminalization of rape within marriage. Within classical conceptions of the civil and the political, this form of state intervention into the private realm of the family was both barely thinkable and largely unwelcome.

A recognition that the spaces of civil society may also be sites of political power joins up with an argument that the boundaries of the state, and formal democratic processes, do not determine the field of political struggle. New social movements based on protest, demonstration and direct action in part reject the procedures and effectiveness of representative government for bringing about social change. For example, environmental movements may have as their aim changes in government policy – through the closure of nuclear power stations, controls on car emissions, or the scrapping of public road-building programmes – but may seek to influence policy through direct action and campaigning. The space of political action is not confined to the ballot-box and the parliamentary chamber, but is to be found in the streets, in public squares, on billboards, along (and over) perimeter fences.

The 'rights' of citizenship

One of the most important criticisms to be levelled at classical theories of civil society concerns the definition of a 'citizen'. Civil society has traditionally been understood, and in quite specific ways, as a community of *men*. An observation that the language of sovereignty and citizenship has either explicitly or through processes of exclusion left women out (see Lloyd 1984) opens onto a wider set of questions about the limits of political rights and **civil liberties**. How should these be defined and who do they include? While women were formerly excluded from citizenship, can it be said that all men enjoyed common rights as citizens? If citizenship has been a partial and often exclusive form of social membership, how might it be extended and deepened? How might we understand ourselves as citizens today?

Debates about citizenship have in recent years assumed an important place in political life, not least because of the efforts of post-communist states to develop and articulate the institutions and liberties of civil society such as political parties, a free press and freedom of conscience (see Keane 1988a; 1988b). In the context of Britain, whose political arrangements provided the setting for the philosophies of Hobbes and Locke, the lack of a written constitution and the endurance of monarchy raise questions as to whether a British person can be considered a citizen in a modern and mature sense, or whether they simply remain the subject of a sovereign power (Hall 1995).

The division between civil society and the state is in part mediated by distinct but interlinked civil liberties and political rights (a distinction especially evident in the works of Paine and Ferguson). Civil liberties (or *civil rights*) concern the rights of the individual in a free society: these are commonly taken to include freedom of speech, freedom of conscience, freedom of movement and association, freedom to own and possess property, and justice before the law. *Political rights*, on the other hand, concern the individual's participation within public life. In modern democracies these include the right to join a political party and to stand for public office, as well as the primary right to vote. These rights form the basis of the citizen's reciprocal relation with the state. In return for the establishment and the protection of their rights, the citizen is obliged to obey the law, to pay taxes to the state, and at times to undertake jury duty or military service.

These civil and political rights, enshrined within the constitutional state, establish the formal equality of citizens. What is more, they mark the boundaries of a shared political community which excludes various categories of person. While the legal status of the citizen is highly meaningful to someone under threat of deportation, it is necessary to question the limits of meaningful citizenship in everyday life. The influential work of Marshall (1950) argued that the necessary conditions for active and equal citizenship extended beyond civil and political rights to *social rights*. His definition of such social rights was broad, but included as a minimum a degree of economic security and welfare, education and a share in a common culture. These rights might be secured through social policy measures. Marshall held that a chief good of the postwar welfare state in Britain was the provision of the social rights which were necessary for people to enjoy the full political rights of citizenship. The state education system produced knowledgeable and informed individuals, while public housing, welfare and health provisions allowed people to participate fully in society as independent actors. In such an account, political measures are employed so that people are enabled to realize their rights as independent citizens. It is evident that a debate on the nature of political citizenship cannot exclude an account of those conditions which prevent different groups and individuals from exercising their rights in an active or equal manner. Marx made this point in relation to economic inequality, but the constraints on meaningful citizenship are not confined to this realm.

Such a conception of social rights opens up the debate on citizenship to take into account the questions which early modern philosophies of civil society tended to exclude. A whole set of material conditions may prevent a person from actively exercising their political rights as citizens. Different people, furthermore, are empowered as citizens in ways which are shaped by their material circumstance, by their mental and physical health, by their age, and by the gender and race relations in which they are placed. For example, differential rights of citizenship are especially clear in the case of lesbian women and gay men, who in many liberal democracies do not possess the same legal status as do heterosexual people (see Evans 1993). The arena of rights is a highly contested one. Do the rights of the citizen extend to the right to a job? If I have a job, do I have the right to strike? Should all women have the right to receive an abortion? At what point does the racist's right to freedom of expression impinge on the rights of the black citizen?

CONCLUSION

These sorts of question appear at the interface between the civil and the political. Social theorists have become quite used to critically examining the dualisms around which sociology and related disciplines have been organized. Such ways of carving up the world have generally had to work quite hard to maintain the divisions which they institute, and to categorize people accordingly. However, the civil/political dichotomy has always been a rather self-conscious one, uncertain of the (divided) ground on which it stands. Liberal forms of government have involved continual deliberation over the proper limits of political authority and the claims of individual freedoms and civil liberties. This boundary between the civil and the political continues to be contested and mutable. Rather than dissolving it altogether, it is possible to use this line of division as the basis for redrawing the map of the political, particularly in terms of politicizing the private realms of economy and society and rethinking the rights of the citizen.

KEY CONCEPTS

CIVIL Sociologists are not always clear about the distinctions they draw between economic, social and political relations. As ideas about the changing relationship between the state, the economy and wider society change so also do views about the civil society. Traditionally the social, symbolic and normative aspects of everyday life constitute the civil society while the rest falls under political economy.

POLITICAL The political realm is that which brings social relations into focus but specifically in terms of their direction, control, management and adjustment to the demands of the state. The social is rarely, if at all, ever apolitical but the politics are not always those mediated by state and party.

State States have varied through history but the modern state is a collection of institutions including the legislature, the executive, the judiciary, central and local administration, the police and the armed forces. The state acts as the institutional system of political domination and can exercise the legitimate use of power.

Citizenship Citizenship describes membership of a state with the concomitant rights and responsibilities. Citizens are not natural but definitely cultural and peculiarly culturally specific. Citizenship speaks of the intense relationship that exists between the individual and the central administration of power within his or her society.

Civil liberties   These are rights that are bestowed upon citizens who are fully membershipped into the state through taxation, franchise and lawful obedience. There are also rights that are contingent upon responsibilities. They vary from state to state: see for example, freedom of speech.

Active/Passive

Chris Jenks

This chapter will introduce you to the debate that exists between sociologists over how they imagine that people are motivated to act in the social world. This can take the form of an active perspective, where it is supposed that people exercise free will and choice, or a passive perspective, where it is supposed that human action is organized by social pressures and constraints that are not of the individual's choosing. In considering the active perspective the chapter will also introduce you to a particular kind of sociological theory called 'symbolic interactionism' and compare it with 'systems theory' and 'structural functionalism'; these approaches are explained more fully in other chapters. Sociologists are involved in a very complex world which is the world of human action. This means that the very thing that they set out to explain and understand, namely how and why human beings behave in the ways that they do once they are members of groups, is itself always emerging, that it is full of meaning and that it carries with it people's choices and their values. Whereas many of the natural sciences investigate things, or phenomena, that are relatively constant, like the geologist's rocks and strata, the physicist's waves and particles, the chemist's elements and combinations of substances, and the mathematician's numbers, sets and forms, the social scientist is confronting a world made up of meaning which changes through time, or history, and according to its different cultural space or location. Now although the activities of natural scientists are by no means as straightforward as my simple sketch might suggest, there is a significant difference in the quality of social phenomena like families, social class, gender, power and ideology, for example, as opposed to rocks, numbers or whatever. Social phenomena have a meaning before sociologists investigate them, they are already 'social', whereas natural phenomena are inactive and meaningless until scientists agree to name them and investigate them. Gravity may have always existed as a constant force in relation to the world but it did not become part of our reality and part of our ways of making sense until Isaac Newton 'discovered' it as a pain in the head, and gravity has never 'known' about itself. Men and women, however, have always 'known' that there is a difference between them; all men and women in all societies have always 'known' that some people are more or less powerful than themselves; and all people 'know' that they are closer to their family than to friends, acquaintances or strangers.

Now the point of this explanation of the differences between social and natural sciences is not to suggest that either has a simpler or more difficult task but to show that they each employ different methods for understanding their chosen worlds, or phenomena. This leads us to our current dichotomy, that between the active and the passive. The active and the passive refer to what sociologists call 'models of the actor'. They are an important, but often undisclosed, component in a sociologist's method. We no longer think of sociological explanation in terms of a naive naturalism or a correspondence theory between what is said and what actually exists; what we look towards is some idea of the theorist's place or responsibility for building social worlds.

In order to best typify the distinction between active and passive models of the actor I shall compare and contrast conventional structural sociology and its theoretical grounds with the assumptions that ground the theory of symbolic interactionism. So what we are looking at here, from two different perspectives, are instances of social methodologies generated in relation to perspectives on human conduct. These perspectives find themselves articulated in social theory through different accounts of 'social control' and 'socialization'.

Aaron Cicourel (1964), when writing about the problems that arise in establishing appropriate forms of method and measurement in sociology, states that 'any attempt at theory or any views on method and measurement in sociology presuppose a certain view of the actor' and he demonstrates this through a review and analysis of different methodologies, like participant observation and content analysis, within sociology. A major point of his thesis is that the initial conception of the actor predisposes the character and form of the subsequent theorizing.

Dennis Wrong (1961), writing particularly about Parsonian systems theory and structural functionalism, which he considered to be the dominant and overwhelming theoretical perspective of that period of the 1950s and 1960s, describes the predisposition of such thinking as being organized in terms of an 'oversocialized conception of man'. By this he means that Parsons's somewhat cybernetic way of supposing that actors' conduct is highly and narrowly determined by the universal and fixed constraints of a social system implies that if such individuals approximate the way that we live in real social life then, far from being free agents, we are rather very rigidly coerced, determined and programmed through our **socialization**, that is, our induction into the rules, the norms and the folkways of modern society. Clearly, Wrong is saying, such 'oversocialized' actors appear to have lost, abandoned or been deprived of the important elements of choice and free will in the world as designed by Parsons. In Parsons's social system it is generally predicted that the limits of the system are the limits of action. What Parsons is generating here, in terms of our original dichotomy, is a passive model of the actor brought about through strict and inflexible views on social control and individual socialization. Rather than choosing and evaluating a situation, the actor within the Parsonian world always behaves or, we might even say, reacts under constraint. Although systems theory and structural functionalism were certainly dominant styles of sociological reasoning for an extended period, and thus the predominant model of the actor in sociology was a passive one, other alternatives do exist and have come to figure largely within modern sociology.

If we view the body of work within the tradition of sociology we will find that although the typical models of the actor exist, in reality, along a spectrum, the two predominant conceptions of the active and the passive have established a formal dichotomy. Any review of the range of theories within our discipline would show that, in general terms, sociologists have tended to focus on either one or the other of these two positions, almost exclusively, for empirical and conceptual reasons. This state of affairs has to some extent given rise to a semblance of an almost sectarian fission in the form of the development of two schools of thought. Active and passive are not equivalent to but do equate with the dichotomy between agency and structure, and in a different context the dichotomy between the philosophies of idealism and materialism.

Instancing this very issue, linking models of the actor with theories of action and philosophies of being, Alan Dawe (1970) suggests that in essence there are 'two sociologies'. The two predominant modes of sociology derive from two distinct social doctrines coming out of the Enlightenment. The first of these he refers to as the 'doctrine of order', which gives life to the sociology of structural functionalism and systems theory and which is committed to treating social action as being derivative of the system or social structure. The second he refers to as the 'doctrine of control', which provides the basis for the sociology contained within an action frame of reference; in this instance we have the mode of theorizing which views social systems and social structures (in whatever form) as the emergent products or depositions of social interaction.

Cicourel, whom we referred to earlier, acknowledges both the active and the passive perspectives within sociology and says that they can be identified more readily as the traditions of 'socio-psychological' sociology and 'classical' sociology, respectively – which I shall, in a short while, compare in the form of 'symbolic interactionism' and 'structural sociology'. Cicourel, unlike Dawe, goes on to suggest that both forms of theorizing stem, in fact, from the same origin; that is, the Hobbesian problem of order. It was Thomas Hobbes's view that the natural disposition of humankind was antagonistic, self-centred and self-seeking, such that if left to their own devices human beings would bring about, inevitably, a war of 'all against all'. Hobbes's solution was to place the control of human action and destiny into the hands of the state, which he symbolized in terms of the ancient mythical giant called 'Leviathan' – the title of his major work. Cicourel expands this original problem and suggests that the problem of order can be negotiated by individuals being constrained from above (passivity) or electing to control themselves by, as it were, contracting into the rules of the society (active). In this way Cicourel sees the problem not so much as a binary choice but as an issue of levels – the levels that modern sociology often refers to as the 'macro' (structure) and the 'micro' (interaction). His work then seeks to link the levels of analysis, while conceding that little other work has been done to demonstrate the relationship between the two levels: he recommends that we might initially describe the measurement problems that arise in attempting to operationalize either or both levels.

Let us now treat these two levels as a binary opposition, that is to say that they are competitive and divergent from one another: this is a more common view in sociology. In this way we can indicate both the strengths and weaknesses and also the appeal of the symbolic interactionists' position (as an active perspective) by showing its distance and difference from more structurally oriented sociologies.

Structural sociologies, like systems theory and structural functionalism, are those which operate, in the broadest terms, with a passive conception of the human actor. Their primary object of analysis is not the individual so much as the totality: they begin with a concern for the wholeness of a society rather than its particular parts. Because of this structural sociologies, those with a passive perspective, start off by arguing that it is social structures or abstract social systems that cause people to act in the way that they do, and similarly they end up explaining the purpose of people's action in terms of what it contributes to, or indeed how it maintains, the social structure or social system. This is partly what Durkheim had in mind when he said that the social should always be explained in terms of the social.

As you might imagine from this passive perspective, if it is supposed that the structure dominates and dictates action then any theory concerning how people learn to act in a social way is highly deterministic: this is what Wrong, whom we looked at earlier, meant by 'oversocialization'. Socialization, within the passive model, is thus treated as a process of 'absorbing', or 'internalizing', or 'programming': it certainly always indicates a forcible pattern of necessary learning for the social actor. As you will remember, in the social world described by Durkheim the actor is socialized and subsequently guided in his or her conduct by the compulsion of the 'social facts'. Similarly the actor in Parsons's social system cannot be seen to be adult or rational until they have internalized the central value system, that is the dominant set of ideas that bind all people's behaviour together into a uniformity. Strangely enough then, sociological theories that operate with a passive perspective have great difficulty in explaining childhood or even adolescence because they assume that everybody is either a competent member of a society or a deviant of some sort. Structural sociologies tend therefore to be populated with readily constituted, competent adult members who embody the needs of the social system. Another feature of socialization within a passive perspective is, as a consequence of the above, that it is well regimented, fairly rapid, and once and for all.

If we look now at an active model of the actor, such as is contained within the theory of symbolic interactionism, then we find a very different set of assumptions. Within the active model, instead of viewing people as if they were constantly determined and prey to the constraint of external factors, here we find the individual actor occupying central stage. This factor is heavily emphasized within the theory: the social actor is treated not as a 'puppet' but as a 'self'. From this framework the practice of socialization takes on a very different significance. Rather than being seen as a necessary but deflecting process it is regarded as absolutely central to the interactionist's concerns, and far from being regarded as a transitory stage it is seen rather as a perpetual and self-renewing process within social life. Adopting an active perspective, the individual is considered to be routinely and yet regularly involved in the practice of engaging in new interactional situations and thus learning as he or she lives. The dual ideas that socialization is ongoing or lifelong, and that the point of continuous interactional exchanges is to successfully negotiate their outcome with other actors, point to the twin theoretical origins of symbolic interactionism itself, namely 'evolutionism' and 'pragmatism'. The conceptualization of socialization as being a continuous or lifelong process has given rise to what the interactionists call 'adult socialization': this is one of their central concepts which appears in many of their studies, particularly their studies of occupations, some of which we shall look at later.

The origins of the symbolic interactionist tradition are to be found in a variety of sources, most notably in the works of Charles Cooley, William Thomas and James Baldwin in the USA, and independently in the works of Georg Simmel and Weber's rational *verstehen* sociology in Germany. Clearly, however, the most significant and comprehensive formulation of the position, in the explicit form of symbolic interactionism, is to be found in the collected papers of the American social psychologist George Herbert Mead, the collection appearing under the title of *Mind, Self and Society*. This body of thought has given rise to the large and flourishing American tradition of symbolic interactionism, spreading mostly through the research and teaching of a group of scholars at the University of Chicago (which is why it is often referred to as the Chicago School) such as Everett C.

Hughes, Herbert Blumer, Howard Becker, Anselm Strauss, Irving Goffman, Blanche Geer, Arnold Rose and Julius Roth.

If we look, for a moment, at the major contribution provided by Max Weber to what we are describing as an active perspective we can see that it was he who most forcefully stressed the absolute uniqueness of human behaviour, but also he whose work systematically advised that the key to understanding society as a whole lay in a detailed understanding of the typical features of individual human action. So, for Weber, the prime concern of sociological investigation is the explanation of meaningful social behaviour. This meaningful behaviour – meaningful in the sense of being intentional or having a purpose – is what has come to be properly referred to as 'social action'. Following Weber, what sociologists mean by social action is human conduct that has a subjective meaning, indeed a motive, for the individual actor.

Resting on this assumption, a sense of rationality is supposed to be active within human conduct. We think about our concerns, problems, values or needs and then act in ways that we have considered to best achieve the ends that we have appointed ourselves. So we are not talking about animal instinct or stimulus–response kneejerk reactions, but about human, rational action. This rationality, for Weber and the active theorists who follow his inspirations, is descriptive of human action but also a continuous and developing feature of that action itself. Now, if we put these ideas in the context of the dichotomy that we started off with, the active/passive, then we can say that within this perspective individuals are not conceptualized as passive objects that are merely reacting under constraint. On the contrary, what we are offered here is an overwhelming concern with human decision-making and human purpose. Within an active perspective what is paramount is the idea of conscious, thinking subjects, actually planning and carrying out courses of action. We could say that, unlike with the passive perspective where people live in a world ordered and controlled by material forms, by objectivities, here the subjective dimension is in the ascendant.

Within the active perspective our theoretical attention is directed from a concern with global explanations to local explanations, from generalities to particularities, from social totalities or structures to individuals. To put that another way we could say that adopting an active model of the actor requires that we theorists should eschew the monolithic structures or systems that began and ended explanation for the passive model and which were supposed to determine the lives of the puppets or prisoners who supposedly populated them. From the active perspective we should cease to construct what Harold Garfinkel has referred to as 'cultural dopes', that is actors who are apparently directed by the rules of a society that they seemingly do not understand, or what Ralph Dahrendorf (1973) has described as *Homo sociologicus*, that is an actor who is essentially comprised of the bundle of role expectations that the sociologist has projected onto him. The overall message is clear: within the active model of the actor our explanations tend to veer away from unidirectional causality, from the singular determinism and inevitable reductionism of structural sociology.

Symbolic interactionism therefore directs us to address individual actors, but not individuals in isolation as this is a sociological not a psychological theory. Individuals are our topic, but individuals as they relate to one another in the process of interaction. More specifically we might say that the source of interest for interactionism is individuals united in an inter-subjective web or network of meaning: this is a much looser, more fluid and potentially changeable concept than that of a social structure. If we remind ourselves that we are now thinking within an active perspective, one concerned with choice and decision-making, we can then anticipate that any social phenomenon, indeed any social situation, will have potentially different meaning and significance for different individuals. That is, we can anticipate that different actors' interpretations of a situation will vary for a whole spectrum of reasons like, for example, their value systems, belief systems, age, gender, class, nationality, education, interests or even according to where they are standing. The sociality of these different individuals resides in the symbolism, the shared signs or meanings, that contrives to unite them within a more or less coherent definition of the situation of which they are a part.

We might say that the interactionists would argue that to generalize about the constituent features of a society's social structure, like its educational system, its occupational system, its system of stratification and so on, in the way that structural functionalism or systems theory would, is to ignore the basic face-to-face mechanisms of social life. In other words, abstract talk and theorizing about systems and structures fails to recognize the startlingly obvious fact that people practically, or concretely, construct meaningful worlds on a person-to-person, day-to-day basis. Structural sociology with its passive perspective fails to recognize or pay sufficient attention to the significance and importance of ordinary everyday people's ability to attach symbolic meanings to things in their world, to other people in their world, and to the action of themselves and other people in that world. The active perspective seeks for an understanding of the basis of social organization in people's obvious and perceived capacity to manage and control their own circumstances. Any individual, or social actor, demonstrates his or her ability to exercise control by the way in which they assess a situation and then place a definition upon that situation. This is not usually a wholly wilful or capricious activity – we cannot choose to define a block of flats as a banana – but some propagandists might have us believe that a dictatorship is a democracy. The point here is that there are certain social conventions – red lights are always perceived as red and therefore indicating warning or stop – but within and also beyond these conventions people are very powerful in controlling and defining their particular situation. Max Weber, in his essays on sociological method, says

267

that the world could be almost anything, it is infinite in its possibilities, but human beings ensure that it is always something and thus produce its stability by defining it and thus exercising control over it. So by defining a situation an actor generates his or her own possibilities, and by so defining that same actor is also exercising control and creating and reproducing the social conditions of control in interaction with other actors.

Meaning, within an active perspective, derives from interpersonal interaction, and it is from this context that the experience of social life as orderly also derives. Actors are not constrained by the search for meaning and thus order at the level of social structure. Actors are not visualized as guessing, or aspiring towards, or acting as automatons in relation to central values or societal norms. In as much as such standards exist they are treated as emerging out of the negotiation and agreement that occurs within interaction. Actors then, are given the responsibility and autonomy of acting according to their own understanding of social life: they are not treated as pawns within a theorist's structural framework. As we have stated before, within the context of conventional sociological terminology, the level of analysis has shifted from the 'macro' to the 'micro', and from the supposed and unavailable to the actual and the available.

So, let us reiterate the two dichotomous positions. The passive model of the actor, contained within structural sociology, takes an idea of a total society as its primary reality, that is, it moves off from a belief in a social reality that has an organic structure to which all individuals, who are members of that society, are subordinate. Society, from this perspective, is treated as a unitary and coherent organization which, for the purposes of analysis within structural functionalism or systems theory, can be broken down into its interrelated constituent parts. Thus when analysing a particular society one might look at the different institutions, the essential relations between them, and their total functional contributions to the maintenance of the society as a whole. However, when analysing different societies and comparing them, each particular society would be seen in terms of its different level of systems development, just like comparing the heights or weights of growing children: thus such sociology develops a language of 'simple' and 'complex' societies, or 'developed' and 'underdeveloped' societies. Beyond this, the more 'advanced' societies, with their functioning systems, are spoken about in terms of their 'convergence', clearly implying an increased tendency towards similarity at the 'macro' level of systems development.

In contradistinction, the active perspective entreats us to take not society but humankind and its ability to choose and perceive as the primary reality for sociological analysis. Within this view of the actor the idea of institutions is grasped and understood but not as fixed and autonomous, albeit functional, entities. Rather, institutions are to be understood in terms of regularized, conventional, crystallized patterns of interaction. To put that another way we might say that for the active perspective institutions are there, they are real, they do contain and constrain human action, but they are there as a result of the history of human interaction, they are embodiments of human choice and perception: they are not 'God-given'.

Within the passive perspective, the question of order is understood from above, that is, with direction, constraint and organizational principles moving downwards from universal standards, social norms and central values to the level of interaction. By contrast, within the active view of the actor, order is addressed almost exclusively with reference to social relationships: thus we would consider how order is achieved through the initiation, maintenance and alteration of face-to-face social encounters.

If we can change our focus for a moment, it is interesting to note that despite the wide divergences between sociologies that are informed by or rest upon models of the actor which are either active or passive, it is nevertheless the case that both seats of sociology also have something in common. They do not regard themselves as merely abstractions; they both have strong senses of the 'real world' and they are both dedicated to getting to grips with the 'real nature of things social'. Thus both perspectives, to some extent, trade on common-sense assumptions about the way things are in the world, they both take their implicit views of the world for granted, and to this degree they can both be understood as forms of 'positivism'. Positivism is discussed elsewhere in greater detail (see 'Subject/Object'), but essentially it can be understood as any form of knowledge which takes the world at face value, which uses direct observation to address the world rather than any intervening conceptual framework, which has little time for any questions of value in relation to the validity of its own statements, and finally which believes that the methods of 'science' best encapsulate all of these principles.

We might go as far as to say that a systems theory, such as that of Talcott Parsons, is marginally less positivistic in as much as it is an abstraction, or what is sometimes referred to as a 'heuristic device' – that is, a concept employed by a theorist to conceptualize the way that things are arranged in the world. Symbolic interactionists, on the other hand, often assume that the ordinary member of society operates exactly like the theorist suggests, that their own theory accurately photographs or perfectly describes the way people act. It would be as if sociologists and all people live together in a state of 'symbolic interaction'.

Before we move on to a consideration of the theory of socialization that stems from an active, symbolic interactionist's perspective, let us finally reform our dichotomy. The passive approach looks at social structure as the object of examination and therefore tends to ignore the significance of meaning and interpretation at the level of the actor. In the active approach, on the other hand, there is a tendency to underplay or assume social structure, quite often in terms of a very diffuse yet highly explanatory concept like the 'definition of the situation' (this, for the interactionists, constitutes the stage upon which action takes place); the concern is rather

269

with approaching social phenomena from the actor's perspective. In many ways one perspective takes for granted what is problematic for the other – or in more formal terms, the dependent variable of one constitutes the independent variable of the other. Perhaps what we should realize, as with the seeming split or irreconcilable gap formed by so many established dichotomies, that the reality lies somewhere in tension between the two poles and that no one argument originating at one end can produce the complete picture. This is a most important point to learn because within the context of this dichotomy active/passive, for example, it often appears that the active perspective has a more sympathetic, subtle, accurate, empowering, and even critical view of the actor and her or his capacity to understand and change the world. The revolution proposed by Karl Marx could not be brought about by actors who were anything but active, critical, conscious, choosing and so on. However, preceding this state of affairs, preceding 'revolutionary consciousness', Karl Marx was required, with telling accuracy, to describe a capitalist society populated by passive, recipient, yielding, ordered and constrained actors who were wholly guided in their thoughts, words and deeds by the systems of dominant values and the structure of functional 'ideological' thought which you will consider elsewhere.

We may now proceed to an investigation of the interactionists' theory of 'socialization' which, as was stated at the outset, along with theories of social control, is always a key to whether a theory is operating with an active or a passive perspective. Socialization, for the symbolic interactionists, is a process of the development and subsequent regeneration of the 'self'. Self is an absolutely central concept. Herbert Blumer has stated that a human being is an organism in possession of a 'self', and what he is meaning here is that the 'self' is a unique property of being human and, indeed, its major distinguishing characteristic. It is the symbolic possession of a self that renders the human being a special kind of actor. The possession of a 'self' transforms the human individual's relation to the world and gives it an original and peculiar character.

In asserting that the individual has a 'self' the symbolic interactionists mean that humankind is able to reflect upon itself, both as a general feature of any situation that it inhabits, and as a particular identity. Animals, it is supposed, do not have this capacity. The human individual is able to regard himself or herself as both an object and a subject in the world: in the terminology of George Herbert Mead, the human 'self' is 'reflexive'. The human actor, as a **reflexive self**, may perceive him/herself, communicate with him/herself, and act towards or in relation to him/herself. In sum, the human actor as a reflexive self is able to become an involved object of his/her own subjective course of action.

Through the capacity of a reflexive self the individual becomes centred and thus stands, knowingly, in relation to personal sensations and thoughts like wants, pains, fears, goals and aspirations, but also in relation to the non-personal like the objects in the world which surround him or her. Most significantly, in terms of social life and social action, through the continuous ability to 'reflect' the individual actor learns to perceive him/herself in relation to the presence of other people, their actions and their expected actions. So, apart from forming a strong and centred sense of his or her own identity the individual learns to classify his or her own form of existence and self-presentation as a reflection of the responses that other people make to his or her behaviour. This is a process that the symbolic interactionists refer to as 'identification' or 'self-definition'. It is a process of collectively constructed self-awareness brought about cumulatively through the responses of others in interaction. The process gives rise to what Cooley has described as the development of a 'looking-glass self', that is, we grow to see ourselves as others see us, we become aware of how we are for others. The mirror metaphor is not, of course, specifically accurate as such reflected images are reversed; however, the point is a good one. We come to know things about our presence in interaction that affect people in predictable ways – but not all!

Through this continual process of interacting with the self, of perceiving directly in relation to the self, but of also seeing the self as others might see it, the individual is strategically placed to plan, organize and carry out his or her own courses of action. The individual actor can act towards others specifically in relation to his or her own presence. As Blumer (1969) has put it: 'Possession of a Self provides the human being with a mechanism of self-interaction with which to meet the world – a mechanism that is used in forming and guiding his conduct.' So the interactionists also seem to be saying that the human capacity to symbolize always instances the otherness of things or other people. Interactionism then is described as a real and practical capacity of human being, it is alive in the minds and practices of real active people; the social world may be regarded as a unified collection of interacting reflexive selves. The manner in which people escape 'solipsism', that is the belief that the self is all that is the case, is through a sustained concentration on defining the self, not in isolation, but as an object in a world of similar objects. It is as if the individual provides for others, the 'outside', from a strong awareness of self, 'the inside'. The development of the reflexive self through socialization is seen to be brought about by two complementary processes, the first being the attainment of a language, learning to speak, and the second being the practical experience of interacting with other people. These two processes can be recognized as the 'symbolic' and the 'interactive': hence 'symbolic interaction'.

The interactionists understand initial or 'primary' socialization taking place through a series of loosely defined stages. It must be emphasized that these stages are theoretically descriptive rather than normatively and chronologically prescriptive in the way that, say, Jean Piaget's steps in human physical and mental development are laid out. At a preparatory stage the human infant is treated as being born non-social. That is, the baby is considered to be an organism, full of potential, but as yet unable to impose sense or meaning upon the world. The infant is initially 'non-reflexive' and passive rather than active. Of course babies have a presence and a series of wants and needs that are expressed as demands, but they are essentially controlled rather than controlling. At the outset the human infant is not able to join in social interaction but, necessarily, that same infant is not born into a vacuum: he or she is born into a social world, a meaningful world, a communicating world, indeed, an environment that is symbolic.

The interactionists are not entirely explicit about the mechanisms by which a child adopts a symbolic repertoire and thus becomes active, but their theory of language acquisition seems to follow rather from the ideas of 'behaviourism', that people learn by responding to particular stimuli. What they suggest is that by virtue of being human and alive the baby will produce a whole range of sounds, gestures and movements, and out of this vast pattern of expressions certain features are selectively encouraged by the parents. In a sense meaning is structured upon them, so, for example, 'ma . . .' and 'da . . .' sounds are applauded and rewarded and become the initial linguistic categories through which the infant attaches meaning to the differentiation between his or her parents.

Following from the 'initial' socialization the interactionists talk about the play stage. It is here that the infant imitates the skills and roles of other people in their immediate environment. By various sets of copying procedures the infant practises all of the regularized patterns of action that are available within the confines of his or her social world. The various roles that the infant plays are unconnected: they consist of diverse aspects of behaviour learned from particular people or 'specific others'. However, within a child's world it is supposed that some individuals will have greater influence on the child than others and these people are referred to as significant others. For the child the most obvious significant others are the parents, but when interactionists are doing studies of adult socialization a significant other might be the person in an occupational situation who teaches a newcomer the important aspects of their new job. Significant others are, then, the most consistently available and strategically important members of one's immediate social world.

At the following stage, which the interactionists refer to as the game stage, the child is seen as becoming more involved, more generally, with other people. By entering into the forms of interaction that are available the child learns, to some degree, what is expected or required of him or her 'generally' by other people. Beyond simply indulging in private imitation of others that he or she has observed, the child is now placed in a position where he or she needs to come to terms with others, to consider others, and to relate to others in the world. It is at this game stage, the stage involving general interaction with others, that the individual finally decentres, abandons solipsism, ceases to regard him/herself as all that there is in the world. The child is required, by demands from the outside, to alter the view that everything and everybody is part of or an extension of his or her ego. The child is, oddly enough, learning to become an active participant in social life but through a necessary acknowledgement of and adjustment to the 'passifying' constraints of other people. Our original dichotomy between the active and the passive now begins to look less like a pair of radical alternatives and more like a contingency, two aspects of a situation in a necessary, and perhaps even tense, relationship. We have an emergent, active, actor who has achieved this status of being able to choose, decide and evaluate situations in order to act upon them, but only through the acceptance of the idea that he or she is merely part of a situation or a world – and that this world is a shared world, it is populated by others, and these others are conscious and active just like him/herself. This recognition of 'otherness' is the way that the interactionists import an idea of social structure back into their theory. You will remember that earlier we talked about systems theory and structural functionalism both operating with a strong, deterministic concept of structure which directed people's behaviour – so much so that Wrong referred to it as producing an 'oversocialized conception of man' and Martin Hollis (1977) referred to it elsewhere as creating an idea of 'plastic man', the malleable or bendable person. Well, what we have in the interactionists' active perspective is a soft concept of structure, an iron hand in a velvet glove. The interactionists rarely talk about structure but say that individual actors organize their behaviour in relation to a generalized other, which is an extremely broad concept meaning, approximately, all other people and their expectations in an interactional context. Another similar passive or structural concept that the interactionists employ is that of a 'definition of the situation', and if we enter into or take on a definition of the situation it means that as active actors we nevertheless assume a taken-for-granted and consensus view of the way things typically happen in situations like this! Our dichotomy looks like a contingency again.

Let us now complete our account of the interactionists' view of the development of the reflexive and essentially active self. Emerging from the game stage the young person is now viewing him/herself as an active part within situations but is also viewing him/herself in terms similar to those which can be applied to others. The child is perceiving him/herself as situated, interacting with others, interacting on the same terms with self: the child is, indeed, becoming 'reflexive'. George Herbert Mead states that the reflexive self comprises two elements – which neatly fit the dichotomy of the active and the passive into the microcosm of the individual actor's personality. These two elements he refers to as the **I** and the **Me**. The 'I' is that inner, personal, essential element of individuality; it is the immediate, continuous and non-reducible different self-consciousness of the particular person. The 'Me' is the organized and routine set of attitudes of other people that each and every individual takes on board through the process of socialization. The 'Me' is that aspect of self which is cumulatively available in the social arena; it is that aspect of ourselves, or outside presentation of self, that is most readily communicated with others in interaction. We are both personal and private and also public and shared; we are both active in our conduct but also passive in our responses. In conclusion, it is interesting to note the parallels between the 'I' and the 'Me' and the 'ego' and the 'superego' that Sigmund Freud was writing about at the same historical period.

KEY CONCEPTS

ACTIVE This concept ties in very closely with the idea of agency discussed earlier. It implies that in the process of becoming social members and when exercising that membership the individual is active rather than re-active or done-to. Such an idea of the person rests on the belief that people are constructive in forging their own destinies, given the constraints placed upon them.

PASSIVE This concept resonates with the dominant idea of structure in sociology. It implies that individuals receive society in a pre-established form and are relatively powerless to shape their own futures. In this sense they are passive in receipt of the constraints that structure places upon them.

Socialization Socialization is a theory concerning how individuals grow and learn into becoming full members of society. Clearly any such theory presupposes a firm grasp of what society is like and it supposes that individuals are brought into that reality whatever their level of activity.

Reflexive self This is a concept which comes from the work of G.H. Mead who suggested that all of life is a continuous practice of socialization. The reflexive self, however, is a state of being and identity when the individual realizes that in a whole series of ways they are just like everybody else and they understand the world like everybody else. This realization enables full and free communication to take place because whatever the other persons differences we can assume that they see the world much as we do.

'I' and 'Me' These two concepts concerning the development of self derive from G.H. Mead also. The 'I' is the private interior which cannot communicate, and the 'Me' is the public exterior which is dedicated to communication. Between them they provide a sense of the private and the public and the ability to move between the two.

Subject/Object

David F. Walsh

That society has a real existence is, of course, the starting point for sociology that provides the basis for its own existence as a discipline. However, the problem for sociology has always been what kind of reality society is, because this also decides the nature of sociology and sociological enquiry. In this respect sociology has to a great extent been divided between a theoretical stance deriving from idealism, which emphasizes the subjective character of society and the social relationships of which it is composed, and a theoretical stance deriving from positivism and materialism, which emphasizes the objective nature of society as a structurally and institutionally based organization of social relationships (often seen as a system) that determines and constrains the lives of its members. With regard to the first position, then, consciousness and meaning are argued to lie at the centre of social life in the sense that social relations are organized around the ideas, interests, values and motives of its members who act and interact with one another in terms of them. Society emerges in and through the processes of action and interaction and is constituted as a reality by their intersubjective and socially meaningful nature. Therein lies the objectivity of society's existence that it is not objective in the sense that the natural world is a world of physical or material objects although society has an empirical reality. On this basis, sociology cannot become nor need it be a science in the manner of the natural sciences, but rather is an interpretive discipline which is based upon an attempt to understand as well as observe social action and social life in an empirical analysis of it. The claim it makes to scientific status, then, is a claim only that understanding and observation are conducted on a systematic basis so that the explanations which this kind of sociology produces are based upon empirical evidence, except that this evidence shows how action and social life find their basis in the meanings, interests, values and motives of the social actors themselves and examines how their actions are determined and organized in these terms. It is the social organization of social relationships at the level of meaning, consciousness and agency that becomes the primary interest of sociologies that focus on the subjective and intersubjective constitution of society. And steadily this condition moves to a treatment of society as a constructed reality rather than a given, pre-existent and determinant world.

Positivistic sociologies, on the other hand, reject this emphasis on society as a socially constructed world of meaningfully organized social interaction in favour of a sense of its essentially objective and factual existence as a reality that exists in its own right and consists of a determinate order of social structures and institutions that are historically and socially conditioned and which organize social relationships, action and life within society. In the classic formulation of society in these terms put forward by Durkheim, society is thing-like, and in this way it has the same degree of objectivity and reality as the world of nature. Structures and institutions empirically exist as themselves and this existence is recognizable and observable in the causal determination and constraint that they impose on social life as they regulate forms which this life, relationships and action take on even to the point of dictating the consciousness of its members. Culture, then, is actively produced by structure and is structurally organized in society at an institutional level. Society, then, can largely be conceptualized as a system of social relationships that is structurally, institutionally and culturally organized in terms of its internal constitution in material, historical and political conditions of its genesis and functioning. Consequently, society can be investigated scientifically as the natural sciences do the world of nature, i.e. objectively through theoretically informed empirical investigation of its structures and institutions which explain them causally and functionally in terms of their empirical characteristics and the conditions which determine this. Positivistic sociologies, then, are premised upon a conception of society which characterizes it as an object world which is external to its members. It is a world of what Durkheim calls social facts that exist in their own right and are subject to their own conditions and organization. On this basis, sociology and its methods of enquiry as well as its explanations are no different from any other science and, ultimately, the aim of sociology like that of science would be to produce a system of high-level, empirically grounded theoretical propositions about the social world which would provide the basis for predictive statements about social phenomena. Within this positivistic framework, of course, much more moderate statements about the scientific capacity of sociology exist too, which focus on a more limited and less totalistic form of historical and empirical enquiry into social structures and institutions and their causal and functional organization and development.

However, the sense of their objective existence as facts which are materially, politically and culturally organized and not intersubjectively constituted at the level of meaning and action alone remains central to this form of sociology. It does not seek to establish a primarily qualitative investigation of social life, although it does entail an investigation of the role that interests, ideas and values play in social activities, but they are treated in terms of their structural location and institutional organization. Positivism, then, creates an essentially structural sociology and, in its ultimate form, it seeks quantitative evidence as the most reliable basis of explanation of the structure and conditions of society.

However, idealism and positivism in their absolute forms pose extremes of subjectivism, which specific sociologists working within either of the two traditions embrace in different ways and to a different extent simply because they face – and ultimately do so empirically – the reality of the social organization of social relationships (Ryan 1970). Society is not only conditioned and structured materially but also enacted by its members consciously and subjectively as actors within it who are agents in respect of their lives. Consequently the objectivity of society extends beyond the intersubjectivity of the social relationships within it since they are framed within and constrained by its material and institutional formations. Yet society is not simply an objective and external world for its members, because social organization and social relationships are ultimately realized in practice by them, and this is done with reference to the sense they have of them and their capacity for action within them in the light of their interests, values and motives in relation to them. Subject and object, then, are mutually interrelated as the social structures of society are played out in action, and action is played out within social structures. This in turn provides for a degree of open-endedness in the shaping and development of both, but the interplay has a social constitution to it – only this sociality is conscious and cultural as well as materially structured. Consequently, the character of the sociological analysis of explanation of society need not be posed as entirely an issue of either qualitative interpretation or hard-nosed science through a subject–object divide. Empirical analysis, which is the hallmark of scientific investigation and explanation generally, can and must be brought to bear upon the study of social relationships in terms of a variety of levels and types of enquiry, since it is empirical evidence which has to be used to sustain both the understanding and the interpretation of the social world and ultimately validates the explanations which sociology generates about it. This then may require different strategies depending on what social phenomenon is being investigated and the complexity of the levels on and in terms of which it exists. For example, Merton's functional analysis of corrupt political power shows how the American Constitution clashes with the need for the concentration of power by the government of a complex society: this the political boss ensures through the manipulation of political patronage and voting in a world of disparate communities.

Merton's analysis squares with Whyte's participant and interactionist study of a slum district of Boston which shows how political corruption thrives in the ways in which the material needs of the members of the community and the possibilities of their social advancement depend on political power and the advantages which accrue to it in the American political and social world. Electoral alliances and pork-barrel politics are the essence of how government funding and legislation are directed towards the distribution of central resources to communities, and there is only a very rudimentary form of welfare state which cannot compensate for the advantages of political patronage as far as the satisfaction of community and individual needs is concerned. So the institutional structure of American society which Merton addresses relates to Whyte's investigation of the way in which, in a particular community, social life is organized at an interactional level between the people within it, and treats this in terms of the interests of its members and the interpersonal basis on which they pursue them and makes this central to an understanding of the nature and existence of the community as a social world.

POSITIVISTIC AND OBJECTIVIST SOCIOLOGIES

The classic formulation of the positivistic conception of sociology is to be found in the early work of Durkheim. Durkheim argues for a view of society which treats it as a reality in its own right which is essentially external to and constraining upon its individual members and which he specifically distinguishes from the psychological and biological levels of human existence. It consists of typical ways of action and thinking which are, because of the external constraint which they exercise upon the social behaviour of individuals, real forces and phenomena with a thing-like character. Society is essentially objective in nature and consists of social facts which exist not only as the material, political and organizational structure of social relationships but also as the institutionalized moral and symbolic system of society, i.e. its collective consciousness of common beliefs, values and norms. Through its material and cultural organization, the social relations of society are structured and regulated and solidarity is produced between its members which gathers them into a community, initially through a completely determining and shared common culture within a segmental social structure (mechanical solidarity) and later, as societies become more complex in the process of social development, through the social division of labour which creates a society of functional relationships of interdependence between its members (organic solidarity).

Individuals enter into and participate in this external order not only through the subjection of their lives to its organization but also through a process of socialization in which the beliefs, values and rules of society are internalized to create a self-constraint that mirrors the external constraint of society and its structures and institutions. So, individuals become social inhabitants of society through these processes of social determination, although, as Durkheim points out, the division of labour in complex societies creates individuality through the specialization of tasks within it that separates and distinguishes people from one another as they engage in them. But still this individuality is socially established by society and, as it meshes in the unique psychological and biological characteristics of the individual, needs to be controlled by society in order to preserve communal existence from the threat of individual egotism. Quite clearly then, the subjective *per se* is rejected in Durkheim's account of the conditions and existence of society which have objective foundation in its structural, institutional and normative organization as social facts.

Moreover, and precisely because social facts are real in terms of their thing-like character, Durkheim argues that they can be systematically studied through the empirical observation of their characteristics as facts and explained in terms of their causal determination and their functions for society. They are, in this sense, no different from the facts of nature and, just as the natural sciences study and explain them, so sociology is able to do the same and in the same way, i.e. sociology is a science. But to do this the common-sense preconceptions of society which its members hold must be abandoned in favour of the empirical observation of social facts themselves. This, for Durkheim, is the first rule of all scientific investigation, but Durkheim's positivism means, of course, that the rule is used to eliminate the subjective element of social life, i.e. the actual meanings, motives and purposes in terms of which the members of society act as agents within it. Instead the issue of meaning is treated in terms of the social structural determination of human consciousness by the epistemological and normative belief system of the society in which they live – a position which structuralism in late-twentieth-century sociologies adopts too.

The problem of this objectivist conception of society surfaces clearly and empirically, however, in Durkheim's positivistic study of suicide. He argues that suicide is a social fact because the official statistics on it show that there is a suicide rate which is a stable and regular occurrence within society and its social groupings, and therefore suicide is a typical form of human behaviour which therefore must be social. So he discounts the motivation of the individual as the real explanation for suicide and sets out to demonstrate instead that it is the nature of the social groupings to which the individual belongs (the family, religion, etc.) and his/her relation to them (the degree and kind of integration of the individual into the group) which causes it. It is society through its structural conditions and organizations which generates suicide, and it does so on a determinate basis because of the nature and workings of these conditions and organizations. But this opens up two objections to Durkheim's entirely positivistic account of suicide. The first is, why do only certain of the individuals who are subject to the same group life and social conditions commit suicide? Surely only the motivation of the individual explains this? But more, suicide is also a social phenomenon in a different way from that in which Durkheim treats it. Suicide is also a culturally formed way of distinguishing, describing and explaining a particular kind of death (matter of social meaning too) which has to be invoked in every instance in which a potential suicide has occurred to make sense of it as suicide. This process of invocation and explanation is undertaken by coroners' courts which arrive at a verdict about a death as suicide by using expert and lay witnesses to reconstruct the circumstances of the death and the intentions of the victim. In this the culture's version of what kind of death a suicide is and how it occurs is central to establishing the fact of suicide, and official statistics are the product of this process of reconstruction. Suicide is not just a thing-like fact but a meaningful event, and the intentionality of the victim to kill himself/herself is central to the social meaning of suicide. The empirical and statistical investigation of suicide to establish social causes is not enough. The meaningful nature of social life, which is part of the nature of the social relationships which form society, cannot then be pushed entirely aside in favour of objective social structures, organization and institutions, because ultimately these have to be enacted. An argument about the structural nature of culture and consciousness which incorporates the individual through socialization and internalization cannot handle the agency of the members of society in their actions and the intentionality of their consciousness as they act in terms of ideas, values, purposes, interests, motives, etc. Action cannot be read off from structures, however constraining they are, because they are objectively and subjectively composed.

This problem arises again in functionalist sociology which, although it examines social structures and institutions in more specifically cultural terms and at the level of their functions rather than their causation, preserves an essentially objectivistic conception of society formulated as a system of socially structured and institutionalized relationships. Functionalism still seeks a positivistic science of society but now the model of the natural sciences which it draws upon is taken from biology, as befits a conception of society as an organized unity (society as a social system) which is located within an environment to which its structures and institutions are adapted culturally in terms of how they function on the basis of their reciprocal interdependence upon and with one another. So structures and institutions are internally adapted to one another too in the same way as and in relation to how the system is adapted as a totality to its environment.

Talcott Parsons provides the most elaborate account of society as a social system in which the structures and institutions of society emerge and function in relation to: an environment of material resources; the organizational necessities and legitimation requirements of the distribution of material and symbolic rewards to the members of society in exchange for their conformity with its dictates; and the psychological and biological needs and dispositions of its members which have to be met through their tailoring to socially determined outlets and satisfactions. This environment represents the conditions which shape the existence of society in the sense that human relationships can only become organized on a social basis (and society become established) in so far as structures and institutions emerge which deal with the environment by functionally resolving the problems that they pose. So society must establish economic structures and institutions which create a material basis for its existence by utilizing scarce material resources; political structures and institutions which govern and direct their allocation to its members; ideological structures and institutions which legitimate this allocation and produce an active acceptance of it on the part of its members; and structures and institutions of socialization which incorporate individuals into society as social creatures engaging in social behaviour. These different spheres of social organization are functionally interrelated to form a system, since ultimately they have to work together with one another, as the social conformity of the members of society on which social life depends can only be achieved if the psychological and biological needs of its members are satisfied through the social rewards it offers them in exchange for conformity. This depends on society being able to reward its members both materially and symbolically through the production and allocation of these resources in a way that is governmentally organized and ideologically legitimated, so that in the final analysis the process of socialization through which social conformity is created can be achieved successfully.

So society is an objective reality which consists of a system of functionally interrelated structures and institutions which direct and organize social life and into which its individuals are socialized. The functional logic of the system determines what society is, how it works, and what is the nature of the structures and institutions through which it does this. As the heart of this system, and as the basis of how its structure and institutions are formed and articulated and its members incorporated into it as social actors acting in terms of them, is a common value system. This is the important place that functionalism gives to culture in its account of society. This acts as a normative order of ideas, beliefs, values and norms through which the structural and institutional roles that individuals occupy in society are regulated, controlled and accepted so that social relationships are created and maintained in this way. Society, then, is an objective world of ordered relationships between its members in which that order has been produced functionally, is maintained consensually and ultimately rests upon its determination as a necessity for the survival of society. Societies vary because their culture, structures and institutions represent different functional and adaptive solutions to the environment in which they are placed, but all are social systems and, as systems, are organized in terms of systemic universal nature, character and logic. The scientific task of sociology is to empirically investigate how social structure and institutions function within the total system of society in relation to one another and the environment within which the society is located. So, for example, Talcott Parsons has argued that the nuclear family is its universal institutional form in modern complex industrial societies because it is functionally adapted to an industrial economy which requires geographical and social mobility and separates work from the home, thereby distinctively gendering men and women into the performance of two primary kinds of activity: instrumental activity (work and men) and expressive activity (the home and women). This instrumental expressive divide is both necessary and complementary since it guarantees the economic survival of the family through the husband's work and its domestic organization through the work of the wife, and together this makes it an effective agent of socialization for children.

That the functionality of social institutions in relation to the wider society of which they are part cannot be denied is a major contribution of functional sociology to the explanation of social life, and functionalism is able to demonstrate that structures and institutions do have an objective reality and that how and why they work in fact has to do with their functionality in relation to social needs and the organization of the other structures and institutions of society. That the particular gendering of social roles which has occurred in the modern industrial world has major effects on women and their place in it, which feminism has demonstrated, does not entirely destroy functionalist arguments about how this has come about. The issue is whether the scientific analysis of the structures and institutions by functionalism in terms of their necessity for the survival of society conceals a ideological celebration of these structures and institutions, because it ignores other possible forms of social organization that could also be functional. And it ignores an alternative but necessary part of a cogent explanation of the structures and institutions of society that examines their historical, political and material causation as well as their functions. Moreover, in addressing society in terms of functional interdependence of its institutions and the normative ordering of society on a consensual basis, functionalism ignores the conflicts and contradictions between structures and institutions (between bureaucracy and democratic government) and disguises the cultural and normative diversity in society that arises with respect to the different social groups and the conflicts and power struggles between them with regard not only to beliefs and values but also to the distribution of symbolic rewards in society. The social order which functionalism proclaims is far from being a consensual order or a completely stable organization of social relationships.

But this raises again the problem of treating society as though it was only an objective and systemic world of structures and institutions in which the agency of its members is simply a matter of determination by them.

Ultimately the scientific explanation of society which is offered by functionalism rests on the argument that action within it is determined by rules and roles in terms of their institutionalized integration with one another, in which socialization into them through internalization is the key to the way in which the members of society come to participate in it on a socially determined basis. Yet an empirical inspection of rules and roles shows that the enaction of the latter in terms of the governance of the former is much more complex than this. Rules can only come to govern action through their interpretation, and roles can only be enacted in the light of this, so ultimately social action depends on this process of interpretation by its members in which they have to take decisions about how to enact social roles and engage in social relationships. Of course this is done against a background of the structural constraints of institutions and institutional settings, not in an automatic fashion but in terms of a sense of what the institution and the purposes, rules and activities are; what the constraints are that impose themselves in these terms and need to be attended to on a practical level; how much scope there is to negotiate action within the situation, and what it would be appropriate to negotiate; and what kind of private or other interests can be served or satisfied within an institutional context. All of this is bound to the contingencies and exigencies of day-to-day existence within the social world which, however orderly, regular and normal are the forms which life takes within it, still has to be encountered on a daily basis and recognized and dealt with as such, which means, in part, routinizing it. It is the processes though which the members of society constantly routinize their world and the actions within it, however much they do this on a taken-for-granted basis, that functionalism ignores in its analysis of the social purposes, values and motives that are entailed on the part of the members of society as they go about their daily lives. The objective forms of culture and structure have to be activated to become the determinants of the organization of society and action within it.

But this, then, raises another primary issue about the objectivity of structures and institutions, which is the issue of power as opposed to culture and meaning. This is central to Marxism and its discussion of social action within society and the possibilities of the agency of the subject in terms of this. For Marx, society emerges in terms of social action but at the level of the social organization of the production of the material conditions of human life. So the mode of production and the material forces on which it is based are the foundation of society and they produce an organized system of structural and institutional social relationships between the members of society which determines the interests and actions of the participants as they enter the system. So human action is understood by Marx in terms of its productive nature and by virtue of the means and mode of its organization. In this sense, then, society is an objective and material reality which exists at the level of the structures and institutions arising from the mode of production which emerges historically in terms of the different means on which it is based and the different forms which it takes. Furthermore, the material and social organization of the mode of production generates a cultural and institutional superstructure of ideas and beliefs, legal and political institutions, etc. which reflect and sustain the mode of production and the organization of social relationships which it engenders.

Consciousness, subjectivity and human agency, then, are largely subordinated by Marx to labour and the act of production which, although they entail creative engagement on the part of the labourer, are practically and socially determined by the organization of production; the social relations this generates between producers; the interests and purposes which the productive relationships create for the producers as they are located within them; and the cultural organization of social consciousness at the level of ideas and values that is established in terms of these interests and purposes. The point for Marx is that in so far as the social organization of the mode of production entails the private ownership of the means of production, it creates social relations of domination and subordination between the producers in terms of this ownership and the power which accrues to it. So every mode of production produces a class structure consisting of a ruling class and a subordinate class which determines the interests of each class and structures the relations between them in terms of power and conflict. The culture of a society emerges as a representation and distillation of these interests in which a dominant culture is created by the ruling class by virtue of its economic position and power and which is an ideological reflection of its interests and position. This is the major role assigned to institutionalized forms of social consciousness by Marx which legitimates and underpins the whole material and social order on which the society is based. In capitalism, the mode of production is based upon labour power and its use to manufacture commodities for profit through their sale within the marketplace. In the capitalist mode of production labour is itself commodified and manufacture entails the extraction of surplus value from its use to create profit. The result, then, is the emergence of a class structure in which a ruling class, the bourgeoisie, own labour power and the profit which is produced through its use in the form of capital and property, and a subordinate class, the proletariat, who live through the sale of their labour under conditions of exploitation and alienation by virtue of its commodification and private appropriation by the bourgeoisie as capital and profit. This, in turn, is institutionalized in a legal and political superstructure which transforms the economic position of the bourgeoisie into a position of power, government and control over society, and a dominant culture of ideas, beliefs and values which performs the ideological function of legitimating the system and their position within it by justifying and disguising the economic and power relations on which it is based and the conditions of exploitation and alienation to which it reduces the proletariat, whose labour is the absolute foundation of the creation of wealth and profit in the capitalist mode of production. Capital and private property, then, which are the heart of capitalism, depend on the commodification, exploitation and alienation of labour on which they are based, according to Marx; and in this sense, capitalism is an inhuman system that denies its members the right to engage in and enjoy the fruits of their labour on a creative and socially co-operative basis.

Now it is in terms of this materialist conception of society as a system of objective and objectified relationships that Marx attempts to establish a scientific sociology which investigates them in empirical terms. However it is, as Marx argues, a dialectical science as opposed to mere positivism, although its empiricism has a positivistic basis. It is dialectical in two senses. Firstly, it is a scientific analysis based in a project for the revolutionary transformation of capitalism to socialism in which the theoretical and empirical investigation of capitalism is designed to act as a critical and real foundation and tool of a political practice which overthrows capitalism and replaces it with socialism. In this it sides with the proletariat and the alienated and exploited life which they lead and treats them, because of the primary role of their labour in capitalist manufacture, as the necessary social agent of revolution since the conditions in which the proletariat exist are the universal and negative conditions of human and social life within capitalism. A new and co-operative organization of the collective forces of labour that capitalism has produced through industrial manufacture, once it has broken the chains of private property and been placed in the hands of the labour force itself, opens instead a classless and human world which is free of exploitation and subordination. Secondly, Marx's analysis is dialectical because it treats society as a totality (system) of interrelated and interpenetrating structures, institutions, relationships and action (albeit stemming from the mode of production) that exists in terms of a dynamic of the contradictions as well as the integration between them, which constantly transforms their nature in terms of revolution as the forces of production change. In the consequent development of new modes of production, new and different classes and structures of ownership and power are created; new class conflicts emerge and are fought within society. All history, as Marx puts it, is the history of class conflict, and therein lies the role of human agency in social life; but it is an agency bound to class, class interests and class conflict which changes in terms of the forces of production, the emergence of new modes of production and contradictions within the mode of production.

It is in this latter sense that Marx's science is positivistic, since it treats society as an objective and real system of structures and institutions that are ultimately lodged in and created by the social organization of production. The subject and human agency emerge practically in relation to this system, and the potential for action on the part of the members of society is shaped and determined by the possibilities of life which it creates. The power that human beings have to create their world lies not in their consciousness *per se* or their individuality but in the collective and practical reorganization of structures and institutions. This too must be done structurally and institutionally to create a new social order of structures and institutions that are essentially communal, albeit ones that may liberate the creative capacities of the individual in terms of the ways in which participation in society is organized and the needs of its members are satisfied. The problem here is that Marxism lacks a theory of the subject because of its commitment to the essential sociality of human life and its critique of bourgeois individualism in capitalism as nothing but a commodification of the person in terms of the ownership of private property which simply extends it to the subject. A sense of what the real subject may be is offered in terms of the creative and unalienated nature of human labour as the essential property of being human, but its collective and social organization remains the central issue for Marx and he locates the human being of human beings in this sociality of labour and production. But also and specifically, too, Marx is scientific in a positivistic manner in terms of the empirical analysis that he conducts into the capitalist system in terms of a distinction between its essence, which is the real organization of its productive relationships, and the structure and institutions of social life which this creates through the commodification of labour at the level of class property and power and the appearance of capitalism. The latter is the dominant idealized and ideological cultural form in which it represents, legitimates and disguises its own exploitative and alienated world as an essential, natural and just form of society; and, through the taken-for-granted acceptance of this dominant culture by the members of society, capitalism both creates their allegiance to it and incorporates them into it as participants who accept their position in it. But it is the scientific and empirical investigation of capitalism which is used to reveal the real structures and institutions of which it consists, and this is how Marx claims to demonstrate its essential nature and so breaks with its ideological appearances. In this sense Marx, like Durkheim, rejects the common sense of the members of society as the necessary condition for a scientific, empirical and objective enquiry that is based upon facts, but facts that provide the empirical and theoretical foundation for a revolutionary political practice in Marx's case. As Marx puts it himself, his socialism is a scientific socialism and not a philosophical and humanistic socialism. Positivism and dialectics fuse in Marx.

Now this distinction between essence and appearance in terms of the treatment of society as a system of social relationships, in which the former is the objective reality of society and the latter is the subjective and cultural representations of itself (the social consciousness) that are structurally produced by and generated within it, is the core of structuralism and structuralist sociology. In this sociology the subject as a person endowed with consciousness, and as an agent of action acting individually or socially in society, disappears altogether. Instead it is the system which is real, but not in the classic empiricist sense of its reality, i.e. simply as a matter of mere observational evidence. Instead reality is understood in terms of the concealed but underlying and structured way that the system generates itself as a system and which produces the institutions, social formations and culture of which it is composed. It is this underlying reality of the system which a structuralist and realist science is directed towards investigating, in terms of how the system composes institutions, social formations and culture through the dynamics of the relations between them which the system creates and which has its own logic of ordering and change. In the anthropology of Lévi-Strauss, his structuralism seizes upon the later work of Durkheim on the moral and symbolic ordering of society by its institutionalized collective consciousness and the semiotic linguistics of Saussure to treat society like a language which has an underlying grammar as rules of organization that determine its social formations and relationships but on a cultural basis. This social and cultural grammar is a grammar of mythology which has its foundation in the universal nature of the human mind itself. All societies are organized through an enculturation in terms of a dominant mythology which, as the collective consciousness and symbolic knowledge of society, generates a collective sense and meaning of human existence for the members of society which structures and institutionalizes their social relationships in particular forms that organize the conditions and resolve the problems which human life and the world of nature entail. All mythologies have the same basis and logic to them in which culture and structure match and mesh and which is synchronic rather than diachronic in its character, so all societies can be understood in terms of how their social relationships are embodied in and organized through the mythological structuring of them by the culture of society, and so society can be explained in terms of how it works on this basis. The individual in society, then, is subjected to and incorporated into it not as a subject in his or her own right who engages consciously in society as an active agent, but as a subject whose subjectivity and consciousness have been unconsciously and collectively determined and constituted by the culture of society, which is a structure that imposes itself on the individual and comes from society. It is society which acts and not the individual, and its action lies in its symbolic organization.

Lévi-Strauss's structuralism is ideational but nevertheless society is objective and real. In Althusser structuralism is now given a materialist character and derives from a realist-structuralist reinterpretation of Marx and the scientific analysis of capitalism in terms of the distinction Marx makes between its essence and its appearance, in which the former is the focus of enquiry and the basis of Marx's explanation of its nature. Althusser treats this scientific analysis of capitalism by Marx as the basis of the objectivity and validity of Marxism and argues that it rests on the recognition by Marx that capitalism is a system of production that generates and organizes the social relationships, social formations and culture of which it is composed in terms of the underlying reality and logic of that system. The scientific and structuralist task for Althusser is to uncover the reality and its logic in terms of the relationships that are generated between production, institutional and social formations and culture and the ways in which they sustain, underpin and contradict one another. In this Althusser moves beyond a simple base/superstructure model of the capitalist system to show how it operates at important interrelated and different levels, in which the state apparatus of capitalist society as it exists in the judiciary, bureaucracy etc. works as coercive management and control of social relationships in favour of its productive and social organization, but in conjunction with the ideological apparatus of society which works through a dominant culture absorbing individuals by shaping and determining their consciousness and incorporating them into it on an unconscious basis so they willingly occupy the positions that the capitalist mode of production has assigned to them. There is, then, no subject as agent in Althusser's structuralist account of capitalism because consciousness and action are structured by society through its institutionalized and ideologically generated culture which is part of its systemic nature. Society is real, the individual is not. The problem, of course, is that in so far as Marxism is a revolutionary position the revolution is left to the breakdown of the capitalist system through its inherent contradictions and the opportunities offered by the objectivity of a scientific analysis of it. But there are no subjects here to organize the revolution and carry it through since Althusser's position denies the possibility of action which depends upon a subject who can be a self-conscious agent of action as opposed to being a vehicle of the collective cultural consciousness. If Althusser's science offers a way out of ideology to revolution it does so through theory and an elitism which leaves the common person trapped in an unconscious collectivism from which there is no form of release in action, because action is stifled by an inevitable and determined incorporation of the individual into the structures of capitalism in which they have no reality and identity as actual subjects and agents. But this is the general problem faced by systemic Marxism of any variety, be it of Marx himself or not.

Precisely because of this Gramsci seeks to offer a different sense of Marx which attempts to restore and emphasize the position of human agency, action, consciousness and culture in its analysis of the capitalist system and the ways in which the system works. Gramsci argues that capitalism, however much it is organized institutionally and structurally at the level of production, depends also upon the ways in which these institutions and structures are institutionalized, legitimized and enshrined in a dominant and hegemonic culture which, as it becomes taken for granted within society as common sense, preserves the status quo. Moreover, Gramsci argues that the development of a hegemonic culture is an absolutely central part of capitalism and its survival which it achieves through economic negotiations between capital, labour and parliamentary government which entails some sharing of power on the part of the ruling class. Revolution can begin only by the proletariat challenging the dominant cultural apparatus to form a consciousness of its own in relation to its conditions within the capitalist system: the proletariat must become agents for revolution to succeed, and only the development of social consciousness on their part provides for this.

Revolutionary action requires collective and political organization. Culture is the arena of critique and struggle for Gramsci and not just a structural, collective and unconscious determinant of subjectivity which incorporates people into capitalist society on a socially constituted, determined and robotic basis. In this Gramsci cites Marx's argument that the revolutionary project depends on class as a form of economic position (class in itself) becoming politically conscious and organized (class for itself), and systemic Marxism completely objectivizes the structures and institutions of society and further reduces them to the material organization of its productive system and the class relationship it generates. But Gramsci too is caught in this, and he leaves no space for other forms of the social organization of action such as politics and administration, government, status, gender and ethnicity. Social action in society has many sources, which is not to deny how structures and institutions condition it, but they are varied in their nature; and the fact that the members of society are grouped and group themselves culturally in their actions in terms of them, and differently so, suggests empirically that any version of society as a system overdraws its objectivity and underestimates social and cultural differentiation and agency within it. It presumes a determined incorporation of the members of society into its structures and institutions which their enactment belies, since these depend for their effect, however much they are taken for granted and lived within by the members of society, on the ways in which members attend to and make sense of them on a practical and conscious basis.

IDEALIST, SUBJECTIVIST AND INTERPRETIVE SOCIOLOGIES

From the critique of positivistic sociology it follows, then, that it is necessary to turn to the issues raised about the nature of social reality by subjectivist and interpretive sociologies. These focus their concern upon action and consciousness, i.e. on the subjective and intersubjective nature of social relationships and the ways in which society and its structures and institutions are to be understood and explained in terms of their organization on this basis.

Weber's sociology of action establishes the foundation of subjectivist sociology, and with it the conception of sociology as an interpretive science; but distinctively his science of action entails a marriage with positivism because of its commitment to the causal explanation of action which makes this the basis of its objectivity. However, for Weber, what society consists of factually is the actions and interactions of individuals which are subjectively meaningful to them in the sense that they are consciously conducted and organize purposively on the basis of the ideas, interests, values and purposes of the actors themselves. Society emerges as subjective meanings develop historically and collectively and become institutionalized intersubjectively on a cultural basis to produce a mutual orientation towards one another on the part of the members of society that structures their relationships with one another on an interactive basis. For Weber, then, it is not that society has no material sources of its organization – it has these in the historical, economic, political, administrative, etc. conditions and factors which are part of its causal development – but that the institutions created in society, however material, are always organized and operative in society at the level of the conscious and meaningful actions of individuals out of which they are really composed. It follows for Weber that the explanation of the social must be based on an internal understanding of the subjective meaning of action, which differentiates the methodology of sociology from the natural sciences. The latter proceed on the basis of the external observation of the facts of nature, which have no meaning in themselves, unlike the facts of society which are meaningful actions and where the object which is society lies in its cultural and material constitution through intersubjective relationships. But for Weber, understanding remains merely the hypothetical interpretation of action until its meaning can be verified and translated into an objective explanation of it, and this is a matter of establishing its causal determination in terms of subjective meaning. And here the positivism enters into Weber's interpretive science of action.

Weber argues that the meaning of action cannot be understood simply on the basis of an empathetic grasp of the actor's position by the sociological observer, because this substitutes emotion for objectivity. Instead the sociological observer must seek a rational understanding of action – an understanding which is objective because it is verifiable – and the causal canons of scientific explanation must be brought into play to do this. This means treating action as purposively organized by the actor in terms of a means–ends relationship in which the meaning of the action can be understood on the basis of how it is motivated by the way in which the actor selectively chooses ends and adopts certain means for their achievement within a situation. Action, then, is capable of objective explanation because it is tested and verified by the empirical observation of the actual course which it takes to see if this latter matches the observer's understanding of it. Consequently the study of action, albeit through the understanding of its motivation, proceeds in terms of the normal scientific procedure of the construction and empirical testing of causal hypotheses about it. But ultimately for the purposes of its scientific explanation this depends on the rational and causal conceptualization of its nature, and that Weber provides in terms of seeing it as organized on a means–ends basis so that different types can be distinguished from which to construct hypotheses about and explicate the reality of particular concrete actions in the social world. These types are ideal types of action which distinguish them in terms of the particular form of the organization of the means–ends relationship which they entail and which provide and clarify the basis on which particular and concrete actions can be understood and explained. Ultimately Weber goes on to argue that different societies have culturally and institutionally organized their social structures and relationships around and in terms of one or more of these particular forms of action: in Western society, it is the instrumentally rational form of action which dominates its structures and social relationships.

For Weber, science can be used to understand and objectively explain action because factually its subjectively meaningful nature consists in its causally motivated determination on a means–ends basis. But it remains an interpretive science because the explanation is one of probability rather than exactitude, and because the sociological observer's values determine what he or she wishes to grasp and understand about the historical formation and structural and cultural motivation and organization of action in the social world. Nevertheless, fact interposes between values and explanation in the form of empirical evidence as the basis of the understanding of meaning, and of causality as the basis of the explanation of action; the problem is whether the rationality of scientific explanation of action can be accepted altogether. Essentially Weber's science of action insists that its intelligibility (meaning) and explicability (causation) lie in its purposive organization on a means–ends basis. But this makes science the arbiter of its meaning and determination, since the ideal-typical formulation of concrete actions in these terms assumes forms of means–ends organization that are scientifically formulated rather than culturally determined and imposes them on the latter organization of action. And this is precisely where phenomenological sociology departs from Weber's science of action.

The issue for phenomenological sociology is not the positivistic empirical investigation of action but the examination of the social basis of its organization at the level of meaning which raises the relevance of a positivistic and causal science to its explanation. It moves, then, much more specifically to the subjective and intersubjective nature of social life and a sociology which is precisely directed to this. In this it joins hands with symbolic interactionism, and both offer a version of sociology whose theories and explanations seek to ground themselves in the empirical character of the social relationships of everyday life as it is actually lived by the members of society.

For phenomenology, human existence has its foundation in the consciousness through which human beings make sense of and act within the world. Through consciousness experience of the world is given meaning, and through this the world is typified and constructed as a taken-for-granted and real world of facts and events in terms of which the individual can engage in action on an individual and purposive basis in the light of their biographical situation within it. In this way the actions of the individual become subjectively meaningful to that individual, and this organizes the way in which they are conducted on an individual basis. The ordinary and everyday consciousness of the individual is not entirely solitary in its nature but entails the sense that it inhabits a world which is shared with other individuals who understand and factually experience it in reality in the same way, so that social relations can be and are created and sustained between individual actors on the same basis. So society emerges through the way in which social relationships are constituted and organized by a shared sense of the world, which is intersubjective and commonsensical in nature and which constructs and establishes the social world as a real world of facts, situations and events which are accepted as common in a taken-for-granted manner by the members of society by virtue of this shared sense of their nature. Social reality as fact, then, is actually constructed by common-sense reasoning, and this is embodied in and uses ordinary language which then acts as the foundation of a common and social consciousness. Using language, the members of society are able to describe and typify their world and its events and scenes in the same way and so experience it as a reality in the same terms as one another. So they organize their actions and relationships on a reciprocal and social basis through what their common sense takes social reality to be – and so it is for the members of society – the objective and factual social environment (society) in which they live. So society is indeed an objective, real communal world for its members, but it is actually constituted from within it on an intersubjective basis by its members through the use of common-sense knowledge, as embodied in language, which they share with one another and bring to bear on one another's actions and social scenes so as to understand and conduct their social life. Society, then, has its foundation in a common culture (common-sense knowledge) which has its own way of making sense of the events and scenes of the social world and actions within it. This gives it a distinctive rationality of its own which organizes and constructs them in its own terms on a practical day-to-day basis. Social structure, then, lies in how the members of a society organize (i.e. structure) their world socially in these terms. And in doing this they are constantly engaged in a process of describing, defining and negotiating the nature of the social scenes of society, and conducting their actions and interactions within them in this way. The social world is produced and organized by their own communal and sense-making activity.

However, the way in which the social world is constructed, organized and negotiated in terms of common-sense knowledge by its members goes unnoticed by them because they treat that knowledge positivistically and unreflexively as fact about social reality and not as constitutive of the facts of social reality. The task of sociology then becomes one of an empirical and reflexive enquiry into the social construction of social reality, which abandons the common-sense view of the social world as fact to examine how its facticity is established by common-sense knowledge itself. In this sociology seeks to understand and explicate how the members of society actually utilize common-sense reasoning and go about the business of constructing their social world as they make sense of its scenes and events and as they act in it on a day-to-day basis. It is concerned then with the practices and practicalities of social organization of society as this is enacted in the socially meaningful activities of its members, in which their sense of the world is the key to its understanding and examination and not the causal rationality of a positivistic science which imposes its own framework of organization and determination upon their activities in terms of society as the external and objective conditions of action within it.

But, in doing so, phenomenology (and symbolic interaction) goes too far in a subjectivist direction. It is true, of course, that social structures and institutions ultimately depend on their enactment for their existence and the strength of the subjectivist position consists of showing how such are articulated from within on the basis of common-sense knowledge in terms of the negotiation and definition of social situations and practical decision-making within them. Social action has, then, a meaningful, subjective and purposive character. But social structures and institutions are not simply reducible to the intersubjective relationships and actions of which they are composed, because they do impose external and objective constraints upon those relationships in terms of the forms in which they have become institutionalized and which have emerged historically on the basis of material, economic, political, technological, administrative, etc. conditions and are sustained in and by the various relationships that structures and institutions enjoy with one another in particular societies. It is the strength of Weber's position to recognize this need for a causal and historical explanation of action and society as well as an examination of its internal constitution at the level of an understanding of culture and meaning. The point is that culture and consciousness have a societal and structural location and action within society emerges in the reflexive and causal engagement between consciousness and structure. Neither the subjectivity of the individual nor the structural conditions of society in themselves determine human action. Objectivist sociologies enshrine the important point about the relationship of consciousness and action, which is how the social location of both means that the content of the consciousness of the individual is largely social, is unconsciously absorbed from society and operates at a taken-for-granted level. But phenomenological sociology makes a similar claim about common-sense knowledge and social action. Both show the reality of the social organization of society. The key question is what degree of agency is entailed in action and how it is achieved.

THE POSTMODERN TURN IN SOCIOLOGY

With postmodernism the whole subject/object debate is abandoned on the grounds that it belongs to and with a mode of thinking and a world order, that of modern society, which no longer exists because the whole world has been radically transformed and reconstituted in terms of a new type of society and culture. Modern society from this point of view is seen as a highly differentiated society structurally in which the capitalist economy dominated, and it is characterized by a complex division of labour, industrialization and urbanization, science and technology, and cultural and ideological values which emphasize political and ethical individualism and a sense of society as a total community which is bound together by a social contract between its members. Modern society, conceived in these terms, is seen as giving rise to sociology and the social sciences generally by establishing the method, interests and agenda for them as an Enlightenment programme which seeks to extend the uses of reason – especially in terms of science, technology and applied science – to promote the growth of a rational civilization. As such sociology, as it has been traditionally conceived, has developed set ideas about the self, society and history, and it is the dominance of these which postmodernism rejects as essentially irrelevant to an analysis of the postmodern world.

These set ideas, as befits science, continuously trade off an absolutist and empiricist knowledge, a version of truth and rationality which science embodies and which distinguishes the objective and real (the rational) from the merely personal and subjective (the non-rational). Postmodernism claims that social science has sought to explain human nature and history and to provide, through that knowledge, the emancipatory means by which personal identity could emerge from instinct and need and be developed in terms of a conscious, purposive, integrated and determining self; society could be successfully organized and regulated in terms of communal and contractual relationships which mutually satisfied the interests of its members; and history could now become the progressive development of society in which human beings could take charge of their future. But this simply confuses the realities of identity, society and history with the rationalistic theories and explanations that science has produced about them in what is, in fact, an attempt to order and control them through science's own absolutist claims to knowledge about the world. But science is itself a socio-historically produced form of knowledge which is therefore culturally relative and constructionist in terms of the rationality with which it explains the world, and the facts which it detects about that world are secured through its own epistemological perspective upon it.

Instead, then, of the empirical certainties of the scientific and institutional structural analysis of society which sociology has traditionally set out to generate – which takes identity as a unified and conscious self, society as an orderly totality, and history as a progressive and determined path of change and development – postmodernism offers a thoroughly historicized view of society. This locates society in the discontinuities of different forms of consciousness, identities, signification, organization, etc. which situate and are situated within a world of highly diversified cultural and social divisions and differences, i.e. an indeterminate and unstable world of heterogeneous groups, alternative social voices and multiple realities in which semiotic structures and cultural processes produce and reproduce organizations and economies of wealth, power and privilege in terms of the location and habitus of the social groupings within it. Culture, language, the sign and discursive practices are the hallmark of the postmodern world and its organizational, if disorganizing and fragmenting, basis. These are constructive of social existence and in that sense are material and real (i.e. objective) but are also ideational and in that sense subjective, not as subjective manifestations of consciousness but as the historico-social and linguistic orders and processes of signification – the structure and practice which create, as they subject and subjugate them, social identity and social reality.

In this context, the ideas of Baudrillard and Foucault have become par-ticularly significant for postmodern sociology. According to Baudrillard, the postmodern world is no longer structured by production and economic exchange but by the symbolic exchange which new technologies and systems of information have created and which generates a heterogeneous cultural world of proliferating signs, images and significations which is inhabited by its members as consumers in relation to them. But signs themselves have now taken on a life of their own and become free-floating so that they replace reality by their own images and so become the primary determinants of social experience. This process, which Baudrillard refers to as a process of simulation, generates a world of hyper-reality in which social structures and boundaries dissolve into a black hole of signs, images, meanings and messages which, as they create social reality, also neutralize one another in a constant and conflicting flow of information urging its consumption on the part of the members of society. But the flood and flux of information which produces a social world of simulacra destroys the subject and human agency within it, since signs and images now control social practice and action can only generate more of the same and with no more claim on reality than any other images and signs and so contribute to the hyper-reality. But this is precisely what is problematic in Baudrillard's sociology. By relativizing science and the sociological tradition of structural enquiry, he is left only with culture and the sign and so is unable to analyse the far from disappearing and objective structural reality which is that of the political and economic organizations, social divisions, technological and administrative practices, etc. of the contemporary social world and which act as the social location for and the basis of signs and signification in society. This structural reality is a readily and demonstrably evident part of the contemporary social world: yet, of course, Baudrillard's whole analysis is underpinned by a version of the underlying structure of the postmodern world in terms of a general technological determinism which focuses upon the place of information systems in its organization. The undoubtedly powerful position of information and the sign in the contemporary world and the role of consumption in the creation of identity and social differentiation and division is overdrawn, because Baudrillard has reduced social divisions of the contemporary world to a cultural diversity, difference and fragmentation that treat this world as having no other foundation. The resulting nihilism in relation to human action and agency depends precisely upon this reduction of the reality of structure to signification and the dissolution of the empirical which this entails, and it follows upon the way in which constructional and deconstructional analysis replaces any version of science and a rational and observational enquiry into the social world which treats it as having an existential and material foundation, which entails forms of symbolic representation as well as being entailed by them.

Foucault maintains the constructionist position, but in a specifically poststructuralist form. He moves away from Baudrillard's concern with the generative power of signs and images in the construction of the contemporary social world to its production through the forms of discipline and governmentality that it exercises. Therein lies its reality as society is organized through discursive practices, i.e. historically, politically and economically located epistemes. These are systems of thought and understanding of the world with their own rationality and which surface and concretize themselves socially as regimes and practices of the government and organization of self and social relationships and so produce society and social and personal existence within it. Discursive practices, then, are forms of power with their own determinative organization, and the epistemes which underpin them emerge historically in terms not of a process of continuous development but of discontinuities and disconjunctions between them. There is no grand structural narrative to history in terms of which the contemporary world has developed or is developing, but only the history of its present form; and science is only the present and historically emergent episteme with its own organizational rationality and not an absolutely valid and universal form of knowledge. As such it constructs and produces the world through its discursive and governmental practices and regimes of power and organization.

For Foucault, the contemporary world can be understood as a carceral society based upon a moral technology of power and a government embodied in Enlightenment and scientific discourses and practices. This submits its members and their bodies to a constant regimentation induced through their minds on the basis of the objective, universal and moral claims of the rationality of science and the practices of governmentality which this creates in terms of the systematic regime of supervision, surveillance and discipline which it enforces on people in society. This regime entails the regulation and scheduling of all social activities spatially, hierarchically and collectively to create a disciplined environment in which order is produced through the control of every fragment of the lives of people both formally and informally to ensure their conformity. It is achieved by creating the docile person through the moral transformation of the individual into a hard-working, conscience-ridden and useful creature that fits the needs of production and warfare in a rational, efficient and technical society. And social science plays its part in this by generating scientific and rationalistic conceptions of normality with reference to identity and sociality that are implemented practically and professionally in the whole varieties of administrative, educational, therapeutic, etc. technologies through which social life is organized in the contemporary world. Moreover, the governmental regime claims the moral right to and does punish people who do not fit into its categories of normality on the grounds of truth claims that are embodied in scientific knowledge. But this disciplinary organization of contemporary society is anonymous, dispersed and comprehensive, and in that sense no one owns it but everyone is subject to it. There are no subjects in society because the individual has no inner essence but is socially conditioned and produced through the discursive technologies of the soul which society enforces on the individual in terms of normality and which the individual internalizes. So the contemporary world is one which differentiates, hierarchicalizes, marginalizes and excludes its members on these terms. Society lies in its governmentality; the governmentality of the contemporary world lies in the regime of carceral, anonymous and disciplinary power; and the members of society are not agents but products of this disciplinary organization which reaches into and forms their identities. This, for Foucault, is the nature of the contemporary social world and the real historical legacy of the Enlightenment and the rationalism of science as it developed from it. The promise of emancipation has turned into a nightmare of discipline and regimentation from which nothing and nobody can escape except through refusal and the deconstruction of the discourse and the rationality on which it is based. So Foucault recommends an archaeology and a genealogy which historically unearth and trace the origins and development of Enlightenment and scientific knowledge, which challenge its absolutist epistemological and moral claims, and which reject the disciplinary technologies of social engineering and normalization that it seeks to enforce.

The problem, however, is whether escape is possible given that Foucault has reduced science to mere discourse and power as opposed to understanding and knowledge; society to discursive formations which have no structural existence; and the subject to the regimented and normalized product of social and scientific technologies of the soul. But this is the empirical case, and in the end Foucault's analysis must stand or fall on evidence which makes it impossible to reject rational and scientific knowledge altogether as merely relativistic and socio-historical discourse, since he is actually making an empirical claim about the nature of contemporary society which entails a demonstration of the truth and validity of this claim in terms of reality, and reality not just as an epistemological object.

And there lies the problem which postmodern constructionism does not overcome, however much it seeks to reformulate the issue of subject and object (i.e. self and society) in terms of the historical, cultural, linguistic, symbolic and discursive constitution, formation and organization of their nature. They are more than just this relativity, and obdurately exert an empirical existence that goes beyond construction. So whereas it is true that power may have become anonymized and decentralized in the contemporary world in a whole variety of ways, it is also true that it is socially located structurally in forms of the social division within society and the hierarchies of ownership and domination on which they are based and in its concentrations in the institutional organizations of society. Moreover, the interactional achievement of social life requires an enactment in terms of interest, purpose and consciousness, which, however social, must assume an autonomy of the self, which an argument about governmentality cannot encompass because it theorizes it out of existence in a sociology which does not empirically investigate what people actually do in society but constantly and analytically asserts what society does to them. For all of its commitment to relativity and difference, the natives are largely and empirically absent from the postmodern analysis of the world since the sociological analysts of this world have abrogated the native's right to speak in anything other than the analytical terms of construction and deconstruction which postmodern sociology has provided for them.

KEY CONCEPTS

SUBJECTIVISM   Society as a subjective phenomenon in which the subject is the individual who is endowed with consciousness and acts in terms of his or her own ideas, values, interests and motives. So the reality of society lies in its nature as the intersubjective organization of relationships and interactions between individuals as subjects which is based on shared beliefs, values and motives.

OBJECTIVISM   Society as an objective phenomenon whose reality consists of the structural and institutional organization of social relationships which determines and constrains the actions of the individual members of it and so shapes the nature of their subjectivity, ideas, values, motives and action.

Image/Text

Paul Filmer

I seemed to learn . . .
That what we see of forms and images
Which float along on minds, and what we feel
Of active or recognizable thought,
Prospectiveness, or intellect, or will,
Not only is not worthy to be deemed
Our being, to be prized as what we are,
But is the very littleness of life.
Such consciousness I deem but accidents,
Relapses from the one interior life
That lives in all things, sacred from the touch
Of that false secondary power by which
In weakness we create distinctions, then
Believe that all our puny boundaries are things
Which we perceive and not which we have made.

William Wordsworth

IMAGE/TEXT AND SOCIOLOGICAL DISCOURSE

The sociological dichotomy between image and text is one which has emerged only recently, though Wordsworth reminds us that it is a much more venerable preoccupation of Enlightenment thought about the dichotomous tension between culture and nature (see chapter 'Culture/ Nature'). As a concern for sociology, however, it is largely a result of the importance of structuralism in twentieth-century social and cultural theories. This relates the dichotomy, both directly and indirectly, to the significance for sociology of concepts and theories of language as a social phenomenon that expresses consciousness intersubjectively. Yet sociology was marked by a reluctance to address language as a topic until the middle of the twentieth century, largely because of the desire of sociologists working within the dominant normative schools to preserve a positivist methodology for a scientific sociology. This involved a commitment to a correspondence version of truth and an attendant version of language as a neutral, correspondential medium of communication and expression. Both versions served well enough the epistemological ambitions for sociology as a science, but neither was able adequately to accommodate the reflexively experiential character of the social world, and the extent to which it was grounded by and for its actors in the negotiated truths of common sense which are established in and expressed through language. Whilst the potential for considering this linguistically constituted character of the social world was available conceptually in the formulation of the individual as social actor (see chapter 'Theory/Practice') and methodologically in the formulation of purposive social action as agency (see chapter 'Structure/ Agency'), the philosophical positivism underlying these conceptions denied them the possibility of being put into operation in terms of the social significance of language as the *basis* of sociological explanation. This gave the image/text dichotomy a history within sociology during this period on other terms, and in related forms: for example, as a dichotomous tension between the differentiated referents and manifestations of symbol and sign, where the sign establishes a concrete and specific (textual) realization of the imaginative possibilities represented by the symbol from which it is derived. It can be seen as implicated also in the idealism/materialism dichotomy, in the sense that a text may stand for an empirically specific, and therefore materially constraining, version of an imagined ideal (see chapter 'Idealism/Materialism'). Most significantly, perhaps, there is a clear sense of the dichotomy which lurks in the discursive sociological differentiation between theoretical images of society as a whole and the constructed texts of empirical sociological data.

The advent and consolidation of structuralist theories of language as a system of signs through the first two-thirds of the twentieth century has turned sociology back from its reluctance to address language and towards a concern with its essentially social character. This is not to suggest, however, a *sociologistic* account of language. On the contrary, it is clear that the origins of human society and language are dialectically interdependent and equally prehistoric. They are not empirically available for historically specific explanation. Instead, sociology addresses language theoretically and conceptually in terms of a phenomenology of the linguistic sign, though it is able to undertake detailed empirical inquiries into the embedded practices of its conventions of usage and the mundane meanings implied in them. Indeed, these conventions and meanings enable some empirical sociologists to claim variously, and quite coherently, that language is a social fact and can be treated functionally as if it is an interactionally natural phenomenon (Giglioli 1972; Boden and Zimmerman 1991).

Image/text relations have become a focus of central contemporary sociological interest as a result of the instatement of language as a topic of serious sociological concern and, following from this, the important interrelations which sociology has developed with other disciplines during the second half of the twentieth century, through adopting in common structuralist methodological approaches to the analysis of contemporary culture (see chapters 'Culture/Nature', 'Modernity/Postmodernity' and 'High/Mass'). The most important of these interrelations have been with cultural studies (Turner 1990; Davies 1993) and literary theory (Eagleton 1976; 1983) and have led to further involvement with contemporary psychoanalytical theory and with critical feminist thought (Milner 1994; see also chapter 'Theory/Practice'). These developments have had significant implications also for the sociology of art (see, for example, Wolff 1981; 1983; Filmer 1998), where they have generated attempts to extend the range of this subdisciplinary area beyond attempts to explain works of visual and literary art in the rather limiting terms of contextually determined *reflections* of their social worlds, into critical analyses of the *reflexive* relations between artistic practices and the social structures in which they are generated and to which they refer (see Natanson 1970; Blum et al. 1974; Bryson 1981). In structuralist terms, the result of these developments has been the elaboration of a series of methodological strategies which involve the treatment of social practices as if they are texts which articulate prior imagistic conceptions and projections of orders of relations (structures) within and between human groups which already exist, but of which members of the groups are not yet conscious, or which may yet be able to be brought into existence. These implicit and imaginary structures are complemented by possible intended meanings (senses) that members of the groups already share or might come to hold in common and which also require articulation in ways that may be treated as texts.

IMAGE, TEXT AND SOCIAL REALITY: THE DIVERSITY OF IMAGE/TEXT RELATIONS

The methodologically strategic, structuralist relation between image and text is quite abstract, and can be formulated clearly as a type of relation between substantive, empirical *absence* and *presence*, with several variants such as: image is absent, text is present; an image exists in consciousness but not as physical substance; a text is a substantive, empirical object; and so on. As Leppert notes, 'what images represent may otherwise not exist in "reality" and may instead be confined to the realm of imagination, wish, desire, dream, or fantasy' (1996: 3), a point made more polemically by Boorstin's (1962) formulation of image as pseudo-event. Roland Barthes (1915–80) offers unequivocally as 'the definition of the image, any image: that from which I am excluded' (1978: 132) and, in writing of privacy, insists that it is 'the absolutely precious, inalienable site where my image is free (free to abolish itself)' (1984: 98), thus offering a further example of the image/text relation as that between private and public. Barthes offers these and other (e.g. 1977) formulations in relation to the social and aesthetic practices that constitute photography, one of the specific sites on which the dichotomous tension between image and text has been addressed recurrently. This dichotomy becomes the more clear in the case of photography because the concept of image is addressed in tension not only with the text, but with a sense that may be seen as extending beyond the text, to a reality which is external to it, and its photographic representation.

This tension, as Sontag (1978) points out, is one which, like the discipline of sociology itself, is a consequence of the Enlightenment. The advances in humanist and scientific thought of the nineteenth century were greeted with the expectation that they would bring within reach ways of representing the real that would be freed from the interpretive mediation of an image. The techniques of photography and film in particular were seen as supporting the progress of scientific research through their capacity to represent things, in full detail, precisely as science had discovered they were constituted and events exactly as they occurred. From the mid nineteenth century, an aesthetic of **realism** developed which argued that the tasks of visual art and literature should be directed to the work of 'mirroring nature' – a task which, though realist artists found it impossible to accomplish, nevertheless continues to sustain a critical rhetorical force (Foster 1980).

Indeed, this tension between the aim of 'mirroring nature' through linking the technology of visual reproduction with the aesthetics of realism relates to a cognate tension (Benjamin 1969; 1979; Gombrich 1956; 1982) between photography and visual art which elaborates the image/text dichotomy still further. A figurative visual art work – for example, a painted portrait or a landscape painting – may be interpreted as presenting an image of the artist's and/or viewer's perception of what it represents to them and as such, to constitute a text (Phillipson 1985). As a text, it can be compared to a photographic text of the same subject in terms of a criterion of verisimilitude, for example. Each text, moreover, can be transformed in each medium of representation to an image of the other: a photograph can be made of the painting, and a painting of the photograph. The latter transformation is a particularly complicated one because of its history as a conventional feature of artistic practice: Courbet, Manet, Monet, Degas and Cezanne, for example, regularly used photographs of their subjects as *aides-mémoires* for their paintings (Macdonald 1979). Far from defining the image more precisely, the continuing development of increasingly sophisticated technologies of visual reproduction has served, with the most creative of ironies, to make more complex the relations between image and text. As Sontag has noted, 'the credence that could no longer be given to realities understood *in the form of* images was now being given to realities understood *to be* images, illusions' (1978: 153). Whereas the post-Enlightenment expectation had been that scientific knowledge would come to supplant the 'magic' of imagistic representation, it came instead to depend upon it as its necessary antithesis (Warnock 1976). Moreover, by the middle of the twentieth century, and notwithstanding the considerable achievements of scientific research and technology, it had been clearly established that the correspondential truth claims of scientific positivism, which depended upon proof, could not themselves be proved absolutely (see, for example, Popper 1962; Kuhn 1970). However, the **hermeneutic** necessity for interpretation of claims to validity that this produced, especially in the social sciences, had already begun to be addressed much earlier, during the nineteenth century, even as the claims of aesthetic realism began to be announced (Hirsch 1967).

Marx's critical analysis of the culture of capitalism, though the materialist character of so much of his argument means inevitably that it comes to be committed almost entirely to realist aesthetics, nevertheless offers an early example of the significance of the concept of image for sociological thought. He is critical, for example, of the process of what he terms *reification*, whereby, for example, the interests of a particular dominant social group, the beliefs and values in terms of which they legitimate their social position and the social structure in which they are located, are all treated as an inevitable, unchangeable, even a 'natural' set of institutional arrangements. Similarly, he criticizes the tendency of capitalist culture towards *fetishization of commodities*, where material objects, like monetary coins, are treated as having intrinsic value rather than representing the value of the goods and services whose exchange they facilitate. In both instances, the practice which is criticized is one which substitutes an image, an illusion, for a reality. Indeed, Marx formulates ideology quite specifically in the imagistic terms of a camera obscura, in which individuals and their relations appear upside down (Mitchell 1980; 1986).

These criticisms invoke also a further sense of image which is sociologically important – that of an **ontology** of the human individual as a member of society (Lyon 1983). All general sociological theories are based upon an implicit or explicit formulation of the essentially social character of human being which informs their major arguments. In Marx's case, both of the imagistic fallacies – of reification and fetishization of commodities – which he sees as perpetrated by the dominant interest groups in capitalist societies are generated by, and in turn contribute to, the substantiation of his ontological concept of the human being as *Homo laborens* – the person who works and, by doing so, produces and reproduces the material conditions required to sustain human existence. Just as human individuals reproduce themselves and their material conditions, so they are the principal and active agents in the production and reproduction of their social world and its constitutive political, economic and legal institutions and practices. In this sense, Marx is arguing that human beings reproduce themselves *in their own image*. The distinctive character of Marx's version of human ontology can be seen by contrasting it with that of his mentor, Georg Friedrich Hegel (1770–1831), for example, whom he later claims to have 'turned on his head'. Like many other philosophers, Hegel argued that the essential character of the human individual was that of *Homo sapiens* – the person who is wise and for whom thought, therefore, determines action. Marx's inversion of Hegel occurs with his contradictory proposition that it is the *material* conditions of human existence that determine consciousness. But both theorists are working with a clearly formulated and distinctive image of the human individual, in terms of which they develop their account of social reality. There is a sense, thus, in terms of which the image/text dichotomy parallels closely that between theory and practice.

This can be seen still more clearly if we consider Durkheim's contribution to the sociological formulation of image as a concept. Whilst Durkheim does not address image specifically, it is clear, as Smith's (1995) discussion implies, that his conceptions both of social fact and of society itself are imagistic and, in the Barthesian terms noted above, substantive absences rather than the empirical presences that his (Durkheim 1938) commitment to positivism would appear to require (Morrison 1995). Yet Durkheim implies a more significant sociological concept of image in his discussions of the relations between symbolism and society. These occur in his late works on *Primitive Classification* (Durkheim and Mauss 1963) and in *The Elementary Forms of the Religious Life* (1915), in the first of which he argues **sociologistically** (see Tiryakian 1962) that the abstract, symbolic categories in terms of which human societies classify their environments and experiences, such as time and space, are generated from the categories in terms of which they classify the structures of their own social relations. Thus space is conceptualized in terms of the segmental unity of a society of clans, each of which is composed of a network of extended families; and time is structured according to the principal events of the societal calendar of continuity, change and renewal. Each symbolic category is represented as an image of the social structures and processes which generate it. This is complemented in the later work on *The Elementary Forms of the Religious Life* by the argument that the sacred objects and ritual practices of religious worship are images of the society in which they are established. They are generated by the society as a reflexive representation of itself, on the grounds that the abstract idea of society can in this way be made cognitively accessible and understandable to its individual members as an emergent whole (see chapter 'Theory/Practice'). Thus the divine image itself (God) is seen by Durkheim as a projection of the collective consciousness, an imagistic representation of society in the form of a symbol which is socially generated. This amounts to a sociologistic inversion of the Judaeo-Christian myth that society is created in the divine image, since Durkheim has argued not only that society has created the image of the divine to represent itself, but also that it has generated the symbols with which to do so (Filmer 1977a). Thus, what he and Mauss term the 'total social fact' of emergent, collective consciousness is a *symbolic* reality, constituted in terms of a reflexive image of the structure of the social relations in which it inheres. The essential human capacity to symbolize which is implied here, and argued in *Primitive Classification*, suggests an ontological conception of the human individual in Durkheim's late work, as one who symbolizes. In the sense in which Durkheim conceptualizes them, moreover, symbols articulate the relation between image and text by representing the absent image as a substantive presence in some categorical or classificatory form (Lukes 1973). This form is conceptualized linguistically, and the symbol thus both articulates and represents a linguistic structuralist relation between image and text.

As a sociological phenomenon, as Leppert points out, 'any image literally exists as an object within the world that it in one way or another engages. When we look at images . . . what we see is the product of human consciousness, itself part and parcel of culture and history . . . images are constructed for the purpose of performing some function within a given sociocultural matrix' (1996: 3). It is to the realization of the possibility of performance of this function that the transformation of image into text is of crucial importance. In order to understand how that process of trans-formation occurs, it is necessary to consider the ways in which language mediates between image and text, and thus to consider some aspects of the textuality of language itself.

IMAGE, TEXT AND LANGUAGE: THE CONTINUITY OF IMAGE/ TEXT RELATIONS

The relations between image and text are structured invariably by lan-guage, and are therefore both **semiotic** and social. They are semiotic because they are constituted in and as signs which textualize the image; and they are social in so far as the textualization of the image makes it meaningful to the human collectivity which authors and shares the system of signs. The semiotic articulation of the image makes it analysable both on its own terms and in terms of the social conventions which make it meaningful. But this very accessibility means that at the very point at which an image is recognizable as a phenomenon in itself, it is made available for analysis: indeed, it is that availability which makes possible the constitution of the image as a phenomenon itself. Without its re-presentation in textual form, the image remains the 'absence' to which Barthes condemns it. The process of analysis begins, thus, with the (re-)production of the image as a text (Barthes 1967a). This is a routine, micro-interactional and interpretive social process and, as such, is deeply embedded in the mundane practices of everyday social life. Like all such practices, however, its routine character belies the complexity which becomes apparent when attempts are made to analyse its structure. That depth of embeddedness makes the semiotics of image/text relations recondite for analysis. But what gives especial complexity to sociological analysis of relations between image and text is that the textualization of an image which makes it analysable involves also a transformational intervention into the conventions of language itself. In translating an image into a text, the language of the text is extended beyond an assembly of potential meanings established by conventions of usage, which are already and relatively unproblematically known to readers, into a quite new and thus potentially problematic configuration of meanings which may not be interpretable in terms of existing linguistic conventions. Altman refers to this as 'doubly articulated language' (1981: 40), a concept which makes it possible to differentiate between what he has termed the linguistic and the textual meaning of a sign. The established, conventional meanings of linguistic signs constitute a primary modelling system which makes sense of the mundane world and enables it routinely to be taken for granted, much as Schutz (1962) proposes when referring to the meanings of everyday words as first-order typifications. Texts contain linguistic signs which carry everyday meanings; but Altman suggests 'that the text's most radical and disconcerting method of making meaning is that which derives from its status as secondary modelling system. The experience of reading draws its special nature from the necessity of learning a new language in the course of reading . . . one must learn the language and construe a message during the same reception' (1981: 42).

Altman's suggestion recalls other formulations of the double articulation of language. He uses himself (1981: 40) the primary morphemic/phonemic relation of general linguistics between sign and sound, the relations between which, in the primary modelling system of everyday language, are arbitrary in their conventionality and are learnt and relearnt, apparently routinely and straightforwardly, as a mundane pattern of common-sense usage. This echoes Saussure's (1959) distinction between signifier and signified as the constitutive relations of the sign, which Saussure also proposes are conventional and arbitrary in character. For Saussure, the primary modelling system of language, termed *la langue*, is different from that of Altman in constituting a basic grammatical system which is generative of the *langage* of everyday life, equivalent to Altman's conception of sound. But again, both formulations hold in common that the conventional relations between signs and the phenomena to which they refer are arbitrary.

But this double articulation of language is expressed, in these formulations, at only a primary level. Schutz (1962) indicates that there is a double articulation between this and a higher level when he complements his concept of the first-order typifications which constitute the taken-for-granted meanings of everyday words and expressions with a concept of the more formal expressions which he terms second-order typifications. The relations between the signs which carry these higher-order typifications, whilst they are both arbitrary and conventional in the sense that there is no *natural* basis for their relations with their referents, are treated nevertheless as governed by a specific *paradigm* of reference which limits their meaning to a specific realm of discourse. They are not, in other words, open to a potentially infinite variety of possible meanings, but are tied to the limits imposed on them by the requirements of particular forms of discourse such as natural and physical or social sciences, philosophy or more specific epistemological disciplines and systematic practices within these forms. They are the terms of critical and reflexive theorizing and their associated methodologies, of concepts and their definitions.

A distinction related to that of Schutz is made by Garfinkel (1963. 4–6), who differentiates between indexical and objective expressions. Indexical expressions are what he terms 'contingent accomplishments of organized artful practices of everyday life' (1967: 11). They refer to phenomena which represent them in the specific uniqueness of their particular and concrete manifestations, and depend for their interpretive meanings strictly upon the contexts in which they are employed (Bar-Hillel 1954; Garfinkel and Sacks 1970: 348–50). Objective expressions, by contrast, are employed to represent the general properties of phenomena and do not depend for their meanings upon the specific contexts of the particular manifestations of those phenomena. Whereas indexical expressions are bound by the contexts in which they are employed, objective expressions are employed as if they are context-free: indeed, Garfinkel sees them as an indispensable basis for the discourses of what he terms the exact sciences. For despite the enormous utility of indexical expressions for mundane interaction, they are inappropriate for formal discourse, which depends, according to Garfinkel, on a clear distinction between and substitution of objective for indexical expressions. Yet this distinction and substitution, Garfinkel notes, remains programmatic and unsatisfied 'in every *particular* case and in every *actual* occasion in which [it] must be demonstrated. In every actual case without exception, conditions will be cited . . . such that in that particular case the terms of the demonstration can be relaxed and nevertheless the demonstration be counted an adequate one' (1967: 6). Garfinkel thus moves beyond Schutz's distinction between first-order and second-order typifications to imply a set of what he terms formal or rational properties of indexical expressions which enable them to offer a practical infinity of potential meanings whilst making possible, through their association in accounts of the phenomena to which they refer, a formal discourse which can be interpreted routinely as meaningful within much narrower limits. This is due, he argues, to the essential reflexivity of language. In accounting for a phenomenon *in a language*, the phenomenon is in effect constituted as meaningful within the interpretive limits represented by the conventions of usage *of that language*. It is the language of discourse for any community that creates the *common* sense of that community (Filmer et al. 1972).

The relation between the semiotic and social character of image/text relations is taken still further by Charles Sanders Pierce (1867–1914) who argues the necessity for categorizing signs on the grounds that 'a sign . . . is an image of its object and, more strictly speaking, can only be an *idea*' (Buchler 1955: 105). Pierce identifies three principal forms of sign – icon, index and symbol – into one or other of which all signs can be classified. He differentiates them as follows: 'an *icon* is a sign which would possess the character which renders it significant, even though its object had no existence . . . an *index* is a sign which would, at once, lose the character which makes it a sign if its object were removed . . . a *symbol* is a sign which would lose the character which renders it a sign if there were no interpretant' (1955: 104). It is on Pierce's concept of index that Garfinkel draws in identifying indexical expressions, as he draws on the concept of icon in identifying objective expressions. Like objective expressions, and Schutzian second-order typifications, iconic signs are abstract categories within which the class of phenomena to which they refer can be collected in terms of their common general characteristics, whatever the specific social, cultural and historical contexts in which they occur. But Pierce's concept of the symbol goes beyond these categories of Garfinkel and Schutz, and returns us to the concept of image and its relation to text. Pierce develops the complex semiotic character of the symbol in terms of its emergent relations with other types of sign, noting that its

> representative character consists precisely in its being a rule that will determine its interpretant . . . A symbol is a law, or regularity of the indefinite future . . . it must *denote* an individual, and must *signify* a character . . . The symbol is connected with its object by virtue of the idea of the symbol-using mind, without which no such connection would exist . . . Symbols grow. They come into being by development out of other signs, particularly from icons, or from mixed signs partaking of the nature of icons and symbols . . . it is only out of symbols that a new symbol can grow . . . In use and in experience, its meaning grows . . . The symbol may, with Emerson's sphynx, say to man, 'Of thine eye I am eyebeam.' (1955: 112–15)

In effect, thus, the symbol is for Pierce both the originary category of sign (the eyebeam of the eye), since it is dependent on the ontological idea of the 'symbol-using mind', and also the highest order of the sign, since it is an emergent development from other signs (see Eco 1981: 175–99). In this it parallels the emergent synthesis of the dialectical interrelation between symbol and society identified by Durkheim. Similarly, in its ability both to synthesize and to authorize the meanings of other signs, it carries what

Garfinkel terms the essential reflexivity of language. For Pierce, 'all words, sentences, books, and other conventional signs are symbols . . . The word itself has no existence although it has a real being, *consisting in* the fact that existents *will* conform to it', and they will do so because they exist 'in the possibly imaginary universe to which the symbol refers' (1955: 102, 112). This is the sense in which the symbol not only is an image of its object but, in being so *strictly speaking*, as Pierce puts it, is no more than an *idea* which requires realization by being transformed into a condition ('real being') in which the phenomena to which it refers will conform to that referentiality. What it requires, in effect, is to be *con-texted*, to be constituted in and as a text. Hence a symbol can be both a word (or other conventional sign), that is, a single unit in a text (which is also a text in itself), and also an assembly of words (or other conventional signs) that constitute a much more elaborate text, such as a sentence or a book. For Saussure, the process of contexting requires limiting what he terms *la parole*, the promise of potential meanings held by the terms of *la langue*, at the point at which it becomes *langage*, language in use. The potential meanings are part of a syntagmatic linguistic system which is quite arbitrarily cross-cultural and trans-historical in character. Signs in a syntagmatic system can be likened to both Durkheim's and Pierce's senses of symbol precisely because they have the potential to mean, and they will mean. But they need to be brought to the condition in which that potential can be realized in and as text. For Saussure, context is a paradigmatic system which orders assemblies of signs from potentially infinite varieties of possible meanings into the 'real being' of actual interpretive meanings fixed by convention. This locates signs reflexively, as texts, in historically and culturally specific social contexts (Barthes 1967b; Guiraud 1975). The contexts, thus, both imply the paradigmatic principle(s) which make texts meaningful and are guaranteed constitutively by the texts to the extent to which they are successful in doing so. This demonstrates, once again, the essential reflexivity of language operating through the structure of image/text relations: the text both realizes and constitutes the paradigmatic image.

In Altman's sense, a text constitutes a paradigmatic condition for itself by establishing limits to the meaning of the terms associated within it through that very structure of association itself. Hence, texts are articulated into two levels which Altman (1981: 40) terms functions and signs. The *signs* of a particular text can have meanings which are prior to their inclusion in that specific text. They may be more or less closely related to the meaning(s) generated by or associated with their meanings in other texts which have already been constructed, or are being created simultaneously, or may be produced in future. But the *functions* of the text limit the meanings of its signs to the limits which the text reflexively and simultaneously generates for them and imposes upon them. This limiting process is the process of textual interpretation. It does not imply that there is one sole meaning to a text, and hence to the functions attributed to its constitutive signs; but it does indicate the manner in which an interpretation makes explicit the text's paradigmatic condition. This is, in effect, both a translation of image into text and, thereby, a concretization of the image, from its private absence from the social world in subjective consciousness, into the social and cultural presence of its public meaningfulness (Eco 1989).

It is important to note, however, that this process of self-constitution of the text at the functional level is only one of three sources of meaning for the text – what Altman (1981: 45) terms its *intratextual* meaning. Another source of meaning is that which derives from the words or other conventional signs of the primary language of the text – its *linguistic* meaning. Finally, all texts derive from their intratextual meaning an *intertextual* meaning which is a crucial feature of their paradigmatic condition. Intertextual meanings parallel, at a higher level of generalizability, the linguistic meanings of texts. Linguistic meanings are effectively denotative, whereas intertextual meanings are connotative, and relate the texts to the most fully elaborated paradigmatic resources for meaning in the cultures in which they are constructed and interpreted. These developed paradigms constitute what can be termed the cosmology of such cultures. As such, they are the most fundamental socio-cultural resources for collective and hence shareable images.

Barthes (1972) endorses this point in his reconceptualization of myth as a *form of speech*, which constructs itself as a higher-order semiological system. He terms this higher-order system *metalanguage*, proposing that it is a second language in the terms of which it is possible to speak about a linguistic system of a lower order. This lower-order system is composed of *language objects* on which myth draws to build its own system. Myth, thus, is in a reflexive relation to its lower-order system of language objects: it both draws on and speaks of them. Metalanguage enables semiologists to treat writing and pictures in the same way because both are conventional signs and hence have the same signifying function in relation to myth, which is to constitute language objects. Mythic speech, for Barthes, is speech which draws on semiotically full signifier/signified relations. The signs constituted by these semiotically full relations are already related to the paradigmatic structures of meaning which constitute cultural cosmologies: it is the contents of these structures which fill them and which give them their mythic status, no matter in which particular epistemological discourse (of art, science, religion, for example) they manifest themselves. And it is these semiotically full relations which represent the fundamental relation between image and text, since the sources of images are the cosmologies which fill the signifier/signified relations with the potential for meanings which can be interpreted within the paradigmatic limits that constitute them and make them recognizable (and interpretable) as texts. Effectively, cosmologies both provide and *provide for* paradigms in the sense that they are both the resource for connotative meanings which can exist in language objects prior to their constitutive incorporation into texts, and the site for the texts whose intratextual meanings enable connotations to be further elaborated.

Barthes's argument that myth is a form of speech echoes that of Lévi-Strauss, for whom the function of signs is to 'transcend the contrast between the tangible and the intelligible . . . [through expressing] the one by means of the other' (1969: 14). If image and text are considered, respectively, as instances of the intelligible and the tangible, then the parallel becomes clear. By giving signification to the intelligible image, the sign makes it tangible and hence textual. This concept of the function of the sign is crucial to Lévi-Strauss's concept of myths, which operate autonomously in the human mind, without the awareness of the human subject, to the extent that he suggests analysing them 'as if the thinking process were taking place in the myths, in their reflection upon themselves and their interrelation . . . myths themselves are based on secondary codes (the primary codes being those that provide the substance of language)'. The structural analysis of myth implies 'a tertiary code, which is intended to ensure the reciprocal translatability of several myths . . . as it were, the myth of mythology . . . each myth taken separately exists as the limited application of a pattern, which is gradually revealed by the relations of reciprocal intelligibility discerned between several myths' (1969: 12–13). From a sociological perspective, the genesis of this concept of myth as tertiary code serves a purpose comparable to that of Barthes's concept of myth as metalanguage: both provide for the conceptualization of culture as generating reflexively, through its constitutive cosmologies, the paradigms which provide for the connotative interpretability of texts (Barthes 1975).

CONCLUSION: IDEOLOGY AND IMAGE/TEXT RELATIONS

One prolific source of images in contemporary culture is the media of broadcast communication – in particular, television – whose discourses provide us with interesting sociological examples of how paradigms provide for the connotative interpretability of texts. In a pluralist political culture, the media carry messages which represent the views of different and divergent interests on the possession of power and the distribution of wealth. These views, whilst divergently different in and of themselves, are views nevertheless of what are treated as common phenomena, such as images of historical events, political and economic institutions and social activities. These phenomena, that is, are represented initially (as news, for example) as if they have *occurred* in the same way for all who are interested in them; but they are open to be *interpreted* and *explained* in quite different ways according to the differences between the interests of those who seek to establish their meaning. It is not actually the case that they are even *represented* initially as if they have occurred in the same way; rather, it is that the connotations of the conventional signs in which they have been represented have not been *addressed* in terms of the particular types of paradigmatic resources from which the signs and their connotations have been drawn. Hall et al. (1980) formulates the processes of interpretive representation and 'reading' of the text of messages broadcast by the media as a disjunctive set of processes of systematically distorted communications (see Habermas 1970) which he terms non-symmetrical encoding/decoding. Messages are encoded according to the distortions of one system of interests and decoded according to those of another.

The systems of shared beliefs and values which underpin common interests on the use of power and the distribution of wealth in any political society are its ideologies (see chapter 'Theory/Practice'). They offer coherent and persuasive accounts of the states of the social world, of the causes, conditions and directions of societies – often as important features of their cultures. Eco notes that

> the human labour of transforming states of the world . . . cannot be performed without organizing such states of the world into semantic systems. In order to be transformed, the states of the world must be *named* and structurally arranged. As soon as they are named, that system of sign systems which is called 'culture' (which also organizes the way in which the material forces are thought of and discussed) may assume a degree of extra-referential independence that a theory of codes must respect and analyse in all its autonomy. (1977: 297)

The process of encoding of broadcast media images is, in effect, one form of organizing interpretively a state of the world into a semantic system; the process of decoding is that of interpretively *reorganizing* that semantic system to generate a different organization of the state of the world. As Eco points out, the interpretive organization of semantic systems is a fundamentally social activity: 'the labour of sign production releases social forces and itself represents a social force. It can produce both ideologies and criticism of ideologies. Thus semiotics . . . is also a form of *social criticism*, and therefore one among the many forms of *social practice*' (1977: 298).

Hall et al. (1980: 136–8) is thus able to suggest three hypothetical positions in terms of which the messages of a televisual discourse which has been encoded in the dominant ideological sign system of a political culture can be decoded in terms of a different sign system. These are, first, the *dominant-hegemonic* position in which the connoted meaning of the message is decoded in the terms of the sign system in which it has been encoded. This is the only sustainable sociological formulation of correspondential communication, in which the intentionally connoted meaning of the communicator is understood and accepted by the recipient of the message. The recipient is thus operating within the dominant code and participating in a process of ideological reproduction at a *global* level. The second position is identified as that of the *negotiated code*, which modifies the dominant hegemonic code of the intended connotations of the message by adapting it to the recipient's specific *local* knowledge and experience. This means that the negotiated position is one of particular exceptions and contradictions to the universality of the dominant code. Because of such contradictions, Hall notes that it is with the deployment of the negotiated code that so-called 'failures' of communication occur from the point of view of professional broadcasters utilizing the dominant code, and 'misunderstandings' from the point of view of the decoders. Thirdly, recipients can decode messages in terms of an *oppositional code* at a global level by replacing the connotative system of the dominant code with a completely different and divergent system of connotations. It is at this point, Hall notes, that 'the "politics of signification" – the struggle in discourse – is joined' (1980: 178). It is at this point, too, that the labour of sign production becomes a social force by generating ideological and social criticism. Just as the dominant code has attempted to reinforce the existing socio-cultural order by connoting its hegemony in broadcast messages, the image of an alternative state of the social world has been connoted as a realizable possibility by being encoded as the text of a different sign system. As social forces, and as practices of social criticism and the criticism of ideologies, thus, the dichotomous semiotic and linguistic structures of relations between image and text are central to contemporary critical sociological inquiry.

KEY CONCEPTS

IMAGE Although an image is a likeness the word has come to suggest a gap between the real and the created (the image). The image is thus more like the imagined, however, as sociologists know, images and imaginings can be real in their consequences so we have to seek to understand the reality both within and behind any image.

TEXT Text is a way of talking about any reality as a series of potential messages. Psychologies, personalities, identities, books, films, social events can all comprise texts that can be read in a variety of different ways. It is critical for the social theorist to understand the rules and interests contained within any particular reading and to justify any reading of their own.

Realism An aesthetic which argues that the role of art is to represent reality. It is developed most fully during the nineteenth century, alongside materialist philosophy and scientific knowledge, and in opposition to philosophical idealism. Amongst its principal consequences is a correspondential theory of linguistic and semiotic representation, according to which the work of art is a reflection of the reality of experience. The structure of social reality is seen, in turn, as determining the work of art.

Hermeneutics   The term was imported from theology into modern philosophy by Wilhelm Dilthey (1833–1911) to characterize the interpretive investigation of essentially intentional human acts of linguistic understanding. It is also used by Heidegger to denote the phenomenology of existence and understanding. Ricouer argues that contemporary hermeneutics is concerned with two principal forms of textual exegesis: by recovery, in which the text is analysed interpretively to reveal a meaning hidden within it; and by suspicion, in which the text is treated as concealing a set of cultural determinations which must be exposed.

Ontology   That part of metaphysics which is concerned with inquiry into the conditions and character of (human) being itself. It has become important for modern philosophy as a result of the phenomenological critique of positivism. Positivism sought to end metaphysical speculation altogether, and subsumed ontology into epistemology, from which it had been traditionally differentiated, thereby proposing to establish being as (human) nature. Phenomenology re-establishes ontology at the centre of philosophical inquiry because of its focus on the reflexive character of consciousness.

Sociologism   A form of reductionist explanation of all human social phenomena in sociological terms. It is most closely associated with Durkheim's sociology, though as Tiryakian (1962) notes, he neither defines nor uses the term. As a type of sociological explanation it depends upon the differentiation of social from all other types of human phenomena, and it insists upon their irreducibility to explanation in terms of other epistemological discourses, such as anthropology, history or psychology.

Semiotics/semiology   The systematic study of signs and their denotative and connotative properties. The term was used by Pierce at the end of the nineteenth century to represent a general theory of the logical function of signs. He proposed that semiotics was effectively another name for logic in its general sense and thus a science of what he termed abstractive observation. Shortly after this, Saussure conceived the term semiology to represent the study of the social character and functions of signs.

Needs/Wants

Don Slater

The concept of 'need', and its distinction from 'want', plays a crucial role in many societies. It is also written profoundly into modern social thought. To say that something is a need is to say that it is essential to the continued existence or identity of a body, person or social order. Thus people talk of 'basic needs' for food, clothing and shelter which if not satisfied will cause death or ill-health: a failure to reproduce a social entity. Basic needs, as defined for example by international aid agencies, may also include such things as health, human rights, control over reproduction: things whose absence would entail living something less than the life to which one is entitled. The list of basic needs can be extended to needs for love or security or creativity or education, indicating that humans are essentially more than bodies and need certain capacities or pleasures in order to be what a community considers really human. Much modern thought has been preoccupied with defining real, basic or essential humanity, or has made assumptions about what real humans are or should be. At the same time there is some recognition that need has a historical dimension. We can talk about needing literacy or a car or a CD player in the sense that these things are now considered essential or normal to living properly in a specific society at a specific time: we might not be considered a full social member or able to participate fully in social life without filling these needs. Much of political life and social critique consists in judging whether current social arrangements meet human needs and produce a way of life which is deemed good.

What we define as needs are attributed the qualities of being essential, objective and compelling (Table 1). I cannot choose to need food, it is a

CORE SOCIOLOGICAL DICHOTOMIES

TABLE 1

Needs	Wants
Objective (not necessarily experienced by the social actor, a potential object of another's knowledge)	Subjective (and subjectively experienced)
Determined, compelled or caused	Chosen or decided by the social actor
Essential: necessary for physical or social 'existence'	Luxurious, dispensable, a matter of arbitrary desire, trivial
Universal, defined at the level of body, species or society as such	Contingent, relative, 'eccentric': defined in terms of the peculiarities of a specific individual, group, community
Existential, pre-cultural	Preferential, stylistic, cultural

requirement of my physical body; and whether or not I *want* food, or choose to eat it, it is a need. Needs appear to be anchored in the objective world, either in the physical human body or in the nature or essence of human life. The case of bodily needs demonstrates a further feature, that needs are often considered universal: a body needs food in any society it might live in. The same universality can apply to other declared needs, like many related 'rights', such as the idea that everyone has a need for and therefore a right to education, security, freedom and so on. This close relationship between needs and rights indicates that needs can involve a strong claim to entitlement. Wanting a cup of coffee does not indicate any obligation on the part of society to provide one; to say that 'people need food', on the other hand, implies a moral or social failure if people do not get enough of it.

'Need' is a powerful concept, then, because it seems to anchor social claims in the realm of necessity or even nature: statements about need are generally based on assumptions about what human beings or bodies 'really are'. For example, scientific definitions of the nutritional requirements for basic health can be used to ground national and international welfare policies: the claim is that 'real needs' can be identified 'scientifically', outside politics, and should govern the actions of political agents. Marx, to take another example, based much of his socio-political perspective on claims about the real nature or 'species being' of the human: he argued that the human's essential need is for conscious and creative human praxis and therefore their most pressing need in modern society is the overcoming of alienation. This notion of need grounds his entire theory and critique of history and practice.

In fact, as we shall discuss below, concepts of need are not objective and outside politics, but are always bound up with social values and value judgements, are matters of culture, not nature. However, in social thought needs are generally counterposed to 'wants' – and related terms such as preferences and desires – and these terms convey the idea of value-laden or culture-bound desires. Whereas needs are defined as objective, wants are largely seen as subjective: they are desires that have to do with how I see myself and the pleasures, aims, motives I define for myself and consciously experience. I need food, whether I consciously want it or not, on the other hand, I might experience an ungovernable desire for chips but that does not mean I need them. Indeed, what I want may be the opposite of what I need; and – as in the case of anorexia – what I need may be subjectively repellent.

Wants are seen as grounded not in human nature and bodies but rather in either the eccentricities of the individual's personality or the peculiarities of their local culture. Wants are therefore not universal but regarded as relative, contingent, pluralistic. By the same token, they are not defined as compelling but rather – unlike needs – are often used to mark out the sphere of human freedom and choice: in both liberal notions of consumer sovereignty and Marxist theory, human progress is identified with moving out of the realm of necessity and the compulsion of animal needs into a realm where choice is dictated by the self-defined cultural desires of individuals. By the same token, however, wants are not regarded as essential but often as actually trivial, mere whim, fashion or fad, and as luxuries: to be able to want something ('I want maple syrup on my waffles') usually indicates a step up from a world in which scarcity anchors needs firmly in nature to an affluence which allows for an open-ended exploration of non-essential, non-existential desires. Finally, because wants are not anchored in the existential reproduction of bodies or identities, they are often characterized as 'insatiable' in that new wants can always be conjured up by the imagination or through social competition.

CULTURE AND CRITIQUE

If needs and wants are distinguished by such things as their objectivity and assumptions about the nature of human subjects and societies, then each term assigns a quite different role and character to social thought and knowledge. If need is deemed to be objective and compelling, it is also a matter of objective knowledge. There are authorities and experts who can tell us what we need independently of our subjective experience: scientific authorities, moral authorities, political authorities who can say that, for example, traditional values, or 2000 calories per day, or nuclear families with a wage-earning father, or a rolling back of the state are *necessary* for a proper human life in society. Such 'expertise' can be institutionalized in, for example, welfare states, medical establishments, churches, or in social science disciplines: each claims that needs are matters not of individual choice, but of the nature of individuals and social wholes. Social knowledge can therefore be closely allied with social power through concepts of need.

On the other hand, concepts of need are fundamental to social critique and opposition to power: social critique generally uses some definition of 'real human need' as a yardstick or independent standard by which to judge the adequacy of existing social arrangements.

Wants, on the other hand, admit of no authority but that of the individual who is experiencing them. I may feel you should not want heroin as opposed to a healthy meal, but if you say that that's what you want it would be hard to dispute you: in Western thought, you are the authority over your wants and desires. One can go further – as in liberalism – and say that you are also the sole authority over the moral value of your wants: if you want heroin (and can pay for it and will not harm anyone else by having it) then no one has a right to deny you it. Notions of consumer sovereignty, inscribed in the idea of *de gustibus non est disputandem* (tastes cannot be disputed), rely on the idea that wants cannot be rationally debated or decided but are up to the individual. It is perfectly proper to answer the question 'Why do you want that?' by saying 'I just do', and the role of social thought then tends to be limited to describing people's tastes and choices (as in market research). In contrast, to the question 'Do you need that?' one would have to raise knowledge claims about cause and effect (what things are necessary to accomplish various ends) as well as value claims about what *must* be done (for example, not only a demonstration that food is necessary to keep people alive, but also an implicit claim that keeping alive is something good or essential).

The opposition between these two concepts and the different roles they map out for social thought have been formative throughout the modern period. The modern age, and modern sociology, start with a deregulation of desire in which wants are asserted almost to the complete exclusion of needs (indeed, for the crucial tradition of liberalism, the distinction virtually disappears). This occurs as part of a socio-economic and intellectual revolution against the *ancien régime* from the late seventeenth century. Prior to that point, needs are largely contrasted with 'luxuries'. Luxury is not simply consumption above basic requirements, it is also consumption 'above one's station'. In premodern Europe, levels and styles of consumption were clearly tied to status or standing, often juridically through sumptuary laws: there were foods one could not eat (the king's deer), clothes one had to wear (for example, livery or guild costume), and restrictions on where one could live. This regulation of consumption was rooted in a strong sense of necessity: one's station and therefore one's appropriate needs and consumption were fixed by the 'great chain of being', in a cosmic hierarchy stretching from God downwards. Hence, to express or indulge wants which were luxurious – above one's station – was to be insubordinate, sinful or even treasonable, to rebel against the social, political and cosmological hierarchy and order (see Berry 1994; Sekora 1977).

Various modern forces dismantled these forms of social regulation, including the regulation of needs. Crucially, with the rise of commerce and capitalism, goods and their consumption are increasingly regulated by economic value alone – the ability to pay – rather than by rules of status and traditional social order. In fact, the triumph of economic value corrodes the old status order to the point that only money talks. What it says is no longer bound by necessity but is elaborated into a consumer culture comprising (in principle) free individual choice amongst an ever more refined selection of things: a culture of wants and of individual choices and preferences. It is often argued that it is the explosion of productive forces in the Industrial Revolution that begins to raise society out of the realm of necessity and compulsion and into that of freely developing wants and desires. In fact, what seems equally important (and even historically prior) are the emerging concepts of the Enlightenment, formalized in liberalism, in which the individual is increasingly thought about in terms of liberty and autonomy from social forces (tradition, status, authority) as well as from natural compulsion. The free individual is seen as the moral, cognitive and political centre of the universe, and is believed properly to pursue its own self-defined interests (its wants and desires, projects and goals) through institutions, such as the market and representative democracy, which are disciplined and directed by the individual's statements of want (expressed as economic demand or political votes) rather than limiting him or her to needs defined by supra-individual forces and institutions.

The early Enlightenment, and early liberalism, optimistically believed that once individuals are freed from authority and superstition to rely on their own reason, they will all arrive at similar conclusions about what is right and proper in the world, including their desires: amongst other things, 'needs' could be rationally defined and identified as part of universalist definitions of the human. This hope wanes over the eighteenth century: it is diversity, disagreement and the limits of reason in defining the human that become more prominent. This hope also comes into conflict with the equally fundamental Enlightenment stress on individual liberty: for liberalism, this overrides all other considerations, above all the urge to rational universal knowledge (or prescription) of needs.

Hence liberalism develops a completely new vocabulary of need and want, one largely evolved through Bentham's utilitarianism. Adam Smith and David Hume had already begun the process of disparaging the notion of luxury; the expansion of desire, they argue, is crucial to prosperity, culture and civilization. Moreover they begin to replace the distinction between needs and wants with terms like 'conveniences of life' which basically take an approving view of middle-class domestic comfort well above the level of basic need (Appleby 1993). Utilitarianism takes a more radical approach. In place of all the multitudinous needs and wants that individuals could conceivably experience, Bentham espouses the highly abstract concept of 'utility' – the capacity of an object to give pleasure or ease pain. This concept is purely formal: it says nothing about the specific needs or wants of social members, let alone about their moral value. Utility is an attribute any object might have for any reason in relation to any desire any individual might have. Utility is entirely in the eye of the beholder. The social analyst need have no knowledge of either the desires of the subject or the capacities of the object: we need only know *that* an individual wanted something (we know this behaviourally: if they bought it, it must have had utility to them). This concept becomes the centrepiece of mainstream economic thought, particularly after the marginalist revolution of the 1870s: there are no wants or needs, only preferences or revealed preferences (revealed through effectively expressed demand).

Crucially, liberal-utilitarian concepts like utility and preferences elide and even collapse the needs/wants distinction: in fact, the distinction largely disappears for most liberalism. It is fundamental to liberalism that knowledge and moral evaluation of desire are matters for individuals only (subject to the classic proviso that the fulfilment of any of their desires does not harm other social members: hence a liberal *could* condemn a preference for private armies, heroin or toxic waste not because there is anything intrinsically wrong with such desires but because their satisfaction might infringe other people's sovereignty). Specifically, the very idea underlying 'need' – that we can talk about necessities which are independent of the individual's volition or even self-knowledge – is anathema to liberalism. Firstly, it infringes the individual's liberty by placing them under moral, political or social authority. One reason the market (and to a lesser extent democracy) is so miraculous for liberalism is that it can allocate and distribute social resources automatically in relation to expressed desires, without making any conscious judgements or decisions about which desires are better or more basic or important, about what people *need*: the 'hidden hand' does it all. Secondly, it is important that liberalism shares the general positivist distinction between facts and values: one can (for example, through market research) collect facts about what people want, but this cannot warrant any conclusions about what they *should* want. Certainly from Hume onwards, human reason cannot arbitrate human desire but is rather the 'slave of passion'. Reason is restricted to the *manner* in which we pursue our self-interests; the interests themselves are irrational (or, better, arational) and it is therefore unwarranted to evaluate them authoritatively as the needs/wants distinction implicitly does (Slater 1997a).

It is interesting, and important, that contemporary postmodernism converges with some of these liberal conclusions: both attack modernist rational and (social) scientific claims to know the truth of people's needs, and fear the forms of social power with which such claims are often complicit. In a word, both distrust claims which go beyond the expressed preferences, tastes, articulated self-interests manifested by individuals. But the differences between the two are also crucial. Liberals see wants as interests which can be subjectively experienced and rationally pursued by coherent individual egos. Postmodernism, on the other hand, tends to disparage the rationality and coherence of individuals as well as of social knowledge, viewing the social subject as a disorganized 'id' dispersed amongst various intersecting discourses. The coherence of a choosing, want-pursuing ego is regarded as no less problematic than the positing of supra-individual needs; the focus is rather on amorphous forms of 'desire' which are more or less socially structured and organized.

If liberalism cast the triumph of utility and preference over needs, wants and luxuries as a triumph of freedom, critics from both the right and the left saw this triumph (and that of liberal-utilitarianism itself) as the victory of a soulless, immoral and violent industrial capitalist modernity. 'Need' was a battle standard raised from both the left and the right, but in each case the enemy was an individualism which threatened social solidarity and social values.

On the one hand there is a range of more or less straightforwardly conservative and even reactionary responses, most of them formulated in terms of notions such as culture, community and tradition: statements about real and proper needs are grounded in the authority not of science but of tradition (sometimes underpinned by religion). In this view, needs are properly formulated within the organic historicity of human communities and their evolving values, hallowed by time and involving commitments to ways of life that transcend individuals and single generations (much of the 'culture and society tradition' mapped out by Raymond Williams 1985 is concerned with these issues). It is presumptuous for individuals to formulate their own wants in opposition to the necessity implied by a way of life that is deemed organic and authentic. Modern industrial and consumer culture, however, replaces such communities with contractual and materially self-interested bonds between individuals – bonds which recognize no obligation save to the transient wants and whims of the individual. The result is a crisis of social value, as well as of social order and solidarity. Left critiques of modernity also disparage the replacement of needs by wants. However, they tend to look to the future rather than the past for those authentic and non-alienated communities in which enduring values rather than ephemeral wants will rule again. Images of post-capitalist or post-industrial society, from Rousseau and Babeuf onwards, associate equality and the end of exploitation with the limitation of wants and their subordination to a collective, democratically determined measure of need. Tradition is replaced by politics as the source of overriding social values that might distribute social resources in relation to a consensus over what is necessary for the good life in society.

NEEDS AND VALUES

So far we have looked at the needs/wants distinction as a distinction between nature and culture, or between universal and individual values or choices. In fact, the distinction is far more complicated than this largely because statements about need are in fact closely bound up with the values and value judgements of particular communities. For example, analytical philosophers note that implicit in the statement 'I need x . . .' is the further statement 'in order to achieve y', and that y always involves some kind of value choice, the choice of a goal or end to which x is a more or less effective means. Even the basic statement that 'I need food in order to live' is only compelling if one argues that life is a good thing (which would not be true, say, if one were on hunger strike for a cause one believed to be more important than one's own life). It is clear in the case of a health service, for example, that implicit in statements about what people need are assumptions about the expected quality and standard of living of different classes of people at different historical moments (Doyal and Gough 1991).

In other words, both needs and wants are bound up with culture, are particular to specific cultures. The cultural nature of both needs and wants has been a major preoccupation of sociology and anthropology for some time now; and this issue again gives the dichotomy a very strategic role in social thought. We can, for example, counterpose two very prestigious arguments (Slater 1997a; 1997b). On the one hand, it is often argued that there are basic needs (either physical like hunger or more general like nurture or security) but that these might take different cultural forms in different societies: cooked insects or cordon bleu cuisine can equally meet the need of hunger, just as different forms of childhood will do for nurture. The different cultural forms are not arbitrary or whimsical like individual wants since they are transmitted through traditions, language, rituals and so on: they are cultural in a fully social sense. However, they still vary, unlike needs. Social thought might then be interested in two things: accounting for cultural variation, and assessing – across cultures – whether real needs are being met, and if not, why not.

However, this means arguing that we can know what a real need is independently of the individual or cultural form it takes. This argument can be difficult to sustain, partly because we cannot empirically observe any need independent of its cultural form: hunger, for example, always takes the form of desire for, say, a sandwich rather than a sheep's bladder. Indeed, every culture has a different definition of what counts as food (edible/inedible) and therefore of what one can be hungry for, as well as when, with whom and in what order (the social rituals of eating), and through which processes of transformation into food (cooking).

Hence, the second kind of argument. It is not correct to say that basic needs take various cultural forms; rather both needs and wants are defined *within* particular cultures, and cannot be defined or identified in the abstract. Culture constitutes both needs and wants (see, for example, Sahlins 1974; 1976). For example, many cultures – perhaps all – make a distinction between needs and wants, between what is objective, essential, compelling and necessary for being a full member of the society, and what is not. But they each define it very differently. The sociological task, then, is not to define a set of invariable basic needs that exist cross-culturally; rather, sociologists should look at the way in which needs and wants are defined internally to a culture. This position can be pluralistic – that we should respect the diversity of needs/wants expressed by individuals and communities and not try to judge them against some universal yardstick of what humans should really want or need, or (to put it another way) that we should not expect people to want what we 'know' they need. There is also the possibility here of a more extreme relativism, culminating in a view that human desire is so entirely a question of culturally specific wants that members of one culture cannot really understand, let alone meaningfully comment upon, those of another. As in liberalism, *de gustibus non est disputandem*: wants are not amenable to rational or even sensible discussion.

The culturalist view, like the liberal stress on preferences as free choice, treats difference as absolute, irreducible and incommensurable. If social thought attempts to reduce these differences to more universal definitions of need, it is not only empirically wrong, but actually infringes fundamental freedoms and cultural autonomy (for example, it may be part of Western imperialism). The universalist response, in favour of a notion of real needs, is that freedom and autonomy are themselves conditional on the meeting of certain needs which are objective in character. For example, in order to have a culture in the first place, or to individually participate in one, it is necessary to have a healthy body and sound mind, the product of particular needs having been met. This approach, it is argued, has the merit of being able to compare different communities or societies as to whether the preconditions of cultural life are being met for the various categories of members, and to provide a critique of societies which do not. (Doyal and Gough 1991 present this argument; see also Soper 1981; 1990 on the politics of need.)

All of these issues become increasingly pressing precisely because modernity and modern social thought seem to be all about the intensification of cultural diversity, pluralism and competition. And this itself is often experienced as arising from the fact that modernity involves (or promises) enormously expanding productive forces, and therefore potentially rising standards of living and increasingly complex and differentiated lifestyles. Both desires and their objects – as well as things like taste, discrimination and style which connect them – become increasingly complex, differentiated and abundant. Marx, for example, worked within the Hegelian tradition in which history is seen as a dialectic between subjects and objects: humans, motivated by forms of need, desire and goals, transform the world through their praxis (Miller 1987). The objective world therefore takes the form of an objectification of their subjective desires. However, this objective culture constitutes the environment in which human subjectivity is formed, and new desires and goals are formulated. In transforming the world, humans therefore transform themselves. For most Marxists (and non-Marxists such as Simmel, who stressed the role of urban life as well as industrialization in this process) this dialectic moves in the direction of increasing complexity and refinement. In fact, Marx defines the goal of human development as the production of individuals who are 'rich in needs', not individuals who are satiated, but those who inhabit and require a stimulating and evolving environment which provokes them to ever greater self-development. Marx associates this richness of needs with a move from the realm of 'animal needs' into a 'realm of freedom' in which, freed from the struggle for mere existence (the meeting of basic needs), humans will have the opportunity and material means to realize their 'species being' (see Heller 1976). Capitalism is in one respect heroic and progressive for Marx, since it involves an explosive discovery and creation of new use values, of new needs and objects; however, exploitative class relations mean that those with money merely satisfy wants (trivial whims and fashions), while those who produce the goods are reduced to a point below animal needs, a point at which 'even the need for fresh air ceases to be a need for the worker' (Marx 1975: 359).

Marx was one of the first to argue that modern affluence and productivity could be used to manipulate people. Because it is tied to the imperatives of capital accumulation and the need to sell ever more goods, this productivity is not related to need (to which capitalists are entirely and in principle indifferent) but rather to wants or – more precisely – effective demand: those desires which can be manifested through the market. Capitalists attempt to create ever more desires through ever more objects, as well as through advertising, marketing, design. The evolution of needs becomes a tool of capitalist accumulation rather than the realization of human potential. In a sense, Marx argues that capitalism creates a vast range of new wants, but fails to satisfy humanity's basic need: the need to express and develop itself through unalienated human praxis. Indeed, the range of wants and goods on offer in consumer society are merely false and frustrating compensations for the fundamental alienation of human labour.

These themes were powerfully developed in the work of Herbert Marcuse. Marcuse (1964; 1973a; 1973b) argues that the development of modern productive forces would allow the satisfaction of all human needs with a minimum of alienated labour, thus permitting the expansion of the realm of human freedom and development. Of course, capitalism could not continue on this basis: it requires both continued labour and ever expanding production and consumption. This is secured by creating or inciting ever more wants in people (which means they have to work more for the cash to buy more goods), wants which – because they involve people in continuing alienated labour – are actually repressive even when they are satisfied. More than this, these new wants are actually internalized by the individual as needs. Needs, for Marcuse, are not biological or other essences, but rather 'vital needs, which, if not satisfied, would cause dysfunction of the organism' (1973b: 26): thus, for example, a car can be a 'vital need' in modern society, without which an organism may not be able to objectively or subjectively function. In this sense, even the most trivial of wants can be experienced as a need, can be installed as 'second nature'. He therefore refers to the commodity system as a counter-revolution at the level of the instincts: individuals are reconstituted around needs for ever more commodities. Instead of goods serving human development, humans are developed to fit the needs of commodity production.

Marcuse's position also exemplifies a central theme of modern critical theory: Marcuse believes that some notion of 'real need' is a *sine qua non* of critical thought and political practice. If the system is able to generate wants for the goods that it is able to produce profitably, and if people come to perceive those wants as essential needs, then they come to identify entirely and happily with the system which satisfies them, without understanding or realizing that this seemingly satisfying arrangement is based on an irrational and repressive deception: whatever the apparent satisfactions, they are based on a system of alienation and slavery to commodity production. The same logic is at work in the non-Marxist Galbraith's critique of advertising and marketing: unless people's needs are defined independently of the system which ostensibly satisfies them, they cannot adequately critique and judge that system: they are rather a part of its smooth functioning. Hence, wants and 'false needs' are associated with conformity, passive manipulation, loss of critical consciousness and failure of political opposition; needs or 'real needs' are the only valid critical vantage point from which the very idea of critique and political opposition can be imagined. This leaves the standard problem of putting forward a principled basis on which real and false needs can be identified or defined independently of the expressed wants of populations. On what basis can Marcuse say that the desire I feel for a car is not a real need, but a want or false need which actually represses me?

INSATIABLE NEEDS AND THE CURSE OF AFFLUENCE

Marcuse's position also reflects another long-term theme: that ever increasing affluence, occasioned by expanded forces of production on the one hand and the deregulation of desire on the other, may promote great social wealth and social dissatisfaction at the same time. This is largely because with the increase of affluence, the meeting of basic needs accounts for a decreasing proportion of social labour and consumption, and the satisfaction of wants becomes the paramount concern of the population. However, whereas needs are limited (they can be satisfied), wants, it is argued, are malleable, insatiable and relative: they are, in effect, inexhaustible because for a variety of reasons new ones can always be dreamed up, whereas ones that have been satisfied are quickly forgotten. A clear example of this logic is provided by 'relational' or 'positional' goods and 'status symbols' (see, for example, Hirsch 1976; Leiss 1976; Leiss et al. 1986): if we eat to satisfy the need of hunger, it is argued, we come to an end when the pangs are sated. However, if we consume in order to demonstrate our cosmopolitan status as knowledgeable consumers of the latest culinary styles or choicest ingredients, then the 'need' at stake is not hunger but status or prestige, and the latter is always provisional. Indeed, this form of consumption is an inevitably zero-sum game, for once too many people have these wants satisfied ('everyone' is eating Mexican this year and makes *fajitas* at home), it is necessarily devalued because it can no longer signify status and social position: 'everyone' has caught up. Thus, ever new wants are generated as people attempt to differentiate position and status – to find a preference and an object with social rarity value. Fashion – a constant revolution in taste structures, a constant hunger for the new – serves both status seekers and commercial interests, but at the cost of a state of permanent dissatisfaction, for unlike needs, there is no end to want. A classic account of this process, and its role in social power, was provided by Thorstein Veblen's theory of conspicuous consumption (Veblen 1953; see also Baudrillard 1981; Campbell 1989; Miller 1987).

In this view, needs are associated as usual with a limited set of rational or natural utilities; wants are associated with unlimited social competition. Indeed, many accounts imply that all wants respond to the one true basic need of humans, the need for prestige, or belonging, or status. Any want is merely the occasion to fulfil a basically competitive social need which grounds all or most social action. Hence wants, or the 'cultural aspect' of needs (the desire to assuage hunger not just by eating food but by eating at the trendiest bistro), are prey to fashion and taste systems, status hierarchies, the commercial production and manipulation of signs and 'commodity aesthetics' (Haug 1986). This view of things goes back to the eighteenth century in the work of Rousseau, for example, and is central to Durkheim. Liberals such as Hume and Adam Smith noted, approvingly, that people do not act or consume purely in relation to utility, in order to functionally meet needs (see Hirschman 1977; Ignatieff 1984; Xenos 1989). Indeed, the progress of civilization as well as its moral order, they believed, rested on the desire for 'consideration on the part of others': we desire to appear in a good light in others' eyes, and we use our imaginative and 'sympathetic' faculties to think about and adjust how we might appear. Hence, our wants are related to sociality and sociability, our desire for esteem, which Hume and Smith regard highly.

Rousseau, on the other hand, believed that this desire for esteem (*amour propre*, mere vanity) was a form of social slavery: as we move out of the state of nature and into society, the good opinion of others becomes tyrannical, and conformity to fashion the only rule. This tyranny is evil because it renders humans inauthentic, untrue to themselves, heteronomous rather than autonomous. In nature, people followed the dictates of *amour de soi*: they naturally and unselfconsciously satisfied their real needs as part of a sensible and limited care for the self and its survival. Society and social comparison, coupled with the unlimited capacity to imagine new desires and new points of comparison, make their life unnatural such that 'to be and to appear became two entirely different things, and from this distinction arose ostentatious display, deceitful cunning, and all the vices that follow in their train' (Rousseau 1984: 119). This line of thought is pursued (by way of Tocqueville) well into twentieth-century sociology with figures like C. Wright Mills and David Riesman.

Durkheim also attacks affluence and the deregulation of desire, from a different direction but towards very similar ends. Human happiness cannot be based on open-ended individual desire. There must be a stable framework of real but limited needs. In Durkheim, this framework is provided not by nature as for Rousseau but by society as a moral order above the level of the individual. Liberal-utilitarian modernity, however, dismantles the traditional institutions and values through which this moral order was sustained, replacing it with mere individual self-interests and the pursuit of industrial prosperity. However, he argues, 'the appetites thus awakened are freed from any limiting authority. By sanctifying these appetites . . . this deification of material well-being has placed them above all human law . . . From the top to the bottom of the scale covetous desires are aroused without it being known where they might level out' (Thompson 1985: 111). The price paid for the shift from needs (defined through a supra-individual moral order) to wants (defined by individuals) occasioned by affluence and liberal deregulation is anomie at the level of the individual (the quote is actually from *Suicide*) and a crisis of solidarity at the level of society.

Again, the distinction between needs and wants is central in assessing the cultural and social crisis of a modernity seemingly characterized by increasing productivity and affluence as well as individual autonomy and freedom, yet which is also uncertain as to what is really socially and ethically valued, real, authentic and satisfying. In the broadest terms, the needs/wants dichotomy marks out the preoccupation of modern thought with the new freedoms and pathologies involved in living in a post-traditional society.

KEY CONCEPTS

NEEDS Needs are a way of speaking about those things in life that are essential to survival. In an elementary form they are made up of food, water, shelter, warmth and so on. As society develops more and more and enculturates more and more of the natural world needs become greater and less fundamental. Now we all 'need' hot water on tap, refrigerators, motor cars, even air-conditioning so the needs seem to alter with the level of social development.

WANTS Wants on the other hand are desires for life in excess of needs. However, with the development of societies and consumer cultures the continuum between wants and needs becomes blurred and in places stretched thin. Not being able to live without a pair of shoes is not the same as not being able to live without that new pair of shoes and so an element of choice in relation to disposable income comes into play when we consider wants. Lifestyles rather than lifeneeds organize wants.

Life/Death

Clive Seale

> The irony that Joe so succinctly captured, that life is after all a terminal illness, is the tragedy of the natural order that we can do nothing to change. But like him, we can so live that, when we depart, we shall have made life that much more bearable for others.
>
> Nelson Mandela at the funeral of Joe Slovo, leader of the South African Communist Party, reported in *The Guardian* 16 January 1995)

This observation from Nelson Mandela summarizes a conclusion reached by thinkers from a variety of backgrounds, religious, philosophical, psychological and sociological, when considering the inevitable fact of human mortality. At a personal level, contemplation of death can provide a remarkable sharpening of one's efforts to live well – as Mandela suggests was demonstrated by Joe Slovo. The purpose of this chapter is to show the central part played by awareness of mortality in human social organization. The chapter will also outline the particular problems posed by death for self-identity in late modern social conditions,[1] where religion and traditional authority no longer provide very effective explanations for death.

It is not pleasant to contemplate our own deaths, particularly if we have no expectation of another life beyond death, as it seems to threaten us with meaninglessness. Indeed, one of the central arguments of this chapter will be that human social organization can be understood as a defence against the flood of despair that can be induced by contemplating death too closely. Just as we avert our eyes from the sun, so we busily fill our minds with matters other than mortality. Paradoxically, however, death is also the source of a fundamental desire to give life meaning. This can be demonstrated by considering how our lives would be if we were immortal.

Jorge Luis Borges has written a story in which he considered just such a state of being, imagining a City of the Immortals, where 'a hundred or so irregular niches . . . furrowed the mountain and the valley. In the sand there were shallow pits; from these miserable holes (and from the niches) naked, grey-skinned, scraggly bearded men emerged' (1970: 138). One of these, it transpires, was Homer, who composed the *Odyssey*. However, knowing his immortality, this achievement had lost all meaning for its author as it became clear to him that 'if we postulate an infinite period of time, with infinite circumstances and changes, the impossible thing is not to compose the *Odyssey*, at least once' (1970: 145). As Bauman, who comments on this story, observes, the composition of the *Odyssey* 'loses its lustre . . . [it is] no longer a unique event, and thus not an act of heroism; it is useless as a vehicle of self assertion' (1992b: 32).

Knowledge of mortality and finitude, then, can be seen as a primary motive for participation in human culture, which offers a series of opportunities for people to claim meaning for their lives. Culture, as was shown in the chapter 'Culture/Nature', can involve the production of great works of art such as Homer's *Odyssey*, or it can consist of much more mundane matters of everyday general knowledge or custom. Achieving membership of a particular social group, learning its rules and values and making them one's own, acting to influence others by creating new meanings and memberships that others may aspire to, constitute participation in culture and social life. Ernst Becker, in his book *The Denial of Death* (1973), has depicted this activity as an organized system for the production of heroic self-identity:

> society is and always has been . . . a symbolic action system, a structure of statuses and roles, customs and rules for behavior, designed to serve as a vehicle for earthly heroism . . . a mythical hero-system in which people serve in order to earn a feeling of primary value. (1973: 4–5)

Hero myths, such as those of Odysseus, are simply extreme ends of the spectrum of activities in which we daily engage. In our education, our jobs, our families, our leisure activities we draw upon culturally available identities and weave them into a personal identity that we like to believe is 'unique', a set of self-defining activities through which we assert our special place in the world.

But before exploring the problems thrown up in late modern social conditions in this organized 'denial' of death by participation in culture, we will consider the way in which death has been experienced in traditional societies. This will serve to highlight specifically modern and late modern means of dealing with mortality that we now face.

DEATH AND SOCIAL ORDER

'Death presents society with a formidable problem not only because of its obvious threat to the continuity of human relationships, but because it threatens the basic assumptions of order on which society rests' (Berger 1969: 32–3). If we accept what is argued in this quotation, then the prevailing distribution of death in a particular society will have profound consequences for the maintenance of order. In premodern (traditional) societies death tends to be common in all age groups, but particularly amongst infants. Most members of society, before they are very old, will see many deaths of people whom they know well. There is a widespread familiarity with the handling of dead bodies. By contrast, in modern or late modern societies, such as the United Kingdom or the USA today, death is primarily confined to the very old because of increases in life expectancy. It occurs behind the scenes of everyday life, so that most people's exposure to death is via their television screens or other media. Associated with these differences between traditional and modern societies are profound differences in the way in which social order is sustained.

Death in traditional societies

The term 'traditional society' groups together societies that may in fact be different from each other in various respects, but it is a convenient umbrella heading to indicate certain common features of 'non-modern' societies. In both medieval European states, for example, and many contemporary hunting and gathering groups, the sort of direct personal knowledge of death described above is common. In small, traditional communities most individuals meet each other regularly and there is a relatively simple division of labour. In hunter-gatherer groups, for example, institutions (such as the Church, the state, medicine and education) are relatively undeveloped and undifferentiated. A single individual may combine the role of chief, priest, healer and educator of the young, or these may be distributed amongst only two or three individuals. The manner in which these roles are carried out will be heavily dependent on the personal idiosyncrasies of individuals, something not easily codified or passed on to others by some method of education or training. Should one of these people die, social order is therefore radically disrupted. Elaborate funeral rituals (described later) are constructed to help repair this damage.

Additionally, the intense grief that we now feel at the death of children is less likely to be allowed to disrupt social order. The death of children in traditional societies is and was far more 'normal' than in modern societies.

A woman could expect to bear ten or fifteen children, and perhaps have fewer than half of them survive to their teenage years. The French historian Philippe Aries has commented on the way in which this was managed in medieval Europe. Then, people did not recognize infants as people until they reached puberty, when they participated in a variety of rituals that affirmed their 'rebirth' as full members of society:

> No one thought of keeping a picture of a child if that child had . . . died in infancy . . . it was thought that the little thing which had disappeared so soon in life was not worthy of remembrance . . . Nobody thought, as we ordinarily think today, that every child already contained a man's personality. Too many of them died. (1962: 38)

A key feature of the death of adults in such societies is that the dead have a social presence. This is revealed in cults of ancestor worship or stories of ghosts and spirits of the dead, which are felt as real. The dead inhabit another world, which may be ordered in a manner similar to the world of the living, reflecting status divisions and involving property rights and so forth. The feelings of the living about the dead vary between fear of their malevolence and pleasure at their benevolence. This is reflected in the treatment of physical remains. At certain points the corpse may be feared as a source of pollution and danger; at others skulls or bones act as protective talismans, as they did for the head-hunters of Borneo, or the religious reliquaries beloved of medieval Catholics.

The task of funeral **ritual** is to transform the malevolence and danger represented by death into something more positive and secure. If the dead can be understood as benevolent spirits who guard and aid the living, death itself is potentially less fearful and disruptive. If they are perceived to lead an orderly life after death, with predictable and controllable relations with the living, they can be integrated into the social order of the living. The void that is left by the person's departure can be filled, at least for a time, with the person's 'spiritual' presence, until such time as a living person can inhabit the role.

Some early Durkheimian sociologists and social anthropologists paid particular attention to funeral rituals in traditional societies, the most original of whom was Hertz, who was himself killed in the First World War. He summarizes the threat posed by death: 'When a man dies, society loses in him much more than a unit; it is stricken in the very principle of its life, in the faith it has in itself' (Hertz 1907: 78). Hertz's study of the Dayak people in Borneo described a feature of their mortuary rites subsequently found to be quite widespread in other parts of the world, that of 'double burial'. Amongst the Dayaks the corpse was initially seen as extremely dangerous, and was sealed in a box for some months until it had decayed (the first burial). The close family of the deceased were also seen as potentially polluting influences, and were considered socially 'dead' for a period, living at a physical distance from the rest of the group, and being obliged to show affection to the corpse by physical contact with its decaying products in order to protect others from its influence.

When the bones were dry, a second burial took place, which was the occasion for a transformation of the identities of both the dead person and the close mourners. A feast was prepared, and this was the point at which it was safe to distribute the dead person's belongings without fear of retribution. The head of the dead person could be kept and fed to maintain the spirit's benevolence. The close family mourners became free of the taint of death, and began to participate once more in social life. For Hertz, such mortuary rites assert social solidarity – a sense of holding together – in the face of death. Illustrating the precarious nature of this solidarity, however, is Hertz's observation that the deaths of chiefs were sometimes kept secret until the bones were dry, as the danger represented by a chief's corpse was too great to be successfully deflected. Today, we may see parallels in the secrecy that still can surround the illness and deaths of political leaders, such as Deng in China. Rumours of their deaths abound as the individual is less frequently seen in public: the assertions of officials that the leader remains healthy are increasingly questioned, but serve to give these officials time to ensure a smooth transition of power.

Hertz further observes that 'In establishing a society of the dead the society of the living regularly recreates itself' (1907: 71–2). Thus, a system of rewards and punishments in the afterlife (heaven and hell) may develop with direct relevance to the moral regulation of the living. Funeral monuments in cemeteries, for example, contain indications of the social status of a person in life by their height, decoration or expense. Traditionally children were buried in undifferentiated graves in less favoured parts of cemeteries; dead strangers, suicides or victims of violent or accidental deaths – all of which have been used to represent particularly threatening forms of death – may be excluded from the burial ground. Hertz comments that 'the sinister way in which some individuals are torn from this world separates them for ever from their relatives' (1907: 86). Such is the origin of stories of ghosts, who wander the earth seeking to deal with the unfinished business of life.

Later social anthropologists have noted the linkage that is often made between death and fertility in various rituals, with themes of rebirth and resurrection (as in the resurrection of Christ) often being evident. Bloch and Parry (1982), for example, argue that many traditional social groups see life as existing in a limited quantity, with individuals engaging in various practices to possess as much of it as possible. If a person's death can be interpreted as a 'good death' by ritual, it can be seen as generating a quantity of life. As an example, Bloch and Parry describe the ritual death of a Dinka 'spearmaster', who transcends fear of death and provides an opportunity for communal regeneration by presiding over his own live burial. Unlike suicide, which is a defeat, this means that the death is 'transformed into regeneration by acting out a victory over . . . the finality and uncontrollability of death' (Bloch and Parry 1982: 18). The actions of Japanese kamikaze pilots or Palestinian 'suicide' bombers have been interpreted by their communities in a similar light. These individuals attain heroic status as having magically transformed a more 'normal' fear of death. They therefore induce in some onlookers a feeling that they too might perform a similar inversion when their time comes.

In these studies of traditional societies by social anthropologists and historians, then, it is evident that death can provoke a major threat to social order, requiring elaborate rituals to manage this threat. These rituals are, as Erving Goffman (1968: 24) once remarked in relation to another topic, one of the 'primal scenes' for the sociologist, marking the boundary between human culture and its annihilation. What could be more fundamental than the joint effort in which we are constantly engaged, to turn away from death towards life? Death rites, as Danforth has stated, can be understood as 'concrete procedures for the maintenance of reality in the face of death' (1982: 31). This chapter will now consider the relationship between death and social order in modern and late modern society, where stable images of a single 'reality' have become increasingly difficult to maintain.

Death in modern society

In modern times death is typically confined to the old, who are largely excluded from meaningful social participation by a variety of procedures, including the enforcement of a retirement age and a degree of segregation and social stigma (sometimes called 'social death'). Social institutions are highly developed and bureaucratized, routinely replacing and training their functionaries by hiring and firing procedures. Knowledge and skills are passed on by codified procedures of education and training that do not depend on the personally held wisdom of a particular individual. The death of a particular individual is therefore less likely to pose a threat to social order, unless that individual represents an unusually symbolic or charismatic authority (as in the assassination of J.F. Kennedy or Martin Luther King). Death is more usually experienced as a private rather than a public loss and grief is understood as a matter of personal psychology rather than a community affair.

Additionally, the dead are truly dead in modern society. Science teaches that death is the material end of being. Religion and beliefs in an afterlife are designated as illusory, since there is no proof of them acceptable to reason. Medicine may battle against death on our behalf, but it is ultimately unsuccessful in all cases. Talcott Parsons (Parsons and Lidz 1967) has argued that the modern management of death rests on a distinction between 'natural' and 'unnatural' death. Painful, premature or violent deaths are designated as unnatural, and a variety of social customs and procedures, including the whole panoply of modern medicine, are devoted to creating a sense of 'natural' death at the end of a similarly 'natural' ageing process. By contrast, in traditional societies, all deaths are 'unnatural' and threaten the group with a sense of evil.

Modern social organizations have the appearance of permanence by comparison with the less developed institutions of traditional societies. Although we learn in school that an institution such as the state, or the education system itself, or the police, the law, medicine and so on each have a 'history', that once they did not exist, that they developed out of something else, it is hard to imagine that they will in the future be different, or that they may one day not exist. They seem 'handed down', given things. This appearance of a hard and objective permanence gives the people who take part in making and sustaining them an opportunity to bid for personal immortality. By taking part an individual contributes part of him or herself to something that will continue beyond the person's own death. This is what Ernst Becker meant in the quote from him given earlier when he described society as a symbolic action system serving as a vehicle for earthly heroism.

Hero myths abound in modern society. The media parade a succession of 'stars' and 'role models' for emulation, superwomen populate the pages of women's magazines, supermen strut across our cinema screens. Mythical qualities of courage, fortitude, sexual success and self-sacrifice are routinely exhibited. The traditional masculine hero has recently been joined by newly liberated female heroes. In clothing, leisure pursuits, jobs and family activities people can draw upon a range of these mythical exemplars to construct an apparently distinct personal narrative of the heroic self, so that they can feel that they have made their mark and will be remembered. Children can be particularly burdened with their parents' desires for immortality, perhaps especially where parents are driven by a sense of personal failure.

Social order is less threatened by death, which is itself increasingly hidden from everyday social experience. The dying are placed in institutions, and bureaucratic systems process bodies and control our contact with the dying and the dead. In Western industrialized countries there has been in the twentieth century a steady rise in the proportion of people dying in hospitals. The medical management of death has more or less replaced the involvement of priests in leading the action and interpreting the meaning of the deathbed (as will be shown later). This has led some social theorists to claim that we live in a 'death denying' society.

The denial of death thesis has been strongly argued by the sociologist Norbert Elias, who links this with his theory of the 'civilizing process' (Elias 1939)[2] which, he believes, involves drawing a veil over the animal-like aspects of human life (e.g. violence, disposal of body matter, sex and death). Elias is basically concerned to argue the case for better treatment of the aged and the dying in modern social conditions. This humanistic perspective is shared by others who espouse the thesis of the denial of death, such as the anthropologist Gorer (1965) who bemoans the fact that the grief of the bereaved is no longer channelled by mourning rituals as the meaning of the funeral has atrophied, or Aries (1976; 1981) who argues that discussion of death is 'forbidden'. Elias conveys the loneliness of the dying in modern times in a book which he wrote in his own old age:

> Closely bound up, in our day, with the greatest possible exclusion of death and dying from social life, and with the screening-off of dying people from others . . . is a peculiar embarrassment felt by the living in the presence of dying people. They often do not know what to say . . . Feelings of embarrassment hold words back. For the dying this can be a bitter experience . . . It is not always easy to show to people on their way to death that they have not lost their meaning for other people . . . If this happens, if a person must feel while dying that, though still alive, he or she has scarcely any significance for other people, that person is truly alone. (1985: 23, 64)

However, there are a number of problems with this perspective as a piece of sociological analysis (as was observed by Parsons and Lidz 1967 as well as later sociologists such as Kellehear 1984 and Walter 1992). While the subjective experience of dying or grieving may be painful in conditions where there is widespread reluctance to discuss death, this masks a central feature of repression: the thing that is repressed from consciousness is determinedly 'present' – perhaps more so than things that do not 'need' to be repressed. The intensity of organized efforts to deny death are themselves indicators of the pressing nature of the topic. A sociological analysis of modern culture, social life and social institutions suggests that a primary use made of these is to help people 'forget' death, which they do with sometimes greater, sometimes lesser success. As Ivan Illich has argued in his analysis of death in modern society: 'We cannot fully understand the deeply rooted structure of our social organization unless we see it as a multi-faceted exorcism of all forms of evil death' (1976: 205).

Additionally, it can be argued that in *late* modernity the designation of death as a taboo topic has been significantly eroded, as a host of revivalist social movements – such as hospices or counselling services for the bereaved – open up the topic once again. The last part of this chapter will consider how the institutions most closely involved in people's management of death – namely medicine and warfare – achieve their effects. Before this, however, we will consider how death is involved in the production of late modern self-identity.

DEATH AND SELF-IDENTITY IN LATE MODERNITY

Modern individuals are from time to time assailed by knowledge that their sense of permanence is illusory. Fantasies about nuclear annihilation, fascination with astronomers' predictions of the end of the world, fears about ecological imbalance and pollution of the environment touch on fundamental anxieties about ultimate meaninglessness. Officially sponsored programmes to combat these things, peace and disarmament initiatives, space travel and ecological initiatives, command widespread support and interest. These suggest that a state of chronic doubt about the truths of modernity – beliefs in the beneficial nature of science, in the possibilities for progress and so on – characterize late modern social conditions. Anthony Giddens (1991) has explored the consequences for self-identity when individuals live in such a climate. Mellor (1993; Mellor and Shilling 1993) has further expanded on Giddens's ideas with specific reference to death.

Giddens argues that there has been a decline in people's capacity to accept authoritative 'answers' to life's questions from either religion or science. This is, in part, because we have become increasingly aware through the media that for every 'answer' there is a corresponding critique. We are, for example, aware that a variety of religious beliefs exist, and so question a blind faith in any single one. We have learned to view science as a potentially destructive force leading, for example, to Hiroshima, the Holocaust and ecological destruction. These have fundamentally eroded our capacity for trust, so that the individual is thrown back on his or her own efforts to gather information about the risks of different actions.

People consult what Giddens calls 'expert systems' such as medicine when they are confronted with situations – such as illness – that demand choices. The competing voices of experts are critically assessed as the individual forms a plan of action. Thus people come to regard themselves as critical consumers of expertise, as is evident in political rhetoric about the advantages of 'consumer choice' across a range of specialist services. There exist also a host of competing 'self-help' guides – often written by psychologists – on how to manage such problems of everyday life as deciding how to raise children, what food to eat, what exercise to take in order to promote a 'healthy' life and avoid unnaturally early death.

Living an increasingly complex and cosmopolitan life, individuals learn that a variety of lifestyles are possible, and the styling of life becomes a consciously managed enterprise, or a 'reflexive' process. Self-identity – that is, a sense of who we are – depends on a continual reordering of narratives of the self, interpreting and reinterpreting one's biography as a series of 'stories' that 'make sense' temporarily before some fateful moment requires that we reorder our lives, gather new information and construct a new personal story to confer meaning upon our biographies. Additionally, the body and its adornment in clothes is increasingly used as a vehicle for the expression of self-identity, fashion allowing people to inscribe upon themselves additional narratives of identity.

Chief amongst the fateful moments that provoke reordering of narratives is the event of death. The death of someone close, or the knowledge that we are terminally ill, provokes the most profound anxiety, threatening the security with which mortality is 'bracketed out'. Where there is great investment in using bodily appearance to construct self-identity, the disintegration of the body in illness and death is very disturbing. These anxieties have been felt perhaps most starkly in the case of AIDS, which poses a particular threat because of its jarring association with sex and youthfulness. AIDS has led to a profound re-evaluation of the place of sex in our lives, threatening the capacity of individuals to appropriate the permissive narrative that had been developing since the 1960s, and encouraging narratives of responsibility and safety. A stream of media accounts of death from AIDS, in which dying individuals are paraded across television screens acting out dramas of heroic confrontation with an 'unfair' fate, has helped forcefully to reorientate these narratives.

But fundamentally, death remains as a constant potential reminder that world-building activities and narrative reorderings are a sham. The late modern individual is unusually exposed to the threat of personal meaninglessness and the dread of personal finitude. Sociology has tended to leave things at this point, content to have exposed a fashionably nihilistic sense of despair, a modish exposition of pointlessness. This chapter will now consider the variety of ways in which modern and late modern social institutions have been fashioned in order to kill death itself.

KILLING DEATH

'Death remains the great extrinsic factor of human existence; it cannot as such be brought within the internally referential systems of modernity. However, all types of event leading up to and involved with the process of dying can be so incorporated' (Giddens 1991: 162). Giddens suggests here that there is indeed no 'solution' to the problem of death. This is hardly surprising, nor is it necessarily regrettable if Borges's point about the impossibility of culture without mortality is taken seriously. The task of sociology in this field must be to document the variety of ways in which defences against this great 'extrinsic factor' are maintained. This does not simply involve the study of people's experience of dying – though this may provide some valuable insights. Death exerts an influence on institutions that are not normally felt to be primarily concerned with the management of dying. In this section, some socially organized practices for killing death will be outlined.

Killing other people

Killing people in warfare has long been used as a means to triumphant assertion of survival against the odds, and therefore against death itself. This is shown in the sentiments of a knight, Jean de Bueil, in 1465:

> War is a joyous thing. We love each other so much in war. If we see that our cause is just and our kinsmen fight boldly, tears come to our eyes. A sweet joy rises in our hearts, in the feeling of our honest loyalty to each other; and seeing our friend so bravely exposing his body to danger . . . we resolve to go forward and die or live with him and never leave him on account of love. This brings such delight that anyone who has not felt it cannot say how wonderful it is. Do you think that someone who feels this is afraid of death? Not in the least! He is so strengthened, so delighted, that he does not know where he is. Truly he fears nothing in the world! (quoted in Elias 1939: 160)

Additionally, in this quote, we see the theme of love, a sense of standing together with others that is the basis of social solidarity.[3] The type of love to which de Bueil refers is clearly generated by the identification and conquest of an enemy. The chapter 'Normal/Pathological' analyses the roots of the desire for membership, and the role of stigma in maintaining it. Warfare is an extreme consequence of tribal stigma; stigma itself is a minor rehearsal for killing.

Zygmunt Bauman (1992b) analyses the formation of tribal identities along these lines. Tribalism – the bonding together of people along territorial and kinship lines to form a cohesive group – frequently involves victorious affirmations of rectitude, won by expelling or killing people identified as polluting the tribe. A variety of racist discourses, for example, serve this purpose. Here, notions of racial hygiene are invoked, defences of the purity of blood lines, a fight against germs, filth or degeneration. These legitimize acts of persecution, making it safe – even desirable – to kill others. The formation of tribes whose members engage jointly in the killing of others reduces the need for individuals to contemplate the terrifying prospect of being left alone in the world once all others have been killed. Tribalism is often identified, in public consciousness, as a 'primitive' or 'uncivilized' affair. Indeed, Norbert Elias (1939) accounts for what he calls the 'civilizing process' which has been undergone by European societies as a rise in the level of empathy and consideration for others' feelings, a spreading throughout society of the values of diplomacy and tact, involving widespread disapproval for acts of violence. The sort of sentiment voiced by the fifteenth-century knight above would be considered barbaric if voiced by a soldier today.

Bauman (1989), however, reminds us that the Holocaust of the Nazi era is a product of modern rationality, the application of technology to create a factory-like process, a production line of death, made possible by the neutralization of the feelings of those directly involved in acts of killing. One of the ironies of Elias's great work on the civilizing process is that it is dedicated to his own parents, one of whom died at a date unknown to him in Auschwitz. In a sense, though, there is no contradiction between these positions. Modern warfare is subject to calculation to a degree that would have been unrecognizable to a medieval knight, for whom fighting was akin to a blood sport. The nineteenth-century theorist of war von Clausewitz described it as 'a continuation of political commerce . . . by other means' (1908: 85). In late modern times one could almost turn this around to say that political commerce is warfare by other means. One sees this in the macro-economic sphere, where apparently 'non-violent' means of economic exploitation have substituted for the battleship diplomacy that once characterized relations between the 'West' and its colonies. The fundamental desire to dominate and conquer others, to have (metaphorically) their lifeblood, remains at the heart of political activity. The urge to power equates with a strategy of survival and this permeates everyday life as modern individuals adopt the 'rat-race' mentality.

The mastery of nature

Science, and in particular medicine, represents one of the best hopes of the modern individual to kill death. This is seen at its most absurd in science fiction fantasies of 'cryogenics' where people place their bodies (or sometimes just brains!) in deep freeze until such time as science discovers the means to create immortal life. At a more mundane level, medical care holds out the promise to anaesthetize suffering by a variety of technical means. Just as creating stigma can be seen as a rehearsal for killing, so pain and the suffering of illness are a rehearsal of our own deaths. Pain makes the body strange, as it acts against our wishes and reminds us of the limitations of bodily existence. Controlling pain is a routine matter for modern medicine, and for many pains we administer medication ourselves. By thus killing pain, medicine enables us to 'forget' our bodies, or once again see them as vehicles for pleasure and self-expression rather than the bearers of our own deaths.

Sociologists (e.g. Illich 1976) have called the widespread resort to medicine and medical explanations in modern societies **medicalization**. It represents the increasing colonization of everyday life by expertise, a reinterpretation of problems previously perceived as religious or moral matters as medical affairs. Illich writes that then death itself becomes the 'ultimate form of consumer resistance' (1976: 210) against organized medicine.

Linked to medicalization is the perception that death is the outcome of disease. It is not, for example, seen as caused by evil, bad luck or mortality. Doctors do not write such things when asked to complete the 'cause of death' section on death certificates. Death is seen as the outcome of a medically defined process of 'dying', each stage of which is subject to medical intervention, or can be influenced by health promoting actions taken by the sick individual. A medico-legal system enquires into deaths that are not produced by 'dying', with coroners and pathologists ruling to guard against 'unnatural' causes such as accidents, murder or other violence (Prior 1989).

One of the consequences of this rational way of thinking about death is that it comes to be understood as the outcome of a calculable chance. Indeed, calculating the chances that a given action will increase or decrease the likelihood of death becomes a way of controlling its fearful unpredictability. This is seen most powerfully in statistical tables that calculate life expectancy. The science of social statistics in its early origins was intimately linked to the calculation of mortality rates for different sections of the population (Hacking 1990). Today's mortality statistics reflect and encourage a way of thinking that sees life as a risk business. There are even enquiries made into the causes of accidents or suicides, identifying 'risk groups' or 'risk factors' that can then be manipulated or avoided. As a result there is a widespread social valuing of 'safety' (car seat belts, safe sex, health and safety regulations, anti-smoking sentiment etc.). The other side to the avoidance of such risky behaviour is the promotion of its opposite: health enhancing activity. Thus we see in late modern society a great emphasis placed on the value of exercise, fitness, proper diet and so on, amounting to a near fanaticism about health. The healthy life has become a metaphor for the good life, previously led under the jurisdiction of religious authorities.

The active planning of life by engaging in health promoting activity, calculating and avoiding risk, and anaesthetizing suffering is increasingly threatened as death approaches. This is seen most evidently in accounts of terminal illness. The responses of individuals told that they have terminal cancer, for example, provide unusual insight into the strategies used at more normal moments to neutralize death. Typically, at such moments, people engage in various forms of life planning, which take on a new tinge owing to awareness of their oncoming deaths. Thus they may plan their funerals, make their wills, say their farewells and otherwise be seen as making their peace with life. The person who 'faces' their death in such a way is generally admired, and awareness and the open 'acceptance' of death is now generally encouraged by medical and nursing staff. This is because it enables the reflexive project of the self to continue unabated, whereas 'denial' that one is dying makes a mockery of such life planning. *Death: The Final Stage of Growth* is the title of a book written by Kubler-Ross (1975) in which she extols a process of dying that portrays it as a continuation of a lifelong project of growing self-awareness.

The ability to plan one's life in the face of death is admired precisely because it suggests a sense of mastery over death. The individual unafraid of the disintegration of the self is apparently untouched by mortality, and we carry the memory of this with us as an inspiration. Thus Becker writes of the death of Freud that he 'faced up to life and to a fatal cancer with a Stoic heroism' (1973: 22). Modern ways of thinking about death also include more direct attempts to control the manner of dying, as is seen in the increasing support for voluntary euthanasia. This represents an attempt to control the capriciousness of death, wresting the body from the control of nature by administering a final anaesthetic.

It is notable that suicide is less stigmatized in late modern society, as its acceptability as one solution to the problems of living increases. Parsons has indicated that in a society with a 'primary cultural pattern of activism . . . there is a suicidal component in a very large proportion of ordinary deaths' (Parsons and Lidz 1967: 164–5). Controlling the manner of death is linked to a similar approach to life.

RESURRECTIVE PRACTICES AND EMOTIONAL LABOUR

Resurrective practices in traditional societies involve quite literal beliefs in the resurrection of the dead, a sense of their physical presence as spirits. The effectiveness of religious promises of an afterlife is confined in late modern society to sects who insulate themselves against prevailing views. Thus the occasional mass suicides of religious cults evoke widespread derision. The effectiveness with which such cults use the elementary forces of tribalism to engender a fearless approach to death is, however, remarkable. The power of this sentiment depends on the identification of those outside the cult as enemies, with especial vilification being exercised on those who attempt to defect. Occasional declarations of war upon the outside world (for example, the recent release of nerve gas by a religious cult on the underground rail system in Tokyo) are indicative of the dynamics involved. Outside such groups beliefs in an afterlife are only weakly held, if at all.

We can now understand that at the root of religious beliefs in the resurrection of the dead is a desire of the living to continue to orientate themselves towards life, and not to give in to the despair of death. A key feature of late modern attempts to resurrect this sense of optimism about continuing in life in the face of death is the belief in the value of care, concern and emotional accompaniment. Routine assertions about the decline in community values, rather like the denial of death thesis, can themselves be understood as incitements to a commitment to the values of a caring community. Government policies of 'community care' recognize this widespread sentiment, although such policies are often experienced as somewhat manipulative. There is a continual public exhortation to care for others, in school programmes that emphasize the values of 'sharing', and in psychotherapeutic expertise devoted to smoothing the stresses of living with others.

Medicine itself has expanded its jurisdiction over the body to include the psychological and social lives of patients (Armstrong 1983; Arney and Bergen 1984). Patient-centred medicine, organized by a host of professionals, increasingly valuing areas previously relegated to a 'natural' female expertise of caring and nurturing, is widespread. It represents a new form of organized emotional labour (Hochschild 1983) in which nurses play an increasingly valued part. The conception of medicine as simply the scientific mastery of nature is increasingly outmoded and routinely condemned, as people become increasingly interested in, for example, alternative therapies where concern with effectiveness is substituted by concerns for the quality of the therapeutic experience itself. These trends can be seen quite explicitly in the communities of care that have arisen around the terminally ill in recent years. Hospices for cancer and AIDS patients enact a drama of accompaniment and care that evokes widespread admiration, supporting individuals' heroic facing of death described earlier. The professional orchestration of love and care in a variety of sectors represents an attempt to resurrect the hopes of the living in the face of death.

CONCLUSION

This chapter has outlined something of the variety of strategies used by people to orientate themselves away from death towards life. In spite of the importance of the human problem of mortality for understanding social organization, analysis of this topic has not been a priority for many sociologists, who have tended to leave it to psychologists and philosophers. Anthropology has made a more significant contribution to an understanding of the consequences of death for human social organization, as was seen in the section on traditional societies. However, anthropologists, though increasingly interested in studying other aspects of modern societies, have otherwise made few contributions. Amongst sociologists there has in recent years been something of an upsurge of interest in death, as described here in the review of contributions made by Bauman and Giddens, and to a lesser extent by Parsons, Illich and Berger. As the millennium approaches, apocalyptic thinking is increasingly likely to turn on matters of life and death. Coupled with the growing perception that much social theory has lost its way, having lost touch with any sense of moral purpose, we may expect a return to consideration of the social arrangements that enable us to cling together on the raft of life.

This chapter has tended to concentrate on the contributions made by sociologists concerned to draw out the consequences of mortality for the management of social life, and has excluded discussion of the burgeoning literature describing institutional practices for the management of death. Such work (e.g. Seale 1995; Glaser and Strauss 1965; Sudnow 1967) is of particular interest in revealing practices that exist but are normally less obvious in other areas of social life. The main purpose of this piece, however, has been to emphasize how awareness of mortality acts as a fundamental motive for human social organization.

KEY CONCEPTS

LIFE The condition of the human being which, for sociologists, is inevitably to be understood within the context of social life. Life itself then, becomes a social phenomenon and we fear mortality and grieve the death of others just as we celebrate their lives.

DEATH The condition of not being but also the fracture in a complex of social relationships which are personal, economic, political and moral and all of which have an impact on the wider society.

Ritual Any conventional and formal actions which complete a set pattern and which express a public or shared meaning through cultural symbols. The concept derives from anthropology and can be used ironically in sociology to imply a social process that is out of date or has forgotten its purpose.

Medicalization A new term to describe the way that modern society often places social processes under medical definitions. People today exercise a whole medical vocabulary of explanation and referral to understand child-rearing, eating, self-care, worry, routine minor illness and all of those states of being that were previously contained within the family or the school or the self image.

NOTES

1 See chapter 'Modernity/Postmodernity' for a definition of these terms.
2 Described in more detail in the chapter 'Normal/Pathological'.
3 Romantic love as a denial of death is analysed by Becker (1973).

High/Mass

Paul Filmer

The terms 'high ' and 'mass' are key terms in the sociological analysis of *vertical* stratification of culture in industrial societies. A significant problem for the sociology of culture, however, is that the terms are also in everyday use, where they often carry strong ideological connotations. When deployed in the sociological analysis of culture, thus, they demonstrate the tension between sociological theory and ideology referred to in the chapter 'Theory/Practice'. Moreover, they are not the only terms important for the sociological analysis of contemporary culture. They are complemented by a series of related terms and concepts which will be discussed with them. Similarly, vertical stratification is not the only form of social structural differentiation and division of contemporary culture. It is complemented by an increasingly significant *horizontal* stratification of culture to be found in the contemporary proliferation of **subcultures** that occur both within and between modern nation-states and which are, in the latter case, an important feature of the process of **globalization** (see chapter 'Local/ Global').

The term 'culture' itself (see chapter 'Culture/Nature') is one which refers to a sociological concept of central analytical importance (Kroeber and Kluckhohn 1952; Kroeber 1963), and yet is in wide everyday use in a variety of descriptive and evaluative senses (Williams 1981; 1984). In his study of the selective tradition of relations between culture and society from the late eighteenth to the mid twentieth century, Williams (1958) identifies culture as one of the two or three most important of the five key words (culture, class, industry, democracy and art) around which that tradition is constellated. The sociological concept refers to the whole way of life of a society, or of a significant group within society (hence the term and concept of subculture) – its beliefs, values, shared meanings, routine practices and artifacts. This sense of the term holds also in everyday use where, however, it is more often used to refer in a selective sense (Snow 1959; Leavis and Yudkin 1962) to the aesthetic and epistemological traditions of the arts, sciences and letters. The relation between these two dominant mundane senses of culture is that the latter is part of the whole that is the former. But it plays an important role in discursive debates over the high/mass dichotomy in the sociology of culture, where it represents *high culture* in the vertical stratification of culture.

This dual sense of culture is constituted in a relation between culture as an articulation of the shared meanings of large-scale social groups and as a representation of the structure of interrelations within and between those groups. It is, moreover, a relation between them which is *reflexive*, in the sense that the shared meanings are constructed to legitimate the structural interrelations. Culture is not autonomous of social structure; it is determined by it and reflexive upon it. Thus, the dichotomy between concepts and processes of high and mass culture refers to the legitimation of dichotomous social structures and the oppositions between their attendant political economies. Inevitably, therefore, a critical explication of the sociological dichotomy involves critical examination also of contrasting political ideologies.

HIGH CULTURE

High culture is invariably the culture of a social minority at or near the political and economic apex of a vertically stratified society. It is, thus, both a minority culture and the culture of an elite. Since it is characteristic of elites, as the Italian sociologist Vilfredo Pareto (1848–1923) has pointed out, to seek to maintain the exclusiveness of their social position, political power and economic advantage, high culture manifests a strong tendency towards social and political conservatism and the concentration of economic wealth (Pareto 1966). T.S. Eliot (1888–1965) has proposed this clearly by contending (1939; 1963) that high culture is most likely to be sustained in a traditional society, in which there is an established religion, an agrarian economy and an aristocracy of extended families, amongst whose members ownership of the means of agrarian production is protected and transferred through primogeniture (inheritance by the first-born son) – a guarantee, whether intentional or not, that such a society would be patriarchal as well as traditional. In its recommendation of physiocracy, Eliot's is an extreme example of the type of social structure that can determine, and in turn would be legitimated by, high culture. But in its recommendation, from the vantage point of a fully developed, high-modern industrial society, of a return to a pre-industrial order, it provides a clear example of how strong a dimension of high culture is its conservatism. The concept depends upon a hierarchically stratified society, of which the major historical instances are caste, feudal, mercantile-class and industrial class societies. As structural types of society, these can be differentiated according to their degree of social openness. The social position of the individual member of a caste society, for example, is fixed ascriptively by birth. This is characteristic of most members of feudal society also, though some mobility through certain estates is possible (Bloch 1961). Class societies, however, are characterized by a degree of social mobility which is intended to be consonant with whatever social philosophy of political equality grounds the dominant legitimating ideology espoused by their ruling groups. Yet in all these types of society are to be found alike selective traditions of high culture manifested in distinctive sets of dominant beliefs, values and communicative and expressive meanings which legitimate and reinforce their hierarchies of social and political order. These traditions are institutionalized in educational academies, religious practices and social rituals to which access is limited, however open the society may purport to be. Eliot, for example, proposes that culture includes 'all the characteristics and interests of a people', suggesting that 'the reader can make his own list' (1963: 31). In making his own version of such a list, however, like most high culture theorists, he recommends the traditional cultural practices of a particular social group as representative of a whole society, in the sense that they are somehow superior to or a more representative selection than those of other groups. Their superiority is real in the sense that, though the practices are differentiated as those of the dominant, ruling upper middle class, they are accepted as representative of those of other class groups, only some of whom also either engage in them or seek to do so (Williams 1958). They are complemented invariably by the intellectual articulation of the traditions through the formal orthodoxies of epistemological codes of discursive method and aesthetic expression.

The Italian Marxist Antonio Gramsci (1891–1937) uses the term **hegemony** (Gramsci 1971; 1985; Williams 1977; Bennett 1986; Bennett et al. 1981) to characterize this reflexive and legitimating interrelation between the social structure and epistemological culture of ruling groups in class societies. He points out that, although it is an interrelation that extends throughout class society and is often manifest in the mundane culture of common sense, it reinforces and is beneficial to the dominant position of the ruling groups. This indicates that the cultures and social structures of non-elite groups are necessary and important sociological correlates of high culture. One clear formulation of this reinvokes imaginatively the allegedly stable socio-cultural conditions of pre- or non-industrial society in the form of an organic community. In this idea of a traditional society, life and work are integrated in unalienated agrarian and craft production. Sound sociological formulations of this type of pre-industrial socio-economic order are to be found in the theories of social change of Durkheim, where it is given the term *mechanical* (as opposed to *organic*) social solidarity, and of Tonnies and Weber, who use the term *Gemeinschaft* or *community* (as opposed to *Gesellschaft* or *association*) (see chapter 'Theory/Practice'). That the non-elite socio-cultural correlates of high culture are usually pre- or non-industrial is a reminder of the socio-political conservatism that underwrites and is legitimated by high culture (see, for example, Williams 1973; 1984; Laslett 1979; Konig 1968). It is a key to the traditionalism that sustains the existing political and economic order and its dominant groups.

But the organic community and its common culture are not only seen as the correlate of *high* culture. An interesting elaboration of the concept of high culture is formulated as *minority culture*, in terms of which an intellectual elite is seen as responsible for safeguarding intellectual culture for its intrinsic worth – for example as a repository of moral values. The literary critic F.R. Leavis (1895–1978) argued that what he termed the 'great tradition' in the English novel, from Dickens to Lawrence, of serious moral concern about the quality of social and cultural life constituted such a repository. To safeguard it required, in Eliot's words, a 'common pursuit of true judgement' (Leavis 1952) by an intellectual minority of critics committed to sustaining the life of a common culture by subjecting its language to the test of literature (Filmer 1969; 1977b). Leavis sees his minority as guardians of and contributors to a selective tradition that originates with Coleridge at the beginning of the nineteenth century, is sustained by Arnold at its close and which constellates in the middle of the twentieth century around himself and his colleagues in the English School at Cambridge University (Milner 1994; Mulhern 1981). This tradition, whilst not anti-industrial in a Luddite sense, is one which insists that the socio-cultural consequences of industrial society have an inevitably subversive effect on the quality of social and cultural life. For all its moral and intellectual tone, the conservatism that ensues is unavoidably political in its implications, arguing as it does that those capable of being entrusted with the stewardship of traditional culture inevitably constitute a minority of artists, critics and educators.

A further instance of a minority committed to the safeguarding of high culture, but one which is not tied to tradition – which seeks, indeed, an outright rejection of tradition as a necessary condition of its own distinct character – is the aesthetic **avant-garde**. It shares with the minority guardians of traditional culture an antipathy towards industrialism, but for the different reasons that stem from the marginalization of the social role of the fine artist. This is seen as resulting from the scientistic materialism from which the processes of industrialization have been generated. The particular targets of the avant-garde's critique of modern society are the industrial capitalist market of production and exchange, and the commoditization of works of art implicated in such an economy by the industrial capitalist bourgeoisie (Benjamin 1991; Lowe 1982). Their commitment to absolute modernity through constant artistic innovation, together with a rejection of both aesthetic tradition and bourgeois convention, is expressed through an espousal of the aesthetics of *modernism* (see, for example, Bradbury and McFarlane 1976), rather than a necessary commitment to a particular social or political theory. Indeed, some of their espousals of social theories and political ideologies have seemed dangerously naive. Such espousals are invariably based upon their need to remain an exclusive minority, but one committed to the overthrow or radical retrenchment of, rather than a stable continuity in, the existing political economic order, which they see as the cause of their social alienation and isolation. But the exclusiveness of their absolute commitment to modernity, and its associated rejection of tradition, make the possibility of sustaining any commitment to social *order* theoretically inconceivable and thus practically impossible. Their orientation to social change, whilst vital to their identity as an elite cultural minority, can generate a version of society no more coherent than that of bohemian anarchy. The political and sociological naivety that is so characteristic of avant-garde high cultural movements exposes a relation between high culture and some theoretical formulations of mass society which will be discussed in relation to the concept of mass in the high/mass dichotomy.

MASS CULTURE

There are two distinct senses of mass culture which are prevalent in sociological discussions of culture: the first is as the culture of *mass society*, the second as the culture of the *mass media audience*.

The phenomenon of mass society, and the conception of the social world that it implies, has been described (Giner 1976: ix–xiii) as an outlook rather than an accomplished type of society. It has a history within Western social thought that stretches back to the earliest systematic reflections on the political order of the societies of the ancient city-states (1976: 1–24), and appears as a focus of debate in social and political thought in the Renaissance, at the turn of the eighteenth and nineteenth and of the nineteenth and twentieth centuries. This debate, indeed, has intensified as a feature of modern Western social and political theory on two distinct occasions during the twentieth century: between the two world wars and from the late 1950s to the early 1970s. Yet whenever, since the late eighteenth century, the features of social structure and process are identified that are alleged to constitute mass society, their interrelation, and thus its outcome – mass society itself – are always immanent rather than actual. The particular form of mass society which is formulated is only ever about to happen and has never quite emerged as a fully developed societal type. Nevertheless, its characteristic features are instructive in reaching an understanding both of the concept of mass itself as a constitutive feature of contemporary social thought, and of the much more substantive practices of cultural stratification that are collected under the term of mass culture.

In the physical sciences, the term 'mass' refers to an incoherent condition of matter – an agglomeration of undifferentiated particles. In all formulations of modern society as mass society since the late eighteenth century, it is this sense of mass that is used to characterize the socio-political condition of the majority of a geopolitical population once they are admitted, through enfranchisement, to individual membership of society. They are treated as if the experience is inevitably bewildering and disorienting. The one exception is Marx's conception of a proletarian mass of the alienated, exploited and dispossessed who recognize, in their common condition of expropriation, a common interest in the revolutionary overthrow of the sources of their oppression – industrial capitalist society and its bourgeois ruling class. The proletariat's realization of their mass identity is seen by Marx as a liberating and revolutionary necessary one, which transforms them from passive victims of material expropriation to active and participating agents of radical and permanent change. But its substantive value is discharged in the accomplishment of the revolution itself and it remains a passing phase in the realization of a new and ideal social and political order. By active participation in revolutionary action, those individuals who make up the mass are able to recover their human integrity as members of a free, open and democratic post-revolutionary society, characterized by equal economic opportunity and the just distribution and exercise of political power.

All other conceptualizations of social majorities as masses are more permanent in character, and are either derogatory or pessimistic in their explicit attributions of, or implications about, the human character of the individual in mass society. From the development of post-feudal and Enlightenment conceptions of republican democracy, which depended on egalitarian theories of popular government, arguments have been put forward repeatedly that popular majorities are composed of individuals who, for largely ascriptive reasons, are seen as cognitively and morally unfit to exercise the judgements necessary for participation in the processes required by responsible government in a modern society. They are seen not yet as masses but as plebs, peasants, crowds, mobs, rabble, the *hoi polloi*, common people (Giner 1976: xi, 28–68). Industrial mass production, particularly under capitalism, lends the sense of massification to this way of formulating the social majority. Industrialization is seen as commodifying human work to the point of automation, and thus reducing workers from the creative craftspeople of pre-industrial society, involved in all stages of the processes of production to which their work contributed, to machine-dominated automata, alienated from the product of their labour. This further depersonalizes individuals into a one-dimensional, anonymous, isolated, immature and amoral condition in which they are easily manipulated by sinister elites who dominate them in order to achieve ulterior goals. The resulting political condition of mass society is unavoidably either authoritarian, justified by the cognitive inability and political incapacity of the majority for the self-determination required by democratic majority government; or totalitarian, in order to realize in institutional practice the extremist (invariably racist, often genocidal) ideologies of the ruling elites. Mass society holds the prospect of a social condition in which the interactional and interdependent relations between structurally differentiated groups such as classes, status groups and their attendant subcultures are replaced by an increasingly inactive, inept and impotent majority subject to the oppression of an anti-social, self-interested and corrupt elite (1976: 189–93).

The overstatement endemic to these formulations is indicative of why mass society is an immanent rather than a real condition of modern society. It explains also why the concept of mass society has not been grounded effectively in social theory and is therefore referred to more correctly as an 'outlook'. But emerging, as it has, at key points in the development of reflexive thought about the changing conditions of modern society, it is very much a part of its culture. This explains, in part, the **teleological** character of some of the formulations of mass culture as the culture (Kornhauser 1959; 1968) or the cultural correlate (Coser 1964) of mass society. Apparently unenlightening though these attempts at definition appear to be, they reinforce the substantive absence of the phenomenon of mass society itself. The constitutive elements of mass culture, by contrast, are seen as increasingly ubiquitous and burgeoning features of mass society.

The first and in some respects determining characteristic of mass culture is that proposed in the second sense noted above – as the culture of the audiences for the mass media of communication. The term 'mass media' collects within its descriptive and definitional range the broadcast media of electronic and print communication. The sense in which these can be referred to as a *mass* media follows from the economic necessity of the large scale of their audiences and readerships. This is accompanied, from the outset of systematic sociological analysis of their socio-cultural structure, by a series of related assumptions about the homogeneity of the social backgrounds and characters of their members, the low intellectual, academic and educational level of their cognitive abilities and the impersonal character of the social relations between them (Bramson 1961; Elkin 1964; Merton and Lazarsfeld 1957; Vidich and Bensman 1958). All of these elements, inevitably, provide for constituting such audiences as masses in a manner which is much more a projection into sociology of political ideology than it is either adequate as a sociological account of their structures or accurate as a social psychological formulation of their likely behaviours. It is related explicitly to the tradition of political conservatism, referred to above and summarized effectively by Giner (1976), which provides for a characterization of the social and cultural majorities of modern societies as crowds, mobs and masses. It is also reinforced by a set of economic practices which require what Williams (1976) refers to as seeing others as masses. Where masses are identified, it is rare that the identifiers include themselves as members of the masses, rather than critics (see Jacobs 1961) or manipulators of them. Even the exception of the Marxian sense of mass noted above tends to disappear in later, critical post-Marxist discussions of mass communication and culture. Indeed, the influential neo-Marxists of the Frankfurt School argued, differently from but not unrelated to Gramsci, that it was the seduction of the working class away from the project of revolution by the mass entertainments and diversions of what they term the 'culture industry' that was in part responsible for the failure of what Marx had proposed as the inevitable revolutionary overthrow of industrial capitalism by socialism (Adorno 1957; Benjamin 1968; 1979; Horkheimer and Adorno 1973a; 1973b; Jay 1973; Marcuse 1964). The production of mass culture had become itself a form of industrial work as well as the focus of the workers' leisure. In this dual capacity, it is seen as serving to legitimate and reinforce the passive and quiescent impotence of workers in the face of a system of production and exchange which exploits them.

The mass media, as part of the culture industry, are deeply implicated in the logic of industrial capitalist political economy (see, for example, Williams 1974). The initial capital investment required to establish a broadcast communications medium has been relatively high for most of the history of its technological possibility. Its current technological sophistication, based upon global satellite communication systems, is so costly that the possibility of ownership is limited either to the governments of nation-states (usually for purposes of national security, and not ownership by capital) or to multinational corporations. These broadcasters use the media for the transmission of some news and related content, but mainly for entertainment programmes designed to attract numerically large audiences. The size of audiences dictates the price that can be charged for the media timeslots available to advertise retail consumer goods and services. The revenue from these charges underwrites the current running costs of the media and, most importantly, provides a return on the large initial investments required to finance them.

There is, thus, an economic pressure of global proportions in the contemporary broadcast communications industries to construct audiences with social characters and cognitive abilities which are as homogeneous as possible – in effect, to see large-scale groups of people as masses. To accomplish the construction of such audiences would provide the widest possible reception for a relatively easily produced and narrow variety of informational and entertainment content. It would also establish a market for a relatively narrow variety of mass-produced goods and services to be advertised on the media for mass consumption, thus playing a significant role in the operation of the global exchange processes in which late industrial capitalist economies are centrally involved (Lash and Urry 1987). They are a part of the processes of globalization of culture (Appadurai 1990; Arnason 1990; Friedman 1990; King 1990; Robertson and Lechner 1985; Robertson 1992; Smith 1990; Wallerstein 1990) discussed below (see also the chapter 'Local/Global'). It is in this sense that a concept of mass culture as the content of the mass media can be identified as the cultural correlate of mass society. For just as the concept of mass society is a recent construction of a tradition of political conservatism, so mass culture is a recent version of some of the changes in political economic orders which are consequences of increased egalitarianism and social mobility (Bauman 1991; Bocock and Thompson 1992; Bourdieu 1984; Kellner 1989; Gans 1974; Haug 1986; Mulgan 1991; Rosenberg 1957; 1971; Thompson 1990).

As the content of the so-called mass media, mass culture is a collection of substantive social phenomena and is thus unlike the idea of mass society. But it is, nevertheless, associated with the unreal character of mass society, because there is no evidential basis to support claims that the audiences that owners and controllers of the broadcast media seek to construct are as socially and cognitively homogeneous as they are required to be to perform the passive and quiescent political conformism required by the mass society outlook. Nor is there any evidence to suggest that they consume everything that is mass produced for them. On the contrary, the sociology of broadcast media audiences suggests that, rather than being a mass culture, they are composed of a variety of socially heterogeneous subcultures (Morley 1992; Hall et al. 1992). The members of these subcultures are not characterized by the social isolation, political impotence, economic exploitation and cultural conformism of individuals in mass society. Confronted by the constraints of a centralized institutional social and political structure, and by uniform material and cultural products for consumption, they respond actively through forms of social resistance and cultural interpretation that reinforce their senses of subcultural identities (Hall and Jefferson 1976; Hebdige 1979) and by customizing a wide range of mass-produced consumer goods and services into artifacts which are expressive of the specific identities and collective interests of particular groups (Forty 1986; Hine 1987; Willis 1990; Wolfe 1966; 1969). They are equipped to respond in these active ways, moreover, because of their continuing membership of traditions of social structural differentiation and division by class, generation, region, gender, age, sex, race, ethnicity and nationality which are the sociological bases for their senses of the varieties of subcultural identities in terms of which they identify themselves.

Thus, although the idea of mass culture, like the outlook of mass society, retains a certain rhetorical force, it does so because it is a gross sociological oversimplification of a social process of cultural differentiation that is far more complex and subtle than derogatory formulations of mass culture can possibly allow. For, upon systematic ethnographic investigation as a feature of what has been termed the *postmodern condition* (Docherty 1993; Foster

1985; Harvey 1990; Jameson 1991; Lyotard 1984; Ridless 1984 and see the chapter 'Modernity/Postmodernity'), what has been proposed as mass culture dissolves into a series of other typical forms of culture which are diverse enough to suggest a challenge to the vertical model of cultural stratification itself. Moreover, once these cultural forms are identified explicitly as the implicit cultural correlate of mass society, they can be seen clearly as one resource for countering the negative sociological prophecies made by the proponents of the mass society outlook. For a brief period in American sociology, for example, mass society comes to be formulated as a new societal order in the sense that the mass of people have become incorporated within a form of structural and institutional societal relations which have traditionally been exclusive (Bell 1961; 1974; 1976; Bensman and Rosenberg 1963; Olson 1963; Shils 1972). This is discussed further below, in relation to the horizontal stratification of culture into centre and periphery.

FURTHER FORMS OF VERTICALLY STRATIFIED CULTURE

There are four more specifically differentiated cultural forms in terms of which sociological discussion of the high/mass dichotomy has been developed: folk culture, popular culture, middlebrow or mid-cult, and common culture. The first two of these forms, folk and popular culture, can be distinguished in terms of their location either side of the watershed in social structural change that occurs with industrialization.

Folk culture is, for many social theorists (e.g. Lessa 1964; Redfield 1953; 1956; Sumner 1906; Tonnies 1955), historically the correlate of high culture in pre-industrial, traditional societies. This is the culture of the organic society, referred to above, which Tonnies terms *Gemeinschaft* and Durkheim *mechanical solidarity*. It is a culture which both legitimates the high culture of such social structures and provides a resource for it. Legitimating in its traditional system of political authority, it accedes to a version of social position based on a hierarchy of ascriptive status and a sacred belief system rooted in myth. Folk culture is a majority culture which integrates a whole way of social life with pre-industrial craft and agrarian modes of production. Its clearest surviving contemporary expressions are in fine craft manufacture, in so far as this can still be differentiated from fine applied arts; in certain forms of youth culture, i.e. some types of traditional popular music and communalist lifestyles; and in the politics of ecology, where these are rooted in an opposition to centrist, corporate economics and large-scale, heavy industrial production.

It is the strength of its traditionalism that leads to the emphasis on folk culture as a resource for minority high culture. In sustaining traditional beliefs, and their oral expression in myth, legend and religious practice, it provides and gradually renews the *prima materia* for a high culture which insists on the necessity of tradition. This insistence is teleological, since it is the means by which the practitioners and beneficiaries of high culture legitimate the vertical stratification of the class or estate society which they claim is necessary to sustain high culture. The legitimating process is reinforced structurally, as indicated earlier in the discussion of high culture, by restricting access to the skills of literacy required to create, represent and communicate high culture beyond a minority. The dominant patterns of social, political and economic development in modern societies have made such restrictions of access difficult to justify in the face of egalitarian philosophies, and counterproductive to the skills required by secondary and tertiary industrialization. Thus, attempts to revive or retain forms of folk culture, on any other than the sorts of marginal and esoteric terms in which their survival has been indicated above, have often been specious representations of social majorities for the purpose of racial or ethnic nationalism and are, as such, linked to pathological features of the mass society outlook, such as fascism (Nolte 1965).

Popular culture emerges as the majority culture of Western society with the dissolution of the traditional societal forms that sustained the firm distinctions between high and folk cultures. Its occurrence is, in effect, coincident with that of modern society itself (Lowenthal 1961), though it is most often associated with the onset of industrialization. But wherever it is identified, it is related to the social majority's conception of itself as a people or populace (Arnold 1960). It is for this reason that some critics (e.g. MacDonald 1957; Tumin 1957; Van Den Haag 1957) treat the term as interchangeable with mass culture. Either the relative affluence and increased leisure that accompany secondary and tertiary industrialization, or the egalitarianism that marks the spread of liberal, social democratic politics, or the progress towards universal literacy and increased educational opportunities that accompany all these processes, are seen as exposing the majority as either uninterested in or somehow unfit for the appreciation of the traditional high culture which is now accessible to them (Inglis 1988). Some of these critics see the situation as exacerbated by claims that such access to minority culture is or should be a right of the majority, and that the means of mechanical industrial mass production are utilized to reproduce fine art and literature. For in doing so, it is proposed, the works of high culture are reduced to the condition of mere commodities, goods for exchange and consumption. Two further contentions are implied by this. The first is that the mass reproduction of works of art predicates the construction of a mass audience, according to a logic directly comparable to that of the economic argument for the necessity of a homogeneous mass media audience, which has been discussed earlier. The second is that the intrinsic aesthetic worth of the works themselves are thereby reduced – deprived, in their mechanically reproduced state, of what Benjamin (1968) terms their *aura*. There is no more evidence to support the first of these contentions than supports the related argument in regard to mass media audiences. But the second contention leads in part to a compounding of the confusion which stems from treating mass and popular culture as equivalent. This occurs with the introduction of the terms *middlebrow culture*, and *mid-cult* (MacDonald 1957) to refer to intermediate orientations in the dichotomy between high and mass culture.

The phenomenon of middlebrow emerges from the democratization and widespread affluence of modern societies. The former extends a participatory status of citizenship to increasing numbers and wider groups of people; the latter provides them with the means to improve their material lifestyles through consumption. As one reaction to these processes, traditionally dominant classes and elites, no longer able to claim ascriptive social and political authority, seek to redifferentiate themselves from the majority by claiming new, implicitly ascriptive qualities of superior insight into, awareness and experience of, and ability to express high culture. As has been noted earlier, they claim to be defending a tradition of epistemology against dilution through popularization, condensation and trivialization, and to constitute an avant-garde of fine artists, intellectuals and critics, devoted to an exclusive modernism in order to preserve the intrinsic meaningfulness of aesthetics against the tide of commercial consumerism that is mass culture. Sociologically, they are an alliance of traditional aristocracy and high bourgeois against the upwardly mobile social aspirations and reductive cultural philistinism of the new middle classes – the middlebrows.

Middlebrow culture is seen as the antithesis of high and folk culture, but it is one form of differentiating popular culture in negative terms as the culture of a majority which aspires to membership of traditionally dominant social groups. Middlebrow culture is seen, in this sense, as the legitimating culture of conformist social aspiration. Middlebrow is the culture of those who are motivated by the ambition to differentiate themselves from the culture of the majority groups from which they have separated and which they consider beneath them. It is also the culture of those who need to dismiss the culture of intellectual minorities because they see it as the culture of the politically and economically impotent (Fiedler 1957). In some cases – the avant-garde, for example – these minorities seek deliberately to generate an epistemological culture which is difficult to understand, and therefore designed to be especially inaccessible to those whom they label middlebrow. This is part of a strategy of response to their perception of the need to defend traditional culture from dilution. It is also a reaction to their sense of dismissal into the social isolation of a marginal relation with the normative, scientist and materialist culture of high and late industrial society, and of their disdain, in turn, for what some of them term the **kitsch** that it produces (Greenberg 1957). The condition of middlebrow, thus, is a fragile and unstable one. It is attacked by those who are sustained by the norms and values of popular culture which ambition has led it to deny, and despised by those committed to the high cultural tradition towards which it is drawn inevitably by its aspirations, but where there is to be found little that is compatible with its own urge to conformity and desire for bland consensus. It is, in effect, a recurrent aberration within the increasing heterogeneity of contemporary popular culture, a manifestation of the continuing volatility of the complex social structures of late industrial societies as they change and reconstellate around the proliferating focuses of interest, association and differentiation.

Confronted with these configurations of societal flux, popular culture demonstrates a coherence and resilience which support its claim to remain the appropriate sociological formulation of the beliefs, values, artifacts and institutional practices of contemporary social majorities. First, it is sustained through a historical continuity which is rooted in communities that have survived through an active engagement with the structural and ecological changes that have characterized industrialization through all its stages. The flexibility of a social structure which has adapted in microcosm to the considerable pressures and constraints that societal and global changes have placed upon it has generated and been reinforced by a reflexive *common culture* of popular beliefs and values. It is a *common* culture because of its genesis within and its reflexive legitimation of a sense of community that is coherent enough to adapt consciously to change as a way of preserving its collective sense of identity. The central experiential value of this common culture is identified by Williams (1958) as solidarity, which he proposes as the central achievement of working-class culture. Hoggart (1957) and Thompson (1968) endorse this in discussing critically the self-consciousness and confidence with which working-class communities and movements have responded to the social changes that have confronted them to produce their reflexive, lived culture. The industrial working class has been, since the mid nineteenth century, the most dominant of the self-conceptions of the social majority that have been characteristic of modern societies. As such, it is a formulation of the *people* as a collectively conscious social majority; and its culture, in the distinctively sociological sense of a whole way of life, is a *popular* culture, whose strength stems from a core of lived values which are held in common (Clarke et al. 1979).

This experiential core to popular culture gives it a coherence which enables it to adapt creatively to the processes of change which constantly confront it in modern society. This is in marked contrast to the unavoidable conservatism of those who are concerned for high culture, for whom change – of which popular culture itself is seen as a manifestation – invariably threatens the coherence and continuity of tradition. Whereas high culture is seen as sustaining a traditional past, popular culture allows for collective orientation to and active engagement with future ways of life. Liberal exponents of the mass society outlook (Shils 1972) argue that the future of what they term mass culture is of participation in and contribution to high and minority cultures, thereby broadening their selective traditions into a lively critique of contemporary experience. This generates the complex, reflexive texts of pop art (Hughes 1991; Williams 1984) and punk

(Hebdige 1979; 1988) which invert the high/mass dichotomy as part of a broad critique of aesthetic and epistemological cultural valuation. These are clear contemporary examples of the processes of cultural hegemony discussed above. The processes which they exemplify are features of the self-differentiation of social majorities into heterogeneous subcultures: social groups organized within and between societies around a considerable variety of focuses of identity and differentiation (Gilroy 1993b). Subcultures are constitutive features of the postmodern condition, and incorporate what Gans (1974) has termed *taste cultures*, to indicate the relatively transitory processes by which they constellate, disband and reform around interests which are quite temporary as well as more sustained. Both subcultures and taste cultures are interrelated with another of the characteristic features of postmodernity, the globalization of culture (Mennell 1990 and see chapter 'Local/Global').

HORIZONTAL STRATIFICATION OF CULTURE: CENTRE AND PERIPHERY AS A DISSOLUTION OF THE HIGH/MASS DICHOTOMY

The type of complex, large-scale contemporary societies that are characterized variously as First World, affluent, developed, late industrial and postmodern have in common, as well as the features implied by these characteristics, a central value system which is shared by the ruling authorities of each society and which is intimately connected with what each society holds sacred (Parsons 1951; Parsons et al. 1961; Shils 1972). If there is a specific location for the dominant, normative culture of these societies, it is to be found in this central value system. It both legitimates and is reinforced by a centralized complex of institutionalized organizational structures which constrain and facilitate the immense variety of patterned actions and interrelations that constitute each society's constant and recurrent processes. Because it is a *normative* system, however, specific social groups are located in differential proximity to the societal centre of the value system and the institutional complex. Indeed, since societies of this type are governed and administered by elites, the majority of their populations find themselves located structurally and culturally in relatively peripheral relations to the centre. As these societies continue to develop in scale and complexity the vertical social stratification between relatively empowered and unempowered classes has been supplanted by a differentiation between elites and majorities, the changing memberships between which have tended to be drawn from wider social bases and have become more mobile, for reasons of meritocracy and egalitarianism that have been legitimated by the central value system. Thus a new mode of stratification begins to emerge, between *centre* and *periphery*.

The designation of the type of society in which these processes are occurring as First World indicates a further distinctive feature of their structures and cultural processes. They are deeply implicated and engaged in what Wallerstein (1974; 1979; 1987) has termed a **world system**, that is, a structure of interrelations between modern societies that is in itself trans-societal. In important political and economic respects, Wallerstein argues that these interrelations, and the system in terms of which they are organized, are more important in their consequences for the societies involved in them than are many of their internal institutional structures. Because of this, he proposes that the preoccupation of much general, comparative sociology since the mid nineteenth century with the geopolitics of the nation-state has been misplaced (see chapter 'Civil/Political') – a contention which is supported to an extent by the initial emergence of modern Western societies in the context of a structure of inter-societal mercantile economic relations. It was on these, in turn, that the capital was developed and concentrated to a sufficient extent to stimulate industrialization as a developmental process. Since the fifteenth century, modern Western societies have been mutually engaged in a structure of political and economic relations which have generated and been legitimated by a set of reflexive cultural values and practices (Elias 1978; 1982). These relations, moreover, have been developed not only between Western societies but, from the outset, with those located in non-Western subcontinents also. Against such an endemic history of global orientations, a preoccupation with the politics of the nation-state seems almost an aberration (see chapter 'Nationalism/Internationalism'). It ignores, moreover, the incipience, throughout the process of Western modernization, of a trans-societal structure of institutions and identities which parallels that of the intra-societal relations between centre and periphery: that of the relations between global and local (Hannerz 1990). Just as the relations between centre and periphery have emerged to destabilize, and perhaps to supplant, the traditional hierarchies of stratification in late industrial societies, so the globalization of economic interests has become manifest in the institutional structures of multicorporate industrial capitalism and has generated parallel movements of trans-societal political federalism. These have had the further effects of generating a self-conscious sense of *local* identity among more particular economic and political interests within the geopolitical limits of traditional nation-states.

It is these movements especially which have generated the reciprocal global/local flux and diversity that is so characteristic of postmodern culture. Globalization has been formulated quite specifically as an essential process of modernity, which translates routine social practices from their local, intra-societal situation into contact with related practices in other societies, thereby transforming them potentially into a globalized environment (Giddens 1990). It is more generally understood as a diffuse process of global interdependence in several different dimensions, of which the economic is the most evident. But it refers also to a process by which particular institutions, and collectivities of interest and belief, develop a sense of inter-societal identity on a global scale. In both a formal and an informal sense, these institutions and collectivities are clearly cultural where, for example, they focus in common on the arts, science, education and religious beliefs and practices, or unite around a set of political goals (Inglis 1993). The cultural consequences of this are those of modernity itself and suggest, therefore, that the sociological coherence of popular culture, as it has emerged and sustained itself over the past two centuries of modernization, is able to engage reflexively with the conditions of postmodernity. The strength and durability of popular culture is in its structural capacity to constellate peripheral and local groups in flexible forms of relation around changing focuses of common interest. The very flexibility of these forms of relation has made the groups increasingly conscious of, and therefore reflexive about, their collective interests and activities. It is what has enabled them to be resilient in the face of their dismissive designation as manipulable political masses or quiescent, passive mass audiences. More importantly, the structural capacity of popular culture to survive the hierarchical constraints of the high/mass dichotomy might come to provide a basis from which the potentially global, heterogeneous social majorities of late industrial societies might construct themselves by transcending the increasingly anachronistic limits imposed by the traditional nation-states.

KEY CONCEPTS

HIGH High culture is that which operates exclusively for the few within society. It contains theatre, opera and classical music, among other forms; it has exclusive access and its appreciation requires training or socialization. To have acquired this training is to possess what Bourdieu calls 'cultural capital'.

MASS Mass culture is that which is not exclusive and accessible to all people. It is, therefore, less highly valued and less highly regarded. The distinction between high and mass culture is also a description of the symbolic hierarchy that constitutes the class system within a society.

Subculture The distinctive way of life of a significant subgroup within a complex society. This will include in particular the beliefs, values, expressive symbolic systems and artifacts, but may also extend to institutional and organizational structures of relations. Subcultures may be deviant from or oppositional towards the normative culture of dominant groups, or they may be constellated around non-normative focuses of social identity and differentiation.

Globalization A series of related processes which are characteristic of the history of *modern* society. These include the development of universalizing concepts of humankind and of the individual, of normal or typical conditions of society (e.g. the nation-state), its political economy (e.g. capitalism, socialism) and its mode of government (e.g. electoral democracy). Globalization itself becomes distinctively recognizable through the emergence of trans-societal relations, initially, perhaps, to facilitate trade and communication, but moving towards creation of a permanent forum to regulate international relations (League of Nations, United Nations). This is complemented by comparable organizations to promote cross-cultural relations (International Olympic Committee, Nobel Prizes).

Hegemony A neo-Marxian concept, implemented initially by Antonio Gramsci, to explain the relation between culture and ideology in everyday life, and the role of that relation in sustaining economic, political and social dominance of a ruling class or other social group in the face of the oppositional interests, practices and beliefs of subordinate groups. The concept seeks to explain in particular how concessions are offered by dominant to subordinate groups in the distribution and exercise of power as a way of subsuming the oppositional beliefs of the latter into the consensual ideologies of the former.

Avant-garde A recurrent grouping of literary and visual artists committed to the modernist aesthetic principle of the intrinsic value of art. The first avant-garde at the turn of the eighteenth and nineteenth centuries were strongly associated with romanticism and revolutionary bourgeois politics. Such movements recurred throughout the nineteenth and the first half of the twentieth century, but became apolitical, seeking to sustain art in the face of commercialization, trivialization and ideological reductionism.

Teleology In the logic of sociological explanation, this term refers to the problematic practice of offering a causal explanation of a social phenomenon, structural process or event in terms of its consequences for the social system in which it is implicated. It is problematic because it produces a self-sustaining explanation, such as that mass culture is the culture of mass society, rather than one which is autonomous and can thus account for the phenomenon to which it refers as a phenomenon in its own right.

Kitsch The antithesis of fine art and traditional culture. Kitsch is seen by critics of mass and popular culture as the deleterious cultural consequence of the linked processes of industrialization, general affluence and democratization. It is transitory, superficial and trivial; it communicates by formula and mechanistically, consisting of false experiences, vicarious sensations and pseudo-events.

World system A mode of analysis of the human condition of modernity which questions the dominant conceptualization of societal organization, the conventional periodization of history and the characteristic differentiations of economic and political systems. Developed by Wallerstein (1974), world systems analysis seeks to argue that the relations between societies that have characterized the history of modernity are more important than the specific intra-societal structures that are typically studied comparatively by social scientists.

Physiocracy The theory of political economy according to which agrarian and mercantile craft production and their corresponding social ecology are a normal condition of human society. The theory was held by influential groups in England and France during the late sixteenth and the seventeenth centuries, when attempts were made to operationalize it in practice through physiocratic movements. It was tied to a naturalistic theory of social and cultural ritual, a cyclical social round of birth, growth, fruition, decline and renewal, whose rhythm was set by the passing of the seasons.

Modernity/Postmodernity

Helen Thomas and David F. Walsh

A major debate has now developed in the cultural and social sciences in consideration of the nature of the contemporary Western world which centres around the argument that it is undergoing processes of transformation which have moved it from a state of modernity to one of postmodernity.

The modern world, it is argued, is a world that emerged in the West largely from the seventeenth century onward in the form of a radical disjunction with traditional societies to become characterized in opposition to them by: a large and heterogeneous population; a high level of industrialization; a primarily capitalist and market economy; highly specific and structurally organized forms of social differentiation and division; a territorial and administrative system based on the nation-state in terms of which both citizenship and civic communal membership are organized and in which political activities and processes are shaped and structured; and an increasing domination by science and technology. Moreover, the forms of culture, belief systems and practices which modernity came to generate, in contrast to traditional societies, are primarily consensual, normative, rationalistic and secular.

This view of the contemporary modern world has recently been called into question. It is argued that, from around the 1960s, but with seeds taking shape at an earlier stage, the whole shape and organization of modern Western society at the levels of the social, the communal, the economic, the administrative and the cultural have been subject to disintegration, transformation and change to produce a postmodern world. Just as modernity constituted a radical departure from traditional societies, so postmodernity, it is argued, represents a fundamental disjunction with modernity. Postmodernity is a globalizing post-industrial world of media, communication and information systems. It is organized on the basis of a market-orientated world of consumption rather than work and production; a fragmented and pluralistic community of heterogeneous groups with diverse cultures and lifestyles; a world in which the nation-state has been shrunk by privatization, marketization, internationalization, and new forms of citizen and civil rights. Increasingly, in postmodernity, political life rejects traditional class- and party-based power politics for micro-political activities and social movements. Social existence and self-identity are seen as being organized primarily in terms of the varied internal rationalities of the languages, knowledge, beliefs, practices and styles of the heterogeneous subgroups that make up a fragmented society which has no distinct boundaries, or highly structured and fixed forms of social organization. That is, it is a world of culture in which tradition, consensual values, normative control, absolutist forms of knowledge and universal beliefs and standards have been challenged, undermined and rejected for hetero-geneity, differentiation and difference. In consequence, it is argued that the very reality of the emergence of a postmodernist world has inevitably set up a new agenda for the social sciences (the agenda of postmodernism and its theoretical stance within and towards this world) since the existing one and its whole set of assumptions, concepts, methods and aspirations are no longer relevant. Its foundations lie in the investigation of and programmatic attempt to direct and control the modern world. What is required now is a new agenda with which to encounter the postmodern world and to engage with and within it.

POSTMODERNISM AND POSTSTRUCTURALISM

Whereas it is possible to describe and characterize with some clarity the empirical and historical social and cultural processes of postmodernization which are argued to constitute the emergence of postmodern society, it is not so easy to establish a precise identity for postmodernism. That is, it is difficult to accurately delineate the thinking, ideas, issues, discourses and sensibility that constitute the new cultural, theoretical and analytical stance within and to postmodernity (the postmodern world) or, in these terms, provide the new agenda for sociology to engage with and analyse its nature. Postmodernism has flourished in a whole variety of discursive arenas including the arts, cultural studies and the social sciences. Because it is still the subject of much contentious discussion and debate, one is immediately confronted with a variety of different levels of meaning and usage of the term itself. But more than this, two other reasons stand out which make for a difficulty of characterization. First, as Huyssen (1986) has noted, the 'post' in postmodernism should provide a caution for those wishing to define what postmodernism *is* within closed boundaries because it indicates its relational character. Consequently postmodernism can only be addressed in terms of its relation to modernity and the modern, in which case it is best seen as 'a slowly emerging cultural transformation that entails a shift in sensibility, practices and discourse formations' (1986: 186). Second, as the processes of postmodernization and the nature of postmodernity have been identified in terms which argue that heterogeneity, differentiation, fragmentation and difference lie at the heart of the postmodern, modernism too may be seen to be implicated in this. On this basis, Boyne and Rattansi (1990: 9) recognize that although postmodernism lacks conceptual coherence (as well as being inescapably fuzzy around the edges in relation to modernism), there is, nevertheless, a certain ironic unity to be found 'in the paradox of a set of cultural projects united by self-proclaimed commitment to heterogeneity, fragmentation and difference'. This relates closely to Jameson's by now classic formulation of the most salient stylistic features of postmodernism, which are: the erosion of 'key boundaries and separations', particularly the high/popular culture divide; 'diversity' as a value in itself; 'pastiche' and 'alliteration' as forms of aesthetic organization; and 'schizophrenia' as a mode of self-being and seeing; all of which are brought about through a reaction against 'established forms of high modernism . . . which conquered the university, the museum, the art gallery, the network and the foundation' (1985: 111). The term 'postmodernism', then, refers to developments in the arts, cultural products and cultural knowledge which are constitutive elements of that social, political and cultural configuration of the postmodern world that is postmodernity.

Although the philosophical roots of postmodernism can be traced to the late nineteenth century to the writings of Nietzsche, the word 'postmodernism' first appeared in the 1930s to point up a slight resistance to modernism (Featherstone 1988). In the late 1950s it was used in literature to denote a concern for the loss of the cutting edge of the modernist movement. As Huyssen (1986) points out, it was taken up in New York in the 1960s by literary critics and artists from different fields (Hassan, Fielder, Sontag, Cage, Rauschenberg, Rainer, etc.) as a response to the institutionalization of modernism in the arts and literature. In America in the 1970s and 1980s the term became commonplace across the arts, encompassing architecture, dance, theatre, painting, films and music. In all this, it confronted the European tradition of modernism with its aesthetic of 'high' art, the unity of forms, the necessarily critical representative, progressive avant-garde role of art, the cult of creative authorship, and the artist as individual genius. However, although American postmodernism originally took shape as a kind of avant-garde protest against the institutionalization of modernism in the form of 'high modernism', this was also a protest against the conservatism of the American socio-political world of the 1960s and part of the general protest movements of that era. By the 1970s, this critical form of avant-garde postmodern art – particularly the iconoclasm of pop – had disappeared under the pressure of commercial culture, the cementing of high/popular culture, and the critique of the naivety of counter-cultural politics to become something different (Huyssen 1986). Now feminism and other minority groups began to explore their 'hidden', 'silenced' traditions which provided a different impetus to the critique of high culture and to the generation of alternative forms of cultural production that served also to open out the original attack on modernity and modernism.

But now, and very central for sociology and the creation of a new agenda, came the emergence of **poststructuralism** and its association with postmodernism. By the 1970s postmodernism travelled to Europe and began to be taken up by writers such as Barthes, Baudrillard, Derrida, Foucoult, Kristeva, and Lyotard in terms of what was being developed by them as poststructuralist thought (being both anti-phenomenological and anti-structuralist: see chapters 'Subject/Object' and 'Idealism/Materialism' for discussions of phenomenology and structuralism). Again, poststructuralism like postmodernism represents a diversity of thought and approaches struggling together under this one umbrella and refers to a number of intellectual initiatives in French thought (literary criticism, philosophy, history) which began to gain ground after the collapse of the socialist-led student revolts in 1968 which swept across Europe. It too, given the 'post' in it, is a relative term which Eagleton has argued 'was a product of the blend of euphoria and disillusionment, liberation and dissipation, carnival and catastrophe, which was 1968. Unable to break the structures of state-power, poststructuralism found it possible instead to subvert the structures of language' (1983: 142). But, despite the differences between the projects and the analyses of the various thinkers who are dubbed as poststructuralists, there are particular suppositions regarding languages, meaning and subjectivity (and the reflexive constructed and constituted nature of the human and the social in these terms) that they share in common.

Central to poststructuralist thought, as McNay (1992) argues, is the critique of the human subject or *cogito* which has dominated Western cultural thought. The mind/body dualism inscribed in Descartes's first principle of philosophy in his *Discourse on Method* (1637), *cogito, ergo, sum*, 'I think, therefore I am' (Hampshire 1956: 68–9), has been of central importance to classical thought and to developments and achievements in scientific thought. For Descartes, the essence or nature of human beings consists only in thinking and is not dependent on any material thing. The human subject is constituted through the mind and the mind is wholly distinct from the body. Western cultural thought since the Enlightenment has been dominated by the privileging of the rational thinking subject and the negation or regulation of the 'other' (i.e. what is not part of the former) to a subservient position. Rationality takes precedence over emotions, idealism over materialism, culture over nature, objectivity over subjectivity.

In poststructural theory the idea of the individual as a self-reflecting, rational, unified, fixed subject is rejected in favour of a dislocated, contradictory, fragmented subjectivity which is not fixed but reconstituted in language on each and every occasion we speak. The subject, in poststructuralist theory, contrary to the dominant Western humanist tradition, is constructed through language. Poststructuralist theory takes its starting point from Saussure's structuralist linguistic theory formulated around the turn of the twentieth century. Language, according to Saussure (1974), is an abstract system of relational signs which are arbitrary and extra-individual. It is a closed system where the signifiers (sounds) and the signifieds (meanings) are arbitrary, and the arbitrary relation of the signifier to the signified is fixed by social convention. Poststructuralism rejects the idea of language as a closed system and the relative fixing of the elements of the sign (which is the structuralism in Saussure's linguistic theory) in preference for the notion that the signifieds of language are never fixed but always in the process of being deferred (in this sense it is poststructuralist), continually breaking apart and reattaching in new combinations (Harvey 1989). So the focus moves away from the 'logocentrism' of the speaking subject (the word) to the 'text' and so the speaking subject is decentred. Cultural existence (and thus social existence too in the end) is seen as a succession of texts which converge with other texts that, in turn, produce other texts. Writers create texts on the basis of all the other texts they have ever come across and readers read texts on the same principle. This 'collage/montage' effect or 'intertextuality' has an existence of its own which gives rise to multiple (unintended) readings and meanings (1989: 49). And this heralds the 'death of the author' traditionally cast as the privileged speaking subject who creates the text and is the sole arbiter of meaning which, in turn, gives rise to the notion of the 'birth of the reader' (the consumer) as deconstructing and combining the elements in any way they like. Thus, the idea of 'real', 'true', 'fixed' meanings is called into question.

From the late 1970s poststructuralism, through initially crossing the Atlantic mainly through the ideas of Barthes and Derrida, has rekindled interest in philosophical pragmatism in philosophy and literary and cultural criticism to join hands in a general postmodernist stance. The battle cry of its discourse has been raised against humanism and the Enlightenment tradition even if, as its critics argue, much of its critical thrust has melted into a form of new conservatism (perhaps most visible in Baudrillard and least in Foucault), because of its anti-realism, its historicist and relativistic stance towards rationalism, and the link to the dialectics of culture and consumption that are seen to institute and enfold the post-modern world. But such criticism depends on what stance is adopted towards the pivotal theme of the modernist/postmodernist debate, particularly with regard to the critique of the Enlightenment project which constitutes the essence of modernity and the consequential issues and notions of intertextuality, difference, plurality and reflectivity. For some, such as Habermas (1985), who wishes to reinstate the emancipatory potential inscribed in the Enlightenment project into late-twentieth-century culture and society, postmodernism and poststructuralism represent neo-conservatism. For others equally critical, such as Jameson (1985), it represents a cultural shift, but one which follows upon and echoes a shift in the global capitalist economic order since 1945 and of which postmodernism is the cultural expression and logic. Jameson rejects the idea that there is a total epochal shift taking place towards post-industrialism or post-capitalism. Instead capitalism has moved into a new and late stage of modernity, *vis-à-vis* international global capitalism, which has developed new energies and strategies. The emergence of postmodernism is closely related to the emergence of this new late movement of capitalism which is a consumer capitalism in which representation has become the central focus of economic activity. Culture has become commonplace: style, images, representations no longer embellish economic products, rather they are themselves products. Postmodernism, then, is wedded to late modernity and the globalization of capitalism and consumer society. This, in turn, produces and undermines its ideological and critical claims to the new and more valid existence. However, for some, the postmodern condition has arrived and must be addressed in its own terms. For Lyotard (1984) this means the 'metanarratives' or **grand narratives** of rationalistic scientific discourse are, and thankfully, at an end. For Foucault (1979b), it requires a history of the present as an address on the discursive order and practices through which the panoptical governmentality of the contemporary world of society and identity in it is produced and sustained and through which it can be subverted. For Baudrillard (Connor 1989), the eruption and expansion of cultural commodities and signs has created a new world of simulation and hyper-reality based on the political economy of the sign, where signs have lost their referential function (as indicators of the economic and of a world outside of them) and instead there is a continuous play of signifiers which have their own existence and logic and which has led to a 'death of the real'.

So the modernism/postmodernism debate in the arts and the wider cultural arena and the modernity/postmodernity debate in the cultural and social sciences has now become a highly contested area with, as Featherstone (1988) has suggested, epochal meaning. Just as modernity refers to the process of development which led to the collapse of feudalism and the emergence and establishment of industrial capitalism in the West, so postmodernity, it is argued, is the process of development through which modernity is collapsing or has collapsed and with it the cultural sensibility, practices and discourse formations of modernism which were central to the constitution of modernity and against which postmodernism mounts a critique on behalf of heterogeneity, fragmentation and difference.

Crucially, the nature and agenda of sociology are caught up in this contest because it was the processes through which the modern world developed and their social consequences that preoccupied sociology in the early stages of its development and which, in turn, shaped its nature and agenda as a discipline. This legacy has maintained a firm hold upon sociology until this present moment of highly charged and contentious debate over and within the contemporary world (although critics may ask whether, at one level, this is very much still the Western world, despite all the talk of it developing on a global basis).

MODERNIZATION, MODERNITY AND MODERNISM

The beginnings of the modern world (i.e. modernity) can be traced most particularly to Western Europe in the seventeenth century, in which a conjunction began between emergent structural changes taking place in society, most specifically in the arenas of its economic and political organization and the social divisions produced by such in association with and as part of new cultural forms and values that began to entail, most of all, a transformation of the nature and basis of knowledge which moved from the religious and theological to the secular and scientific. Central figures in the development and creation of this new scientific and rational knowledge and its application to the world are Bacon, Galileo, Hobbes and Machiavelli, but most particularly Descartes, because it was he who was the first to establish a thoroughgoing foundation for the rational knowledge of the world which distinguished between what was objective and true as opposed to merely subjective, and this original foundation has remained the primary basis of modern Western thought ever since. The foundation of rational knowledge, according to Descartes, had to be a rigorous methodo-logical objectivity which was that of radical doubt, in which the human enquirer set aside the human body and all subjective qualities for the use of faculties of the mind alone, through its disinterested reason, to discover the data of physical reality which are all that objectively exists in the world.

This commitment to reason, rational knowledge and science began to flower into an extensive movement and unity of thought during the eighteenth century in Europe in what is referred to as the Enlightenment. Enlightenment thought is an essential and constitutive part of the process of modernization through which the modern world came into being and established itself culturally, intellectually and ideologically in association with the structural changes that were occurring in the processes of capitalist industrialization from (but with much earlier roots) the seventeenth century onwards.

What, then, constituted Enlightenment thought and how is it constitutive of modernization and modernity? It can be seen as having a fundamental set of characteristics which centre around reason as the basis of true knowledge which is tied to a project for the reconstruction of the world and the emancipation of the individual in terms of the application of the powers of reason and scientific knowledge to these tasks. It is this project which is absolutely central to an understanding of modernity since it functions as the knowledge, values and ideology in terms of which the modern Western world has defended and legitimated its whole existence: its strictures and institutions, its culture and forms of life and its sense of human identity.

What the Enlightenment entailed as thought and project, as Hollinger (1995) puts it, was a belief in a universal and objective knowledge which was generated through a rational epistemology which all human beings can share together: a moral unity of humankind in which universal rational moral principles are binding on all human beings as rational creatures and which provide absolute standards for conduct and judgement. Any impediment in thought, action and institutions which prevents the growth of universal knowledge or the moral unity of humankind hinders human progress and happiness and must be swept aside for a society based on science and universal values. Only the truth can make human beings free and happy, and the more we know scientifically about the world and ourselves the better human life will become; it is ignorance that causes immorality and unhappiness, and scientific knowledge will abolish ignorance to create progress and emancipation. So what occurred in the Enlightenment through its project was not just the consolidation of science, but also the birth of the social sciences in conjunction with the processes of industrialization taking place during this period; the birth of sociology as the science of 'man' engaged in an empirical and diagnostic enquiry into the newly emerging industrial and modern world using the rational methods of science and geared to the aim of providing the means for the reorganization of society and the reconstruction of morality through scientific sociological knowledge. Central to this sociology was the concept of structure which was viewed as constituting the essential nature of the reality of society (i.e. that social relationships have an objective and particular order and pattern of organization to them): that human social behaviour is structurally generated and that society and its structures can be empirically observed and scientifically explained in terms of their causal determination and valid and universal theories constructed about the nature of society and social life on this basis. This, in many ways, has remained the agenda of sociology until the present day but with considerable variations in its application at the level of theorizing, methodologies and aims that largely revolve around what social structures consist of and how social action is determined by them. But most, if not all, traditional sociologies are wedded to empirical and rational enquiry that attempts a separation between fact and value and so is committed to science, although not necessarily to the particular theories and methods of the natural sciences. But if sociology is implicated in modernity by its rational and scientific nature as a discipline, how has its agenda been set by modernity and the processes of modernization that it set out to tackle, analyse and explain? In what sense is it possible to call classical sociology a sociology of modernity in these terms? Moreover, is it the case that the relevance of classical sociology and its agenda for the analysis of social life has been overtaken by the transformation of events that are claimed to have generated a new and different postmodern social world?

In terms of its substantive theories of society and the topicalized structure and cultural analyses of the historical and empirical social processes of its constitution, classical sociology is undoubtedly a sociology of modernity. Its theories seek to establish the nature and foundations of social reality in terms of the primary issues of social order and stasis, of the organization of social relationships and conditions and processes through which they change, but always within the historical and empirical context of the structures, institutions, culture and self and social identities of the modern world and in terms also of a diagnostic examination of the problems and possibilities of that world. Moreover, the modern world is typically treated as a higher and more developed (if not progressive) state in a general and teleological process of social evolution, change and transformation which all societies are subject to and part of and in terms of which they can be placed relative to one another which strengthens the concern with modernity by making it the inevitable fate of society generally. Other than in this development societies can only become arrested, go into decline or die. Three major theories of modernity have been dominant within classical sociology, namely those of Marx, Durkheim and Weber and the adherents to and extensions of such. Each of these theories thematizes and explains the nature of modernity in terms of a particular and central condition and processes which pose oppositions between them, yet the analyses of the structure, institutions and culture of the modern world which they generate are very much interlinked and have become more so in the contemporary development and uses of these theoretical perspectives in sociology. Crook et al. (1992) and Waters (1994) clarify how each is a theory of societal transformation and so a theory of modernization and modernity which understands the constitutive processes that produce the modern world in its own specific topicalization and explanation of it.

Marxism

For Marx and Marxism the process of modernization is a process of the commodification of the social relationships of society which is generated by the emergence and development of capitalism and its material organization of the mode of production of capitalist society. The capitalist mode of production entails the manufacture of commodities to be sold in a market for a profit which transforms production and products from use value to exchange value. But the basis of capitalist production is the use of labour power as its major force of production, and it entails its commodification through the sale of labour by the labourer for a wage to the manufacturer (entrepreneur) who uses it to manufacture commodities for sale in the market. The surplus value extracted from the labour of the labourer in this process, in terms of the difference between the cost of labour and the value of the commodities produced by it, constitutes the basis of profit. In turn this establishes a structure of social relationships within capitalist society which is one of class, in which a ruling class (the bourgeoisie) emerge as the owners of labour power in the form of capital and private property, and a subordinate class (the proletariat) can merely sell their labour. Capitalist society, then, is a class society and one which is inherently grounded and organized in the process of commodification which the capitalist system of production entails. In it, the labourer loses control of his or her own labour by virtue of its sale and use in the division of labour that is entailed in the industrial process of capitalist manufacture. This produces a state of alienation because he or she is divorced from their own human being which lies in their capacity for creative and self-directed labour. Moreover, the labourer is exploited because the profit and capital, in the form of private property, which gives the bourgeois their ruling position in society is nothing more that the congealed fruits of the labour power of the proletariat which has been acquired through the extraction of the surplus from its ownership and use by the capitalist manufacturer. So the system of production which is capitalism, and the modern world which it creates, is a world of commodified, exploitative and alienated social relationships between its members that are structured in terms of class. The political life of society is simply a reflection of this, whereby parliamentary democratic politics only enshrines and preserves the power of the bourgeoisie through institutionalizing and representing its interests and control over the levers and forms of public power in society. The state is nothing more than its executive and collective means of administration of the ruling class in society. Moreover, capitalism produces a dominant and hegemonic culture which ideologically legitimates and reproduces this class structure and the power relationships which it entails by presenting the market, and so the interests of the bourgeoisie which it serves, as the natural and necessary conditions for economic production. This disguises how it is a historically and socially determined form of production that depends on a particular organization of social relationships between producers that is essentially dehumanizing because of the commodity form which it takes.

Note, then, how the whole theory of modernization and the nature of the modern world is understood by Marx and Marxism in terms of the capitalist system of production and the commodified form which it takes. Consequently it focuses on how the social relationships of the modern world are structured and differentiated primarily in terms of class on a divisive basis by virtue of the central position of labour and property in the productive organization of the capitalist market system, and where culture and the other institutions of society (e.g. the state, the legal system) are generated as the superstructural ideological and hegemonic manifestations of it, and self and identity take the form of possessive individualism. Capitalism creates a modern world based on commodity and possession which ultimately possesses its members and commodifies their lives precisely as such, and it is this which gives it its particular nature as a system that is the modern world of capitalist society.

Weber and neo-Weberianism

For Weber, the process of modernization consists of the rationalization of society in terms of the organization of action within it in terms of calculability and impersonality. In this, not only is tradition replaced as the basis of action, but an ethical foundation for action in terms of a commitment to moral values is replaced by the instrumental organization of action in terms of its costs and benefits. Through this the whole social and cultural organization of society changes because the worth and character of human activities are instrumentalized by subjecting them to criteria of measurement to determine their value. So work is measured by income and not creativity; education by qualifications and not learning; and art and literature by their contribution to leisure and relaxation and not their transcendental value and meaning. Culturally, rationalization changes the nature of consciousness, knowledge and ethics in the modern world. In terms of consciousness, a new kind of subject emerges which is no longer governed by traditional customs and unthinking habit but instead weighs up the means and ends of action before engaging in it. In these terms rational action is based upon knowledge which in modern society takes the rationalistic form of positivistic science and technology which achieves an almost total and singular legitimacy to the point of replacing religion. The result is that the world is intellectualized and demystified and with it a concern with discovering a meaning for life is replaced by the discovery of facts. Finally, this rationality of knowledge moves on to invade the ethical sphere of human existence to produce a value system that is committed to formal and instrumental ethics of work and duty. This rationalization of culture is tied to a thoroughgoing rationalization of the structure and social organization of society in the modern world of which the culture is a constitutive foundation and expressive product. In the sphere of economic activity and production, the modern world is based on industrial capitalism which is orientated to the market and profit and creates economic relationships between the members of society that are based on money, property, formally free and contracted labour and technological knowledge. Capitalism is the epitome of rationalization at an institutional level since it is a system of production based on a finely tuned calculation of the cost–benefit use of resources to achieve the maximum profitability of the industrial enterprise and the rational organization of work and the workforce in

373

the activity of production. For Weber, capitalism is the major theatre in the rationalization of modern life, not only because of its structural organization but because, as the material foundation of modern society, the market enhances and constrains life chances in society in terms of inequalities of power in the ownership and control over market resources, and so is the nexus of social stratification within it. In this Weber stands in agreement with Marx. The market creates classes in terms of common life chances and the sale of labour.

But more important for Weber than class is the development of status as the major form of social stratification in modern society as a hierarchical rank order of prestige based on patterns of consumption and social enclosure by merit which is closely linked to but not determined by the market in the sense that market position may be dictated by status (e.g. ethnic minorities) and status by market position (e.g. professional groups who control their market position through qualifications). For Weber status stratification and not class had become the more important element in the social and political organization of modern society, particularly with the rise of administrative, managerial and white-collar workers who constitute highly solidaristic social groupings within it. In terms of politics and the administration, the rationalization processes that characterize modernization lead to the rise of the state and bureaucracy (although bureaucratization is characteristic of the development of industrial capitalism too).

Orderly exchange in the market needs governmental organization which depends on the creation of formal and abstract law. With it there emerged a political system based on a form of domination that was lodged in terms of legal-rational authority that is embodied in the state as a compulsory organization that possesses a monopoly of violence in society. So the administration of society is centralized in terms of the emergence of the state which accrues to itself control over the political organization and, through the granting of citizen rights and obligations and the creation of political institutions, governs and regulates the activities of the members of society. But crucial to the modern state is its machinery of administration, namely bureaucracy, that is administration by trained administrators. Bureaucracy, then, entails trained experts administrating society on the basis of expert knowledge with a high degree of machine-like efficiency and instrumentality in which there is a distinction between the bureau and the official which produces the separation between public and private life that is a distinctive characteristic of modern society. But more important for modern society, bureaucracy monopolizes the knowledge needed to run society and the technical efficiency with which bureaucracy administrates in terms of knowledge makes it indispensable for social organization. In these terms politics now becomes an autonomous centre of power and social division in society. So bureaucracy produces the dictatorship of the official within a coercive bureaucratic state in association with its managerial form of control in industry. The result is to increase the impersonalization of life in society and produce a machine-like participation in it. Crucially then, for Weber, the modern world is a rational and impersonal world in both the political and the economic sphere. In this respect Weber like Marx is talking about the modern world as a dehumanized and alienated world of social existence. In these terms, then, the modern world entails the technical rationalization of social relationships and the technical control over the world in which human beings are disciplined to conform with the instrumental needs of centrally organized industrial and administrative systems. These control individual actions through calculability and the empirical measurement of achievement, and instil obedience to their dictates through a commitment to materialistic consideration and duty which rejects transcendental values as a basis for giving meaning to life in favour of instrumental results.

What distinguishes Weber's theory of modernization from that of Marx is the focus upon the political organization of modern society and its autonomy from interpenetration with the economic organization of it. But otherwise the analysis of the rationalization of modern society is very close in many ways to Marx's discussion of commodification.

Durkheim and functionalism

For Durkheim, modernization is a process of differentiation brought out by the emergence and development of the social division of labour which creates a new complex and solidaristic (organic) organization of social relationships, in which society is structured and organized through the functional interdependence of highly differentiated and specialized activities and institutional spheres. Social relations become relationships of contractual exchange between the members of society; and culture, as a common overarching and consensual normative and cognitive system, underpins and cements the whole social order. What threatens the creation and maintenance of social order in the modern world is anomie which emerges if the division of labour is not accompanied by consensual and integrative norms (i.e. a common culture), because then the differentiation which it produces creates fragmentation instead of interdependence (a complete and chaotic heterogeneity of differences in the social world with nothing to bind them into a unity) and the egotism that is released when specialization separates out and autonomizes the individual but there are no societal normative controls over their desires as individuals (which precipitates excessive demands within a conflictual competition between them). The point for Durkheim is that it is social control (through a common culture of society) that is needed to ensure that individuals rein in their individual desires in favour of community and reciprocal obligations to one another, and to turn the complexity of differentiation and specialization of activities which the division of labour produces into an orderly and structured web of interdependence and institutional organization. Ultimately this can be achieved only if the economic activity of the capitalist market is socially regulated. This requires that the state represents the collective interests of all members of society; occupational specialization is tied to the natural ability in terms of which people fill occupations and not to inherited wealth and class position; and individual subjectivity is channelled into social participation and constrained by social commitment. The aim of Durkheim's scientific sociology is to utilize the objective scientific analysis of society – and modernization at the level of knowledge is seen by him as producing science as its cognitive system in opposition to religion – to supply, on the basis of factual understanding, the normative and integrative common culture that the modern world requires so as to create social participation and commitment and thereby resolve the anomic tendencies produced by the division of labour.

Functionalism picks up this Durkheimian position to argue that the modern world can be understood as an adaptive and advanced evolutionary response to the existential conditions of the environment within which society exists that has occurred through the reproduction of structural specialization and differentiation.

The shift in the Durkheimian–functionalist picture of modernity is to bring culture more centrally into the organization of the modern world as a constitutive basis of its institutional formation and social relationships, such that it generates a social order out of the complexity of differentiation and specialization which characterize them. Modernity and modernization represent the social and institutional nature of society and the processes and conditions of its emergence, establishment and development. Modernism, however, is the particular cultural and aesthetic movement which was generated within it towards the end of the nineteenth century. But it was a movement, as Kumar (1995) points out, which already had part of its roots in the romanticism that appeared with the birth of the modern world as a product of the revolution which was modernity in terms of the formal artistic innovations of romantic art, its largely utopian and political outlook and its emphasis on the ideal of the autonomous and self-making individuals, but challenging the whole socio-cultural basis on which the modern world stood by pitting imagination against reason, feeling against thought, the natural against artifice, spontaneity against calculation, the subjective against the objective, the visionary against the mundane and the supernatural against science. In this sense, then, romanticism represents not only a cultural and artistic movement on which modernism could draw to create its own aesthetic of avant-gardism with its emphasis on change, relativity and presentness but also a counter-cultural sensibility that actively subverted the rational, rationalist, commodified and institutionalized social order of the modern world.

Modernity already brought with itself from the beginning, then, a critical and complex cultural reaction to itself in which its official and dominant

376

values and socio-economic structures of social relationships were subjected to challenge from within. Modernism can be seen as an artistic and cultural movement that articulates this reaction to modernity in a complex relationship of both affirmation through its absolute commitment to modernity and attack on tradition, and denial through the way it splits modernity as a social and political project of science, reason and industrialism (i.e. bourgeois modernity) from an aesthetic conception which rejects this for reflexivity, sentiment, intuition and the free play of imagination, albeit with many of the means that modernity placed, both of understanding and of technique, at its disposal in a restless and ceaseless quest for the new that rejects all tradition. Modernism, then, as it manifests itself in the artistic work of poets such as Eliot, Yeats, Mallarmé and Rilke; dramatists such as Ibsen, Strindberg, Pirandello and Brecht; musicians like Schoenberg, Berg and Webern; painters and sculptors like Picasso, Dali and Duchamp; and architects like Sullivan, Wright, Le Corbusier and Mies Van de Rohe, has a highly diverse nature. Though its works were an intensely living expression of its own modern times, it represents a complex reaction to them that reveals the split soul in the modernism of its aesthetic stance in which its eagerness to dissect and understand everything (the very essence of the modern outlook) is accompanied by a profound attack upon the modern age and the desire and need to overcome it. This ambivalence came now to find an echo in late-nineteenth-century and early-twentieth-century social thought which resonated with it in terms of a critical reassessment of modernity and the modern world in which the whole idea of reason and rationality (the Enlightenment project of progress and emancipation which is based upon it) began to be challenged and undermined. Leading thinkers here are Simmel, Weber and Pareto in sociology, Sorel and Mosca in politics, Nietzsche and Heidegger in philosophy, and Bergson, James and Le Bon in psychology, but most of all, perhaps, Freud whose ideas challenge the whole conception of the 'modern man' emancipated by reason from an originally primitive mentality, and 'modern civilization' as a progressive development of society in association with this, which form the essential basis of the idea of modernity and the legitimation and justification of the modern world.

There has been a tendency for the advocates of cultural postmodernism and postmodernity to present a one-dimensional view of modernism and modernity. Generally speaking, postmodernism's assault on modernism is targeted on the aesthetic of 'high modernism' which operated in terms of a minimalist canon celebrated by the influential art critic Greenberg in the 1950s. This aspect of modernism is best exemplified in painting by abstract expressionism and in architecture by the streamlined, stark, functionalist buildings of Le Corbusier and his followers. Although the rejection of tradition has been a major driving force of aesthetic modernism from its inception in the latter part of the nineteenth century, by the 1950s modernism was no longer in the avant-garde: ironically, it had become a tradition. High modernism had become the establishment high art and culture, a prime target for debunking. But high modernism represents only one side of the story of modernism, albeit one that has gained ascendancy and was appropriated by conservative hegonomic forces during the era of the Cold War.

Baudelaire's famous essay on 'The Painter of Modern Life' published in 1863 offers a more complex view of modernism (Baudelaire 1981). Modernity is defined by Baudelaire as 'the transient, the fleeting, the contingent; it is one half of art, the other being the eternal and the immutable' (Harvey 1989: 10). High modernism is situated on the eternal and immutable side of modernism. As the previous discussion shows, this side of modernism was already inscribed in the scientific basis of classical sociology as reflected in the work of Marx, Weber and Durkheim which was concerned to ground the understanding of the process of modernization in terms of the generalized principles of rational scientific enquiry. Science provided the tools to comprehend and thus control the fragmentary, ephemeral, chaotic world that characterized life. But it also needs to be recognized that even though all three thinkers insisted upon the absolute universal and authoritative nature of science, the scientific optimism of Marx had become a qualified enthusiasm in Durkheim, while it had reduced to a considerable degree of ambivalence and scepticism in Weber.

The tension between these two elements – the fragmentary, transitory, chaotic anti-tradition side of modernism where, as Marx noted, 'all that is solid melts into the air' (Berman 1983: 13), and the desire to find a common ground or language that would transcend the limitations of this 'tradition of the new' – is a useful way of not only understanding the complexity of modernism (and its problematic relation with rationality and modern industrial and social life) but also illuminating postmodernism's narrow view of modernism. The history of cultural modernism, as Harvey (1989) has noted, has oscillated between these two sides, and this has led to a variety of contradictory discourses, practices and cultural products that can lay claim to the features that modernism in its wider sense gives rise to: 'an aesthetic self-consciousness and reflexiveness; a rejection of narrative structures in favour of simultaneity and montage; an exploration of the paradoxical, ambiguous and uncertain nature of reality' (Featherstone 1988: 202). So the very features that are said to be central markers of postmodernism and the basis of its critique of modernism may also be seen to be inscribed in particular elements of postmodernism's despised other, modernism.

POSTMODERNIZATION, POSTMODERNITY AND POSTMODERNISM

The problem of the way in which postmodernism was founded on a specific image of modernism which is also encapsulated in itself makes it questionable whether it is appropriate to speak of postmodernism as a social, aesthetic and cultural configuration that is distinct and oppositional to modernism. However, its penetration into the discourses of the social sciences, philosophy, cultural analysis and feminism is characterized by one distinct trend running through these frameworks which is, as Boyne and Rattansi argue, a series of 'crises of representation' where:

> older modes of defining, appropriating and recomposing the objects of artistic, philosophical, literary and social scientific languages are not credible and in which one common aspect is the dissolution of the very boundary between language and its object, this in turn being related to the acceptance of the inevitability of a plurality of perspectives and the dissolution of various older polarities (popular/elite forms, subject/object) and boundaries (for instance between disciplines such as philosophy, sociology, history and psycho-analysis). (1990: 12)

But these crises, in turn, can be understood, as Crook et al. (1992) have set out to demonstrate, as tied to and integral with what is argued to be the nature of the emergent postmodern world (i.e. postmodernism itself) and the processes which are constitutive of society, self and identity that compose it (i.e. the process of postmodernization). These processes can be said to centre around five kinds of configural transformations.

Structure

The first is the dissolution of structure. The modern world has typically been conceived and treated by sociology as a bounded and organized system of interdependent institutions of structured social relationships. Central to this organization of the modern world is the role of production and its government of social processes generally (and particularly as the basis of social stratification and social divisions in society) and of the political and cultural arenas of society specifically. However, capitalism has now moved from being geared to production to being geared to consumption, and consumption in turn has moved from the material to the ideistic. The result is a destructuring of the market in favour of its enculturation in which mass production based on mechanical means of production for a mass market is replaced by flexible and niche production based on media, communication and informational technologies and systems using intensive advertising and focused marketing to maintain a continuous and innovatory relation with and response to consumer tastes and demands. The argument is that the economic predatory pricing practices, control of labour costs, protectionism and government subsidy to eliminate competition and create a command relationship with consumers are transformed now into global but decentralized networks of production units which subcontract out more and more in their highly differentiated manufacturing activities, and where consumer choice begins to have a large degree of autonomy in dictating what they produce. In turn, that has changed the organization of work and production in manufacture. Not only is it the case that industrial manufacture is increasingly replaced by service industry (in part an outcome of the West's inability to compete with Third World industry) which creates administrative, managerial and white-collar work, but the technological organization of production has itself begun to change particularly as a result of information, intellectual and automated technologies. Instead of Taylorist management practices which treat labour as just another factor of production to be rationally manipulated like any other raw material, and **Fordist** mass production on the basis of the factory assembly line, batch production seeks to enhance and flexibly utilize labour skill which expands the capacity of workers to participate in the organization of production, although this also (together with subcontracting) produces a large reserve army of unskilled and part-time workers. At the same time, management, as part of this, is moving away from a bureaucratic hierarchical structure of organization to a flattened collegial structure that disperses organizational authority and responsibility by consolidating expertise and freeing organizational segments of the company to establish an autonomous contact with and effect a rapid response to market developments. So economic life generally, in the postmodern world, is becoming more and more decentralized as it is geared to a continuously changing consumer market which forces flexibility and breaks down production and the organization of labour into a whole mixture of forms of ownership, owner–worker relationships, production units and management and work practice.

But as economic life has changed so too, it is argued, has political life. What characterizes the political-administrative organization of late modernity is the corporate nation-state. The late modern corporate state with the bureaucratic organization and administration of society grew up as a response to the spectre of revolution, world war and economic depression which propelled welfare reforms, economic regulation and defensive nation-building on a societal scale. Warfare consolidated the major social forces of society, leading to the formation of their representation through political parties, trade unions and employees' organizations and the generation of state intervention and regulation (and their social acceptance) in the creation of war economics. What emerged was an elitist society operating under the aegis of the state which internally stabilized society through the mediation of industrial conflict and the regulation, co-ordination and harmonization of the economy including the creation of an infrastructure and training to sustain and organize it. In turn, too, the corporatist state consensually legitimated and mobilized mass support for its existence through the creation and extension of civil and political citizen rights into social rights and entitlements, which were defined as belonging to the domain of state power and state responsibility and could only be fulfilled through the concentration of state authority and the massive extension of the bureaucratic apparatus. Finally, the state preserved the external stability of society by safeguarding the national socio-political order through military and political bloc arrangements and treaties. So the state corporatist society of late modernity is one in which the state controls and regulates capitalism and private corporations by partial nationalization, control over credit, currencies and legal regulation, whilst simultaneously socially and politically enfranchising organized labour through its incorporation into government and economic administration in exchange for abandoning revolutionary programmes, tempering demands and respecting the rules. In this way, then, the state becomes the centralized and bureaucratic executive of society which preoccupies itself with economic planning and the overall co-ordination of internal social activities and external national relationships, in terms of the ideological and political control over interest articulation in society and the corporate brokerage of its articulation through the creation of functional power blocs which it licenses to take part in centralized decision-making as official representatives of capital, labour and the like. So in these terms, political life in the corporate state and society is established institutionally, structurally and culturally in terms of class and the class organization of society, and politics is the elite power and party politics of class conducted in terms of market interests within an ideology of social consensus and economic growth and according to political rules of the game which all the parties accept and in which political decisions are made pragmatically through intra-elite deals and where, consequently, there is a low degree of mass involvement and participation in them. Because it works through pragmatism, persuasion and the elitist and party mediation and management of interests, and not by coercion, so the state is tolerant of dissent and respects individual freedoms; and because it organizes through brokerage and regulation it doesn't seek total control of the economy but establishes itself in relation to and works within the market matrix as an administrative agent.

But it is argued that the corporate state is now beginning to break down and withdraw as the controlling apparatus of society for a variety of reasons. Firstly, the territorial sovereignty on which the state is based is being undermined by the globalization and internationalization of the economy and the polity and by the development of nuclear weapons which turn warfare into the threat of total destruction, so the state is forced to surrender its power and sovereignty internally and externally. Secondly, the expansion of the state has led to a spiral of spending, welfare expectations and taxation that is now too costly to maintain, and this, together with globalization, has forced the state into a position of retrenchment and decentralization which involves the privatization and marketization of formerly state-administered activities in which workforce replaces welfare and social provision is devolved from the state to the market, turning people from clients into consumers. Thirdly, and in turn, this has ideo-logically delegitimized the state. On the one hand, its failure to deliver on welfare and peace has produced the realization that the state cannot make people free, happy, safe, equal and rich. On the other hand, the enfran-chisement of the population and the extension of civil rights has produced a better educated, informed and organized body of claimants who define their rights no longer in terms of state guardianship but in terms of human rights to freedom, personal development and the quality of life which are increasingly defined and protected in terms of international laws, con-ventions and agencies. Fourthly, the welfare state has inevitably shifted political conflict from class to a conflict between claimants and providers in which it is not just a question of the educated and informed who articulate political demands about the quality of life but also a matter that involves the empowering of politically and economically marginalized groups. Finally, as the market replaces the state and power shifts to the former whilst responsibility remains with the latter, the two are separated, with the state bearing the brunt of the conflict over resources, turning the market into an invisible agent that is not subject to pressure. So the state has reached a point of crisis to which it can only respond through decentral-ization, fragmentation, privatization and minimalization which destroys its autonomy and reunites it with the other economic, communal and cultural social domains of society.

But the result of all this is to reconstruct the political life of society in terms of these other domains in a way that decouples political conflict and cleavage from class and party politics (as evinced in the decline of class voting and the erosion of support for mass political parties) and associates it with political forces that are focused around issues, rights and social movements and which largely reject traditional politics and the structures of conventional politics (namely centralized state authority of government, bureaucratic parties, leadership and electoral competition) for mass rep-resentation and political activism using the media as their major instrument both as a means of mobilization and as a vehicle for action.

The point about this new politics is that it does not fit into the traditional categories of 'left' and 'right', nor is it structurally generated in terms of class and class interest. Essentially it sees this as a block upon its concerns. It is socio-cultural in nature and articulates itself generationally and culturally. What it entails is value- and issue-orientated cleavages that identify, in group terms, only like-minded people united and contingently generated through shared formative experience of either a social or a cultural character, focusing not so much on segmental economic interests and rights. Its concerns are moral; its politics is anti-elitist; its shape is iconic and symbolic; its instrument is the media; its organization is grass-roots; its activism is spectacle and drama; and its constituents are potentially and often global. What the new politics demands is a new society which rejects bureaucratic organization, and to this end it entails a constant convergence and interrelationship across social and cultural boundaries and divisions in a fluid politics of issue-orientated formation and reformation activated and amplified through grass-roots organization, direct action and media campaigns with a constituency that joins and disengages with it as the political context and personal circumstances change.

But its basis lies not simply in the dissolution of the corporate state but in the more central dissolution and decomposition of the whole organized and structural social divisions and inequalities that characterize modern society. The capitalist system of production originally generated, through the privatization of the means of production and the sale of labour, a class structure which radically distributed rewards and power unequally between capital and labour and produced a society organized around this class division and in terms of which gender relations were largely based on the disjunction between the domestic and public spheres of social existence which gave women a subordinate role in society. However, the development of organized capitalism fragmented ownership by separating it from control through the emergence of the joint stock company; created a whole new middle class of managers and professionals in terms of this fragmentation, and white-collar workers in the move to tertiary industry; and decomposed the working class through deskilling and machine control. To this, the rise of the state added wholly new classes of elite administrators, middle-level bureaucrats and state dependents. The result of all this was a highly complex pattern of class and status stratification in late modern society which dissolved capital–labour relations and which entailed a further process of increasing social differentiation as women too entered the labour market as another social group within it which transformed patriarchy into virarchy. However, and despite the structural complexity of this pattern of social division and differentiation in late modernity, it is a structure that has a generational and material basis in the system of production. The postmodern argument is that this structure has now decayed to the point where divisions of class, status and gender have disappeared into more fluid cultural patterns of social differentiation in which social membership is neither material nor structural but one of symbolic and imagined associations and community (that has a large media determination in it). It is no longer production but consumption that gives shape to society and, as a result, social differentiation moves from the social sphere to the cultural sphere with the shift from life chances to lifestyles that consumption entails. Moreover as consumption moves from goods to signs and signs are no longer representations but codes, so social groupings based upon them are founded in shared systems of meaning that operate in terms of fashion, media messages and information which are entirely self-referential and without material foundation. In this way consumption and cultural differentiation in terms of it detaches from structural constraint to create imagined communities which arise, not from a shared situation or interpersonal network of relations, but from media-induced versions of communities with common ascriptive characteristics, tastes, habits and concerns that foster what is a simulated version of fellowship and communal identity. Furthermore, just because they are media simulations, so they are created and mobilized by the media and find expression through media-directed market and political demands and representation in terms of media images and spectacles. They are culturally produced communities without any concrete referent in terms of any group or type of person and they produce a politics of social movement in terms of their simulated characteristics and interest and, with the globalization and destatization of society, they become transnational communities too. So social differentiation in the postmodern world becomes a fluid mosaic of media-simulated and media-imagined multiple status identities which are based, not on location in society or work, but in consumption and access to codes which display themselves in mass participation and social movement politics.

Culture

The dissolution of structure points to the second and crucial transformation which it is argued characterizes postmodernity: the salience of culture and the creation of a discursive world on this basis. Prior to the mid 1970s sociologists who were interested in the arts and culture were situated on the margins of the discipline and there was little crossover between the sociology of art and culture and literary criticism, aesthetics and cultural history. Now, there is a visible shift in sociology towards the theorization of culture and the relaxing of traditional disciplinary boundaries. Culture is the common thread that runs through the range of meanings which prevail under the banner of postmodernism. In its armoury, the conceptual tools and justificatory strategies for analysing and critiquing texts are aesthetic and its models for life are organized around the aesthetics of life, but this is precisely because the salience of culture in the postmodern world constitutes, as Simmel (Frisby 1985) originally argued, a development in late modernity: that is, the aestheticization of everyday life, or art as life and life as art, as Featherstone (1991) puts it. Although these cultural questions and aesthetic issues have been forced to the centre of sociology by this new salience of culture which is postmodernism, it is important to note that feminism, psychoanalysis, semiotics, late Marxism and cultural studies have also contributed to the topicalization and analysis of culture. What the postmodern transformation argues, however, is more. Postmodernism constitutes a movement which makes culture the constitutive basis of social life which replaces structure and its determinations. What then is ushered in by this is a world, the postmodern world, which exists at the level of surface and appearance; which is depthless and spatial rather than historical and temporal; where identity is simulated, heterogeneity is without substance, and action consists of variations on the theme of consumption; and where tradition and the past have no value or reality apart from that of a cultural emporium of styles and taste. Moreover, in this world of culture there are no universalistic and hierarchical criteria in terms of which its products can be organized, evaluated and ranked. Rather, the danger is that 'anything goes'.

Body

The third transformation which is indicative of the emergence of a post-modern world is the rediscovery of the body. This crucially affects the whole idea of the mass which, as Huyssen (1986) argues, has traditionally been the other of modernism and has been used to establish the identity of women through the location and representation of them in terms of their bodies. What the rediscovery of the body entails is a positioning of it as the central site of discourses and social control which objectify and subjectify it, which, in these terms, played a major part in creating and sustaining the social order of the modern world. Instead, postmodernism, with its emphasis on difference, and postmodernity, which is generated and emerges through heterogeneity, opens up the possibility for other (and once marginal) voices to be heard and accepted as legitimate. A crucial voice, here, is that of the body and with it, most specifically, the voice of women which modernity suppressed in terms of socially and culturally institutionalized patriarchy. Thus, poststructuralist feminists like Irigaray and Cixous insist on a rewriting of the body on the grounds that the feminine has been devalued and repressed through the logocentric structure of language in patriarchal culture (Weedon 1987). More generally, the rediscovery of the body entails rescuing it from the position it has been given in modernity through its dichotomization of nature and culture as an organic system which externally constrains the human actor and his/her action, towards a sense of the lived body and its symbolic significance to the interactional order of society. It also recovers it from the ways in which its institutionalized regulation became central in the growth of civilization which, as Featherstone et al. (1991) argue, 'required the restraint of the body and the cultivation of character in the interests of social stability'. Such regulation peaks, as Foucault (1979b) argues, in the Enlightenment and with the instrumentally rational modern world that it brought, which requires the disciplined suppression of desire to establish the governmentality that resolves its industrial needs. But now the body is in a process of release as a combination of many factors: the collapse of bourgeois morality, particularly in regard to sex; the commercial and consumerist interest in the body focused around health, beauty, keeping fit and the fight against age; the control of the use of erotic advertising; the feminist address of biology and gender; the psychoanalytic discovery of the unconscious; and the demographic transformation of the population in contemporary

Western societies, which has produced an ageing population and consequently thrust the body into the centre of attention and raised a whole series of questions about it in terms of medical treatment and death. In all these ways, then, the body has moved into a central position in the contemporary world to constitute, it is argued, a central part of the move into a postmodern state.

Self

The rediscovery of the body is tied to a fourth configural transformation which is constitutive of the postmodern, and that is the decentring of the self. Modernity is associated with humanism and its conception of the self, which is further sustained and expanded by the structural developments of modernization, namely free market capitalism and political liberalism, and their associated values, namely autonomy, privacy and the rule of law, to create the modern individual. It is dependent on a conception of human nature established largely by Descartes in which the human self is a subject defined by specific properties of which consciousness, free will and rationality are the most crucial and which give it a centred identity and a goal-directed and purposive conception of the self. But postmodernism and poststructuralism attack the logocentrism which this entails on the grounds that it rests on a series of unsupportable dualisms which privilege identity over difference, being over negation, presence over absence, nature over culture, male over female and, most of all, reason over anything that is 'other' to it. This normative hierarchy of binary oppositions not only marginalizes the other, but has also led to what Heidegger (1975) calls a 'Europeanization of Thought' in which its concepts and categories have ethnocentrically dominated all other systems of thought and thereby have played a major part in the Western conquest of the world. As Derrida (1979) argues, these are productive of the ideas of racism, sexism, colonialism and normality which violate the 'other' and force it into its own privileged mode of rationality. As such, then, the logocentric self creates a mythology about its consciousness and reason that becomes a form of appropriation and domination that makes everything and everyone the same as itself and establishes itself the master of all things. Instead, and following on from Nietzsche (1966) and Heidegger (1975), postmodernism and poststructuralism argue that identity is a function of difference. It is multiple and not fixed and always under construction. It has no overall blueprint since it is constituted by the play of its multiplicities at any given time. Particularly, as in Nietzsche, Lacan (1977) and Deleuze and Guattari (1984), this multiple self is seen in terms of a tension between the Dionysian excess of desire and the Apollonian principle of order in which they insist on the need for the liberation of the former in terms of the body, sexuality, play and difference, which has been repressed or sublimated by the

Apollonian dimension as an 'iron cage' (to quote Weber) that constrains and disables the possibilities of self-existence and action. In Foucault (1979b) this release of desire is married to an argument that the self has become a subjugated subject produced by the technologies of governance and discipline that emerged from Enlightenment reason and thought and specifically scientific rationality. These need to be replaced by the ancient idea of the care of self as the art of living. In these terms, then, the human nature of the self is no longer to be seen as governed by natural and universalistic laws which are determining. Neither is it to be seen as structurally determined in its nature by the institutions of society, even when it is historically and culturally located. But in this latter respect we need to distinguish Foucault's argument that the social construction of self and identity in the contemporary world is the product of a disciplinary society in which historically contingent and particular knowledge/power discursive practices have become hegemonic, but which can be defeated by transgressing their limits; Derrida's (1979) deconstruction of logocentric thought; feminist critiques of phallocentricism; and Baudrillard's (1988) argument that the very existence of society and the social has become problematic in the postmodern world of consumption, simulation and hyper-reality. For the last this world of consumerism has now itself become the basis of self as people use or are seduced into constructing their identities in terms of the consumption of codes, images, media and information. This ideational commodity fetishism has freed people from the old structures of society, replacing the social in the formation and construction of self through signification, albeit at the cost of the death of reality through its subsumption by the sign. This conflicts, of course, with those celebrants of the postmodern world who see the cultural heterogeneity and difference in which consumption is freedom, choice and self-expression in these terms and who argue that the new information and media systems and technologies of this world are enabling and liberating for its members.

Nature/culture

Finally, one more configural transformation is presented as a characteristic of modernity which ties to all of the others and this is the breakdown of the nature/culture division in regard to the social world. A central part of the project of modernity has been the technical mastery of the world on behalf of culture, with science and scientific knowledge as the agent for its achievement. So the modern world has seen a vast and exponential growth of science and scientific knowledge in terms of a system of research and teaching establishments, roles, networks, etc. which is interlocked with the government and economy of society in terms of resources, practices and agendas, but which also constitutes a community with a considerable degree of autonomy and norms of cognition in its own right. The problem in the late twentieth century is that this system is now under attack because of the sheer cost of funding it, particularly 'big' theoretical scientific activity, and because the promise of a total control of nature which it once seemed to offer is no longer a real prospect. With regard to the former, science policy and science funding in the contemporary world have now become tied to choosing between research priorities and cost-effectiveness in relation to practical economic and social problems of the use of science as an instrument of economic growth, which imposes an instrumental government and commercial agenda that destroys the autonomy of science as science and the validity of any internal sense of the scientific project in terms of its knowledge. But more problematic is the now recognizable fact that the degree of knowledge of nature which science possesses is limited, that its use to tamper with nature can have malignant and irreversible effects, and that it creates a considerable degree of damage in its own right. All of this has become much more problematic as science and technology have moved into directly and actively supplanting nature with their own practices, such as, for example, genetic engineering. The result is that the whole metanarrative on which science has based its legitimacy has come into question. Science has become publicly challenged in terms of its results because nature has re-entered culture in a whole series of problematic and potentially disastrous ways (e.g. ecological crises, AIDS) which science and technology are unable to control and often actually precipitate. But paradoxically, just as nature has re-entered culture in this way (and made scientific and technological control problematic), so other things which were once conceived of as cultural have now been naturalized, such as unemployment, crime and poverty, and are seen as unavoidable, if unfortunate, conditions of human social life. Either way, the nature/culture divide which was characteristic of modernity and the modern world has been breached, and social life cannot be anything but affected in its economic, political and communal existence and its contours redrawn by this as the activities which compose these spheres are reconditioned and come into new relationships with one another that break down the old boundaries between them. Instead of this old divide between nature and culture, a new interpenetration has appeared. It is clear that there is a two-way dialectic in which social processes have natural consequences and natural processes have social consequences and the postmodern world is rooted in their interlock.

A SOCIOLOGY OF THE POSTMODERN OR A POSTMODERN SOCIOLOGY?

Given the above discussion, there are three routes that sociology could take with regard to postmodernism. It could espouse that it is of no value, and thus ignore it. As we have shown, postmodernism offers an all too singular view of modernism, which is largely characterized by 'high modernism'. But as we have also seen, its presence is ubiquitous and it will not simply disappear. Moreover, as the preceding discussion indicates, postmodernism offers insights into the analyses of the contemporary social world that are both exciting and challenging. As Featherstone (1988) points out, it invites us to question how analytic models are constructed, the ideas that underpin them, and the authorial voice (the sociologist) that speaks of and on behalf of the 'other'. Thus, it requires to be examined and explained, not masked in a veil of silence as the body has been in sociological discourse. Moving to the other end of the spectrum, sociology might be tempted to take on the mantle wholesale and generate, as some propose, a postmodern sociology. Such a venture, however, we suggest, is not useful either. The very idea of postmodern sociology is a contradiction in terms. No matter how blurred sociology has become round the edges in recent years, it is nevertheless a product of modernity, part of the Enlightenment legacy, postmodernism's reviled other. As Featherstone (1988) argues, any attempt to construct a postmodern sociology is ultimately doomed to failure because it could not be other than a flawed attempt to construct another set of grand narratives. From a slightly different angle, as Featherstone further notes, the attachment of postmodern to sociology could only signal the dissolution of the discipline in as much as it would have to abandon its 'generalizing social science ambitions'. The position taken here is that, ultimately, neither of these two extremes is useful. Rather, on the basis of the preceding discussion and in agreement with Featherstone (1988) and Bauman (1992a), we take the position that, in order to understand the changes in contemporary culture, it is necessary to forgo the pitfalls and the allure of a postmodern sociology in favour of the development of a sociology of postmodernism.

KEY CONCEPTS

MODERNITY   Once a term of critique modernity has now become a way of describing not only the contemporary but also that which has become improved through the advent of our epoch. Given the background of capitalism and industrialization the advent of modernity in cultural forms has meant greater critical and reflexive self awareness. This is a description of our times.

POSTMODERNITY   There is a major debate in the social sciences that modernity has run its course and that the methods, desires, aspirations and thought patterns that have sustained the accomplishments of our times have come to an end. This end, if it be so, heralds the era of the postmodern, a time of uncertainty and competing claims for validity.

Poststructuralism   This complex body of theory arose out of the disappointment with the modern Marxist project and with its failure to secure a change in the social structure. Poststructuralism denies the commonality of human consciousness and seeks out difference as the political cause for the future. Identity politics is one of the developments that follows from poststructuralism.

Grand narrative   These are the methods, desires, aspirations and thought patterns of modernity referred to in 'postmodernity' above.

Fordism   This refers to the kind of economic base within a society that is based on uniform production and uniform provision. It also speaks of a society where people are differentiated by their relationship to the means of production. Post-Fordism implies that identity is established through consumption and consumption exercises the principles of difference and choice.

Work/Leisure

Don Slater

Commonsensically, work and leisure are opposites: leisure is time off work, off school, either at play or at rest. It is in many respects a 'residual' category in modern thought and experience, labelling what is left when work time is subtracted from the day (evening), week (weekend), year (holiday) or even lifetime (youth or retirement). At the same time, leisure labels *kinds* of social time, space and activity which are different from or opposed to work. Primarily, work belongs to a public domain of social institutions and obligations whereas leisure belongs to a private sphere of the individual or family. This accounts for much of the different character ascribed to each. Leisure is thought to comprise intrinsic pleasures, activities done for their own sake rather than to achieve some extrinsic end (to produce things, earn money, gain status); leisure is therefore enjoyable rather than irksome; it is also free and uncompelled, a matter of individual or at least private choice, whereas we have no choice but to work if we can get it, while life at work is governed by rules, obligations and pressures. This view of leisure has been important to our view of modern life: the private freedoms and pleasures of leisure (like consumption) are regarded as the payoff for the intensive structuring of public economic and political life. By the same token, however, because leisure is seen as a private affair it is reckoned to take place off the social stage and to have far less social importance than work. It has consequently received far less serious attention from sociology. Historically it has only entered the sociological field of vision when it has entered the public stage as a social problem, as when the non-work time of youth takes unruly forms in public places (for example, football violence, subcultural affronts to 'normal', 'workaday' society).

At the same time, the work/leisure distinction is not as straightforward as common sense would have it. The way in which the two are distinguished depends on the way in which they have been socially separated in modern times and this separation has been a complex and variable achievement. It has also been experienced quite differently by different sectors of the population. Most crucially, a rigorous separation between work and leisure is bound up with employment in paid work outside the home. It has therefore been more characteristic of men's experience than women's, and can become problematic if 'paid work outside the home' becomes less central to the structure of everyday life (as with mass unemployment or increasing self-employment).

Finally, even for those whose time and activities neatly divide into work and leisure, the values ascribed to each can be confused and overlapping. For example, leisure is often associated with play: as in the case of sports and games, we are talking of bounded activities undertaken for their own intrinsic pleasures. But if leisure is active, it can take on many of the properties of work: for example, hobbies and sports can be exceedingly goal-orientated, competitive, methodical, labour-intensive. They can also be encouraged not for their own pleasures, but because they are therapeutic or 'recreate' the person and their energies so that they can continue carrying out their public functions: they therefore become forms of work, or extensions of work. Moreover, when leisure is not overtly active (watching TV, lying on a beach) it may still not be the opposite of work but may rather replicate the boredom and passivity of much modern labour (it can be programmed into schedules or package holidays).

WORK, LEISURE AND MODERNITY

Strictly speaking, the distinction between work and leisure is not new or modern; it is the social *separation* of the two that has taken new forms. Distinctions between being at work and at rest, and related ones such as being engaged in productive or unproductive activities, are fairly widespread. They were fundamental to ancient thought and experience: 'work' meant 'non-leisure' in Greek (Arendt 1958). Just as in contemporary life, however, leisure in ancient Greece did not mean idleness but the pursuit of qualitatively different sorts of activity. In the Greek case, work was identified with those activities that involve securing the necessities of life: people engaged in such activities were considered unfree in spirit (and were in fact generally slaves or women) whereas being a citizen required that one was freed from such necessities and therefore able to pursue the good, to achieve perfected form in body, in speech and (ironically) in the promotion of justice in the *polis*. Non-workers, men of leisure, were therefore identified with culture and spirit rather than necessity and material gain.

The Greek example demonstrates a view of work and leisure as not only dichotomous but also inversely related: in conditions of social inequality, my (free) leisure depends on others' (unfree) work. Pleasure and pain, as well as freedom and unfreedom, are socially distributed. In the famous concept of Thornstein Veblen (1953), ruling classes generally take the form of a 'leisure class' which indicates its superiority by 'conspicuous leisure' and consumption, a wastage of time and goods which demonstrates its freedom from having to engage in productive labour, and its ability to live off the labour of others. In fact, Veblen argues that gender division is at the basis of social inequality: men engage in sport, exploit and warfare to accentuate their distance from (and command over) the *work* of domestic reproduction as done by women. The ideal demonstration of superiority would be pure leisure in the sense of doing absolutely nothing at all. However, as total inactivity is irksome even to the most effete aristocrat, they learn to fill their time with a multitude of leisure (non-productive, non-necessary, literally useless) activities which come to be understood as 'cultured': for example, bourgeois and upper-crust men and women are rushed off their feet learning dead languages, doing charity work, acquiring 'accomplishments', or maintaining refined behaviour in 'society'. However much those who engage in leisure believe that they enjoy it and pursue it (especially in the form of culture) for its intrinsic pleasures, they are nevertheless, Veblen believes, *really* just engaged in status competition through the use of status symbols. Veblen's argument involves a critical reversal of the Greek valuation of leisure and work: for Veblen it is not leisure and culture but work – the productive and useful application of skills to materials (he calls it 'workmanship') – that gives human beings their true ethical dignity and personal integrity.

Though the distinction is ancient, modernity – specifically industrialization and capitalism – introduced a more fundamental and pervasive separation of the two spheres. The basic story is fairly clear: labour becomes separated from rest and pleasure in order to intensify it (make it more productive, efficient, cheap). The rise of industrial capitalism is associated with wage labour: in exchange for a wage, the worker is meant to work (the wage does not pay for idleness during working hours), while private ownership of capital increasingly excludes workers from control over the work process. Intensification of work is associated with separating it both temporally and spatially. Temporally, work hours, work days, work weeks and work years ruled by clock and calendar are delineated (and fought over). Getting to work on time, keeping a steady rate of work within that time, reducing to a minimum those activities which do not contribute to productivity (socializing, eating, resting, going to the toilet): these are central to what is known as 'labour discipline', which in turn is deemed essential to modern forms and relations of production. Negotiations over the limits of this discipline have been historically important struggles, involving unions, management and the state, over labour contracts that define, for example, the length of the working day or conditions at work. However, the primary issue was settled early in the nineteenth century: industry required that the time and pace of labour should be fixed and predictable; and that the payment of a wage for labour entitled the employer to minimize moments of leisure at work (Braverman, 1974).

The same issues arise in relation to the spatial segregation of work from leisure. Work came increasingly to be seen as a rational and technical process which requires complete control over all its elements, including labour. For example the division of labour within the factory or office implies a central plan which allocates tasks to all those involved. This requires that work time is dictated by the flow of work tasks. It has also tended to imply that work flow has to be spatially controlled: people have to be where the machines and materials are. Factory and office buildings therefore physically separate acts of work from the enjoyment of leisure, social labour from domestic activity. Conversely, the work/leisure distinction is possibly beginning to blur again because, it is argued, the electronic nature of new work processes and products (for example, information) allow it to be spatially distributed while still maintaining the temporal intensity and discipline of work.

By the same token these developments physically remove work from the social and communal contexts where it was formerly carried out. Though it would be very wrong to romanticize the arduousness or length of premodern labour, much of it was carried out within cultural contexts which asserted values and obligations other than productivity – indeed, values which we now associate with leisure. For example, premodern agricultural labour was interspersed on a daily basis with eating and rest periods; on a seasonal basis, the work was punctuated by a large number of feasts and saints' days, fairs, market days, and so on. Similarly, guilds combined the regulation of crafts with various forms of social life and consumption. The strength of this integrity of work/leisure can be measured by the extent of the battle of early capitalists to remove these non-work traditions from the work calendar by reducing 'leisure' at work: the classic clash was over 'Saint Monday', whereby workers maintained traditional schedules of work (taking Monday off) despite all employers' efforts (Thompson 1967; 1971).

Temporal and spatial separation of work from leisure was probably most clearly registered in the separation of work from the family. Families have never been self-sufficient, but until fairly late into modern times 'domestic labour' included not just cooking and cleaning but a far more extensive range of domestic production which could involve men, women and children: growing food, rearing animals, brewing, making cloth and clothes. In the premodern household, work and leisure, production and reproduction, were consequently integrated to a now surprising extent. Work could be arduous in the extreme for all members of the household (again there is nothing to romanticize here), but it was carried out in the context of a family's customs and values rather than treated as an abstract productive capacity. Again, this meant that non-work activities which we now hive off to leisure time were then part of the same time and space as work: socializing, celebrating, learning and so on.

Conversely, once work had been sequestered to certain public times and places, the private household came to be associated with leisure (as well as consumption): a space of non-utilitarian values, of emotional rather than rational relationships, of rest and enjoyment rather than effort and discipline. However, this characterization depends on quite particular definitions of work: work came to be identified entirely with paid employment outside the household. It was therefore an activity with a primarily public status (even when it was domestic labour in someone else's home) in that it involved a contractual wage relationship. Moreover, work was increasingly defined as productive labour, which came to mean labour which produced goods for the market, or accomplished public goods such as the management of institutions. *Reproductive* labour was unpaid and domestic (and was also unpaid *because* it was reproductive rather than productive) and therefore was not defined as work.

This gives rise to the clearest problem with the entire work/leisure distinction: it does not recognize unpaid labour in the home (Crowley 1992; Deem 1986; Green et al. 1990). This obviously casts most women's experience into a sociological void: given that most women bear the responsibility for domestic *re*production, the home is for them a place of work, not leisure, despite the absence of payment (indeed there have been campaigns for 'wages for housework' that aim at validating as well as simply recompensing women's labour). Women who do have paid jobs carry out a 'double shift' (public production and domestic reproduction) and therefore have, if anything, *less* leisure. The question is really whether women can be said to have any leisure at all, or whether the entire term rests precisely on a distinction (*paid* work versus non-work) that merely reflects men's experience of and position within modernity. For example, many men feel they can come home from work and indulge in a form of leisure in which they 'do nothing' but watch TV and be a couch potato. Most women, on the other hand, experience the home as a place of work (even if they have just come home from a job) and feel guilty and unsettled as well as straightforwardly hassled by the outstanding duties and demands that confront them in the home: few women feel they can 'just watch television' (Morley 1986; 1992).

On the other hand, it could be argued that women can get much enjoyment as well as ethical dignity from domestic labour, caring, shopping, crafts like sewing or knitting. Indeed, they can experience in them the kinds of pleasures associated with 'leisure'. The issue is whether women's work and leisure can be separated out *in* the home the way men's can be separated out *between* work and home. If a 'housewife' finds knitting or shopping pleasurable, is she then doing work or enjoying leisure? Does she herself know or see things in terms of this distinction?

Finally, because the work/leisure relationship has been bound up with struggles over contractual arrangements such as the length of the working day, it has also been closely bound up with labour organization and representation (trade unions, but also political parties). Women and children have been in a weak position in such spheres (as have immigrant and ethnic communities), and where their terms and conditions of work have eased (for example, reduction of hours) this has had less to do with successful demands for more leisure and more to do with being seen as competing for men's work. Similarly, men's domination over paid labour increasingly meant that wages meant 'family wages'. Women as non-earners did not have their own money to spend on leisure (and spending on oneself is widely experienced as a guilty pleasure by women with families); while women earners received wages that were regarded as supplementary to men's. Family levels of domestic reproduction, consumption and leisure were set through men's participation in paid work.

THE SOCIAL ORGANIZATION OF WORK AND LEISURE

It is obvious to most people that work is socially organized: it takes place in institutions (firms, factories, offices) which are organized in relation to final products and organizational aims (profit, efficiency, etc.). Leisure, on the other hand, like consumption, is less evidently social in character: the very fact that we often call it 'free time' indicates that it is meant to be individual, subjective and undetermined – not structured by social forces. Leisure is ostensibly private, individual and free as opposed to work which is public, social and regulated.

However, leisure is very definitely socially organized, and its structure is clearly bound up with the organization of work. Firstly, as we have seen, modern leisure arises when it becomes socially segregated from work (at least from paid public employment). Secondly, leisure has been structured around the same two features that have structured work itself: commodification and rationalization.

Commodification

We are accustomed to think that capitalism arose on the basis of the increasingly mechanized production of material goods. In fact the commodification of leisure played an important role in the rise of capitalism: early entrepreneurs rapidly realized that forms of play, entertainment, sport and spectacle could be organized as commercial enterprises and transformed into commodities.

On the one hand, material commodities could replace or supplement domestic forms of leisure. For example, toy-making became a major industry from the seventeenth century, linked to a new location of children (at least those of the middling and upper crust) in the world of play rather than labour. So too did popular literature including novels and periodicals from the eighteenth century, which linked a reading public of 'leisured' ladies to the private, non-work world of the home. These were significantly large industries in their own right, they linked to the general development of consumer goods markets in early modernity, and alongside them were pioneers of the art of dealing with large, geographically spread markets of anonymous consumers. The workers in many of these industries were a new type: wage workers who could constitute a consumer market for commodities made by other waged workers (Thirsk 1978).

On the other hand – and to some extent more widespread – was the transformation of many leisure activities into commodities by organizing them commercially and then charging admission by ticket. Much of this was pioneered in the eighteenth century with the entrepreneurial development of events such as masquerades, concerts, theatre, pleasure gardens like Vauxhall and Ranelagh, construction of local halls for subscription dance and ball seasons, and the transformation of sporting events like races and boxing into advertised and ticketed events held at regular times. This is intensified in the early nineteenth century with the rise of theatre (especially melodrama, magic shows), circuses, menageries and other travelling spectacles (Cunningham 1977; Plumb 1973; 1983).

Leisure activities still provide major opportunities for commodification and the creation of new markets. For example, from the 1880s onwards photography was transformed through technological and marketing changes from an expensive craft pursued by professionals or wealthy amateurs into a mass market. That market comprised both snapshooting (in which photography was defined as an essential accompaniment to all leisure activities – the family at play on holiday, at Christmas and other reunions as recorded generally by the woman of the family) and amateur photography (a form of active leisure which generally involved men lusting after ever more technical goods – new types of film and processing, lenses, motor drives, flash, new electronic components). Similar developments can be traced for film and video. It is possible that with the digitization of photography, snaps, amateur photography, video, sound, computer games and interactive multimedia programs can all be integrated as leisure activities through the home computer, which itself can be plugged into the Internet (Slater 1991; 1995).

Many argue that the commodification of leisure (as of consumption) is a counterpart to the commodification of labour. Under modern arrangements, all needs are to be met through the market. Workers go to the labour market to get wages and to consumer markets for consumer and leisure goods. The fact that production is carried out for the market gives both the opportunity and the necessity for the commodification of leisure: workers have neither the time nor the skills for domestic production, while capitalist firms need ever more opportunities to sell things to people – or, in the case of leisure, to sell activities to people in the form of things.

Regulation

While work involves discipline, it is often assumed that leisure is all one's own: a sphere of freedom. In reality, the very fact that people could be free or unregulated in non-work time meant that it was a source of considerable worry to political, social and religious authorities, as well as to many employers who feared that licentious behaviour outside work hours would erode labour discipline within. Hence, the non-work time of workers (as well as the behaviour of non-workers such as the unemployed) became as obsessive a focus for regulation as was their work time.

Workers out of work had always been associated with disorder. Traditional society could contain this precisely through the way it mixed work and celebration: it could license and manage all sorts of periodic disruptions in the form of fairs, festival, carnivalesque events. The separation of work from its various cultural contexts (home and community) – especially when it took the form of mobile workers flooding into the anonymous cities, freed from communal surveillance – served to deregulate time out of work. Early modernity was disrupted by riots and mob actions which combined political protest, economic desperation, and simple criminality and drunken mayhem (the classic examples are the Gin Riots and the Gordon Riots of the eighteenth century; see Rude 1970). Ironically, both the working class and the aristocracy were considered prone to disorderly leisure (both alone and together), especially to drunkenness in the context of games and leisure pursuits such as boxing, horse racing, gambling. Hence many attacks on leisure, as on consumer and popular culture, began as bourgeois attacks on the traditional, premodern activities of both the upper and lower orders, whose lifestyle seemed more appropriate to life on the land than in the factory or office. The aim was to extend a methodical and sober lifestyle across the work/leisure divide.

Leisure was to be 'cleaned up' in a wide variety of ways. Above all it was to be brought into line with evolving bourgeois codes of order and respectability. This could involve purging leisure time of immoral activities which were considered both evil in themselves and unconducive to economic and civil order: above all drink, gambling, gaming, prostitution. The list could be extended – depending on prevailing levels of strictness and passing moral panics – to such things as theatre, films, amusement parks, bathing in public, comic books, and now videos, computer games and the Internet. But leisure could also be disciplined in various ways which closely paralleled the rationalization of work (Haywood et al. 1995). Firstly, it was first banned from public spaces and then spatially restricted to designated locations. Primarily, leisure was to be focused as far as possible in the home and within the bosom of the family; in so far as it took place in public it should occupy ordered spaces such as the park, the playing field, the swimming bath. Secondly, leisure activities were temporally organized (events held at fixed times, from the ninety-minute form of the football game as it developed in the 1880s to the programmed flow of television). Thirdly, various forms of rationalization developed: leisure activities came increasingly to be rule-governed and organized through formal institutions which could enforce them. This regulation also involved what Elias terms a 'civilizing process' that includes the progressive elimination of (unauthorized) violence from games and other leisure.

Finally, leisure was regarded not only as a problem but also as holding a potential for 'educating' people outside work, for making their non-work time productive of social order and moral behaviour as well as of productive skills. Leisure could be made respectable and orderly by giving it worthy aims and even making it conform to a work ethic that condoned only purposeful behaviour. Hence, there is a history of first emptying leisure time of its traditional, non-domestic and volatile activities through temperance, anti-gambling, Sunday school and Sabattarian movements and then filling it again with 'rational recreations' and improving activities such as crafts, adult education, paramilitary groups (like the Boy Scouts) and organized sports which produced team spirit, patriotism and discipline. The contemporary descendant of this rational recreation is probably the 'hobby'.

WORK, LEISURE AND ALIENATION

As we have seen, the different values placed on work and leisure can change, veering for example between a work ethic and a leisure or hedonistic ethic. It is also possible to regard the very distinction itself as a social problem. The clearest example of this is the Hegelian tradition, most radically expressed through Marxism. In this tradition, praxis or practical activity is fundamental to human identity and progress. Through our activity we transform the world and create human-made environments which, in turn, radically transform our own subjectivity and consciousness. Praxis, in this sense, is very far from modern work in which people sell labour time in exchange for wages. Indeed, it looks rather like play, creativity, artistic transformation: the kinds of activities that – for Marx no less than the Greeks – represent a freedom from the realm of necessity that allows the development of a human realm of freedom (culture). In the Marxian tradition, human transformative capacity – the human essence or species being itself – is considered to have been 'alienated' in the form of labour power: we sell it as a commodity, and place it at the disposal of employers. We do not identify ourselves with this labour or with its products. What free time and energy is left to us – leisure – is a poor and insignificant imitation of praxis. Moreover, it is itself highly commodified and regulated.

In fact the picture is even more complicated because the alienated forms of work and leisure, it is argued, partly arise on the basis of a third feature: consumption. Modern productivity means that every hour worked produces far more goods than before and this presents individuals and communities with an obvious choice: they can either keep working, or even work harder, in order to produce yet more material wealth and consumer goods; or they can choose to work less, being now able, through productivity gains, to fulfil the same wants and needs with less time and effort. They could thus reap the modern harvest in *time* (leisure) rather than *goods* (consumption) so long as they decide to limit their needs and wants. In fact this choice is not theoretical, nor was its outcome inevitable: it has been historically decided at various times (Campbell 1989; Cross 1993; Sahlins 1974).

A central argument here, well represented by Marcuse's (1964) work, is that although capitalism has attained the technological capacity to satisfy most needs, it requires that needs never be satisfied or that new ones be constantly created. If needs were satisfied, people would neither work longer to produce more wealth, nor consume more and therefore buy up the goods that are produced. There would be a crisis of production and profit. Marcuse therefore argues that capitalism promotes consumerism and the inculcation of false needs and wants, of ever new desires, so that we will keep working for the money to *buy* more, rather than stop working in order that we may *do* more. The result, for Marcuse, is that work and leisure remain alienated because they are restricted, through consumer culture, to a false necessity. Hence, for authors like Lefebvre, the very triviality yet pathos of 'leisure', as well as the indignity and exploitation of work, reside in the fact that the essence of humans – their activity – has been reduced to hobbies like gardening and building model railways at best, passively watching TV at worst. Even the most active forms of leisure can be nothing but a slim compensation for the alienation of the best part of ourselves in wage labour.

Moreover, it is argued that even this small compensation has become *functional* to capitalism. In fact, it has become multi-functionalized. Firstly, leisure time is seen by critical theory as a time of recuperation, of literal re-creation of labour power. Modern labour has become so rationalized through the factory system, Fordism and Taylorism that there is no moment of rest: leisure is the unpaid time in which you rest for the next day's labour. Secondly, as recuperation from work, leisure is structured in fairly specific ways: above all, it is characterized by escapism, and that fits well with mass culture and consumerism. Leisure is associated by critical theorists with, for example, television and Hollywood films which follow entertainment formulas that can be passively, effortlessly consumed; that allow one to forget the workday world; that do not involve critical thought or challenges to that world. Even active forms of leisure (hobbies) can be seen as escapist (finding great importance in the safe little world of one's garden or darkroom) and passive (gardening and photography can mainly comprise buying consumer goods such as seeds, implements, lenses and using them in conventional, formulaic ways). Thirdly, leisure is intensively commodified and therefore fills the need to sell more goods. Finally, leisure itself is ideologically sold to us as a sphere of freedom from work, from public responsibilities and obligations: the very *concept* of leisure becomes functional to capitalist economy. Ideologically, it is part of a deal that – in exchange for all this 'freedom' and 'pleasure' – secures docile workers and citizens.

Hence, critical theories of leisure tend to be connected to theories and valuations of 'mass culture', 'popular culture', 'consumer culture'. Moreover, leisure and these related terms can be understood in terms of functions at the highest systemic levels, as in theories of Fordism (Aglietta 1979): leisure and consumerism appear as part of a trade-off which secures both more peaceful, disciplined labour and more commodity consumption for capitalism. Fordism is associated with assembly-line production of standardized mass-produced goods. It therefore involves extreme rationalization of the production process and normally a deskilling of the workforce with a corresponding increase in alienation and the discipline demanded at work. At the same time the output of the system is an overwhelming quantity of goods that need to be sold. Fordism represents an ongoing historic compromise in which organized business, labour and government agree on labour discipline and worker loss of control over workplace organization in exchange for a steadily rising consumption standard and the wages that will fund it. The premise of the whole deal is an absolute separation of work and leisure (discipline) but also an absolute association of leisure with the consumption of the commodities produced by work.

TRANSFORMATIONS

The distinction of work and leisure arises in modern times as a result of new ways of organizing labour. It is therefore possible that it might be eroded if modern forms of labour change in fundamental ways. Unsurprisingly, then, arguments that have gathered steam from around the 1950s onwards about a transition to post-industrial, post-Fordist or – latterly – postmodern society have often focused on the increasing confusion between work and leisure.

Firstly, it has often been argued that precisely the expansion of consumption (new needs, new goods and therefore lots more work) at the expense of leisure has reached various limits: boredom with consumer society (or its inability to recompense for increasingly alienating labour), the saturation of crucial consumer markets and inability to find new ones, ecological limits to consumption, limits to the productivity of labour. There might be an increasing preference for leisure rather than consumption and work. This is sometimes expressed in rather utopian terms (small is beautiful, new men who would rather spend more time with their families) which can themselves be intensively commodified.

Secondly, and more importantly, there have been major changes in the structure of employment. This includes mass unemployment and the expectation that full employment will never return; it also includes 'looser' labour contracts, such as temporary labour, freelancing, self-employment and subcontracting. Work has become much less definite than having or not having a job, and there is an expectation that more or most people will *not* be working all of their lives but will start later, or end earlier, or work intermittently owing to 'flexible' labour arrangements. The meaning of free time consequently changes too. A lot of one's life might be taken up with time which is free but – because of the continuing valuation of work, because of material poverty, and because of constant uncertainty about one's future – can hardly be called leisure. It is much like an out-of-work actor claiming to be 'resting'.

A significant factor here is that in modern times one's moral worth and dignity derives from one's (paid) labour. This is obviously an aspect of the Protestant ethic: that leisure comes second and is earned through work. Hence unemployment is understood and experienced as threatening not only one's material comfort but also ethical dignity and social identity. One's social standing depends on labour not leisure (again this is a matter not only of money but also of identity). Attempts therefore to pass off leisure pursuits such as hobbies, adult education, and so on as substitutes for work (as well as claims that the unemployed have somehow 'chosen' a life of leisure rather than labour) have been met with derision and anger by the unemployed: 'free time' activities do not mean the same things when uncoupled from work time status and resources. Yet it is precisely this uncoupling that many theorists are claiming to be necessary and desirable (Frankel 1987; Gorz 1982; 1989): work (doing what is necessary for the material reproduction of society) should be minimal; social resources should be dedicated to facilitating meaningful activity in the time formerly known as leisure. This requires that all have good incomes which are not related to the amount of work done; and that leisure time involves activity rather than mere consumption of more commodities.

Finally, there is a range of arguments associated with the concepts of postmodernism and post-Fordism, both of which foresee an increasing merging, or 'dedifferentiation', of work and leisure. This is associated firstly with a transition from predominantly manufacturing to service or 'non-material' industries: more of the work that the employed do is bound up with servicing the leisure (or at least non-work) time and activities of people through a huge range of occupations spanning the media and entertainment, through forms of education, community work, and so on. In this sense, leisure becomes more important not only to our non-work identities but also to the identity of work itself. This development has been heralded since at least the 1950s when authors like Riesman argued that work would increasingly concern the management of people, personality and experiences through services rather than the transformation of materials through industry.

At the same time, work might be becoming less fixed and less differentiated in terms of time and space. Increased unemployment (especially at the beginning and end of the 'working life'), erosion of job security through various forms of restructuring, increased home working or work in small business based at home: all these erode the idea of a job that spans a life and happens at a factory or an office. For those in employment, new technologies (mobile phones, e-mail, fax) mean that one can always be at work, wherever one is and whatever time it is. This might mean no leisure (the damned phone is always ringing) or a new integration of work and leisure which for some evokes images of premodern lifestyles.

Finally, many of these changes are claimed to be part of a transition in which people's sense of identity is rooted primarily in their non-work rather than work life. Not only has meaning and identity become rooted, as we have seen, in private, domestic life, and therefore in leisure and consumption, but it may well be that leisure and consumption rather than jobs or careers are the constants in most people's lives. Moreover, absence of job security means that people act more like entrepreneurs than employees, managing their life as a project or enterprise. In this new perspective, leisure, work and consumption activities and choices tend to be inextricably entwined.

KEY CONCEPTS

WORK In the days of a production based economy work was the determinant of identity and the regulator of social experience. Work was also the zone where the public most vividly engaged with the private sphere. People became who they were and established their form of life through work. This is not so clearly the case in a late-modern society where production is not the measure of work.

LEISURE   In earlier economies, described under 'work' above, leisure, if at all, was time from work for rest and recuperation. Now leisure has developed into an aesthetic and a form of consumption through which individuals can achieve a different identity. It is also a section of social life that requires more and more management as it is occupying greater sections of peoples lives.

References

Abrams, P. (1982) *Historical Sociology*. Shepton Mallett: Open Books.

Adam, I. and Tiffin, H. (eds) (1991) *Past the Last Post: Theorizing Post-Colonialism and Post-Modernism*. London: Harvester Wheatsheaf.

Adorno, T. (1957) 'Television and the Patterns of Mass Culture', in B. Rosenberg and D. White (eds), *Mass Culture: The Popular Arts in America*. Glencoe, IL: Free Press.

Adorno, T. (1976) *The Positivist Dispute in German Sociology*. London: Heinemann.

Aglietta, M. (1979) *A Theory of Capitalist Regulation: The US Experience*. London: Verso.

Albrow, M. (1990) *Max Weber's Construction of Social Theory*. London: Macmillan.

Alexander, J.C. (1987) *Twenty Lectures: Sociological Theory since World War II*. New York: Columbia University Press.

Alter, P. (1989) *Nationalism*. London: Edward Arnold.

Althusser, L. (1971) *Lenin and Philosophy and Other Essays*, trans. B. Brewster. London: New Left Books.

Altman, C. (1981) 'Intratextual Rewriting: Textuality as Language Formation', in W. Steiner (ed.), *The Sign in Music and Literature*. Austin, TX: University of Texas Press.

Anderson, B. (1983) *Imagined Communities: Reflections on the Origins and Spread of Nationalism*. London: Verso.

Anderson, B. (1991) *Imagined Communities*, 2nd edn. London: Verso.

Anim-Addo, J. (1995) *The Longest Journey: A History of Black Lewisham*. London: Deptford Forum.

Appadurai, A. (1990) 'Disjuncture and Difference in the Global Cultural Economy', *Theory, Culture and Society*, 7 (2–3): 295–310.

Appadurai, A. (1995) 'The Production of Locality', in R. Farndon (ed.), *Counterworks: Managing the Diversity of Knowledge*. London and New York: Routledge.

Appleby, J. (1993) 'Consumption in Early Modern Social Thought', in J. Brewer and R. Porter (eds), *Consumption and the World of Goods*. New York: Routledge. pp. 162–73.

Arendt, H. (1958) *The Human Condition*. Chicago: University of Chicago Press.

Aries, P. (1962) *Centuries of Childhood: A Social History of Family Life*. New York: Knopf.

Aries, P. (1973) *Centuries of Childhood*. Harmondsworth: Penguin.

Aries, P. (1976) *Western Attitudes Towards Death*. London: Marion Boyars.

Aries, P. (1981) *The Hour of Our Death*. Harmondsworth: Penguin.

Armstrong, D. (1983) *The Political Anatomy of the Body: Medical Knowledge in Britain in the Twentieth Century*. Cambridge: Cambridge University Press.

Armstrong, J. (1982) *Nations before Nationalism*. Chapel Hill, NC: University of North Carolina Press.

Arnason, J.P. (1990) 'Nationalism, Globalization and Modernity', *Theory, Culture and Society*, 7 (2–3).

Arney, W.R. and Bergen, B.J. (1984) *Medicine and the Management of Living: Taming the Last Great Beast*. Chicago: University of Chicago Press.

Arnold, M. (1960) *Culture and Anarchy* (1875), ed. J. Dover Wilson. Cambridge: Cambridge University Press.

Ashcroft, B., Griffiths, G. and Tiffin, H. (1989) *The Empire Writes Back*. London: Routledge.

Back, L. (1996) *New Ethnicities and Urban Culture: Racisms and Multiculture in Young Lives*. London: UCL College Press.

Back, L., Keith, M. and Solomos, J. (1996) 'The New Modalities of Racist Culture: Technology, Race and Neo-Fascism in a Digital Age', *Patterns of Prejudice*, 30 (2).

Balibar, E. and Wallerstein, I. (1991) *Race, Nation, Class: Ambiguous Identities*. London: Verso.

Banton, M. (1983) *Racial and Ethnic Competition*. Cambridge: Cambridge University Press.

Bar-Hillel, Y. (1954) 'Indexical Expressions', *Mind*, 63: 359–79.

Barrett, M. (1988) *Women's Oppression Today: The Marxist/Feminist Encounter*. London: Verso.

Barth, F. (1969) *Ethnic Groups and Boundaries*. Oslo, London: Scandinavian University Books.

Barthes, R. (1967a) *Writing Degree Zero*, trans. A. Lavers and C. Smith. New York: Hill and Wang.

Barthes, R. (1967b) *Elements of Semiology*, trans. A. Lavers and C. Smith. London: Jonathan Cape.

Barthes, R. (1972) *Mythologies*. London: Jonathan Cape.

Barthes, R. (1975) *S/Z*, trans. R. Miller. London: Jonathan Cape.

Barthes, R. (1977) *Image–Music–Text*, trans. S. Heath. London: Fontana.

Barthes, R. (1978) *A Lover's Discourse: Fragments*, trans. R. Howard. New York: Hill and Wang.

Barthes, R. (1984) *Camera Lucida: Reflections on Photography*. London: Fontana.

Bateson, G. and Mead, M. (1942) *Balinese Character: A Photographic Analysis*, vol. 2. New York: Special Publications of the New York Academy of Sciences.

Baudelaire, C. (1981) *Selected Writing on Art and Artists*. London: Penguin.

Baudrillard, J. (1981) *For a Critique of the Political Economy of the Sign*. St Louis, MO: Telos.

Baudrillard, J. (1988) *Selected Writings*. Cambridge: Polity.

Bauman, Z. (1989) *Modernity and the Holocaust*. Cambridge: Polity.

Bauman, Z. (1991) *Modernity and Ambivalence*. Cambridge: Polity Press.

Bauman, Z. (1992a) *Intimations of Postmodernity*. London: Routledge.

Bauman, Z. (1992b) *Mortality, Immortality and Other Life Strategies*. Cambridge: Polity Press.

Becker, E. (1973) *The Denial of Death*. New York: Free Press.

Becker, H.S. (1953) 'Becoming a Marihuana User', *American Journal of Sociology*, 59: 235–42.

Becker, H.S. (1963) *Outsiders: Studies in the Sociology of Deviance*. New York: Free Press.

Bell, D. (1961) *The End of Ideology*. New York: Collier.

Bell, D. (1974) *The Coming of Post-Industrial Society: A Venture in Social Forecasting*. London: Heinemann.

Bell, D. (1976) *The Cultural Contradictions of Capitalism*. London: Heinemann.

Benjamin, A. (1991) *Art, Mimesis and the Avant-Garde*. London: Routledge.

Benjamin, W. (1968) *Illuminations*. New York: Harcourt, Brace and World.

Benjamin, W. (1969) *Illuminations*. New York: Schocken.

Benjamin, W. (1979) *One-Way Street and Other Writings*. London: New Left Books.

Bennett, T. (1986) 'Introduction: Popular Culture and "The Turn to Gramsci"', in T. Bennett et al. (eds), *Popular Culture and Social Relations*. Milton Keynes and Philadelphia: Open University Press.

Bennett, T., Martin, G., Mercer, C. and Woollacott, J. (eds) (1981) *Culture, Ideology and Social Process: A Reader*. London: Batsford and Open University Press.

Bensman, J. and Rosenberg, B. (1963) *Mass, Class and Bureaucracy: The Evolution of Contemporary Society*. Englewood Cliffs, NJ: Prentice-Hall.

Benton, T. (1975) *The Philosophical Foundations of the Three Sociologies*. London: Routledge.

Berger, P.L. (1966) *An Invitation to Sociology*. Harmondsworth: Penguin.

Berger, P.L. (1969) *The Sacred Canopy*. London: Faber and Faber. Published 1973 as *The Social Reality of Religion*. Harmondsworth: Penguin.

Berger, P.L. and Luckmann, T. (1966) *The Social Construction of Reality: A Treatise in the Sociology of Knowledge*. New York: Doubleday.

Berman, M. (1983) *All That Is Solid Melts into Air: The Experience of Modernity*. London: Verso.

Berry, C.J. (1994) *The Idea of Luxury: A Conceptual and Historical Investigation*. Cambridge: Cambridge University Press.

Bhaba, H. (ed.) (1990) *Nation and Narration*. London: Routledge.

Bhaba, H. (1994) *The Location of Culture*. London: Routledge.

Bierstedt, R. (1959) 'Nominal and Real Definitions in Sociological Theory', in Llewellyn Gross (ed.), *Symposium in Sociological Theory*. New York: Harper and Row.

Bierstedt, R. (1978) 'Theories of Progress, Development, Evolution', in Tom Bottomore and Robert Nisbet (eds), *A History of Sociological Analysis*. London: Heinemann Educational.

Bingham, F. (1915) *The Official Guide to the Metropolitan Borough of Deptford*. London: Deptford Borough Council.

Birdwhistell, R. (1973) *Kinesics in Context*. Harmondsworth: Penguin.

Blau, P. and Schoenherr, R. (1971) *The Structure of Organizations*. New York: Basic Books.

Bloch, M. (1961) *Feudal Society*. London: Routledge.

Bloch, M. and Parry, J. (eds) (1982) *Death and the Regeneration of Life*. Cambridge: Cambridge University Press.

Blum, A. (1970) 'The Corpus of Knowledge as a Normative Order', in John C. McKinney and Edward A. Tiryakian (eds), *Theoretical Sociology: Perspectives and Developments*. New York: Appleton-Century-Crofts.

Blum, A., McHugh, P. and Raffel, S. (1974) *On the Beginning of Social Inquiry*. London: Routledge.

Blumer, H. (1956) 'Sociological Analysis and the "Variable"', *American Sociological Review*, 21: 633–60.

Bock, G. and James, S. (1992) *Beyond Equality and Difference: Citizenship, Feminist Politics and Female Subjectivity*. London: Routledge.

Bocock, R. and Thompson, K. (1992) *Social and Cultural Forms of Modernity*. Cambridge: Polity.

Boden, D. and Zimmerman, D. (eds) (1991) *Talk and Social Structure*. Cambridge: Polity.

Boorstin, D. (1962) *The Image*. London: Weidenfeld and Nicolson.

Borges, J.L. (1970) 'The Immortal', in D.A. Yates and J.E. Irby (eds), *Labyrinths: Selected Stories and Other Writings*. Harmondsworth: Penguin.

Borough of Lewisham (1905) *Souvenir of the Opening of the Town Hall*. London: Gaylard.

Bottomore, T.B. and Rubel, M. (1956) *Karl Marx: Selected Writings in Sociology and Social Philosophy*. London: Penguin.

Bourdieu, P. (1984) *Distinction: A Social Critique of the Judgement of Taste*, trans. R. Nice. London: Routledge and Kegan Paul.

Boyne, R. and Rattansi, A. (eds) (1990) *Postmodernism and Society*. London: Macmillan.

Bradbury, M. and McFarlane, J. (eds) (1976) *Modernism 1890–1930*. Harmondsworth: Penguin.

Bramson, L. (1961) *The Political Context of Sociology*, 2nd edn. 1970. Princeton: Princeton University Press.

Braverman, H. (1974) *Labour and Monopoly Capital: The Degradation of Work in the Twentieth Century*. New York: Monthly Review Press.

Breuilly, J. (1982) *Nationalism and the State*. Manchester: Manchester University Press.

Brownmiller, S. (1975) *Against Our Will: Men, Women and Rape*. New York: Simon and Schuster.

Brubaker, R. (1984) *The Limits of Rationality*. London: Allen and Unwin.

Bryman, A. (1988) *Quantity and Quality in Social Research*. London: Unwin Hyman.

Bryson, N. (1981) *Word and Image*. Cambridge: Cambridge University Press.

Buchler, J. (1955) *Philosophical Writings of Pierce*. New York: Dover.

Buckley, W. (1967) *Sociology and Modern Systems Theory*. Englewood Cliffs, NJ: Prentice-Hall.

Campbell, C. (1989) *The Romantic Ethic and the Spirit of Modern Consumerism*. Oxford: Basil Blackwell.

Chambers, I. (1994) *Migrancy, Culture, Identity*. London: Routledge.

Chirot, D. (1994) *How Societies Change*. Thousand Oaks, CA: Pine Forge.

Cicourel, A. (1964) *Method and Measurement in Sociology*. New York: Free Press.

Clarke, J., Critcher, C. and Johnson, R. (1979) *Working Class Culture: Studies in History and Theory*. London: Hutchinson.

Clavarino, A., Najman, J. and Silverman, D. (1995) 'Assessing the Quality of Qualitative Data', *Qualitative Inquiry*, 1 (2).

Cobban, A. (1970) *The Nation-State and National Self-Determination*. New York: Thomas Crowell.

Comte, A. (1975) *Physique Sociale. Cours de philosophie positive*, Leçons 46 à 60. Paris: Hermann.

Conrad, J. (1990) *Heart of Darkness and Other Tales*. Oxford: Oxford University Press.

Cohen, A. (ed.) (1974a) *Urban Ethnicity*. London: Tavistock.

Cohen, A. (1974b) *Two-Dimensional Man*. London: Tavistock.

Cohen P. (1968) *Modern Social Theory*. London: Heinemann.

Connor, S. (1989) *Postmodernist Culture: An Introduction to Theories of the Contemporary*. Oxford: Basil Blackwell.

Connor, W. (1984) *The National Question in Marxist-Leninist Theory and Strategy*. Princeton: Princeton University Press.

Connor, W. (1994) *Ethnonationalism: The Quest for Understanding*. Princeton: Princeton University Press.

Coser, L. (1964) 'Mass Culture', in J. Gould and W.L. Kolb (eds), *A Dictionary of the Social Sciences*. London: Tavistock Press and UNESCO. pp. 411–12.

Coulter, J. (1990) *Lewisham and Deptford in Old Photography*. Stroud: Alan Sutton.

Cousins, M. and Hussain, A. (1984) *Michel Foucault*. London: Macmillan Education.

Crook, S., Pakulski, J. and Waters, M. (1992) *Postmodernization: Change in Advanced Societies*. London: Sage.

Cross, G. (1993) *Time and Money: The Making of Consumer Culture*. London: Routledge.

Crowley, H. (1992) 'Women and the Domestic Sphere', in B.R. and K. Thompson (eds), *Social and Cultural Forms of Modernity*. Cambridge: Polity.

Cuff, E.C. and Payne, G.S. (1979) *Perspectives in Sociology*. London: Allen and Unwin.

Cunningham, H. (1977) 'The Metropolitan Fairs in the Nineteenth Century', in A.P. Donajgrodzki (ed.), *Social Control in Nineteenth Century Britain*. London: Routledge.

Dahrendorf, R. (1973) *Homo Sociologicus*. London: Routledge and Kegan Paul.

Dahrendorf, R. (1959) *Class and Class Conflict in Industrial Society*. Stanford: Stanford University Press.

Daly, M. (1978) *Gyn/Ecology: The Metaethics of Radical Feminism*. Boston: Beacon Press.

Danforth, L. (1982) *The Death Rituals of Ancient Greece*. Princeton: Princeton University Press.

Darwin, C. (1969) *The Expression of the Emotions in Man and Animals* (1872). Chicago: Chicago University Press.

Davidson, B. (1992) *The Black Man's Burden: Africa and the Curse of the Nation-State*. London: James Curry.

Davidson, D. (1986) 'On the Very Idea of a Conceptual Scheme', in E. LePore (ed.), *Truth and Interpretation: Perspectives and Philosophy of Donald Davidson*. Oxford: Blackwell.

Davies, I. (1993) 'Cultural Theory in Britain: Narrative and Episteme', *Theory, Culture and Society*, 10 (3).

Dawe, A. (1970) 'Two Sociologies', *British Journal of Sociology*.

Dawkins, R. (1976) *The Selfish Gene*. Oxford: Oxford University Press.

de Beauvoir, S. (1972) *The Second Sex*. London: Penguin.

Deem, R. (1986) *All Work and No Play? The Sociology of Women and Leisure*. Milton Keynes: Open University Press.

Deleuze, G. and Guattari, F. (1984) *Anti-Oedipus: Capitalism and Schizophrenia*. London: Athlone Press.

Demerath III, N.J. and Peterson, Richard A. (eds) (1967) *System, Change and Conflict*. New York: Free Press.

Denzin, N. (1970) *The Research Act in Sociology*. London: Butterworth.

Denzin, N. and Lincoln, Y. (eds) (1994) *Handbook of Qualitative Research*. London: Sage.

Derrida, J. (1978) *Writing and Difference*, trans. A. Bass. Chicago: University of Chicago Press.

Derrida, J. (1979) *Spurs: Neitzsche's Styles*. Chicago: University of Chicago Press.

Dews, N. (1971) *The History of Deptford*. London: Conway Maritime.

Dickens, D. and Fontana, A. (1994) *Postmodernism and Social Enquiry*. London: UCL Press.

Docherty, T. (ed.) (1993) *Postmodernism: A Reader*. Hemel Hempstead: Harvester Wheatsheaf.

Douglas, M. (1970) *Purity and Danger*. Harmondsworth: Penguin.

Douglas, M. (1973) *Natural Symbols*. Harmondsworth: Penguin.

Douglas, M. (1975) *Implicit Meanings: Essays in Anthropology*. London: Routledge and Kegan Paul.

Doyal, L. and Gough, I. (1991) *A Theory of Human Needs*. London: Macmillan.

Du Bois, W.E.B. (1989) *The Souls of Black Folk* (1903). New York: Bantam.

Durkheim, E. (1897) *Suicide: A Study in Sociology*. London: Routledge and Kegan Paul, 1952.

Durkheim, E. (1915) *The Elementary Forms of the Religious Life*. London: Allen and Unwin.

Durkheim, E. (1933) *The Division of Labour in Society*, trans. G. Simpson. New York: Macmillan.

Durkheim, E. (1938) *The Rules of Sociological Method*, trans. S.A. Solvay and J.H. Mueller, ed. G.E.G. Catlin. Chicago, IL: University of Chicago Press.

Durkheim, E. (1947) *The Division of Labour in Society*. New York: Free Press.

Durkheim, E. (1964a) *The Division of Labour in Society*. New York: Free Press.

Durkheim, E. (1964b [1912]) *The Elementary Forms of the Religious Life*. London: Allen and Unwin.

Durkheim, E. (1973) 'Individualism and the Intellectuals', in *Emile Durkheim on Morality and Society*, ed. R.T. Bellah. Chicago: University of Chicago Press.

Durkheim, E. (1974a) 'The Determination of Moral Facts', in *Sociology and Philosophy*. New York: Free Press.

Durkheim, E. (1974b) 'Value Judgements and Judgements of Reality', in *Sociology and Philosophy*. New York: Free Press.

Durkheim, E. (1976) *The Elementary Forms of the Religious Life* (1915), 2nd edn. London: Allen and Unwin.

Durkheim, E. (1982) *The Rules of Sociological Method and Selected Texts on Sociology and its Method*. London: Macmillan.

Durkheim, E. and Mauss, M. (1963) *Primitive Classification*. Chicago, IL: University of Chicago Press.

Dworkin, A. (1981) *Pornography: Men Possessing Women*. New York: Perigee.

Eagleton, T. (1976) *Criticism and Ideology*. London: New Left Books.

Eagleton, T. (1983) *Literary Theory*. Oxford: Basil Blackwell.

Eco, U. (1977) *A Theory of Semiotics*. London: Macmillan.

Eco, U. (1981) *The Role of the Reader: Explorations in the Semiotics of Texts*. London: Hutchinson.

Eco, U. (1989) *The Open Work*, trans. Anna Cancogni. London: Hutchinson.

Efron, D. (1972) *Gesture, Race and Culture*. The Hague: Mouton.

Eibl-Eibesfeldt, I. (1972) 'Similarities and Differences between Cultures in Expressive Movements', in R.A. Hind (ed.), *Non-Verbal Communication*. Cambridge: Cambridge University Press.

Ekman, P. (1977) 'Biological and Cultural Contributions to Body and Facial Movement', in J Blacking (ed.), *The Anthropology of the Body*. London: Academic Press.

Elias, N. (1939) *The Civilizing Process*. Oxford: Blackwell, 1994.

Elias, N. (1978) *The Civilizing Process. Vol. 1: The History of Manners*. Oxford: Basil Blackwell.

Elias, N. (1982) *The Civilizing Process. Vol. 2: State Formation and Civilization*. Oxford: Basil Blackwell.

Elias, N. (1985) *The Loneliness of the Dying*. Oxford: Blackwell.

Eliot, T.S. (1939) *The Idea of a Christian Society*. London: Faber.

Eliot, T.S. (1963) *Notes Towards the Definition of Culture*. London: Faber.

Elkin, F. (1964) 'Mass Media', in J. Gould and W.L. Kolb (eds), *A Dictionary of the Social Sciences*. London: Tavistock Press and UNESCO. pp. 412–13.

Elshtain, J.B. (1981) *Public Man, Private Woman*. Princeton, NJ: Princeton University Press

Eriksen, T.H. (1993) *Ethnicity and Nationalism*. London: Pluto.

Eslea, B. (1981) *Science and Sexual Oppression: Patriarchy's Confrontation with Woman and Nature*. London: Weidenfeld and Nicolson.

Esman, M.J. (1994) *Ethnic Politics*. London, Ithaca, NY: Cornell University Press.

Evans, D. (1993) *Sexual Citizenship: The Material Construction of Sexualities*. New York: Routledge.

Featherstone, M. (1988) 'In Pursuit of the Postmodern: An Introduction', *Theory, Culture and Society*, 5 (2–3): 195–216.

Featherstone, M. (1991) *Consumer Culture and Postmodernism*. London: Sage.

Featherstone, M., Hepworth, M. and Turner, B.S. (eds) (1991) *The Body: Social Processes and Cultural Theory*. London: Sage.

Ferguson, A. (1978) *An Essay on the History of Civil Society* (1767). Edinburgh: Edinburgh University Press.

Fiedler, L. (1957) 'The Middle against Both Ends', in B. Rosenberg and D. White (eds), *Mass Culture: The Popular Arts in America*. Glencoe, IL: Free Press.

Fielding, N.G. and Fielding, J.L. (1986) *Linking Data*. London: Sage.

Filmer, P. (1969) 'The Literary Imagination and the Explanation of Sociocultural Change in Modern Britain', *European Journal of Sociology*, X (2): 271–91.

Filmer, P. (1977a) 'Durkheim, Jung and Symbolism: On the Necessity for a Sociology of the Unconscious', *Harvest*, no. 23.

Filmer, P. (1977b) 'Literary Study as Liberal Education and as Sociology in the Work of F.R. Leavis', in C. Jenks (ed.), *Rationality, Education and the Social Organization of Knowledge: Papers for a Reflexive Sociology of Education*. London: Routledge.

Filmer, P. (1998) 'Analysing Literary Texts', in C. Seale (ed.), *Researching Society and Culture*. London: Sage.

Filmer, P., Phillipson, M., Silverman, D. and Walsh, D. (1972) *New Directions in Sociological Theory*. London: Collier-Macmillan.

Firestone, S. (1970) *The Dialectic of Sex*. New York: Bantam.

Firth, A.E. (1991) *Goldsmiths' College: A Centenary Account*. London: Athlone Press.

Forty, A. (1986) *Objects of Desire: Design and Society, 1750–1980*. London: Thames and Hudson.

Foster, H. (ed.) (1985) *Postmodern Culture*. London: Pluto.

Foster, H. (ed.) (1988) *Vision and Visuality: Dia Art Foundation Discussions in Contemporary Culture*, number 2. Seattle: Bay Press.

Foucault, M. (1967) *Madness and Civilization: A History of Insanity in the Age of Reason*. London: Tavistock.

Foucault, M. (1972) *The Archaeology of Knowledge*, trans. A.M. Sheridan. London: Tavistock.

Foucault, M. (1976) *The Birth of the Clinic*. London: Routledge.

Foucault, M. (1977) *Discipline and Punish*. Harmondsworth: Penguin.

Foucault, M. (1979a) *The History of Sexuality Vol 1: Introduction*. Harmondsworth: Penguin.

Foucault, M. (1979b) 'On Governmentality', *Ideology and Consciousness*, 6.

Foucault, M. (1984) *The Foucault Reader*, ed. P. Rabinow. Harmondsworth: Penguin.

Frankel, B. (1987) *The Post-Industrial Utopians*. Cambridge: Polity.

Freidson, E. (1970) *Profession of Medicine*. New York, London: Harper and Row.

Friedman, J. (1990) 'Being in the World: Globalization and Localization', *Theory, Culture and Society*, 7 (2–3).

Frisby, D. (1985) *Fragments of Modernity*. Cambridge: Polity.

Fryer, P. (1984) *Staying Power: A History of Black People in Britain*. London: Pluto.

Fuss, D. (ed.) (1991) *Inside/Out: Lesbian Theories, Gay Theories*. London: Routledge.

Gans, H.J. (1974) *Popular Culture and High Culture: An Analysis and Evaluation of Taste*. New York: Basic Books.

Garcia, S. (ed.) (1993) *European Identity and the Search for Legitimacy*. London: Pinter.

Garfinkel, E. (1967) *Studies in Ethnomethodology*. Englewood Cliffs, NJ: Prentice-Hall.

Garfinkel, H. (1963) 'A Conception of, and Experiments with, "Trust" as a Condition of Stable Concerted Actions', in O.J. Harvey (ed.), *Motivation and Social Interaction*. New York: Ronald.

Garfinkel, H. and Sacks, H. (1970) 'On Formal Structures of Practical Actions', in J. McKinney and E. Tiryakian (eds), *Theoretical Sociology*. New York: Appleton-Century-Crofts.

Gatens, M. (1991) *Feminism and Philosophy: Perspectives on Difference and Equality*. Cambridge: Polity.

Geertz, C. (1973) *The Interpretation of Cultures: Selected Essays*. New York: Basic Books.

Geertz, C. (1993) *Local Knowledge*. London: Fontana.

Geertz, C. (1995) 'Unabsolute Truths', *New York Times Magazine*, April 1995.

Gellner, E. (1974) 'Cause and Meaning: The New Idealism in Social Science', in A. Giddens (ed.), *Positivism and Sociology*. London: Heinemann.

Gellner, E. (1983) *Nations and Nationalism*. Oxford: Blackwell.

Giddens, A. (1976) *New Rules of Sociological Method*. London: Hutchinson.

Giddens, A. (1984) *The Constitution of Society*. Cambridge: Polity.

Giddens, A. (ed) (1986) *Durkheim on Politics and the State*. Stanford, CA: Stanford University Press.

Giddens, A. (1989) *Sociology*. Cambridge: Polity.

Giddens, A. (1990) *The Consequences of Modernity*. Cambridge: Polity.

Giddens, A. (1991) *Modernity and Self-Identity*. Cambridge: Polity.

Giddens, A. (1993) 'Max Weber on Facts and Values', in *The Giddens Reader*. London: Macmillan.

Giddens, A. and Turner, J. (eds) (1987) *Social Theory Today*. Cambridge: Polity.

Giglioli, P. (ed.) (1972) *Language and Social Context*. Harmondsworth: Penguin.

Gilbert, N. (ed.) (1993) *Researching Social Life*. London: Sage.

Gillborn, D. (1995) *Racism and Antiracism in Real Schools*. Buckingham, Philadelphia: Open University Press.

Gilroy, P. (1993a) *Small Acts: Thoughts on the Politics of Black Cultures*. London: Serpent's Tail.

Gilroy, P. (1993b) *The Black Atlantic: Modernity and Double Consciousness*. London: Verso.

Giner, S. (1976) *Mass Society*. London: Martin Robertson.

Glaser, B.G. and Strauss, A.L. (1965) *Awareness of Dying*. Chicago: Aldine.

Glaser, B. and Strauss, A. (1967) *The Discovery of Grounded Theory*. Chicago: Aldine.

Goffman, E. (1967) *Interaction Ritual*. New York: Doubleday Anchor.

Goffman, E. (1968) *Stigma: Notes on the Management of Spoiled Identity*. Harmondsworth: Pelican.

Goffman, E. (1972) *Relations in Public*. Harmondsworth: Penguin.

Gombrich, E. (1956) *Art and Illusion: Studies in the Psychology of Pictorial Representation*. Princeton, NJ: Princeton University Press.

Gombrich, E. (1982) *The Image and the Eye: Further Studies in the Psychology of Pictorial Representation*. Oxford: Phaidon.

Good, B. (1994) *Medicine, Rationality and Experience*. Cambridge: Cambridge University Press.

Gorer, G. (1965) *Death, Grief and Mourning in Contemporary Britain*. London: Cresset.

Gorz, A. (1982) *Farewell to the Working Class: An Essay on Post-Industrial Socialism*. London: Pluto.

Gorz, A. (1989) *Critique of Economic Reason*. London: Verso.

Gouldner, A. (1967) *Enter Plato: Classical Greece and the Origins of Social Theory*. London: Routledge and Kegan Paul.

Gouldner, A. (1971) *The Coming Crisis of Western Sociology*. London: Heinemann.

Gouldner, A. (1973) *For Sociology*. London: Allen Lane.

Gramsci, A. (1971) *Selections from the Prison Notebooks of Antonio Gramsci*. London: Lawrence and Wishart.

Gramsci, A. (1985) *Selections from Cultural Writings*. London: Lawrence and Wishart.

Green, E., Hebron, S. and Woodward, D. (1990) *Women's Leisure, What Leisure? A Feminist Analysis*. London: Macmillan.

Greenberg, C. (1957) 'Avant-Garde and Kitsch', in B. Rosenberg and D. White (eds), *Mass Culture: The Popular Arts in America*. Glencoe, IL: Free Press.

Greenfeld, L. (1992) *Nationalism: Five Roads to Modernity*. Cambridge, MA: Harvard University Press.

Gubrium, J. (1988) *Analyzing Field Reality*. Newbury Park, CA: Sage.

Guillaumin, C. (1991) '"Race" and Discourse', in M. Silverman (ed.), *Race, Discourse and Power in France*. Aldershot: University of Leeds.

Guiraud, P. (1975) *Semiology*. London: Routledge and Kegan Paul.

Guthrie, W.C. (1971) *The Sophists*. Cambridge: Cambridge University Press.

Habermas, J. (1970) 'Toward a Theory of Communicative Competence', in H. Dreitzel (ed.), *Recent Sociology, No. 2: Patterns of Communicative Behaviour*. London: Collier-Macmillan.

Habermas, J. (1985) 'Modernity: An Incomplete Project', in H. Foster (ed.), *Postmodern Culture*. London: Pluto.

Habermas, J. (1987) *The Philosophical Discourse of Modernity*, trans. F. Lawrence. Cambridge, MA: MIT Press.

Habermas, J. (1991) *The Structural Transformation of the Public Sphere: An Inquiry into a Category of Bourgeois Society.* Cambridge, MA: MIT Press.

Hacking, I. (1990) *The Taming of Chance.* Cambridge: Cambridge University Press.

Halfpenny, P. (1979) 'The Analysis of Qualitative Data', *Sociological Review,* 27 (4): 799–825.

Hall, E. (1969) *The Hidden Dimension.* Garden City, NY: Anchor.

Hall, J. (1995) *Civil Society: Theory, History, Comparison.* Cambridge: Polity.

Hall, S. (1980) 'Encoding/Decoding', in S. Hall et al. (eds), *Culture, Media, Language.* London: Hutchinson.

Hall, S. (1991a) 'The Local and the Global', in A.D. King (ed.), *Culture, Globalisation and the World System.* London: Macmillan.

Hall, S. (1991b) 'Old and New Identities, Old and New Ethnicities', in A.D. King (ed.), *Culture, Globalisation and the World System.* London: Macmillan.

Hall, S. (1992a) 'The Question of Cultural Identity', in S. Hall, D. Held and T. McGrew (eds), *Modernity and its Futures.* Cambridge: Polity.

Hall, S. (1992b) 'The New Ethnicities', in J. Donald and A. Rattansi (eds), *'Race', Culture and Difference.* London: Sage.

Hall, S. and Gieben, B. (1992) *Formations of Modernity.* Buckingham: Open University Press.

Hall, S. and Jefferson, T. (eds) (1976) *Resistance through Rituals: Youth Subcultures in Postwar Britain.* London: Hutchinson.

Hall, S., Hobson, D., Lowe, A. and Willis, P. (1980) *Culture, Media, Language.* London: Hutchinson.

Hall, S., Held, D. and McGrew, T. (eds) (1992) *Modernity and Its Futures.* Cambridge: Polity.

Hamilton, P. (1973) *Talcott Parsons.* London: Fontana.

Hammersley, M. (1990) *Reading Ethnographic Research: A Critical Guide.* London: Longman.

Hammersley, M. (1992) *What's Wrong with Ethnography? Methodological Explorations.* London: Routledge.

Hammersley, M. and Atkinson, P. (1983) *Ethnography: Principles in Practice.* London: Tavistock.

Hampshire, S. (1956) *The Age of Reason: The 17th Century Philosophers.* New York: Mentor.

Hannerz, U. (1990) 'Cosmopolitans and Locals in World Culture', *Theory, Culture and Society,* 7 (2–3).

Haraway, D. (1990) 'A Manifesto for Cyborgs: Science, Technology and Socialist Feminism in the 1980s', in L. Nicholson (ed.), *Feminism/Postmodernism.* London: Routledge.

Haraway, D. (1991) *Simians, Cyborgs and Women: The Reinvention of Nature.* New York: Routledge.

Harvey, D. (1989) *The Condition of Postmodernity.* Oxford: Basil Blackwell.

Harvey, D. (1990) *The Condition of Postmodernity.* Oxford: Blackwell.

Haug, W.F. (1986) *Critique of Commodity Aesthetics: Appearance, Sexuality and Advertising.* Cambridge: Polity.

Hayes, C. (1931) *The Historical Evolution of Nationalism.* New York: Smith.

Hayes, N. (1994) *Foundations of Psychology.* London: Routledge.

Haywood, L., Kew, F., Bramham, P., Spink, J., Capenhurst, J. et al. (1995) *Understanding Leisure*. Cheltenham: Stanley Thornes.

Hebdige, D. (1979) *Subculture: The Meaning of Style*. London: Methuen.

Hebdige, D. (1988) *Hiding in the Light: On Images and Things*. London: Routledge.

Heidegger, M. (1975) *The End of Philosophy*. London: Souvenir Press.

Heller, A. (1976) *The Theory of Need in Marx*. London: Allison and Busby.

Hennis, W. (1988) *Max Weber: Essays in Reconstruction*. London: Allen and Unwin.

Heritage, J. (1984) *Garfinkel and Ethnomethodology*. Cambridge: Polity.

Hertz, R. (1907) *Death and the Right Hand*. Glencoe, IL: Free Press, 1960.

Hertz, R. (1973) 'The Pre-Eminence of the Right Hand: A Study in Religious Polarity' (1909), in R. Needham (ed.), *Right and Left*. Chicago: Chicago University Press.

Hilbert, R. (1984) 'The Acultural Dimensions of Chronic Pain: Flawed Reality Construction and the Problem of Meaning', *Social Problems*, 31 (4): 365–78.

Hindess, B. (1973) *The Use of Official Statistics in Sociology*. London: Macmillan.

Hine, T. (1987) *Populuxe*. New York: Knopf.

Hirsch, E. (1967) *Validity in Interpretation*. New Haven, CT and London: Yale University Press.

Hirsch, F. (1976) *Social Limits to Growth*. Cambridge, MA: Harvard University Press.

Hirschman, A. (1977) *The Passions and the Interests*. Princeton, NJ: Princeton University Press.

Hirst, P. and Woolley, P. (1982) *Social Relations and Human Attributes*. London: Tavistock.

Hobsbawm, E. (1990) *Nations and Nationalism since 1870*. Cambridge: Cambridge University Press.

Hobsbawm, E. and Ranger, T. (eds) (1983) *The Invention of Tradition*. Cambridge: Cambridge University Press.

Hochschild, A.R. (1983) *The Managed Heart: Commercialization of Human Feeling*. San Francisco: University of California Press.

Hoggart, R. (1957) *The Uses of Literacy: Aspects of Working-Class Life with Special Reference to Publications and Entertainments*. London: Chatto and Windus.

Hollinger, D. (1995) *Postethnic America: Beyond Multiculturalism*. New York: Basic Books.

Hollis, M. (1977) *Models of Man*. Cambridge: Cambridge University Press.

Horkheimer, M. and Adorno, T. (1973a) *Dialectic of Enlightenment*. London: Allen Lane.

Horkheimer, M. and Adorno, T. (1973b) *Aspects of Sociology*. London: Heinemann.

Hroch, M. (1985) *Social Preconditions of National Revival in Europe*. Cambridge: Cambridge University Press.

Hughes, H. Stuart (1974) *Consciousness and Society*. St Albans: Paladin.

Hughes, R. (1991) *The Shock of the New*. London: Thames and Hudson.

Hume, D. (1961) *Enquiries*, ed. L.A. Selby Bigge. Oxford: Oxford University Press.

Hume, D. (1967) *A Treatise of Human Nature*, ed. L.A. Selby Bigge. Oxford: Oxford University Press.

Huyssen, A. (1986) *After the Great Divide: Modernism, Mass Culture, Modernism*. London: Macmillan.

Ignatieff, M. (1984) *The Needs of Strangers*. London: Hogarth Press.

Illich, I. (1976) *Limits to Medicine: Medical Nemesis: The Expropriation of Health*. Harmondsworth: Penguin.

Inglis, F. (1988) *Popular Culture and Political Power*. Brighton: Harvester Press.

Inglis, F. (1993) *Cultural Studies*. Oxford: Blackwell.

Jacobs, N. (ed.) (1961) *Culture for the Millions?* Princeton, NJ: Van Nostrand.

James, M. (1994) 'Hysteria', in C. Seale and S. Pattison (eds), *Medical Knowledge: Doubt and Certainty*. Buckingham: Open University Press.

Jameson, F. (1985) 'Postmodernism and Consumer Society', in H. Foster (ed.), *Postmodern Culture*. London: Pluto.

Jameson, F. (1991) *Postmodernism, or The Cultural Logic of Late Capitalism*. London: Verso.

Jay, M. (1973) *The Dialectical Imagination: A History of the Frankfurt School and the Institute for Social Research, 1923–1950*. London: Heinemann.

Kant, I. (1964) *The Groundwork of the Metaphysics of Morals*, ed. H. Paton. London: Hutchinson.

Kapferer, B. (1988) *Legends of People, Myths of State*. Washington, DC: Smithsonian Institution Press.

Keane, J. (1988a) *Civil Society and the State*. London: Verso.

Keane, J. (1988b) *Democracy and Civil Society*. London: Verso.

Kellehear, A. (1984) 'Are We a "Death Denying" Society? A Sociological Review', *Social Science and Medicine*, 18 (9): 713–23.

Kellner, D. (1989) *Critical Theory, Marxism and Modernity*. Cambridge: Polity.

King, A. (ed.) (1990) *Culture, Globalization and the World System*. Binghamton, NY: State University of New York Press.

Kirk, J. and Miller, M. (1986) *Reliability and Validity in Qualitative Research*. London: Sage.

Kohn, H. (1944) *The Idea of Nationalism*. New York: Collier.

Konig, R. (1968) *The Community*. London: Routledge.

Kornhauser, W. (1959) *The Politics of Mass Society*. Glencoe, IL: Free Press.

Kornhauser, W. (1968) 'Mass Society', in *International Encyclopaedia of the Social Sciences*. New York: Cromwell, Collier and Macmillan. Vol. 10, pp. 58–64.

Kroeber, A. (1952) *The Nature of Culture*. Chicago: Chicago University Press.

Kroeber, A. (1963) *Anthropology: Culture Patterns and Processes*. New York: Burlingame, Harcourt, Brace and World.

Kroeber, A. and Kluckhohn, C. (1952) *Culture: A Critical Review of Concepts and Definitions*. New York: Vintage.

Kubler-Ross, E. (ed.) (1975) *Death: The Final Stage of Growth*. Englewood Cliffs, NJ: Prentice-Hall.

Kuhn, T. (1970) *The Structure of Scientific Revolutions*. Chicago: Chicago University Press.

Kumar, K. (1995) *From Post-Industrial to Postmodern Societies*. Oxford: Blackwell.

La Barre, W. (1978) 'The Cultural Basis of Emotions and Gestures', in T. Polhemus (ed.), *Social Aspects of the Human Body*. Harmondsworth: Penguin.

Lacan, J. (1977) *Ecrits A Selection*. London: Tavistock.

Lash, S. and Urry, J. (1987) *The End of Organized Capitalism*. Cambridge: Polity.

Laslett, P. (1979) *The World We Have Lost*, 2nd edn. London: Methuen.

Layder, D. (1994) *Understanding Social Theory*. London: Sage.

Leavis, F.R. (1952) *The Great Tradition*. London: Chatto and Windus.

Leavis, F.R. and Thompson, D. (1933) *Culture and Environment: The Training of Critical Awareness*. London: Chatto and Windus.

Leavis, F.R. and Yudkin, M. (1962) *Two Cultures? The Significance of C.P. Snow*. London: Chatto and Windus.

Leiss, W. (1976) *The Limits to Satisfaction: On Needs and Commodities.* Toronto: University of Toronto Press.

Leiss, W., Kline, S. and Jhally, S. (1986) *Social Communication in Advertising: Persons, Products and Images of Well-Being.* London: Methuen.

Lemert, C. (ed.) (1993) *Social Theory. The Multicultural and Classic Readings.* Boulder, CO: Westview.

Leppert, R. (1996) *Art and the Committed Eye: The Cultural Functions of Imagery.* Boulder, CO and Oxford: Westview.

Lessa, W. (1964) 'Folk Culture', in J. Gould and W. Kolb (eds), *A Dictionary of the Social Sciences.* London: Tavistock Press and UNESCO.

Lessnof, M. (1974) *The Structure of Social Science.* London: Allen and Unwin.

Lévi-Strauss, C. (1969) *The Raw and the Cooked: Introduction to a Science of Mythology: I,* trans. J. and D. Weightman. New York and Evanston, IL: Harper and Row.

Levitt, T. (1983) *The Marketing Imagination.* London: Collier Macmillan.

Linebaugh, P. (1991) *The London Hanged: Crime and Civil Society in the Eighteenth Century.* London: Penguin.

Lipset, S.M., Trow, M. and Coleman, J. (1962) *Union Democracy.* Garden City, NY: Anchor, Doubleday.

Llobera, J.R. (1994a) *The God of Modernity: The Development of Nationalism in Western Europe.* Oxford: Berg.

Llobera, J.R. (1994b) 'Durkheim and the National Question', in W.S.F. Pickering and H. Martins (eds), *Debating Durkheim.* London: Routledge.

Llobera, J.R. (1994c) 'Anthropological Approaches to the Study of Nationalism in Europe: The Work of Van Gennep and Mauss', in V. Goodard, J.R. Llobera and C. Shore (eds), *The Anthropology of Europe.* Oxford: Berg.

Lloyd, G. (1984) *The Man of Reason: 'Male' and 'Female' in Western Philosophy.* London: Methuen.

Locke, J. (1988) *Two Treatises of Government* (1690). Cambridge: Cambridge University Press.

Lowe, D. (1982) *History of Bourgeois Perception.* Brighton: Harvester.

Lowenthal, L. (1961) *Literature, Popular Culture and Society.* Englewood Cliffs, NJ: Prentice-Hall.

Lukes, S. (1973) *Émile Durkheim: His Life and Work: A Historical and Critical Study.* Harmondsworth: Penguin.

Lynch, M. (1984) *Art and Artifact in Laboratory Science.* London: Routledge.

Lyon, D. (1983) *Sociology and the Human Image.* Leicester: Inter-Varsity Press.

Lyotard, J.-F. (1984) *The Postmodern Condition.* Manchester: Manchester University Press.

MacDonald, D. (1957) 'A Theory of Mass Culture', in B. Rosenberg and D. White (eds), *Mass Culture: The Popular Arts in America.* Glencoe, IL: Free Press.

Macdonald, G. (1979) *Camera: A Victorian Eyewitness.* London: Batsford.

MacIntyre, A. (1970) 'The Idea of a Social Science', in B.R. Wilson (ed.), *Rationality.* Oxford: Blackwell.

Malinowski, B. (1922) *Argonauts of the Western Pacific.* London: Routledge.

Malvery, O.C. (1907) *The Soul Market.* London: Hutchinson.

Mandelbaum, M. (1982) 'Subjective, Objective and Conceptual Relativisms', in M. Kraus and J. Meiland (eds), *Relativism, Cognitive and Moral.* Notre Dame, IN: University of Notre Dame Press.

Marcuse, H. (1964) *One Dimensional Man.* London: Abacus. Boston: Beacon.

Marcuse, H. (1973a) *Eros and Civilisation* (1955). London: Abacus.

Marcuse, H. (1973b) *An Essay on Liberation* (1969). Harmondsworth: Penguin.

Marsh, C. (1982) *The Survey Method*. London: Allen and Unwin.

Marshall, C. and Rossman, G. (1989) *Designing Qualitative Research*. London: Sage.

Marshall, T. (1950) *Citizenship and Social Class*. Cambridge: Cambridge University Press.

Martin, E. (1989) *The Woman in the Body: A Cultural Analysis of Reproduction*. Milton Keynes: Open University Press.

Marx, K. (1975) *Early Writings*. Harmondsworth: Penguin/New Left Review.

Marx, K. (1977) *Selected Writings*, ed. D. McLellan. Oxford: Oxford University Press.

Massey, D. (1991) 'A Global Sense of Place', *Marxism Today*, June: 25–26.

Mauss, M. (1973) 'The Techniques of the Body' (1934), *Economy and Society*, 2 (1): 70–88.

McHoul, A. and Grace, W. (1993) *A Foucault Primer*. Melbourne: Melbourne University Press.

McLuhan, M. (1964) *Understanding the Media*. London: Routledge and Kegan Paul.

McNay, L. (1992) *Foucault and Feminism: Power, Gender and the Self*. Cambridge: Polity Press.

Mead, M. (1935) *Sex and Temperament in Three Primitive Societies*. New York: William Morrow.

Mellor, P. (1993) 'Death in High Modernity: The Contemporary Presence and Absence of Death', in D. Clark (ed.), *The Sociology of Death*. Oxford: Blackwell.

Mellor, P. and Shilling, C. (1993) 'Modernity, Self Identity and the Sequestration of Death', *Sociology*, 27 (3): 411–31.

Mennell, S. (1990) 'The Globalization of Culture as a Very Long-Term Process: Elias's Theory', *Theory, Culture and Society*, 7 (2–3).

Merton, R.K. (1957) *Social Theory and Social Structure*. Glencoe, IL: Free Press.

Merton, R. and Lazarsfeld, P. (1957) 'Mass Communication, Popular Taste and Organized Social Action', in B. Rosenberg and D. White (eds), *Mass Culture: The Popular Arts in America*. Glencoe, IL: Free Press.

Miles, M. and Huberman, A. (1984) *Qualitative Data Analysis*. London: Sage.

Miller, D. (1987) *Material Culture and Mass Consumption*. Oxford: Basil Blackwell.

Mills, C.W. (1959) *The Sociological Imagination*. New York: Oxford University Press.

Mills, C.W. (1970) *The Sociological Imagination*. Harmondsworth: Penguin.

Milner, A. (1994) *Contemporary Cultural Theory: An Introduction*. London: UCL Press.

Minh-ha, T.T. (1989) *Woman, Native, Other: Writing, Postcoloniality and Feminism*. Bloomington, IN: Indiana University Press.

Minogue, K.R. (1967) *Nationalism*. London: Methuen.

Mitchell, W. (ed.) (1980) *The Language of Images*. Chicago and London: University of Chicago Press.

Mitchell, W. (1986) *Iconology: Image, Text, Ideology*. Chicago and London: University of Chicago Press.

Mommsen, W.J. (1974) 'Power, Politics, Imperialism and National Emancipation', in T.W. Moody (ed.), *Nationality and the Pursuit of National Independence*. Belfast: Appletree.

Mommsen, W.J. (1984) *Max Weber and German Politics*. Chicago: University of Chicago Press.

Morley, D. (1986) *Family Television: Cultural Power and Domestic Leisure*. London: Comedia.

Morley, D. (1992) *Television, Audiences and Cultural Studies*. London: Routledge.

Morris, D. (1976) *The Naked Ape*. London: Jonathan Cape.

Morris, D. (1979) *Intimate Behaviour*. Hertfordshire: Panther.

Morrison, K. (1995) *Marx, Durkheim, Weber: Formations of Modern Social Thought*. London. Sage.

Mulgan, G. (1991) *Communication and Control*. Cambridge: Polity.

Mulhern, F. (1981) *The Moment of Scrutiny*. London: Verso.

Nairn, T. (1977) *The Break Up of Great Britain*. London: New Left Books.

Natanson, M. (1970) *The Journeying Self: A Study in Philosophy and Social Role*. Reading, MA: Addison-Wesley.

Navarro, V. (1976) *Medicine under Capitalism*. New York, Prodist.

Needham, R. (1973) *Right and Left*. Chicago: University of Chicago Press.

Nimni, E. (1991) *Marxism and Nationalism*. London: Pluto.

Nicholson, L.J. (ed.) (1990) *Feminism/Postmodernism*. New York: Routledge.

Nietzsche, F. (1966) 'Thus Spake Zarathustra', in W. Kaufmann (ed.), *The Portable Nietzsche*. London: Viking Press.

Nisbet, R.A. (1966) *The Sociological Tradition*. New York: Basic Books.

Nolte, E. (1965) *Three Faces of Fascism*. London. Weidenfeld and Nicholson.

Oakley, A. (1974) *Sex, Gender and Society*. London: Temple Smith.

Oakley, A. (1977) *Housewife: High Value, Low Cost*. Harmondsworth: Penguin.

Olson, P. (ed.) (1963) *America as a Mass Society*. London: Collier Macmillan.

Omi, M. and Winant, H. (1994) *Racial Formation in the United States from the 1960s to the 1990s*. New York,. London: Routledge.

Ortner, S. (1974) 'Is Female to Male as Nature is to Culture?', in M. Rosaldo and L. Lamphere (eds), *Women, Culture and Society*. Stanford, CA: Stanford University Press.

Outhwaite, W. (1987) *New Philosophies of the Social Sciences*. London: Macmillan.

Paine, T. (1984) *Rights of Man* (1791–2). Harmondsworth: Penguin.

Pareto, V. (1966) *Selected Writings*, ed. S.E. Finer, trans. Derick Mirfin. London: Pall Mall Press.

Parsons, T. (1937) *The Structure of Social Action*. New York: McGraw-Hill.

Parsons, T. (1951) *The Social System*. Glencoe, IL: Free Press.

Parsons, T. (1966) *Societies: Evolutionary and Comparative Perspectives*. Englewood Cliffs, NJ: Prentice-Hall.

Parsons, T. and Smelser, N.J. (1956) *Economy and Society: A Study in the Integration of Economic and Social Theory*. London: Routledge and Kegan Paul.

Parsons, T. and Lidz, V. (1967) 'Death in American Society', in E. Schneidman (ed.), *Essays in Self Destruction*. New York: Science House.

Parsons, T., Shils, E., Naegele, K. and Pitts, J. (eds) (1961) *Theories of Society: Foundations of Modern Sociological Theory*, 2 vols. Glencoe, IL: Free Press.

Pflanze, O. (1966) 'Nationalism in Europe, 1848–1871', *Review of Politics*, 28: 129–43.

Phillips, D. (1974) *Abandoning Method*. San Francisco and London: Jossey-Bass.

Phillipson, M. (1985) *Painting, Language and Modernity*. London: Routledge and Kegan Paul.

Plumb, J.H. (1973) *The Commercialisation of Leisure in Eighteenth-Century England*. London: Hutchinson.

Plumb, J.H. (1983) 'Commercialization and Society', in N. McKendrick, J. Brewer and J.H. Plumb (eds), *The Birth of a Consumer Society: The Commercialization of the Eighteenth-Century*. London: Hutchinson.

Polhemus, T. (1975) 'Social Bodies', in J. Benthall and T. Polhemus (eds), *The Body as a Medium of Expression*. London: Allen Lane.

Popper, K. (1959) *The Logic of Scientific Discovery*. New York: Basic Books.

Popper, K. (1962) *Conjectures and Refutations*. London: Routledge.

Popper, K. (1976) *The Positivist Dispute in German Sociology*. London: Heinemann.

Porter, R. (1994) *London: A Social History*. London: Hamish Hamilton.

Prior, L. (1987) 'Policing the Dead: A Sociology of the Mortuary', *Sociology*, 21 (3): 355–76.

Prior, L. (1989) *The Social Organization of Death: Medical Discourse and Social Practices in Belfast*. London: Macmillan.

Procter, M. (1993) 'Analysing Survey Data', in N. Gilbert (ed.), *Researching Social Life*. London: Sage.

Rabinow, P. (ed.) (1984) *The Foucault Reader*. London: Penguin.

Rabinow, P. (ed.) (1991) *The Foucault Reader: An Introduction to Foucault's Thought*. Harmondsworth: Penguin.

Radcliffe-Brown, A.R. (1948) *The Andaman Islanders*. Glencoe, IL: Free Press.

Redfield, R. (1953) *The Primitive World and Its Transformations*. Ithaca, NY: Cornell University Press.

Redfield, R. (1956) *Peasant Society and Culture*. Chicago: Chicago University Press.

Rediker, M. (1987) *Between the Devil and the Deep Blue Sea: Merchant Seamen, Pirates, and the Anglo-American Maritime World*. Cambridge: Cambridge University Press.

Rex, J. (1973) *Key Problems in Sociological Theory*. London: Routledge.

Rich, A. (1976) *Of Woman Born: Motherhood as Experience and Institution*. New York: Norton.

Ridless, Robin (1984) *Ideology and Art: Theories of Mass Culture from Walter Benjamin to Umberto Eco*. New York: Peter Lang.

Robertson, R. (1992) *Globalization: Social Theory and Global Culture*. London: Sage.

Robertson, R. and Lechner, F. (1985) 'Modernization, Globalization and the Problem of Culture in World Systems Theory', *Theory, Culture and Society*, 2 (3).

Robins, K. (1991) 'Tradition and Translation: National Culture in a Global Context', in J. Corner and S. Harvey (eds), *Enterprise and Heritage: Crosscurrents of National Culture*. London and New York: Routledge.

Rorty, R. (1972) 'The World Well Lost', *The Journal of Philosophy*, 69.

Rose, N. (1989) *Governing the Soul: The Shaping of the Private Self*. London: Routledge.

Rose, S., Lewontin, R.C. et al. (1987) *Not in Our Genes: Biology, Ideology and Human Nature*. Harmondsworth: Penguin.

Rosenberg, B. (1957) 'Mass Culture in America', in B. Rosenberg and D.M. White (eds), *Mass Culture: The Popular Arts in America*. Glencoe, IL: Free Press. pp. 3–12.

Rosenberg, B. (1971) 'Mass Culture Revisited I', in B. Rosenberg and D.M. White (eds), *Mass Culture Revisited*. New York: Van Nostrand Reinhold. pp. 3–12.

Rosenhan, D.L. (1973) 'On Being Sane in an Insane Place', *Science*, 179: 250–8.

Rousseau, J.-J. (1972) *Émile*, trans. A. Bloom. New York: Basic Books.

Rousseau, J.-J. (1973) *The Social Contract* (1762), trans. G.D.H. Cole. London: Dent.

Rousseau, J.-J. (1984) *A Discourse on Inequality* (1755). London: Penguin.

Rude, G. (1970) *Paris and London in the 18th Century: Studies in Popular Protest*. London: Collins.

Runciman, W.G. (1978) *Max Weber: Selected Essays in Translation*. Cambridge: Cambridge University Press.

Runciman, W.G. (1983) *A Treatise on Social Theory. Volume I: The Methodology of Social Theory*. Cambridge: Cambridge University Press.

Ryan, A. (1970) *The Philosophy of the Social Sciences*. London: Heinemann.

Sahlins, M. (1974) *Stone Age Economics*. London: Tavistock.

Sahlins, M. (1976) *Culture and Practical Reason*. Chicago: University of Chicago Press.

Said, E.W. (1978) *Orientalism*. New York: Pantheon.

Said, E. (1993) *Culture and Imperialism*. London: Chatto and Windus.

Saussure, F. de (1959) *Course in General Linguistics*, trans. W. Baskin. New York: McGraw-Hill.

Saussure, F. de (1974) *Course in General Linguistics*. London: Fontana.

Schutz, A. (1962) *Collected Papers*, vol. I. The Hague: Martinus Nijhoff.

Schutz, A. (1964a) *Studies in Social Theory*. Hague: Nijhoff.

Schutz, A. (1964b) 'The Stranger: An Essay in Social Psychology', in *Studies in Social Theory*. The Hague: Martinus Nijhoff. pp. 91–105. Reprinted in B.R. Cosin (ed.) (1971) *School and Society: A Sociological Reader*. London: Routledge and Kegan Paul, Open University.

Schutz, A. (1971) *Collected Papers I: The Problem of Social Reality*. The Hague: Martinus Nijhoff.

Schutz, A. (1972) *The Phenomenology of the Social World*. London: Heinemann.

Schwartz, H. and Jacobs, J. (1979) *Qualitative Sociology: A Method to the Madness*. New York: Free Press.

Seale, C.F. (1995) 'Dying Alone', *Sociology of Health and Illness*, 17 (3): 378–94.

Sekora, J. (1977) *Luxury: The Concept in Western Thought, Eden to Smollet*. Baltimore: Johns Hopkins University Press.

Selltiz, C., Jahoda, M., Deutsch, M. and Cook, S. (1964) *Research Methods in Social Relations*. New York: Holt, Rinehart and Winston.

Sennett, R. (1977) *The Fall of Public Man*. Cambridge: Cambridge University Press.

Seton-Watson, H. (1977) *Nations and States*. London: Methuen.

Seton-Watson, H. (1986) 'State, Nation and Religion', in J. Alpher (ed.), *Nationalism and Modernity*. New York: Praeger.

Shaw, P. and Wong, P. (1990) *Genetic Seeds of Warfare*. London: Unwin Hyman.

Shilling, C. (1993) *The Body and Social Theory*. London: Sage.

Shils, E. (1972) *The Constitution of Society*. Chicago and London: University of Chicago Press.

Silverman, D. (1975) 'Accounts of Organizations: Organizational Structures and the Accounting Process', in J. McKinlay (ed.), *Processing People: Cases in Organizational Behaviour*. London: Holt, Rinehart and Winston.

Silverman, D. (1981) 'The Child as a Social Object: Down's Syndrome Children in a Paediatric Cardiology Clinic', *Sociology of Health and Illness*, 3 (3): 254–74.

Silverman, D. (1984) 'Going Private: Ceremonial Forms in a Private Oncology Clinic', *Sociology*, 18: 191–202.

Silverman, D. (1989) 'Telling Convincing Stories: A Plea for Cautious Positivism in Case-Studies', in B. Glassner and J. Moreno (eds), *The Qualitative–Quantitative Distinction in the Social Sciences*. Dordrecht: Kluwer.

Silverman, D. (1993) *Interpreting Qualitative Data: Methods for Analysing Talk, Text and Interaction*. London: Sage.

Singleton, R., Straits, B., Straits, M. and McAllister R. (1988) *Approaches to Social Research*. Oxford: Oxford University Press.

Slater, D.R. (1991) 'Consuming Kodak', in J. Spence and P. Holland (eds), *Family Snaps: The Meaning of Domestic Photography*. London: Virago.

Slater, D.R. (1995) 'Domestic Photography and Digital Culture', in M. Lister (ed.), *The Photographic Image in Digital Culture*. London: Routledge.

Slater, D.R. (1997a) 'Consumer Culture and the Politics of Need', in M. Nava, A. Blake, I. MacRury and B. Richards (eds), *Buy This Book: Contemporary Issues in Advertising and Consumption*. London: Routledge.

Slater, D.R. (1997b) *Consumer Culture and Modernity*. Cambridge: Polity.

Smith, A.D. (1971) *Theories of Nationalism*. London: Duckworth, 1983.

Smith, A.D. (ed.) (1976) *Nationalist Movements*. London: Macmillan

Smith, A.D. (1979) *Nationalism in the Twentieth Century*. Oxford: Martin Robertson.

Smith, A.D. (1981) *The Ethnic Revival in the Modern World*. Cambridge: Cambridge University Press.

Smith, A.D. (1986) *The Ethnic Origins of Nations*. Oxford: Blackwell.

Smith, A.D. (1990) 'Towards a Global Culture?', *Theory, Culture and Society*, 7 (2–3).

Smith, A.D. (1991) *National Identity*. London: Penguin.

Smith, J. (1995) 'Three Images of the Visual: Empirical, Formal and Normative', in C. Jenks (ed.), *Visual Culture*. London: Routledge.

Snow, C.P. (1959) *The Two Cultures and the Scientific Revolution*. Cambridge: Cambridge University Press.

Solomos, J. and Back, L. (1996) *Racism and Society*. Basingstoke and London: Macmillan.

Sontag, S. (1978) *On Photography*. London: Allen Lane.

Soper, K. (1981) *On Human Needs: Open and Closed Theories in a Marxist Perspective*. Brighton: Harvester.

Soper, K. (1990) *Troubled Pleasures: Writings on Politics, Gender and Hedonism*. London: Verso.

Spender, D. (1980) *Man Made Language*. London: Routledge.

Spivak, G.C. (1988) 'Can the Subaltern Speak?', in C. Nelson and L. Grossberg (eds), *Marxism and the Interpretation of Culture*. London: Macmillan.

Sreberny-Mohammadi, A. (1991) 'The Global and the Local in International Communications', in J. Curran and M. Gurevitch (eds), *Mass Media and Society*. London: Edward Arnold.

Steele, J. (1993) *Turning the Tide: The History of Everyday Deptford*. London: Deptford Forum.

Strauss, L. (1953) *Natural Right and History*. Chicago.

Strong, P. (1979) *The Ceremonial Order of the Clinic*. London: Routledge.

Sudnow, D. (1967) *Passing On: The Social Organization of Dying*. Englewood Cliffs, NJ: Prentice-Hall.

Sudnow, D. (1968) *Passing On: The Social Organization of Dying*. Englewood Cliffs, NJ: Prentice-Hall.

Sumner, G. (1906) *Folkways*. Boston: Beacon.

Suny, R.G. (1993) *The Revenge of the Past: Nationalism, Revolution and the Collapse of the Soviet Union*. Stanford, CA: California University Press.

Swingewood, A. (1975) *Marxism and Modern Social Theory*. London: Macmillan.

Sydie, R.A. (1987) *Natural Women, Cultured Men*. London: Methuen.

Taylor, C. (1994) 'Neutrality in Political Science', in M. Martin and L.C. McIntyre (eds), *Readings in the Philosophy of Social Science*. Cambridge, MA: MIT Press.

Tester, K. (1992) *Civil Society*. London: Routledge.

Thirsk, J. (1978) *Economic Policy and Projects: The Development of a Consumer Society in Early Modern England*. Oxford: Clarendon.

Thomas, H. (1995) *Dance, Modernity and Culture: Explorations in the Sociology of Dance*. London: Routledge.

Thomas, W. and Znaniecki, F. (1927) *The Polish Peasant in Europe and America*. New York: Knopf.

Thompson, E.P. (1967) 'Time, Work-Discipline and Industrial Capitalism', *Past and Present*, 38: 56–97.

Thompson, E.P. (1968) *The Making of the English Working Class*. Harmondsworth: Penguin.

Thompson, E.P. (1971) *The Making of the English Working Class*. London: Penguin.

Thompson, J.B. (1990) *Ideology and Modern Culture*. Cambridge: Polity.

Thompson, K. (ed.) (1985) *Readings from Emile Durkheim*. London: Ellis Horwood/ Tavistock.

Tilly, C. (ed.) (1990) *The Formation of National States in Western Europe*. Princeton, NJ: Princeton University Press.

Tiryakian, E. (1962) *Sociologism and Existentialism*. Englewood Cliffs, NJ: Prentice-Hall.

Tocqueville, A. de (1994) *Democracy in America* (1835/40). London: Everyman.

Tong, R. (1994) *Feminist Thought: A Comprehensive Introduction*. London: Routledge.

Tonnies, F. (1955) *Community and Association*. London: Routledge.

Tracey, M. (1988) 'Popular Culture and the Economics of Global Television', *Intermedia*, 16: 2.

Truzzi, M. (1971) *Sociology: The Classic Statements*. New York: Random House.

Tumin, M. (1957) 'Popular Culture and the Open Society', in B. Rosenberg and D. White (eds), *Mass Culture: The Popular Arts in America*. Glencoe, IL: Free Press.

Turner, B.S. (1984) *The Body and Society: Explorations in Social Theory*. Oxford: Basil Blackwell.

Turner, B.S. (1987) *Medical Power and Social Knowledge*. London: Sage.

Turner, B.S. (1991) 'Recent Developments in the Theory of the Body', in M. Featherstone, M. Hepworth and B.S. Turner (eds), *The Body: Social Processes and Cultural Theory*. London: Sage.

Turner, B.S. (1992) *Regulating Bodies*. London: Routledge.

Turner, G. (1990) *British Cultural Studies: An Introduction*. London: Unwin Hyman.

Tylor, E.B. (1958) *Religion in Primitive Culture*. New York: Harper and Row.

Tyryakian, E.A. and Rogowski, R. (1985) *New Nationalisms of the Developed West*. London: Allen and Unwin.

Van den Berghe, P.L. (1981) *The Ethnic Phenomenon*. New York, Oxford: Elsevier.

Van den Haag, E. (1957) 'Of Happiness and Despair We Have No Measure', in B. Rosenberg and D. White (eds), *Mass Culture: The Popular Arts in America*. Glencoe, IL: Free Press.

Van Gennep, A. (1909) *The Rites of Passage*. Chicago: University of Chicago Press, 1960.

Veblen, T. (1953) *The Theory of the Leisure Class: An Economic Study of Institutions* (1899). New York: Mentor.

Vidich, A. and Bensman, J. (1958) *Small Town in Mass Society*. Princeton, NJ: Princeton University Press.

von Clausewitz, K.M. (1908) *On War*. London: Routledge and Kegan Paul.

Wallerstein, I. (1974) *The Modern World-System*, 2 vols. New York and London: Academic Press.

Wallerstein, I. (1979) *The Capitalist World-Economy*. Cambridge: Cambridge University Press.

Wallerstein, I. (1987) 'World-Systems Analysis', in A. Giddens and J. Turner (eds), *Social Theory Today*. Cambridge: Polity.

Wallerstein, I. (1990) 'Culture as the Ideological Battleground of the Modern World-System', *Theory, Culture and Society*, 7 (2–3).

Walter, T. (1992) 'Modern Death: Taboo or Not Taboo?', *Sociology*, 25 (2): 293–310.

Walton, J.K. (1992) *Fish and Chips and the British Working Class 1870–1940*. Leicester: Leicester University Press.

Warnock, M. (1976) *Imagination*. London: Faber and Faber.

Waters, M. (1994) *Modern Sociological Theory*. London: Sage.

Weber, M. (1930) *The Protestant Ethic and the Spirit of Capitalism*, trans. Talcott Parsons. London: Allen and Unwin.

Weber, M. (1947) *The Theory of Social and Economic Organization*, ed. Talcott Parsons. New York: Oxford University Press.

Weber, M. (1949) *The Methodology of the Social Sciences*, ed. Edward A. Shils and Henry A. Finch. Glencoe, IL: Free Press.

Weedon, C. (1987) *Feminist Practice and Post-Structuralist Theory*. Oxford: Blackwell.

Weeks, J. (1991) *Against Nature: Essays on History, Sexuality and Identity*. London: Rivers Oram.

Williams, B. (1972) *Morality: An Introduction to Ethics*. New York: Harper and Row.

Williams, R. (1958) *Culture and Society: 1780–1950*. London: Chatto and Windus.

Williams, R. (1973) *The Country and the City*. London: Chatto and Windus.

Williams, R. (1974) *Television: Technology and Cultural Form*. London: Collins.

Williams, R. (1976) *Communications*, 3rd edn. Harmondsworth: Penguin.

Williams, R. (1977) *Marxism and Literature*. Oxford: Oxford University Press.

Williams, R. (1981) *Culture*. Glasgow: Fontana.

Williams, R. (1984) *Keywords*, new edn. New York: Oxford University Press.

Williams, R. (1985) *Culture and Society: 1780–1950*. Harmondsworth: Penguin.

Willis, P. (1990) *Common Culture: Symbolic Work at Play in the Everyday Cultures of the Young*. London: Westview.

Wilson, E.O. (1975) *Sociobiology: The New Synthesis*. Cambridge, MA: Harvard University Press.

Winant, H. (1994) 'Racial Formation and Hegemony: Global and Local Developments', in A. Rattansi and S. Westwood (eds), *Racism, Modernity, Identity*. Cambridge: Polity.

Winch, P. (1958) *The Idea of a Social Science*. London: Routledge and Kegan Paul.

Winch, P. (1970) 'Understanding a Primitive Society', in B. Wilson (ed.), *Rationality*. Oxford: Basil Blackwell.

Winch, P. (1978) 'Nature and Convention', in R. Beehler and A. Dregson (eds), *The Philosophy of Society*. London: Methuen.

Wittgenstein, L. (1968) *Philosophical Investigations*. Oxford: Basil Blackwell.

Wolfe, T. (1966) *The Kandy-Kolored, Tangerine-Flake Streamline Baby*. London: Jonathan Cape.

Wolfe, T. (1969) *The Pump House Gang*. New York: Bantam.

Wolff, J. (1981) *The Social Production of Art*. London: Macmillan.

Wolff, J. (1983) *Aesthetics and the Sociology of Art*. London: Allen and Unwin.

Wollstonecraft, M. (1975) *A Vindication of the Rights of Woman* (1792). New York: Norton.

Wrong, D. (1961) 'The Oversocialized Conception of Man in Modern Sociology', *American Sociological Review*, 26.

Xenos, N. (1989) *Scarcity and Modernity*. London: Routledge.

Young, C. (1994) *The African Colonial State in Comparative Perspective*. New Haven, CT: Yale University Press.

Young, R.C. (1995) *Colonial Desire: Hybridity in Theory, Culture and Race*. London: Routledge.

Name index

Subject index